ÖSTERREICHISCHE AKADEMIE DER WISSENSCHAFTEN
PHILOSOPHISCH-HISTORISCHE KLASSE
DENKSCHRIFTEN, 362. BAND

LH III C CHRONOLOGY AND SYNCHRONISMS II
LH III C MIDDLE

PROCEEDINGS OF THE INTERNATIONAL WORKSHOP HELD AT
THE AUSTRIAN ACADEMY OF SCIENCES AT VIENNA
OCTOBER 29ᵀᴴ AND 30ᵀᴴ, 2004

Edited
by
SIGRID DEGER-JALKOTZY AND MICHAELA ZAVADIL

Vorgelegt von w. M. Sigrid Deger-Jalkotzy in der Sitzung am 13. Oktober 2006

Coverdrawing:
Fragment of a Krater from Kynos: Courtesy of Fanouria Dakoronia
(Drawing by Marion Frauenglas after a photography by Stephanos Alexandrou)

Coverlayout: Hannes Weinberger

Die verwendete Papiersorte ist aus chlorfrei gebleichtem Zellstoff hergestellt,
frei von säurebildenden Bestandteilen und alterungsbeständig.

Alle Rechte vorbehalten
ISBN 978-3-7001-3787-0
Copyright © 2007 by
Österreichische Akademie der Wissenschaften
Wien
Grafik: Marion Frauenglas
Grafik, Satz, Layout: Angela Schwab
Druck: Holzhausen Druck & Medien GmbH
Printed and bound in Austria
http://hw.oeaw.ac.at/3787-0
http://verlag.oeaw.ac.at

CONTENTS

Contents 5

Preface 7

Abbreviations 9

Programme of the Workshop 11

List of Participants 13

Eva ALRAM-STERN, Characteristic Small Finds of LH III C
    from Aigeira and their Context 15

Maria ANDREADAKI-VLAZAKI – Eleni PAPADOPOULOU, Recent Evidence for the
    Destruction of the LM III C Habitation at Khamalevri, Rethymnon 27

Elisabetta BORGNA, LM III C Pottery at Phaistos: An Attempt to Integrate
    Typological Analysis with Stratigraphic Investigation 55

Joost H. CROUWEL, Pictorial Pottery of LH III C Middle and its Antecedents 73

Anna Lucia D'AGATA, Evolutionary Paradigms and Late Minoan III.
    On a Definition of LM III C Middle 89

Fanouria DAKORONIA, LH III C Middle Pottery Repertoire of Kynos 119

Sigrid DEGER-JALKOTZY, Defining LH III C Middle at the Cemetery
    of Elateia-Alonaki in Central Greece 129

Katie DEMAKOPOULOU, Laconia and Arcadia in LH III C Middle:
    Pottery and other Finds 161

Elizabeth FRENCH, Late Helladic III C Middle at Mycenae 175

Birgitta P. HALLAGER, Problems with LM/LH III B/C Synchronisms 189

Reinhard JUNG, LH III C Middle Synchronisms across the Adriatic 203

Penelope A. MOUNTJOY, A Definition of LH III C Middle 221

Tobias MÜHLENBRUCH, The Post-Palatial Settlement in the
    Lower Citadel of Tiryns 243

Michalis PETROPOULOS, A Mycenaean Cemetery at Nikoleika
    near Aigion of Achaia 253

Jeremy B. RUTTER, How Different is LH III C Middle at Mitrou?
    An Initial Comparison with Kalapodi, Kynos, and Lefkandi 287

Elizabeth V. SCHOFIELD †, Lefkandi in Late Helladic III C Middle 301

Marina THOMATOS, *Koine* and subsidiary *Koines*: Coastal and Island Sites
    of the Central and Southern Aegean during LH III C Middle 315

Peter M. WARREN, Characteristics of Late Minoan III C from the
   Stratigraphical Museum Site at Knossos 329

Report on the Final General Discussion 345

Dedicated to the Memory of Elizabeth V. Schofield

PREFACE

On October 29th and 30th, 2004 the second workshop on "LH III C Chronology and Synchronisms" took place. As a matter of fact, it was already the third workshop of the project "End of the Mycenaean culture"[1] within the framework of the special project group SCIEM 2000 ("The Synchronisation of Civilisations in the Eastern Mediterranean in the 2nd Millennium B.C."): The second meeting went under the disguise of a section on "Mycenaeans and Philistines in the Levant", when in 2003 the crucial questions concerning the ongoing research in Eastern Mediterranean chronology were discussed at the 2nd EuroConference of SCIEM 2000 in Vienna. Thirteen of the papers presented at this section, which was headed by Sigrid Deger-Jalkotzy, have been included in the Proceedings of the EuroConference.[2]

At the first workshop on "LH III C Chronology and Synchronisms" the chronological problems of the post palatial Mycenaean period were treated in a more general way. However, many questions and discussions focussed on the end of LH III B, as well as on the transition to LH III C and on the definition of the earliest phase of the post palatial period. Therefore the 2004 workshop was dedicated to LH III C Middle. We are glad that, with very few exceptions, the leading scholars in this field accepted our invitation. Due to the outstanding quality of the papers and to the lively discussions which followed them, in our opinion this workshop contributed greatly to a better understanding of the stylistic developments of LH III C Middle pottery and of the historical development of the period.

Once more our special thanks are due to Jeremy B. Rutter who chaired the final session and subsequently compiled a catalogue of subjects which had been treated. This catalogue was distributed to all participants who were invited to reformulate their earlier statements or to give further comments. Some authors sent their contributions which have been collected in the report on the final discussion at the end of this volume. Others preferred to include their considerations into the final version of their paper.

The death of Elizabeth Schofield in 2005 was a great loss to the scholarly world, and a great sorrow to all those who knew her. Her paper on the LH III C pottery sequence from Lefkandi was of essential importance to the deliberations of the workshop. Our special thanks are due to those colleagues and friends who have accompanied her manuscript through the process of printing.

---

[1] The aims of this project have been described in the foreword to the proceedings of the first workshop: S. DEGER-JALKOTZY – M. ZAVADIL (eds.), *LH III C Chronology and Synchronisms. Proceedings of the International Workshop Held at the Austrian Academy of Sciences at Vienna, May 7th and 8th, 2001* (DenkschrWien 310 = Veröffentlichungen der Mykenischen Kommission 20 gemeinsam mit SCIEM 2000). Vienna 2003, 7f.

[2] M. BIETAK – E. CZERNY (eds.), *The Synchronisation of Civilisations in the Eastern Mediterranean in the Second Millennium B.C. III. Proceedings of the SCIEM 2000 – 2nd EuroConference, Vienna 28th of May–1st of June 2003* (Denkschriften der Gesamtakademie 37 = Contributions to the Chronology of the Eastern Mediterranean 9), Vienna 2007, 501–629.

It is our pleasant duty to express our sincere thanks to the following persons and institutions: The Austrian Academy of Sciences, the Federal Ministry for Education, Science and Culture, the Austrian Science Fund and SCIEM 2000. – Ministerialrat Dr. Alois Söhn and Mag. Gottfried Prinz (Federal Ministry for Education, Science and Culture); Generalsekretär Prof. Dr. Herwig Friesinger, Lisbeth Triska, Dr. Martina Milletich, Mag. Bernhard Plunger, Hannes Weinberger and Robert Püringer (Austrian Academy of Sciences); Prof. Dr. Manfred Bietak, Dr. Angela Schwab and Mag. Marion Frauenglas (SCIEM 2000). Nicola Nightingale B.A. kindly corrected the English versions of some papers.

Vienna, February 2007   The Editors

BIBLIOGRAPHICAL ABBREVIATIONS

This list includes abbreviations of frequently quoted monographs, series and periodicals which are not included in the list of abbreviations published in the *American Journal of Archaeology*.

ArchEphem	*Αρχαιολογική Εφημερίς*
Ariadne's Threads	A. L. D'AGATA – J. MOODY – E. WILLIAMS (eds.), *Ariadne's Threads. Connections between Crete and the Greek Mainland in Late Minoan III (LM III A2 to LM III C). Proceedings of the International Workshop Held at Athens, Scuola Archeologica Italiana, 5–6 April 2003* (Tripodes 3). Athens 2005.
GSE II	E. HALLAGER – B. P. HALLAGER (eds.), *The Greek-Swedish Excavations at the Agia Aikaterini Square, Kastelli, Khania 1970–1987. Vol II. The Late Minoan IIIC Settlement* (Skrifter utgivna av Svenska Institutet i Athen, 4°, 47:2). Stockholm 2000.
GSE III	E. HALLAGER – B. P. HALLAGER (eds.), *The Greek-Swedish Excavations at the Agia Aikaterini Square, Kastelli, Khania 1970–1987 and 2001. Vol. III. The Late Minoan IIIB:2 Settlement* (Skrifter utgivna av Svenska Institutet i Athen, 4°, 47:3). Stockholm 2003.
Late Minoan III Pottery	E. HALLAGER – B. P. HALLAGER (eds.), *Late Minoan III Pottery. Chronology and Terminology. Acts of a Meeting held at the Danish Institute at Athens, August 12–14, 1994* (Monographs of the Danish Institute at Athens 1). Athens 1997.
LH III C Chronology and Synchronisms	S. DEGER-JALKOTZY – M. ZAVADIL (eds.), *LH III C Chronology and Synchronisms. Proceedings of the International Workshop held at the Austrian Academy of Sciences at Vienna, May 7th and 8th 2001* (Veröffentlichungen der Mykenischen Kommission Band 20). Vienna 2003.
MDP	P. A. MOUNTJOY, *Mycenaean Decorated Pottery. A Guide to Identification* (SIMA 73). Göteborg 1986.
Meletemata	PH. P. BETANCOURT – V. KARAGEORGHIS – R. LAFFINEUR – W.-D. NIEMEIER (eds.), *Meletemata. Studies in Aegean Archaeology presented to Malcolm H. Wiener as He enters His 65th Year* (Aegaeum 20). Liège – Austin 1999.
RMDP	P. A. MOUNTJOY, *Regional Mycenaean Decorated Pottery*. Rahden/Westf. 1999.
Wace and Blegen	C. ZERNER – P. ZERNER – J. WINDER (eds.), *Proceedings of the International Conference 'Wace and Blegen: Pottery as Evidence for Trade in the Aegean Bronze Age 1939–1989' Held at the American School of Classical Studies at Athens, December 2–3, 1989*. Amsterdam 1993.

ABBREVIATIONS

EH	Early Helladic	LG	Late Geometric
EM	Early Minoan	LH	Late Helladic
EPG	Early Protogeometric	LM	Late Minoan
FM	Furumark Motif	MG	Middle Geometric
FS	Furumark Shape	MH	Middle Helladic
FT	Furumark Type	MPG	Middle Protogeometric
IA	Iron Age	OSJ	Octopus Stirrup Jar
LBA	Late Bronze Age	PG	Protogeometric
LC	Late Cypriot	SM	Subminoan

PROGRAMME OF THE WORKSHOP

The sessions took place at the Austrian Academy of Sciences at Vienna,
Dr. Ignaz-Seipel-Platz 2, Clubraum.

Friday, 29th October 2004

9.15	Opening Session: Address by Herwig FRIESINGER, Secretary General of the Austrian Academy of Sciences

Definitions: LH III C Middle

9.30	E. FRENCH: *LH III C Middle at Mycenae and the Granary Reassessed.*
10.00	P. A. MOUNTJOY: *A Definition of LH III C Middle.*
10.30	E. SCHOFIELD: *Lefkandi in LH III C Middle.*
11.00	Coffee-break

Definitions: LM III C Middle

11.30	B. P. HALLAGER: *Problems with LM/LH Synchronisms.*
12.00	A. L. D'AGATA: *On a Definition of LM III C Middle.*
12.30	Discussion
13.00	Lunch

The Peloponnese

14.30	T. MÜHLENBRUCH: *The Post-Palatial Settlement in the Lower Citadel of Tiryns.*
15.00	K. DEMAKOPOULOU: *Laconia and Arcadia in LH III C Middle: Pottery and Other Finds.*
15.30	E. ALRAM-STERN: *Characteristic Small Finds of LH III C from Aigeira and their Contexts.*
16.00	Coffee-break
16.30	I. MOSCHOS (read by M. Petropoulos): *Regional Styles and LH III C Middle at Western Achaia According to New Cemeteries' Material. A New Approach to the Middle Phase.*
17.00	M. PETROPOULOS: *The Mycenaean Cemetery at Nikoleika near Aigion*
17.30	Discussion
18.15	Dinner at the "Zwölf-Apostel-Keller"

Saturday, 30th October 2004

Central Greece

9.00	J. B. RUTTER: *How Different is LH III C Middle at Mitrou? An Initial Comparison with Kalapodi, Kynos and Lefkandi.*
9.30	F. DAKORONIA: *LH III C Middle Pottery Repertoire of Kynos.*
10.00	S. DEGER-JALKOTZY: *A First Glance at LH III C Middle from Elateia.*
10.30	Discussion
11.00	Coffee-break

Crete

11.30	P. WARREN: *Characteristics of LM III C from the Stratigraphical Museum Site, Knossos.*
12.00	M. ANDREADAKI-VLAZAKI – E. PAPADOPOULOU: *New Evidence for the Destruction of LM III C Habitation at Khamalevri, Rethymnon.*
12.30	E. BORGNA: *LM III C Pottery at Phaistos: An Attempt to Integrate Typological Analysis with Stratigraphic Investigation.*
13.00	Lunch

Special Topics

14.30	J. CROUWEL: *Pictorial Pottery of LH III C Middle and its Antecedents.*
15.00	M. THOMATOS: *Regionalisms and Inter-Connections: Coastal and Island Sites of the Central and Southern Aegean during LH III C Middle.*
15.30	R. JUNG: *LH III C Middle Synchronisms across the Adriatic.*
16.00	Coffee-break

General Discussion until 18.00

LIST OF PARTICIPANTS

ALRAM-STERN, Eva
Österreichische Akademie der Wissenschaften, Mykenische Kommission, Dr. Ignaz-Seipel-Platz 2, A – 1010 Wien

ANDREADAKI-VLAZAKI, Maria
25th Ephorate of Prehistoric and Classical Antiquities, Stoa Vardinogianni, 4th floor, GR – 731 34 Chania

BORGNA, Elisabetta
Dipartimento di Storia e Tutela dei Beni Culturali, Università di Udine, Palazzo Caiselli, vicolo Florio 2, I – 33100 Udine

CROUWEL, Joost
University of Amsterdam, Research Group Amsterdam Archaeological Centre, Nieuwe Prinsengracht 130, NL – 1018 VZ Amsterdam

D'AGATA, Anna Lucia
Instituto per gli Studi Micenei ed Egeo-Anatolici, Via Giano della Bella 18, I – 00162 Roma

DAKORONIA, Fanouria
Kariotaki 7, GR – 11 141 Athens

DEGER-JALKOTZY, Sigrid
Österreichische Akademie der Wissenschaften, Mykenische Kommission, Dr. Ignaz-Seipel-Platz 2, A – 1010 Wien

DEMAKOPOULOU, Katie
Pyrgotelous 10–12, GR – 11 635 Athens

EDER, Birgitta
Albert-Ludwigs-Universität Freiburg, Archäologisches Institut, Fahnenbergplatz, D – 79085 Freiburg i. Br.

FRENCH, Elizabeth
26 Millington Road, UK – Cambridge CB3 9HP

HALLAGER, Birgitta
Danish Institute at Athens, Herefondos 14, Platia Aghias Aikaterinis, GR – 105 58 Athens

JUNG, Reinhard
Österreichische Akademie der Wissenschaften, Mykenische Kommission, Dr. Ignaz-Seipel-Platz 2, A – 1010 Wien

MOSCHOS, Ioannis
6th Ephorate of Prehistoric and Classical Antiquities, 197 Alex. Ypsilantou str., GR – 261 10 Patras

MOUNTJOY, Penelope
British School at Athens, Odos Souidias 52, GR – 10676 Athens

MÜHLENBRUCH, Tobias
Philipps-Universität Marburg, Seminar für Vor- und Frühgeschichte, Biegenstraße 11, D – 35032 Marburg

PAPADOPOULOU, Eleni
25th Ephorate of Prehistoric and Classical Antiquities, Stoa Vardinogianni, 4th floor, GR – 731 34 Chania

PETROPOULOS, Michalis
39th Ephorate of Prehistoric and Classical Antiquities, 8 Evaggelistrias str., GR 22100 – Tripolis

RUTTER, Jeremy
Dartmouth College, Classics Dept., 6086 Reed Hall, Hanover – New Hampshire, 03755 – 506, USA

SCHOFIELD, Elizabeth †
Cambridge

THOMATOS, Marina
British School at Athens, Odos Souidias 52, GR – 10676 Athens

WARREN, Peter
University of Bristol, Department of Archaeology and Anthropology, 43 Woodland Road, UK – Bristol BS8 1UU

Organisation:

ZAVADIL, Michaela
Österreichische Akademie der Wissenschaften, Mykenische Kommission, Dr. Ignaz-Seipel-Platz 2, A – 1010 Wien

EVA ALRAM-STERN

CHARACTERISTIC SMALL FINDS OF LH III C FROM AIGEIRA AND THEIR CONTEXT*

This contribution to the conference deals with the Mycenaean finds from the acropolis of Aigeira in Achaia excavated by the Austrian Archaeological Institute from 1975 until 1980, which is part of the project no. 14 "End of the Mycenaean Civilisation" of SCIEM. Since ancient Aigeira is situated on the north coast of the Gulf of Corinth in Achaia on the border to Corinthia its finds have to be seen in the light of the research carried out in eastern Achaia and coastal Corinthia. The small Mycenaean settlement is situated on a flat, rocky outcrop of about 750 m² which covers the highest point of a hill, rising directly from sea level to 415 m. Its agricultural potential includes an area of more gently sloping fields, which are currently terraced, in the north, as well as a steep narrow valley, watered by a spring, leading to the south into the interior of the Peloponnese (ALRAM-STERN 2003b, 437–438).

In this article the small finds belonging to the LH III C settlement strata of the acropolis area of Aigeira will be considered with regards to their date and context (ALRAM-STERN – CARTER – LABRIOLA – LANG 2006). Objects datable to the pre-Mycenaean habitation levels have already been treated separately (ALRAM-STERN 2003b, 447–449). The findings belonging to the post-Mycenaean period will be subject to additional study.

The main groups of objects found on the plateau of Aigeira are identical to other Mycenaean sites. Objects for spinning (spindle whorls, so-called conuli) will receive less attention in this article, since due to their size as well as their non-specific place of use it is difficult to determine whether they are in situ finds (CARINGTON SMITH 1992, 674). Bronze tools (knives, sickles, tweezers) as well as lead objects are important for the interpretation of working areas. An interesting group are the Mycenaean terracotta figurines (ALRAM-STERN 1987). Most of the female figurines belong to the Late Psi type A, B and D as defined by E. French (FRENCH 1971. – WEBER-HIDEN 1985), while the animal figurines are mostly of Linear type 2 and Spine type 1 and their variants (WEBER-HIDEN 1990).

Since the western part of the plateau shows a good LH III C habitation sequence (ALRAM-STERN 2003a) many finds may be dated by their stratigraphical position. The earliest habitation, Phase Ia dating to LH III C Early (DEGER-JALKOTZY 2003, 55–58, 65–67), was identified in the central part of the plateau directly above the stereo or above a dark brown layer containing mainly pre-Mycenaean finds respectively. The architectural remains consist of two half-timbered houses separated by a passage, of which the southern one is equipped with a hearth. Since its destruction layer was extremely thin and consisted mainly of parts of floors and a thin ashy layer virtually no small finds may be associated with this phase, and in situ finds are very uncertain.

---

* I am grateful to S. Deger-Jalkotzy who is responsible for the publication of the pottery and who has supplied me with the important information about the pottery.

After the destruction of the house north of the passage a pottery kiln was set in its ruins. Contemporary with this stage of the settlement is a storage room in the north central part of the plateau, the latter bordering a court with a fire place or an oven. Phases Ia and Ib are not in all parts of the plateau discernible. Further west there was another storage room which was built directly on the stereo. In the south-eastern part of the plateau there must have been a forge. While the destruction layer of the first phase was very thin, the thick burnt destruction debris of Phase Ib had a depth of up to 50 cm consisting of burnt mud-bricks, daub, fragments of carbonised timber and ashes. The debris of this habitation phase covered the whole plateau and was rich in pottery and small finds. However since the distribution of the pottery sherds shows that the debris of this phase had been dispersed over a larger area it must be postulated that only a few of the small finds were found in situ. This phase has been dated by Sigrid Deger-Jalkotzy to the latest part of LH III C Early and III C Developed (DEGER-JALKOTZY 2003, 58–67).

Over this destruction layer another floor level, called Phase II, was identified in some parts of the plateau. It was sometimes covered by a reddish, partly ashy layer which shows that this phase, too, must have been destroyed by fire. Walls dug into the destruction layer of Phase Ib show that the plateau must have been covered by larger building units, displaying a new concept. According to the pottery finds Phase II should be dated to LH III C Advanced (DEGER-JALKOTZY 2003, 67–73). Unfortunately practically no small finds of this phase may be associated with a closed context.

As already mentioned small finds attributable to Phase Ia are very rare. Two shanks of a tweezer (MARINATOS 1967, B 35), a fragmented sickle as well as a small conulus were found on the floor layer close to the north central half-timbered building.

In contrast, the destruction layer of Phase Ib was rich in small finds. The objects of bronze, comprising eight knives of Sandars class Ia and b (SANDARS 1955, 175–179), four sickles of Deshayes type D2b (DESHAYES 1960, 343–344) or Catling type Ea (CATLING 1964, 83–84) which are clearly discernible from knives by their curved back, their parallel edge and their short tang with one rivet only (Fig. 2:1–2), are of extreme interest. Compared to other much larger sites like Tiryns, where not more than three sickles are known (RAHMSTORF 2001, 35–36 nos. 582/694, 596, 613) the bronze objects comprise a high number. This may be the result of the fact that on the acropolis bronze objects were produced, which is proven by the existence of a mould probably for a spearhead in a heap of fired clay in the south-eastern part of the plateau (Figs. 1:18; 2:6). Furthermore, the high amount of bronze objects, but also of lead may be interpreted in terms of the history of the site. It shows that after the fire-destruction of Phase Ib the inhabitants were probably not able to return to the site and take away most of the valuable objects. The next generation of settlers who built their houses after having levelled the area did not know about the existence of these objects. So it seems probable that the generation inhabiting the houses of Phase II was not identical to the settlers of Phase I. This interpretation is supported by the changes in the layout of the settlement (ALRAM-STERN 2003a, 19). Of the three knives found close to the floor of Phase Ib one was deposited in a pithos east of the north central storage room, the other in a storage bin of unburnt clay in the western storage room (Fig. 1:1–2). So these two knives may be connected with assemblages of storage activity in Phase Ib and had probably fallen from some board into the vessels. The two almost complete sickles also come from Phase Ib contexts (Fig. 1:3–4).

During Phase Ib concentrations of lead in the northern area probably attest to places for lead processing comparable to certain areas in Tiryns (MOSSMAN 1993, 238–241, 245. – MOSSMAN 2000, 88, 98–99). As in other places, lead was also mainly used in Aigeira for mending pots. One concentration with a larger piece as well as drops of lead were found in the same western storage room as one of the knives (Fig. 1:5–6). In the same context there was also a krater with ivy decoration (DEGER-JALKOTZY – ALRAM-STERN 1985, 413, fig. 15:1), which was restored in LH III C Early with a lead clamp. Further east two sheets of lead were located which could have derived from boxes or architectural components as at Gla (MOSSMAN 2000, 90–91. – IAKOVIDIS 1998, 165–169) but could also have been stored for reuse (Fig. 1:7–9). According to another heap of lead, processing may have also taken place close to the pottery kiln (Fig. 1:10).

Most of the figurines were found in Phase Ib assemblages, and so, according to the pottery, they should be dated to a late phase of LH III C Early as well as to III C Developed. The leg of a wheelmade animal figurine from a mixed context is of special interest, since it shows that during this period there must have been further cultic activity on the plateau (Fig. 3:1. – FRENCH 1985, 236–252). As already mentioned most of the figurines were distributed with the destruction debris all over the plateau, and in only a few cases they were situated in situ.

This is possibly the case for a figurine of the Late Psi type B (Fig. 3:3. – FRENCH 1971, 135–136) with irregular crossing lines, and crosses on the top of the polos and the base with analogies in Tiryns (WEBER-HIDEN 1990, 47 no. 34) and Delphi (DEMANGEL 1926, 19, fig. 22:4–6). It was found under the floor of the Phase Ib storage room situated in the central area in an ash layer, which was probably part of the destruction debris of Phase Ia which was levelled before the construction of the Phase Ib buildings (Fig. 1:11). So either it is an item belonging to Phase Ia and preceding Phase Ib, or it was deposited for some cultic reason in this place before constructing the storage room of Phase Ib. From the Ib-level above the figurine a large amphora with irregular patches of paint derives as well as a small rounded alabastron (DEGER-JALKOTZY – ALRAM-STERN 1985, 416, fig. 16:7). The unit which was found near to the figurine above and in its level shows a clear LH III C Early context. As elsewhere, FS 284 bell-shaped deep bowls with flaring rim and monochrome paint are dominant, and cups FS 215 with monochrome interior paint and a medium lip band are abundant. Furthermore, there is also a Group A deep bowl with two thin lip bands on its exterior, a ring-based krater FS 282 with panel decoration and semicircles (comparable to DEGER-JALKOTZY 2003, 59, fig. 3:4) and a closed vessel with joining semicircles.

Further west of the central storage room of Phase Ib in the area of the hearth or oven north of the pottery kiln an almost complete animal figurine of a variant of Linear type 2 (FRENCH 1971, 155–156. – WEBER HIDEN 1990, 56), decorated with horizontal lines (Fig. 3:4), was found in the destruction layer of Phase Ib. It was discovered quite close to the floor level, and therefore close to its original position (Fig. 1:12). Unfortunately this area did not produce many other significant finds. The pottery consists mainly of monochrome deep bowls FS 284 as well as sherds of unpainted or banded closed vessels. There is also a sherd from a medium band bowl FS 215, the shoulder of a small closed vessel with N-pattern and the lip of a small closed vessel, possibly a lekythos.

A miniature Psi-figurine (Fig. 3:2) came from an ashy and stony layer and must have been deposited as refuse (TZONOU-HERBST 2002, 54–55). This layer must have been the substructure of a passage which was in use during the earliest two phases Ia and Ib of the settlement and which separated the northern building area of the plateau from the south (Fig. 1:13. – ALRAM-STERN 2003b, 19). With its minimal paint in the form of a few vertical lines along the arms the figurine belongs to Late Psi type D (FRENCH 1971, 139) and is comparable to a figurine found in the Amyklaion (DEMAKOPOULOU 1982, 50, pl. 23:64). The layer of the passage was especially rich in pottery. In addition to the pottery, well-known from other contexts, there were several finds which date this assemblage to the earliest settlement of LH III C Early; several sherds, such as the shoulder of a closed vessel with whorl-shell decoration FM 23, a Group A deep bowl with zigzag design and a Group B deep bowl with spiraloid design point to a LH III B tradition.

Further, several bottoms of bowls and cups show concentric circles in their interior, and one bottom of a bowl has an interior reserved circle and a reserved band along its base on the exterior.

Further east of it, close to a pile of mud-bricks which must derive from a fallen wall, another completely preserved Psi-figurine was found in the destruction debris of Phase Ib, close to the floor level (Fig. 1:14). This figurine with short vertical wavy lines and a necklace consisting of a band bordered by two rows of pearls should be associated with French Late Psi type A (Fig. 3:5. – FRENCH 1971, 134–135). A figurine of Late Psi Type A which came from the same context is actually a miniature. We have to be aware of the fact that the destruction layer of this area has been disturbed by building activities during historical times. Thus the pottery from this area shows typical items dating to LH III C Developed such as an open vessel with octopus design, a basin and a banded bowl. However, there is also a possibly intrusive sherd of a krater with an elaborated running spiral, similar to a piece in Korakou, dating to LH III C Advanced (RUTTER 1974, 226, fig. 99:4). Aside these two figurines the destruction layer of this area produced a larger amount (seven items) of fragmented figurines as well as the foot of the wheel-made animal figurine. It is possible, therefore, that this part of the plateau also comprised an area of special cultic activity.

In the same area an interesting assemblage of Phase I came from a small stone wall and a base of clay. It consisted of two worked horns of a deer (Fig. 1:15), an unpainted cup FS 215 and a kylix FS 274. Moreover, one of the two sickles from the southern part of the plateau derived from this area (Figs. 1:3; 2:2). Close to the base there was an, admittedly fragmented, animal figurine of Linear type 2 (Figs. 1:16; 3:6). It is not certain if this assemblage is cultic. It is comparable to building VI, room 130 in Tiryns, where a sickle was found in context with small open vessels (deep bowl, kylix, two cups), two rhyta, and two awls (KILIAN 1982, 403). For Aigeira, however, it also has to be considered that the area further south brought to light an assemblage of larger closed vessels which could derive from a storeroom of liquids.

An enigmatic object of soapstone, which may have been a pommel (Fig. 1:17), was found close to the assemblage with the base of clay. Its form harks back to a large spindle whorl of shanked type (FURUMARK 1941, 89) with a central hole tapering towards its end (Fig. 2:4). It is fragmented and was probably not found in situ but was dispersed with the debris of the destruction layer of Phase Ib. Though this item differs from the well-known complete sceptres in Cyprus (KOUROU 1994) Sigrid Deger-Jalkotzy has suggested – in analogy with finds of pommels from Perati (IAKOVIDIS 1969/70, 349–350) and Ialysos (BENZI 1992, 205–206, 265 [T. 17/66], pl. 183), that it should be interpreted as a head of a sceptre (DEGER-JALKOTZY 1994, 20). In this case it would be an emblem of a person of high social rank. The pottery in this context consisted mainly of vessels well-known from the Phase Ib destruction layer such as monochrome deep bowls FS 284, medium band cups FS 215, a deep bowl with monochrome paint on its interior and spiral decoration on its exterior as well as a basin with banded decoration. On the other hand the bowl with monochrome interior paint, a lip band and a broad band or even monochrome paint in the lower part of the vessel could already be a later sign. So this vessel would correspond to the krater with concentric semicircles high up in the decoration zone which Deger-Jalkotzy has dated to LH III C Developed (DEGER-JALKOTZY 2003, 60, fig. 4:9).

In connection with the pommel a conulus (IAKOVIDIS 1977) of steatite with incised decoration of concentric circles on its sides as well as on the base should be mentioned (Fig. 2:3). According to its size and its hollow base (BALFANTZ 1995b. – IAKOVIDIS 1969/70, vol. 2, 280, type 6) it has to be interpreted as a spindle whorl. It came to light in the eastern part of the plateau close to the bedrock, unfortunately in an area with major disturbances. So far only a few comparable whorls from Mycenae, Tiryns, Dimini, Perati, and Ialysos (RAHMSTORF 2001, 170–171) are known. Best known is the ivory spindle from Perati (IAKOVIDIS 1969/70, vol. 1, 56; vol. 2, 350–351, fig. 155). Interestingly enough the same sort of decoration has been used on the pommels in Ialysos and Perati (see above) as well as on jewellery (e.g. DIMAKI 1999, 207, figs. 13–15). Decorated spindle whorls with linear design are also well-known from North-Western Anatolia (BALFANTZ 1995a) as well as from Cyprus (CREWE 1998, 43–52), but since their design is linear it is not certain whether there was a direct influence from this area, as Rahmstorf has argued (RAHMSTORF 2005). In any case, according to the written sources (Hom. *Il*. IV 122. – Hom. *Od*. 4 121–136), whorls of precious material as well as decorated whorls should be interpreted as symbols of status of their user and thus a high value object of a woman of higher rank in the community. As Borgna has pointed out this development may mainly be dated to the post-palatial period and could thus be seen in relation to the emergence of a self-sufficient oikos-economy (BORGNA 2003). For Aigeira it could be argued that it was wool which was locally produced. This hypothesis is consistent with the high proportion of ovicaprids in the animal bone material (FORSTENPOINTNER – PUCHER – WEISSENGRUBER – GALIK 2006) as well as with the hillside situation of the site.

In summary, during Phase Ib the site of Aigeira must have played a major role in the production and storage of goods. Aside pottery production in a kiln and the repairing of it with lead clamps there is evidence for bronzeworking and wool production. On the other hand sickles, grinding stones and storage rooms demonstrate the importance of agriculture and the storage of agricultural goods. Concerning religious activities, with the exception of the foot of a wheelmade figure, there are no indications for cultic activities exceeding popular cult within households and storage units.

Unfortunately, no small finds from closed contexts of Phase II, which is dated to LH III C Advanced, exist. In spite of this fact several finds of this phase demonstrate that economic and cultic activities did not cease during this period. Four low fired clay spools, of which three have rounded ends (Fig. 2:5), are extremely unattractive. Since none of them were found in the rich destruction layer of Phase I but exclusively in the strata of Phase II, they are most probably to be connected with this phase. This situation corresponds with observations by Carington Smith (CARINGTON SMITH 1983, 290) and Rahmstorf (RAHMSTORF 2003, 400–402), that similar low fired clay spools are not found in early and palatial Mycenaean contexts but in strata of LH III C Advanced. Thus these objects have to be connected with a technology introduced during the post-palatial period. Two concurring interpretations exist. On the one hand it is argued that such spools were used in pottery kilns for separating the pots (KARAGEORGHIS 1969, 467–469. – See also CARINGTON SMITH 2000, 228). This interpretation seems very unlikely since the spools are extremely low fired, and their rounded form does not seem useful for keeping space. On the other hand another interpretation says that they could have been used as loom weights (SCHLIEMANN 1886, 136–137. – CARINGTON SMITH 1983, 291, – BARBER 1991, 98. – RAHMSTORF 2003, 402). This idea is supported by finds in Tiryns and Ashkelon where assemblages of spools were found in connection with weaving activity. Thus the low fired spools could be interpreted as evidence for weaving activity during Phase II and possibly even the use of a new type of loom could be connected with it. On the contrary, evidence for weaving activity is missing for Phase I which, compared to other sites, was especially rich in spindle whorls (CARINGTON SMITH 1992, 675).

Unfortunately, there is little evidence for cultic activity. Aside some figurines which derive from Phase II contexts but which could also have been displaced from a Phase I layer the body of an animal figurine shows a decoration with concentric arcs (Fig. 3:7), a motif also known from Close Style pottery and with a good parallel in Tiryns (WEBER-

HIDEN 1990, 60 no. 86). It was discovered in an ashy layer south of the central storage house which was above the destruction layer of Phase Ib and contained material of Phase II. So this fragment most probably synchronises to the group of pottery from the uppermost Mycenaean level of the acropolis in LH III C Advanced.

Bibliography

ALRAM-STERN, E.
1987 "Die mykenischen Idole von Aigeira", 4–7 in: POCHMARSKI – SCHWARZ – HAINZMANN 1987.
2003a "Aigeira – Acropolis: The Stratigraphy", 15–21 in: *LH III C Chronology and Synchronisms*.
2003b "The Acropolis of Aigeira before the Mycenaean Settlement", 437–454 in: BIETAK 2003.

ALRAM-STERN, E. – T. CARTER – L. LABRIOLA – F. LANG
2006 "Die Kleinfunde", 103–167 in: ALRAM-STERN – DEGER-JALKOTZY 2006.

ALRAM-STERN, E. – S. DEGER-JALKOTZY (eds.)
2006 *Die österreichischen Ausgrabungen von Aigeira in Achaia. Aigeira I. Die mykenische Akropolis, Faszikel 3* (Veröffentlichungen der Mykenischen Kommission 24). Vienna.

ALZINGER, W. UND MITARBEITER
1985 "Aigeira-Hyperesia und die Siedlung Phelloë in Achaia. Österreichische Ausgrabungen auf der Peloponnes 1972–1983. Teil I: Akropolis", *Klio* 67, 389–451.

BALFANZ, K.
1995a "Eine spätbronzezeitliche Elfenbeinspindel aus Troia VIIA", *Studia Troica* 5, 107–116.
1995b "Bronzezeitliche Spinnwirtel aus Troia", *Studia Troica* 5, 1995, 117–144.

BARBER, E. J. W.
1991 *Prehistoric Textiles. The Development of Cloth in the Neolithic and Bronze Ages with Special Reference to the Aegean*. Princeton.

BENZI, M.
1992 *Rodi e la Civiltà Micenea* (Incunabula Graeca 94). Rome.

BIETAK, M. (ed.)
2003 *The Synchronisation of Civilisations in the Eastern Mediterranean in the Second Millennium B.C. II. Proceedings of the SCIEM 2000 – EuroConference, Haindorf, 2nd of May – 7th of May 2001* (Österreichische Akademie der Wissenschaften. Denkschriften der Gesamtakademie 29 = Contributions to the Chronology of the Eastern Mediterranean 4). Vienna.

BORGNA, E.
2003 "Attrezzi per filare nella tarda età del Bronzo italiana: connessioni con l'Egeo e con Cipro", *Rivista di Scienze Preistoriche* 53, 519–548.

CARINGTON SMITH, J.
1983 "The Evidence for Spinning and Weaving", 287–291 in: MCDONALD – COULSON – ROSSER 1983.
1992 "Spinning and Weaving Equipment", 674–711 in: MCDONALD – WILKIE 1992.
2000 "The Spinning and Weaving Implements", 207–263 in: RIDLEY – WARDLE – MOULD 2000.

CATLING, H. W.
1964 *Cypriot Bronzework in the Mycenaean World*. Oxford.

CREWE, L.
1998 *Spindle Whorls. A Study of Form, Function and Decoration in Prehistoric Bronze Age Cyprus* (SIMA-Pb 149). Jonsered.

DEGER-JALKOTZY, S.
1994 "The Post-Palatial Period of Greece: An Aegean Prelude to the 11th Century B.C. in Cyprus", 11–30 in: KARAGEORGHIS 1994.
2003 "Stratified Pottery Deposits from the Late Helladic III C Settlement at Aigeira/Achaia", 53–75 in: *LH III C Chronology and Synchronisms*.

DEGER-JALKOTZY, S. – E. ALRAM-STERN
1985 "Die mykenische Siedlung", 394–426 in: ALZINGER UND MITARBEITER 1985.

DEMANGEL, R.
1926 *Le sanctuaire d'Athèna Pronaia (Marmaria)* (Fouilles de Delphes II:5). Paris.

DEMAKOPOULOU, K.
1982 *Το μυκηναϊκό ιερό στο Αμυκλαίο και η ΥΕ ΙΙΙ Γ περίοδος στη Λακονία*. Athens.

DESHAYES, J.
1960 *Les outils de bronze de l'Indus au Danube (IVe au IIe millénaire)* (Bibliothèque archéologique et historique 71). Paris.

DIMAKI, S.
1999 "Νεκροταφείο Ελάτειας: Περιδέραια από στεατίτη", 203–214 in: *Περιφέρεια*.

FORSTENPOINTNER, G. – E. PUCHER – G. E. WEISSENGRUBER – A. GALIK
2006 "Tierreste aus dem bronzezeitlichen Aigeira – Befunde und funktionelle Interpretationen", 171–188 in: ALRAM-STERN – DEGER-JALKOTZY 2006.

FRENCH, E.
1971 "The Development of Mycenaean Terracotta Figurines", *BSA* 66, 101–187.
1985 "The Figures and Figurines", 209–280 in: RENFREW 1985.

FURUMARK, A.
1941 *The Chronology of Mycenaean Pottery*. Stockholm.

GILLIS, C. – C. RISBERG – B. SJÖBERG
2000 *Trade and Production in Premonetary Greece. Acquisition and Distribution of Raw Materials and Finished Products. Proceedings of the 6th International Workshop, Athens 1996* (SIMA-Pb 154). Jonsered.

IAKOVIDIS, S. E.
1969/70 *Περατή. Το νεκροταφείον* (Βιβλιοθήκη της εν Αθήναις Αρχαιολογικής Εταιρείας 67). Athens.
1977 "On the Use of Mycenaean 'Buttons'", *BSA* 72, 113–119.
1998 *Γλας ΙΙ. Η ανασκαφή 1981–1991* (Βιβλιοθήκη της εν Αθήναις Αρχαιολογικής Εταιρείας 173). Athens.

KARAGEORGHIS, V.
1969 "Chronique des fouilles et découvertes archéologiques à Chypre en 1968", *BCH* 93, 431–569.

KARAGEORGHIS, V. (ed.)
1994 *Proceedings of the International Symposium Cyprus in the 11th Century B.C.* Nicosia.

KARAGEORGHIS, V. – H. MATTHÄUS – S. ROGGE (eds.)
2005 *Cyprus. Religion and Society from the Late Bronze Age to the End of the Archaic Period. Proceedings of an International Symposium on Cypriote Archaeology, Erlangen, 23–24 July 2004*. Möhnesee-Wamel.

KILIAN, K.
1982 "Ausgrabungen in Tiryns 1980. Bericht zu den Grabungen", *AA*, 393–430.

KOUROU, N.
1994 "Sceptres and Maces in Cyprus before, during and immediately after the 11th Century", 203–227 in: KARAGEORGHIS 1994.

KYPARISSI-APOSTOLIKA, N. – M. PAPAKONSTANTINOU (eds.)
2003 *Η περιφέρεια του Μυκηναϊκού κόσμου. Β' διεθνές διεπιστημονικό συμπόσιο, 26–30 Σεπτεμβρίου, Λαμία 1999*. Athens.

MARINATOS, S.
1967 "Haar- und Barttracht", in: *ArchHom I, Kapitel B*. Göttingen.

MCDONALD, W. A. – W. D. E. COULSON – J. ROSSER (eds.)
1983 *Excavations at Nichoria in Southwest Greece. Vol. III: Dark Age and Byzantine Occupation*. Minneapolis.

MCDONALD, W. A. – N. C. WILKIE (eds.)
1992 *Excavations at Nichoria in Southwest Greece. Vol. II. The Bronze Age Occupation*. Minneapolis.

MOSSMAN, S. T. I.
1993 *Mycenaean Lead: Archaeology and Technology* (unpublished Ph.D. thesis). Birmingham.
2000 "Mycenaean Age Lead: A Fresh Look at an Old Material", 85–119 in: GILLIS – RISBERG – SJÖBERG 2000.

Περιφέρεια
1999 Η περιφέρεια του Μυκηναϊκού κόσμου. Α᾽ διεθνές διεπιστημονικό συμπόσιο, Λαμία, 25–29 Σεπτεμβρίου 1994. Lamia.

POCHMARSKI, E. – G. SCHWARZ – M. HAINZMANN (eds.)
1987 Berichte des 2. Österreichischen Archäologentages im Schloss Seggau bei Leibnitz vom 14. bis 16. Juni 1984 (Mitteilungen der Archaeologischen Gesellschaft Graz, Beiheft 1). Graz.

RAHMSTORF, L.
2001 Kleinfunde aus Tiryns aus Terrakotta, Stein, Bein und Glas/Fayence vornehmlich spätbronzezeitlicher Zeitstellung (unpublished Ph.D. thesis). Heidelberg.
2003 "Clay Spools from Tiryns and Other Contemporary Sites. An Indication of Foreign Influence in LH III C?", 397–415 in: KYPARISSI-APOSTOLIKA – PAPAKONSTANTINOU 2003.
2005 "Ethnicity and Changes in Weaving Technology in Cyprus and the Eastern Mediterranean in the 12th Century BC", 143–169 in: KARAGEORGHIS – MATTHÄUS – ROGGE 2005.

RENFREW, C.
1985 The Archaeology of Cult. The Sanctuary at Phylakopi (BSA Suppl. 18). London.

RIDLEY, C. – K. A. WARDLE – C. A. MOULD (eds.)
2000 Servia I. Anglo-Hellenic Rescue Excavations 1971–73 Directed by Katerina Rhomiopoulou and Cressida Ridley (BSA Suppl. 32). London.

RUTTER, J. B.
1974 The Late Helladic III B and III C Periods at Korakou and Gonia in the Corinthia (Ph.D. dissertation, University of Pennsylvania [Ann Arbor Nr. 48106]).

SANDARS, N. K.
1955 "The Antiquity of the One-Edged Bronze Knife in the Aegean", Proceedings of the Prehistoric Society, N. S. 21, 174–197.

SCHLIEMANN, H.
1886 Tiryns. Der prähistorische Palast der Könige von Tiryns. Ergebnisse der neuesten Ausgrabungen. Leipzig.

TZONOU-HERBST, I. N.
2002 A Contextual Analysis of Mycenaean Terracotta Figurines (unpublished Ph.D. thesis). Cincinnati.

WEBER-HIDEN, I.
1985 "Zur Datierung mykenischer Idole", Archäologisches Korrespondenzblatt 15, 307–312.
1990 "Die mykenischen Terrakottafigurinen aus den Syringes von Tiryns", 35–85 in: Tiryns. Forschungen und Berichte 11. Mainz.

Fig. 1 Distribution of small finds of Phase Ib contexts in the western part of the plateau of the acropolis of Aigeira (Drawing: Marion Frauenglas)

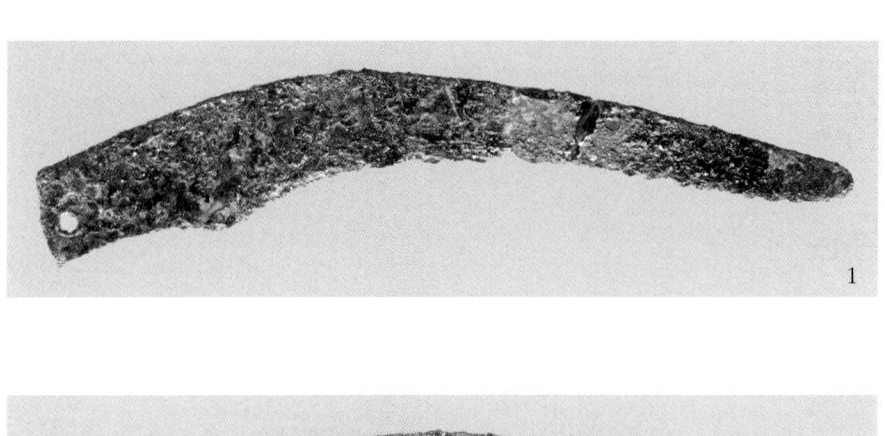
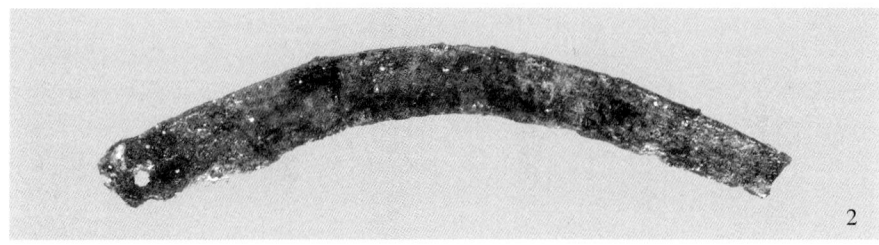

Fig. 2 Small finds from the acropolis of Aigeira (Photos: Rudolf Goth, Thomas Römer)

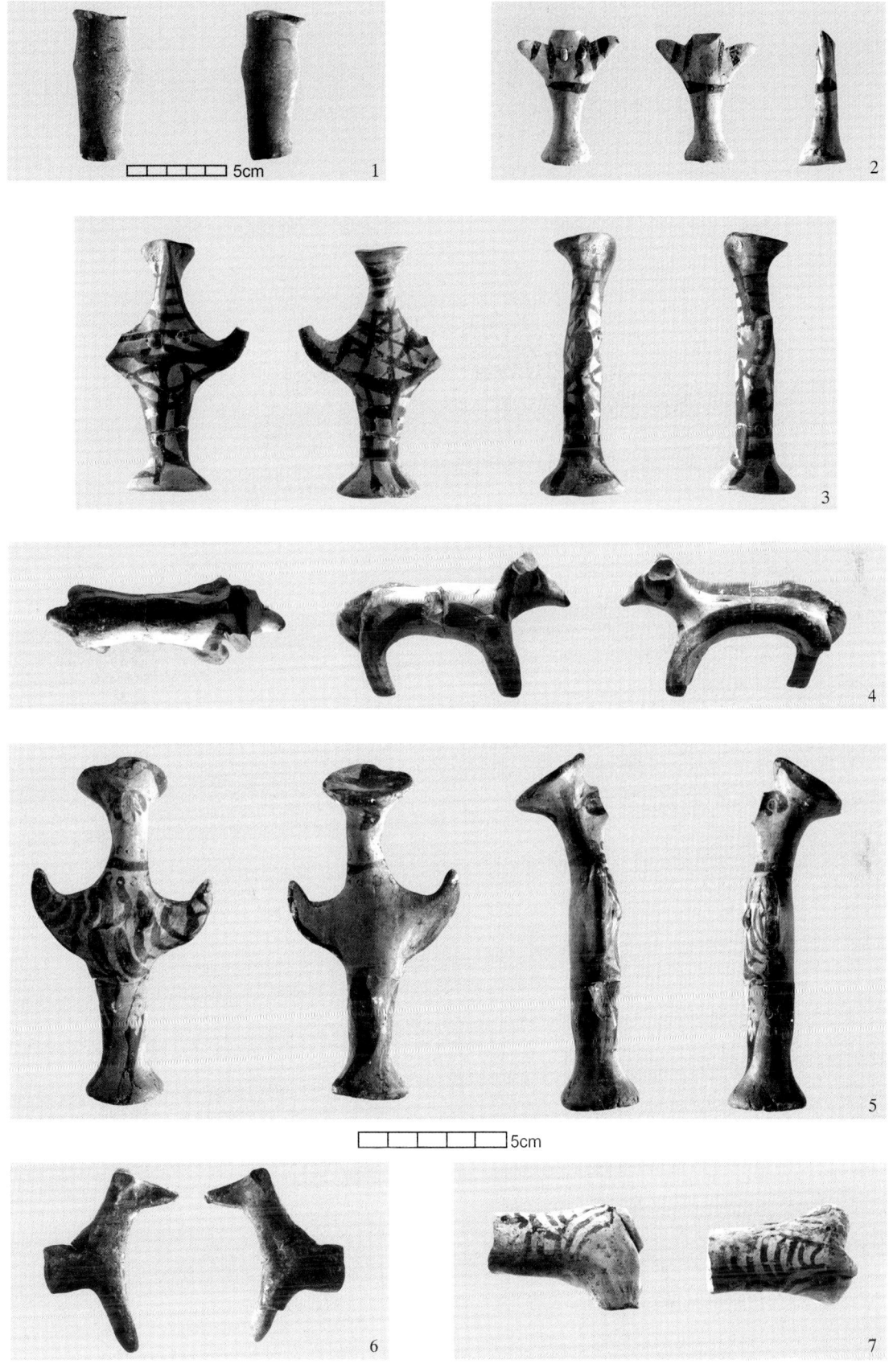

Fig. 3 Figurines from the acropolis of Aigeira
(Photos: Rudolf Goth, Thomas Römer, Klaus-Valtin von Eickstedt)

MARIA ANDREADAKI-VLAZAKI, ELENI PAPADOPOULOU

RECENT EVIDENCE FOR THE DESTRUCTION OF THE LM III C HABITATION AT KHAMALEVRI, RETHYMNON*

In April 2003, during the conference entitled "Ariadne's Threads", which was held at the Italian Archaeological School of Athens, we presented, for the first time, LM III C pottery derived from the excavations in several fields of the Khamalevri area. Khamalevri is situated 12 km east of Rethymnon, in a northerly coastal fertile plain (HOOD – WARREN – CADOGAN 1964, 50–52, 62–66. – SCHIERING – MÜLLER – NIEMEIER 1982, 15–47. – ANDREADAKI-VLAZAKI – PAPADOPOULOU 2005, 353–397, with further references). From this initial general documentation we realised the urgent need to bring forward the excavation of one of the building complexes already mentioned, in depth and extent, for two reasons: a) to identify the different LM III C phases, according to the evidence available, and b) to obtain more information on the circumstances of the establishment as well as the abandonment of the LM III C settlement.

The most recent excavation was carried out during the first half of 2004 at the Pateras site and in particular in the Defteraios field, where the most complete stratified sequence of LM III C habitation had been identified (ANDREADAKI-VLAZAKI – PAPADOPOULOU 2005, 357–361, fig. 1 [field no. 2]). The research was difficult as the archaeological layers had been severely damaged by long-term cultivation and, in particular, by deep ploughing over the past decades. The LM III C strata have been revealed in a very poor state, just below the surface level and quite often parts of the walls have entirely disappeared. Only a team, small in number and extremely skilled, could conduct such an excavation.[1]

THE ARCHITECTURE (Fig. 1)

The archaeological research once again confirmed two main phases in the LM III C Pateras installation, limited to the first half of the 12th century. It also revealed, in every possible detail, the architectural settlement pattern in part of the building complex. It has already been quoted that the "ceremonial" or ritual pits possess an area of at least 50 m² from north to south, including those in the Bolanis site (ANDREADAKI-VLAZAKI 1996. – ANDREADAKI-VLAZAKI 1997. – ANDREADAKI-VLAZAKI 1998. – ANDREADAKI-VLAZAKI 1999b. – ANDREADAKI-VLAZAKI – PAPADOPOULOU 2005, 365, figs. 1 [field no. 1, D. Stratidakis field]; 18) just to the north. The first pits had been dug as soon as the shift from the Kakavella (west hill) to the Tsikouriana (east hill) took place, at the onset of the 12th century B.C., in the so-called "transitional LM III B/C" phase. As we are not sure of the use of these pits, similar to the ones on the Sybrita hill in the Amari valley

---

* We are deeply grateful to Prof. S. Deger-Jalkotzy and to Dr. M. Zavadil for the invitation to participate in this international workshop on LH III C/LM III C Middle, held in Vienna in October 2004.

[1] The head of the group of workers, which was small in number, was the chief craftsman of the Ephorate, Manolis Tsitsirides.

to the south, we can only suggest special ceremonies at least at the time of the arrival of the new inhabitants and later on, in accordance with the activities of the settlement (ANDREADAKI-VLAZAKI 1999a, 734. – VLASAKI – HALLAGER 1995, 255. – D'AGATA 2001, 50, 57–59. – D'AGATA 2003, 23–25). It seems that the pits were dug and used over a short span of time, during the course of a single ritual event (ANDREADAKI-VLAZAKI – PAPADOPOULOU 2005, 376, 392. – D'AGATA 2003, 25).

Contemporary with the first "ceremonial pits" in Pateras seems to be the erection of a building to their west in phase I, in an area now covered by an arbitrary modern house. Later on, in the Ib stage (or intermediate phase I–II), Room ΣΤ was added to this early building and a pottery kiln (ANDREADAKI-VLAZAKI – PAPADOPOULOU 2005, 361, fig. 15, with further references) with its accompanying installations was established to the east. Even later, in phase II, more rooms were added, thus covering much of the old open-air space N+M. Some modifications within the new annex indicate a considerable duration of the latter phase. The same can also be said for phase I, as is indicated by the existence of more than one floor level. All the floors are made of beaten earth with small pebbles and pieces of limestone. The foundation walls, with a width of 0.45–0.50 m, are built of semi-worked stones and earth mortar. The foundation walls of Rooms E, ΣΤ and H are better constructed, following the "sandwich type" technique (*GSE II*, 127). Analytically:

The earliest of the excavated rooms is **Room ΣΤ**, built some time within phase I, as an annex to the building to the west or as a separate dwelling. It has an entrance from the open-air space N+M with the pits, and its west wall seems to be a double one, according to the evidence available. Three floor layers have been revealed. On the deepest one (floor αα4), quite a few traces of ashes and charcoal are still visible, together with an extensive spot with burning remains towards the north part of the room. Slabs and small stones, a few of them in a vertical position, border an area adjacent to the west side of the room. On the same floor quite a few small finds have been collected: part of a clay bovine figurine, a simple bronze ring, a spindle whorl (part of the stem of a kylix), a fragment of a stone vase, a pumice stone and a stone pounder-grinder. A residential character of the room could be implied by the above-mentioned findings. On the second floor (floor αα3), which is just a repair of the previous one, only burned patches were found, mainly towards the east entrance. The third floor (floor ατ) lies 13 cm above the second and belongs to phase II. Two vases, a jar (A 52) and a handleless conical cup (A 53), were the only finds on the floor surface (Fig. 5:15–16).

The same floor arrangement was noticed in the open-air space **N+M**. The upper surface of the "ceremonial pits" fits well with the earliest floor γ (phase I), when the floor was repaired (floor β) the top of the pits (phase Ib) was sealed. An extensive burnt layer, ashes, sandy burnt earth and broken vases (basins, cooking basins, pithos fragments) characterises mainly the north part of floor γ, in connection with the use of the pits. 10 cm above it, a third layer (floor α) of phase II was laid, and thus the pits were completely forgotten (Fig. 1 [section A–A]).

During the excavation of 2004, six more "ceremonial pits" – not only of phase I, but also of phase II (pits Aκ and Aλ) – came to light, scattered around Room ΣΤ, all of them full of dark grey to black burnt earth. Obsidian blades were found in pits Aκ, Aη and Aθ; the latter also contained a few animal bones. In pit Aλ an interesting bronze sickle was found together with a clay spindle whorl. Just east of Room ΣΤ, the pits Aε and Aζ contained small schist stones and pebbles, bones, two small fragments of stone bases and a clay bobbin. Pit Aι in the east is quite different in manufacture. Built of small stones, it has a funnel-like shape and its interior was filled with fine, black earth, bones, seashells and an obsidian blade.

The floor around the pits has different numbers, since it has been divided into several parts according to the digging in each room. Most of the floors (αα6, αα10, αα13 and its repairs αα5 and αα7) were partly covered by ashes and burnt soil.

Just outside Room ΣΤ, between the two pits Αε and Αζ, a free standing carved stone is of special interest. It stands up to 0.30 m above the earliest floor αα6, with vertical grooves along its three sides, the west one remaining roughly chiselled. Two square *τόρ-μοι*, high up on the north and south façades, point to the use of the stone as a stand, for example, to support a wooden pole.[2] The stone seems to belong at least to phase I, before the construction of Room Z. It still remained visible up to 20 cm above the second floor αα5, while it stood only 10 cm above the upper floor αψ, which is the only one that belongs to Room Z.

The five Rooms E and Z–I as well as the small part of a sixth Room K belong to the LM III C Khamalevri phase II, where Room ΣΤ of phase Ib was also incorporated. The deepest floors below the rooms belong to the earliest floors γ and β of the open-air space N+M (phase I).

In **Room E** floor ασ is the earliest of the room, with many burnt, black patches on its surface. The two "ceremonial pits" Ακ and Αλ are connected with this floor (phase II). The upper floor απ is a repair layer of ασ; a burnt clay layer, surrounded by small stones on the west side, indicates traces of a hearth. The deepest floor αα13 belongs to space N+M.

Although only a very small part of **Room K** has been preserved, it was enough for us to recognise two floor layers (αν and αα11) while a deeper third one, αα12, belongs to space N+M. Two broken vases were still resting on this last floor: a handleless spouted cup (A 42 = Π27077, Fig. 10:28) and pieces of a cooking pot (A 43).

On the upper floor αψ of **Room Z** the traces of burning were very strong and probably have to do with the use of the room (as a kind of workroom). Obsidian blades, clay spindle whorls, a stone pounder-grinder and four vases (part of a jar, two jugs and a cup: A 48–51) were found in situ along the east side of the floor. Two door openings towards Rooms H and I were closed sometime during phase II. The two earlier floor layers αα5 and αα6 belong to the intermediate stage Ib and to Ia (space N+M), together with the three "ceremonial pits" in this area (Αε, Αστ, Αζ).

Room H to the south was a storeroom. The earliest floor, αα9, belongs to the open-air space N+M (phase Ib) below the room, while the two upper ones (αα8 and αω) belong to Room H (phase II). Pieces of tripod pots, basins, pithoid jars and a small krater (A 54) were concentrated on the last floor together with a few schist slabs and seashells. A decorated pyxis has been reconstructed from fragments collected from both floor layers αα8 and αω. During the last phase, a door opening to Room Z was closed and another was opened towards the west.

Room Θ has a similar shape and communicates with Room Z through a door in its north-western corner. On its upper floor αα1, a burnt clay layer was recovered and two clay spindle whorls, a stone pounder-grinder, an obsidian blade, and a piece of rock crystal were found on its surface. For the construction of this floor a rough layer of different kinds of stones was used in order to create a flat level. Below this, floor αα10 came to light, together with a "ceremonial pit" Αθ, both belonging to the early open-air space N+M of phase I.

Room I to the north-east has been greatly destroyed by the deep ploughing. The floor layer αα14 belongs to the earlier open-air space (phase I), together with pit Αη, while the upper one αα2 was used as the floor of Room I in phase II. Two obsidian

---

[2] Interior supports in rooms are quite common at Vronda, Kavousi: DAY 1997, 391–392.

blades, a clay spindle whorl, a stone weight and a clay horn of an animal figurine were found on this last floor. A door opening in its south-east corner leads outside the building.

Four meters to the south of this building complex, a narrow stone passage has been revealed between the two long walls 50 and 46, indicating the existence of another structure.

The main features of the architecture of the LM III C Khamalevri settlement have been recognised once more at this building complex: spacious rooms with no traces of any staircase, walls built entirely of stone, often in sandwich type technique, floors of beaten earth, hearths – mainly in the form of burned patches – at the level of the surrounding floor, and door positions either at the corner or along the wall (ANDREADAKI-VLAZAKI – PAPADOPOULOU 2005, 375. – *GSE II*, 127–134. – DAY 1997, 391–394. – HAYDEN 1990, 209–213). The grey to black and ashy earth, which characterises the LM III C layers, both in the dwellings and the pits, is a phenomenon frequently observed in Khania, Sybrita, Pediada Kastelli and Knossos, as far as we know (HATZAKI 2005, 86. – RETHEMIOTAKIS 1997, 307–308). An explanation could be that it may indicate wooden roofs for the houses and this could explain the severe traces of fire on the various floors. Concerning the pits, we would also propose a new habit of burning garbage and not just burying it, as was usual in earlier times. A plague could be the reason to start burning. A possible increase of the temperature would explain an urgency to adopt such drastic steps (ANDHREADHAKI VLASAKI 1991, 421–422. – MOODY 2005, 464. – ANDREADAKI-VLAZAKI – PAPADOPOULOU 2005, 393).

THE POTTERY

A main feature, characteristic of the various pottery groups dated to the first part of LM III C, deriving from several sites in Crete, is the ascertainment of the subtle, almost imperceptible evolution of the pottery within this period. This has been noticed in the pottery from Kavousi Kastro, Palaikastro Kastri, Karphi, Pediada Kastelli, Phaistos, Kastrokephala, Sybrita, Khania Kastelli and Knossos (MOOK – COULSON 1997, 337–365. – SACKETT – POPHAM – WARREN 1965, 269–314. – RETHEMIOTAKIS 1997, 305–326. – BORGNA 1997. – KANTA 2003a, 168. – KANTA 2003b, 537. – KANTA – KARETSOU 2003. – D'AGATA 1999. – WARREN 2005, 100) and indicates a homogeneous development throughout the island in LM III C. The same can be said for the pottery from the different floor layers of the LM III C building in the Pateras site of Khamalevri.

Thus, concerning the bulk of the pottery, there are only slight differences among the two main phases (I and II). It is primarily the stratigraphical variation that leads us to separate it. We are using the term "phase" to describe stratigraphical phasing initially, and stylistic differentiation afterwards.

Ceramic material from Khamalevri, ranging from the MM I to LM III A1, LM III B/C and LM III C periods, has been sampled for petrographic analysis.[3] The main issue was to establish the variability of the local production throughout time. According to the preliminary results, the main local fabrics in the LM III C period for skyphoi, cups, kraters and small jars, seem to be "overfired" greenish (2.5Y 7/3–7/4) and orange brown (5YR 6/6–7/6) to pale brown (10YR 8/4–7/4). The majority of the cooking-, coarse-, and semi-coarse wares belong to a variety of gritty fabrics in a colour ranging from orange

---

[3] The samples were selected by Dr. J. Moody in autumn 2003, after the completion of the study of macroscopic fabrics, and the petrographic analysis was carried out by Dr. E. Nodarou at the INSTAP Study Center for East Crete. We are grateful to both of them for this preliminary information.

(5YR 5/8) to red (2.5YR 4/8) or dark brown (2.5YR 3/4). Pithoi are also of a buff brown (10YR 8/3–4) gritty fabric and pinkish orange (2.5YR 6/6–8) paste, which seems to be a combination of the above ones. The coarse wares were produced using similar fabrics according to different recipes/versions for the production of different types of vessels. It seems that there was a relationship among fabric, shape and function.

The decoration is matt, in a red or brown colour and rarely has a metallic sheen.

It is worth noting that pottery from the surface levels is quite often worn, while the strokes of the paint are visible and the slip tends to be thinner than in earlier strata. To a point, this could be attributed to the wear and tear of time from the long-term exposure of the material to weathering conditions; however, it may represent a technological change, which could be interpreted as a dating feature for an advanced stage of the LM III C period (Fig. 4:30).

Phase I

Phase I includes the pottery from most of the "ceremonial pits" and the floor γ of the open-air space N+M (as well as the floors αα6, αα10, αα13, and αα14 below the Rooms Z, Θ, E, and I, respectively).

The predominant vessel, the *deep bowl* (BETANCOURT 1985, 179. – BORGNA 1997, 276–287. – *GSE II*, 139–142. – D'AGATA 1999, 188–201. – DAY 1997, 395)[4] is current in several forms in Khamalevri. Pateras phase I: examples of the new type with straight walls and a plain or slightly everted rim prevail (Figs. 2:1,3–1,17; 3:4; 4:28; 7:1,5; 9:3–4), sometimes with a slight carination (Fig. 3:7) or with an outward inclination of the walls (Figs. 2:16; 3:1,3,17; 7:2–3), while specimens with a curving, rounded profile and an everted rim remind us of the LM III B examples and justify phase I as a very early III C phase (Figs. 3:6; 4:27; 5:5; 7:6).[5] A small group of bowls with slightly convergent walls is also present (Figs. 2:2; 3:2; 9:5. – BORGNA 1997, 279, fig. 6:4. – ANDREADAKI-VLAZAKI – PAPADOPOULOU 2005, figs. 5 [second row left]; 35 [second row left]). The rim diameter varies between 10 and 17 cm. The base is raised and mostly flat or slightly depressed underneath (Figs. 2:1; 4:28; 9:6. – ANDREADAKI-VLAZAKI – PAPADOPOULOU 2005, fig. 5); a reserved band around its edge sometimes appears (Fig. 9:6). The reserved band seems to have been introduced on the interior of the rim during Khamalevri phase I, although rare in the beginning (ANDREADAKI-VLAZAKI – PAPADOPOULOU 2005, fig. 30:Π15993, ΧΑΜ 92/1/39) (it is only present in the Ib deposits of Pateras).

All kinds of bowls have a monochrome painted interior, often with a reserved disk at the bottom (Figs. 2:1; 9:6). The open style decoration is favoured for isolated and widely spaced motifs, though thin lines, fringes or dots sometimes outline them. Button hook spirals, tricurved streamers, running spirals, shell chains, concentric semicircles, alternating arcs, lozenges, triangular patches, wavy and zigzag lines are among the current motifs on deep bowls (Figs. 2:2,4,16–17; 3:1,3–4,6; 7:1–3; 9:3–5); the first two are new motifs. Furthermore, some bowls are decorated with flowers (Figs. 2:3; 3:7; 4:27–28 – ANDREADAKI-VLAZAKI – PAPADOPOULOU 2005, figs. 23 [bottom row, left]; 31:Π15994; 34 [first row, left]. – See also *GSE II*, 141, fig. 31:80-P0524, pls. 35; 69:f.3). Panelled patterns are present as well but not dominant (Figs. 2:1; 3:5).

---

[4] MOUNTJOY 1999, 511 believes that the Minoan version has no connection to the Mycenaean bell-shaped deep bowl FS 284; for a different opinion see KANTA 2003b, 526.

[5] For more examples of deep bowls of phase I: ANDREADAKI-VLAZAKI – PAPADOPOULOU 2005, figs. 23; 28–30; 34–35.

The blob decorated bowls are popular in phase I (Figs. 3:2; 7:5. – See also ANDREADAKI-VLAZAKI – PAPADOPOULOU 2005, fig. 7. – MOOK – COULSON 1997, 347, figs. 8:25; 11:29).

The *shallow bowl*, with a horizontal rim and two horizontal handles set on it, is a rare shape in LM III C Khamalevri. One plain example has been found in Pateras, pit A (phase Ia) (Fig. 2:20). Another example from pit B has a deeper body, monochrome painted interior and strokes on the rim (ANDREADAKI-VLAZAKI – PAPADOPOULOU 2005, fig. 24 [middle]).

The deep bowl and the *krater* seem to be the most common and distinctive vases in the Khamalevri pottery material, just as in every LM III C site all over Crete (BORGNA 1997, 288–294. – ANDREADAKI-VLAZAKI – PAPADOPOULOU 2005, 381). The majority of the krater examples from both phases belong to the new straight-sided type or type with outwards leaning walls (Figs. 3:13; 10:1. – See also ANDREADAKI-VLAZAKI – PAPADOPOULOU 2005, figs. 35 [middle, right]; 44), while the globular krater is still present in phase I (Fig. 10:2–3). According to the restorable examples, the rim diameter is of around 25 cm. Smaller specimens, similar to the large deep bowls, also coexist with the normal sized krater (Fig. 2:5).

In contrast to the LH III C pottery, the Cretan pictorial style and an early version of the Cretan close and fringed style (KANTA 2003b, 536) are well represented from the very beginning; birds are the most popular theme (Fig. 10:3. – ANDREADAKI-VLAZAKI – PAPADOPOULOU 2005, figs. 21 [chest-shaped vessel]; 44).

The *kylix*, though quite rare at this building complex, is a well attested shape from the rest of the Khamalevri assemblages (Fig. 2:6–7. – ANDREADAKI-VLAZAKI – PAPADOPOULOU 2005, fig. 46:ΧΑΜ91/1/26, ΧΑΜ91/1/27). It is an important shape of the period, since its evolution provides chronological criteria for the LM III C stages. An example from phase I has a rounded body, a type current in the LM III B period (Fig. 9:8).

Various bases and body fragments of the *one-handled footed cup* have been identified in these Khamalevri pottery groups (Figs. 3:9–10; 6:6; 7:7–8). Although they look plain, it is probable that some of them could have been blobbed.[6]

A number of *one-handled cups* have been found in phase I and II deposits. The most frequent shape is with flaring profile and everted rim, while a few of them have straight walls and plain rims (ANDREADAKI-VLAZAKI – PAPADOPOULOU 2005, fig. 24 [bottom]). Bases are raised and depressed underneath. Most of the examples are blobbed, as Π27075 (Fig. 9:2) and Π27076 (Fig. 10:5).

Handleless undecorated cups are still in use, though rare. Π27113 has a broad, everted rim and a narrow, raised and flat base (Fig. 9:1).

The medium-coarse *lekane* or *basin* and *tub*, with a distinct groove and ridge below the protruding rim, are a common shape for both phases (Fig. 2:9). The decoration is restricted to bands, wavy bands and tentacles (Fig. 9:7). The *kalathos*, in various sizes, with the typical everted rim, usually flat on top, has the same decoration (Fig. 3:14) or is plain (Fig. 2:14. – See also *GSE II*, pl. 45:80-P1500).

The finely decorated, closed vases in the Pateras LM III C strata are not as many as the open shapes. There are a few recognisable medium sized examples of the *stirrup jar* of the globular type. The shoulder of one example is decorated with a floral design in panel arrangement.[7] The *storage stirrup jar* is also testified, preserving mostly flat bases and glob-

---

[6] For an early example decorated with a stemmed spiral from Tzambakas, pit E: ANDREADAKI-VLAZAKI – PAPADOPOULOU 2005, 384, fig. 35:ΧΑΜ94/10/2.

[7] ANDREADAKI-VLAZAKI – PAPADOPOULOU 2005, 385–387, fig. 49:ΧΑΜ93/2/3. See also IBID., figs. 21 (bottom, left); 50:ΧΑΜ91/1/7, ΧΑΜ94/10/20 for other examples from Khamalevri phase I. The painted semicircles on the false spout are a feature limited only to phase I. See also MOOK – COULSON 1997, fig. 17:37 (phase I).

ular to ovoid body fragments, occasionally decorated with bands. Bands encircle the bases of the handles, spout and false spout (Fig. 3:15. – ANDREADAKI-VLAZAKI – PAPADOPOULOU 2005, fig. 51). The top of a false spout is covered by a spiral (Fig. 3:16).

The semi-coarse *jug* and *amphora*, as well as the *juglet* and the *amphoriskos* are usually globular in shape, with a cylindrical neck and a rounded and flaring rim (Fig. 2:12). Their body is banded, and sometimes simple curvilinear motifs (scroll, wavy band) cover the shoulder of the vase (ANDREADAKI-VLAZAKI – PAPADOPOULOU 2005, 387–388, figs. 36–37).

A *thelastron* with globular banded body and a wavy band[8] on the shoulder was found in the "ceremonial" pit B (Fig. 2:8. – ANDREADAKI-VLAZAKI – PAPADOPOULOU 2005, 388, fig. 6:Π15260).

A number of coarse cooking vessels, most of them burnt, were recovered in Pateras, phase I. The *tripod cooking pot* is the predominant shape with a globular body, flat or round bottom, horizontal or vertical handles, a collar-waisted neck and everted rim (Figs. 2:15; 9:9). The round-sectioned legs are decorated with thumb impressions or deep vertical slashes (Figs. 3:8; 9:10. – See also ANDREADAKI-VLAZAKI – PAPADOPOULOU 2005, 388, figs. 8; 12; 24). Apart from the traditional Minoan tripod cooking pot with horizontal handles, there is the pot with vertical handles, not very deep body, an everted rim and clumsy legs attached not far from the handles, as well as the Mycenaean-type cooking jar and jug, all shapes attributed to the Mainland and connected with a different cooking tradition to that of Minoan Crete.[9] A *cooking jar* with vertical handles, of the Mycenaean type (Π27339), was found in the "ceremonial" pit Αη[10] (Fig. 10:4). Apart from the legs, the shape and the dimensions are identical to those of the tripod cooking pot.

The shallow *cooking tray* profile is not rare (Figs. 2:18; 3:12; 7:4). A few of them are tripodal, occasionally with finger impressions (ANDREADAKI-VLAZAKI – PAPADOPOULOU 2005, 388, figs. 22; 53. – *GSE II*, pl. 46).

A few rim fragments of *cooking dishes* were found, with a tall or short rim (MOOK – COULSON 1997, 351, fig. 17:41–42), preserving only the beginning of the rounded thick bottom (Fig. 2:10,21–22).

Fig. 9:11 is part of a flat base and the beginning of a stand of a coarse vessel (cf. *GSE II*, 92, pl. 49:87-P0032).

Many fragments of at least four different pithoi were found in level 3 of Room H, above floor αα9 of the open-air space N+M. All the preserved rim sherds were rectangular and the bases flat. The body decoration consists of relief bands with an incised herring-bone pattern or straight lines, as well as narrow ridges with small diagonally incised lines or finger impressions.

Stage Ib (intermediate I/II)

The pottery of the advanced phase I – wherever it was possible to be distinguished by the stratigraphy – is called "Ib" and characterises the intermediate stage between phases I and II. It includes the pottery from the kiln and its adjacent pits P and Ω, the floor β of the open-air space N+M, as well as floors αα3 of Room ΣΤ, αα5 below Room Z, αα9 below Room H, and αα7 of Trench 43.

---

[8] For an extended application of the horizontal wavy band to a series of shapes see RUTTER 2003, 197–198, figs. 8; 10.

[9] KANTA 2003b, 515, 526, fig. 9. – *Ariadne's Threads*, 301–302 (discussion Hallager – Mountjoy). – See also ANDREADAKI-VLAZAKI – PAPADOPOULOU 2005, fig. 24 (top) for one more Khamalevri example.

[10] For almost identical examples see *GSE II*, 159–160, pl. 45. – See also RETHEMIOTAKIS 1997, fig. 8. – KANTA 2003b, 526–527, fig. 9.

In phase Ib the *deep bowl* remains the same size (ANDREADAKI-VLAZAKI – PAPADOPOULOU 2005, figs. 13 [bottom, right]; 14; 31). The examples with an outward inclination of walls and a plain or slightly flaring rim (*GSE II*, 139, pl. 35) form the majority (Figs. 3:18; 4:3–4,18; 5:2–3; 7:11,14–16,18; 8:2–4) and coexist with the least popular straight-sided form (Figs. 4:1–2; 7:19). The shape with the convergent walls still exists (Figs. 2:25; 5:4; 7:17; 8:1). The reserved rim band becomes more frequent (Figs. 5:2–3; 7:19; 8:2–3). The flat base is less popular (Fig. 7:11) and there is a strong preference for a raised hollowed base (Figs. 4:7; 8:9); the ringed one also appears (Figs. 3:22; 4:13; 5:9). In the monochrome painted interior, a reserved base circle is always present (Figs. 4:7; 5:9; 8:9). The reserved band around the edge of the base also occasionally occurs in decorated bowls (Fig. 8:9). The open style decoration continues.

More fragments of blobbed bowls or cups are now apparent (Figs. 3:19,21; 5:6,11–12; 8:6. – See also ANDREADAKI-VLAZAKI – PAPADOPOULOU, fig. 31 [bottom, middle]), mainly of the type with the leaning outward walls.

An example of the banded *shallow bowl* was found on floor αα9 of open-air space N+M, below Room H (Fig. 8:5). The *one-handled footed cup* is represented by several feet, most of them have a concave profile (Figs. 3:9–10,20; 4:9; 7:7–9), sometimes blobbed (Fig. 4:8). The fragment in Fig. 8:8 belongs to the *one-handled cup*, which in phase Ib has a tall body with a narrow base. The *kylix* is now rare; in this context, it is represented by a banded stem fragment of the solid Mycenaean type (Fig. 4:19).

The straight-sided *krater* prevails (Fig. 3:23–24. – See also ANDREADAKI-VLAZAKI – PAPADOPOULOU 2005, fig. 25:XAM91/1/34). The everted rim is more numerous than the rounded one, while dashes on its top and heavy curvilinear motifs make their first appearance (Figs. 3:23; 4:14). The handles belong to the common roll-type and the retained bases are of the ring or low pedestal form (Fig. 4:11). The interiors are monochrome painted, occasionally with a reserved base circle. The reserved rim band seems to be an exception in the Khamalevri material (Fig. 5:1). Apart from the already published LM III C Khamalevri krater examples decorated in the pictorial style (ANDREADAKI-VLAZAKI – PAPADOPOULOU 2005, figs. 40; 44–45), a vase from phase Ib (Fig. 5:1) is decorated with birds and fish as the main motifs in a wide decorative scene, probably in a heraldic position, with triglyphs and panels between them.

Sherds of *jars, amphorae, amphoriskoi, jugs* and *juglets* (Figs. 2:26; 3:25; 4:10; 5:10) usually have very worn surfaces, though traces of bands are preserved all over the body. Wavy bands cover the shoulder of Fig. 4:10 and a dotted band covers the shoulder of Fig. 2:26.[11] The vertical handles of the amphorae, with an oval section, often have a vertical, wavy band (Fig. 3:25. – See also ANDREADAKI-VLAZAKI – PAPADOPOULOU 2005, fig. 32 [bottom, right]). Two twisted, painted handles have been found (Fig. 8:11). This handle type, common in jugs or amphorae, is also present in Athens in LH III C Early (*RMDP*, 567).

Two fine-ware examples of the medium sized *stirrup jar* are imports.[12] The first one preserves the ringed base and half of the globular belly with an elaborate octopus design (Fig. 5:8); the other one is a small sherd of the shoulder of a Kydonian product decorated with concentric arcs (Fig. 7:13).[13]

---

[11] For the wavy bands see PROKOPIOU 1997, 378, fig. 19a; for the dotted shoulder bands see *RMDP*, fig. 456:136 (LH III C Middle – Kos).

[12] For one further sherd of a stirrup jar decorated with an octopus design: ANDREADAKI-VLAZAKI – PAPADOPOULOU 2005, fig. 14 (bottom, right).

[13] A small stirrup jar of the straight-sided type found in Bolanis, well Ξ, is dated to phase Ib (I/II): ANDREADAKI-VLAZAKI – PAPADOPOULOU 2005, 385, fig. 32:XAM92/1/47. An example from Kavousi is also dated to Kastro phase I: MOOK – COULSON 1997, fig. 17:35.

Apart from the well-known Minoan *cooking pots* (Figs. 2:23; 4:17; 8:16), two characteristic examples of the Mycenaean tripodal type have been found (Figs. 3:28; 4:15); the second one, from pit Ω, in the area of the pottery kiln, has a peculiar and squat body[14] and may indicate potters with a different potting tradition. The piercing of the upper part of the heavy leg probably means an attempt to relieve the pressure on this weak point, like the slash or thumb impressions on the legs of the Minoan pots (*GSE II*, 173).

Medium-coarse *basins* and *tubs* of various sizes (Figs. 2:24; 3:26–27; 4:16; 5:7; 8:13–14) seem to be more numerous in this advanced stage than in early phase I. The decoration of the finer examples consists of horizontal bands (see also ANDREADAKI-VLAZAKI – PAPADOPOULOU 2005, fig. 26). Fig. 8:12 is a basin or *kalathos* (cf. *GSE II*, pl. 54:71-P1378 with the same profile) and Fig. 8:15 a small kalathos, monochrome painted outside.

The upper part of a *pithos* with relief and incised decoration was found in the mouth of the firing chamber of the kiln (pit Ψ) (ANDREADAKI-VLAZAKI – PAPADOPOULOU 2005, fig. 17).

During the petrographic analysis by E. Nodarou, three groups of imported pottery were isolated in Khamalevri, Pateras phase Ib. The first two are probably products of a workshop in Southern Crete (Messara plain) and are represented here by a few sherds from kraters and closed vessels. The krater foot (Fig. 4:11) was constructed by two coils, the lower one coarser (red clay: 2.5 YR5/6). The third group of imported pottery is represented by a body fragment of a fine krater (Fig. 4.12), which is considered to be imported from North-Central Crete (Knossos),[15] The clay is reddish yellow (5 YR 6/6–8).

Phase II

Phase II includes the pottery from the floor layers ασ, αψ, αω, αα8, αα1, αα2, and αν of Rooms E and Z–K, the upper floor ατ of Room ΣΤ, the floor α of the open-air space N+M, the "ceremonial pits" Aκ and Aλ, and the upper levels 1 and 2.

In Khamalevri phase II, there is a tendency for bigger *deep bowls* with an average diameter of 13 to 19 cm (Figs. 4:29; 6:2–3,9–12,15; 7:20,22,26; 10:7–9,12,23). The forms continue to be the same at this last stage with a tendency towards bell-shaped examples. The leaning outwards, flaring walls prevail. Apart from the everted rim already known, a new shape of a squared lip is also apparent (Fig. 7:20. – MOOK – COULSON 1997, 353, fig. 18:55. For similar spiral decoration see RETHEMIOTAKIS 1997, fig. 27:1). The flat base has almost disappeared (Fig. 10:18); there is a tendency for narrower, raised and hollowed underneath examples, in a very few cases almost conical (Figs. 7:22; 8:21–22,31; 10:26), whilst the ringed ones now become more frequent (Fig. 10:17). The flat ledge underneath the base, which is apparent in isolated fragments, provides a chronological criterion for an advanced stage of LM III C (Fig. 10:17). The reserved band around the edge of the base is more popular now (Figs. 8:22,31; 9:17). The open style decoration of phase I is still in use, but the motifs are sometimes executed in an imprecise and more stylised way (Figs. 4:29–30; 6:15; 7:22; 10:12). In Fig. 4, the deep bowls nos. 27–30, found in levels 1 and 2, show the gradual evolution of the type, from the vases 27 and 28 (recon-

---

[14] Its rim profile is identical to the Aeginetan pots but there is neither mica in the clay nor potter's marks on the preserved vertical loop handle: RUTTER 2003, 196–197, fig. 7. For similar pots from Mycenae see TZEDAKIS – MARTLEW 1999, 196, no. 181 (LH III B). – KANTA 2003b, 526, fig. 9D and from Khania see *GSE III*, 240, pl. 74:71-P0833 (LM III B Late). For pots of Khamalevri phase Ib (I/II) see also ANDREADAKI-VLAZAKI – PAPADOPOULOU 2005, figs. 9; 33.

[15] The krater P 2469 from Knossos (see WARREN this volume, fig. 6) almost has an identical decoration.

structed by sherds found in different deposits) of phase I, which recall LM III B examples, to the large carinated vase no. 29 from the beginning of phase II and finally, to the carinated bowl no. 30 of a type close to the bowls of the latest Khania deposits and to the Kavousi Vronda bowls of an advanced LM III C stage (*GSE II*, 139, pl. 35. – DAY 1997, fig. 3:1–2. – KANTA 2003b, 519, fig. 4D–E).

The blob decorated bowls multiply in number, often with the paint trickling on the surface (Figs. 5:13; 7:24; 10:6).

Concerning the *krater* (Figs. 6:1,4,7,13–14; 7:21,25; 8:28–29; 10:10–11,13–14, 21,24–25) the straight-sided type always prevails; the triangular and squared lips, current in Crete, are generally very restricted in Khamalevri assemblages (Fig. 8:28). Various base types can be distinguished in the phase II material: mainly ringed (Fig. 10:16), raised and depressed underneath (Fig. 9:15); there is also an advanced example, a torus-disk fragment (Fig. 7:30). Dashes on the outer rim top are frequent (Fig. 10:14,21) and the decorative zone tends to be more elaborate (Figs. 4:22–23; 6:14; 10:21. – ANDREADAKI-VLAZAKI – PAPADOPOULOU 2005, figs. 40; 45). In a Pleonastic (MOUNTJOY 1999, 513) or Cretan Close Style, quatrefoils, ivy leaves, wavy lines, dots, hatched lozenges and tongues are used together, often in panel arrangement, and fill every available space. This feature characterises the kraters of phase II and provides the final date of this phase at around the Middle of LM III C, in accordance with the kraters of Khania Kastelli, Sybrita, Knossos, Pediada Kastelli, Palaikastro Kastri and Kavousi Kastro (KANTA 2003b, 514, fig. 10, 515, 522. – *GSE II*, 146, pls. 38–39. – KARETSOU 2003, 65–57, fig. 7. – WARREN 1982/83, 73–74, fig. 59. – RETHEMIOTAKIS 1997, figs. 33–34 [phase II]. – MOOK – COULSON 1997, fig. 32 [phase III]).

In phase II, the *kylix* profile is of the new deep conical type with a sharp carination and everted rim. The preserved handle is small, typical LM III C (Fig. 10:27). The Mycenaean-type solid foot (Fig. 2:31) is slightly bulgy. One more example from level 1 (and rubbish pit H) has a bulging stem (Fig. 4:24). The monochrome base of a kylix is depicted in Fig. 9:19, probably of the advanced Kavousi Vronda type (DAY 1997, 398–399, fig. 5). The decoration consists of tricurved streamers or their derivatives, spirals, cross-hatched lozenges and hatched loops (Figs. 4:24–25; 5:14; 8:19; 10:27). The interior of the body is monochrome painted, occasionally with a reserved rim band or with a spiral in the bottom.[16]

The bases of the *one-handled footed cup* no longer have the concave profile and are often higher than in phase I (Fig. 6:5–6,8; 9:18).

The body of the *one-handled cup* is tall and narrow in diameter, like the example from the floor αψ of Room Z (Fig. 7:23). An open vase, probably a large cup (Fig. 8:32) with a wavy line on the shoulder, looks similar to a LH III C spouted cup from Lefkandi (*RMDP*, 712). It was found on the upper floor αω of Room H.

A *handleless undecorated cup* has been found on the upper floor ατ of Room ΣΤ (Fig. 5:15) and another fine example with a pulled out rim on floor αν of Room K (Fig. 10:28). They are taller than the examples of phase I and their body turns to bell-shaped, with a plain or flaring rim and a narrow base, flat or depressed underneath.

The *lekane* or *basin* usually has a narrower base than the older ones and the bands multiply in the interior (Figs. 2:33; 8:17; 9:1. – ANDREADAKI-VLAZAKI – PAPADOPOULOU 2005, 384, fig. 39). The *kalathos* seems to obtain a narrower body and sometimes a groove below the rim, like the basin (Figs. 8:23; 9:13). Fig. 10:19 may belong to either a kalathos or a basin.

---

[16] See also ANDREADAKI-VLAZAKI – PAPADOPOULOU 2005, figs. 10; 46–48. In fig. 47, only kylikes of phase II are depicted and the subtitle "phases I and II" is due to a printing error. – HALLAGER 1997, 38, fig. 34. – RETHEMIOTAKIS 1997, 313, 316, fig. 24.

The basket-handled *pyxis* is one of the most characteristic shapes of LM III C pottery (*GSE II*, pl. 54:71-P0609). The example from Pateras, Room H (floors αα8 and αω) belongs to phase II (Fig. 8:34).[17] Its Close Style decoration in panelled pattern reminds one of the outstanding imported tripod pyxis (Π25380) from the Khatzametis pottery group (ANDREADAKI-VLAZAKI – PAPADOPOULOU 2005, 384–385, fig. 41). A similar motif arrangement can also be identified on the krater with the birds from the Arismari-Khatzametis area (Π23708) (ANDREADAKI-VLAZAKI – PAPADOPOULOU 2005, 382, fig. 45. – See also EDER 2005, 404–405), which, on stylistic grounds of the decoration, seems to be a little earlier than the pyxis.

The top of a hollowed false spout – characteristic of phase II – of a *storage stirrup jar* is decorated with two curving bands (Fig. 9:12).[18]

The semi-coarse *jug* and *amphora* are common vessels in Khamalevri phase II (Figs. 5:16; 7:27–28). The globular body sometimes turns to squat and is always decorated with groups of horizontal bands. The base is broad and flat or slightly depressed with a shallow groove running around the edge of the underside.[19] The amphora rim is sloping, a characteristic feature of phase II (Fig. 8:26–27. – *GSE II*, pl. 43:80-P0347). The vertical handle of the medium-sized jug A50 (Π27066), which was found on floor αψ of Room Z, is attached to the shoulder, a very rare arrangement on the cylindrical necked jug. The second jug A49 (Π27069) of the same floor, seems to have a similar handle.

At least one *cooking jar* with horizontal handles has been recognised (Π27073), only because it preserves the base (Fig. 7:29). It was found on floor αψ of Room Z.

Although examples of the *tripod cooking pot* are absent from the Pateras material in phase II, the *cooking tray* is always common (Fig. 8:24. – See also ANDREADAKI-VLAZAKI – PAPADOPOULOU 2005, fig. 42), as well as the *cooking dish* (Fig. 8:18).

The coarse *disc-like lid* has a strong presence in the LM III C Khamalevri phase II deposits (ANDREADAKI-VLAZAKI – PAPADOPOULOU 2005, 388, fig. 43). Here, only one example has been revealed, the central knob of the lid (Fig. 4:21). A small fragment of the handle of a *scuttle* was found on floor αα2 of Room I (Fig. 10:20).

A relatively large number of *pithoid* and *large basin* sherds was uncovered, mainly from phase II in Room H (Fig. 8:25,33). The rim is rounded or squared, while the common pithos decoration is the relief band with an incised net or herringbone pattern, vertical lines, finger impressed bands and the rope pattern. A finger impressed band encircles the base of one example (Fig. 8.25).

GENERAL REMARKS

Viewed from the angle of pottery analysis, it can be pointed out that there are no striking differences between phases I and II. On the contrary, both phases indicate a slow development and typological progress during a period without any radical changes. The same is obvious from the stratigraphical and architectural analysis. Nevertheless, according to the various changes we remarked on in both phases of the building constructions of Pateras, it took much time even for this slight evolution. Could such a sub-

---

[17] For the solid quatrefoils in a panelled pattern see MOOK – COULSON 1997, 354, fig. 18:55 (Kastro, phase II). – *GSE II*, pls. 40:73-P0491; 52:70-P0234. – ANDREADAKI-VLAZAKI – PAPADOPOULOU 2005, fig. 40 (phase II).

[18] See also ANDREADAKI-VLAZAKI – PAPADOPOULOU 2005, figs. 51–52 and fig. 50:XAM95/3/674, XAM94/3/216, XAM97/17/61 for disk examples of fine stirrup jars from Khamalevri phase II, as well as IBID., fig. 49 for decorated bodies (the two examples at the top belong to phase I).

[19] A feature common to Kastro Kavousi, phase II: MOOK – COULSON 1997, 354.

tle development have anything to do with the results of the fall of the palaces, in a period without strong central authority to accelerate the development?

In the first study of the LM III C material of Khamalevri it has already been mentioned that the absence of monochrome deep bowls with conical feet, the appearance of a low cone on the false disk of stirrup jars but never an air hole, as well as the presence of small swellings on the stems of kylikes, restrict the settlement to the first half of the period and date the abandonment towards the middle of it (ANDREADAKI-VLAZAKI – PAPADOPOULOU 2005, 391. – See also *GSE II*, 173 n. 340). According to the LM III B features that still exist in phase I, together with the first appearance of the reserved rim band in deep bowls, the beginning of the settlement could be the earliest stage of LM III C Early. This means that phase II began some time later, still in Early III C, according to Cretan terminology (since most scholars divide the LM III C period only into two phases, Early and Late). According to this theory, the Khamalevri settlement can only belong to the Early phase, with its abandonment at the end of the period, at the same time with the abandonment of Khania Kastelli, Phaistos, Pediada Kastelli and Palaikastro Kastri. On the contrary, we prefer to call phase II, i.e. the stage between Early and Late III C, LM III C Middle,[20] in correspondence with the three LH III C phases. We shall sum up some of the characteristic features of this second phase as seen from the Khamalevri pottery:

1. There are no examples harking back to the LM III B repertoire.
2. The deep bowls with flaring walls, everted rim and reserved rim band form the majority.
3. There is a tendency for larger deep bowls.
4. The blob decorated deep bowls increase in number.
5. The one-handled cup is taller and narrower in diameter.
6. The straight-sided krater prevails.
7. The kylix has a deep body with a sharp carination, small handles and usually slightly bulging stem.
8. The base diameter of the basin is now smaller.
9. The paint and the decoration cover more of the surface of the body. The decorative style is more complex, towards a Close Style increase (KANTA 2003b, 515, 517, 522, 526) and the pictorial subjects are more stylised. The characteristic vase of the final date of this phase is the krater decorated in the Cretan Close Style.

LM III C is a period characterised by the reduction of direct imports from the Greek Mainland (RUTTER 2003, 199–200. – KANTA 2003b, 513. – RUTTER 2005, 42–43). The possible Helladic imports into Khamalevri material are also limited. It is noteworthy that most of them were found in contexts closer to the phase II, i.e. a period when the Mycenaean centres show an artistic renaissance after the destruction of the palaces (RUTTER 1992, 62 n. 3, 67). The most important among them seem to be a carinated cup, two stirrup jars and a pyxis (ANDREADAKI-VLAZAKI – PAPADOPOULOU 2005, 384–385, 392, figs. 25:XAM91/1/33α,β; 41; 49:XAM91/1/36, XAM94/3/287). The carinated cup with high-swung handle (FS 240) is a new shape in LH III C Early: Rutter's phase 2, which also continues to III C Middle (*MDP*, 134. – *RMDP*, figs. 74:182–184 [LH III C Early

---

[20] See also RETHEMIOTAKIS 1997, 321, 324–325 and the interesting discussion on pp. 327–336 for Pediada Kastelli phase II. – MOOK – COULSON 1997, 357 for Kavousi Kastro phase II.

Korinthia]; 274:71 [LH III C Middle developed Euboea]). Our example was found in a rubbish pit of phase Ib (I/II) (Bolanis site, section II). The one stirrup jar may be a LH III C Early or Middle developed import (RUTTER 2003, 199–200 ns. 23–24, fig. 14:1), made by the new joining technique, which was in use on the Greek Mainland at least from LH III A2 onwards. Our example was found in a rubbish pit of phase II (Khatzametis site). The second stirrup jar with the dot rosettes on the shoulder may be an import from Attica, where this particular kind of stirrup jar seems to prevail in LH III C Early (RUTTER 2005, 42–44, figs. 9–10). Our example was found in level 1 of the area of the phase I "ceremonial pits" at the Bolanis site. The excellent miniaturist and delicate Close Style execution in the decoration of the outstanding tripod basket-handled cylindrical pyxis suggests a LH III C origin, probably of the Middle developed phase (MOUNTJOY 1999, 513), a *terminus post quem* for the end of phase II in Khamalevri.[21] The pyxis was found in level 2 of Room 2 at the Khatzametis excavation (Psomas field), dated to phase II.

By trying to synchronise the two Khamalevri phases with the corresponding phases of the LH III C pottery we notice the following:

In LM III C pottery there is a combination of Minoan and Mycenaean elements (POPHAM 1965, 334. – D'AGATA 2003, 25–26). The pictorial scenes and the Minoan flowers in several versions are accompanied by motifs familiar in the Aegean "koine", such as running and antithetic spirals, concentric semicircles, triangular patches, s-shaped quirk and wavy line. The Mycenaean-type heraldic compositions and the panelled patterns (Mycenaean triglyphs) are quite frequent. Among the features in Khamalevri LM III C pottery, common both in the Minoan and Mycenaean repertoire, quite a few appear earlier in LM III pottery than in LH III, such as:

1. The reserved rim band (LM III C Early – LH III C Middle) (MOUNTJOY 1999, 513. – KANTA 1997, 97. – KANTA 2003b, 515, 522. – MOOK – COULSON 1997, 351. – *GSE II*, 173).
2. The reserved disk at the bottom of the deep bowl (LM III A2 – LH III B2/III C Early) (MOUNTJOY 1999, 514–515. – *RMDP*, fig. 77:197. – RUTTER 2003, 195, 199, fig. 13:5).
3. The close and fringed style in the decoration (LM III C Early – LH III C Middle) (KANTA 2003b, 536).
4. The clay bobbin or spool (earlier in LM III) (KANTA 2003b, 515, 522. – ANDREADAKI-VLAZAKI – PAPADOPOULOU 2005, 392, fig. 54).

Other features appear earlier in LH III pottery than in LM III, such as:

1. The joining technique of the fine stirrup jars (LH III A2 – LM III B Late/III C Early) (*GSE II*, 144–145 n. 68).
2. The antithetic spiral (LH III B1 – LM III B Late) (*MDP*, 95, fig. 114:24. – *GSE III*, 207–208, fig. 49).
3. The twisted (or rope) handles on closed vessels (LH III B2 – LM III C Early) (*RMDP*, 145 no. 278, fig. 37).

In addition to the above mentioned similarities, the majority of the pottery (as well as the date and context of the imports) indicate a development along similar lines within the "Aegean koine", i.e. a synchronism between the Early, Middle and Late stages. This can be seen, for example, in the following:

---

[21] For an artistic renaissance and an extensive exchange of pottery during LH III C Middle see RUTTER 1992, 65, 67.

1. The predominance of the deep bowl and the scarcity of the kylix from LM/LH III C Early.
2. The increasing popularity of solidly coated interiors on open vessels in LM/LH III C Early (Rutter 2003, 197, 200).
3. The parallel appearance of the deep bowl with vertical upper body and plain rim in LM/LH III C Early.[22]
4. The continuation of the one-handled footed cup in LM/LH III C (Kanta 2003b, 524).
5. The gradual reduction of the plain ware from LM/LH III C Early.
6. The popularity of the straight-sided krater towards LM/LH III C Middle (*MDP*, 175, fig. 225).
7. The carinated profile of the kylix and its slightly bulging, often solid, stem (LM/LH III C Middle).[23]
8. The occasional appearance of a low cone on the disk of the false mouth of the fine stirrup jar (*MDP*, 144–145. – Andreadaki-Vlazaki – Papadopoulou 2005, 385–386).
9. The appearance of the scroll motif on the shoulder of the amphora from LM/LH III C Early.[24]
10. The use of the motif of the tricurved streamer, which seems to appear earlier in Crete (Kanta 2003b, 517), from LM/LH III C Early.[25]
11. The appearance of the necklace motif on the shoulder of the jug from LH/LM III C Middle.[26]
12. The establishment of the Mycenaean-type cooking vessels from LM III B and more intensively from LM III C Early (Kanta 2003b, 526).

During the pan-Cretan cultural homogeneity in LM III C, the connections between Crete and the Mycenaean world, and especially Attica, have already been recognised by several scholars, regarding the pottery assemblages (D'Agata 2003, 33. – Rutter 2003, 193–197). For such a cultural flourishing, a centre is necessary in the island to mediate the influence of the Aegean koine to the regional sites and workshops. This centre could be Knossos, which seems to be a forefront of the developments in LM III C and its relations with Attica are well-known in the mythological sphere.

---

[22] Transitional LH III B2/LH III C Early Laconia: *RMDP*, 279, 282 nos. 176–179, fig. 95. Messenia: *RMDP*, 352 nos. 109–113, fig. 120. – See also Rutter 2003, 197–198, fig. 11. LM III C Early Khamalevri: Figs. 2:1,3; 4:28. – Andreadaki-Vlazaki – Papadopoulou 2005, figs. 5:Π23750; 27; 29; 30:Π15993; 31:Π15994; 34 (upper row, left). Sybrita: D'Agata 1999, 192 (type 1), fig. 4:3.11–3.13. There is, of course, a difference in the base between the flat version in Khamalevri and the ringed one on the Greek Mainland.

[23] Korinthia: *RMDP*, 236 no. 208, fig. 78. Khamalevri: Figs. 2:31; 4:24–25; 5:14; 10:27. Pediada Kastelli: Rethemiotakis 1997, fig. 23g–h (phase II). Vrokastro: Kanta 2003b, 526, fig. 8L.

[24] Attica: *RMDP*, 567 no. 322, fig. 209. Khamalevri: Andreadaki-Vlazaki – Papadopoulou 2005, 374, fig. 36. Sybrita: D'Agata 2003, 27, fig. 2.1. See also Eder 2005, 400–402.

[25] Southern Peloponnese: Rutter 2003, 199, fig. 11. Korinthia: *RMDP*, 234 no. 197, fig. 77. On the Mainland, this motif is rare in the early deposits, usually in an inverted type (Kanta's tricurved arch: Kanta 2003b, 522), while in Crete it is common from the onset of LM III C. In Khamalevri, the version of this motif as an elaborate flower is familiar in both phases: Figs. 5:2; 7:12,21; 8:2,19. See also Andreadaki-Vlazaki – Papadopoulou 2005, figs. 27; 46. – Mook – Coulson 1997, figs. 11:31; 31:136. – Rethemiotakis 1997, figs. 23g–h; 33b. – Kanta 2003b, fig. 8L.

[26] Attica: *RMDP*, 585 no. 416, fig. 217. Khamalevri: Fig. 4:26. Sybrita: D'Agata 2003, 28–29, fig. 2:3.

Index to illustrations

Fig. 1   Khamalevri. Pateras. Ground plan and section A–A of the excavation
Fig. 2   Open air-space N+M. **1–14**: "ceremonial pit" B (Ia). **15**: pit I (I). **16–22**: "ceremonial pit" A (Ia). **23–27**: on floor β (Ib). **28–33**: on floor γ (Ia)
Fig. 3   Open air-space N+M. **1–16**: "ceremonial pit" Δ (Ia). **17**:"ceremonial" pit ΣΤ (Ia). **18–28**: "ceremonial pit" Γ (Ib)
Fig. 4   Area of the pottery kiln and *varia*. **1–11, 14–15**: rubbish dumps P+Ω (Ib). **12**: firing chamber – pit Ψ (Ib). **13**: on the grid (Ib). **16–20**: open air-space N+M, on floor αα7 (II). **21**: trench 45, level 1 (II). **22–23**: trench 44, level 2 (II). **24**: trench 7, level 1, and pit H (II). **25–26**: trench 9, level 1 (II). **27**: trench 7, level 2 (I). **28**: trench 7, level 1, level 2, and pit H + trench 8, level 2 (I). **29**: trench 22, level 1 (II). **30**: trench 43, level 1 (II)
Fig. 5   Room ΣΤ. **1–7**: in floor αα3 and on floor αα4 (Ib). **8–12**: on floor αα3 (Ib). **13–14**: in floor ατ (II). **15–16**: on floor ατ (II)
Fig. 6   Room E. **1–3**: "ceremonial pit" Αλ (II). **4–5**: "ceremonial pit" Ακ (II). **6**: on floor αα13 (I). **7–8**: in floor ασ (II). **9–15**: on floor ασ (II)
Fig. 7   Room Z. **1–2, 4**: "ceremonial pit" Αε (Ia). **3**: "ceremonial pit" Αζ (Ia). **5–6**: on floor αα6 (Ia). **7–8**: level 4 (Ia). **9–10**: in floor αα5 (Ib). **11–19**: on floor αα5 (Ib). **20**: in floor αψ (II). **21–29**: on floor αψ (II). **30**: level 2 (II)
Fig. 8   Room H. **1–16**: on floor αα9 (Ib). **17–25**: in floor αω and on floor αα8 (II). **26–33**: on floor αω (II). **34**: on floor αω and in floor αω/on floor αα8 and in floor αα8 (II)
Fig. 9   Room Θ. **1**: "ceremonial pit" Αθ (I). **2–7**: on floor αα10 (I). **8–11**: level 3 (I). **12–19**: in floor αα1 (II)
Fig. 10 Room I. **1–4**: "ceremonial pit" Αη (I). **5**: on floor αα14 (I). **6–9**: in floor αα2 (II). **10–20**: on floor αα2 (II). **21–22**: level 2 (II). Room K, **23–26**: in floor αν (II), **27–28**: on floor αν (II)

Bibliography

ANDHREADHAKI VLASAKI, M.
1991   "The Khania Area, ca. 1200–700 B.C.", 403–423 in: MUSTI ET AL.

ANDREADAKI-VLAZAKI, M.
1996   "Χαμαλεύρι. Αγρός Δημ. Στρατιδάκη", *ArchDelt* 46, 1991 [1996], Chron 426–429.
1997   "Χαμαλεύρι. Θέση Μπολάνης (αγρός Δημ. Στρατιδάκη)", *ArchDelt* 47, 1992 [1997], Chron 584–590.
1998   "Χαμαλεύρι. Αγρός Δημ. Στρατιδάκη (θέση Μπολάνης)", *ArchDelt* 48, 1993 [1998], Chron 482.
1999a "Χαμαλεύρι. Αγρός Γεωργ. και Στ. Δευτεραίου (θέση Πατέρας)", *ArchDelt* 49, 1994 [1999], Chron 730–734.
1999b "The Production of Aromatic and Pharmaceutical Oils in Minoan Crete: The Case of Chamalevri", 48–49 in: TZEDAKIS – MARTLEW 1999

ANDREADAKI-VLAZAKI, M. – E. PAPADOPOULOU
2005   "The Habitation at Khamalevri, Rethymnon, during the 12th Century BC", 353–397 in: *Ariadne's Threads*.

BETANCOURT, PH. P.
1985   *The History of Minoan Pottery*. Princeton NJ.

BIETAK, M. (ed.)
2003   *The Synchronisation of Civilisations in the Eastern Mediterranean in the Second Millennium B.C. II. Proceedings of the SCIEM 2000 – EuroConference, Haindorf, 2nd of May – 7th of May 2001* (Österreichische Akademie der Wissenschaften. Denkschriften der Gesamtakademie 29 = Contributions to the Chronology of the Eastern Mediterranean 4). Vienna.

BORGNA, E.
1997   "Some Observations on Deep Bowls and Kraters from the 'Acropoli Mediana' at Phaistos", 273–298 in: *Late Minoan III Pottery*.

D'AGATA, A. L.
1999 "Defining a Pattern of Continuity during the Dark Age in Central-Western Crete: Ceramic Evidence from the Settlement of Thronos/Kephala (Ancient Sybrita)", *SMEA* 41, 181–218.
2001 "Ritual and Rubbish in Dark Age Crete: The Settlement of Thronos/Kephala (Ancient Sybrita) and the Pre-Classical Roots of a Greek City", *Aegean Archaeology* 4, 1997–2000 [2001], 45–59.
2003 "Late Minoan III C–Subminoan Pottery Sequence at Thronos/Kephala and its Connections with the Greek Mainland", 23–35 in: *LH III C Chronology and Synchronisms*.

DARCQUE P. – R. TREUIL (eds.)
1990 *L'habitat Égéen préhistorique. Actes de la Table Ronde internationale organisée par le Centre National de la Recherche Scientifique, l'Université de Paris I et l'École française d'Athènes (Athènes, 23–25 juin 1987)* (BCH Suppl. 19). Paris.

DAY, L. P.
1997 "The Late Minoan III C Period at Vronda, Kavousi", 391–406 in: DRIESSEN – FARNOUX 1997.

DRIESSEN, J. – A. FARNOUX (eds.)
1997 *La Crète Mycénienne. Actes de la Table Ronde internationale organisée par l'École française d'Athènes, 26–28 Mars 1991* (BCH Suppl. 30). Paris.

EDER, B.
2005 "Response to Maria Andreadaki-Vlazaki and Eleni Papadopoulou, 'The Habitation at Khamalevri, Rethymnon, during the 12th Century BC'", 399–408 in: *Ariadne's Threads*.

HALLAGER, B. P.
1997 "Terminology – The Late Minoan Goblet, Kylix and Footed Cup", 15–47 in: *Late Minoan III Pottery*.

HATZAKI, E.
2005 "Postpalatial Knossos: Town and Cemeteries from LM III A2 to LM III C", 65–95 in: *Ariadne's Threads*.

HAYDEN, B. J.
1990 "Aspects of Village Architecture in the Cretan Postpalatial Period", 203–213 in: DARCQUE – TREUIL 1990.

HOOD, S. – P. WARREN – G. CADOGAN
1964 "Travels in Crete, 1962", *BSA* 59, 50–99.

KANTA, A.
1997 "LM III B and LM III C Pottery Phases. Some Problems of Definition", 83–101 in: *Late Minoan III Pottery*.
2003a "The Citadel of Kastrokephala and the Date of the Minoan Refuge Citadels", 167–182 in: *LH III C Chronology and Synchronisms*.
2003b "The First Half of the Late Minoan III C – Correlations among Cretan Sites with Reference to Mainland and Cypriote Developments", 513–538 in: BIETAK 2003.

KANTA, A. – A. KARETSOU
2003 "The Acropolis of Kastrokephala and its Pottery", 145–165 in: *LH III C Chronology and Synchronisms*.

KARETSOU, A.
2003 "Juktas Peak Sanctuary. Notes on 12th Century Material", *AM* 118, 49–65.

MOODY, J.
2005 "Unravelling the Threads: Climate Changes in the Late Bronze Aegean", 443–470 in: *Ariadne's Threads*.

MOOK, M. – W. COULSON
1997 "Late Minoan III C Pottery from the Kastro at Kavousi", 337–365 in: *Late Minoan III Pottery*.

Mountjoy, P. A.
1999 "Late Minoan III C/Late Helladic III C: Chronology and Terminology", 511–516 in: *Meletemata*.

Musti, D. – A. Sacconi – L. Rocchetti – M. Rocchi – E. Scafa – L. Sportiello – M. E. Giannotta (eds.)
1991 *La transizione dal Miceneo all'Alto Arcaismo. Dal pallazzo alla città (Atti del Convegno Internazionale, Roma 14–19 marzo 1988)*. Rome.

Popham, M. R.
1965 "Some Late Minoan III Pottery from Crete", *BSA* 60, 316–342.

Prokopiou, N.
1997 "LM III Pottery from the Greek-Italian Excavations at Sybritos Amariou", 371–394 in: *Late Minoan III Pottery*.

Rethemiotakis, G.
1997 "Late Minoan III Pottery from Kastelli Pediada", 305–326 in: *Late Minoan III Pottery*.

Rutter, J. B.
1992 "Cultural Novelties in the Post-Palatial Aegean World: Indices of Vitality or Decline?", 61–78 in: Ward – Joukowsky 1992.
2003 "The Nature and Potential Significance of Minoan Features in the Earliest Late Helladic III C Ceramic Assemblages of the Central and Southern Greek Mainland", 193–216 in: *LH III C Chronology and Synchronisms*.
2005 "Southern Triangles Revisited: Lakonia, Messenia, and Crete in the 14th–12th Centuries BC", 17–50 in: *Ariadne's Threads*.

Sackett, L. H. – M. R. Popham – P. M. Warren
1965 "Excavations at Palaikastro VI", *BSA* 60, 248–315.

Schiering, W. – W. Müller – W.-D. Niemeier
1982 "Landbegehungen in Rethymnon und Umgebung", *AA*, 15–54.

Tzedakis, Y. – H. Martlew (eds.)
1999 *Minoans and Mycenaeans. Flavours of Their Time. National Archaeological Museum, 12 July–27 November 1999*. Athens.

Vlasaki, M. – E. Hallager
1995 "Evidence for Seal Use in Pre-Palatial Western Crete", *CMS Beiheft* 5, 251–270.

Ward, W. A. – M. S. Joukowsky (eds.)
1992 *The Crisis Years: The 12th Century B.C. from beyond the Danube to the Tigris (International Conference at Brown University, Providence, on May 16–19, 1990)*. Dubuque.

Warren, P. M.
1982/83 "Knossos: Stratigraphical Museum Excavations, 1978–82. Part II", *AR* 29, 63–87.
2005 "Response to Eleni Hatzaki, 'Postpalatial Knossos: Town and Cemeteries from LM III A2 to LM III C'", 97–103 in: *Ariadne's Threads*.

Fig. 1 Khamalevri. Pateras. Ground plan and section A–A of the excavation

Fig. 2 Open air-space N+M

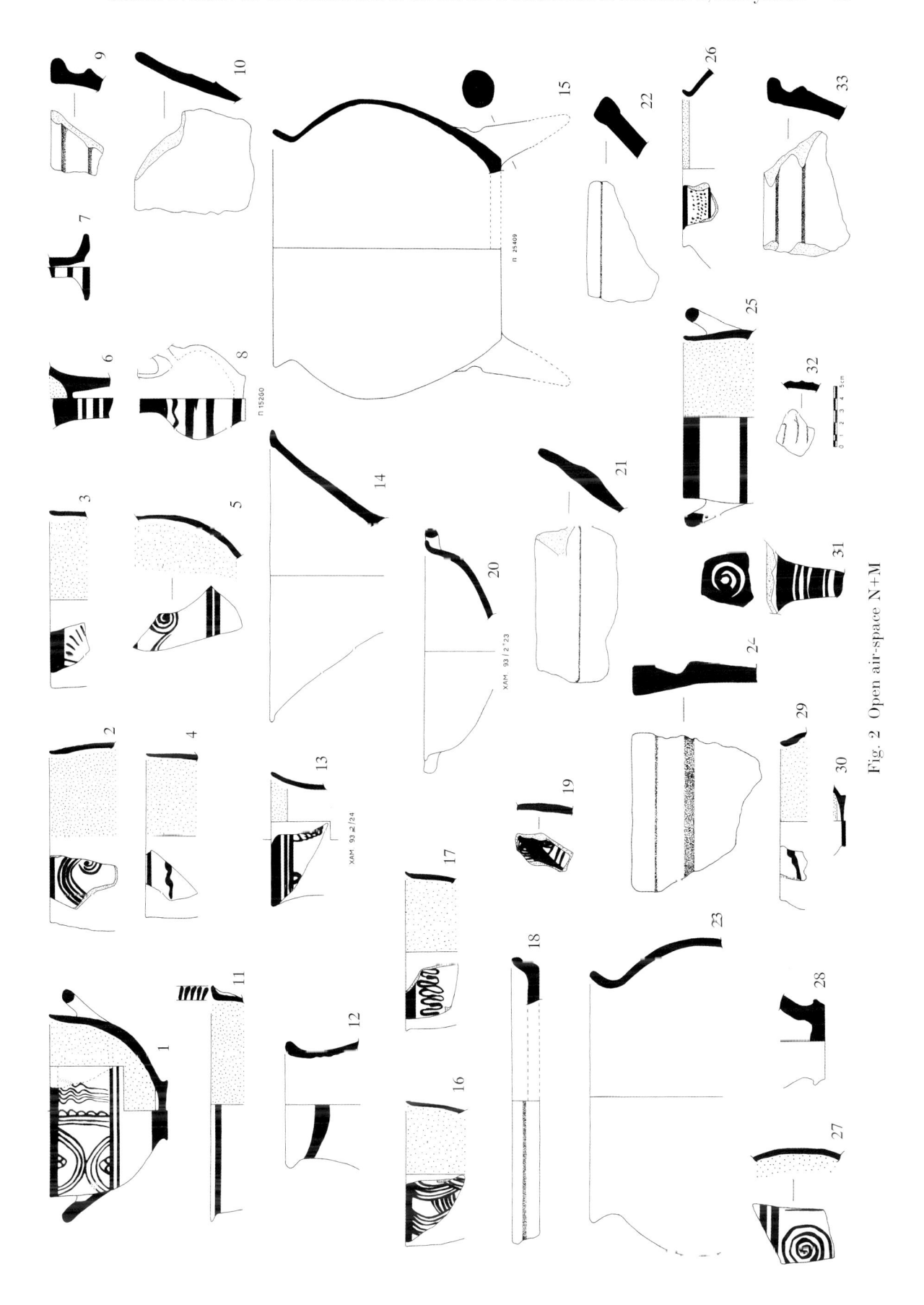

Fig. 3 Open air-space N+M

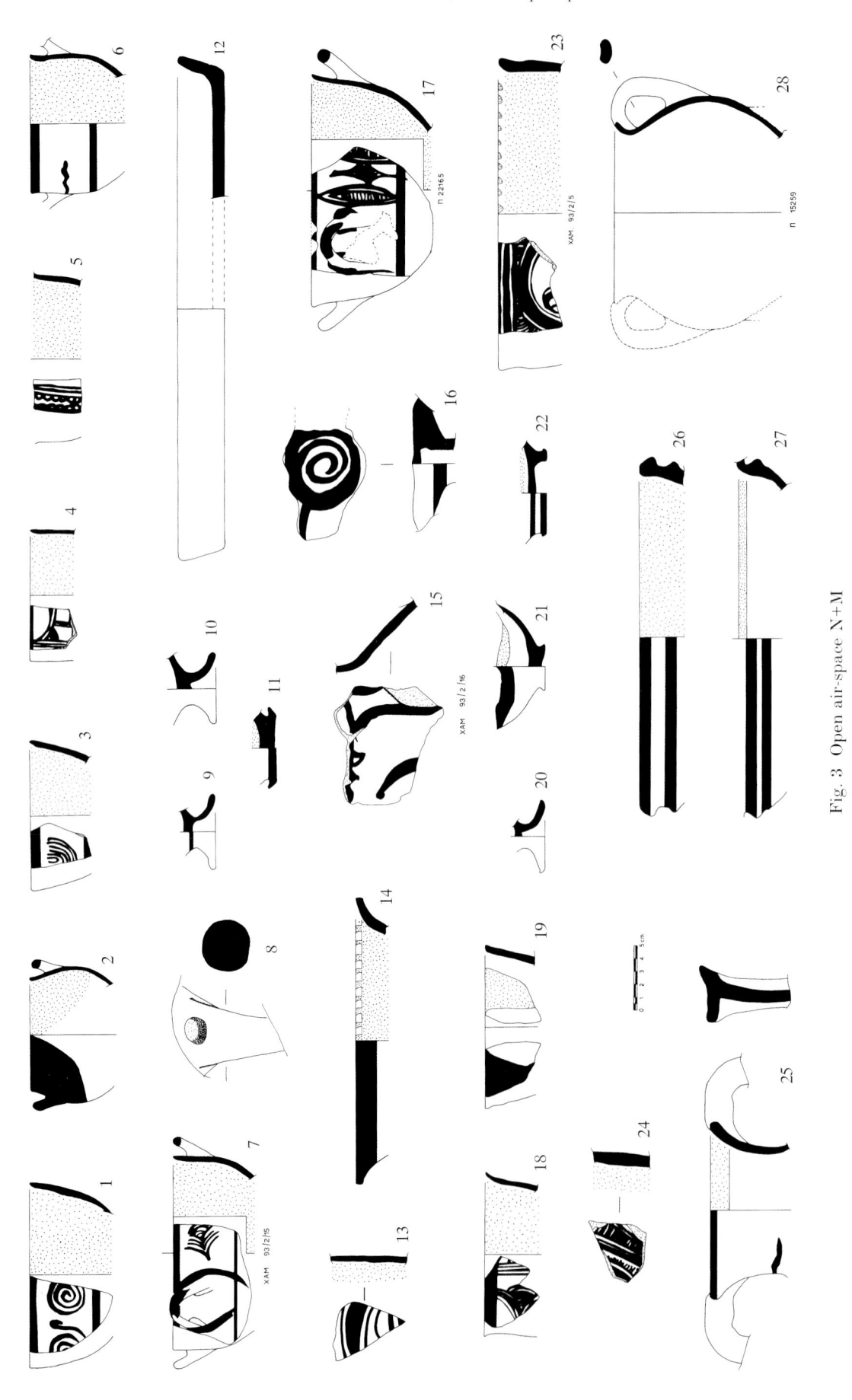

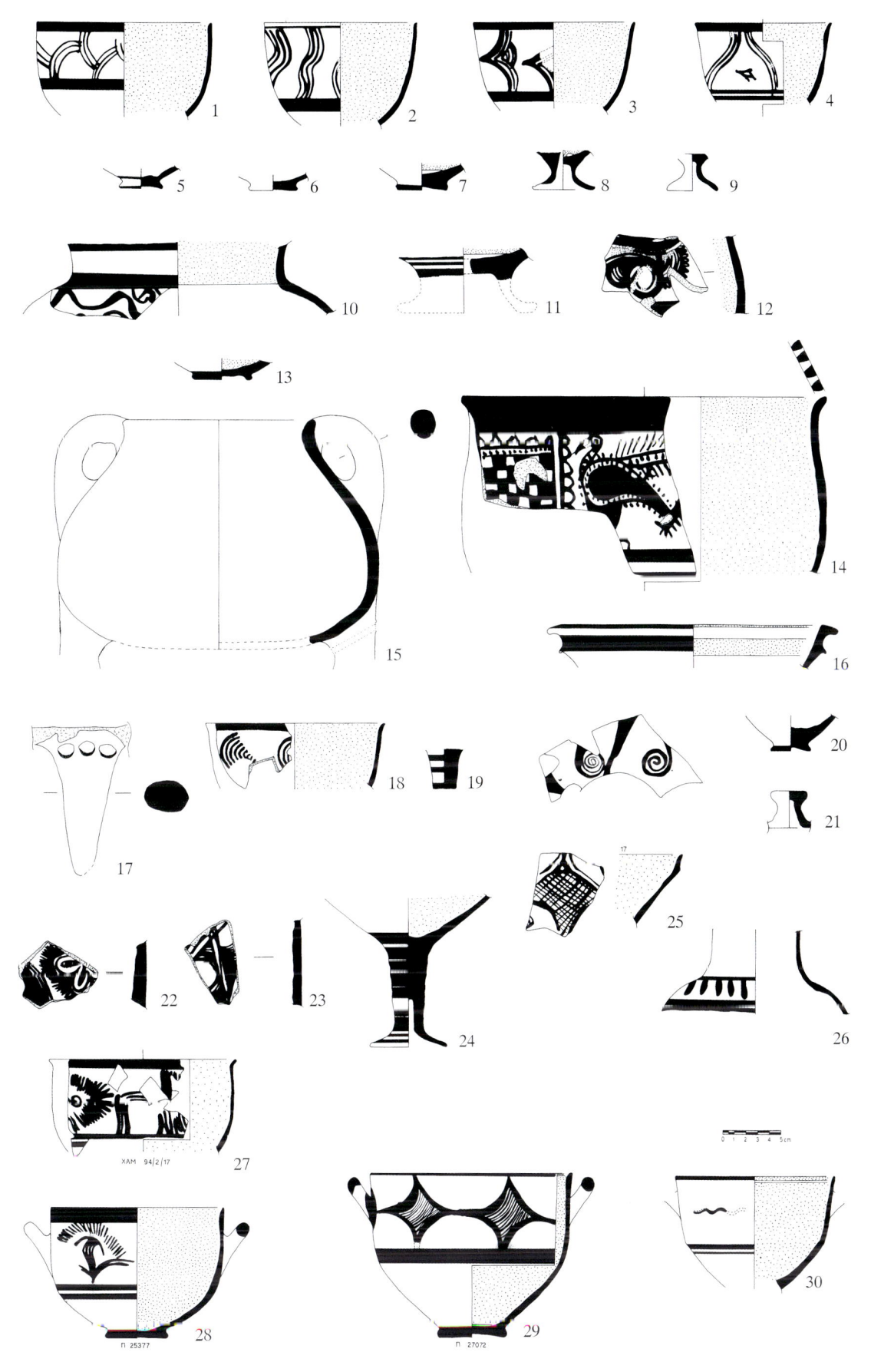

Fig. 4 Area of the pottery kiln and *varia*

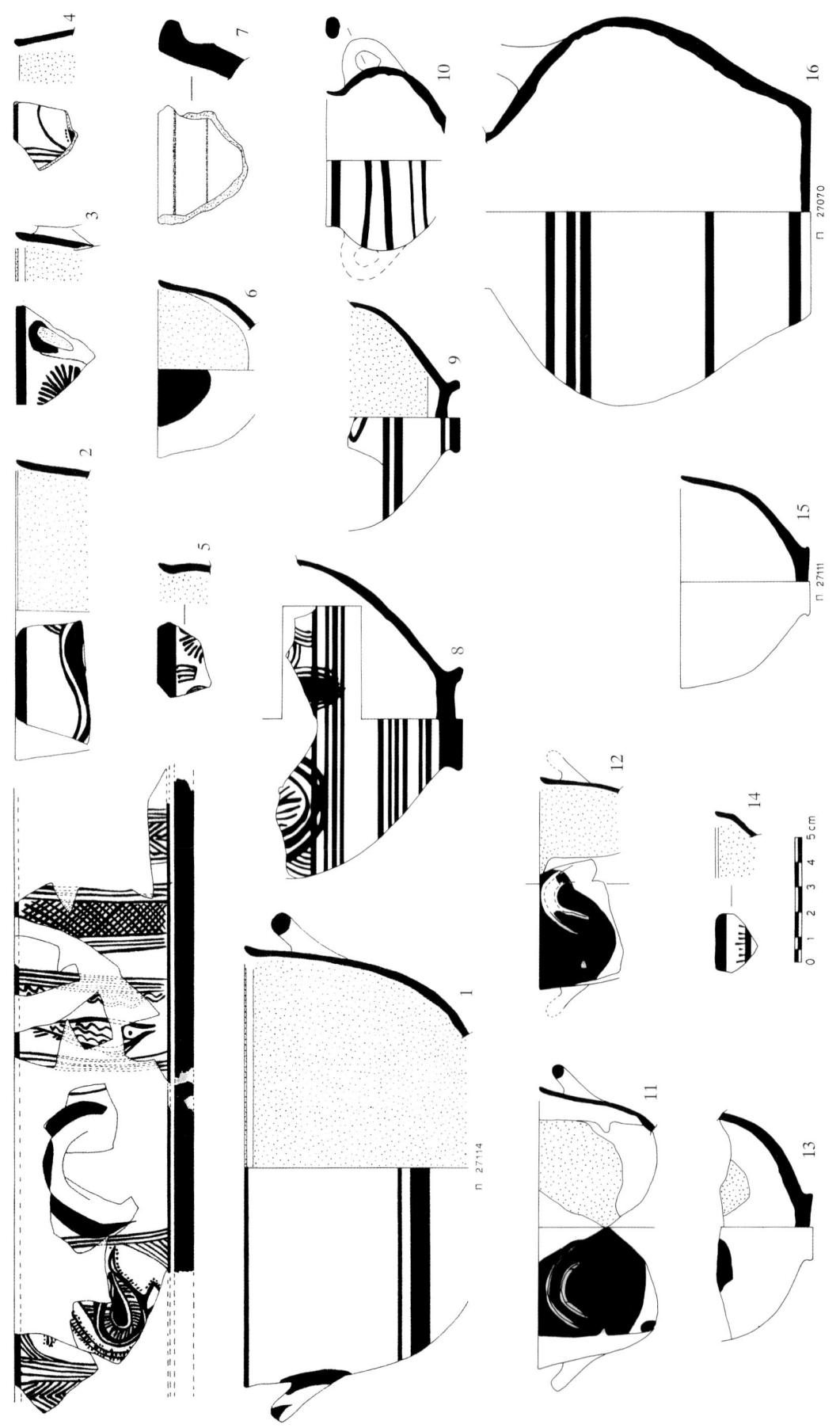

48 Maria Andreadaki-Vlazaki, Eleni Papadopoulou

Fig. 5 Room ΣΤ

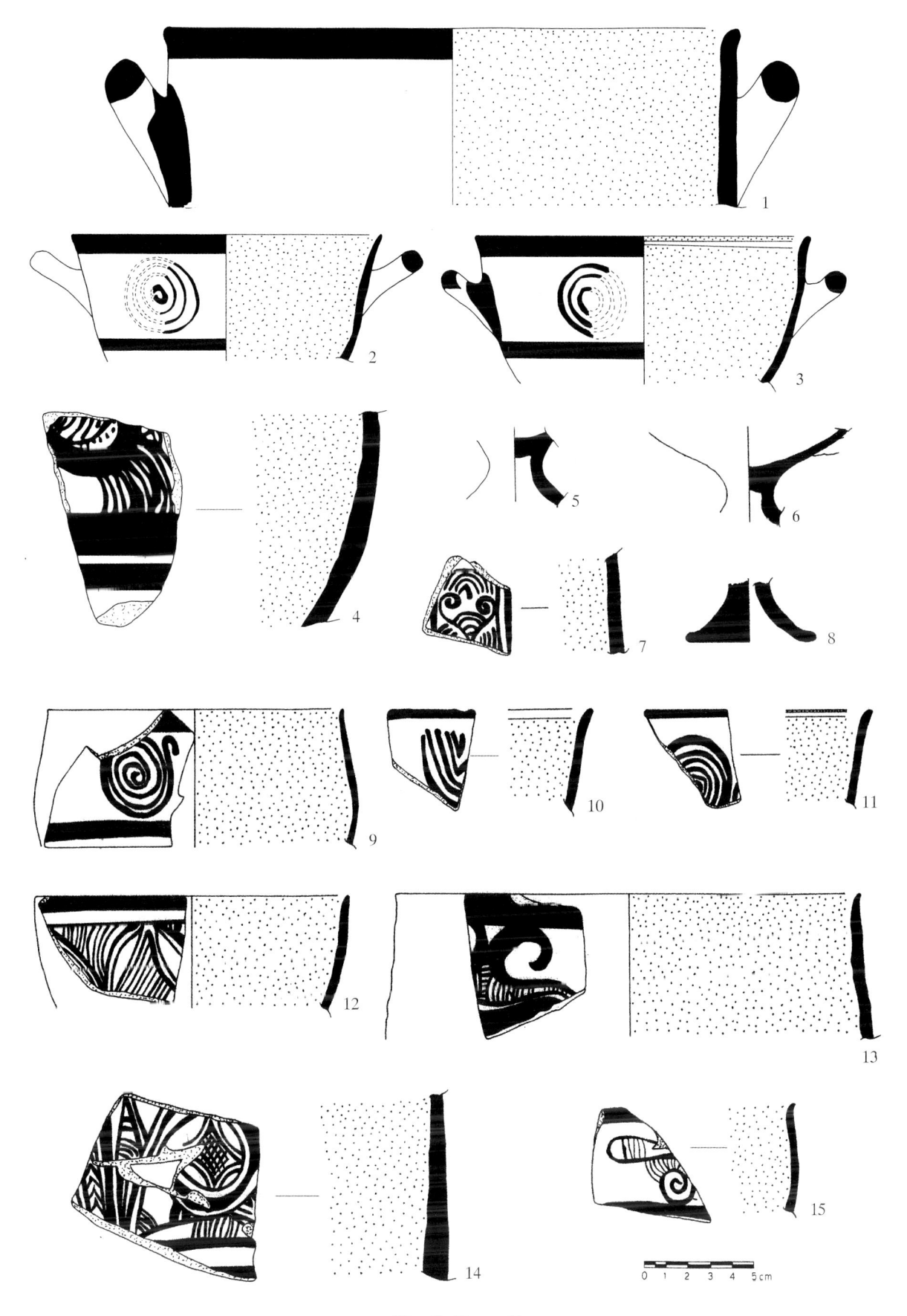

Fig. 6 Room E

Fig. 7 Room Z

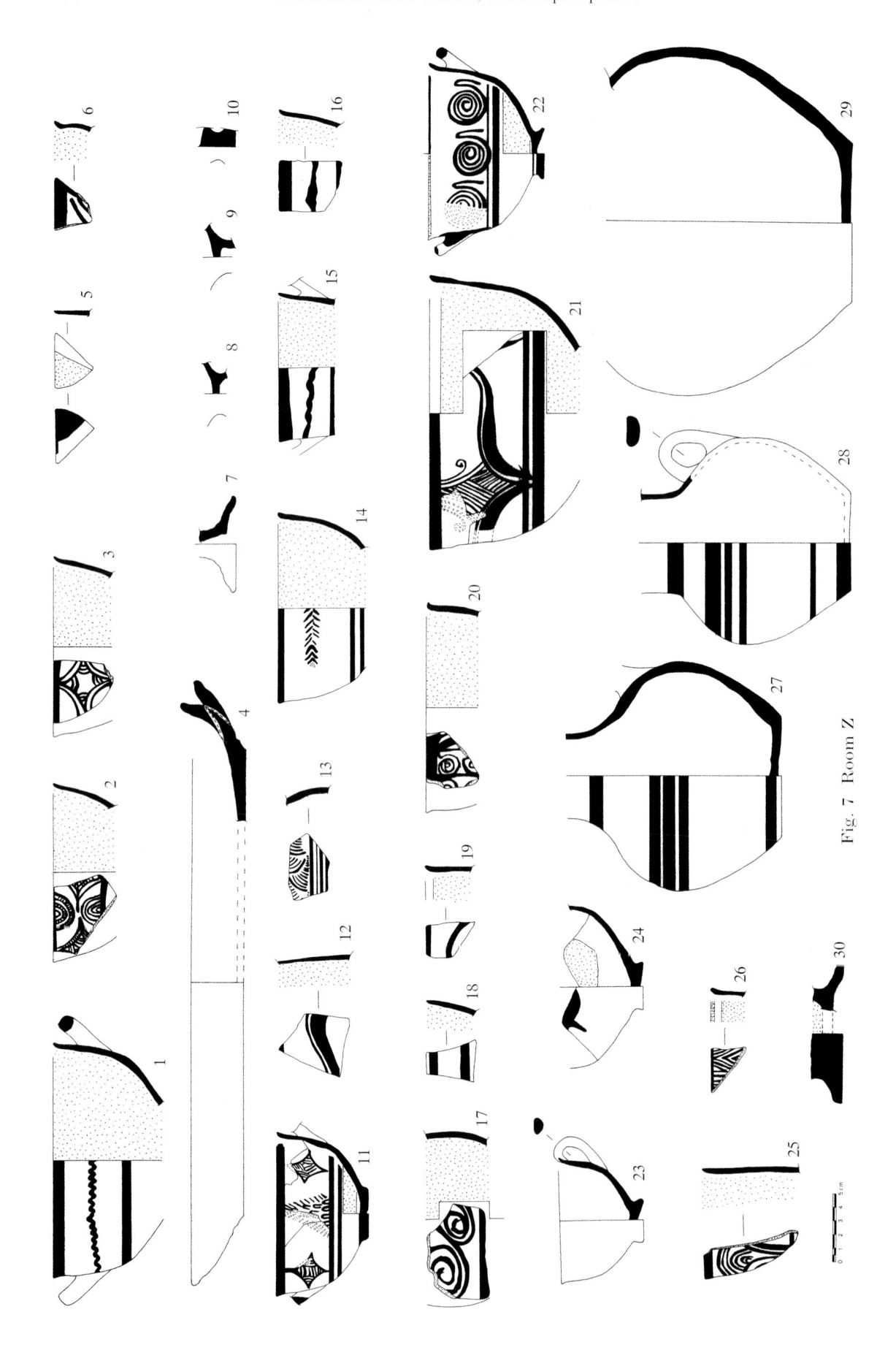

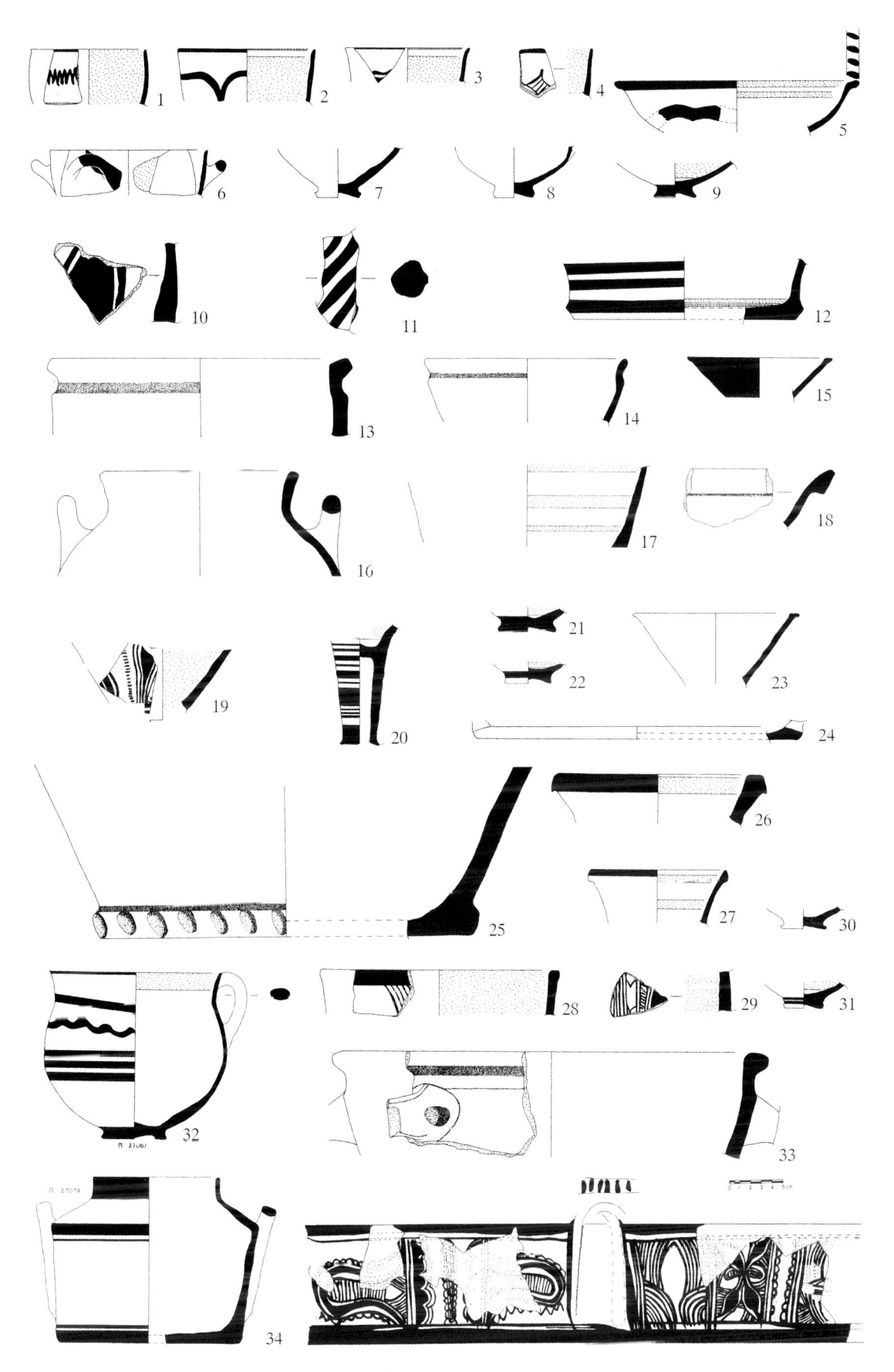

Fig. 8 Room H

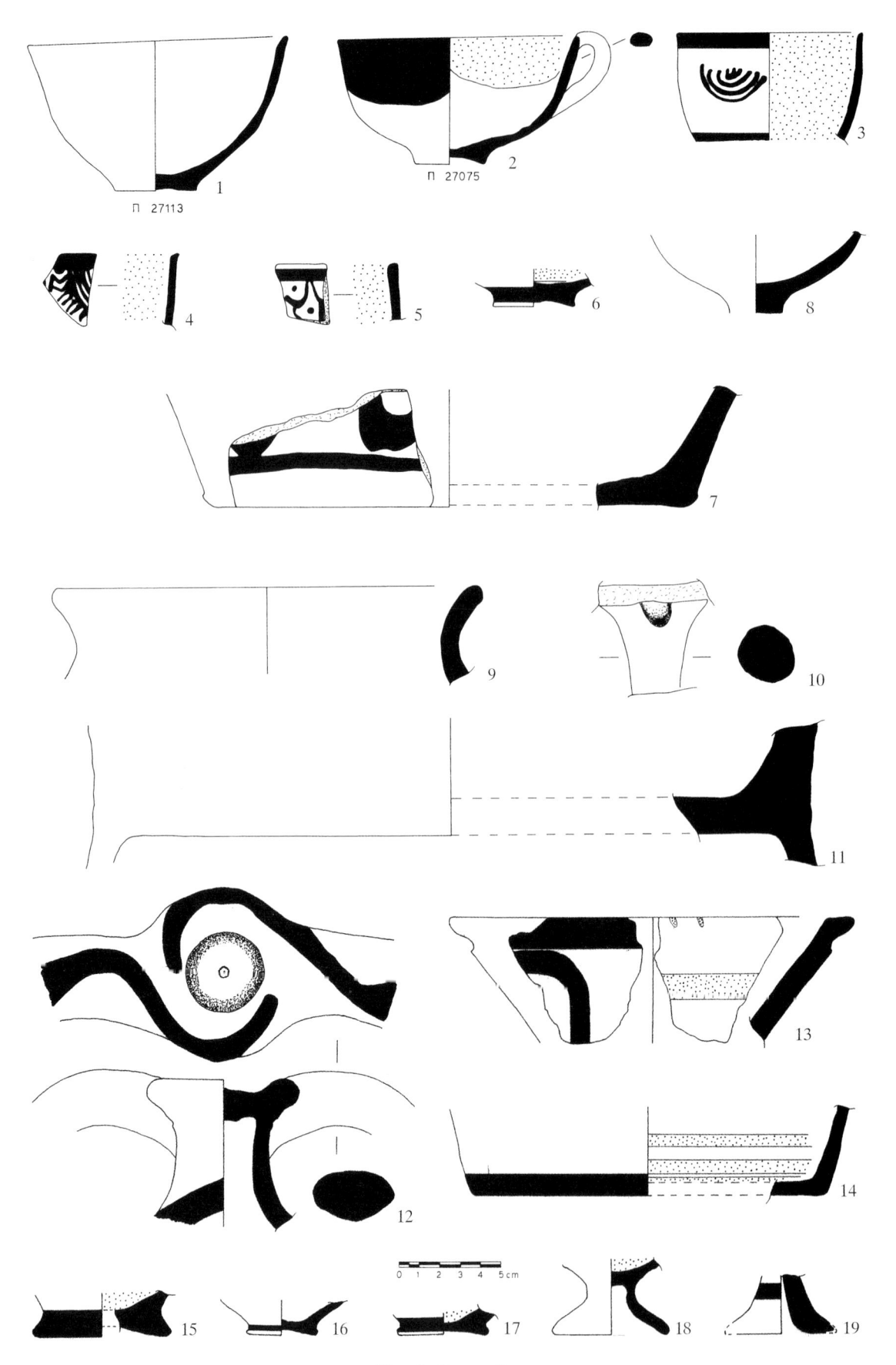

Fig. 9 Room Θ

Fig. 10 Room I and Room K

ELISABETTA BORGNA

LM III C POTTERY AT PHAISTOS: AN ATTEMPT TO INTEGRATE TYPOLOGICAL ANALYSIS WITH STRATIGRAPHIC INVESTIGATION*

Late Minoan III Phaistos is known in the literature only through preliminary, incomplete publications of pottery coming from old excavations, first by L. Pernier and later by D. Levi.[1] Large quantities of pottery lie on the shelves of the Stratigraphical Museum at Phaistos, as well as in the Archaeological Museum, Heraklion, where they are waiting to be systematically edited (see e.g. KANTA 1980, 96–101).

I tried to fulfil such a task with my work on the material of the "Acropoli Mediana", which has been finally published (BORGNA 2003a). On that occasion I attempted to establish a pattern for the diachronic, cultural and functional dynamics which characterised the development of the settlement of Phaistos in the post-palatial period from the point of view of its eminent acropolis.

This plot was submitted to a rescue excavation, which hindered the excavators from recording any indications that might help to correlate the stratigraphy and the huge deposit of pottery which was brought to light (see in particular LEVI 1956). Therefore, for the study of the ceramics, I have tried to construct internal typologies in order to build up a reliable sequence of the Phaistos productions, which I have tested by undertaking a thorough review of LM III B–III C edited pottery. The pottery, which was mostly discarded during a series of possibly ritual actions, seemed to represent a period lasting from the end of III B until somewhere in the middle of III C, with a few indications of later occupation.

The recent edition of the stratified pottery, from both the III B late and the III C settlements at Chania, strongly supports at least some of my proposals, which could not be based on either stratigraphic or contextual data (*GSE II*. – *GSE III*).

It now seems clear that the Minoan-Mycenaean interaction within the pottery system began well before the beginning of LM III C, as seems to be demonstrated by the occurrence of deep bowls imitating Mycenaean types already in LM III B2 (cf. KANTA 2003a, 168). At that time, the Mycenaean stylistic component seems to have been represented by both imports and imitations of Mainland types of the FS 284 deep bowl, as well as by the adoption of such decorative patterns as antithetic spirals and panels. Such a stylistic component was, however, still clearly separated from the local stylistic tradition detectable in other types of deep bowl, in particular the hemispheric, the rounded

---

* I would like to express my warm thanks to Sigrid Deger-Jalkotzy and Michaela Zavadil for inviting me to participate in the workshop. The drawings are by Giuliano Merlatti and belong to the archive of the Scuola Archeologica Italiana; I am grateful to its Director, Emanuele Greco, for permitting their publication.

[1] For the history of the investigations and literature on LM III Phaistos see BORGNA 2003a, 29–41. – BORGNA 2006.

or deep-bellied, and the distinctly articulated or angular bowls – all vessels that are well-rooted in the Minoan tradition, as well as the choice of the decorative language.[2]

Small dimensions, low walls, and unarticulated or only slightly distinct, small rims are features that distinguish III B bowls (BORGNA 2003a, pls. 2:1–2; 5:33–36; 15:164–165);[3] in time, the hemispheric exemplars are characterised by higher straight walls, while the rounded deep-bellied ones, which seem to have derived their shape from the repertoire of LM III cups, become much larger and show everted or flaring rims and convex walls (BORGNA 2003a, pls. 2:3–10; 5:38–39; 6). Both the type of the hemispheric bowl and the articulated one with a conical body, whose shape also depends on earlier cups, are recognisable at the beginning of LM III C by the marked outward inclination of their walls, which gives them an angular profile (BORGNA 2003a, pls. 3:11–15; 4:16–23),[4] corresponding to the carinated type of B. Hallager at Chania (*GSE II*, 138, pl. 35). At the same time, the Mycenaean repertoire of deep bowls is increased by the appearance of various other types, including both bowls with sinuous walls and high flaring rims (BORGNA 2003a, pls. 8–9. – *GSE III*, 208), and articulated bowls with a conical body and straight walls (BORGNA 2003a, 184–187, pls. 10–11).[5]

The III B chronology of a discrete variety of kraters is verified at Chania as well: the specimens which were dated earlier at Phaistos find strict comparisons in the III B2 settlement, in particular a globular type with a distinct, mostly rounded rim, and an articulated one with straight walls which seems to derive from Mainland patterns (FS 281) (BORGNA 2003a, pls. 30:2; 35:42; 60:1. – *GSE III*, 218–220, 262. – HALLAGER 2003, 109. – KANTA 2003a, 171).

Besides a few indications of III B late occupation, the bulk of the Acropoli material, however, points to a flourishing III C settlement. Due to the lack of a detailed stratigraphy, subdivisions within the LM III C pottery were obviously very difficult to detect, all the more so when we consider that III C phases are not definitely assessed in Crete on the basis of pottery, which is generally divided into an earlier and a later III C horizon (KANTA 2003b. – D'AGATA 2003, in particular 26–29. – See the discussion in this volume).

On the basis of the Acropoli evidence, I have provisionally considered as belonging to an advanced phase of III C, possibly III C "Middle", such vessels as: later types and varieties of deep bowls, in particular slightly-articulated vessels with high convex or convergent walls, namely vessels pointing to a complete integration of models belonging either to the Minoan or the Mycenaean tradition (BORGNA 2003a, pls. 6:40; 12–14; 17); articulated kraters, which are close to the late Mainland typological FS 282 varieties, such as kraters with biconical profile and walls inclined inwards, and angular or carinated kraters with ridges below the rim (BORGNA 2003a, pls. 37:51,53; 38:64–66; for com-

---

[2] On the problem of distinct stylistic components and their integration see BORGNA 1997b. – Cf. *GSE III*, 208.

[3] On the typology of deep bowls and their diachronic evolution see BORGNA 2003a, 176–219, on earlier local types and their origin IBID., 181–184, 187–188.

[4] I have constructed the morphological typology of the Acropoli pottery by assuming, as a relevant principle, the basic difference between articulated and unarticulated profiles: in the manufacture of articulated shapes the basic parts of the vessel, such as body, walls and rim, are well-defined components apparently linked organically – whether connected by a continuous profile or marked by angular junctions; by contrast, unarticulated shapes seem to have been conceived by the producers as a whole without clear partitions; cf. BORGNA 2003a, 22–23, 180.

[5] These bowls seem to be very close to Type 3 deep bowls of the LH III B–III C Transitional phase (MOUNTJOY 1997, 111, fig. 11:65–72).

ments and comparisons see IBID., 176–219, 269–287. – Cf. BORGNA 1997b). The articulated stemmed kraters with a continuous profile, provided with slightly everted or rounded rims, which are very similar to huge stemmed bowls, have been kept as indicators of a possibly developed III C phase as well (BORGNA 2003a, pls. 32:14–16; 33).

Regarding the most recent evidence within the Acropoli pottery, I have tentatively attributed to a "late" III C phase a few isolated vessels, such as a pilgrim flask and an elongated stirrup jar decorated with cross-hatched triangles (BORGNA 2003a, 293–295, pls. 41:2.1; 76:5).

Though the criteria used for distinguishing different III C phases within the Acropoli pottery are not objective, and therefore not completely reliable, the indications of a continuous occupation during an earlier part of III C are indisputable. The correlation I have tried to suggest between the end of this occupation – namely the sealing of the deposit on the Acropoli – and an earlier part of III C Middle on the Mainland (III C Middle developed) (BORGNA 1999a, 360), seems now to be encouraged by the dynamics that have been put forward for the occupation of several Cretan III C sites. These, according to A. Kanta and other scholars, flourished during an earlier part of III C and possibly lasted up to the middle of the period, namely until the beginning of a new pottery horizon, which was characterised by the appearance of elaborately decorated kraters (KANTA 2003b, in particular 526–529. – KANTA 2003a, 168). Patterns of cultural and social unity, together with continuity in the pottery production, seem to mark this settlement phase, which would have come to an end towards an advanced III C date, possibly coinciding with dramatic gaps in the island settlement patterns as a consequence of change and disturbance (BORGNA 2003b).

A kind of continuity in pottery productions from the beginning of III C well into III C Middle (developed, according to Mainland subdivisions) has already been inferred in other Aegean contexts as well, as for example in Rhodes, where, according to P. A. Mountjoy, III C Early vessels cannot be easily distinguished from III C Middle developed products (*RMDP*, 45).

On the present occasion I would like to offer a deeper insight into the pottery system of post-palatial Phaistos by verifying by the way of stratigraphic support the previous results that had been obtained on a purely typological basis. A careful review of the structural growth and the stratigraphy of the "Casa a ovest del Piazzale I" – an important LM III building on the western edge of the palatial site and at the foot of the Acropoli (Fig. 1:1) – has enabled me to find grounds for testing the evolution of the pottery during a sequence of sub-phases beginning with LM III B2 and ending with LM III C Late or Subminoan (see already LAVIOSA 1977. – BORGNA 2001, with literature).

The building was excavated in the 1960s by the Italian School under the direction of D. Levi and the supervision of C. Laviosa. Obviously the methods and criteria then adopted for both the fieldwork and the processing of the findings do not meet present-day expectations. The location of the building on a slope which was intensely inhabited in both previous Neopalatial and later Hellenistic times makes it clear that reading and comprehending the stratigraphy are very difficult and subjectivity cannot be avoided.

To go into detail, the most recent floors were most probably removed in Hellenistic times, so the upper layers are not to be considered as closed deposits; nor is the southern part of the building, including the walls founded on the lower part of the slope, retrievable. Furthermore, the structural and depositional dynamics that affected the building seem to account for the lack of reliable floor deposits such as homogeneous associations of vessels. These could attest short spans of time and be used as chronological markers of limited sub-phases. In very few cases sherds can be considered as found in situ on a floor. The pre-depositional frameworks have been thoroughly modified by means of continuous interventions and structural changes – in particular the raising of the floors, which were based on thick layers of broken ceramics mostly belonging to previous phases of inhabitation. When nothing was added something was removed, so that we are obliged to suppose that drastic clearances took place, which the huge deposits of discarded pottery, together with architectural and structural remains, would seem to confirm.

In short, a careful, albeit provisional and not definitive, revision of the stratigraphy indicates that the building seems to have developed in several phases which may be summarised as follows:

- at some point in LM III B the earliest rooms were founded, as seems to be attested by the sherds beneath the lowest floors, at least as far as the eastern sector is concerned, namely Rooms 1, 2, 4 and possibly 3;
- the life of the building in the period that immediately succeeded the foundation is not directly attested by material in situ, but only by considerable amounts of III B2 ceramics which were included in the deposits created in order to raise the floor levels;
- such floors were most probably laid at the beginning of LM III C, as a small percentage of the material (Room 1) seems to indicate. At the time of such rebuilding, the western sector of the house (future Rooms 5 and 6) was possibly an outdoor space, paved with pebbles;
- as for the III C Early occupation, we have no in situ evidence at all, as the floor deposits are mostly not preserved and most material which looks III C Early is included in the upper layers along with many more recent sherds;[6]
- a huge amount of III C Early broken vessels, which were found in the relatively small Room 4, together with remains of removed floors, point to a break in the depositional growth, involving some kind of clearance and discarding of pottery. This huge deposit consists mostly of ceramics whose style is markedly consistent with a III C Early date, and includes a few possibly later vessels which could date the sealing of the deposit a little further into III C. The consideration of some significative joins from different locations in the building, together with the finding of a cluster of removed pebbles within the deposit, help to clarify the dynamics of clearance and removal, including the outdoor pebbled floor in the western sector (Rooms 5 and 6) and, in Room 4, the III C Early floor, which seems to be attested by remains of unconnected stone slabs at the bottom of the huge deposit. Perhaps not a single but a series of discards, ritual in origin, might have brought about the deposition of the pottery and the final closing of the deposit during a span of time which may be correlated with the chronology of the "Acropoli Mediana" assemblage, itself an outcome of a series of possibly ritual discards during a period which was tentatively dated to III C Early and the earlier part of III C Middle;[7]
- as for the "Casa a ovest" we may conclude that well into III C an important reorganisation of the area took place, which, together with the discard in Room 4, implies the addition of a large new room provided with a continuous floor taking in both Rooms 5 and 6 on the western side of the building, and the foundation of new floors in the eastern sector, at least for Rooms 2 and 4;

---

[6] The floor in Room 1 may be considered an exception, though the material which was recorded in association with it may hardly be considered as a part of a set of vessels in situ.

[7] For ritual activities in both places see BORGNA 1997a. – BORGNA 2003a, 354–371. – BORGNA 2004a. – BORGNA 2004b.

- though the occupation in this III C Advanced phase is only scantily attested in the "Casa a ovest" on a stratigraphic and architectural basis, some evidence has been preserved thanks to the subsequent foundation of Room 5, which entailed the raising of the floor level in the residual part of Room 6, as well as the sealing of some broken pottery which had been used on the floor beneath. By comparing these sherds with those which have been classified as most recent in the deposit of Room 4, and, furthermore, with some other relevant evidence coming from the upper layers in the other Rooms (1–4), an advanced III C phase seems recognisable and distinguishable from a still later phase;
- more recent evidence comes, in particular, from the uppermost floor of Room 6 and the layers relating to the use of Room 5, whose late chronology has already been commented upon on a previous occasion (BORGNA 2001, 285–288).

On this basis I would like to introduce the most relevant pottery that will support the diachronic pattern which I have proposed for the building. From a pottery point of view in particular, such diachronic development may be discerned by visualising a sequence of five phases.

In the first phase, which is represented by the pottery underneath the lowest floors, the eastern sector of the building was constructed. At that moment bowls provided with low walls, mostly hemispheric or provided with a globular, deep-bellied body,[8] but also bowls with a much more sinuous profile, which are very close to the Mycenaean types of deep bowls,[9] and furthermore globular or hemispheric fine deep cups, shallow cups with low straight walls,[10] large bowls or kraters, provided with articulated profiles, very simple everted rims and flat bases[11] – all point to a date still well into LM III B. As for closed shapes, it is worth mentioning the presence of fine medium-sized globular belly-handled amphorae.[12] The clear connections of such pottery not only with the productions of the III B late settlement of Chania but also with some III B earlier assemblages, such as the one recently published from the South House at Knossos by P. A. Mountjoy (MOUNTJOY 2003: for deep bowls: 148, fig. 4:42 nos. 783–784, 796–797; for cups: 148, fig. 4:42 nos. 779, 781), might indicate that the "Casa a ovest" at Phaistos was founded not very late into III B2. Decorative patterns, such as chains of quirks, semicircles, and bivalve shells seem to find resemblances within III B assemblages, as is possible to detect at Chania (*GSE III*, 206–207, fig. 49, 262) and Kommos (WATROUS 1992, figs. 45–46; 52; pl. 36). Other features such as, from a technological point of view, the irregular manufacture and thickness of the walls and the uncertain outline of many drawn patterns

---

[8] BORGNA 2001, 289, fig. 8; see above. – Cf. e.g. at LM III B Malia: FARNOUX 1997, 264, 266, figs. 5; 7. Chania: *GSE III*, pls. 49–50, in particular pl. 49:71-P0813. Kommos: WATROUS 1992, nos. 1247, 1557. Knossos, Unexplored Mansion: POPHAM 1984, pl. 179:1. For more detailed comments and comparisons cf. BORGNA 2003a, 181–184.

[9] Phaistos: BORGNA 2003a, pl. 9. Cf. Chania: *GSE III*, pl. 51. Kommos: WATROUS 1992, no. 1155. – RUTTER 2003, fig. 14:2. The common occurrence of solidly painted inner walls is not to be considered a chronological marker in Central Crete: cf. HALLAGER 2003, 109.

[10] BORGNA 2001, 289, fig. 8, 291, fig. 9:2. For III B deep cups with comparisons: BORGNA 2003a, 220–237. – Cf. WATROUS 1992, no. 1431. – POPHAM 1970a, pl. 49b. – POPHAM 1984, pls. 179:1; 180:3. – WARREN 1997, fig. 32. – *GSE III*, pls. 45–46. For low-walled cups BORGNA 2003a, 226–227 with literature.

[11] BORGNA 2001, 289, fig. 8:4–5. Chania: *GSE III*, pls. 58:84-P0950, 73-P1071; 59:80-P0472. – KANTA 1997, fig. 3:2 ("Mycenaean import" in level 11 of Kastelli).

[12] See for comparisons in particular a typical shape of the "italo-micenea" ware from Broglio di Trebisacce and Termitito: VAGNETTI – PANICHELLI 1994, 402–403, no. 13, fig. 132:3. – VAGNETTI 1982, pl. 22:1.

(BORGNA 2001, 290), and the presence of particular coarse ware shapes, such as incense-burners or pedestal bowls and wide-mouthed pots[13] among the kitchen ware may be considered as indicators of an early chronology as well.

The second phase is represented by the layers which may be interpreted as filling deposits suitable for the preparation of new floors, in particular in Rooms 1, 2 and 3. In such deposits, several features may be isolated as relevant for defining a ceramic horizon still rooted in LM III B: the as yet limited occurrence of Mycenaean types of deep bowls, which belong almost exclusively to either a type with high vertical walls or a type provided with only slightly flaring walls and everted rims (Fig. 1:2. – See at Chania *GSE III*, pl. 51:73-P0581, 84-P1451, 80-P0478); the occurrence of both hemispheric and globular bowls with low walls (Fig. 1:3); the persistence of a technological horizon that we are tempted to define as "experimental" or "formative" as regards both manufacture and decoration – which is particularly manifest in the field of a new shape, namely the deep bowl. These are the most significant features, together with the almost general absence of bowls with inner reserved band, as well as of linear deep cups resembling the Mainland FS 215 cup (RUTTER 2003, 197), and of typical III C decorative patterns such as streamers, hooked spirals and elaborate motifs (except some uncertain instances) (*GSE II*, 140–141, fig. 31). Kraters, mainly globular with an everted rounded rim, but also slightly articulated with vertical walls and a simple everted rim,[14] as well as decorated cups and footed bowls,[15] seem to point to III B productions as well. The most helpful comparisons for such pottery are to be found in LM III B late contexts, as we may verify at Chania, Malia and Kommos, in particular for the articulated bowls with straight walls and everted rims,[16] and also at Kommos for hemispheric bowls with high walls and deep-bellied ones (*GSE III*, pl. 50. – WATROUS 1992, figs. 56:1483; 61:1648. – Cf. also WARREN 1997, 173, fig. 28 row 2); at III B Knossos we find a good comparison for the shallow bowl (Fig. 1:4. – WARREN 1997, fig. 22 row 3). A few vessels which seem to be closer to III C products, such as an amphoriskos with dotted rim and a globular krater with a markedly everted rim, find reliable comparisons in LM III B Late contexts as well, in particular at Chania.[17] However, some isolated pieces, which seem to be actually datable to III C, such as a large articulated deep bowl or an unarticulated one with high convex walls and decorated with inner reserved band and streamers, may be explained either as intrusive on stratigraphic grounds (as they were mostly found at points where later structural interventions are documented, for instance the foundation of stairs built at the cost of earlier deposits) or as chronological markers of the sealing of such deposits at the beginning of LM III C for laying the new floors. Both an isolated rim with inner reserved band and an elaborately decorated sherd from a krater seem to point to such a date.[18] As has

---

[13] Both shapes do not seem to be typical of III C coarse assemblages, which are mostly characterised by pots provided with restricted openings; cf. BORGNA 1997a. – KANTA 2003a, 173–177. For incense-burners see e.g. POPHAM 1970b, 192, fig. 1. – *GSE III*, 243.

[14] Chania: *GSE III*: for globular shapes with rounded rims: pls. 58:71-P0417; 59:80-P1457; for articulated rims with straight walls: e.g. pl. 59:80-P1429, 84-P0531, 80-P0482, 01-P0656.

[15] For footed bowls cf. KARANTZALI 1986, 63, fig. 12, 70. – HALLAGER 1997, 408 B 4. – *GSE III*, 198, fig. 48 no. 11, 209; cf. at Malia: FARNOUX 1989/90, 31, fig. 17.

[16] Chania: *GSE III*, pl. 52:71-P0761. Kommos: WATROUS 1992, no. 1557. Malia: FARNOUX 1992, 210, fig. 14.

[17] For the krater: *GSE III*, pl. 59:82-P0167. For the dotted rim and coated neck of the amphoriskos see at Sklavoi: KANTA 1980, fig. 76:1 (piriform jar, III B).

[18] For the sporadic occurrence of bowls with inner reserved bands at III B Chania see, however, *GSE III*, 210.

already been suggested, however, only a very low percentage of the material from this second phase may be classified as III C Early, while most of the pottery seems to be consistent with an earlier chronological horizon, namely the lifespan of the building from its initial construction until the first rebuilding. The inclusion of III B sherds within the walls which, on stratigraphic grounds, are supposed to have been raised at the beginning of III C, seems to support such a conclusion.

The chronological interpretation of this pottery horizon is subject to much dispute as, according to some scholars – in particular on the basis of clear connections with III B2 Chania – the pottery horizon without reserved bands and elaborate style would be consistent with a LM III B2 date;[19] according to others, however, the appearance of both bowls with reserved bands and the elaborate or noble style only after the beginning of III C would support an attribution of such pottery to the very beginning of III C Early.[20] This seems to be the case, for example, at Kastelli Pediada and at Thronos/Sybrita.[21] The stratigraphic position of the Phaistian deposit, which seems to include mostly pottery used immediately after the foundation of the house, would perhaps fit better with a chronology still late in III B. Comparisons and connections for such pottery may be found, however, not only in pure III B contexts but also within possibly later assemblages, such as the LH III B–C Early Transitional ones, according to the terminology of P. A. Mountjoy, which might be useful for establishing Mainland-Cretan chronological correlations (MOUNTJOY 1997. – See in particular *RMDP*, 36–38).[22]

As for the third phase, we have to turn to the huge amount of pottery discarded in Room 4. There, together with some undisputedly earlier – namely III B – and a few possibly later ceramics, to be dated well into III C, we recognise a typical III C Early pottery horizon, which fits in very well with the bulk of the material from the "Acropoli Mediana".

As for deep bowls, the inner reserved band occurs sporadically: the "Mycenaean" stylistic connection is now shown by more types of deep bowls, such as bowls with markedly sinuous walls and high flaring rims (Fig. 1:5)[23] together with articulated bowls with a conical body and straight walls (Fig. 1:6),[24] while types well-rooted in the Minoan tradition include hemispheric bowls with high walls inclined outwards (Fig. 1:7).[25] Some hybrid shapes, namely bowls with convex walls, which cannot be easily attributed to either the Minoan or the Mycenaean tradition, occur as well (see BORGNA 2003a, 181, type B 5). Bowls are mainly decorated with chains of linear motifs belonging to both the Minoan and the Mycenaean stylistic languages, but a discrete variety of more complex motifs occurs, which expresses an impressively rich and lively stylistic milieu, much

---

[19] In particular *GSE II*, 147, 172–173 for the beginning of III C with the appearance of bowls with inner reserved bands and the elaborate style.

[20] KANTA 1997. – KANTA 2003a, 176–178 in particular for the reserved bands; for the occurrence of vessels decorated with the elaborate style already in III C Early layers see IBID., 179.

[21] Kastelli Pediada: RETHEMIOTAKIS 1997, phase 1 (consider however the discussion on pp. 327–336). Thronos/Sybrita: D'AGATA 1999, 192–193. – D'AGATA 2001, 54, fig. 5. – D'AGATA 2003, in particular 28 for the appearance of both reserved bands and a more complex decorative style on deep bowls.

[22] For a more articulated chronological assessment of the deposits included in Mountjoy's Transitional phase see however VITALE 2006. I am very grateful to S. Vitale for permitting me to read his work when it was still unpublished.

[23] See e.g. *GSE II*, pl. 36:84-P0689; for the typological classification of LM III C deep bowls depending upon Mycenaean influence see BORGNA 2003a, 181–189, types B 2–4.

[24] *GSE II*, pl. 36:70-P0160. – KANTA 2003a, 168–171, fig. 1a. – D'AGATA 1999, 189, fig. 4:3.10. Cf. also the Type 3 bowl of Mountjoy's Transitional phase, e.g. *RMDP*, 282 no. 164, fig. 94.

[25] "Carinated" bowls according to the terminology adopted at Chania: *GSE II*, pl. 35 (e.g. 71-P0728).

influenced by Mainland patterns. Typical Minoan III C motifs, such as streamers, are very common as well. The elaborate style participates in the creation of such a milieu, but it is mainly limited to kraters (Fig. 2:1). Kraters have now the typical III C look as regards not only decoration but also shape, which is mostly articulated and provided with triangular or other clearly distinct rims (Fig. 2:2. – *GSE II*, 146–147, pls. 40–41. – In general, with literature: BORGNA 2003a, 273, 277–279. – KANTA 2003a, 171). As for other open vessels, while the ornamental style is exclusively adopted for deep bowls, blob cups and champagne cups occur (BORGNA 2003a, 229. – KANTA 1997, 96. – *GSE II*, 137. – D'AGATA 1999, 190–191, figs. 5:3.17; 6:3.1 [phase 1, III C Early]) together with many deep linear cups similar to FS 215 (Fig. 2:3) or cups decorated with wavy bands. Apart from hemispheric, globular and articulated cups with conical body and straight walls, which are well-rooted in the earlier local tradition, the occurrence of both deep cups provided with profiles very similar to deep bowls and monochrome carinated cups or FS 240 might be considered as diagnostic (Fig. 2:4).[26] The occurrence of some typical Mycenaean shapes, such as the linear basin or shallow bowl (FS 294–295) (Fig. 2:5), which seems to have been very common in the Aegean during LH III C Early and Middle (BENZI 1993. – Aigeira, LH III C Early: DEGER-JALKOTZY 2003, 56. – Cf. *MDP*, 153. – *RMDP*, 43, 49. – RUTTER 2003, 197), could also help to establish chronological correlations and connections. For the time being, the most manifest connections seem to be detectable in some III C Early Mycenaean peripheral assemblages, such as those in Laconia (*RMDP*, 282–287) and in the Aegean islands, particularly in III C Early (and possibly Middle developed) Phylakopi and Rhodes (*RMDP*, 912–927, figs. 374–375 [Melos] and 1027–1066 [Rhodes]), but also in III C "Früh" Tiryns (PODZUWEIT 1978, in particular 475, fig. 28. – PODZUWEIT 1979, 416, fig. 37). As for Crete, the LM III C settlement at Chania provides us once again with the closest comparisons (*GSE II*).

Some evidence in the III C pottery discarded in Room 4 might, on a stylistic and typological basis, be dated later in the period: some deep bowls provided with very high walls, whose profile is a mixture of the local Minoan and the Mycenaean traditions, such as vessels with a very low body and high vertical or slightly convex walls (Fig. 2:6) together with very deep bowls with expanded rounded body and markedly convex walls, as well as bell-like exemplars with an expanded rounded body and restricted mouths (BORGNA 2001, 286, fig. 7:2); in addition, some bowls with complex but roughly executed patterns. All are features that seem to anticipate a more advanced III C stylistic horizon and find comparisons in LM III C "Late" contexts, such as at Chalasmenos (COULSON – TSIPOPOULOU 1994, pl. 12:6. – See now TSIPOPOULOU 2004 [III C "Middle"]), Kavousi Vronda (DAY 1997) and the Kephala tomb near Knossos (CADOGAN 1967, 260, fig. 2:11,14. – See also D'AGATA 2003, 30, fig. 3:2).

Cups with high flaring rims (Fig. 2:7),[27] small or miniature bell-shaped cups with a wavy band immediately below the rim (Fig. 2:8),[28] narrow raised or slightly hollowed bases or low conical feet for open vessels[29] are further features which might indicate that the deposit in Room 4 was definitively sealed at some point later than III C Early, and

---

[26] For the carinated cup in LH III C Early assemblages see e.g. DEGER-JALKOTZY 2003, 57, fig. 2:12 (Aigeira). – Cf. *RMDP*, 230 no. 182, fig. 74 (Rutter phases 2 and 3). – RUTTER 2003, 197.

[27] Kavousi Vronda: DAY 1997, 400, fig. 6:2. Kavousi Kastro: MOOK – COULSON 1997, fig. 18:80 (Phase II). Thronos: D'AGATA 2003, fig. 2:6.

[28] See in particular in III C "Entwickelt" Tiryns: PODZUWEIT 1981, 209, fig. 58:5. – *RMDP*, 169 no. 358, fig. 48.

[29] KANTA 1997, 86, fig. 1. – Cf. D'AGATA 2003, 29, as a feature of LM III C "Late" contexts.

possibly at the same time when pottery included in our next phase (4) was circulating. Also the isolated occurrence of the monochrome deep bowl might be considered as an indicator of a later date as well as an indication of chronological correlations with LH III C Middle contexts.[30]

In particular the depositional situation at the top of the deposit, where a cluster of removed stones was recorded by the excavators, might indicate that the deposit of pottery in Room 4 is to be interpreted as the result of a series of discards, and the upper level might have been created from a later clearance of the supposed outdoor pebble floor under Rooms 5 and 6.

For the definition of phase 4 we can adopt only a negative perspective by trying to enucleate from the upper non-closed layers the features that are not attested in the earlier deposits and are very likely to reveal a later III C pottery phase, possibly the one dating the sealing of the deposit in Room 4.

For such a task we also have at our disposal the pottery abandoned on the surface that constitutes the lower floor of Room 6, which was possibly created immediately after the huge discard in Room 4 and was modified after a while by raising its floor and creating Room 5.

A notable feature of this phase – which is, however, very difficult to isolate within the stratigraphy of the building – might be the appearance of huge bell-shaped bowls with a high, rounded conical body and sinuous walls, slightly restricted mouth and high flaring rims (Figs. 2:9–10; 3:1).[31] These bowls are associated with highly complex decorative systems, pointing to the "vulgarisation" or diffusion of the elaborate style,[32] which is adopted for decorating many different vessels; an intensely creative and free stylistic language is perceivable in the use of decorating differently the two faces of a single vessel. As for kraters, we record the occurrence of huge kraters or storage jars provided with highly articulated or quasi-squared rims with ridges or ropes below.[33] Also articulated kraters with carinated walls or inclining walls, with everted or squared rims, are possibly to be attributed to the same phase (BORGNA 2003a, 271, types C 3–4). Stemmed kraters with a continuous profile, provided with straight or slightly everted rims (Fig. 3:2. – In the "Acropoli Mediana" deposit: BORGNA 2003a, 270, types B 1–3) might also be considered widespread in this advanced III C phase, not only on internal stratigraphic grounds but also on the basis of external comparisons. Comparable elaborately decorated kraters, which do not seem to occur frequently at LM III C Early Chania, are very well attested in some advanced III C Cretan contexts, as at Thronos pit 36, Karphi, Mouliana, possibly Knossos SEX and Vrokastro, though they seem to be known from III C

---

[30] For the treatment of the foot with reserved lines cf. *MDP*, 178, fig. 229; in Crete, cf. D'AGATA 2003, 29 with literature.

[31] For comparisons and correlations consider e.g. the appearance of "larger dimensions of deep bowls" in phase 2 at Kavousi Kastro: MOOK – COULSON 1997, 353; see now MOOK 2004, 169: III C "late". On the Mainland see the "bulged" shape of deep bowls in some LH III C Middle contexts, such as at III C "Entwickelt" Tiryns: PODZUWEIT 1979, 426–427, fig. 43:12, 429, fig. 45; and in particular III C Fortgeschritten: PODZUWEIT 1983, 369, figs. 3:12; 4:9–11; Lefkandi, Phase 2: POPHAM – MILBURN 1971, 339, fig. 4:1.

[32] For Close Style deep bowls in III C Middle advanced or III C Mitte–Fortgeschritten in Greece see e.g. PODZUWEIT 1983, 371–372; for a "late type" of Close Style decoration in Crete see KANTA 2003b, 519.

[33] E.g. BORGNA 2001, 284, fig. 6. For a possible correlation with LH III C Middle pottery: *MDP*, 175, fig. 225 (squared rims FS 282 kraters in III C Middle advanced or Rutter phase 4b in Greece). – Cf. PODZUWEIT 1979, 428, fig. 44:7 (III C "Mitte–Entwickelt"). In Crete cf. in particular SACKETT – POPHAM – WARREN 1965, 292, fig. 12 (Palaikastro Kastri). – KANTA 2003b, 523, fig. 7H. For the occurrence of ridges below the rims of many shapes already in LM III C Early see, however, KANTA 2003a, 171.

Early contexts as well.[34] Monochrome or blob-decorated bowls occur in these later layers as well, and their late diffusion seems to be confirmed in other sites, such as at Chania, Thronos/Sybrita, and Chalasmenos.[35] Conical feet for bowls, cups and carinated kylikes provided with a high carination just below the rim seem to complete this advanced III C repertoire.[36]

Some correlations with LH III C Middle advanced pottery may be proposed, especially as regards the style of both kraters and deep bowls, as is suggested, in particular, by the decoration with huge solid streamers with a linear outline (Fig. 3:1), which finds a direct comparison in Lefkandi, Phase 2a (POPHAM – MILBURN 1971, 343, fig. 6:2, pl. 55:1–2).[37]

Phase 5 is best represented in the western sector of the building, including the later Rooms 5 and 6. Here the depositional processes have brought about a better preservation of the stratigraphic sequence, which elsewhere was more radically interrupted by the later Hellenistic building activity. Room 5 seems to be a later addition towards the end of III C, when the level of Room 6 was raised by creating a new floor. The evidence of the material included within the stones of both the southern and the western walls of Room 5 seems to show that this last building activity is later than the III C horizons so far considered. The upper level excavated in Room 1, albeit not closed, may be considered a rather homogeneous and reliable indicator of an on-the-spot activity, contemporary with the life of Rooms 5 and 6. Only here, as well as in the upper layers of Rooms 5 and 6, are we able to record the occurrence of some very late pottery such as angular and bell-like cups, with very high flaring walls and rims, which are treated with a simple linear decoration (Fig. 3:3) or, more rarely, with very roughly executed decorative patterns as well (Fig. 3:4). Such cups invite particular comparison with some Subminoan products at Knossos, Stratigraphical Museum Site (WARREN 1982/83, 85, fig. 60a,b. – Knossos SM: POPHAM 1992, pl. 43) and at Thronos/Sybrita (D'AGATA 1999, 197, fig. 9:31.5, 203, fig. 14:41.5). Monochrome deep bowls include a range of solutions, such as monochrome coating with an inner reserved band under the rim, with a reserved lower part or with a reserved window under the handles (Fig. 3:5), all of these solutions may be compared to Subminoan contexts such as Knossos, Thronos/Sybrita, and Chalasmenos.[38]

---

[34] Thronos: D'AGATA 1999, 199, fig. 10. Karphi: SEIRADAKI 1960, fig. 15:1. Mouliana: XANTHOUDIDIS 1905. Knossos: WARREN 1982/83. – See WARREN this volume in particular for stage III. – POPHAM 1965, 332, fig. 9, pl. 84a. Vrokastro: HAYDEN 2003, fig. 13:67–68. – Cf. KANTA 2003a, 170–171, fig. 2 (in particular a,b,g): most dated to "the middle of the period". Other III C evidence at Kastelli Pediada: RETHEMIOTAKIS 1997, in particular 322, fig. 33b, 323, fig. 34a. Palaikastro Kastri: SACKETT – POPHAM – WARREN 1965, 292, fig. 13. – Cf. also KANTA 2003a, 171 for the intensification of the use of dashed rims in "later LM III C stages".

[35] At Chania bowls with a blob decoration appear in the pits related to a later III C occupation: GSE II, 94, no. 82-P1084, pl. 73:e8, cf. p. 141. Thronos/Sybrita: D'AGATA 1999, 200, fig. 11:20.2. Chalasmenos: COULSON – TSIPOPOULOU 1994, fig. 19:3.

[36] For conical feet see above, n. 29; furthermore KANTA 2003b, 526. For kylikes, cf. e.g. at Karphi: SEIRADAKI 1960, 26, fig. 18:1–2. Chalasmenos, Tomb A: COULSON – TSIPOPOULOU 1994, fig. 8:1. – TSIPOPOULOU 2004, 121, fig. 8.13:94-180. Kavousi Kastro, phase 1: MOOK – COULSON 1997 (for a chronology of this phase possibly a little later into III C see the discussion, pp. 366–370). Vrokastro: HAYDEN 2003, fig. 8:53. See also Kavousi Vronda, Building B, "later phase": DAY – SNYDER 2004, 72, fig. 5.11.

[37] For a correlation of Lefkandi 2a with III C Middle advanced see now RMDP, 696; see furthermore RMDP, 599, fig. 223 (LH III C Middle in Attica). In Crete see in particular the decoration of the elaborate kraters at Kastelli Pediada (Church's plot): RETHEMIOTAKIS 1997, 322, fig. 33 ("III C Middle"?).

[38] Knossos: WARREN 1982/83, 86, figs. 62; 64–65. Thronos: D'AGATA 1999, 202, fig. 13:41.6 (SM I); for a window reserved under the handles IBID., 204, 206, fig. 16:2.23 (SM II). Chalasmenos: COULSON – TSIPOPOULOU 1994, 75, fig. 10, 78, fig. 13:7, 79, fig. 14; see also DAY 1997, 396, fig. 3:8. For several varieties of monochrome bowls and cups at Kavousi Vronda: IBID., 400, fig. 6.

Monochrome bowls provided with a narrow zone reserved for a wavy line-pattern (Fig. 3:6) find Cretan comparisons at Knossos and Kephala[39] and Mainland Greek ones in several III C Late and Submycenaean assemblages – such as III C "Spät" Tiryns and "Final Mycenaean" Asine in the Argolid (PODZUWEIT 1983, 398, fig. 16:6. – SANTILLO FRIZELL 1986, fig. 16:139. – Cf. *RMDP*, 634 no. 652, fig. 244 ["III C Late" and "SM"]) and Kynos and Kalapodi in Phocis (DAKORONIA 2003, 46, fig. 18. – JACOB-FELSCH 1996, pls. 6:418; 45:418). In addition to high-footed bowls, also deep bowls with linear inner walls, together with bell-like bowls with a very low rounded articulation between the body and the walls (Fig. 3:7), seem very late in the post-palatial period, as comparisons to clusters dated to the Subminoan period at Thronos seem to suggest (D'AGATA 1999, 206, fig. 16 [SM II]). As for kraters, bell-shaped exemplars, which look very similar to huge bowls (Fig. 3:8), fit well with the evidence of Karphi (SEIRADAKI 1960, figs. 15:2; 16:3), Subminoan Knossos (POPHAM 1992, pl. 44) and Thronos/Sybrita (D'AGATA 2003, 32 [SM]. – D'AGATA 1999, 205, fig. 15:2.15 [SM II]), while large weighed-down bowls or kraters decorated with double wavy bands (Fig. 3:9) find comparisons within a wider Aegean area including Mainland Greece, as seems to be attested at III C Late Kalapodi (JACOB-FELSCH 1996, pls. 11:264; 38:264).[40] Hard, over-fired fabrics and uneven manufactures can be observed, which match the evidence of other late productions, such as at Thronos/Sybrita (D'AGATA 1999, 198).

As for correlations with the Mainland, besides the monochrome deep bowls with a reserved zone for the decorative patterns, we may mention the occurrence of a new shape in the Phaistian repertoire, namely the tray (Fig. 3:10).[41] In Crete this is already attested at both Karphi (SEIRADAKI 1960, fig. 6:8) and Subminoan Knossos (POPHAM 1992, 63), while in the Aegean it seems to have been diffused since at least III C Middle advanced (*RMDP*, 928 no. 204, fig. 379 [Melos], 1066 no. 252, fig. 436 [Rhodes]). Finally, it is worth mentioning some close comparisons regarding decorative patterns, such as the ladder pattern from III C Fortgeschritten at Kalapodi (Fig. 3:8).[42]

We may add to this very late III C documentation some pieces coming from the nearby Room 7, an area most probably belonging to the "Casa a ovest del Piazzale I" but completely unstratified: huge deep bowls with a reserved lower part and a ribbed-stemmed kylix (BORGNA 1999b, 200, fig. 2, with comments and discussion. – *RMDP*, 53 [III C Late]), for example, seem to fit with a SM chronology in Greece.

The state of our evidence does not permit, however, a thorough description of ceramic sets used in III C Late or Subminoan Phaistos, as this late pottery comes mostly from unclosed filling deposits and is mixed with earlier pottery dating from III C Early and even III B.

From the framework that I have tentatively introduced, it emerges that the "Casa a ovest del Piazzale I" seems to have had a long life, beginning somewhere in the middle of LM III B and lasting most probably until the very end of the Bronze Age. As for

---

[39] Knossos Kephala: CADOGAN 1967, 260, fig. 2:14. Knossos SEX: WARREN 1982/83, 86, fig. 62:2. – See also BORGNA 2001, 286, fig. 7.

[40] Cf. PODZUWEIT 1983, 380–381, for the appearance of "Doppelwellenband" decoration in III C Mitte–Fortgeschritten.

[41] BORGNA 2001, 286, fig. 7:6. FS 322: *MDP*, 155 (III C Middle/Rutter 4a). – *RMDP*, 49 (III C Middle advanced); cf. at III C Late Lefkandi: *RMDP*, 721, fig. 277:97. – JACOB-FELSCH 1996, pl. 12 (Schicht 8: III C Fortgeschritten).

[42] JACOB-FELSCH 1996, pl. 34.209; on a bell-shaped krater see at SM Knossos: POPHAM 1992, pl. 46c, no. 4; also for impressed patterns on the rim of pithoi cf. JACOB-FELSCH 1996, pls. 21:414; 45:414.

the middle phase of LM III C, whose definition constitutes the main purpose of this conference, we should concentrate our attention on phase 4, though it does not succeed in emerging as a well-defined phase marked by new appearances and novelties as regards the pottery system. By contrast, we may recognise a continuous evolution of shapes and decorations during an earlier part of III C, possibly over a rather long span of time. Some evidence, however, such as highly decorated and intensely elaborated stemmed kraters, may be considered as a link to certain new trends and developments which participated in the formation of a new pottery milieu towards the middle of III C. At that moment in the history of Crete, many clusters of pottery seem to have been discarded and many deposits been sealed, possibly coinciding with some important events involving major gaps in settlement patterns and changes in the social life of post-palatial Crete. Among the pottery, which occurs in stratigraphic contexts, to be considered as either contemporary with or immediately following upon these events, we may mention later varieties of articulated kraters, including huge storage jars with squared rims and ridged walls, huge bell-like deep bowls with a bulged body, a restricted mouth and high flaring rims, hollowed bases and conical feet for bowls and cups, as well as the intensification and deterioration of the elaborate style, which is then often associated with deep bowls; otherwise both bowls and cups are monochrome or dipped. Other features possibly relating to such a phase – such as marked hollowed lips of jars, carinated kylikes, the application of hooked patterns underneath the handles of jugs (cf. *RMDP*, 49 [III C Middle]), which are attested in the "Casa a ovest" and might be useful for a thorough definition of the LM III C Middle pottery – need a more detailed assessment.

Whether Phaistos phase 4 may be called "LM III C Middle" preceding an actual III C Late(/SM? Phase 5?) horizon or is to be defined as "III C Late" followed by a pure SM sequence, is a problem of terminology, which we should try to solve by comparing the results presented at this conference and by exploring the Dark Ages contexts at Phaistos more closely.

Index to illustrations

Fig. 1 "Casa a ovest del Piazzale I" at Phaistos: isometric reconstruction (after R. Oliva); pottery from phase 2 (2–4: deep bowls from Rooms 3 and 2; shallow bowl from Room 2) and phase 3 (5–7: deep bowls from Room 4)

Fig. 2 "Casa a ovest del Piazzale I": pottery from phase 3 (1–5: kraters from Room 2–4 and 4: cups and shallow bowl from Room 4); and phase 4 (6–10: deep bowls and cups from Room 4; deep bowl [9] from Room 3)

Fig. 3 "Casa a ovest del Piazzale I": pottery from phase 4 (1–2: deep bowl from Room 4 and krater from Room 6) and phase 5 (3–10: cups from Rooms 1 and 6, deep bowls from Rooms 4, 1, and 6; bell-kraters from Rooms 1 and 6; tray from Room 5)

Bibliography

BENZI, M.
1993 "The Late Bronze Age Pottery from Vathy Cave, Kalymnos", 275–288 in: *Wace and Blegen*.

BIETAK, M. (ed.)
2003 *The Synchronisation of Civilisations in the Eastern Mediterranean in the Second Millennium B.C. II. Proceedings of the SCIEM 2000 – EuroConference, Haindorf, 2nd of May – 7th of May 2001* (Österreichische Akademie der Wissenschaften. Denkschriften der Gesamtakademie 29 = Contributions to the Chronology of the Eastern Mediterranean 4). Vienna.

BORGNA, E.
1997a "Kitchen-Ware from LM III C Phaistos. Cooking Traditions and Ritual Activities in LBA Cretan Societies", *SMEA* 39, 189–217.

1997b "Some Observations on Deep Bowls and Kraters from the 'Acropoli Mediana' at Phaistos", 273–298 in: *Late Minoan III Pottery*.
1999a "Central Crete and the Mycenaeans at the Close of the Late Bronze Age: The Evidence of the 'Acropoli Mediana' at Phaistos", 353–370 in: Περιφέρεια.
1999b "Circolazione della ceramica nello scambio cerimoniale tra mondo miceneo palaziale e Creta tardominoica: la prospettiva di Festòs nel TM III", 199–205 in: LA ROSA – PALERMO – VAGNETTI 1999.
2001 "Il periodo Tardo Minoico III B–C: La Casa ad Ovest del Piazzale I", 273–298 in: *I cento anni dello scavo di Festòs*.
2003a *Il complesso di ceramica Tardominoico III dell'Acropoli Mediana di Festòs* (Studi di Archeologia Cretese 3). Padua.
2003b "Regional Settlement Patterns, Exchange Systems and Sources of Power in Crete at the End of the Late Bronze Age: Establishing a Connection", *SMEA* 45, 153–183.
2004a "Aegean Feasting: A Minoan Perspective", 127–159 in: WRIGHT 2004.
2004b "Social Meanings of Drink and Food Consumption at LM III Phaistos", 174–195 in: HALSTEAD – BARRETT 2004.
2006 "Observations on LM III A and III B Pottery from Phaistos and the Problem of the Reoccupation of the Palatial Site", 105–121 in: Πεπραγμένα Θ' διεθνούς κρητολογικού συνεδρίου, Ελούντα 1–6 Οκτοβρίου 2001. Iraklio.

CADOGAN, G.
1967 "Late Minoan III C Pottery from the Kephala Tholos Tomb near Knossos (Knossos Survey 8)", *BSA* 62, 257–265.

I cento anni dello scavo di Festòs
2001 *I cento anni dello scavo di Festòs. Giornate Lincee, Roma, 13–14 dicembre 2000* (Atti dei Convegni Lincei 173). Rome.

COULSON, W. – M. TSIPOPOULOU
1994 "Preliminary Investigations at Halasmenos, Crete, 1992–93", *Aegean Archaeology* 1, 65–86.

D'AGATA, A. L.
1999 "Defining a Pattern of Continuity during the Dark Age in Central-Western Crete: Ceramic Evidence from the Settlement of Thronos/Kephala (Ancient Sybrita)", *SMEA* 41, 181–218.
2001 "Ritual and Rubbish in Dark Age Crete: The Settlement of Thronos/Kephala (Ancient Sybrita) and the Pre-Classical Roots of a Greek City", *Aegean Archaeology* 4, 1997–2000 [2001], 45–59.
2003 "Late Minoan III C–Subminoan Pottery Sequence at Thronos/Kephala and its Connections with the Greek Mainland", 23–35 in: *LH III C Chronology and Synchronisms*.

DAKORONIA, F.
2003 "The Transition from Late Helladic III C to the Early Iron Age at Kynos", 37–51 in: *LH III C Chronology and Synchronisms*.

DAY, L. P.
1997 "The Late Minoan III C Period at Vronda, Kavousi", 391–406 in: DRIESSEN – FARNOUX 1997.

DAY, L. P. – M. S. MOOK – J. D. MUHLY (eds.)
2004 *Crete beyond the Palaces: Proceedings of the Crete 2000 Conference* (Prehistory Monographs 10). Philadelphia.

DAY, L. P. – L. M. SNYDER
2004 "The 'Big House' at Vronda and the 'Great House' at Karphi: Evidence for Social Structure in LM III C Crete", 63–79 in: DAY – MOOK – MUHLY 2004.

DEGER-JALKOTZY, S.
2003 "Stratified Pottery Deposits from the Late Helladic III C Settlement at Aigeira/Achaia", 53–75 in: *LH III C Chronology and Synchronisms*.

DRIESSEN, J. – A. FARNOUX (eds.)
1997 *La Crète Mycénienne. Actes de la Table Ronde internationale organisée par l'École française d'Athènes, 26–28 Mars 1991* (BCH Suppl. 30). Paris.

FARNOUX, A.
1989/90 "Malia à la fin du Bronze Récent", *ActaArchLov* 28/29, 25–33.
1992 "Malia et la Crète à l'époque mycénienne", *RA*, 201–216.
1997 "Quartier Gamma at Malia Reconsidered", 259–272 in: *Late Minoan III Pottery*.

FELSCH, R. C. S. (ed.)
1996   *Kalapodi. Ergebnisse der Ausgrabungen im Heiligtum der Artemis und des Apollon von Hyampolis in der antiken Phokis. Vol. I*. Mainz.

HALLAGER, B. P.
1997   "LM III Pottery Shapes and Their Nomenclature", 407–417 in: *Late Minoan III Pottery*.
2003   "Late Minoan III B2 and Late Minoan III C Pottery in Khania", 105–116 in: *LH III C Chronology and Synchronisms*.

HALSTEAD, P. – J. C. BARRETT (eds.)
2004   *Food, Cuisine and Society in Prehistoric Greece* (Sheffield Studies in Aegean Archaeology 5). Sheffield.

HAYDEN, B. J.
2003   *Reports on the Vrokastro Area, Eastern Crete. Vol. 1: Catalogue of Pottery from the Bronze and Early Iron Age Settlement of Vrokastro in the Collections of the University of Pennsylvania Museum of Archaeology and Anthropology and the Archaeological Museum, Herakleion, Crete* (University Museum Monograph 113). Philadelphia.

JACOB-FELSCH, M.
1996   "Die spätmykenische bis frühprotogeometrische Keramik", 1–213 in: FELSCH 1996.

KANTA, A.
1980   *The Late Minoan III Period in Crete. A Survey of Sites, Pottery and Their Distribution* (SIMA 58). Göteborg.
1997   "LM III B and LM III C Pottery Phases. Some Problems of Definition", 83–101 in: *Late Minoan III Pottery*.
2003a "The Citadel of Kastrokephala and the Date of the Minoan Refuge Citadels", 167–182 in: *LH III C Chronology and Synchronisms*.
2003b "The First Half of the Late Minoan III C – Correlations among Cretan Sites with Reference to Mainland and Cypriote Developments", 513–538 in: BIETAK 2003.

KARANTZALI, E.
1986   "Une tombe du Minoen Récent III B à la Canée", *BCH* 110, 53–87.

LA ROSA, V. – D. PALERMO – L. VAGNETTI (eds.)
1999   επί πόντον πλαζόμενοι. *Simposio italiano di Studi Egei dedicato a Luigi Bernabò Brea e Giovanni Pugliese Carratelli. Roma, 18–20 febbraio 1998*. Rome – Athens.

LAVIOSA, C.
1977   "La casa TM III a Festòs: osservazioni sull'architettura cretese in età micenea", 79–88 in: *Antichità cretesi. Studi in onore di Doro Levi. Vol. 1* (CronCatania 12, 1973). Catania.

LEVI, D.
1956   "Attività della Scuola Archeologica Italiana di Atene nell'anno 1955", *BdA* 41, 238–271.

MOOK, M. S.
2004   "From Foundation to Abandonment: New Ceramic Phasing for the Late Bronze Age and Early Iron Age on the Kastro at Kavousi", 163–179 in: DAY – MOOK – MUHLY 2004.

MOOK, M. S. – W. D. E. COULSON
1997   "Late Minoan III C Pottery from the Kastro at Kavousi", 337–365 in: *Late Minoan III Pottery*.

MOUNTJOY, P. A.
1997   "The Destruction of the Palace at Pylos Reconsidered", *BSA* 92, 109–137.
2003   *Knossos. The South House* (*BSA* Suppl. 34). London.

Περιφέρεια
1999   *Η περιφέρεια του Μυκηναϊκού κόσμου. Α´ διεθνές διεπιστημονικό συμπόσιο, Λαμία, 25–29 Σεπτεμβρίου 1994*. Lamia.

PERONI, R. (ed.)
1982   *Ricerche sulla protostoria della Sibaritide, 2* (Cahiers du Centre Jean Bérard 8). Naples.

PERONI, R. – F. TRUCCO (eds.)
1994   *Enotri e Micenei nella Sibaritide. I. Broglio di Trebisacce II. Altri siti della Sibaritide* (Magna Grecia 8). Taranto.

PODZUWEIT, C.
1978   "Ausgrabungen in Tiryns 1976. Bericht zur spätmykenischen Keramik", *AA*, 471–498.

1979 "Ausgrabungen in Tiryns 1977. Bericht zur spätmykenischen Keramik", *AA*, 412–440.
1981 "Ausgrabungen in Tiryns 1978. 1979. Bericht zur spätmykenischen Keramik", *AA*, 194–220.
1983 "Ausgrabungen in Tiryns 1981. Bericht zur spätmykenischen Keramik. Die Phasen SH III C Fortgeschritten bis Spät", *AA*, 359–402.

POPHAM, M. R.
1965 "Some Late Minoan III Pottery from Crete", *BSA* 60, 316–342.
1970a "Late Minoan III B Pottery from Knossos", *BSA* 65, 195–202.
1970b "A Late Minoan Shrine at Knossos", *BSA* 65, 191–194.
1992 "Sub-Minoan Pottery", 59–66 in: SACKETT 1992.

POPHAM, M. R. (ed.)
1984 *The Minoan Unexplored Mansion at Knossos* (BSA Suppl. 17). London.

POPHAM, M. R. – E. MILBURN
1971 "The Late Helladic III C Pottery of Xeropolis (Lefkandi): A Summary", *BSA* 66, 333–352.

RETHEMIOTAKIS, G.
1997 "Late Minoan III Pottery from Kastelli Pediada", 305–326 in: *Late Minoan III Pottery*.

RUTTER, J. B.
2003 "The Nature and Potential Significance of Minoan Features in the Earliest Late Helladic III C Ceramic Assemblages of the Central and Southern Greek Mainland", 193–216 in: *LH III C Chronology and Synchronisms*.

SACKETT, L. H. (ed.)
1992 *Knossos. From Greek City to Roman Colony. Excavations at the Unexplored Mansion* II (BSA Suppl. 21). London.

SACKETT, L. H. – M. R. POPHAM – P. M. WARREN
1965 "Excavations at Palaikastro VI", *BSA* 60, 248–315.

SANTILLO FRIZELL, B.
1986 *Asine II. Results of the Excavations East of the Acropolis 1970–1974. Fasc. 3: The Late and Final Mycenaean Periods* (Skrifter utgivna av Svenska Institutet i Athen, 4°, 24:3). Stockholm.

SEIRADAKI, M.
1960 "Pottery from Karphi", *BSA* 55, 1–37.

TSIPOPOULOU, M.
2004 "Halasmenos, Destroyed but not Invisible: New Insights on the LM III C Period in the Isthmus of Ierapetra. First Presentation of the Pottery from the 1992–1997 Campaigns", 103–123 in: DAY – MOOK – MUHLY 2004.

VAGNETTI, L.
1982 "Ceramica micenea e ceramica dipinta dell'età del bronzo", 99–113 in: PERONI 1982.

VAGNETTI, L. – S. PANICHELLI
1994 "Ceramica egea importata e di produzione locale", 373–454 in: PERONI – TRUCCO 1994.

VITALE, S.
2006 "The LH III B–LH III C Transition on the Mycenaean Mainland", *Hesperia* 75, 177–204.

WARREN, P. M.
1982/83 "Knossos: Stratigraphical Museum Excavations, 1978–82, Part II", *AR*, 63–87.
1997 "Late Minoan III Pottery from the City of Knossos: Stratigraphical Museum Extension Site", 157–184 in: *Late Minoan III Pottery*.

WATROUS, V. L.
1992 *Kommos III. The Late Bronze Age Pottery*. Princeton.

WRIGHT, J. C. (ed.)
2004 *The Mycenaean Feast* (= *Hesperia* 72:2). Princeton.

XANTHOUDIDIS, S. A.
1905 "Ἐκ Κρήτης", *ArchEph* 1904 [1905], 1–56.

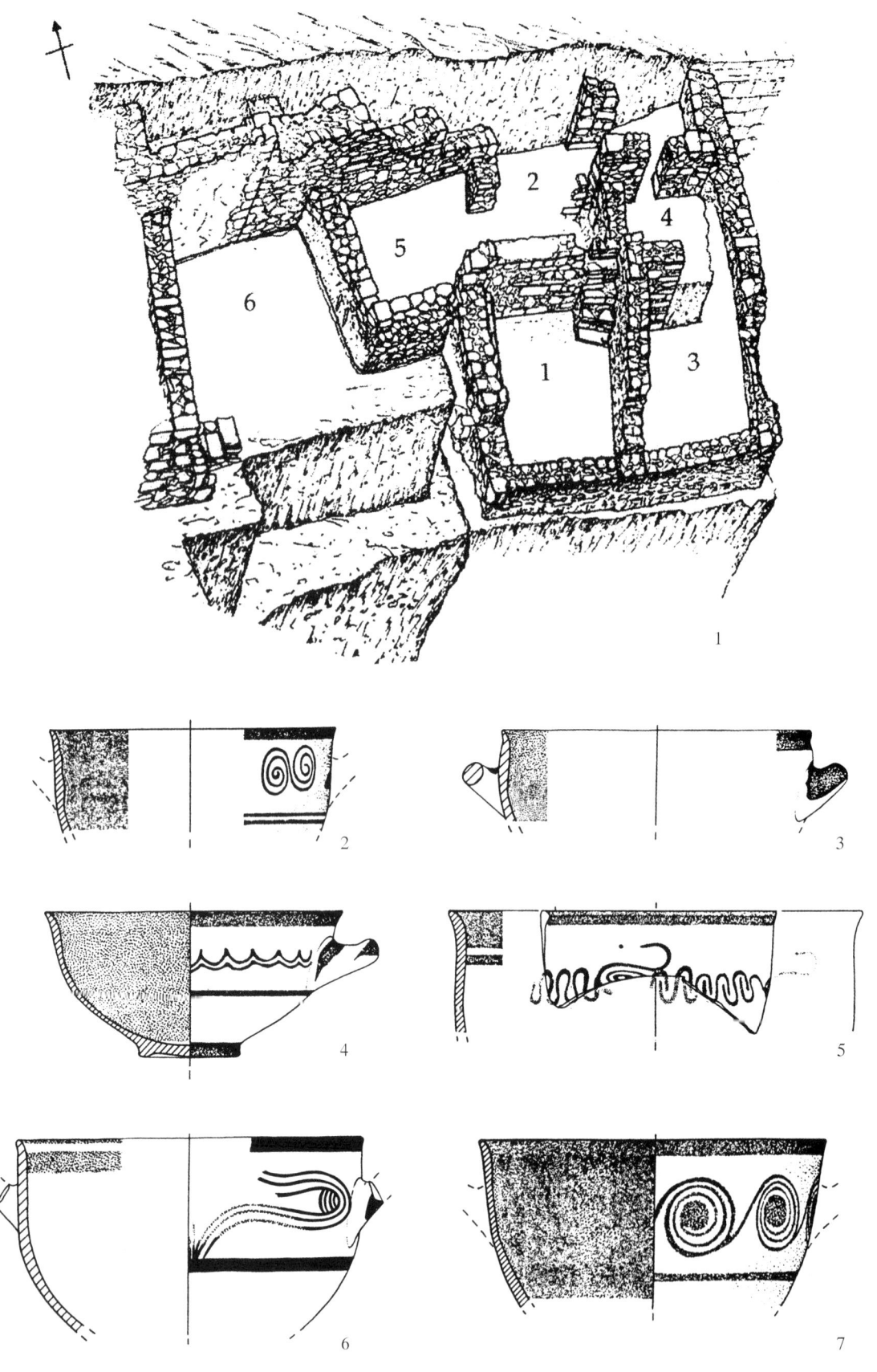

Fig. 1 "Casa a ovest del Piazzale I" at Phaistos: isometric reconstruction.
Pottery from phase 2 and phase 3 (1:3)

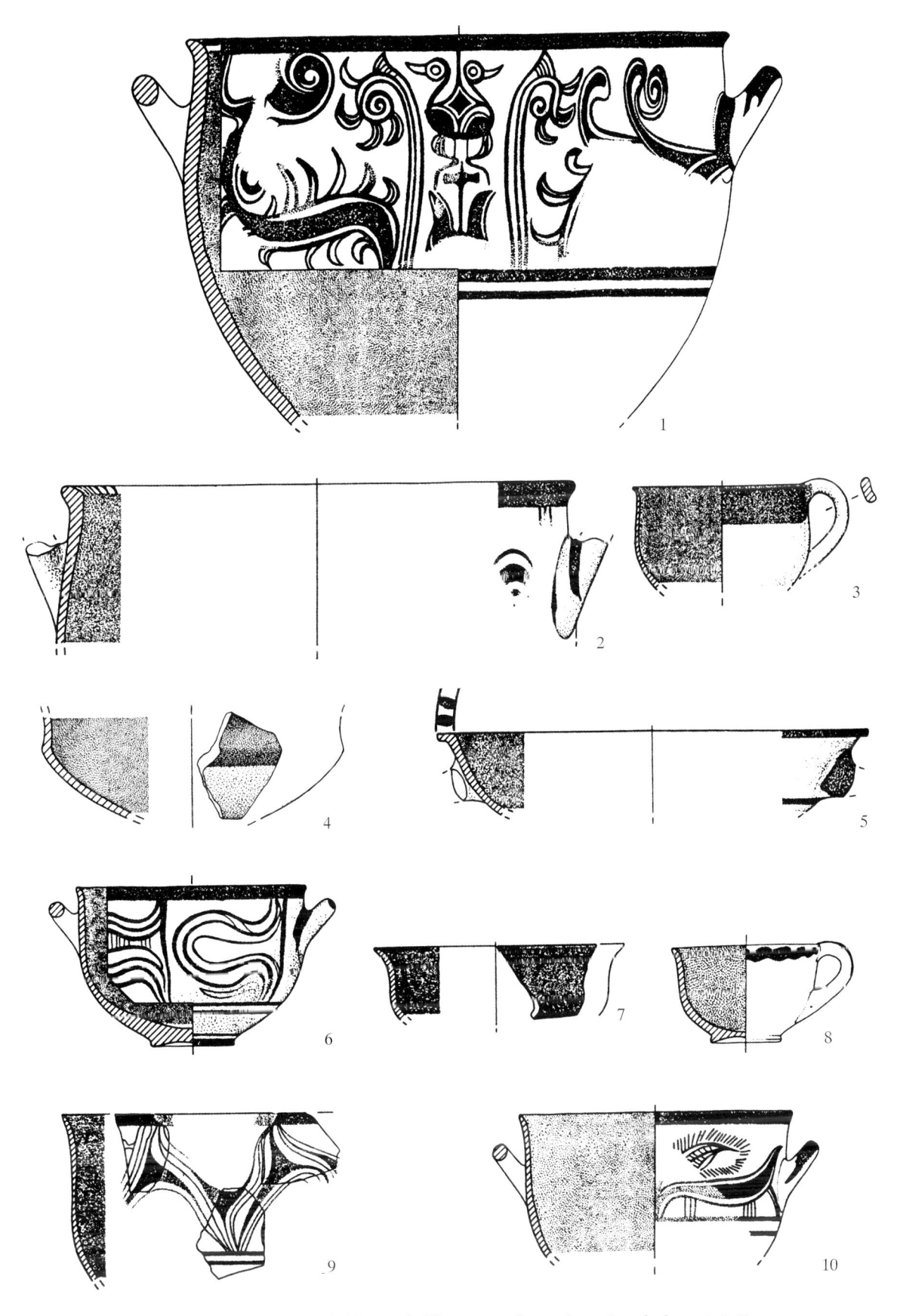

Fig. 2 "Casa a ovest del Piazzale I": pottery from phase 3 and phase 4 (1:3)

Fig. 3 "Casa a ovest del Piazzale I": pottery from phase 4 and phase 5 (1:3)

JOOST H. CROUWEL

PICTORIAL POTTERY OF LH III C MIDDLE AND ITS ANTECEDENTS*

The subject of this paper is the painted Mycenaean vessels with pictorial decoration that can be attributed on stratigraphical and/or stylistic grounds to the relatively short period of LH III C Middle (ca. 1150/1140–1100/1090 B.C.). In fact, only a selection of these pictorial vessels will be considered, focusing on what is new about them and on what has antecedents in earlier Mycenaean vase painting or other artistic media. The examples selected come mainly from settlement contexts at Mycenae and Tiryns in the Argolid, and Lefkandi on Euboea, the three sites that have up until now yielded the largest collections of pictorial material of this date.[1]

Among the pottery vessels belonging to a floor deposit in the East Basement of the so-called Granary within the citadel of Mycenae is a deep bowl with pictorial decoration consisting of a row of birds (Fig. 1. – WACE 1921–23, 52, pl. 7b [p. 48–55, for the East Basement, lower level]. – VERMEULE – KARAGEORGHIS 1982, no. XI.110. – *RMDP*, 174 no. 365, fig. 49 [pp. 47, 49, 61, 76, for the East Basement, lower level]). The pottery from this deposit firmly dates to LH III C Middle, as defined by P. A. Mountjoy and E. S. Sherratt (*MDP*, 155–180. – *RMDP*, 38–41, 47–50 with tables I and II. – MOUNTJOY this volume. – SHERRATT 1981).[2] The birds and the subsidiary ornaments are rendered in the so-called Close Style, which was produced in the Argolid. By far the most published examples of this class of pottery come from Mycenae (for what follows, see esp. *RMDP*, 50, 77–78. – CROUWEL 1991, 17–18, 22–23, 28–29, 32. – FRENCH this volume).[3] In other parts of Greece it only appears as (mostly rare) imports, or in imitations of birds or abstract motifs.

The Close Style may be defined as a miniaturist, highly ornate class of pottery, with carefully drawn, detailed motifs filling all or nearly all available spaces. It occurs mainly on small vessels of fine, thin fabric, representing a limited number of open and closed shapes. The motifs are mostly abstract, but birds and fish arranged in friezes

---

* This paper is a prelude to a larger study of late Mycenaean pictorial pottery (see also CROUWEL 2006b). Many thanks are due to the following friends and colleagues who have helped with information, supplied photographs or allowed me to study material under their care: Dr. K. Demakopoulou, Dr. E. French, Dr. W. Güntner, the late Dr. K. Kilian, Dr. P. A. Mountjoy and the late M. R. Popham.

[1] Much material of this date from Mycenae and Tiryns is included in VERMEULE – KARAGEORGHIS 1982, chapter XI. – SAKELLARAKIS 1992. – SLENCZKA 1974. – CROUWEL 1991. – GÜNTNER 2000. For the material from Lefkandi, see CROUWEL 2006a, and, previously, POPHAM – SACKETT 1968, 19, figs. 35, 37–46. – POPHAM – MILBURN 1971, 340, pls. 53:6; 54; 57:3. – VERMEULE – KARAGEORGHIS 1982, nos. XI.37–39,51,61–62,65–66,91.

[2] At the major sites of Mycenae and Tiryns the period comprises the two phases called Developed/Entwickelt and Advanced/Fortgeschritten.

[3] The elite of the LH III C Middle is described in DEGER-JALKOTZY 2002, 58–63 as a warrior aristocracy.

or panels also appear. The Close Style clearly represents a ceramic phenomenon, independent of wall paintings or other non-ceramic sources. While the pictorial elements are usually no more than "a kind of calligraphic substitute for abstract ornament" (quoted from KOPCKE 1977, 33), an example of more complex pictorial decoration can be seen on a fragmentary deep bowl from the Citadel House Area, not far from the Granary at Mycenae (Fig. 2. – CROUWEL 1991, no. G 3. – Also *MDP*, 176, fig. 228:3 [one sherd]). This vessel, called the "Goats and Fish Bowl", bears panelled decoration, with antithetically placed goats feeding on a leaved triglyph, and fish filling the spaces above the goats. A similar arrangement, involving goats, a leaved triglyph or actual tree but without the fish, is seen on fragments of two other Close Style deep bowls from Mycenae (VERMEULE – KARAGEORGHIS 1982, nos. IX.73–74, their dating corrected in CROUWEL 1991, 17, 22) and a contemporary krater from Lefkandi (CROUWEL 2006a, no. C 1. – POPHAM – MILBURN 1971, pl. 54:1. – VERMEULE – KARAGEORGHIS 1982, no. X.85). As regards panelled decoration, this is well-known in Mycenaean vase painting of LH III B and III C, particularly on deep bowls and ring-based kraters. The panels mostly have abstract motifs, but pictorial ones also occur (*RMDP*, 33, 35, 44, 49).

One of the friezes on a fragmentary Close Style stirrup jar from an unknown location at Mycenae carries a row of birds (Fig. 3. – VERMEULE – KARAGEORGHIS 1982, no. XI.118. – SAKELLARAKIS 1992, no. 174). The birds are quite differently rendered from those on the deep bowl from the Granary, but resemble the two creatures depicted on the well-known "Warrior Krater" from a nearby building within the citadel of Mycenae (Fig. 4. – VERMEULE – KARAGEORGHIS 1982, no. XI.42. – IMMERWAHR 1990, 149–151, pls. 85–87. – SAKELLARAKIS 1992, no. 32 [with bibliography]). On this ring-based krater the birds are placed antithetically under the twisted horns of a frontal bull's head which form the double-arched handles. The large spaces between the handles display files of marching warriors, in one case together with a female figure standing at the rear. In sharp contrast to the small, delicately potted and painted Close Style vessels, the "Mycenae Warrior Krater" is a large, robust vessel, made in the coarse, heavy, so-called oatmeal fabric which is new in LH III C Middle. Its decoration is polychrome, combining dark brown with pale yellow and added white. At the same time, the "Warrior Krater" is linked to the Close Style vessels by the rendering of the birds.

Close Style birds can also be seen on fragments of other kraters and vases of different shapes, including a large four-handled jar of "oatmeal" fabric from the Granary at Mycenae (WACE 1921–23, 46, pl. 9b [probably from the West Basement]. – VERMEULE – KARAGEORGHIS 1982, no. XI.119. – SAKELLARAKIS 1992, no. 184. – CROUWEL 1991, 23, 28. – *RMDP*, 159). So a picture emerges of a large workshop of LH III C Middle, presumably situated at Mycenae and producing both fine Close Style pottery and robust kraters, along with other large vessels of similar heavy fabric, such as the jar from the Granary and the so-called Horses and Birds Jar from the Citadel House Area (Fig. 6. – VERMEULE – KARAGEORGHIS 1982, no. XI.13. – CROUWEL 1991, no. G 2 ["Horses and Birds Jar"]).

The "Warrior Krater" from Mycenae has other significant connections as well. First, there is the much noted close link with the Painted Stele which was found in one of the many chamber tombs in the Mycenae area (Fig. 5. – TSOUNTAS 1896. – VERMEULE – KARAGEORGHIS 1982, no. XI.43. – XENAKI-SAKELLARIOU 1985, 203–204 with frontispiece [Kato Pigadi, tomb 70]. – IMMERWAHR 1990, 150–151, My No. 21, pl. 84. – See now also *Archaeological Atlas*, 36 [called Alepotrypa, tomb 70]). This sandstone stele was clearly reused, as its original carved decoration was covered in plaster and subsequently painted polychrome. One long side has three horizontal registers, including one with a file of soldiers closely similar to those seen on the "Warrior Krater" and presumably painted by the same hand.[4] Another register shows a row of deer, with a hedgehog filling the space above one of them. The scene in the upper, third register is only partly preserved: part of a seated figure in a long dress facing a man, with a trace of a possible other figure behind him.

The technique in which the Painted Stele was plastered and painted is very similar to that of the paintings of the walls of the palace and other LH III B buildings at Mycenae. This suggests that the artist was trained as a wall painter or copied the technique of wall paintings that were still visible well after the destruction of the palace and other buildings.[5]

The "Warrior Krater" from Mycenae is also linked by details of its shape and elaborate pictorial decoration to other ring-based kraters, most of which are only preserved in fragments. These have been found not only at Mycenae, but also at nearby Tiryns and various sites in other parts of Mainland Greece, as well as on Euboea, Melos and Naxos (CROUWEL 2006b).

Of particular interest is an example from Lefkandi which may be called the "Warrior and Horses Krater" (VERMEULE – KARAGEORGHIS 1982, no. XI.59. – CROUWEL 2006a, no. G 1a–b). Unfortunately, only fragments of it remain, but these include a double bull's head handle like those of the "Warrior Krater" from Mycenae. The one, partially preserved armed man on the Lefkandi krater (Fig. 7) wears a short fringed tunic, greaves or leggings and laced boots, again like the soldiers on the "Warrior Krater" from Mycenae. On the other hand, he is not carrying a spear and shield but is armed with a sword in a tasselled scabbard, while raising one arm up in front. On its other side the "Warrior and Horses Krater" from Lefkandi featured a number of horses which were not harnessed to chariots, as on other kraters, but roamed freely, as on the contemporary "Horses and Birds Jar" from Mycenae mentioned above (Fig. 6).

The fragments of the "Warrior and Horses Krater" come from contexts belonging to Lefkandi LH III C Phase 2a, which firmly dates to LH III C Middle (*RMDP*, 694, 696. – SCHOFIELD this volume). Much more pictorial pottery of this phase was found in the limited area of the Xeropolis site at Lefkandi that was excavated in the 1960s. Other such finds are reported from the large-scale excavations that started there in 2003.[6]

Apart from links with the pictorial pottery from the north-east Peloponnese, there are connections with finds, again mainly krater fragments, from nearer sites, such as Kalapodi in Phocis (*RMDP*, 815 nos. 27–28, fig. 325), Volos in Thessaly (VERMEULE – KARAGEORGHIS 1982, nos. XI.57–58. – IMMERWAHR 1987) and Kynos (also called Kynos Livanates, Livanates, or Pyrgos Livanaton) on the East Locrian coast, opposite

---

[4] See, most recently, GÜNTNER 2000, 358–359, where two items are also attributed to his Stele-Painter: a fragmentary krater with panelled decoration involving antithetic birds from the Unterburg at Tiryns (IBID., 111, Tiryns *Vogel* 63 = 273, *Vogel* 438 with pl. 50a–d), and a krater fragment with part of a bird from Mycenae (IBID., 272, *Vogel* 401. – See also VERMEULE – KARAGEORGHIS 1982, no. VIII.24. – SAKELLARAKIS 1992, no. 220).

[5] There is controversy over the LH III C date that has been attributed, as yet without full contextual evidence, to a wall painting called "Lady with a Lily" from the Greek excavations in the Cult Centre at Mycenae, see KRITSELI-PROVIDI 1982, 73–76 no. G-1, 80–89, 111, fig. 8, pls. B; 24. – IMMERWAHR, 1990, 119–120, 148 with n. 5, 191 (My No. 5). – RUTTER 1992, 65 with n. 10.

[6] For the earlier finds, see supra n. 1; for new ones from Phase 2, see WHITLEY 2003/04, 39, fig. 54 (krater sherd with part of a warrior), WHITLEY 2004/05, 51, fig. 90 (krater sherd with rowers on board of a ship).

Euboea. The pictorial pottery from the latter site comes from a well-defined destruction level of LH III C Middle (DAKORONIA this volume).[7]

Altogether, the pictorial material datable to III C Middle presents a considerable variety of motifs, compositions and styles, as well as (levels of) draughtsmanship. The rich iconography comprises armed men on foot, in chariots or aboard ships, as well as unarmed human figures, animals of various species, birds, fish and fantastic creatures engaged in a variety of activities. The shapes used are mainly ring-based kraters, but pictorial deep bowls, kalathoi and other open shapes also occur, along with stirrup jars, other types of jars and other closed shapes. Let us now examine to what extent the pictorial repertoire of LH III C Middle was an original creation and in how far it had antecedents.

By LH III C Middle pictorially decorated pottery had had a long history in Mycenaean Greece, going back to LH I and II (for what follows, see esp. VERMEULE – KARAGEORGHIS 1982, chapters III–X. – ÅKERSTRÖM 1987. – GÜNTNER 2000, 323–332. – CROUWEL – MORRIS 1996). Originally strongly influenced by Minoan prototypes as regards shapes and iconography, Mycenaean pictorial pottery subsequently went through a process of conventionalisation and standardisation. For a considerable time it was primarily a phenomenon of the Argolid, with finds concentrated in the palatial centres of Mycenae, Tiryns and Midea and in the production centre of Berbati.[8] In LH III B, the pictorially decorated vessels were mainly kraters of a new, ring-based type, which usually carried rows of chariots, bulls and other animals. Other shapes, such as deep bowls, jugs and (stirrup) jars, were mostly decorated with birds or fish. The range of shapes, motifs and compositions is well illustrated by the substantial body of finds from the LH III B2 destruction horizon within the citadel of Midea (MCMULLEN FISHER 1998. – MCMULLEN FISHER – GIERING 1998. – DEMAKOPOULOU forthcoming). All in all, the depictions are often repetitive, taken from a stock repertoire, though more original ones do also occur. It is important to note that the pictorial material of this and any other Mycenaean period constitutes only a tiny fraction (probably less than 1% at any given time) of the total amount of patterned pottery. It is also of note that pictorial Mycenaean pottery displays the same techniques of manufacture as non-pictorial, patterned vessels.

The history of pictorial pottery in LH III C Early, a period of some 50 years (ca. 1185/1180–1150/1140 B.C.) after the destruction of the Mycenaean palaces, is rather controversial. As we shall see below, there is little material from stratified deposits of this time, with the apparent exception of Tiryns. On the other hand, a fairly large number of pieces has been attributed on stylistic grounds to LH III C Early in a recent authoritative study by Wolfgang Güntner (GÜNTNER 2000).

Among the sizeable corpus of pictorial pottery from the British excavations in the Citadel House Area at Mycenae, its stratified deposits running from LH III B to LH III C Late, only two fragments could be firmly assigned to LH III C Early by their find contexts and style. They belong to a single deep bowl with a spiral pattern which was pictorialised into a bird's head (Fig. 8. – CROUWEL 1991, no. E 27).[9]

At Lefkandi on Euboea, where LH III B is not well represented, LH III C Phases 1 to 3 cover the entire length of this period as recognised on the Greek Mainland. Among

---

[7] Pictorial material of this period may also be expected from the current excavations at Mitrou, another coastal site in East Locris just 10 km south of Kynos; see RUTTER this volume.

[8] For the potter's workshop at Berbati, see most recently SCHALLIN 2002.

[9] I am grateful to Dr. E. French for letting me have a revised list of the dating of the find contexts of the pictorial material from the Citadel House Area that was presented in CROUWEL 1991.

the 93 catalogued pieces from the 1960s excavations only three have definite find contexts of Phase 1, which dates to LH III C Early: a deep bowl (?) sherd showing a horse's head (Fig. 10), two fragments from a krater with remains of two birds, and another krater sherd also preserving part of a bird (CROUWEL 2006a, nos. A 12, E 10, E 17). In addition, six krater fragments, with remains of a horse, birds and unidentified pictorial motifs, less certainly derive from Phase 1 contexts (CROUWEL 2006a, nos. A 7, E 9, E 12, E 15, H 2, H 17).

The large-scale excavations by Klaus Kilian in the Unterburg at Tiryns, where the occupation levels include LH III B and all of LH III C, have produced much pictorial material. All in all, 46 pieces have been recorded from (as yet not fully published) find contexts of LH III C Early. Most of these fragmentary pictorial pieces were assigned by Wolfgang Güntner to LH III B or earlier on stylistic grounds (GÜNTNER 2000, 16, 19–20 [Tiryns *Wagen* 5, 12–13], 32–33 [*Mensch* 13–15], 40, 43–44, 46, 49, 51–58, 62 [*Stier* 3, 12, 14B, 15, 22, 33, 36, 42B, 43B, 44B, 44G, 44L, 45C, 48, 53D], 65, 68 [*Hirsch* 2C, 8], 69–71 [*Ziege* 1, 3D], 91, 96–100, 102–103, 105 [*Vogel* 19, 34A, 34F, 34R, 34U, 34Z, 34AA, 34AB, 34AC, 34AD, 34AE, 34EF, 42, 46, 53C]). These "throw-ups" present a variety of motifs, including chariot, human figure, bovid, deer and goat, and mainly bird. One fragment with a small part of a chariot team actually belongs to the so-called Tiryns Sphinx Krater of which many other fragments were found in scattered contexts of LH III B and III C Middle. The original krater must then date back to LH III B (PODZUWEIT 1979, 434 with fig. 38:5. – GÜNTNER 2000, 21 [Tiryns *Wagen* 15], 181 [*Wagen* 180], 194, 357–358 ["Tiryns Sphinx Painter"] with pl. 4:1a–b).

Only four pictorial pieces from LH III C levels, preserving a horse's head (Fig. 9), a deer and (twice) birds, were assigned by Güntner to this period itself, again for stylistic reasons (GÜNTNER 2000, 23 [Tiryns *Wagen* 22], 69 [Tiryns *Hirsch* 11], 107 [Tiryns *Vogel* 56], 109–110 [Tiryns *Vogel* 62C] with pl. 50:2, 182 [*Wagen* 196] with pl. 6:1, 245 [*Hirsch* 11] with pl. 31:10, 271 [*Vogel* 367] with pl. 49:3).

To these pieces may be added a remarkable document in the form of a restored bull-shaped figure from the Unterburg at Tiryns (Fig. 13. – KILIAN 1992, 21 n. 136, pl. 3:2. – VERMEULE – KARAGEORGHIS 1982, no. XI.85.1. – GUGGISBERG 1996, 46 no. 111, pl. 8:1–4. – GÜNTNER 2000, 252, 256 [*Ziege* 56], 322). It is well stratified, coming from the LH III C Early shrine Room 117, which in III C Middle was overbuilt and replaced by shrine Room 110.[10] This bull-figure is so far unique in having (incompletely preserved) pictorial decoration on all four sides of its body involving male goats and fish. The goats are mostly raised on their hind legs, which are alternately painted solid and patterned, but at least one appears to be shown leaping. The pair of goats depicted on the back of the bull's body are walking to the right while holding long sticks, which suggests a supernatural setting. Assuming that the bull is not an heirloom from LH III B,[11] it offers an example of elaborate pictorial pottery of LH III C Early which is not decorative but rather carries a specific meaning.

Elsewhere, only a few pictorial pieces can be attributed to LH III C Early. They include a fragmentary ring based krater, with apparently rather simply drawn birds in panels, belonging to a floor deposit of this date at Korakou in the Corinthia (*RMDP*, 230, 234 no. 190, fig. 76; cf. no. 192, a contemporary fragmentary krater with fish [?]). Also

---

[10] For the shrine Rooms, see esp. ALBERS 1994, 105–106. – Also MÜHLENBRUCH this volume.

[11] As was suggested at the Vienna Workshop by E. French on the basis of the shape of the bull's feet. It may be noted that the bull figures found in the sanctuary at Phylakopi on Melos, although contextually late Mycenaean, may stylistically date to LH III B or even earlier; see FRENCH 1985, 238–239, 279–280.

belonging here is a stirrup jar from Perati in east Attica (Fig. 15. – IAKOVIDIS 1969/70, vol. 1, 434–435 no. 892; vol. 2, esp. 139, 150, 181, fig. 65; vol. 3, pl. 129γ. – VERMEULE – KARAGEORGHIS 1982, no. XI.83. – SAKELLARAKIS 1992, no. 113. – *RMDP*, 572). The vessel was locally made and comes from chamber tomb 124 which has been assigned to the cemetery's Phase I, corresponding to LH III C Early (*RMDP*, 497). The elaborate pictorial design, which is unparalleled, includes a goat eating from a palm tree, as well as what looks like a big stylised plant and many birds of different sizes.

In addition, Wolfgang Güntner attributes to LH III C Early a good number of pictorial pots or fragments that have no find context of this date. These pieces, presenting a variety of both simple and elaborate motifs and compositions, come not only from the Unterburg but also from other parts of Tiryns, as well as from Mycenae and elsewhere. Here again the arguments are stylistic (GÜNTNER 2000, esp. 323–333 with table 7, also 182, 195–196 [*Wagen* 182–200], 203, 212–213 [*Mensch* 106–115], 252, 255–256 [*Ziege* 54–60], 289–291 [*Vogel* 357–399], 296, 303–304 [*Fisch* 66–92]).

Yet when we examine more closely the stylistic criteria used by Güntner, they appear rather vague and inconclusive. This concerns both his distinction between pictorial pottery of LH III C Early and III B, and his distinction between pictorial pottery of LH III C Early and Middle. At a general level, Güntner observes two tendencies among the material attributed by him to LH III C Early: one towards simplification, after the more complex motifs and compositions of LH III B, the other towards the detailed motifs seen in LH III C Middle. A problem here is that, while the first tendency is paralleled by the contemporary non-pictorial, patterned pottery of Mainland Greece and Euboea, the second one is clearly not. Indeed, it is the commonly held view that there was a clear fall-off in the production of pictorial and other elaborately decorated pottery in these parts of the Aegean world after the demise of the palaces (for general assessments, see *MDP*, 134–154. – MOUNTJOY 1993, 90–91. – *RMDP*, 41–47. – SHERRATT 1981. – RUTTER 1992, 65–66).

On a more specific level, Güntner regards as typical of LH III C Early, apart from the rendering in perspective of the hind legs of running animals, the often observed contrast between solidly painted and reserved or patterned body parts of animals and human figures. The latter feature, however, can also frequently be seen among the pictorial finds from Lefkandi Phase 2a, which dates to LH III C Middle.

To confuse matters further, Güntner notes the overall decline in the production of pictorial pottery after the end of LH III B and also admits that stylistically it is hard to distinguish between pictorial pottery of LH III C Early and that of the end of LH III B. In this case he even speaks of a transitional style.[12]

All in all, at Tiryns and elsewhere on the Greek Mainland and Euboea, it is clearly difficult to date pictorial pottery to LH III C Early on purely stylistic grounds, without the backing of stratigraphical evidence, and to confidently assess how far the rich repertoire of pictorial pottery datable to LH III C Middle has antecedents in the immediately preceding years. For the time being, there must remain considerable doubt as to whether Güntner is correct in attributing to LH III C Early rather than Middle such elaborate pieces as, for instance, the well-known jar fragments with a chariot race and a seated female figure holding up a kylix (Fig. 11. – KILIAN 1980. – VERMEULE – KARAGEORGHIS 1982, no. XI.19.1. – GÜNTNER 2000, 22 [Tiryns *Wagen* 17], 182 [*Wagen* 190], 195, pl. 5:1a–b), and the fragments of a krater with a dog pursuing fleeing deer from

---

[12] GÜNTNER 2000, 332–333, recalling the "transitional period" discussed in VERMEULE – KARAGEORGHIS 1982, chapter X. – Cf. CROUWEL 2003.

Tiryns (Fig. 12. – SLENCZKA 1974, no. 139. – GÜNTNER 2000, 37 [another fragment, Tiryns *Jagd* 2], 217 [*Jagd* 12], 219–220, pl. 14:2 = KNELL – VOIGTLÄNDER 1980, pl. 69:167. – Also IMMERWAHR 1990, 153, pl. 89) to LH III C Early rather than Middle.

Things seem to have been different in the eastern Aegean, where, as recent research suggests, pictorial pottery may have been more common in early LH III C. Among the pieces attributed to this time are an extraordinary, very large fragmentary krater with a naval battle, recently found at Bademgediği Tepe in western Anatolia, and a long-known three-legged mug with birds and fish from Miletus. In general, the LH III C pottery from the eastern Aegean displays clear regional characteristics and did not pass through the same stylistic developments as took place in the Argolid and other parts of Mainland Greece or nearby Euboea (MOUNTJOY 1998, 51–63. – MOUNTJOY 2004 [including a discussion of the mug from Miletus]. – MOUNTJOY 2005 [the new ship krater]).

To focus again on LH III C Middle, it is a period of increased prosperity and contacts throughout the Aegean world. This prosperity is reflected in a new demand for elaborately and imaginatively decorated pottery, such as the Close Style of the Argolid which represents a table ware of very high quality (for general assessments of the pottery of LH III C Middle, see *MDP*, 155–180. – MOUNTJOY 1993, 97–108. – *RMDP*, 47–51. – SHERRATT 1981. – RUTTER 1992, 66–67, 69). LH III C Middle also marks the hey-day of the well-known Octopus stirrup jars, many of which at this time feature birds, fish or other additional pictorial motifs. In contrast to the Close Style, these distinctive jars were widely used in the Aegean and had several production centres, mainly on islands but also in Attica (RUTTER 1992, 63–64. – VLACHOPOULOS 1997. – *RMDP*, 50–51, etc.).

The pictorial pottery of LH III C Middle may be described as a mixture of old and new. With regard to the vessel shapes used, the favourite, ring-based type of krater first appeared in LH III B and remained in use throughout LH III C. The shape obviously for a long time appealed to vase painters and their patrons, offering as it did relatively large surfaces for elaborate designs in the handle zones. Besides, the kraters are large and impressive-looking. For instance, the "Warrior Krater" of LH III C Middle from Mycenae and another pictorial example from Grotta on Naxos, presumably of similar date, have rim diameters of ca. 0.50 and 0.65 m respectively.[13] Such mixing bowls of water and wine must have been commissioned by male elites and used primarily as centre pieces in wine drinking sets, both in LH III B and later (see STEEL 1999). A new feature of kraters, attributable to LH III C Middle and attested at various sites, are the plain or slashed ridge(s) below the rims (JACOB-FELSCH 1996, 32–33. – *RMDP*, 49, etc.). New at that time are also the occasional bull's head handles of kraters,[14] as is the heavy "oatmeal" fabric that was used at Mycenae, and apparently also at Tiryns, for kraters as well as some other large vessels. Other shapes favoured for pictorial decoration, such as the deep bowl, kalathos and stirrup jar, like the krater go back to LH III B.

As regards the iconography, many motifs were known before, including chariots, animals like goats and deer, birds and fish, as well as fantastic creatures such as griffins and sphinxes. In contrast, bovids and their protomes, which had been quite popular motifs in LH III B vase painting, no longer seem to occur in LH III C Middle.

---

[13] Cf. supra p. 74 (Mycenae "Warrior Krater"). VLACHOPOULOS 1999. – VLACHOPOULOS 2003, 225, fig. 10 (Naxos krater). The rim diameter of the new ship krater from western Turkey (see above) falls within the same range.

[14] Apart from the Mycenae "Warrior Krater" and the "Warrior and Horses Krater" from Lefkandi, there is a krater fragment with such a handle from Athens; see BRONEER 1939, 353–354, fig. 27g. *RMDP*, 598. According to HALLAGER this volume, the double handles were adopted from kraters on Crete, where there are examples from LM III B at Chania and from LM III C Early contexts at sites in the east.

Traditional motifs were often used in novel, imaginative ways, free from the conventions of the past. For instance, the slow-moving chariots of old now often carry warriors and not civilians.[15] Similar heavily armed men are shown marching on foot, as on the Painted Stele and the "Warrior Krater" from Mycenae, in the latter case juxtaposed with a – unique – female figure. Yet other such military men are seen on board of ships, where they are sometimes clearly engaged in battle (DAKORONIA this volume. – CROUWEL 1999. – WEDDE 1999, 467, 470 nos. A 4–6, C 9).[16] The latter subject may have a predecessor in the stylistically very different krater from western Anatolia that was mentioned above.

As regards animal scenes, there are quite a few involving dogs pursuing or attacking deer or wild boar. The theme of hunting was of course not unknown in LH III B vase- and wall paintings which include the Boar Hunt Tableaux from Tiryns and Orchomenos (VERMEULE – KARAGEORGHIS 1982, no. V.60 [ring-based krater from Aradippo, Cyprus]. – Cf. MYLONAS 1975, pl. 124β. – SAKELLARAKIS 1992, no. 98 [fragments of two kraters from Mycenae with deer hit by spears]. – IMMERWAHR 1990, 129–130, pl. 70 [Ti No. 6], 132 [Or No. 3]). But it is treated in a particularly lively and sometimes even dramatic way on kraters and fragments thereof datable to LH III C Middle. As an example is illustrated a krater fragment in "oatmeal" fabric from Mycenae which preserves the head of a fierce dog and part of a hind leg of a fleeing deer (Fig. 14).[17]

Other animal scenes include one of goats mating, a subject that is otherwise known only from a much earlier Minoan gold ring (KENNA 1967, no. 68). Equally new in vase painting is the presence of a foal among horses seen roaming freely on the "Horses and Birds Jar" from Mycenae (Fig. 6). On the other hand, the several scenes of goats feeding from trees or leaved triglyphs in panel compositions (Fig. 2), original as they are, ultimately derive from the theme of antithetic goats feeding on "the tree of life" that was adopted much earlier in Bronze Age Aegean iconography from the Near East (CROUWEL 1991, 17, 22. – CROUWEL 2006a, no. C 1. – ÅKERSTRÖM 1987, 2, 60. – VERMEULE – KARAGEORGHIS 1982, 23 no. III.26, 55 no. V.110. – For the Near East itself, see GENGE 1971). Among the other animals, hedgehogs are depicted for the first time (Fig. 5. – CROUWEL 1991, no. C 22. – GÜNTNER 2000, 257–258).

As to the many representations of birds dating to LH III C Middle, krater fragments from Lefkandi may be singled out. They illustrate young birds in nests or flying up to a parent (Fig. 16. – CROUWEL 2006a, nos. E 2a–c, E 1 = POPHAM – SACKETT 1968, fig. 45. – POPHAM – MILBURN 1971, pl. 54:4. – VERMEULE – KARAGEORGHIS, no. XI.141) – subjects which are rare in earlier Aegean iconography.[18]

A different family group, consisting of a parent sphinx standing over its wingless young, is depicted on a krater fragment also from Lefkandi (Fig. 17. – CROUWEL

---

[15] Among these chariot scenes is, in my view, a fragmentary krater from Tiryns which was attributed by Güntner to LH III C Early on vague stylistic grounds: GÜNTNER 2000, 23 (Tiryns *Wagen* 23), 182 (*Wagen* 197), 195, pl. 6:2a–c. – SLENCZKA 1974, nos. 115–116. – VERMEULE – KARAGEORGHIS 1982, no. XI.16. – IMMERWAHR 1990, 152–153, pl. 90.

[16] Add the fragments reported from the resumed excavations at Lefkandi (supra p. 75).

[17] CROUWEL 1991, no. G 5A with pl. 3, also nos. G 4, 5B, and G 1 with fig. 7 and pl. 4 (larnax fragment). Cf. a possible hunting scene on krater fragments from Lefkandi, CROUWEL 2006a, no. G 3a–b. – POPHAM – SACKETT 1968, 19, fig. 46. – POPHAM – MILBURN 1971, pl. 54:6. – VERMEULE – KARAGEORGHIS 1982, no. XI.79.

[18] Birds feeding in nests are seen on a LH III A2 amphoroid krater from Maroni in Cyprus (VERMEULE – KARAGEORGHIS 1982, no. IV.38) and possibly on an undated fragment from Mycenae (SAKELLARAKIS 1992, no. 122). Swallows feeding in a nest are depicted on a wall painting from Akrotiri on Thera, see DOUMAS 1992, 128, pls. 97–99.

2006a, no. G 2. – POPHAM – SACKETT 1968, fig. 37. – POPHAM – MILBURN 1971, pl. 53:6. – VERMEULE – KARAGEORGHIS 1982, no. XI.65). The two sphinxes are looking in opposite directions, recalling various earlier scenes of mother cows and other animals suckling their young in different artistic media of the Aegean Bronze Age (see e.g. SAKELLARIOU 1966, 49–50). The sphinxes wear beret-like caps in two tiers. Similar headdresses, but usually plumed, are commonly worn by the sphinxes in earlier Mycenaean vase paintings and other representations.[19] On the Lefkandi krater fragment the group of sphinxes is shown side by side with a standing or walking human figure wearing a long, richly patterned robe in combination with cross-hatched boots such as are seen in other contexts on the Mycenae "Warrior Krater" and the "Warrior and Horses Krater" from Lefkandi (Figs. 4; 7).[20] It remains uncertain what the long-robed person, who carries a jug, is doing beside the sphinxes. There seems to be no obvious relationship with earlier representations of human figures associated with sphinxes.[21] The decorated long robe recalls those worn in cultic contexts on wall paintings of the Mycenaean palaces.[22]

Three family groups can be distinguished on the well-known, completely preserved alabastron from Lefkandi which is painted in white-on-dark rather than in the common dark-on-light (Fig. 18. – CROUWEL 2006a, no. G 1. – POPHAM – SACKETT 1968, fig. 35 and cover. – POPHAM – MILBURN 1971, pl. 53:6. – VERMEULE – KARAGEORGHIS 1982, no. XI.65. – DEMAKOPOULOU 1988, no. 68. – IMMERWAHR 1990, 152, pl. 88). One of these groups consists of two griffins feeding their young in a nest – a theme known in connection with birds in LH III C Middle and earlier (Fig. 16), but unique in the extensive repertoire of griffin representations in the Aegean Bronze Age. The latter are all earlier (DELPLACE 1967. – POURSAT 1977, 64–68. – MORGAN 1988, 49–54).[23]

The second group is formed by three goats, quite probably a (larger) parent facing its two young which are placed one above the other. There are no obvious parallels for the lively composition of the three goats, nor for their individual rendering.

The third family group consists of two deer, with an antlered parent looking back at a fawn standing on its back and facing in the opposite direction. Exactly the same poses can be seen on some LH III B ring-based krater fragments, but not earlier nor later (SLENCZKA 1973, no. 43, pl. 35:1a [Tiryns]. – VERMEULE – KARAGEORGHIS 1982, no. IX.48 [Menelaion]). On the other hand, the antlered deer and its young with its incipient antlers on the Lefkandi alabastron do not share the characteristic wavy line body fill of the earlier vase representations. The spotted hide of the fawn rather recalls the deer on the contemporary Painted Stele from Mycenae.

---

[19] VERMEULE – KARAGEORGHIS 1982, nos. V.27–28, VIII.30 (= SAKELLARAKIS 1992, no. 248), VIII.31 (= SAKELLARAKIS 1992, nos. 245–247), X.42. – CROUWEL 1991, no. D 1, fig. 3. – GÜNTNER supra p. 77 (the name piece of his "Tiryns Sphinx Painter"). For sphinxes in Aegean art, see DESSENNE 1957. – POURSAT 1977, 61–64. It may be noted that a fragment of a Close Style deep bowl from Mycenae may well show a mother goat standing over her young facing in the same direction; see CROUWEL 1991, 17 no. C 19, fig. 3.

[20] The two kraters with their different subject matter from Lefkandi may well be by the same painter, see CROUWEL 2006a, 246.

[21] SAKELLARIOU 1966, 49–50. – POURSAT 1977. – DESSENNE 1957. Add two LH III B larnakes from Tanagra, SPYROPOULOS 1981, pl. 20β (Dendron, tomb 115). – IMMERWAHR 1990, 156–157, pl. 92 (Ledeza, tomb 51).

[22] See e.g. men and women at Pylos, LANG 1969, pls. D; N (no. 50 H nws); 125–126 (nos. 43 H 6 and 44a H 6). See also the long-robed figures on Tanagra larnakes such as those mentioned supra n. 21.

[23] There is only one other Mycenaean vase painting with griffins, a LH III B ring-based krater from Enkomi, see VERMEULE – KARAGEORGHIS 1982, V.27.

There seems to be no obvious, meaningful relationship between the deer and the single sphinx opposite them on the Lefkandi alabastron. The sphinx with its ruffled hair has no close parallels among the many representations of this kind of fantastic creature in Aegean Bronze Age art, including the contemporary krater fragment with a parent and baby sphinx also from Lefkandi (see above).

The alabastron from Lefkandi with its juxtaposition of family groups is a good example for the practice of vase painters of LH III C Middle to use traditional motifs, such as chariot, deer, goat, bird, fish, griffin and sphinx, and to treat and combine these in such a way as to create a variety of whole new pictures of marked originality.

After the abundance, variety and quality of pictorial pottery of LH III C Middle there is a sharp decline in this and other elaborately decorated ceramics in the Aegean world. What pictorial pottery there is in LH III C Late, and its possible antecedents, should be a subject to be considered at another Workshop in Vienna!

Index to illustrations

Fig. 1 after *RMDP*, 174 no. 365, fig. 49
Fig. 2 after CROUWEL 1991, fig. 8, no. G 3
Fig. 3 photograph K. Demakopoulou
Fig. 4 photograph J. L. Benson
Fig. 5 after XENAKI-SAKELLARIOU 1985, frontispiece
Fig. 6 photograph J. de Vries
Fig. 7 photograph M. R. Popham
Fig. 8 photograph J. de Vries
Fig. 9 after GÜNTNER 2000, pl. 6:1
Fig. 10 photograph M. R. Popham
Fig. 11 after GÜNTNER 2000, pl. 5:1a
Fig. 12 photograph E. Slenczka
Fig. 13 after KILIAN 1992, pl. 3:2
Fig. 14 photograph J. de Vries
Fig. 15 after IAKOVIDIS 1969/70, vol. 2, fig. 65
Fig. 16 photograph M. R. Popham
Fig. 17 photograph M. R. Popham
Fig. 18 drawing S. Bird

Bibliography

ÅKERSTRÖM, Å.
1987 *Berbati. Vol. 2. The Pictorial Pottery* (Skrifter utgivna av Svenska Institutet i Athen, 4°, 36:2). Stockholm.

ALBERS, G.
1994 *Spätmykenische Stadtheiligtümer. Systematische Analyse und vergleichende Auswertung der archäologischen Befunde* (BAR-IS 596). Oxford.

Archaeological Atlas
2003 *Archaeological Atlas of Mycenae* (The Archaeological Society at Athens Library 229). Athens.

BRAUN-HOLZINGER, E. A. – H. MATTHÄUS (eds.)
2002 *Die nahöstlichen Kulturen und Griechenland an der Wende vom 2. zum 1. Jahrtausend v. Chr. Kontinuität und Wandel von Strukturen und Mechanismen kultureller Interaktion. Kolloquium des Sonderforschungsbereiches 295 "Kulturelle und sprachliche Kontakte" der Johannes Gutenberg-Universität Mainz, 11.–12. Dezember 1998.* Möhnesee.

BRONEER, O.
1939 "A Mycenaean Fountain on the Athenian Acropolis", *Hesperia* 8, 317–433.

CROUWEL, J. H.
1991 *The Mycenaean Pictorial Pottery* (Well Built Mycenae 21). Oxford.
1999 "Fighting on Land and Sea in Late Mycenaean Times", 455–460 in: LAFFINEUR 1999.
2003 "Review of W. Güntner, Figürlich bemalte mykenische Keramik aus Tiryns (Tiryns. Forschungen und Berichte 12). Mainz 2000", *AJA* 107, 298–299.
2006a "Late Mycenaean Pictorial Pottery", 233–255 in: EVELY 2006.
2006b "Late Mycenaean Pictorial Pottery: A Brief Review", 15–22 in: RYSTEDT – WELLS 2006.

CROUWEL, J. H. – C. E. MORRIS
1996 "The Beginnings of Mycenaean Pictorial Vase Painting", AA 93, 197–219.

DAVIS, E. N. (ed.)
1977 Symposium on the Dark Ages in Greece. New York.

DEGER-JALKOTZY, S.
2002 "Innerägäische Beziehungen und auswärtige Kontakte des mykenischen Griechenland in nachpalatialer Zeit", 47–74 in: BRAUN-HOLZINGER – MATTHÄUS 2002.

DELPLACE, C.
1967 "Le griffon créto-mycénien", AntCl 36, 49–86.

DEMAKOPOULOU, K.
2006 "Mycenaean Pictorial Pottery from Midea in the Argolid", 31–43 in: RYSTEDT – WELLS 2006.

DEMAKOPOULOU, K. (ed.)
1988 Das mykenische Hellas. Heimat der Helden Homers. Berlin.

DESSENNE, A.
1957 Le sphinx. Étude iconographique. Paris.

DOUMAS, C. G.
1992 The Wall Paintings of Thera. Athens.

EVELY, D. (ed.)
2006 Lefkandi IV. The Bronze Age. The Late Helladic III C Settlement at Xeropolis (BSA Suppl. 39). London.

FELSCH, R. C. S. (ed.)
1996 Kalapodi. Ergebnisse der Ausgrabungen im Heiligtum der Artemis und des Apollon von Hyampolis in der antiken Phokis. Vol. I. Mainz.

FRENCH, E.
1985 "The Figures and Figurines", 209–280 in: RENFREW 1985.

FRONING, H. – T. HÖLSCHER – H. MIELSCH (eds.)
1992 Kotinos. Festschrift für Erika Simon. Mainz.

GENGE, H.
1971 "Zum 'Lebensbaum' in den Keilschrifturkunden", Acta Orientalia 33, 321–334.

GÜNTNER, W.
2000 Figürlich bemalte mykenische Keramik aus Tiryns (Tiryns. Forschungen und Berichte 12). Mainz.

GUGGISBERG, M. A.
1996 Frühgriechische Tierkeramik. Zur Entwicklung und Bedeutung der Tiergefäße und der hohlen Tierfiguren in der späten Bronze- und frühen Eisenzeit (ca. 1600–700 v. Chr.). Mainz.

IAKOVIDIS, S. E.
1969/70 Περατή. Το νεκροταφείον (Βιβλιοθήκη της εν Αθήναις Αρχαιολογικής Εταιρείας 67). Athens

IMMERWAHR, S. A.
1987 "Some Pictorial Fragments from Iolkos in the Volos Museum", ArchEphem 124, 1985 [1987], 85–94.
1990 Aegean Painting in the Bronze Age. University Park – London.

JACOB-FELSCH, M.
1996 "Die spätmykenische bis frühprotogeometrische Keramik", 1–213 in: FELSCH 1996.

KENNA, V. E. G.
1967 Die englischen Museen II (CMS VII). Berlin.

KILIAN, K.
1980 "Zur Darstellung eines Wagenrennens aus spätmykenischer Zeit", AM 95, 21–31.
1992 "Mykenische Heiligtümer der Peloponnes", 10–25 in: FRONING – HÖLSCHER – MIELSCH 1992.

KNELL, H. – W. VOIGTLÄNDER
1980 "Die Ergebnisse in den Quadranten V 2 und VI 2", 118–155 in: Tiryns. Forschungen und Berichte 9. Mainz.

KOPCKE, G.
1977 "Figures in Pot-Painting before, during and after the Dark Age", 32–50 in: DAVIS 1977.

KRITSELI-PROVIDI, I.
1982   Τοιχογραφίες του θρησκευτικού κέντρου των Μυκηνών. Athens.

LAFFINEUR, R. (ed.)
1999   *Polemos. Le Contexte Guerrier en Égée à l'âge du Bronze. Actes de la 7e Rencontre égéenne internationale, Université de Liège, 14–17 avril 1998* (Aegaeum 19). Liège – Austin.

LAFFINEUR, R. – E. GRECO (eds.)
2005   *Emporia. Aegeans in the Central and Eastern Mediterranean. Proceedings of the 10th International Aegean Conference/10e Rencontre égéenne internationale, Athens, Italian School of Archaeology, 14–18 April 2004* (Aegaeum 25). Liège – Austin.

LANG, M. L.
1969   *The Palace of Nestor at Pylos in Western Messenia. Vol. II: The Frescoes*. Princeton.

MCMULLAN FISHER, S.
1998   "The Mycenaean Pictorial Pottery", 100–109 in: WALBERG 1998.

MCMULLAN FISHER, S. – K. L. GIERING
1998   "The Pictorial Stirrup Jar", 109–113 in: WALBERG 1998.

MORGAN, L.
1988   *The Miniature Wall Paintings of Thera. A Study in Aegean Culture and Iconography*. Cambridge.

MOUNTJOY, P. A.
1993   *Mycenaean Pottery. An Introduction*. Oxford.
1998   "The East Aegean–West Anatolian Interface in the Late Bronze Age: Mycenaeans and the Kingdom of Ahhiyawa", *AS* 48, 33–67.
2004   "Miletos: A Note", *BSA* 99, 189–200.
2005   "Mycenaean Connections with the Near East in LH III C: Ships and Sea Peoples", 423–427 in: LAFFINEUR – GRECO 2005.

MYLONAS, G. E.
1975   "Ανασκαφή Μυκηνών", *Prakt* 1973 [1975], 99–107.

PODZUWEIT, C.
1979   "Ausgrabungen in Tiryns 1977. Bericht zur spätmykenischen Keramik", *AA*, 412–440.

POPHAM, M. R. – E. V. MILBURN
1971   "The Late Helladic III C Pottery of Xeropolis (Lefkandi): A Summary", *BSA* 66, 333–352.

POPHAM, M. R. – L. H. SACKETT
1968   *Excavations at Lefkandi, Euboea, 1964–66. A Preliminary Report*. Oxford.

POURSAT, J.-C.
1977   *Les ivoires mycéniens. Essai sur la formation d'un art mycénien* (BEFAR 230). Paris.

RENFREW, C.
1985   *The Archaeology of Cult. The Sanctuary at Phylakopi* (BSA Suppl. 18). London.

RUTTER, J. B.
1992   "Cultural Novelties in the Post-Palatial Aegean World: Indices of Vitality or Decline?", 61–78 in: WARD – JOUKOWSKY 1992.

RYSTEDT, E. – B. WELLS (eds.)
2006   *Pictorial Pursuits: Figurative Painting on Mycenaean and Geometric Pottery. Papers from two Seminars at the Swedish Institute at Athens in 1999 and 2001* (Skrifter Utgivna av Svenska Institutet i Athen, 4°, 53). Stockholm.

SAKELLARAKIS, J. A.
1992   *The Mycenaean Pictorial Style in the National Archaeological Museum of Athens*. Athens.

SAKELLARIOU, A.
1966   Μυκηναϊκή σφραγιδογλυφία. Athens.

SCHALLIN, A.-L.
2002   "Pots for Sale: The Late Helladic III A and III B Ceramic Production at Berbati", 141–155 in: WELLS 2002.

SHERRATT, E. S.
1981   *The Pottery of Late Helladic III C and its Significance* (unpublished Ph.D. thesis). Oxford.

SLENCZKA, E.
1974   *Figürlich bemalte mykenische Keramik aus Tiryns* (Tiryns. Forschungen und Berichte 7). Mainz.

SPYROPOULOS, TH. G.
1981   "Ανασκαφή Μυκηναϊκής Ταναγρας", *Prakt* 1979 [1981], 27–36.

STAMPOLIDIS, N. C. (ed.)
1999   *Φως Κυκλαδικόν. Τιμιτικός τόμος στη μνήμη Νίκου Ζαφειροπούλου*. Athens.

STEEL, L.
1999   "Wine Kraters and Chariots: The Mycenaean Pictorial Style Reconsidered", 803–811 in: *Meletemata*.

TSOUNTAS, C.
1896   "Γραπτή στήλη εκ Μυκηνών", *ArchEphem*, 1–22.

VERMEULE, E. – V. KARAGEORGHIS
1982   *Mycenaean Pictorial Vase Painting*. Cambridge (Mass.) – London.

VLACHOPOULOS, A.
1997   "Ψευδόστομος αμφορέας του Πολυποδικού ρυθμού στο Μουσείο της Πύλου", *ArchEphem* 134, 1995 [1997], 247–256.
1999   "Ο Κρατήρας της Γρόττας. Συμβολή στη μελέτη της ΥΕ ΙΙΙ Γ εικονιστικής κεραμεικής της Νάξου", 74–95 in: STAMPOLIDIS 1999.
2003   "The Late Helladic III C 'Grotta phase' of Naxos. Its Synchronisms in the Aegean and its Non-Synchronisms in the Cyclades", 217–234 in: *LH III C Chronology and Synchronisms*.

WACE, A. J. B.
1921–23 "Excavations at Mycenae § VII. – The Lion Gate and Grave Circle Area. 2. The Granary", *BSA* 25, 38–61.

WALBERG, G.
1998   *Excavations on the Acropolis of Midea. Results of the Greek-Swedish Excavations under the Direction of Katie Demakopoulou and Paul Åström. Vol. I: The Excavations on the Lower Terraces 1985–1991*. Stockholm.

WARD, W. A. – M. S. JOUKOWSKY (eds.)
1992   *The Crisis Years: The 12th Century B.C. from beyond the Danube to the Tigris (International Conference at Brown University, Providence, on May 16–19, 1990)*. Dubuque.

WEDDE, M.
1999   "War at Sea: The Mycenaean and Early Iron Age Oared Galley", 465–476, in: LAFFINEUR 1999.

WELLS, B. (ed.)
2002   *New Research on Old Material from Asine and Berbati in Celebration of the Fiftieth Anniversary of the Swedish Institute at Athens* (Skrifter utgivna av Svenska Institutet i Athen, 8°, 17). Stockholm.

WHITLEY, J.
2003/04 "Archaeology in Greece 2003–2004", *ARepLond* 50, 1–92.
2004/05 "Archaeology in Greece 2004–2005", *ARepLond* 51, 1–118.

XENAKI-SAKELLARIOU, A.
1985   *Οι θαλαμωτοί τάφοι των Μυκηνών. Ανασκαφής Χρ. Τσούντα (1887–1898). Les tombes á chambre de Mycènes. Fouilles de Chr. Tsountas (1887–1898)*. Paris.

Fig. 1 Mycenae. Close Style deep bowl

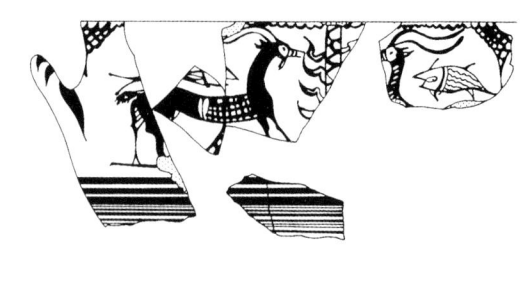

Fig. 2 Mycenae. "Goats and Fish Bowl"

Fig. 3 Mycenae. Close Style stirrup jar

Fig. 4 Mycenae. Detail of the "Warrior Krater"

Fig. 5 Mycenae. Painted Stele

Fig. 6 Mycenae. "Horses and Birds Jar"

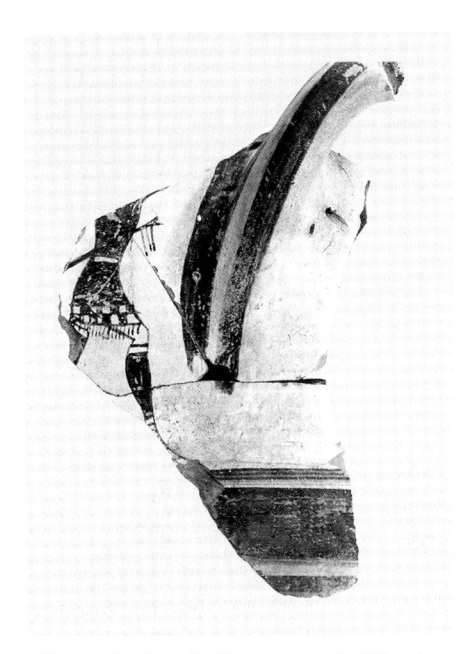

Fig. 7 Lefkandi. Fragment of "Warrior and Horses Krater"

Fig. 8 Mycenae. Deep bowl fragments

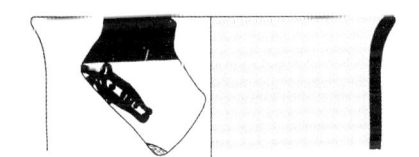

Fig. 9 Tiryns. Deep bowl (?) fragment. Horse's head

Fig. 10 Lefkandi. Deep bowl (?) fragment. Horse's head

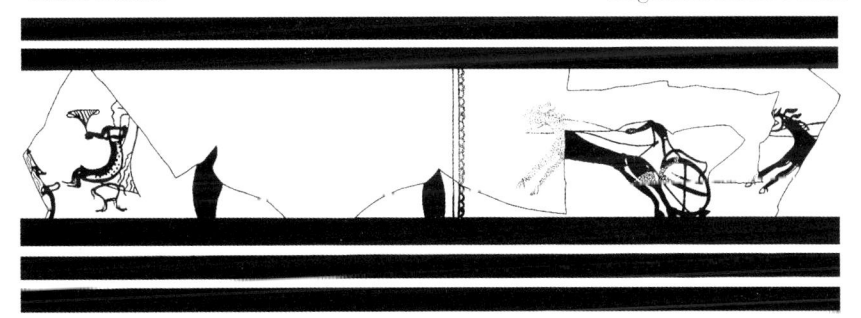

Fig. 11 Tiryns. Jar fragments

Fig. 12 Tiryns. Krater fragment

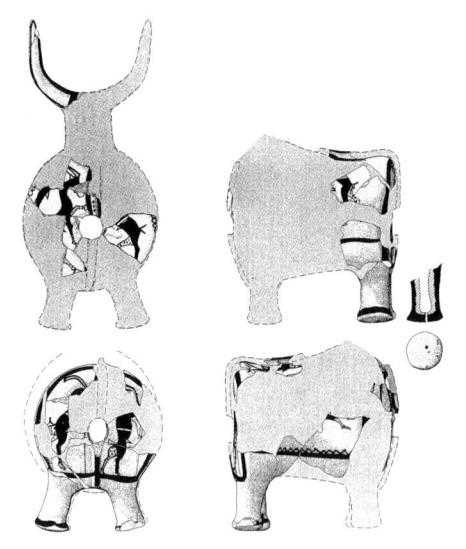

Fig. 13 Tiryns. Restored bull-figure

Fig. 14 Mycenae. Krater fragment

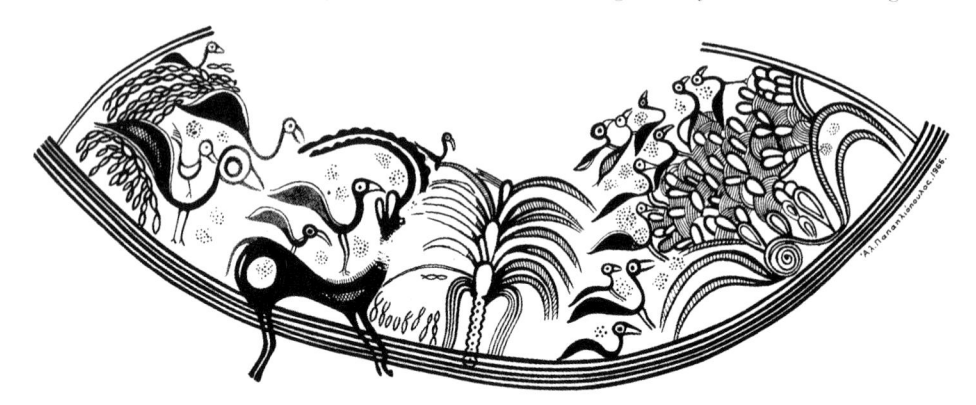

Fig. 15 Perati. Detail of stirrup jar

Fig. 16 Lefkandi. Krater fragment

Fig. 17 Lefkandi. Krater fragment

Fig. 18 Lefkandi. Detail of alabastron

ANNA LUCIA D'AGATA

EVOLUTIONARY PARADIGMS AND LATE MINOAN III. ON A DEFINITION OF LM III C MIDDLE*

INTRODUCTION

The aim of this article is to identify the pottery phase in Crete coeval with LH III C Middle (Advanced). In the following pages it will be seen that the material and contexts corresponding to LH III C Middle Advanced are those defined as LM III C Late (Table 3) in the case of Crete.

Studies on Minoan pottery make no use of the notion of LM III C Middle, for which there is in fact no archaeological definition, and I, too, prefer not to apply it. Rather than drawing a formal terminological correspondence between the Greek Mainland and Crete, labelling as LM III C Middle what had hitherto been referred to as LM III C Late, I find it more fitting to retain the current usage in order to avoid the confusion such a change could generate.

Moreover, it hardly seems justifiable on the sole basis of a formalistic need for uniformity to draw a forced parallel between the subdivisions of Late Minoan pottery in Crete and those applied on the Mainland. Finally, it is worth recalling that the terminology used to refer to the pottery phases is of purely indicative rather than substantive value.

It is to Arthur Evans that we owe the tripartite format of chronology (Early I–III, Middle I–III and Late I–III), still closely adhered to in studies on Bronze Age Crete (MACGILLIVRAY 2000, 234. – PAPADOPOULOS 2005, 105–106). This system of subdivision, which Evans devised to embrace the birth, maturity and decline of each single phase, derives from the evolutionary archaeology which preceded the formulation of an historical view of prehistory and was based on belief in the unilinear development of human society (TRIGGER 1989, 145–147).

All the phases (Early, Middle and Late) of Bronze Age Crete have retained their tripartite structure to this day, and in some cases even sub-phases, identified only at a later stage, have been divided in the same way.

LM III C, however, departs from this scheme. Unlike LH III C, which is divided into Early, Middle and Late, LM III C fell into the bipartite scheme of LM III C Early and LM III C Late from the very outset. It is difficult to identify clear transformations in the Cretan pottery repertory at the close of the Bronze Age to account for a tripartite division. However, bipartition into Early and Late together with the assumed Subminoan/Submycenaean correspondence led to the conviction that Early and Late were coeval with the continental phases of LH III C Early and LH III C Late. This in turn, together with the need to establish the tripartite format, gave rise to the quest for a LM III C Middle.[1]

---

* Thanks are due to Penelope Mountjoy for her comments on a draft of this paper.
[1] See e.g. KANTA 2003 and BORGNA 2004, where division of LM III C into Early, Middle and Late is taken for granted, but not fully explained.

The first to manifest this need explicitly was Fritz Schachermeyr, who proposed a tripartite division of Cretan III C in 1979 (SCHACHERMEYR 1979a. – SCHACHERMEYR 1979b) (Table 2). The Austrian scholar took Middle III C to refer to a central phase, thus corresponding to a time of floruit, characterised by a style that was much the same throughout the Aegean basin. It is of course true that establishing synchronisms between Crete, Cyprus and Greek Mainland is a matter of great moment, but Schachermeyr's attempt fell short in that the subdivision he proposed was based solely on stylistic considerations, with the result that neither a certain number of consistent assemblages was ascribed to the phase, nor were precise and clearly recognisable characteristics identified for it.

Again in purely stylistic terms, but fully aware that stratified deposits are needed to verify her idea, Penelope Mountjoy recently suggested a criterion that could be used to define LM III C Middle, i.e. the presence of a specific type of deep bowl characterised by a raised concave base and a carinated bowl (MOUNTJOY 1999, 511–512): this type, which Mountjoy exemplifies, citing for comparison a vase from Phaistos (MOUNTJOY 1999, pl. 113:b3), is in fact recurrent in the assemblages attributed both to LM III C Late and, in the case of Khania, to LM III C Early. Hence it clearly cannot be applied as the sole criterion to define the phase subsequent to LM III C Early.

What I hope to demonstrate in this paper is that the complexes attributable to LM III C Late, on the basis of the definitions supplied by Desborough and Popham, appear to be coeval with complexes ascribed to LH III C Middle advanced on the Greek Mainland (see also D'AGATA 1999, 195–196. – D'AGATA 2001. – D'AGATA 2003), and that the subsequent phase on Crete, corresponding to LH III C Late, is to be sought in what is now attributed to Subminoan, which actually comprises at least two phases, corresponding to the phases known on the Greek Mainland as LH III C Late and Submycenaean.

Minoan Scholarship on Late Minoan pottery never included, explicitly, a LM III C Middle, and one may well wonder, therefore, why we should also adopt a tripartite division into Early, Middle and Late for Crete, too. It would in fact entail the need for a radical change in terminology with all the consequent risks of confusion and incomprehension, above all for those lacking work experience on Crete. The possibility is not to be ruled out that one or more intermediate phases between LM III C Early and LM III C Late may be identified in the future, and that these phases may rightly be classified as LM III C Middle. It is, however, quite likely that the thus identified LM III C Middle is a phase which corresponds to the end of LH III C Early and/or an initial phase of LH III C Middle (D'AGATA 1999, 195–196).

As for Subminoan, I myself have divided it into two phases: SM I and II (on Subminoan, see D'AGATA forthcoming). In fact, the traditional nomenclature adopted for Knossos includes single forms and contexts that have been defined as Subminoan but which may be considered coeval with LH III C Late.[2] A crucial point here is the possibility to identify artefacts on the basis of which synchronisms can be established with the continental sequence, and so to draw up a clear grid of equivalences in order to tie in firmly the Cretan sequence with the continental sequence (cf. D'AGATA 2003).

LM III C PHASE SEQUENCING HISTORY (Tables 1–2)

The first clear definition of internal phase sequencing within LM III C was given in the 1960s by Mervyn Popham.

---

[2] As I already did in D'AGATA 1999. – D'AGATA 2003.

	DESBOROUGH 1964	
LM III C, first half	Mavrospelio, St Jar Isopata Tomb, St Jar	LH III C Early
Latter stage of LM III C, or Subminoan, or Intermediate	Karphi Mouliana Kephala ThTomb Gypsades Ayios Ioannis Fortetsa Tomb P Spring Chamber Deposit Liliana Tombs	LH III C Late and Submycenaean

	POPHAM 1965, 1992
LM III C Early (first half)	Palaikastro Kastri
LM III C Late or Advanced (second half)	Karphi Gypsades Tombs VIA, VII, IX
Subminoan	Spring Chamber Dep Knossos NorthCem

	KANTA 1980	
LM III C Early (first half)	Palaikastro Kastri	LH III C Early
LM III C Late or Advanced (second half)	Karphi Mouliana Tombs	LH III C Late
Subminoan	Karphi	

Table 1

Following on from the detailed analysis of the island's complexes carried out by Vincent Desborough (DESBOROUGH 1964, 14–15, 166–195) (Table 1), Popham was able to draw a sharp distinction between the first half of the period, to which he assigns the assemblages from Palaikastro Kastri and also some material from Vrokastro, and a later or advanced phase, to which the material recovered in the settlement of Karphi belongs (Table 1). At Palaikastro Kastri Popham pointed out that kylikes with bulbous stems and stirrup jars with an air hole are absent (SACKETT – POPHAM – WARREN 1965, 280–282 – POPHAM 1965, 334). Moreover, these two phases are kept quite distinct from Subminoan (cf. POPHAM 1992); in this respect Popham differs from Desborough, who had considered the final phase of the Bronze Age on Crete as divided in two parts, one corresponding to LM III C Early, the other belonging "to a latter stage of LM III C (whether called sub-Minoan or Intermediate) until such time as it gives way to Protogeometric ..." (DESBOROUGH 1964, 179). Thus Desborough took Subminoan to be an integral part of LM III C, constituting the final stage.

In the very same period a further contribution to the debate appears to have been offered by the deposits of reuse in the tholos tomb on the Kephala at Knossos, published by Gerald Cadogan (CADOGAN 1967). Three single vases were found in the dromos area and in the north side chamber (Fig. 3). Inside the main chamber, however, different deposits were identified stratigraphically and assigned, respectively, to an ancient and late phase of LM III C (Figs. 1–2. – CADOGAN 1967, 259–261). The quantity of material recovered was limited but the difference in the vases which make up the two deposits is evident. However, the presence of a monochrome deep bowl with S-shaped profile and conical foot (Fig. 2.1. – CADOGAN 1967, fig. 2:14) indicates that the latest burial is assignable to a date post-LM III C Late (see below).

	SCHACHERMEYR 1979a,b
III C Early	Palaikastro Kastri
III C Middle	Palaikastro Kastri Karphi (Nobelware of Eastern Crete) Mouliana Tomb B Isopata Tomb, St Jar
III C Late/SM	Karphi Mouliana Tomb A Vrokastro Tomb V Spring Chamber
SM/PG	Fortetsa

	WARREN 1982/83 WARREN – HANKEY 1989	MOOK – COULSON 1997	DAY 1997	HALLAGER 2000	DAY – SNYDER 2004	
LM III C Early	Palaikastro Kastri	KavKastro I		Khania, GSE, AgAikat		LH III C Early
LM III C Middle	KnStratMusExc	KavKastro II KnStratMusExc		Khania, GSE, AgAikat, Pit in Room I	KavKastro II KavVronda I	LH III C Middle
LM III C Late	Kephala ThTomb Mouliana Dreros Tomb I Karphi	KavKastro III KavVronda Karphi	KavKastro III KavVronda	KavKastro III KavVronda Khalasmenos Knossos-Subminoan	KavKastro III KavVronda II Karphi, Great House	LH III C Late
Subminoan	KnStratMusExc Spring Chamber Fortetsa Tomb P				Karphi	Submycenaean

Table 2

In 1980 Athanasia Kanta's book *The Late Minoan III Period in Crete* – i.e. the first substantial contribution to LM III beyond Knossos – was published, confirming Popham's distinction between an ancient and late phase (KANTA 1980, *passim*. – See also KANTA 2003). Kanta's work is still fundamental in the publication and dating of many groups of material. Nevertheless, she makes no further progress in defining a phase sequence for the period (Table 1).

A preliminary report on the Stratigraphical Museum Excavations at Knossos was published in 1983 (WARREN 1982/83). Peter Warren attributed the material recovered to a middle phase of III C, explicitly stating that this phase is situated between the early phase attested by Palaikastro Kastri and the late one documented by Karphi (WARREN 1982/83, 73–74. – WARREN – HANKEY 1989, 90–92) (Table 2). Since this hypothesis would seem to be based mainly on the conviction – then widely held – that the reserved band on deep bowls and kraters was an element of Mainland derivation which appeared in a late phase of LM III C (WARREN 1982/83, 71), it is clear that this complex needs to be examined in the light of more recent acquisitions.[3] In fact, the reserved band has recently been recognised as a Cretan feature already appearing in LM III C Early (KANTA 1997, 97. – TZEDAKIS – KANTA 1978, 15–16. – MOUNTJOY 1999. – HALLAGER 2000, 139).

---

[3] WARREN this volume, where the existence of more "stages" on the basis of the stratigraphic evidence is suggested.

At the end of the 1990s some progress was made with the publication of *Late Minoan III Pottery* and *La Crète Mycénienne* (DRIESSEN – FARNOUX 1997). In the preliminary publication of the material from Kavousi Kastro (MOOK – COULSON 1997), Margaret Mook and William Coulson distinguished three phases based on three different stratigraphic levels.

Phase I is attributed to LM III C Early and appears to be characterised by the introduction of the reserved band on deep bowls, kylikes and kraters, and by the presence of material in LM III B tradition. Phase III is considered to be LM III C Late and coeval with Vronda and Karphi. Fabrics are softer now, the reserved band more common, blob cups with raised bases the most common types of cup, while the deep bowls show straight profiles. Some elements are, however, missing: identified in Karphi, these elements – kylikes with swollen stems, and stirrup jars with knob on the disk – are deemed to be characteristic of the late phase of the period. Phase II definition is even more uncertain. The characteristics considered new are the appearance of basins with inset rim, a larger diameter for deep bowls and a greater frequency of cups. Mook and Coulson themselves state that this phase is difficult to define and cannot be judged on the evidence of single pieces but on the basis of the material as a whole. Nevertheless, they conclude by saying that this is the same period as the one indicated by Warren in the deposits from the Stratigraphical Museum Excavations and defined as "mid-III C" (MOOK – COULSON 1997, 357). In fact, the Kavousi Kastro material is extremely fragmentary and the definitions of Phases II and III are ambiguous in archaeological terms (Table 2).

It is with the preliminary publication of the Kavousi Vronda settlement (DAY 1997) that the characteristics of LM III C Late become clearer. Although different floor levels were identified in many rooms, Leslie P. Day did not consider it possible to define chronological phases for the ceramic assemblages recovered: eventually all of them were attributed to "a late phase of LM III C, later than the earliest remains on the Kastro and contemporary with Karphi" (DAY 1997, 390) (Table 2). At Vronda, the deep bowl with straight sides and raised base is the most common fine shape, with zigzag and wavy lines as the most popular decoration. The number of decorative motifs appears limited, and the monochrome deep bowl makes occasional appearances. Cups and champagne cups may have a carinated profile, and are usually decorated with blobs. Kylikes with deep angular bowls are popular. Kalathoi, kraters and stirrup jars are frequently decorated in a somewhat elaborate style.

Recently a chronological sequence for the material from Building B of Vronda was offered by Day, who now distinguishes two phases on the basis of stratigraphic analysis of the deposits. The older phase is identified in an early deposit in Room 4 and in the lower deposit of Room 7. Attributed to this phase, which is contemporary with Phase II at Kavousi Kastro (DAY – SNYDER 2004, 69) (Table 2), are the deep bowls with straight sides and conical feet, champagne cups with blob decoration, kalathoi and octopus stirrup jars (Fig. 4). Kylikes with deep angular bowls and kalathoi (Fig. 5) are attributed to a later phase, isolated in Room 3 and in Room 7, upper layer. According to Day, instead of the deep bowls and champagne cups we now find kylikes of exceptionally large proportions, and this phase, she holds, is also to be identified at Karphi, in the Great House (DAY – SNYDER 2004, 73). This should correspond to Phase III of Kavousi Kastro and LM III C Late. The main phases at Vronda and Karphi are to be attributed to LM III C Late (DAY forthcoming).

---

[4] On SM I types see below.

As for Karphi (PENDLEBURY H. – PENDLEBURY J. – MONEY-COUTTS 1937/38. – SEIRADAKI 1960), however, no homogeneous groups of material can at present be identified. The material published indicates that there are both LM III C Late carinated cups (SEIRADAKI 1960, fig. 14 [Cup 1]), and SM I material including deep bowls with an S-shaped profile (SEIRADAKI 1960, fig. 14:2),[4] while LM III C Early material is also present (Leslie Day, pers. comm.).

The recent publication of the LM III C settlement of platia Agia Aikaterini in Khania (Greek-Swedish Excavations) contributes to the phase definition of the period (HALLAGER 2000). Here most of the material is from LM III C Early, and, as we all know, this is a complex of great importance, not only because of its exemplary presentation, but also because it originates from a stratigraphic sequence. Birgitta Hallager uses the term "mid LM III C" (HALLAGER 2000, 173) to identify the few complexes that stratigraphically follow on from LM III C Early levels, i.e. material from three rubbish pits, the most significant of which is the one cut in Room I (HALLAGER E. – HALLAGER B. 2000, 39–44). Here, when compared with typical material of the III C Early phase from the site, two elements may be noted: 1. the predominance of deep bowls and kraters with straight to carinated profile; 2. the presence of a small stirrup jar with a knob on the disk (Fig. 6. – HALLAGER E. – HALLAGER B. 2000, 41, 71-P 0738, pl. 38. – HALLAGER 2000, 146).

Hallager attributes this material to a phase later than III C Early but earlier than III C Late (Table 2), because characteristics of the latter – such as conical feet on deep bowls and stirrup jars, swollen stems of kylikes, and air holes close to the neck and the handles of stirrup jars – were not identified. It is true, however, that this is a rather limited quantity of material, and it appears so similar to the Kavousi Vronda material that it is difficult to assign it to a different phase, or to create a phase on the basis of it. It should, therefore, be taken as belonging to LM III C Late:[5] if this is in fact true, then it is Khania that to date provides the best stratigraphic indication for the succession of the two phases known on Crete as LM III C Early and LM III C Late.

The preliminary publication of the material from the ritual pits of Thronos Kephala – which I myself was responsible for – also provides a contribution to a phase definition of the period. As I have pointed out on more than one occasion (D'AGATA 1999. – D'AGATA 2001. – D'AGATA 2003), the material recovered from the pits on the summit of Kephala – even though not found in stratified levels – affords the opportunity to follow the features of local ceramic production at the transition between the Late Bronze and Early Iron Age. It also provides evidence to ascribe local development within LM III C, to reassert the existence of a Subminoan phase within the domestic context, and to link this chronological development to precise reference points on the Greek Mainland.

Three groups of material which exemplify the sequence are:

1. Material from Pits 3 and 5, of LM III C Early, with cups, kylikes, footed cups and deep bowls of known types.

2. Material from Pits 36 and 20, of LM III C Late (Figs. 8–9). To be noted: the conical feet of deep bowls; deep bowls with straight to carinated profile; a reduction in the decorative motifs and the appearance of monochrome among the deep bowls; irregularities in the manufacture of open vessels such as spattering and turning of the bases. At Thronos Kephala correspondence can be found between material from the pits and strat-

---

[5] The stirrup jar from the pit in Room I, characterised by a knob on the stirrup and a decorated band on the belly with a zigzag finds an excellent comparandum in a vase from Atsipadhes (Fig. 7) not earlier than LM III C Late (AGELARAKIS – KANTA – MOODY 2001, 75, fig. 13). For an LM III C Early example of the same kind of stirrup jar, with a decorated band on the belly, see WARREN this volume.

ified material from the dwelling area. Layer 194, which was excavated in 1999 inside Building 2, was the filling of an irregular cut below the earliest floor of Building 2 and may be assigned to LM III C Late. Correspondence with the material from Pits 36 and 20 is clear, and I would also like to underline its correspondence with some vases from the higher deposits of reuse in the Kephala Tholos Tomb at Knossos (cf. Figs. 10; 2).

3. Material from Pit 41 belonging to the earliest phase of Subminoan (Fig. 11a–b): here the most diagnostic shapes are the wavy-band cup 41.5 and the S-shaped monochrome deep bowls (41.22+2, 41.6). The latter constitute the earliest appearance of what Popham called bell-skyphos for an advanced phase of Subminoan: according to the British scholar, in the monochrome version, it was "well represented in SM and EPG deposits and may have served as the standard eating vessel" (POPHAM 1992, 62. – COLDSTREAM – EIRING – FORSTER 2001, 51). Fig. 12 brings together examples of LM III C Early (Fig. 12:1), SM I (Fig. 12:2) and SM II (Fig. 12:3–5) wavy-band cups to show the typological sequence. To date no LM III C Late example has been published. The vase from Thronos Kephala Pit 41.5 (Fig. 12:2) belongs to a rarer type: a couple of very good parallels from the Argolid, dated to LH III C Late, show that the vase from Thronos must be assigned to a coeval phase on Crete (SM I) (*RMDP*, 186 nos. 427–428, fig. 56 [FS 216]. – D'AGATA 2003, 31). Later examples of SM II date (Fig. 12:4–5) are known from Knossos, and have good comparanda with Submycenaean vases.

In short, the existence of a sequence including III C Early, III C Late, and SM I is certain at Thronos Kephala, while the possibility of defining an intermediate phase on stratigraphical bases between LM III C Early and LM III C Late is still hypothetical, as I have already had occasion to stress.[6] Nor does the attempt to do so at Kavousi Kastro seem to have met with success, since Phase II was defined on the basis of marginal characteristics and not the appearance of a coherent assemblage that was at least partially new in comparison with the preceding phase and made up of clearly identifiable types.

LM III C LATE: ARCHAEOLOGICAL DEFINITION AND SYNCHRONISMS WITH THE MAINLAND

On the basis of our present knowledge, it must be concluded that an intermediate phase between LM III C Early and LM III C Late can be identified neither stratigraphically nor as a group of complexes of material whose stylistic features are homogeneous and clearly definable.

Thus, coming to the theme of this workshop, which is the phase in correspondence with LH III C Middle?

On the basis of the synchronisms identified for Thronos Kephala, which I presented at the previous Vienna Workshop (D'AGATA 2003), we can compare the Cretan sequence with the Mainland one. The phases can be summarised as follows:

LM III C Early	LH III C Early/Middle developed
LM III C Late	LH III C Middle advanced
SM I	LH III C Late
SM II	Submycenaean

---

[6] An intermediate phase between LM III C Early and LM III C Late was tentatively considered synchronic with an initial phase of LH III C Middle, D'AGATA 2003, especially table 1 on p. 32. – See also D'AGATA 1999, 195–196.

The phase we are concerned with here is LM III C Late, which comes immediately after III C Early and roughly corresponds to LH III C Middle advanced in Mainland terms. The characteristics of LM III C Late may be summarised as follows:

- conical foot (or concave raised base) on bowls, cups and stirrup jars;
- predominance of deep bowls with straight to carinated profile;
- presence of carinated cups, kraters with angular or carinated profile, and dipped cups with carinated profile;
- appearance of monochrome deep bowls.

As for the cone on the disk of fine stirrup jars, air holes on the neck of stirrup jars, and kylikes with swollen stems – which seem to be a popular characteristic above all in Eastern Crete – it should be noted that these are elements found only occasionally, and not systematically, in the complexes belonging to this phase. Their presence cannot be generalised.

Let us now go on to analyse some contexts which allow us to broaden this definition of LM III C Late. We will begin with the eastern area of the island and Tomb A and B at Mouliana.

Tomb A at Mouliana was discovered in 1903 and referred to by Xanthoudidis as early as 1905 (XANTHOUDIDIS 1905, 22–38). It is a small, square tholos tomb which has yielded a substantial amount of material, including: a krater decorated with figured scenes; a cylindrical pyxis; a deep bowl and a large flask – all found to the left of the entrance (Fig. 13). This material is probably connected with the cremation found within the krater. To the right of the entrance the following objects were found: three stirrup jars, two bronze swords and fragments of a third, a pin of the type without head and with oval boss on the shaft, two fibulae, two spearheads, several bronze plaques, and remains of bronze vases. Furthermore, a gold ring, a small bone disk, and iron fragments were also recovered. The remains of at least one skeleton were discovered in the tomb.

Kanta published the photographs of two deep bowls, similar but not identical, from the Mouliana tombs. The one from Tomb A (Fig. 13:5), reproduced in the report by Xanthoudidis (XANTHOUDIDIS 1905, fig. 6. – KANTA 1980, pl. 83:1), appears very similar to LH III C Middle deep bowls.[7] If not an import, the vase from Mouliana could have been produced under the influence of Mycenaean (Cycladic?) workshops. The other vase (Fig. 13:6. – KANTA 1980, pl. 81:6) looks like a monochrome deep bowl of the carinated type, whose profile is well known in LM III C: comparison can, for example, be made with the LM III C Late deep bowls from Thronos Pit 36 (Fig. 8:36.1), Pit 20 (Fig. 9:20.2) and Layer 194 (Fig. 10.THK99/2).[8]

The presence of the large globular flask (Fig. 13:2. – XANTHOUDIDIS 1905, 26–27, fig. 6) can also be attributed to the link between the Cyclades and Eastern Crete. The majority of the comparanda are from LH III C Middle, and those from Naxos in particular seem the most similar to our piece.[9] The vase is rare on Crete and known only in the

---

[7] According to Mountjoy, this shape often has a dark ground with a reserved band below the interior rim, cf. *RMDP*, 959, fig. 391:67–70 (from Naxos).

[8] Cf. MOUNTJOY 1999, pl. 113:b3 – it corresponds to the type of deep bowl which, as already noted, Mountjoy thinks it may be typical of a middle phase of III C on Crete. The carinated deep bowl is, however, known from LM III C Early, cf. e.g. a vase from Khania in HALLAGER 2000, pl. 35:70-P0755, and continues in SM I, cf. an example from Thronos, Pit 41 (Fig. 11a:41B/7+36).

[9] Cf. *RMDP*, 957 nos. 52–53, fig. 390 (Naxos), no. 52 has nipples on one side of the spout. Melos: *RMDP*, 928 no. 200, fig. 379. Rhodes: *RMDP*, 1084 no. 278, fig. 440. Kalymnos: *RMDP*, 1136 no. 25, fig. 466 (nipple on each side, concentric circles on the body).

eastern part of the island. A similar flask appears to have been discovered in the sanctuary of Kato Symi (cf. *Late Minoan III Pottery*, 103).

The large pictorial krater with carinated profile has a new element under the rim, namely a raised band with white painted strokes (Fig. 13:1. – XANTHOUDIDIS 1905, 32, pl. 3). In LM III C Early, a triangular profile moulding may be present under the rim of straight-sided kraters, as, for instance, in an example from House K at Palaikastro Kastri (SACKETT – POPHAM – WARREN 1965, 299 KP32, fig. 12), but its transformation into a raised and decorated band could be a development of LM III C Late. The same feature also appears on a pithoid krater from a tomb at Kria Sitia (Fig. 14:1. – DAVARAS 1984, 337. – DAVARAS 1981, 116–117, pl. 23. – KANTA – DAVARAS 2004, 151, fig. 5) and on two clay larnakes: one from Mouliana, Tomb B (Fig. 14:2. – XANTHOUDIDIS 1905, 39–42, fig. 9. – KANTA 1980, pl. 81:5), another one from Tourloti (Fig. 14:3. – TSIPOPOULOU – VAGNETTI 1999). On kraters and larnakes from East Crete of LM III C Early date the raised band with strokes is missing (cf. TSIPOPOULOU – VAGNETTI 1997, pls. 180–188). This element is well known as a feature of continental kraters assigned to LH III C Middle advanced (*RMDP*, 170), in the form of a raised band with incised strokes.

The larnax from Tourloti has to be mentioned with respect to the evolution of the Cretan pictorial style. The difference between the depiction of birds in the examples from Khamalevri (ANDREADAKI-VLAZAKI – PAPADOPOULOU 2005, 381–382, figs. 44–45), Khania (HALLAGER 2000, pl. 53:78-P0069, 77-P0116/0117 [+71-P 1015]) and Kastelli Pediada (RETHEMIOTAKIS 1997, 411, figs. 14–15), all dating from LM III C Early and showing an impressionistic, but still naturalistic appearance (Fig. 15), and those on the larnax – in a quasi-geometric style – which must be considered one of the latest manifestations of the pictorial style of LM III C (Fig. 14:3), may be useful in asserting a development in the rendering of birds on vases and larnakes at the very end of the Late Bronze Age in Crete.

We can conclude that at least the burial assemblage found in Mouliana, Tomb A to the left of the entrance and including the pictorial krater may be considered LM III C Late.

Tomb B at Mouliana (XANTHOUDIDIS 1905, 38–50) is a tholos tomb with a square ground plan. It was found a few metres to the south of Tomb A and contained two burials, one of them inside a clay larnax. The larnax shows the raised band with painted strokes which we have just analysed. Two stirrup jars, three shield bosses and a sword were attributed to the burial inside the larnax. There were two stirrup jars, one of them decorated in Octopus Style, a second sword, two spearheads, the remains of a gold mask, and two small ivory plaques in the tomb. The burial inside the larnax should also belong to LM III C Late.

Few Minoan octopus stirrup jars have been fully published, so the development of this typical East Cretan product is unknown. We must therefore exclude them from our discussion, suffice it to note that stirrup jars in this style are almost certainly to be found in contexts of both LM III C Early and LM III C Late. On the other hand, we have no certainty that the style remained in use in the subsequent phase.

The presence of Naue type swords in both Tombs A and B at Mouliana, however, provides an important link between the two complexes, and also with the warrior tombs common in western Greece, especially in LH III C Middle advanced (EDER – JUNG, pls. 107–108). Likewise, the gold rings with granulations from Mouliana Vroulia (XANTHOUDIDIS 1905, 50, fig. 13), Praesos Photula and the Tiryns treasure, which have recently been taken into consideration together (MARAN 2005, 426. – MARAN 2006), could be of help in defining a synchronism between Crete and the Mainland. In this respect, we must take into account the presence of a gold ring in Tomb A of Mouliana (Fig. 13:7. – XANTHOUDIDIS 1905, 37, fig. 8), albeit of a different type, with simple bezel, if we wish to understand whether such a concentration of similar, high-quality objects in the same area and in tombs displaying common characteristics is to be attributed to one and the same phase (see also EDER – JUNG 2005, 488).

Moving on, now, to Central Crete, two rather important complexes are Tombs VII and VIA of Gypsades at Knossos (HOOD – HUXLEY – SANDARS 1958/59, 205–208). Their chronology has given rise to some controversy: Desborough considered them Subminoan, meaning by this, as we have seen, a phase corresponding to a late phase of LM III C, preceding the Protogeometric.[10] Popham dated them to "advanced LM III C", while Catling assigned the vases from Tomb VIA to Subminoan, and recently Mountjoy described the stirrup jars recovered there as examples of Subminoan style (POPHAM 1965, 333 n. 36. – CATLING 1996, 309. – *RMDP*, 194 n. 1018).

Tomb VII at Gypsades is a chamber tomb preceded by a long dromos. Apart from a group of older and stratigraphically separate material, two burials were recovered: the first is associated with material found inside and outside the larnax; the second was identified slightly to the east.

The larnax, decorated with wavy bands, leant against the eastern wall, contained the remains of a skeleton and an iron knife with bronze rivets. There was a group of vases to the south-east of the larnax (HOOD – HUXLEY – SANDARS 1958/59, 247–248 nos. 1–3, 7, fig. 27:VII.1–2 [amphorae], 3, 7 [small stirrup jars]) comprising two belly-handled amphorae, each with a small stirrup jar close to its mouth (Fig. 16:1–4). Three stirrup jars leant against the southern wall (HOOD – HUXLEY – SANDARS 1958/59, 248 nos. 4–6, figs. 27:VII.5–6; 29:VII.4), and on the floor near to the vessels there were four bronze pins of the type without head and with an elliptical boss on the shaft (HOOD – HUXLEY – SANDARS 1958/59, 249 nos. 13–16, fig. 60a, pl. 34). Vases and pins were linked to the burial inside the larnax.

The belly-handled amphorae belonging to this burial (Fig. 16:1–2) should be dated to LM III C Late. They have a globular body, and VII.1 (Fig. 16:1) has two small nipples on its shoulder. It may be useful in asserting synchronisms between Crete and the Mainland to compare them to a vase from Asine, which corresponds to FS 58 and has been assigned to LH III C Middle (*RMDP*, 159 no. 323, fig. 42). A fragmentary vase belonging to a similar type was recovered from one of the later pits from the Agia Aikaterini settlement in Khania (HALLAGER 2000, 38–39, 151, pl. 43:77-P1935a). A vertical handle has, however, been attributed to it.

In Crete the form develops towards a biconical profile, in which the lower part of the body becomes conical and the shoulder tends to be less slanted, as in the amphorae from a tomb in Agios Ioannis (HOOD – COLDSTREAM 1968, 211 no. B.1, pl. 53), and Tomb D at Liliana (SAVIGNONI 1904, 643, fig. 111) (Fig. 16:5–6). On the strength of this, Amphora 112.1 from Knossos, North Cemetery (COLDSTREAM – CATLING 1996, 163, 303, fig. 121), with its globular body, could still be assigned to LM III C Late, and not to Subminoan. And the same consideration may perhaps be made for another Knossian vase, F 67 from Tomb 5.1 (COLDSTREAM – CATLING 1996, 287, 303, pl. 262).

A different burial inside Gypsades VII is represented by three pieces found in the eastern part of the chamber: a stirrup jar, a trefoil-mouthed jug, and a bronze ring (Fig. 17. – HOOD – HUXLEY – SANDARS 1958/59, 248–249 nos. 8–9, 17, figs. 27:VII.8–9; 33:VII.17). The definition VIA in Gypsades refers to a group of vases leaning against the rock, that was found about a metre beneath the modern-day ground level and interpreted as the remains of a burial. These comprise a stirrup jar and fragments of a sec-

---

[10] DESBOROUGH 1964, 182. For the meaning of Subminoan in Desborough, see supra.

ond, a small neck-handled amphora, and a neck-handled amphora with scroll decoration (Fig. 18. – HOOD – HUXLEY – SANDARS 1958/59, 247 nos. 1–4, fig. 28:VIA.1–4).

Both the burial in the eastern part of Gypsades Tomb VII, and Gypsades VIA contained vases of small dimensions. In fact, from LM III C Late onwards, small amphorae and small flasks, oinochoai, and side-spouted jars became popular (cf. D'AGATA 2003, 30–31). The small side-spouted jars from Karphi, and the amphora from Thronos Kephala Pit 35 are probably of LM III C Late date (Fig. 19:1–3). The latter shows an irregular decoration of the dipped type. The trefoil-mouthed jug with rising handle of Gypsades Tomb VII (Fig. 19:6. – HOOD – HUXLEY – SANDARS 1958/59, fig. 27:VII.9) apparently constitutes the first phase in the evolution of a vase which was widespread at Knossos in SM II (Fig. 19:9). The typological evolution from a rounded body to a squat one veering towards the biconical is evident. The decorative style also changes in Subminoan, becoming prevalently of the dipped type. The same tendencies are to be found in the neck-handled miniature amphora. Transition from a type with an oval body (SM I) to a type with a squat profile body (SM II) can be observed (Fig. 19).

The neck-handled amphora with scroll decoration appears in Crete in LH III C Early, as examples from Thronos Kephala and Khamalevri (D'AGATA 2003, 28, fig. 2:1. – ANDREADAKI-VLAZAKI – PAPADOPOULOU 2005, 374, fig. 36) may show (Fig. 20:1–2). In this phase its body has an oval profile with handles rising above the rim. The amphora with tassel from Palaikastro Kastri seems to represent an example of a very similar type (SACKETT – POPHAM – WARREN 1965, 299 KP28, fig. 16 [wrongly numbered KP31]). In LM III C Late the shape becomes oval and, occasionally, has twisted handles: vases from Gypsades, Tomb VIA, Vrokastro Settlement and, perhaps, Karphi should belong to this phase (Fig. 20:3–5. – HOOD – HUXLEY – SANDARS 1958/59, 247 VIA.4, fig. 28. – HAYDEN 2003, 38 no. 70, fig. 14). The evolution of the shape in SM I and SM II is indicated in Fig. 20:6–8. In SM II the body becomes longer and the twisted handles a stable feature. The comparison between the example from Gypsades Tomb VIA and LH III C Middle examples from Naxos (*RMDP*, 946 no. 21, fig. 385) reveals a strong affinity between the two groups.

Bearing this in mind, the amphora from Tomb 200, North Cemetery (Fig. 20:6. – COLDSTREAM – CATLING 1996, 193, fig. 128:200.4) which is part of the group of tombs identified by Catling as belonging to the earliest phase of Subminoan, could be attributed to SM I, corresponding to LH III C Late. Many details on this vase – i.e. shape, decorative motif and linear decoration, and the swirl on the body under the handles – may be found on coeval vases from Thronos Kephala, Pit 41 (Figs. 11b:41B/32; 20:7). Again with regard to Tomb 200 of Knossos North Cemetery, it might be interesting to compare stirrup jar 3 (COLDSTREAM – CATLING 1996, 193, fig. 123:200.3) with the one imported from Crete, recovered in Naxos, Kamini, and attributed to a LH III C Early /Middle context (Fig. 21:1–2. – VLACHOPOULOS 1999, 306, fig. 8. – VLACHOPOULOS 2001, 223, fig. 6). Apart from the general similarities between the two vases, the same detail can be observed: a festoon decoration – near the shoulder. The two vases cannot be too far apart chronologically: LM III C Late for the one recovered in Naxos, SM I for the Knossian one, and they might even have come from the same workshop.

CONCLUSION

In order to establish a sequence parallel to the one established for the Mainland, and on the basis of stratigraphic evidence, LM III C–SM pottery may be divided into four phases (Table 3):

- the first, which corresponds to LM III C Early;
- the second, which is usually called LM III C Late;

- the third, which may be called SM I;
- the fourth, which may be called SM II.

The possibility of defining an intermediate phase on stratigraphic bases between LM III C Early and LM III C Late is, as we have said, still hypothetical. One candidate might possibly be Khamalevri, Phase II: this is a second structural phase identified in the LM III C village of Khamalevri in the Rethymnon area. Within a pottery context that appears very close to III C Early, a decorated trypod pyxis (ANDREADAKI-VLAZAKI – PAPADOPOULOU 2005, 384–385, fig. 41. – ANDREADAKI-VLAZAKI – PAPADOPOULOU this volume), which is considered an import by the excavators, finds comparanda in LH III C Middle vases from Attica (*RMDP*, 585 no. 413, fig. 216, from Perati). However, more data are needed on the context of phase II before we can understand which continental phase of III C Middle (developed or advanced) it is to be synchronised with.

Table 3 lists, in chronological order, some significant Cretan contexts of the LM III C–SM II sequence. The adjacent column shows the continental contexts that have yielded Minoan imports, offering the possibility to link the Cretan with the Mainland sequence.

SM I and SM II seem to correspond to LH III C Late and Submycenaean respectively. Thus, the definition of LM III C Late also emerges from analysis of the successive phases. This analysis, however, goes beyond the scope of this paper and will be presented elsewhere (D'AGATA forthcoming).

Index to illustrations

Fig. 1 Pottery from the lower levels of reuse in the Kephala Tholos Tomb at Knossos
1) H. 9.8; D. rim 13.2 (after POPHAM 1978, 185, fig. 1e); 2) H. 9.4; D. rim 15.3 (after CADOGAN 1967, 261 no. 8, fig. 2); 3) H. 10.2 (after CADOGAN 1967, 261 no. 2, fig. 4); 4) H. 28.5 (after CADOGAN 1967, 265 no. 13, fig. 5)

Fig. 2 Pottery from the upper levels of reuse in the Kephala Tholos Tomb at Knossos
1) H. 9.4; D. rim 11 (after CADOGAN 1967, 265 no. 14, fig. 2); 2) H. 8.3; D. rim 12–13 (after CADOGAN 1967, 261 no. 4, fig. 2); 3) H. 12.4; D. rim 16 (after CADOGAN 1967, 263 no. 11, fig. 2); 4) H. 10.8 (after CADOGAN 1967, 261 no. 1, fig. 4)

Fig. 3 Pottery from the dromos and the side chamber of the Kephala Tholos Tomb at Knossos
1) H. 7 (after CADOGAN 1967, 261 no. 3, fig. 3); 2) H. 10.5 (after CADOGAN 1967, 263 no. 9, fig. 3); 3) H. 22.2 (after CADOGAN 1967, 265 no. 12, fig. 3)

Fig. 4 Pottery from early deposits in Vronda, Building B, Rooms 4 and 7 (after DAY – SNYDER 2004, fig. 5:6)

Fig. 5 Pottery from later deposits in Vronda, Building B, Room 3 (after DAY – SNYDER 2004, fig. 5:11)

Fig. 6 Pottery from Khania, GSE, LM III C settlement, Pit in Room I (after HALLAGER 2000, pls. 35; 38–39)

Fig. 7 Jug from Atsipadhes (after AGELARAKIS – KANTA – MOODY 2001, 75, fig. 13)

Fig. 8 Pottery from Thronos Kephala, Pit 36

Fig. 9 Pottery from Thronos Kephala, Pit 20

Fig. 10 Pottery from Thronos Kephala, Layer 194

Fig. 11a–b Pottery from Thronos Kephala, Pit 41

Fig. 12 LM III C–SM Wavy-Band Cups
1) H. max. 7.3; D. 12. From Thronos Kephala, Pit 5.1; 2) H. 8; D. 10.7. From Thronos Kephala, Pit 41.5; 3) H. 6.3; D. 6.2. From Knossos, North Cemetery, Tomb 40 (after COLDSTREAM – CATLING 1996, 88, fig. 83:19); 4) H. ca. 7.4. From Knossos, Spring Chambers (after POPHAM 1992, pl. 50b); 5) H. ca. 10.8; D. rim ca. 11.1. H. ca. 12; D. rim ca. 12. From Knossos, Stratigraphical Museum Excavations (after WARREN 1982/83, fig. 60a–b)

Fig. 13 Mouliana, Tomb A, pictorial krater burial context
1) Mouliana, Tomb A, pottery (after XANTHOUDIDIS 1905, pl. 3); 2) Mouliana, Tomb A, pottery (after XANTHOUDIDIS 1905, fig. 6); 3) Mouliana, Tomb A, stirrup jar HM 3480 (after KANTA 1980, fig. 82:5); 4) Mouliana, Tomb A, stirrup jar HM 3477 (after KANTA 1980, fig. 82:4); 5) Mouliana, Tomb A, deep bowl HM 3484 (after KANTA 1980, fig. 83:1); 6) Mouliana, Tomb A?, deep bowl HM 3485 (after KANTA 1980, fig. 81:6); 7) Mouliana, Tomb A, gold ring (after XANTHOUDIDIS 1905, fig. 8)

		Cretan Imports in LH III C –SubMyc contexts	LH III C Imports on Crete	
LM III C Early	Khania, GSE, AgAikat (HALLAGER 2000) Khamalevri I–II Thronos, Pit 54 (D'AGATA 2003) Kephala ThTomb, lower dep. (Fig. 1:1–3) Kavousi Kastro I–II Palaikastro, House K, floor KnStratMusExc (Kavousi Vronda, Building B)	Tiryns, Lower Town, St Jars (MARAN 2005), III C Early context Epidauros Limera, St Jar (*RMDP*, 283 no. 189), III C Early context Patras, 2 St Jars (*RMDP*, 421), III C Early context Agrapidochori, St Jar (*RMDP*, 390 no. 70, fig. 135), III C Early context	Kommos, III B or C Early St Jar (RUTTER 2005, fig. 9a) Kommos, III C Early St Jar (RUTTER 2005, fig. 9b) Khamalevri, III C Early St Jar (ANDREADAKI-VLAZAKI– PAPADOPOULOU 2005, fig. 49:94/3/287) Khania, III C Early or Middle conical bowl (HALLAGER 2000, 171, 77-P0088, pl. 78:e5)	LH III C Early/ Middle developed
LM III C Late	Khania, GSE, AgAikat, Pit in Room I (Fig. 6) Khamalevri II' Atsipadhes Cemetery? Thronos Kephala, Pit 36 (D'AGATA 1999) Thronos Kephala, Pit 31 (D'AGATA 1999) Thronos, NP, Layer 194 (D'AGATA 2003) KnStratMusExc Isopata Tomb, St Jar Kephala ThTomb, higher dep. (Fig. 2:2–4) Gypsades Tomb VII (Fig. 16:1–4) Khalasmenos? Kavousi Vronda, Building B (Fig. 5) Kavousi Kastro III Karphi Settlement Kria Sitia, Tomb XXIV Tourloti, clay larnax with birds (Fig. 14:3) Mouliana Tomb A, burial with krater (Fig. 13) Mouliana Tomb B, burial with clay larnax Vrokastro, Chamber Tomb V	Epidauros Limera, St Jar (*RMDP*, 290 no. 222, fig. 99) Perati II, St Jar (*RMDP*, 592)	Khamalevri II, III C Middle advanced (?) pyxis in Close Style (ANDREADAKI-VLAZAKI – PAPADOPOULOU 2005, fig. 41)	LH III C Middle advanced
Subminoan I	Thronos, Pit 41 (D'AGATA 1999) Pantanassa ThTomb KnStratMusExc Gypsades VIA (Fig. 18) Gypsades Tomb VII, burial in the eastern part (Fig. 17) Knossos NorthCem, Tomb 200 Knossos NorthCem, Tomb 112 Kephala ThTomb, vases from higher dep. (Fig. 2:1) and in dromos (Fig. 3:1–2) Karphi Settlement	Pellana, St Jar (*RMDP*, 293 no. 242, fig. 100) Epidauros Limera, St Jar, (*RMDP*, 293 no. 241, fig. 100) Argos, St Jar (*RMDP*, 184 no. 423, fig. 56) Salamis, St Jar (*RMDP*, 619 no. 585, fig. 237)		LH III C Late
Subminoan II	Thronos, Pit 2 (D'AGATA 1999) Thronos, Pit 20 (D'AGATA 1999) KnStratMusExc Knossos, Spring Chamber Deposit Knossos, Fortetsa Tomb P Knossos NorthCem, Tomb 40 Knossos NorthCem, Tomb 121 Phatsi Droggara	Tiryns, Tomb XIIIb.5, flask (*RMDP*, 194 no. 464, fig. 60)		Submycenaean

Table 3

Fig. 14 Clay krater and larnakes of LM III C Late date
   1) Krater from Kria Sitia, Tomb XXIV (after Davaras 1981, pl. 23a); 2) Mouliana, Tomb B, clay larnax (after Xanthoudidis 1905, fig. 9); 3) Tourloti, clay larnax (after Tsipopoulou-Vagnetti 1999, 127, fig. 5a)

Fig. 15 Pictorial pottery of LM III C date
   1) (after Andreadaki-Vlazaki – Papadopoulou 2005, fig. 44); 2) (after Hallager 2000, pl. 53:77-P0116/0117 (+71-P1015)); 3–4) (after Rethemiotakis 1997, fig. 15)

Fig. 16 Pottery from Gypsades Tomb VII, Agios Ioannis, reused Minoan tomb, and Liliana Tomb D
   1) H. 41. From Gypsades Tomb VII (after Hood – Huxley – Sandars 1958/59, 208, 247, fig. 27:VII.1, pl. 56); 2) H. 39.4. From Gypsades Tomb VII (after Hood – Huxley – Sandars 1958/59, 208, 247, fig. 27:VII.2); 3) H. 13.3. From Gypsades Tomb VII (after Hood – Huxley – Sandars 1958/59, 208, 247, fig. 27:VII.3); 4) H. 10.2. From Gypsades Tomb VII (after Hood – Huxley – Sandars 1958/59, 208, 248, fig. 27:VII.7); 5) H. 44. From Agios Ioannis, reused Minoan tomb (after Hood – Coldstream 1968, pl. 53); 6) From Liliana, Tomb D (after Savignoni 1904, fig. 111)

Fig. 17 Pottery from Gypsades Tomb VII, burial in the eastern part
   1) H. 13.5 (after Hood – Huxley – Sandars 1958/59, 248, fig. 27:VII.8); 2) H. 11.8 (after Hood – Huxley – Sandars 1958/59, 248, fig. 27:VII.9)

Fig. 18 Pottery from Gypsades VIA
   1) H. 15 (after Hood – Huxley – Sandars 1958/59, 247, fig. 28:VIA.1); 2) (after Hood – Huxley – Sandars 1958/59, 247, fig. 28:VIA.2); 3) H. 10.8 (after Hood – Huxley – Sandars 1958/59, 247, fig. 28:VIA.3); 4) H. 38 (after Hood – Huxley – Sandars 1958/59, 247, fig. 28:VIA.4)

Fig. 19 LM III C Late–SM small jugs and amphorae
   1) H. 7.3. From Thronos Kephala, Pit 35.1; 2–3) From Karphi, settlement (after Seiradaki 1960, 16, fig. 10); 4) H. 10.8. From Gypsades VIA (after Hood – Huxley – Sandars 1958/59, 247, fig. 28:VIA.3); 5) H. 7. From Knossos, Kephala Tholos Tomb (after Cadogan 1967, 261 no. 3, fig. 3); 6) H. 11.8. From Gypsades Tomb VII, burial in the eastern part (after Hood – Huxley – Sandars 1958/59, 248, fig. 28:VII.9); 7) H. 15.5. From Knossos, North Cemetery, Tomb 40 (after Coldstream – Catling 1996, 88, fig. 83:17); 8) H. 10.5. From Knossos, North Cemetery, Tomb 121 (after Coldstream – Catling 1996, 165, fig. 117:121.7); 9) H. 10.6. From Knossos, North Cemetery, Tomb 40 (after Coldstream – Catling 1996, 88, fig. 83:18); 10) H. 10.4. From Tiryns, Tomb XIIIb. 5 (after *RMDP*, 194 no. 464, fig. 60)

Fig. 20 LM III C–SM neck-handled amphorae
   1) H. max. 18. From Thronos Kephala, Pit 54.16 (after D'Agata 2003, fig. 2:1); 2) H. ca. 20. From Khamalevri (after Andreadaki-Vlazaki – Papadopoulou 2005, fig. 36); 3) H. 38. From Gypsades VIA (after Hood – Huxley – Sandars 1958/59, 247, fig. 28:VIA.4); 4) H. 41. From Vrokastro, settlement (after Hayden 2003, fig. 14); 5) From Karphi (after Seiradaki 1960, fig. 8:4); 6) H. 49. From Knossos, North Cemetery, Tomb 200 (after Coldstream – Catling 1996, 193, fig. 128:200.4); 7) H. max. 28. From Thronos Kephala, Pit 41B.32; 8) H. 52. H. 50.5. From Knossos, North Cemetery, Tomb 207 (after Coldstream – Catling 1996, 198, fig. 128:50–51)

Fig. 21 Knossian (?) stirrup jars of LM III C Late and SM I date
   1) From Naxos, Kamini (after Vlachopoulos 1999, 307, fig. 8); 2) H. 19.7. From Knossos, North Cemetery, Tomb 200 (after Coldstream – Catling 1996, 193, fig. 123:3)

Bibliography

Agelarakis, A. – A. Kanta – J. Moody
2001   "Cremation Burials in LM III C–Sub Minoan Crete and the Cemetery at Pezoulos Atsipadhes, Crete", 69–82 in: Stampolidis 2001.

Andreadaki-Vlazaki, M. – E. Papadopoulou
2005   "The Habitation at Khamalevri, Rethymnon, during the 12th Century BC", 353–397 in: *Ariadne's Threads*.

Bietak, M. (ed.)
2003   *The Synchronisation of Civilisations in the Eastern Mediterranean in the Second Millennium B.C. II. Proceedings of the SCIEM 2000 – EuroConference, Haindorf, 2nd of May – 7th of May 2001* (Österreichische Akademie der Wissenschaften. Denkschriften der Gesamtakademie 29 = Contributions to the Chronology of the Eastern Mediterranean 4). Vienna.

BORGNA, E.
2004 "Social Meanings of Food and Drink Consumption at LM III Phaistos", 174–195 in: HALSTEAD – BARRETT 2004.

CADOGAN, G.
1967 "Late Minoan III C Pottery from the Kephala Tholos Tomb near Knossos (Knossos Survey 8)", *BSA* 62, 257–265.

CATLING, H. W.
1996 "The Subminoan Pottery", 295–310; "The Subminoan Phase in the North Cemetery at Knossos", 639–649 in: COLDSTREAM – CATLING 1996.

COLDSTREAM, J. N. – H. W. CATLING (eds.)
1996 *Knossos North Cemetery: Early Greek Tombs* (BSA Suppl. 28). London.

COLDSTREAM, J. N. – L. J. EIRING – G. FORSTER
2001 *Knossos Pottery Handbook. Greek and Roman* (BSA Studies 7). London.

D'AGATA, A. L.
1999 "Defining a Pattern of Continuity during the Dark Age in Central-Western Crete: Ceramic Evidence from the Settlement of Thronos/Kephala (Ancient Sybrita)", *SMEA* 41, 181–218.
2001 "Ritual and Rubbish in Dark Age Crete: The Settlement of Thronos/Kephala (Ancient Sybrita) and the Pre-Classical Roots of a Greek City", *Aegean Archaeology* 4, 1997–2000 [2001], 45–59.
2003 "Late Minoan III C–Subminoan Pottery Sequence at Thronos/Kephala and its Connections with the Greek Mainland", 23–35 in: *LH III C Chronology and Synchronisms*.
forthc. "Subminoan: A Neglected Phase of the Cretan Pottery Sequence", *SMEA* 2008.

D'AGATA, A. L. – A. VAN DE MOORTEL – M. B. RICHARDSON (eds.)
forthc. *Archaeologies of Cult: Essays on Ritual and Cult in Crete* (Hesperia Suppl. 42).

DAVARAS, C.
1981 "A Double Axe-Design (?) from Vrokastro", *ArchEphem* 1979 [1981], 114–117.
1984 "Κρυά Σητείας", *ArchDelt* 32, 1977 [1984], Chron 336–339.

DAY, L. P.
1997 "The Late Minoan III C Period at Vronda, Kavousi", 391–406 in: DRIESSEN – FARNOUX 1997.
forthc. "Ritual Activity at Karphi: A Reappraisal", in: D'AGATA – VAN DE MOORTEL – RICHARDSON forthcoming.

DAY, L. P. – M. S. MOOK – J. D. MUHLY (eds.)
2004 *Crete Beyond the Palaces: Proceedings of the Crete 2000 Conference* (Prehistory Monographs 10). Philadelphia.

DAY, L. P. – L. M. SNYDER
2004 "The 'Big House' at Vronda and the 'Great House' at Karphi: Evidence for Social Structure in LM III C Crete", 63–79 in: DAY – MOOK – MUHLY 2004.

DEGER-JALKOTZY, S. – I. S. LEMOS (eds.)
2006 *Ancient Greece: From the Mycenaean Palaces to the Age of Homer* (Edinburgh Leventis Studies 3). Edinburgh.

DESBOROUGH, V. R. D'A.
1964 *The Last Mycenaeans and Their Successors. An Archaeological Survey c. 1200–c. 1100 B.C.* Oxford.

DRIESSEN, J. – A. FARNOUX (eds.)
1997 *La Crète Mycénienne. Actes de la Table Ronde internationale organisée par l'École française d'Athènes, 26–28 Mars 1991* (BCH Suppl. 30). Paris.

EDER, B. – R. JUNG
2005 "On the Character of Social Relations between Greece and Italy in the 12th/11th c. BC", 485–495 in: LAFFINEUR – GRECO 2005.

HALLAGER, B. P.
2000 "The Late Minoan III C Pottery", 135–174 in: *GSE II*.

HALLAGER, E. – B. P. HALLAGER
2000 "The LM III C Settlement", 34–126 in: *GSE II*.

HALSTEAD, P. – J. C. BARRETT (eds.)
2004 *Food, Cuisine and Society in Prehistoric Greece* (Sheffield Studies in Aegean Archaeology 5). Oxford.

HAYDEN, B. J.
2003 *Reports on the Vrokastro Area, Eastern Crete. Vol. 1: Catalogue of Pottery from the Bronze and Early Iron Age Settlement of Vrokastro in the Collections of the University of Pennsylvania Museum of Archaeology and Anthropology and the Archaeological Museum, Herakleion, Crete* (University Museum Monograph 113). Philadelphia.

HOOD, M. S. F. – J. N. COLDSTREAM
1968 "A Late Minoan Tomb at Ayios Ioannis near Knossos", *BSA* 63, 205–218.

HOOD, M. S. F. – G. HUXLEY – N. SANDARS
1958/59 "A Minoan Cemetery on Upper Gypsades (Knossos Survey 156)", *BSA* 53/54, 194–262.

KANTA, A.
1980 *The Late Minoan III Period in Crete. A Survey of Sites, Pottery and Their Distribution* (SIMA 58). Göteborg.
1997 "LM III B and LM III C Pottery Phases. Some Problems of Definition", 83–101 in: *Late Minoan III Pottery*.
2003 "The First Half of the Late Minoan III C – Correlations among Cretan Sites with Reference to Mainland and Cypriote Developments", 513–538 in: BIETAK 2003.

KANTA, A. – C. DAVARAS
2004 "The Cemetery of Krya, District of Seteia. Developments at the End of the Late Bronze Age and the Beginning of the Early Iron Age in East Crete", 149–157 in: STAMPOLIDIS – IANNIKOURI 2004.

LAFFINEUR, R. – PH. P. BETANCOURT (eds.)
1997 *TEXNH. Craftsmen, Craftswomen and Craftsmanship in the Aegean Bronze Age. Proceedings of the 6th International Aegean Conference/6ᵉ Rencontre égéenne internationale, Philadelphia, Temple University, 18–21 April 1996* (Aegaeum 16). Liège – Austin.

LAFFINEUR, R. – E. GRECO (eds.)
2005 *Emporia. Aegeans in the Central and Eastern Mediterranean. Proceedings of the 10th International Aegean Conference/10ᵉ Rencontre égéenne internationale, Athens, Italian School of Archaeology, 14–18 April 2004* (Aegaeum 25). Liège – Austin.

MACGILLIVRAY, J. A.
2000 *Minotaur. Sir Arthur Evans and the Archaeology of the Minoan Myth*. London.

MARAN, J.
2005 "Late Minoan Coarse Ware Stirrup Jars on the Greek Mainland. A Postpalatial Perspective from the 12th Century BC Argolid", 415–431 in: *Ariadne's Threads*.
2006 "Coming to Terms with the Past: Ideology and Power in Late Helladic III C", 123–150 in: DEGER-JALKOTZY – LEMOS 2006.

MOOK, M. S. – W. D. E. COULSON
1997 "Late Minoan III C Pottery from the Kastro at Kavousi", 337–365 in: *Late Minoan III Pottery*.

MOUNTJOY, P. A.
1999 "Late Minoan III C/Late Helladic III C: Chronology and Terminology", 511–516 in: *Meletemata*.

PAPADOPOULOS, J. K.
2005 "Inventing the Minoans: Archaeology, Modernity and the Quest for European Identity", *JMA* 18, 87–149.

PENDLEBURY, H. W. – J. D. S. PENDLEBURY – M. B. MONEY-COUTTS
1937/38 "Excavations in the Plain of Lasithi. II", *BSA* 38, 1–56.

Περιφέρεια
1999 *Η περιφέρεια του Μυκηναϊκού κόσμου. Α΄ διεθνές διεπιστημονικό συμπόσιο, Λαμία, 25–29 Σεπτεμβρίου 1994*. Lamia.

POPHAM, M. R.
1965 "Some Late Minoan III Pottery from Crete", *BSA* 60, 316–342.
1978 "Notes from Knossos, Part II", *BSA* 73, 179–187.
1992 "The Subminoan Pottery", 59–66 in: SACKETT 1992.

Relations between Cyprus and Crete
1979 *Acts of the International Archaeological Symposium "The Relations between Cyprus and Crete, ca. 2000–500 B.C.", Nicosia 16th April–22nd April 1978*. Nicosia.

Rethemiotakis, G.
1997 "A Chest-Shaped Vessel and Other LM III C Pottery from Kastelli Pediada", 407–421 in: Driessen – Farnoux 1997.

Rutter, J. B.
2005 "Southern Triangles Revisited: Lakonia, Messenia, and Crete in the 14th–12th Centuries BC", 17–50 in: *Ariadne's Threads*.

Sackett, L. H. – M. R. Popham – P. M. Warren
1965 "Excavations at Palaikastro VI", *BSA* 60, 248–315.

Sackett, L. H. (ed.)
1992 *Knossos. From Greek City to Roman Colony. Excavations at the Unexplored Mansion* II (BSA Suppl. 21). Oxford.

Savignoni, L.
1904 "Scavi e scoperte nella necropoli di Festòs", *MAL* 14, 501–666.

Schachermeyr, F.
1979a "The Pleonastic Pottery Style of Cretan Middle III C and its Cypriote Relations", 204–214 in: *Relations between Cyprus and Crete*.
1979b *Die Ägäische Frühzeit. Vol. 3: Kreta zur Zeit der Wanderungen vom Ausgang der Minoischen Ära bis zur Dorisierung der Insel* (SBWien 355 = Mykenische Studien 7). Vienna.

Seiradaki, M.
1960 "Pottery from Karphi", *BSA* 55, 1–37.

Stampolidis, N. C. (ed.)
2001 Πρακτικά του Συμποσίου 'Καύσεις στην Εποχή του Χαλκού και την Πρώιμη Εποχή του Σιδήρου', Ρόδος, 29 Απριλίου – 2 Μαΐου 1999. Athens.

Stampolidis, N. C. – A. Iannikouri (eds.)
2004 Το Αιγαίο στην Πρώιμη Εποχή του Σιδήρου. Πρακτικά του διεθνούς συμποσίου, Ρόδος, 1–4 Νοεμβρίου 2002. Athens.

Trigger, B. G.
1989 *A History of Archaeological Thought*. Cambridge.

Tsipopoulou, M. – L. Vagnetti
1997 "Workshop Attributions for Some Late Minoan III East Cretan Larnakes", 473–479 in: Laffineur – Betancourt 1997.
1999 "A Bath-Tub Larnax from Tourloti (Sitia), East Crete", *SMEA* 41, 123–143.

Tzedakis, I. – A. Kanta
1978 Καστέλλι Χανιών 1966. Αναλυτική μελέτη της κεραμεικής από τη στρωματογραφημένη τάφρο Β και το πηγάδι (Incunabula Graeca 66). Rome.

Vlachopoulos, A.
1999 "Η Νάξος κατά την ΥΕ III Γ περίοδο. Η φυσιογνωμία και ο χαρακτήρας ενός ακμαίου νησιωτικού κέντρου", 303–314 in: *Περιφέρεια*.
2001 "The Late Helladic III C 'Grotta Phase' of Naxos. Its Synchronisms in the Aegean and its Non-Synchronisms in the Cyclades", 217–234 in: *LH III C Chronology and Synchronisms*.

Warren, P. M.
1982/83 "Knossos: Stratigraphical Museum Excavations, 1978–82. Part II", *AR* 29, 63–87.

Warren, P. M. – V. Hankey
1989 *Aegean Bronze Age Chronology*. Bristol.

Xanthoudidis, S. A.
1905 "Εκ Κρήτης", *ArchEphem* 1904 [1905], 1–56.

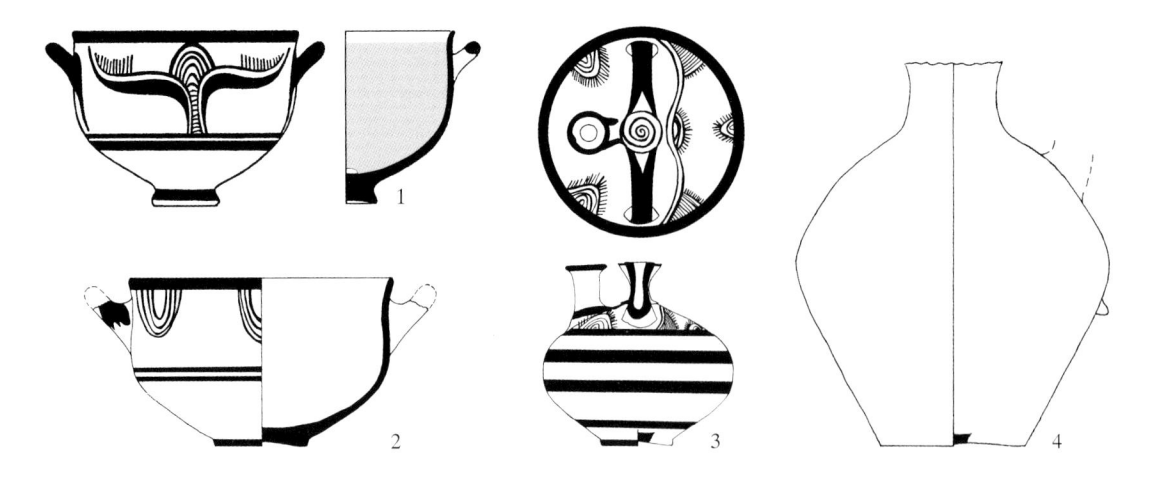

Fig. 1 Pottery from the lower levels of reuse in the Kephala Tholos Tomb at Knossos (not to scale)

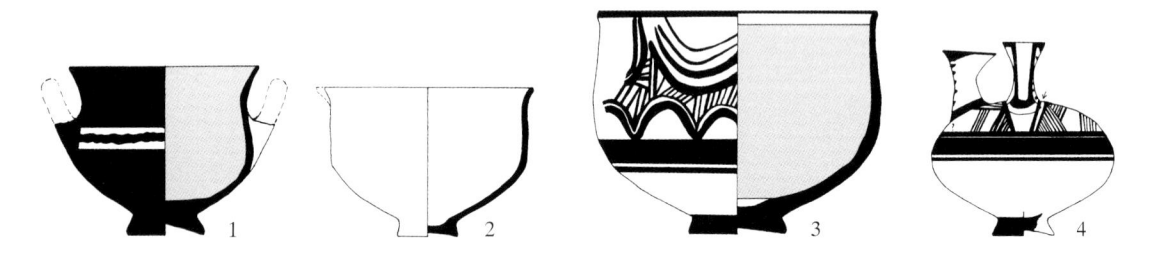

Fig. 2 Pottery from the upper levels of reuse in the Kephala Tholos Tomb at Knossos (not to scale)

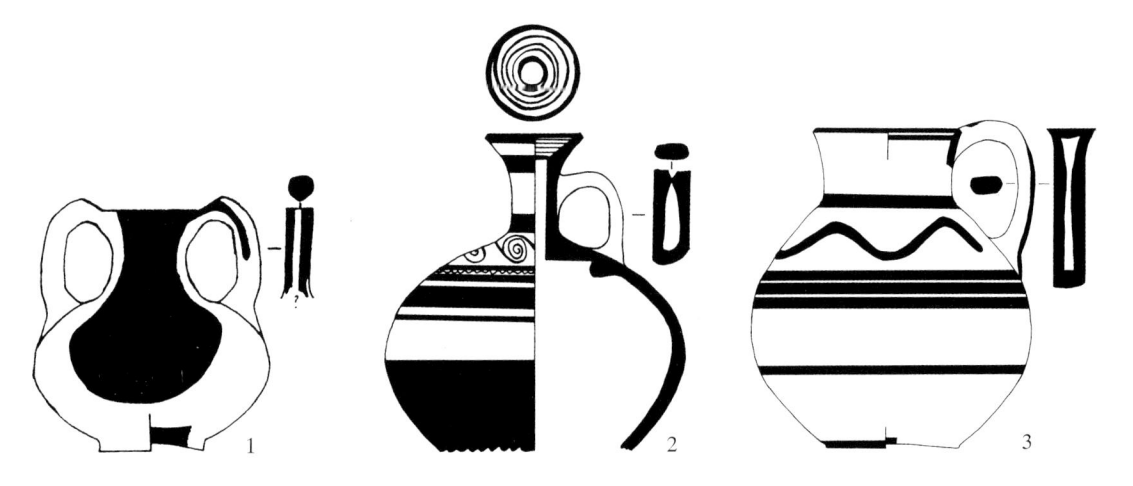

Fig. 3 Pottery from the dromos and the side chamber of the Kephala Tholos Tomb at Knossos (not to scale)

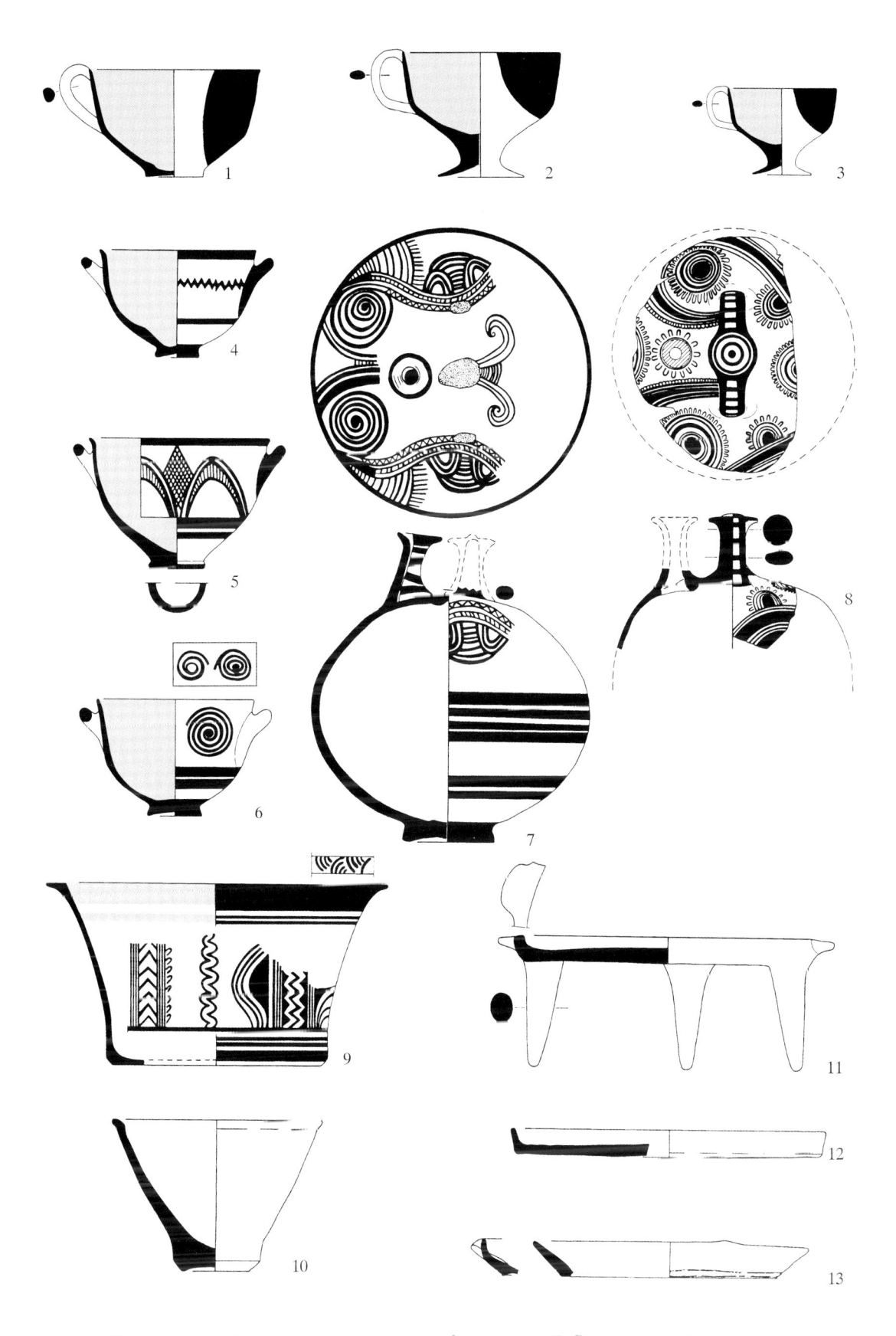

Evolutionary Paradigms and Late Minoan III. On a Definition of LM III C Middle 107

Fig. 4 Pottery from early deposits in Vronda, Building B, Rooms 4 and 7 (not to scale)

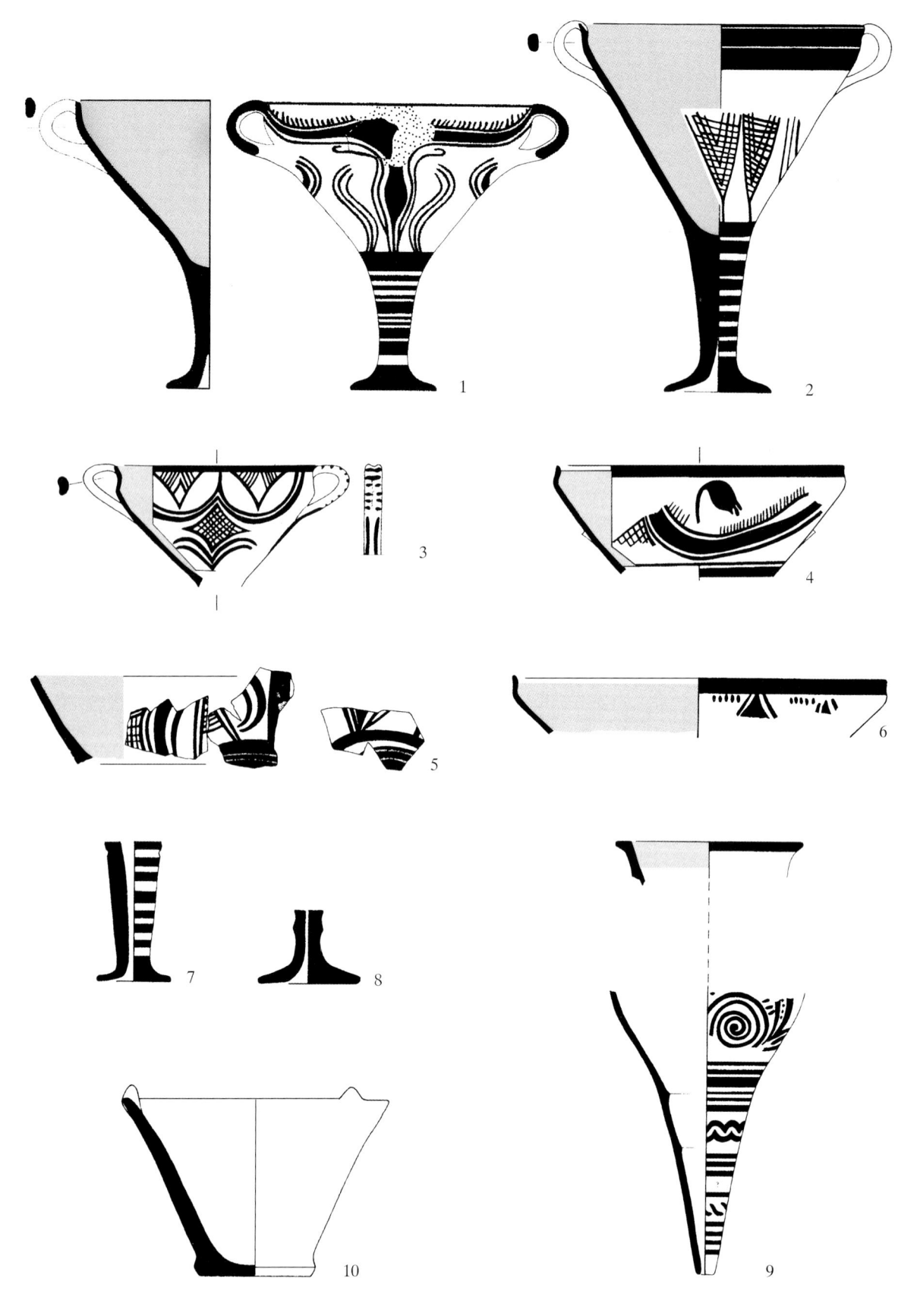

Fig. 5 Pottery from later deposits in Vronda, Building B, Room 3 (not to scale)

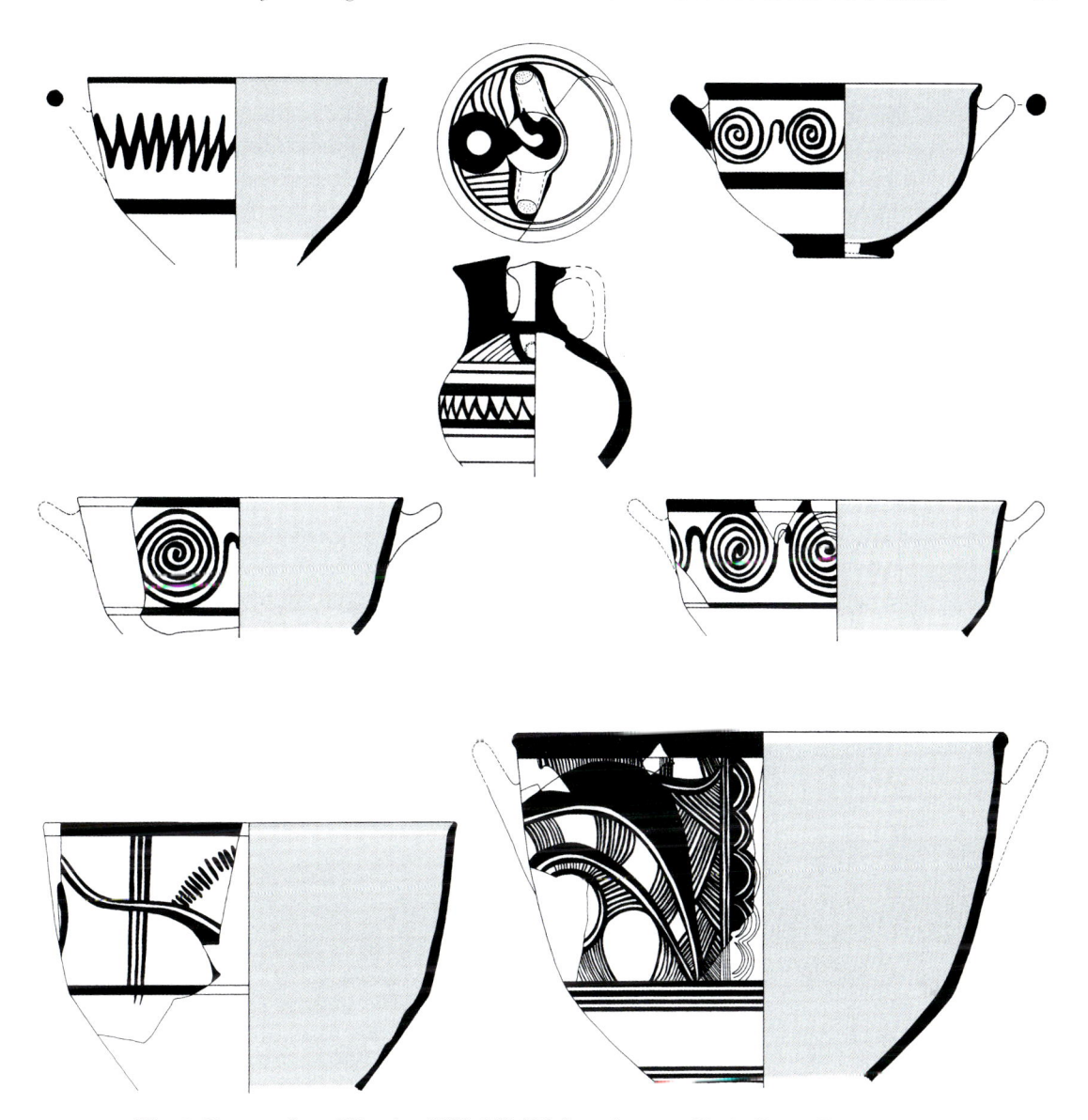

Fig. 6 Pottery from Khania, GSE, LM III C settlement, Pit in Room I (not to scale)

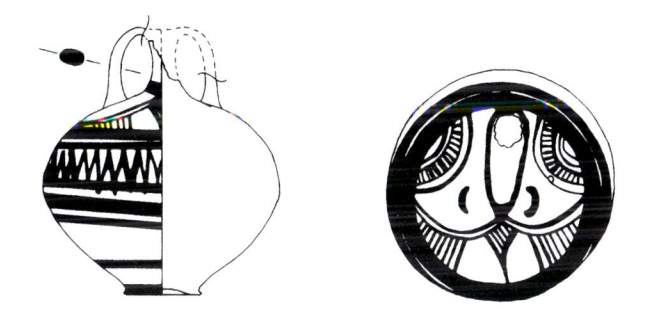

Fig. 7 Jug from Atsipadhes (not to scale)

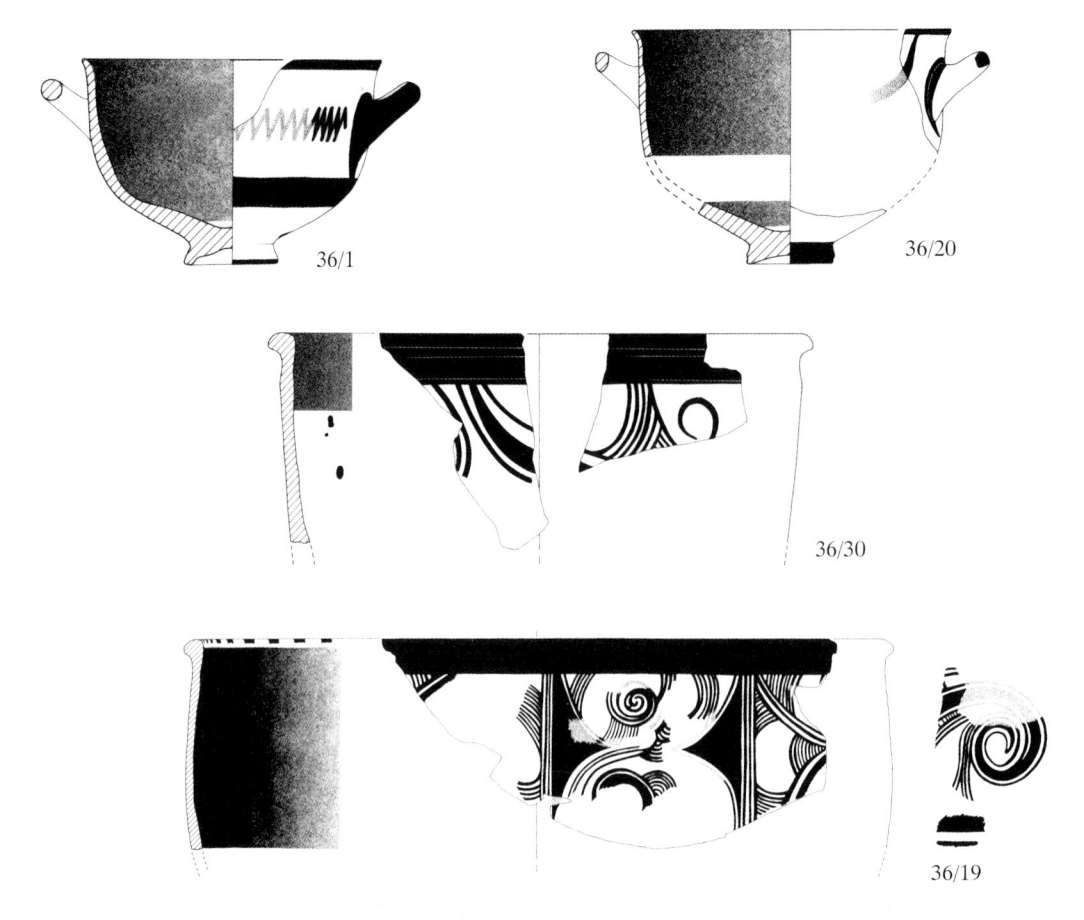

Fig. 8 Pottery from Thronos Kephala, Pit 36 (not to scale)

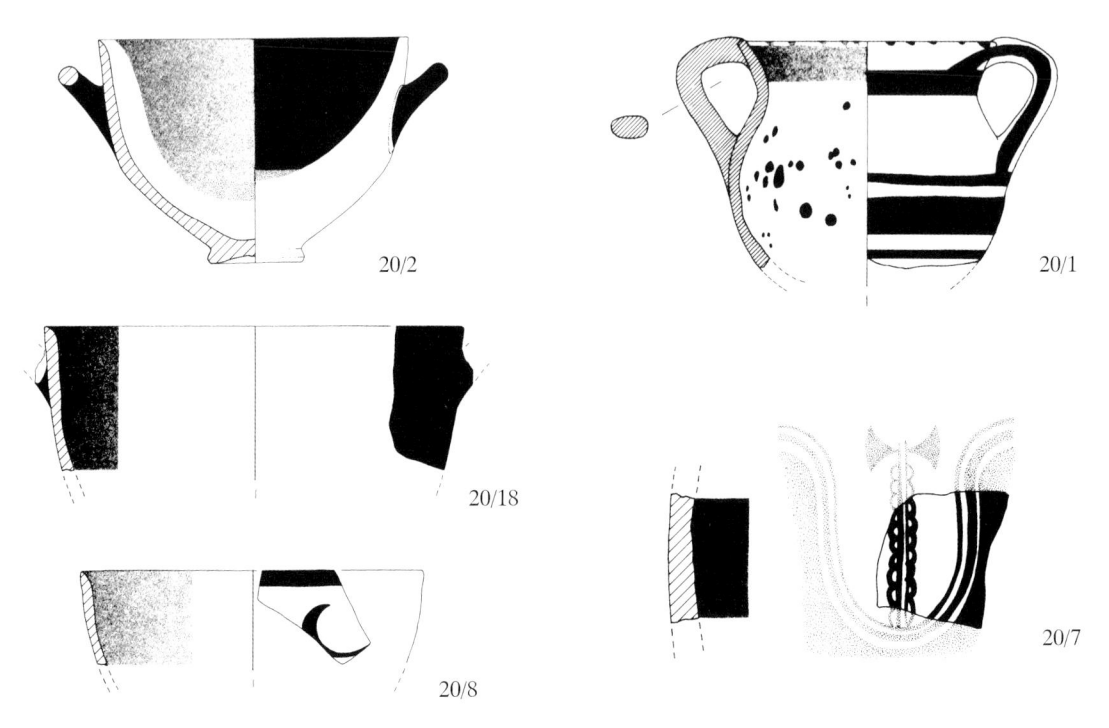

Fig. 9 Pottery from Thronos Kephala, Pit 20 (not to scale)

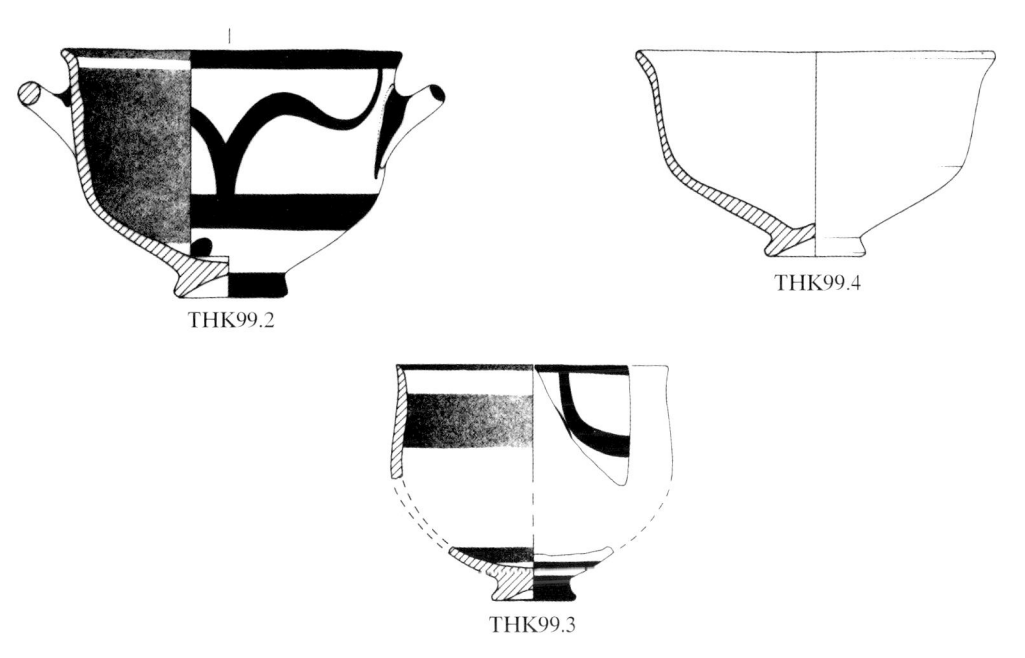

Evolutionary Paradigms and Late Minoan III. On a Definition of LM III C Middle 111

Fig. 10 Pottery from Thronos Kephala, Layer 194 (not to scale)

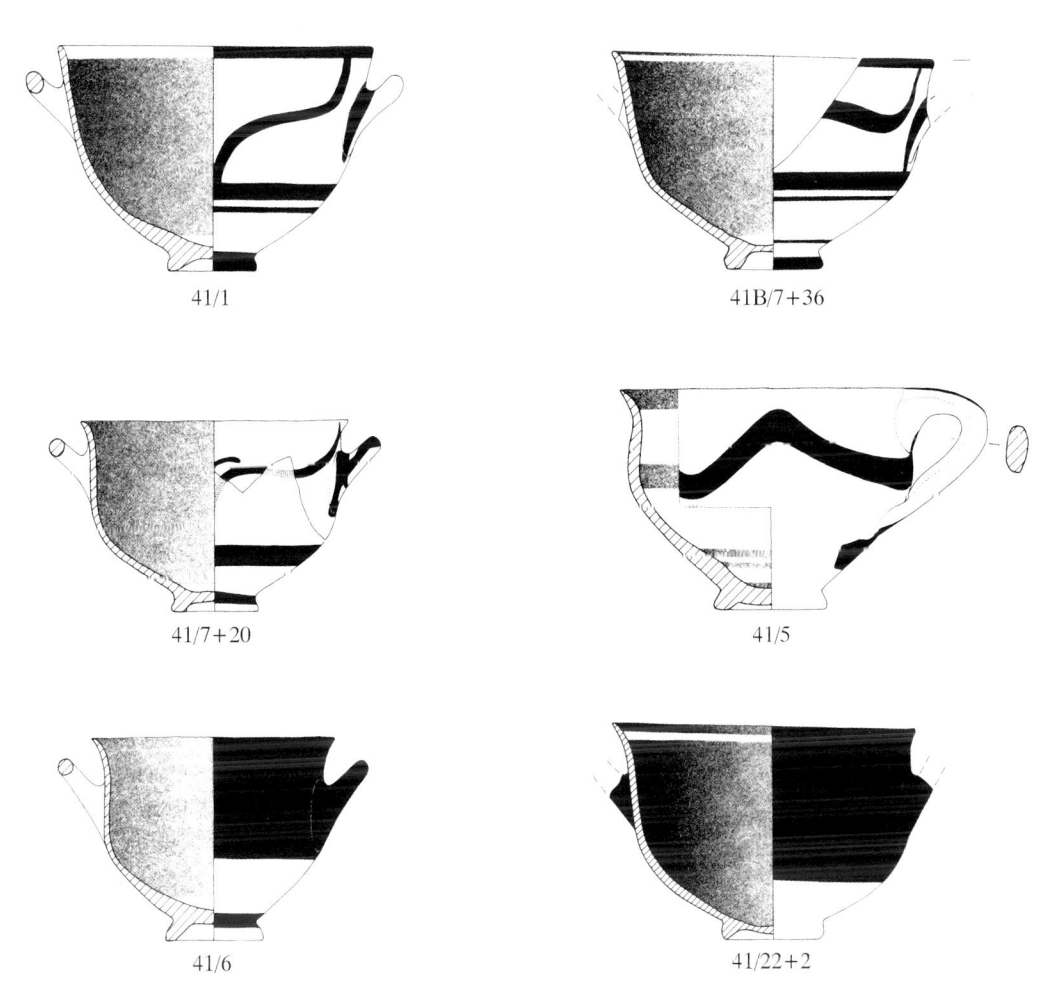

Fig. 11a Pottery from Thronos Kephala, Pit 41 (not to scale)

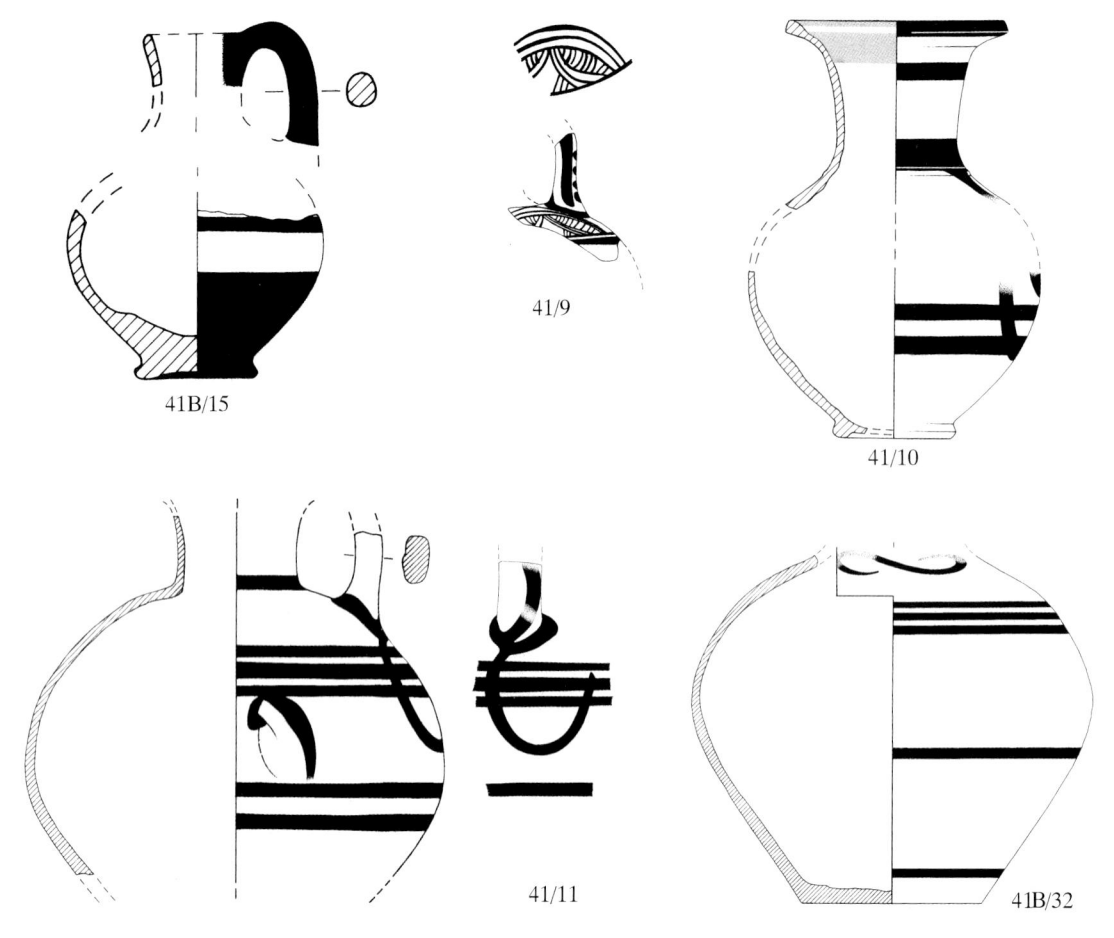

Fig. 11b Pottery from Thronos Kephala, Pit 41 (not to scale)

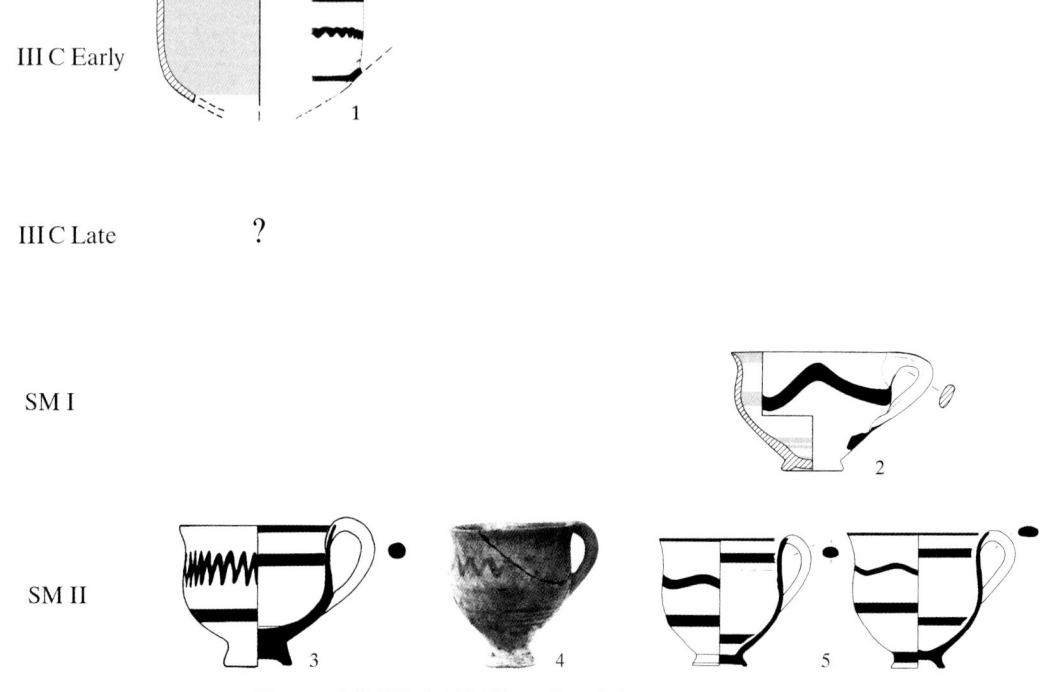

III C Early

III C Late   ?

SM I

SM II

Fig. 12 LM III C-SM Wavy-Band Cups (not to scale)

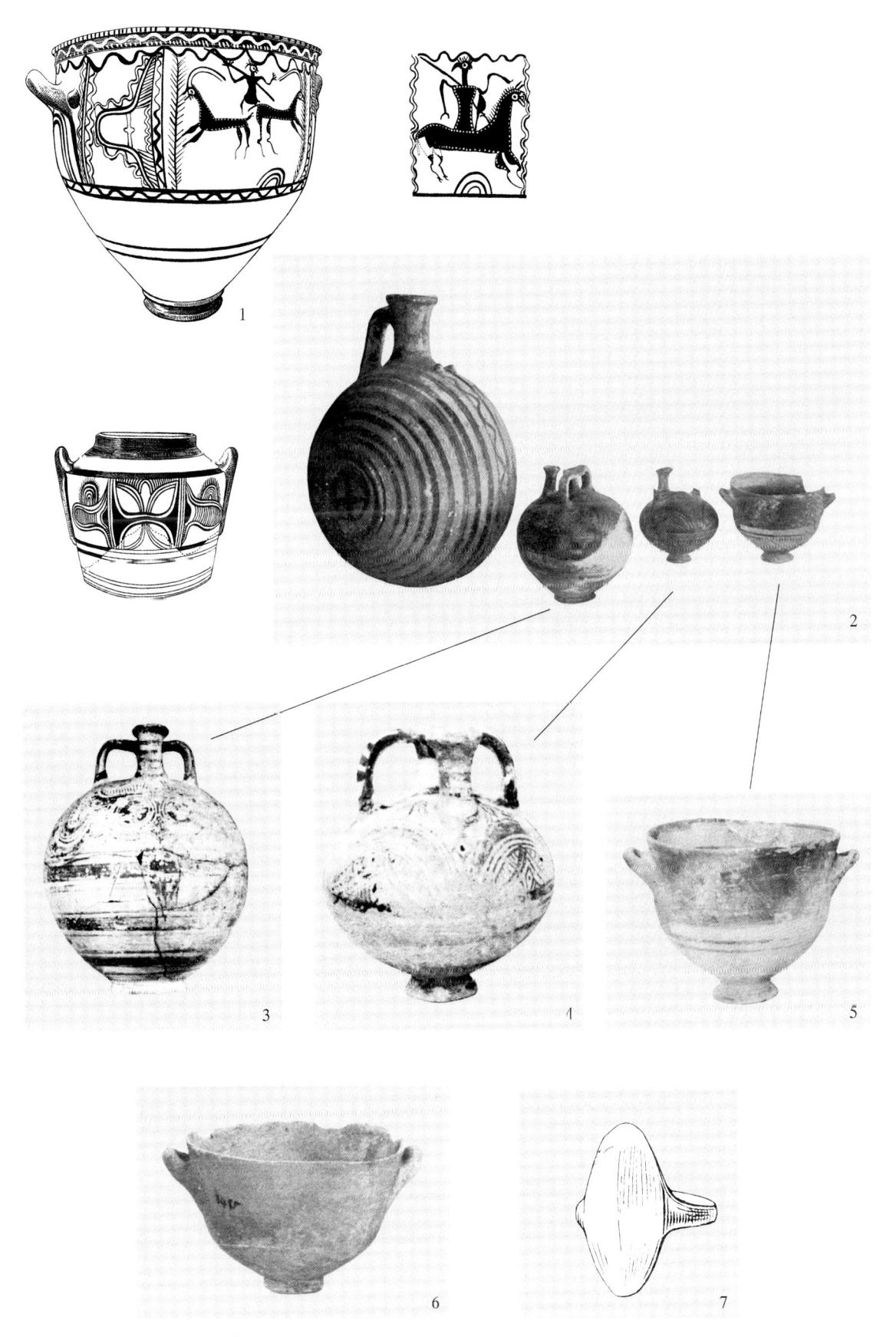

Fig. 13 Mouliana, Tomb A, pictorial krater burial context (not to scale)

Fig. 14 Clay krater and larnakes of LM III C Late date (not to scale)

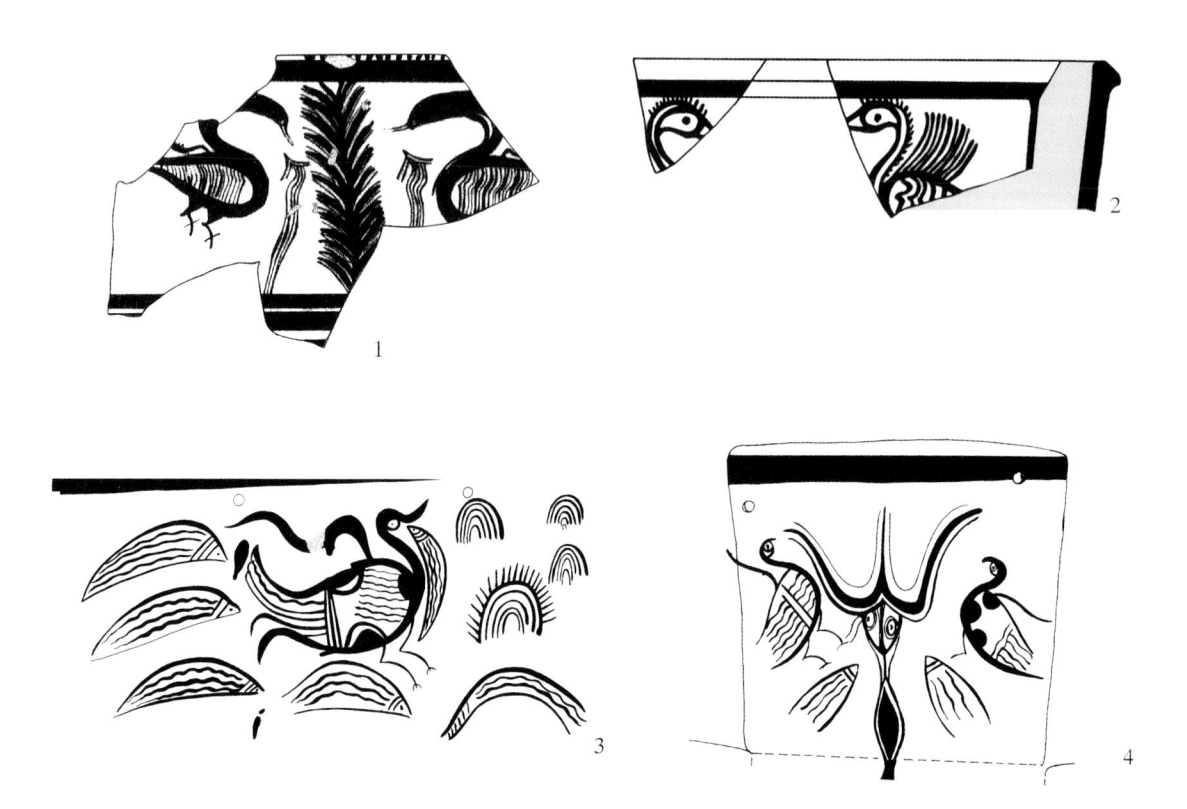

Fig. 15 Pictorial pottery of LM III C date (not to scale)

Evolutionary Paradigms and Late Minoan III. On a Definition of LM III C Middle 115

Fig. 16 Pottery from Gypsades Tomb VII, Agios Ioannis, reused Minoan tomb, and Liliana Tomb D (not to scale)

Fig. 17 Pottery from Gypsades Tomb VII, burial in the eastern part (not to scale)

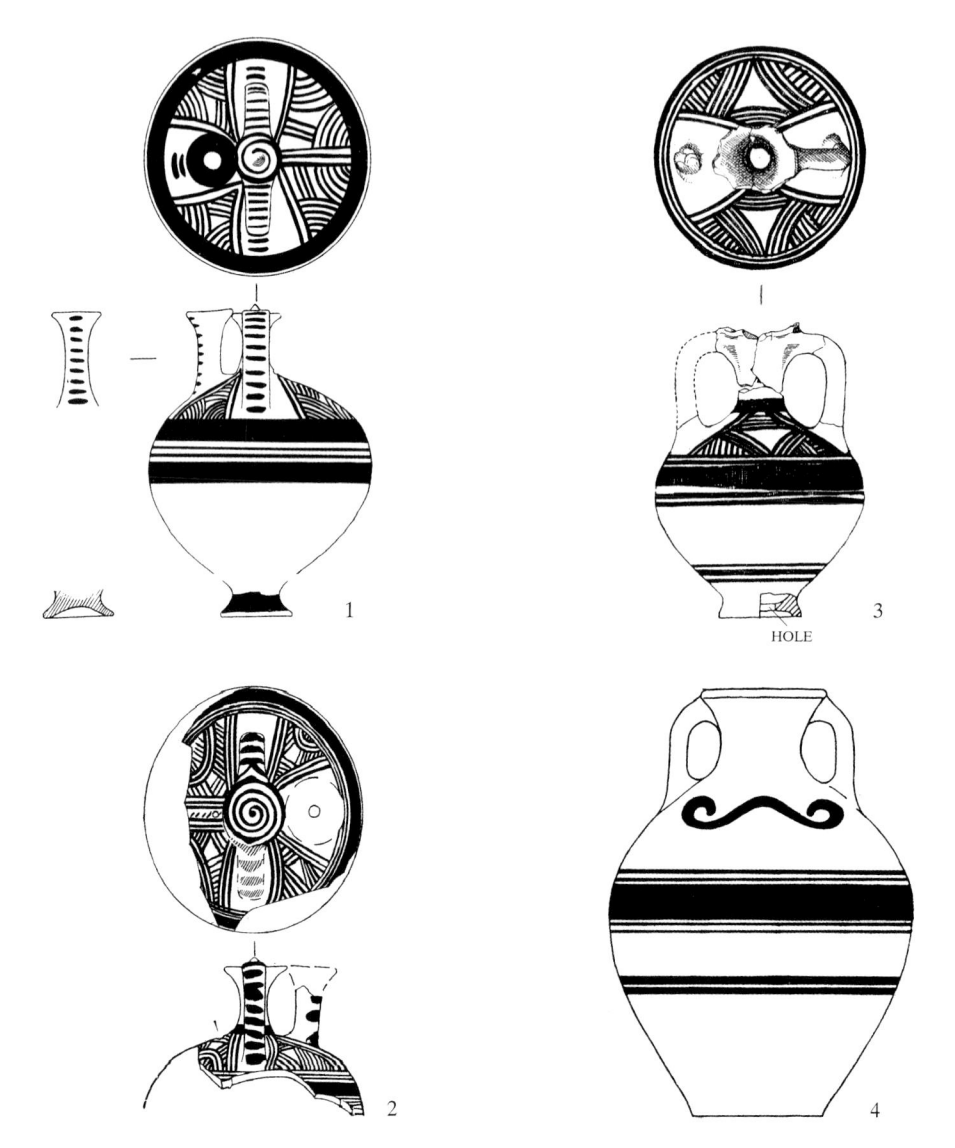

Fig. 18 Pottery from Gypsades VIA (not to scale)

Evolutionary Paradigms and Late Minoan III. On a Definition of LM III C Middle

LM III C Late

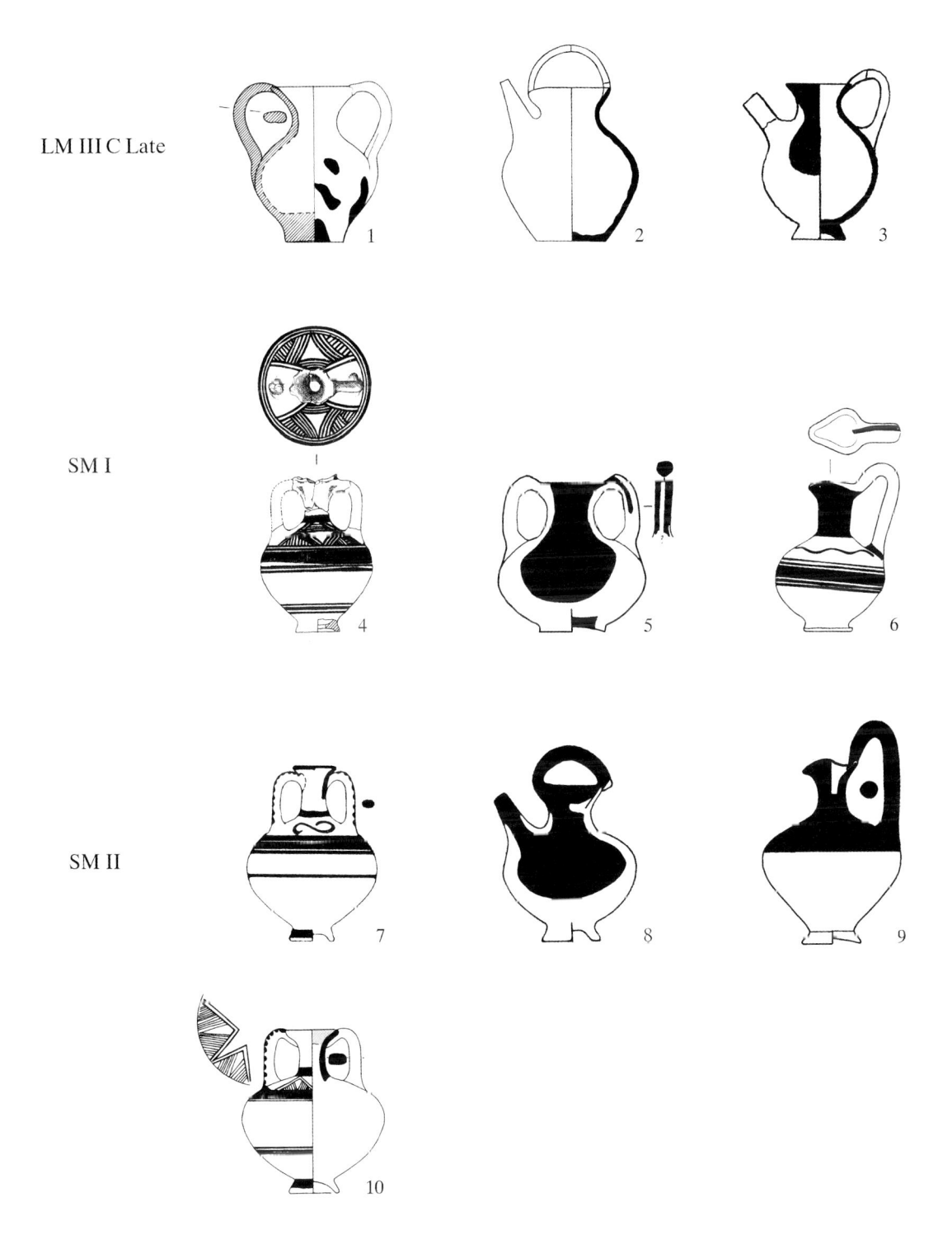

SM I

SM II

Fig. 19 LM III C Late-SM small jugs and amphorae (not to scale)

LM III C Early

LM III C Late

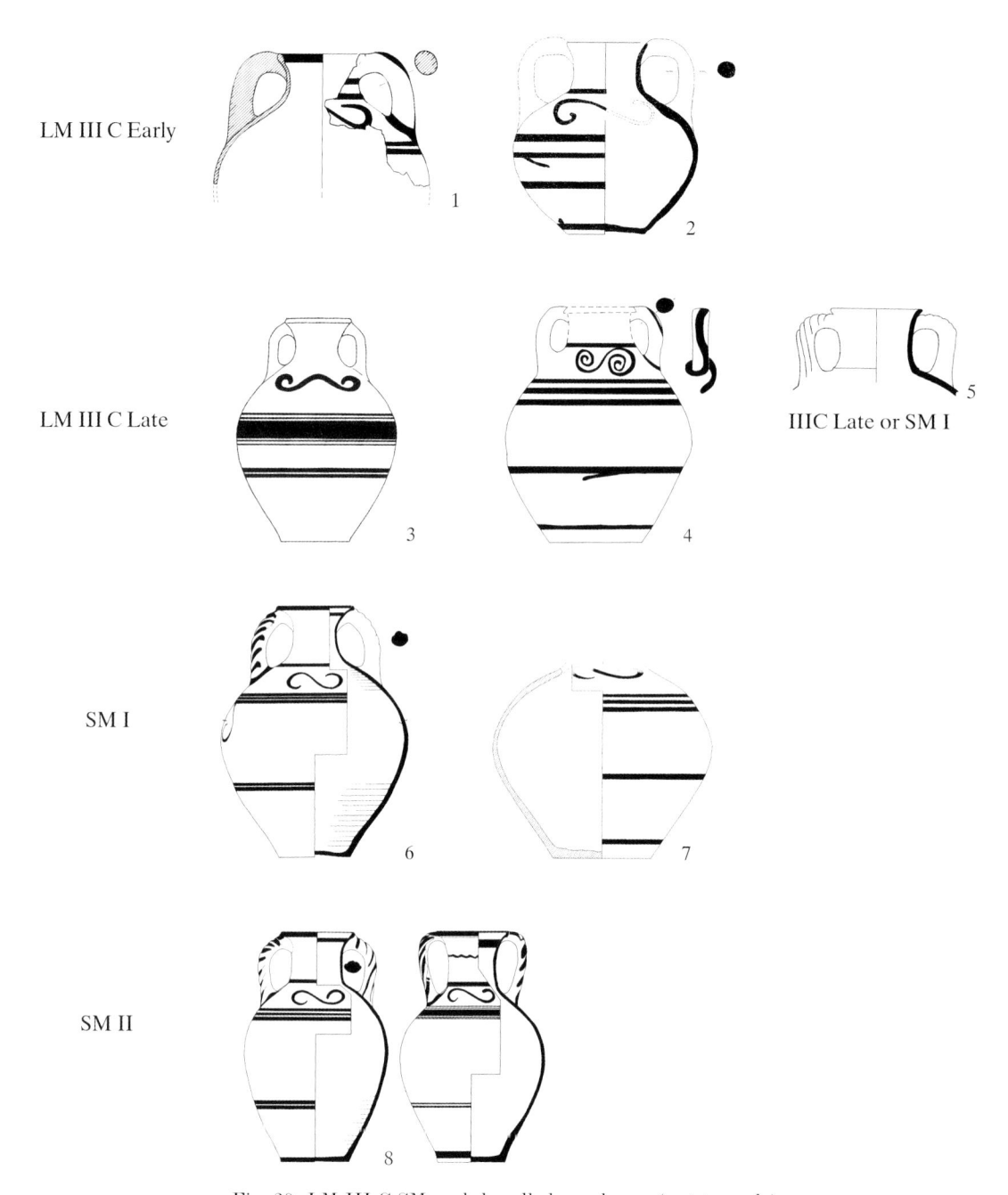

IIIC Late or SM I

SM I

SM II

Fig. 20 LM III C-SM neck-handled amphorae (not to scale)

Fig. 21 Knossian (?) stirrup jars of LM III C Late and SM I date (not to scale)

FANOURIA DAKORONIA

LH III C MIDDLE POTTERY REPERTOIRE OF KYNOS

Since detailed information about the site, the excavation and some of the findings of Kynos have already been presented in various publications (DAKORONIA 2003. – DAKORONIA 2006. – DAKORONIA 1993) this paper will not repeat them.

The LH III C settlement suffered an earthquake, followed by a fire and a huge seawave ("tsounami") which covered the site leaving behind sand, pebbles and seashells. The result of this event was the destruction of the buildings which happened at a time when pottery, characteristic of LH III C Middle, was being produced (DAKORONIA 1996). Immediately after the destruction the inhabitants levelled the debris, repaired the buildings or rebuilt them and continued their lives there. Much of the debris was thrown into a small alley between the buildings and the present paper is the result of the evaluation of the sherds stemming from this debris.

The study of the material is far from being complete but the picture we have so far obtained from the pottery evaluated will not change concerning LH III C Middle as is shown by the stratigraphy (DAKORONIA 2003, 45–47). The pottery we are dealing with was collected from a layer of about 2 m thickness, which, as is the case for the whole excavation, has been excavated in layers of 10 cms. No differentiation of the soil has been distinguished between the successive layers; this fact is mirrored on the mended pottery, as for example the well known sea-battle krater whose sherds come from different depths, different spots of the alley and from different dates (DAKORONIA 1990, 118–119. – DAKORONIA 1999, 123). The majority of the debris consisted of sherds, pieces of clay idols, animal bones, sand and ashes. Sometimes there were sherds more than there was soil.

Kynos' LH III C Middle pottery displays some "abnormal" characteristics. The term "abnormal" refers to the fact that the relevant vases do not always fit in with the picture of the LH III C Middle pottery we have in the Argolid, Attica, Achaia, Lefkandi, and so on. This reflects the characteristic and consistent development towards regionalism in the LH III C period (*MDP*, 134. – RUTTER 1977).

The most indisputable shape of the LH III C Middle pottery is the krater in its various versions. All types of the krater such as the one with a tall stem (Fig. 1:1. – *MDP*, 170, fig. 218), ring-based kraters (*MDP*, 172–174, fig. 223), carinated kraters (*MDP*, 174, fig. 224), kraters with a straight upper body (*MDP*, fig. 226), ring-based kraters with squared rim (Fig. 1:2. – *MDP*, fig. 225), sometimes with a rib below the lip, which can be plain (Fig. 1:3) or rope-like (Fig. 1:4) are found. Concerning the decoration of the kraters Kynos displays a large variety of pictorial kraters as well as ones with wavy lines, festoons, streamers, elaborated triangles, running spiral, triglyphs, etc.

Regarding the pictorial pottery of Kynos it should be stressed that the majority of the vases decorated with pictorial topics are kraters. Narrative scenes are displayed exclusively on this shape (DAKORONIA 2006). There are only few examples of other shapes, mainly kalathoi and plates, with a pictorial decoration consisting of fish and birds. So far no other shape has been distinguished among the evaluated sherds bearing a pictorial decoration.

A characteristic of Kynos' kraters is that the majority of them have a banded interior and are not monochrome as seems to be the rule elsewhere and as can be concluded from the examples already published. Rarely, however, some examples are also monochrome inside. The types described above are present in all layers, therefore can be concluded that the layers can be dated to the same period. The rest of the pottery found in the same context should also be dated to LH III C Middle. The pottery is wheelmade pure hard clay of good quality, well-fired and its core colour ranges between various shades of red and brown. No sign of Handmade Burnished Pottery can be detected in this context. The domestic pots, wheel-turned, without any slip or decoration display coarse well-fired red clay. This category of pottery is not very abundant and is represented by tripod-cooking pots (*chytrae*) and open-mouthed jugs. Some of them have traces of fire. Some of the jugs bear a rope-like rib around the base of their wide necks (Fig. 1:5).[1]

Clay analysis on a number of sherds has proven that the majority of the Kynos' pottery, including the pictorial, is produced locally (MOMMSEN – HEIN – ITTAMEIER – MARAN – DAKORONIA 2001). Apart from the usual local clay, however, a substantial number of vases of Kynos belong to the so-called White Ware category (*MDP*, 158. – POPHAM – SACKETT 1968. – POPHAM – MILBURN 1971, 342, 344). It is too early to determine whether they were imported as vases or whether it was just the raw material which was imported. The White Ware pottery from Kynos is not only represented by large closed shapes but also by smaller open vases (POPHAM – SACKETT 1968. – POPHAM – MILBURN 1971) such as semiglobular cups (Fig. 1:6. – *MDP*, 171, fig. 219), and carinated ones (Fig. 1:7. – *MDP*, 171, fig. 220).

Except for the White Ware fabric, sherds of another kind of clay can be distinguished among the pottery samples of LH III C Middle at Kynos. The clay resembles that of the White Ware one, as it is hard, not quite pure, with some small inclusions, mostly white in colour, with a coarse surface but red in colour. The vases of this category are covered by a thin, pale slip obviously to achieve a smoother surface and a well treated appearance. Using dark brown paint they painted onto this slip the various motifs they chose to decorate the vases. The relevant sherds belong both to closed and open shapes (Fig. 1:8). The description of the clay of the so-called "ceramica rustica" (MORRICONE 1975, 296–298, 319) from Kos as well as that of some vases found at Skyros (PARLAMA 1984, 245–247), which are all considered by the scholars to be of local production also seems to apply to the examples from Kynos, too.

Another example of "alien" pottery has been detected among the LH III C Middle sherds. These sherds form part of a black glazed skyphos decorated with spirals in the light-on-dark technique (Fig. 2:9). The clay of this skyphos is very fine, well fired and grey in colour. The decoration has been painted with diluted clay. The technique resembles the "west slope" one. During a lifetime of work as an archaeologist and excavator in Central Greece it is the first time that a specimen like this has been found. The search for parallels has proven how rare the light-on-dark pottery of LH III C Middle date is.

The place closer to Kynos where vases of this kind have been discovered is Euboea, where they appeared in graves at Chalkis (PAPAVASILEIOS 1910, 27, fig. 27) and at Lefkandi.[2] Examples of dark-on-light pottery are also known from Mycenae, but the

---

[1] Rope-like ribs are a very common decorative element of Kynos' vases and appear not only on kraters but both around the base of the neck of closed vases as well as on jugs of a coarse fabric. They are almost a hallmark of Kynos' workshop.

[2] The well-known pyxis with the griffin: POPHAM – SACKETT 1968, 18, fig. 35.

technique seems to be more familiar in the Dodecanese, Kos (MORRICONE 1975, 191, fig. 77) and Rhodes (MARKETOU 1988, 27–33, figs. 30–31), as well as in Asia Minor[3] and the Near East (YON – KARAGEORGHIS – HIRSCHFELD 2000, 95 no. 120: Stirrup jar: LH/LM[?] III A1). Open and closed vases are rendered in this technique, which strongly recalls the Middle Minoan light-on-dark relevant category of Crete (BETANCOURT 1985, 68–69), which in the writer's opinion is the ancestor of the light-on-dark pottery of LH III C Middle. It seems that the Middle Minoan light-on-dark vases were exported to Dodecanese where they were produced continuously until at least as late as LH III C Middle, the subject of this conference. It is through commercial enterprises or other kinds of communication that this kind of pottery reached Kynos and Euboea. It should be pointed out, however, that at no time and nowhere, according to the published examples, this pottery was very popular. The same route should also have taken the "ceramica rustica" to Kynos. Future clay analysis will perhaps supply an answer for the question of origin of the above mentioned "alien" pottery of Kynos.

With regards to the shapes the study of the pottery completed so far shows that open and closed vases are equally represented.

A fairly good proportion of the total pottery collected at Kynos belongs to good quality finished vases made of pure hard clay, which were left unpainted on purpose and which were obviously for domestic every day use. The vases of this category are either of closed or open shape and of large or small dimensions, such as the ladle (Fig. 2:10–11), a shape not often met among the repertoire of Kynos.

Among the closed vases from Kynos the majority are large containers such as hydrias, belly-handled amphoras, collar-necked jars and jugs. Since, however, the sherds did not always join together to make a whole vase we cannot conclude which of the above shapes prevails. With the exception of collar-necked jars all other vases have hollow rims, and they are decorated with bands, wavy lines, concentric semicircles, running spirals, loops, and tassels. Tassels seem to be the most popular motif of the period. The necks of the vases under discussion are always banded inside except the ones of the collar-necked jars which have a cylindrical neck painted all over.

Among the handles of the large closed vases the majority are horizontal ones, a fact that speaks for hydrias and belly-handled amphoras being popular. Neck-handled amphoras as well as amphoras with handles from the lip to the shoulder are fairly well represented and also the large jugs. What is still missing from the repertoire of LH III C Middle pottery from Kynos is the trefoil-mouthed jug. At least no certain sign of this vase has been attested, except for two twisted vertical handles, a handle type often applied on such a shape.

Jugs of medium size are rare and so is the small version, represented so far only by one example.

Although the pottery is of a settlement the stirrup jar is strongly represented. They are all of small or medium size, of fine well-fired clay, and they are decorated either with groups of thin lines around the belly, or with elaborated triangles on the shoulder or with a degenerated pleonastic octopus motif (DAKORONIA 2003, 48, fig. 26). Other motifs such as flower and bivalve shell are also known but are not common. To come to an end with the closed shapes it should be stated that among them a few examples of amphoriskoi, exclusively with linear decoration, are present and one sherd from a straight-sided alabastron. The lekythos is missing completely.

---

[3] I owe this information to Dr. P. Mountjoy whom I warmly thank.

A remark should be made concerning the decoration of the closed vases according to personal experience based on the results from the evaluation of the Kynos pottery. The thin line between broad bands, usually around the belly of the vases, seems to be a device of the LH III C Middle period, at least at Kynos.

Concerning the open shapes of Kynos we can observe that the dominating shape is the deep bowl (*skyphos*), always two-handled and in all possible versions, among which the most prominent belongs to the many variations of the monochrome deep bowl: totally monochrome, monochrome with a reserved disc on the bottom of the inner side, monochrome with reserved disc and base, with reserved lower body and disc, with reserved band on the edge of the lip, with reserved band on the interior below the lip, monochrome on the interior with reserved disc and banded on the exterior. Almost all of the monochrome bowls display a reserved area between the handles and only a couple of handles are totally monochrome. The bowls with reserved lip with dots are also rare. Deep bowls of the so-called Group A are also present.

Three cases of deep bowls are worth special attention. One is a stemmed bowl in the same context as all the above mentioned shapes (Fig. 2:12). It is obvious from the relevant material so far published that the stemmed bowls ceased to be abundant as early as LH III C Early. However, the sample of Kynos shows a revival of the shape in a later period, a phenomenon otherwise not unknown for the Lokrian ceramic production. A second unusual characteristic for Kynos are the almost vertical walls of a monochrome bowl (Fig. 2:13), a characteristic found once more among the pottery of Kynos but unusual for the rest of it.[4] A third case for probable future discussion are the reserved metopes or zones between the handles of monochrome deep bowls, a device counted among the later decoration fashion (*MDP*, 192, fig. 254:6.8) which at Kynos, however, already appears in a LH III C Middle context (Fig. 2:14).

The presence of conical bowls is uncertain. Even if at the end of the evaluation it is proven that a handful of sherds come indeed from conical bowls, the number of them is limited, thus showing that this shape was never popular at Kynos.

The other prevailing shape, collected in a large number, is the semiglobular cup (Fig. 2:15) which remains almost unchanged throughout the whole LH III C period and was produced until as late as the Submycenaean period. It displays a monochrome interior which always had a reserved disc on the bottom, an unpainted exterior with a band around the edge of the lip and the handle.

The two shapes described above, the deep bowl and the cup, are very popular throughout the entire LH III C and Submycenaean at Kynos. They appear in great numbers and almost always had a reserved disc on the bottom, practically as a "hallmark".

With regards to the cups a few remarks should be made on the carinated ones (Fig. 2:16. – *MDP*, 171, fig. 220) appearing at Kynos, either monochrome or unpainted. The monochrome ones are less frequent than the unpainted ones and usually display a reserved lip with dots. Yet, some carinated cups of Kynos are of White Ware fabric and execution.

Angular bowls (*MDP*, 179, fig. 233) are represented by a handful of hardly recognisable sherds.

Kylikes do not appear in great numbers and are either monochrome with a reserved disc, or with broad unpainted zones on the exterior and a monochrome interior or totally unpainted. Stems found among the sherds are either cylindrical or swollen.

---

[4] A similar example from Aigeira has been shown during this workshop.

Two other well represented open shapes are the bridge spouted basin (Fig. 2:17. – *MDP*, 153, fig. 196:2) as well as the simple basin, always with a linear decoration (Fig. 3:18).

Kalathoi (Fig. 3:19. – *MDP*, 179, fig. 232) decorated with chevrons on the lip, concentric arcs, net, elaborate triangle, etc. are also well attested. The kalathos is the only other shape, besides the kraters, with pictorial decoration consisting exclusively of fish.

Trays (Fig. 3:20. – *MDP*, 180, fig. 234) are also present, either with linear decoration or with a more elaborate and fine decoration such as festoons, spirals, etc.

The rest of the shapes present at Kynos are the lid (Fig. 3:21. – *MDP*, 154, fig. 199), linear or with monochrome exterior, the mug (Fig. 3:22. – *MDP*, 147, fig. 184), a shape not common during LH III C Middle, which always has a monochrome interior and some kind of decoration usually spirals, and a small sherd from a small alabastron with a nipple on its shoulder (Fig. 3:23).

Since the pottery described comes from the debris of a destruction and is preserved in a fragmentary condition there are, among the sherds, some where it cannot be determined which shape they come from.

Concluding the only date which can be proposed for the pottery described from the debris at Kynos is LH III C Middle in general. At the present stage of the evaluation and study of the pottery of Kynos it is neither possible nor advisable to define sub-phases like, for example, Lefkandi 1a, 1b, 2a, 2b, etc. or Advanced, Developed, Final, since elements which characterise some phases are either present at Kynos and absent elsewhere or absent at Kynos and dominant elsewhere as is the case, for example, for the Close Style, which cannot be detected yet among the Kynos material as well as in Lefkandi, too.

In the author's opinion according to the material so far evaluated the pottery discussed moves between Lefkandi 2a–2b, Rutter Phase 4 early to Phase 4 late and Mycenae Developed–Advanced. Sometimes, however, this material seems to "flirt" with the final period, too, exhibiting some features which otherwise are considered to be characteristic of LH III C Late.

On the other hand it is often difficult to give an exact date, on the basis of special elements, since if a local workshop adopted them, the potters adapted them to the taste of the area and to their ability and once this happened they continued to produce them either unchanged or with minor alterations for a long period.

So, in order to establish a reliable synchronism among the regional styles of pottery we should look for the sources of inspiration of the various styles and the mechanisms through which fashions spread, for example the grade of independence or dependence of one region from another.

Bibliography

BASSIAKOS, Y. – E. ALOUPI – Y. FACORELLIS (eds.)
2001 *Αρχαιομετρικές μελέτες για την Ελληνική προϊστορία και αρχαιότητα. Archaeometry Issues in Greek Prehistory and Antiquity*. Athens.

BETANCOURT, PH. P.
1985 *The History of Minoan Pottery*. Princeton NJ.

DAKORONIA, F.
1990 "War–Ships on Sherds of LH III C Kraters from Kynos" 117–122 in: TZALAS 1990.
1993 "Homeric Towns in East Lokris: Problems of Identification", *Hesperia* 62, 115–127.
1996 "Earthquakes of the Late Helladic III Period (12th Century BC) at Kynos (Livanates, Central Greece), 41–44 in: STIROS – JONES 1996.
1999 "Representations of Sea-Battles on Mycenaean Sherds from Kynos", 119–128 in: TZALAS 1999.
2003 "The Transition from Late Helladic III C to the Early Iron Age at Kynos", 37–51 in: *LH III C Chronology and Synchronisms*.
2006 "Mycenaean Pictorial Style at Kynos, East Lokris", 23–29 in: RYSTEDT – WELLS 2006.

DAVIS, E. N. (ed.)
1977 *Symposium on the Dark Ages in Greece*. New York.

DIETZ, S. – I. PAPACHRISTODOULOU (eds.)
1988 *Archaeology in the Dodecanese, Symposium, Copenhagen April 7th to 9th, 1986*. Copenhagen.

MARKETOU, T.
1988 "New Evidence on the Topography and Site History of Prehistoric Ialysos", 27–33 in: DIETZ – PAPACHRISTODOULOU 1988.

MOMMSEN, H. – A. HEIN – D. ITTAMEIER – J. MARAN – F. DAKORONIA
2001 "New Mycenaean Pottery Production Centres from Eastern Central Greece Obtained by Neutron Activation Analysis", 343–354 in: BASSIAKOS – ALOUPI – FACORELLIS 2001.

MORRICONE, L.
1975 "Coo – scavi e scoperte nel 'Serraglio' e in località minori (1935–1943)", *ASAtene* 50/51(= N. S. 34/35), 1972/73 [1975], 139–396.

PAPAVASILEIOS, G. A.
1910 *Περί των εν Ευβοία αρχαίων τάφων*. Athens.

PARLAMA, L.
1984 *Η Σκύρος στην εποχή του χαλκού*. Athens.

POPHAM, M. R. – E. V. MILBURN
1971 "The Late Helladic III C Pottery of Xeropolis (Lefkandi): A Summary", *BSA* 66, 333–352.

POPHAM, M. R. – L. H. SACKETT
1968 *Excavations at Lefkandi, Euboea, 1964–66. A Preliminary Report*. Oxford.

RUTTER, J. B.
1977 "Late Helladic III C Pottery and Some Historical Implications", 1–20 in: DAVIS 1977.

RYSTEDT, E. – B. WELLS (eds.)
2006 *Pictorial Pursuits: Figurative Painting on Mycenaean and Geometric Pottery. Papers from two Seminars at the Swedish Institute at Athens in 1999 and 2001* (Skrifter utgivna av Svenska Institutet i Athen 4°, 53). Stockholm.

STIROS, S. – R. E. JONES (eds.)
1996 *Archaeoseismology* (Fitch Laboratory Occasional Paper 7). Athens.

TZALAS, H. (ed.)
1990 *Tropis II. 2nd International Symposium on Ship Construction in Antiquity, Delphi, 27, 28, 29 August 1987*. Athens.
1999 *Tropis V. 5th International Symposium on Ship Construction in Antiquity, Nauplia, 26, 27, 28 August 1993*. Athens.

YON, M. – V. KARAGEORGHIS – N. HIRSCHFELD
2000 *Céramiques mycéniennes d'Ougarit*. (Ras Shamra-Ougarit 13). Paris – Nicosia.

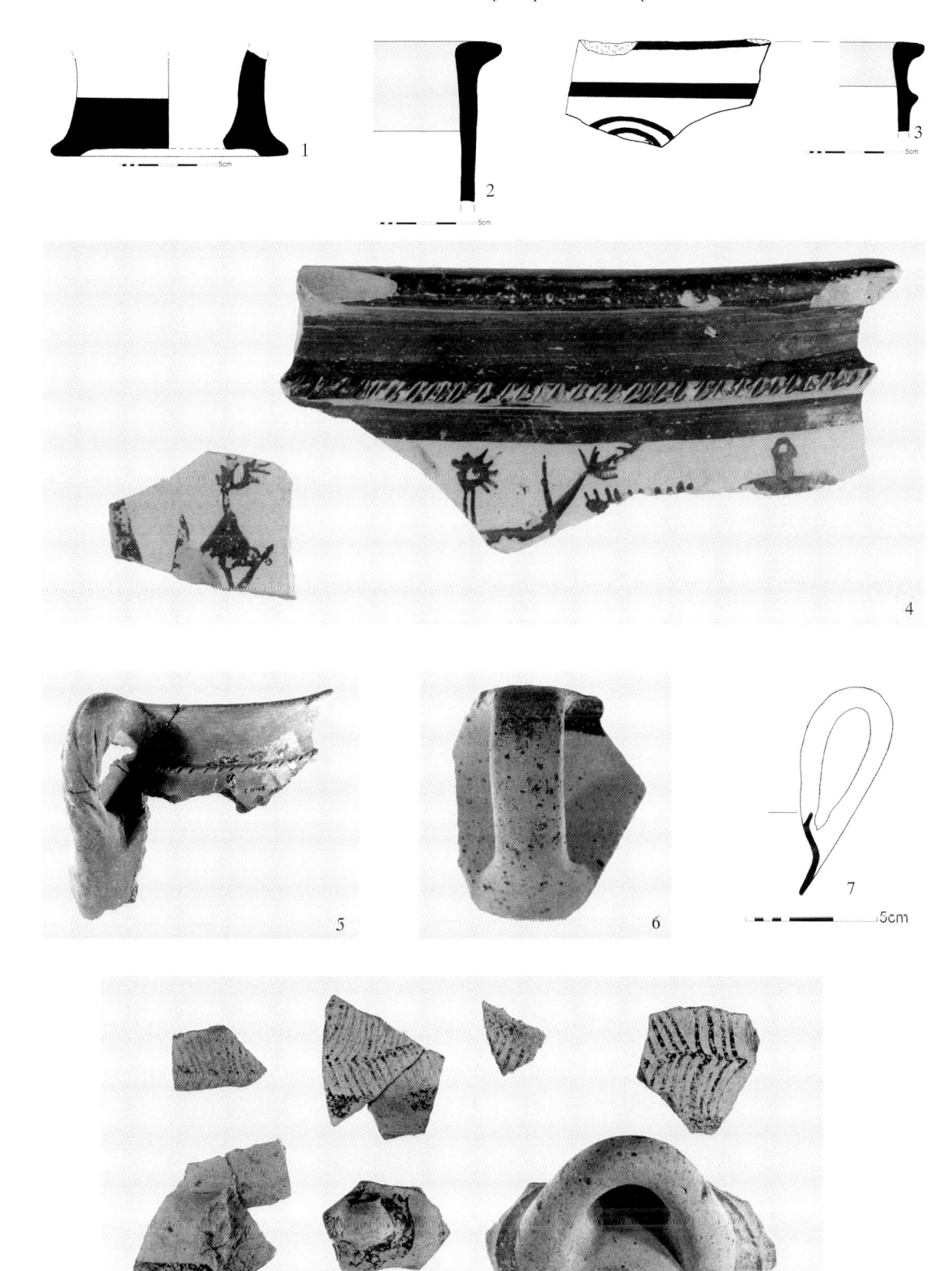

Fig. 1

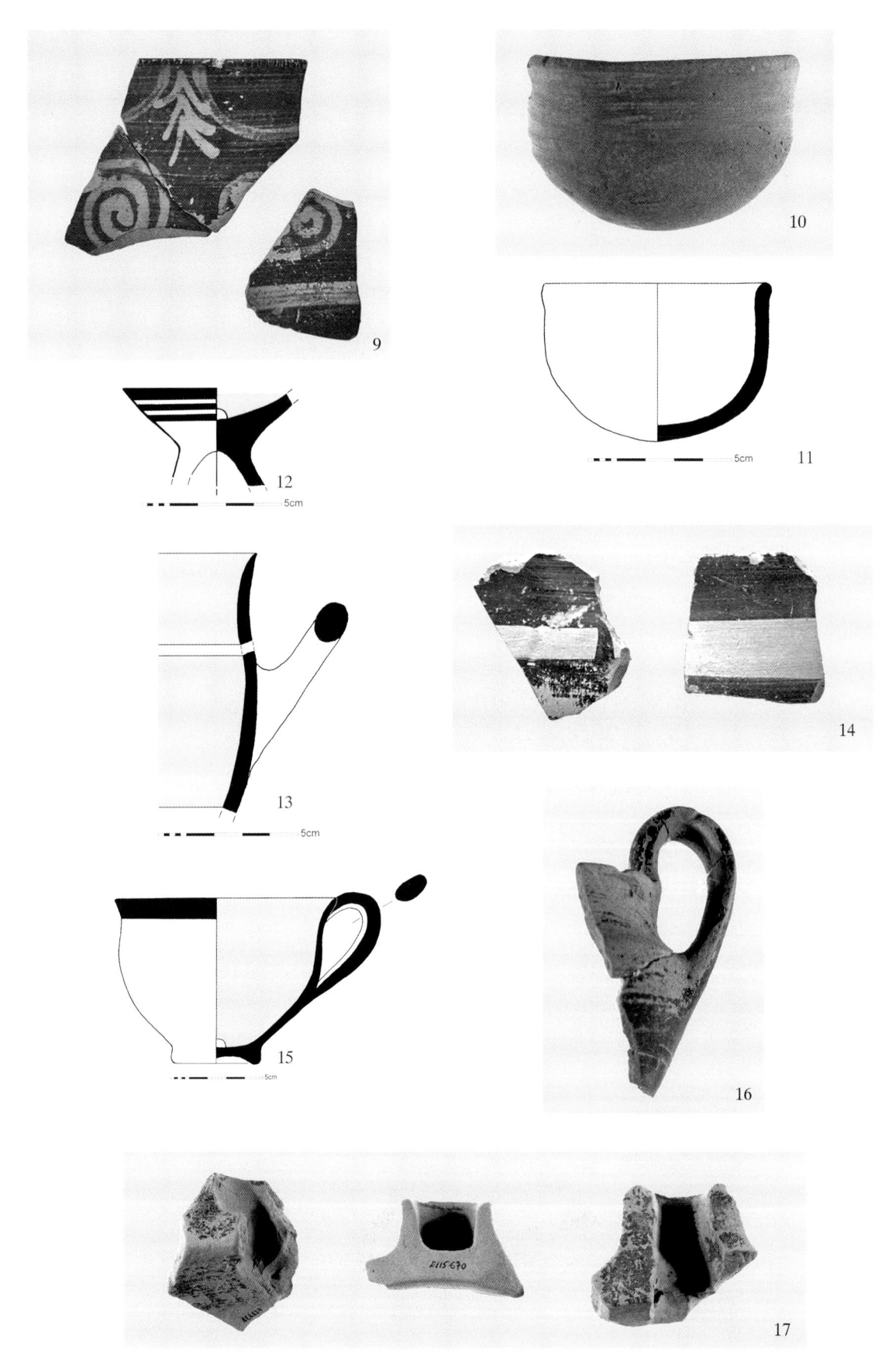

Fig. 2

LH III C Middle Pottery Repertoire of Kynos

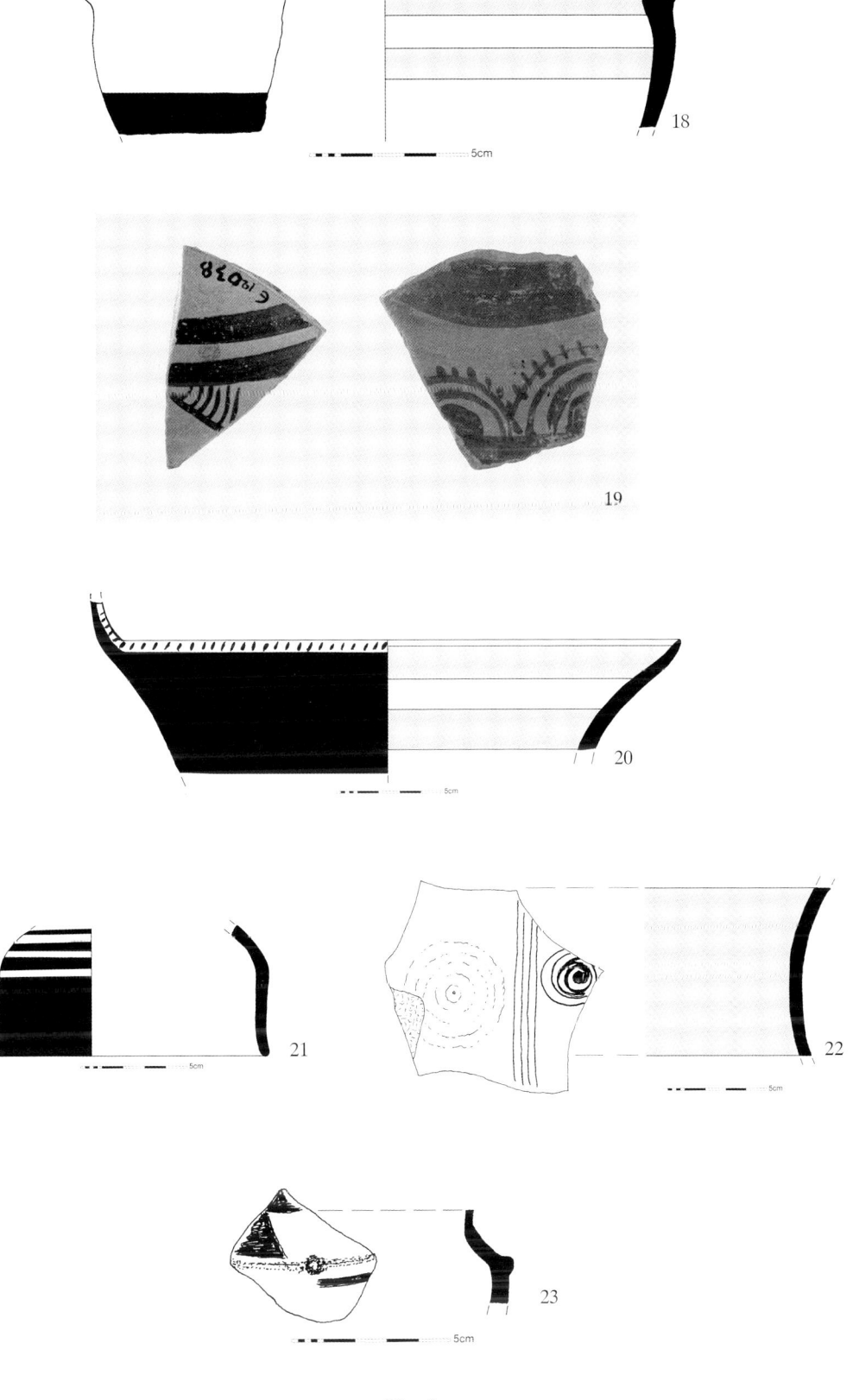

Fig. 3

SIGRID DEGER-JALKOTZY

DEFINING LH III C MIDDLE AT THE CEMETERY OF ELATEIA-ALONAKI IN CENTRAL GREECE

The Mycenaean chamber tombs at Elateia-Alonaki[1] were used from LH III A1 to Early/Middle Geometric (DEGER-JALKOTZY – DAKORONIA 1991. – BÄCHLE 2000. – DEGER-JALKOTZY 2004). Such a long use of a Mycenaean cemetery may be called sensational; however, it has the disadvantage that almost no Mycenaean burials were found in situ. Except for a few burials dating from LH III C Late, all remains of Mycenaean burials including the vases were found either pushed aside to the walls and corners of the chambers, or deposited in floor pits of the chambers and dromoi[2] (DEGER-JALKOTZY 1999, 195). Moreover, according to the anthropological investigation of the skeletal remains the numbers of individuals buried in the tombs were generally high. Therefore it is only for the last phase(s) of the cemetery that pottery seriation based on the sequence of burials can be applied. In most other cases the Mycenaean ceramics from Elateia have to be dated by stylistic analysis.

During LH III A and III B the potters of Elateia followed the general conventions of the time, even if their products already exhibited some distinctive local features (BÄCHLE 2000. – BÄCHLE 2003). During LH III B Late and LH III C Early a considerable number of tombs do not appear to have been used, yet the cemetery was not abandoned: Although it is admittedly difficult to define the characteristics of LH III C Early with burial vases, there is material which can be assigned with confidence to that period (BÄCHLE 2003, 118–120, 121 tab. II). The same is true of several fragments of deep bowls and craters found in the dromos fills (WEISS 1993). The crater fragments of our Fig. 10:3,5 may also have been of that date, even if we prefer to assign them to LH III C Middle.

In contrast to the partial abandonment of the cemetery during the closing years of the palace period and in LH III C Early, the use of the tombs increased again during the subsequent phases of LH III C. In fact, it then reached a pinnacle which lasted until the Early Protogeometric period. During that stretch of time most of the older tombs continued to be in use or were re-used, and new tombs were cut into the Alonaki slope. These facts may certainly be interpreted in terms of a rise in population (DEGER-JALKOTZY 2004). Moreover, from the wealth of the burial gifts – particularly of metal objects, jewellery and a wide variety of small finds (DAKORONIA 2004) – it may be concluded that the people of Elateia then enjoyed a period of considerable prosper-

---

[1] On the situation of the site and the history of the excavations see DEGER-JALKOTZY – DAKORONIA 1991.

[2] The dromoi of the Elateia-Alonaki cemetery frequently display a special kind of recipients for secondary burials which may be called "niche-and-pits". They were cut into the walls and, at the same time, into the floor of the dromos, next to the stomion or at the dromos entrance (sometimes at both sides). Their closures mostly consisted of dry stone masonry similar to that of the stomion.

ity. The number of burial vases, too, is rather high. About 470 vessels were deposited from LH III C Middle through Early and Middle Protogeometric.

Moreover, the burial gifts include an impressive range of imported objects such as amber (EDER 2003), metal ornaments and weapons (DAKORONIA 2004). Prestigious pottery was also imported. These vases are important as they indicate both the geographical range of the external relations of the community and provide a clue to the chronology of the burial contexts.

VASES IMPORTED DURING LH III C MIDDLE AND LATE

1. The Close Style stirrup jar **T. XLIX/16m** (Fig. 1:1) was found in Tomb XLIX/89. This vase is chronologically significant since it was found in a defined context which also included the cylindrical stirrup jar Fig. 3:2 (see below).[3] A date in *LH III C Middle/Advanced* of T. XLIX/16m is suggested by the monochrome lower part of the body with reserved thin lines (cf. PODZUWEIT 1992, chapter "Kleine Bügelkanne"), by the rosette on the domed disc, by the lozenge decoration on the handles and by the airhole on the shoulder. The vase had presumably been imported from a region where the Close Style was at home. It may perhaps not have been made at Mycenae since it does not come up to the refined decoration and the outstanding quality of the Close Style vases from that place.[4] However, a provenance from the Argolid in general cannot be excluded in view of the excellent execution of the decoration.[5]

2. The fragment **T. LIII/31b** (Fig. 1:3) had once been part of another Close Style stirrup jar. The decoration of shoulder, handle and false neck can be compared to stirrup jars from Mycenae (FURTWÄNGLER – LOESCHCKE 1886, pl. XXXVIII no. 393) and from Rhodes (cf. *RMDP*, fig. 439:270; for the decoration of the disc see also *RMDP*, fig. 439:271). At Mycenae and Tiryns the mature Close Style is commonly assigned to *LH III C Middle/Advanced*, and this same date has also been suggested for the Rhodian parallels. Therefore the fragment from Elateia should also be assigned to that period.

3. Close Style decoration also appears on the narrow-necked amphoriskos[6] **T. XXXVIII/9g** (Fig. 1:2). The shape is not alien to the local repertoire at Elateia-Alonaki so that a local imitation of the Close Style cannot be excluded. Moreover, a Close Style stirrup jar found at Delphi in neighbouring Phocis has recently been classified as a local copy (cf. *RMDP*, 783, fig. 308:250). On the other hand the decorative scheme of T. XXXVIII/9g – a combination of triangular patch, running spiral and reserved lines on the monochrome lower part of the body – is very similar to that of an amphoriskos from the Kolonaki cemetery at Thebes, said to have been an Argive import (cf. *RMDP*, 687, fig. 264:205). Moreover, the fabric of T. XXXVIII/9g differs from the local clays of Elateia, so that for the time being we prefer to consider this vase as an import. Clay analysis will solve the matter. Chronologically the vase should be assigned to *LH III C Middle/Advanced*. This date may be used in turn as a clue to the chronology of a few vases which were found in the same context, among them the stirrup jar T. XXXVIII/10d (Fig. 3:3).

---

[3] Tomb XLIX/89 was used from LH III C Middle to Early Protogeometric.

[4] This point was raised by E. French in the discussion which followed after the presentation of this paper.

[5] It should be mentioned that many vases from Elateia-Alonaki were affected by concretion, owing to the unfavourable physical conditions of the bedrock in the tombs. This is also true of the stirrup jar under discussion so that its quality may well have been much better at the time when it was deposited in the tomb.

[6] The shape is called "two-handled jug" in IAKOVIDIS 1969/70, vol. 2, 230–232.

4. The stirrup jar **T. XV/A5** (Figs. 1:7; 2:5) is a remarkable representative of the Octopus Style. The very pale clay betrays a foreign provenance of the vase which, by its shape and decoration, should be dated to *LH III C Middle*. The shape is a well balanced globular-conical version of FS 175; it has tall handles and a tall false neck with a slightly domed disc. The spout did not touch the disc (Fig. 1:7).[7] Unfortunately, the surface of the vase is badly worn, and some parts of the body have not been preserved at all. Therefore it is difficult to understand the decorative scheme. There was obviously no division between shoulder and body zone. Three pairs of outlined and fringed tentacles with rolled tops coil on the shoulder at both sides of the spout (Fig. 2:5). As they emerge from underneath the spout they suggest that the animal's body – perhaps small-sized – was placed still further down (for octopus bodies placed underneath the spout cf. e.g. IAKOVIDIS 1969/70, vol. 2, colour pls. II–III. – PERDRIZET 1908, 9, fig. 26). One tentacle (fat and outlined, but not fringed) undulates round the belly to the opposite part of the vessel (cf. Fig. 1:7), comparable to the (fringed) tentacles painted on the famous[8] stirrup jar from Skyros (PARLAMA 1984, pl. 62) and on an OSJ from Ialysos (OT. 10, cf. *RMDP*, fig. 429:189). There are no filling motifs between the tentacles, but below the handle there is a framed loop with semicircles. Opposite the spout an apparently most remarkable creature had been depicted on the shoulder. It may have been a very schematic – or ill designed? – octopus with enormous eyes and two leg-like tentacles protruding from the head (cf. Fig. 2:5). However, not much has been left of the decoration on this side of the vase. The handles are monochrome, while the disc is decorated with garlands of semicircles and a zigzag band. A most unusual addition to the painted decoration consists of several faience beads set across the disc and along both handles. The only instance known to me of a Mycenaean clay vessel with faience inlays is a LH III C Middle composite vase from Ag. Triadha in Elis. It consists of three small vases, one true and two "quasi" stirrup jars. Their shoulders, as well as the top of the basket handle which unites them, carry inlays of glass beads (VIKATOU 1999, 243–244, fig. 12a–b). However, its painted decoration – evenly spaced bands all down the bodies and fringed concentric circles on the shoulders – is typical of LH III C Middle and Late closed shapes from Achaia.[9]

Vases decorated with the octopus motif and dated to LH III C Middle have been found at other sites of Central Greece, as well (Delphi: PERDRIZET 1908, 9, fig. 26. Kalapodi: JACOB-FELSCH 1996, 125–126, pl. 25:40). However, these instances provide no stylistic parallels for the OSJ from Elateia, since the animals and the tentacles are painted in a different way.[10] Therefore one is inclined to ascribe the OSJ from Elateia to a region where the Octopus Style was at home. Moreover, "Mycenaean" type (FS 175) octopus stirrup jars with tall and slender handles and false spout were produced in the islands and in coastal areas of the Aegean.

---

[7] Unfortunately, the spout is now lost, see Fig. 2:5.

[8] The opposite side of this vase carries the representation of a ship (PARLAMA 1984, fig. 32, pl. 62).

[9] Phases 3–6 in the chronological scheme presented by I. Moschos (cf. below, n. 17). – Birgitta Eder kindly reminded me of to two more vases (apparently stirrup jars) from Ag. Triadha which have also been mentioned as carrying inlays of glass beads (VIKATOU 1999, 244). However, nothing more has been reported about them.

[10] The decoration of a stirrup jar fragment from Kynos (see further below) also includes a fat and outlined, undulating band which resembles the fringeless tentacle on the OSJ from Elateia (DAKORONIA 2003, fig. 26). However, the Kynos vase is no OSJ. Its decorative system rather bears a resemblance to the two "Cretan style" stirrup jars T. VIII/A7 and T. VIII/A8 (see below).

However, it cannot be excluded that the octopus stirrup jar from Elateia came from or via the Northwest Peloponnese. As recently reported by I. Moschos, several Minoan style vases of LH III C Middle and Late were found in the cemetery of Portes in Achaia (Moschos forthcoming). They are all made of very pale clay, and several of them carry the hallmarks of the Octopus Style. According to Moschos these vessels were the products of a "Mainland Minoan workshop" which operated "somewhere in mountainous Elis, perhaps in the area of Olympia" (Moschos forthcoming). During LH III C Middle this workshop employed craftsmen who had come from Crete or who had been trained in Crete.[11] The products apparently were regarded as luxury objects since they were distributed as far as Spaliareika, Clauss, Chalandritsa in Achaia and Palaiokastro in Arcadia. Moreover, nearly all specimens found in the cemetery of Portes came from an exceptionally rich warrior tomb.[12] – During the later phases of LH III C the workshop continued to produce vases decorated in the Cretan style, but the craftsmen were no longer experienced in executing the Minoan decorative system. Direct Minoan influence had apparently subsided.

In view of the pale clay and the idiosyncratic rendering of the octopus decoration, the OSJ from Elateia may well have been a product of the "Mainland Minoan workshop" as described by I. Moschos. Moreover, the glass bead inlays of the stirrup jar from Elateia and those of the composite vases from Ag. Triadha (see above) may well have derived from the same source of inspiration: Ag. Triadha was situated in the area where the "Mainland Minoan workshop" operated. As a matter of fact, several vessels of the workshop were found at this site, too. However, clay analysis will have to reveal whether or not our presumption is correct.

The octopus stirrup jar was found in a niche in the dromos of Tomb XV/86, together with five more vases. Its date in LH III C Middle may serve as a clue to the chronology of this group (see further below).

5.–7. Tomb VIII/86 yielded three imported stirrup jars. Their find contexts are not clear because the burials had been disturbed by the collapse of the tomb.

The two stirrup vases **T. VIII/A7** (Fig. 1:5) and **T. VIII/A8** (Fig. 1:6) have much in common. They are of globular-conical shape with a wide diameter and flattened shoulder, providing ample space for decoration. The discs of the false mouths have a high cone. The spouts are tall, that of T. VIII/A8 is even taller than the false mouth. The everted rims of the spouts touch the discs. The base-ringed feet are raised. Except for their lower parts, both vases are densely covered with pleonastic decoration. The intricate patterns are composed of large curved triangles and vertical panels filled with cross-hatched lozenges, triangles and angle-fillings, as well as with concentric arcs. Below the decorative zone and around the foot both vases are banded. The discs are decorated with spirals. The handles of T. VIII/A7 carry cross-bars, while those of T. VIII/A8 are monochrome. The spout in both cases is decorated with cross-bars. False neck and spout in each case are separately banded.

At first sight these two vases appear to represent Minoan stirrup jars of the so-called "Cretan Close Style" of the later part of LM III C. In fact, they do resemble some stirrup jars from Central East and East Crete either in decoration (Kanta 1980, figs. 33:9 [Kera]; 82:4 [Mouliana]) or in the deep decorative zone (Kanta 1980, fig. 24:1 [Erganos]).

---

[11] I am most grateful to I. Moschos for having supplied me with more detailed information about this new and surprising facet of the ceramics from Achaia which certainly will shed a new light on the development of the mature LH III C style in West Achaia.

[12] Personal communication I. Moschos. On the warrior tomb from Portes, with references, cf. Deger-Jalkotzy 2006.

However, on closer inspection the shoulder decorations of most LM III C vases generally do not stretch to below the belly zone.[13] In fact, among the Minoan stirrup jars published so far there is no convincing parallel for the two vases from Elateia.[14] Moreover, a certain resemblance can be detected between the two stirrup jars from Elateia and the stirrup jar fragment already mentioned from Kynos (DAKORONIA 2003, fig. 26).[15] The patterned decoration of this vase covers almost three quarters of the surface, and the lowest part of the body is banded. Moreover, the space enclosed by the undulating, "tentacle-like" fat and outlined band mentioned earlier (see above, n. 10) is filled with motifs and patterns that bear a striking resemblance to those of the two stirrup jars from Elateia (cf. our Fig. 1:5–6 with DAKORONIA 2003, fig. 26). The decoration of the vase from Kynos may well have been inspired by pottery products from Crete, and the same applies to the "Minoanising" motifs enclosed by the waves of the "tentacle". However, the piece itself was made in the East Locris (MOMMSEN – HEIN – ITTAMEIER – MARAN – DAKORONIA 2001). This explains why the octopus design was clearly misunderstood. In view of the close resemblance between these filling motifs and the decorative patterns of the two stirrup jars from Elateia, it cannot be excluded that the latter had been imported not from Crete, but from East Locris, or from another region where "Cretan style" stirrup jars were produced. Local production cannot be excluded either,[16] even if it seems rather unlikely. Again clay analysis will perhaps provide the answer.

The fragment from Kynos has been dated to LH III C Middle (DAKORONIA 2003, 45 and n. 22). As for the two vases from Elateia, a date in LH III C Middle/Advanced is suggested by their form and decorative system.

Despite its poor state of preservation **T. VIII/A3** (Fig. 1:4), the third imported stirrup jar found in Tomb VIII/86 clearly was imported from West Achaia. It has a wide ring base and a slightly sloping shoulder, and the largest diameter is placed high on the body. The shoulder decoration consists of fringed concentric semicircles flanking the spout and a fringed triangle with scale pattern on the main face. Except for its lowest part, the body is covered with a close evenly spaced banding. Stirrup jars of this kind have been dated by P. A. Mountjoy to LH III C Late (MOUNTJOY 1990, 267–270). However, according to I. Moschos (pers. comm.) this type already started in LH III C Middle. In fact, a good parallel for our vase is provided by two stirrup jars from Voudeni assigned by Moschos to his Phase 4, *LH III C Advanced–LH III C Late*.[17] Like the vase from Elateia, they are not banded all down the body, and the shoulders are decorated with homogeneous and well balanced patterns.[18] Therefore a similar chronology may be assigned to T. VIII/A3. This date comes close to that of the two "Cretan Style" stirrup jars which were also found in Tomb VIII (see above).

---

[13] This also applies to the Mouliana stirrup jar illustrated in KANTA 1980, fig. 82:4.

[14] This also applies to the Laconian stirrup jar dated to LM III C Late/Subminoan by P. A. Mountjoy (*RMDP*, fig. 100:242). It is no parallel at all for the two vases from Elateia (*pace RMDP*, 818).

[15] I would like to thank Birgitta Eder and Reinhard Jung for drawing my attention to this fragment and for discussing with me the two stirrup jars from Elateia.

[16] A Minoanising stirrup jar from Balitis on Skyros apparently also was a local product. The vase is similar to the two stirrup jars from Elateia in shape and decorative syntax, even if its appearance is more provincial (PARLAMA 1984, fig. 33, pl. 65:10).

[17] These vases were illustrated in the handout to the paper of I. Moschos, pl. 11:1.3. – I. Moschos was not able to attend to the workshop *in persona*. He sent his paper – which kindly was read by M. Petropoulos – and the handouts accompanying the paper. Mr. Moschos is preparing an extended version of his paper for publication with the proceedings of the next workshop.

[18] *RMDP*, 404 also considers a date in LH III C Middle for banded vases with a reserved lower part of the body.

8. The large two-handled amphora **T. XII/A4** (Fig. 1:8) found in Tomb XII/87 came from Achaia, too. It has a globular-conical shape with a low and very wide ring base; the tall and straight neck has an everted rim with flat lip. The hard and dark brownish red fabric is a typical product of Achaia (DEGER-JALKOTZY 2003, 64). The vase is covered with dark paint, except for a small zone on the shoulder decorated with flat concentric arcs and the reserved lip decorated with cross bars. According to the settlement evidence from Aigeira monochrome large vessels already occur in LH III C Early (DEGER-JALKOTZY 2003, 61). However, the present vessel should be assigned to *LH III C Late* on account of its shape and of its decorative system. It may be assigned to Phase 5, "Late Achaia Style", dated by I. Moschos to LH III C Late (MOSCHOS handout [cf. n. 17], pl. 12:11–12. – See also PAPADOPOULOS 1978/79, figs. 62d; 63a; 64b).

Thus the evidence of the imported pottery implies that the external relations of Elateia had not come to a close at the end of the 13th century B.C. They were renewed during LH III C Middle, at the latest, and then obviously continued into LH III C Late.

LOCAL POTTERY OF LH III C MIDDLE AT ELATEIA

I. General observations

I.1. As already stated more than 470 *burial vases* found in the tombs of Elateia cover the span of time from LH III C Middle through Early and Middle Protogeometric. Of these 430 were wheelmade. Closed shapes predominate by far. The most frequent shapes among the burial vases were amphoriskos (28,6%), small jug (22,5%) and stirrup jar (17%). Open shapes are exceedingly rare. Two kalathoi and one tray, all dating to LH III C Late, were found complete, and a few fragments had been left from further specimens of these shapes.

In contrast, the pottery remains found in the *dromos fills* predominantly belonged to open shapes such as craters, kylikes, cups and bowls. Several of them have been treated by A. Weiss (WEISS 1993). Otherwise this material is still under study. Some fragments from craters of LH III C Middle are illustrated in Figs. 10–11. Fragments of closed shapes found in the dromos fills almost invariably came from burial vessels which had been either transferred from the chamber to a secondary burial in the dromos (see above, p. 129 and n. 2), or thrown away.

I.2. The pottery production of Elateia did not follow the general stylistic developments of LH III C Middle in every respect. For instance, the monochrome amphoriskoi FS 59 faithfully mirrored the over-regional developments of this decorative scheme in LH III C Middle and Late (see further below, p. 136). In contrast, the characteristic styles of LH III C Middle were not adopted although they were known from imported vessels. This is particularly true of the Close Style and the Octopus Style, as we have seen. Knowledge of the Pictorial Style is occasionally reflected by several crater fragments from the dromos fills, carrying motifs such as fish (Fig. 10:2) and bird (WEISS 1993, fig. 25:177). A motif painted on the crater fragment Fig. 10:4 may vaguely recall the tentacles of an octopus, but it certainly cannot be assigned to the Octopus Style. It cannot even compare with the octopus depicted on a crater from neighbouring Kalapodi (JACOB-FELSCH 1996, 125–126, pl. 25:40). Moreover, narrative pictorials such as the dramatic fighting scenes depicted on the craters from Kynos (DAKORONIA 1999) did not occur on such vessels,[19] although a fair amount of pottery seems to have been imported from that place (cf. Figs. 10:1,6; 11; on the stirrup jars T. VIII/A7–A8 see above, p. 132–133).

---

[19] Only two sherds have been found which seem to show pictorial representations of a narrative character involving chariots. They are under study by Fanouria Dakoronia.

I.3. Under these premises the synchronisation of the local pottery with the general phasing system(s) as proposed for LH III C Middle and Late meets with difficulties. Imported vases therefore prove useful, particularly in well defined contexts. They may indicate the chronological setting of the local vessels associated with them. As we have seen, they mostly date to LH III C Middle/Advanced and III C Late.

A group of vases found in *niche Z* in the western dromos wall of Tomb XV/86 (Fig. 2) may serve as an example. The six vases come from a closed context. Apart from the imported octopus stirrup jar T. XV/5 (Fig. 2:5) datable to LH III C Middle (see above, p. 131–132), there were three darkground amphoriskoi with reserved zones and/or reserved lines (A1–A3: Fig. 2:1–3), a stirrup jar with evenly spaced banding of the body (A4: Fig. 2:4), and a based straight-sided alabastron decorated with what may be called a local elaborate style (A6: Fig. 2:6). For this group some authors might advocate a date in LH III C Late. However, the chronological framework is set by the stirrup jar T. XV/5 of LH III C Middle. Moreover, in terms of the four-part chronological system of the Argolid the monochrome amphoriskoi would qualify for a date in LH III C Middle/Advanced (Fig. 2:1.3) or LH III C in general (Fig. 2:2, see further below). On balance, it appears adequate to assign the group to LH III C Advanced. It should also be added that the locally made vases of this group correspond to the bulk of LH III C funerary pottery at Elateia. Thus their date of LH III C Advanced has a certain bearing on the general chronology of the Elateia-Alonaki cemetery, too.

II. Specific features of LH III C Middle pottery at Elateia

While the pottery from LH III A through III C Early from Elateia has been published by Anna Bächle (see BÄCHLE 2000. – BÄCHLE 2003. – BÄCHLE 2006), the pottery of the subsequent periods is still under study. Therefore our observations should be regarded as a preliminary. At the present stage of investigation the pottery of LH III C Middle appears to be characterised by the following features.

II.1. Pottery shapes

As mentioned previously, in LH III C the most frequent pottery shapes were the amphoriskos FS 59, the small jug FS 115 and the stirrup jar (mainly FS 175). The small jugs are of little chronological significance except for the fact that monochrome specimens became predominant during the closing phases of LH III C Late (cf. DAKORONIA – DEGER-JALKOTZY – REUER-FABRIZII 2002, figs. 2; 7). As for amphoriskoi and stirrup jars, the exact percentages have not yet been established. It may turn out that amphoriskoi became more numerous in LH III C Late and Submycenaean than they had been during the previous period. Nevertheless, in LH III C Middle they already seem to have been equal in frequency to the stirrup jar. In this respect Elateia compares well with e.g. Ialysos on Rhodes where almost equal numbers of stirrup jars and amphoriskoi of LH III C were found (MEE 1982, 30–38). In the cemeteries in Kephallonia, too, amphoriskoi were generally numerous in LH III C, coming third in frequency after small jars and the stirrup jars (SOUYOUZOGLOU-HAYWOOD 1999, 64–67). On the other hand, the evidence from Elateia sharply contrasts with that from Medeon in neighbouring Phocis (MÜLLER 1995), as well as from the cemeteries of Achaia (PAPADOPOULOS 1978/79. – See also PETROPOULOS this volume) and of Skyros (PARLAMA 1984, 368–371), where amphoriskoi were by far outnumbered by stirrup jars and other shapes. Even among the finds from the tombs at Perati the ratio between amphoriskoi and stirrup jars was about 1:2 (IAKOVIDIS 1969/70, vol. 2, 153, 198).

Therefore the **remarkable frequency of amphoriskoi** may be defined as a characteristic feature of LH III C Middle at Elateia. The prevalent shape is **FS 59**. It has a raised base ring and a sharply everted neck. The neck is commonly narrow, while wide necks (cf. Figs. 2:1; 9:2) may have been a reminiscence of LH III C Early shapes. However, the shaping of the body is no longer dumpy. It is always well proportioned, varying from globular-biconical to depressed globular. The largest diameter is never placed below the middle of the vase. As already pointed out by C. Podzuweit, shape and position of the handles are of no chronological relevance (PODZUWEIT 1992, chapter "Amphoriskos"). – The rate between lightground and darkground decorated types is about 50:50.

II.1.1. **Amphoriskoi with darkground decoration.** – Completely monochrome amphoriskoi are extremely rare. One piece has been assigned to LH III C Developed rather than to III C Early on account of its slightly depressed globular body and sharply everted neck (BÄCHLE 2003, 21, fig. 8:80 = our Fig. 7:1). – In most other cases the lower part of the body is left unpainted (cf. Figs. 2:1,3; 9:4). In addition (or alternatively) there is a narrow zone between the handles which carries simple patterns such as stripes (Fig. 2:1), dots (Figs. 2:2; 9:2) and joining semicircles (Figs. 2:2; 9:1). Several reserved lines may be added below the neck (Fig. 9:2). Reserved rims may be dotted or decorated with vertical strokes (Fig. 9:3–4).

In the Argolid these features are said to have been characteristic of open and closed shapes of LH III C Middle/Advanced (PODZUWEIT 1983, 392. – PODZUWEIT 1992, chapters "Monochromer Skyphos", "Amphoriskos", "Kleine Bügelkanne"). Therefore this date would appear appropriate for the three amphoriskoi A1–A3 from Tomb XV/86 (Fig. 2; on A2, however, see below), as well as to the vases of Fig. 9.

However, some monochrome amphoriskoi with reserved zones such as T. XXXVI/38b (Fig. 9:2), T. XV/A2 (Fig. 2:2) and T. XXIV/23g (Fig. 9:1) may well have been produced earlier. The reserved fields between the handles are decorated with simple patterns that had already been in use in LH III C Early. Moreover, these vessels are coated all down the body. The small reserved band at the very edge of the foot of T. XXXVI/38b is a feature that already occurs in Lefkandi Phase Ib (cf. POPHAM – MILBURN 1971, pl. 51:1) and Aigeira Phase Ib (DEGER-JALKOTZY 2003, fig. 4:2), both now re-dated to LH III C Early–Developed (*RMDP*, 714 n. 487. – DEGER-JALKOTZY 2003, 67). – In addition, T. XXIV/23g has a stemmed conical foot, borrowed perhaps from the stemmed bowl (BÄCHLE 2003, 24). The closest parallels are provided by lightground decorated stemmed amphoriskoi from Kladeos/Trypes in Elis (*RMDP*, fig. 136:73. – BÄCHLE 2003, 24–25) and from Perati (IAKOVIDIS 1969/70, vol. 3, pl. 63α), all dated to LH III C Early.[20]

The stylistic development of the darkground amphoriskos FS 59 with reserved zones, fields and bands is illustrated in Fig. 9. As has been argued above, there are a number of reasons to assign the pieces of Fig. 9:1–2 (and Fig. 2:2) to LH III C Middle in general. In contrast, the amphoriskoi of Fig. 9:3–4 (and Fig. 2:1,3) exhibit stylistic features which clearly point to LH III C Advanced and may well have continued into an early phase of LH III C Late. During the later part(s) of LH III C Late the well proportioned shapes disintegrated, and vessels assumed a baggy appearance (cf. Fig. 9:5). The clay of these late vases is often pale, the fabric poor.

In conclusion it should be pointed out again that, while the flamboyant decorative styles of LH III C Middle were not adopted at Elateia (see above, p. 134), the monochrome decoration of amphoriskoi generally followed the over-regional stylistic developments.

II.1.2. **Pattern decorated amphoriskoi.** – Like the monochrome amphoriskoi, their lightground decorated counterparts are characterised by well balanced shapes. Accord-

---

[20] The region of Achaia has produced a considerable number of stemmed stirrup jars (cf. PAPADOPOULOS 1978/79, figs. 104a; 107d; 113d) which can be assigned to Phase 3 (LH III C Developed and Advanced) of the chronological scheme put forward by I. Moschos (cf. above, n. 17).

ing to A. Bächle the vessels of Fig. 7 (= BÄCHLE 2003, fig. 8:80,23,62,50) should be assigned to the earlier part of LH III C: The shapes are globular biconical rather than depressed, the ring bases are slightly raised (note, however, that Fig. 7:2 still has a concave base), the necks are sharply everted. Moreover, the shoulder decoration extends to below the zone of the largest diameter, and large broad wavy lines (Fig. 7:4) did not occur until LH III C Middle (PODZUWEIT 1992, chapter "Amphoriskos"). On the other hand decorative motifs such as linear patterns (Fig. 7:2), running spirals (Fig. 7:3) and FM 57 "net" (BÄCHLE 2003, fig. 8:208) still hark back to LH III C Early and even earlier. On balance, a date in LH III C Developed of these vases, as proposed by Anna Bächle, stands to reason (BÄCHLE 2003, 21–23, with comparisons).

Throughout LH III C Middle and Late the light ground decoration of amphoriskoi remained unassuming, if not dull. Motifs were limited to wavy line, net, lozenges, chevrons and concentric arcs. Intricate patterns are absent. Altogether it is obvious that the production of these vessels was not inspired by the LH III C Middle pleonastic styles of other regions.

However, it cannot be denied that in several cases a fine interplay between shape and decoration was achieved. A good example is provided by the vessels of Fig. 8:4–6. Their shape now is truly depressed globular, the handles are set on the belly, and a heavy decorative system covers two thirds of the surface of the vase: The neck is monochrome in and out, and the zone between the handles is filled with the net pattern FM 57 framed by broad bands above and below. In addition, the uppermost part of the shoulder below the neck may also be filled with further bands (Fig. 8:4), isolated concentric semicircles (Fig. 8:6), or yet another net pattern (Fig. 8:5). The net pattern of the handle zone extends to the largest diameter of the vessel, so that the bands underneath partly enclose the lower part of the body.

Amphoriskoi of this type are quite numerous at Elateia. In contrast, convincing parallels from other regions are sought in vain. Thus, unless more relevant materials from neighbouring regions or from further afield will be revealed, these vases may be regarded as a characteristic feature of the local pottery of LH III C. The earliest piece has been attributed to LH III C Middle/Developed by A. Bächle (BÄCHLE 2003, fig. 8:208). However, the majority should generally be dated to LH III C Middle. Moreover, the decoration of T. XXXVI/38d1 (Fig. 8:6) shows a feature which precludes any chronology of earlier than LH III C Advanced: The two sides of the vase are decorated with different patterns (net pattern vs. stacked zigzag) in the zone between the handles. A darkground amphoriskos from Naxos-Kamini dated to LH III C Middle displays the same feature (*RMDP*, fig. 384:8).

A further group of pattern decorated amphoriskoi is covered with evenly spaced bands down to the lower part of the body (cf. Figs. 5.2, 8.3). However, this decorative system is not confined to this shape. It will therefore be discussed in the following paragraph.

II.2. Vases decorated with evenly spaced stripes

The LH III C Middle pottery of Elateia shows a general predilection for covering the body of closed shapes with evenly spaced stripes/bands. Of course, this decorative system was practised in many other regions, too. However, the ceramic production of Elateia stands out by the remarkably high number of vessels decorated in this way, and by the fact that this decorative pattern was firmly incorporated into the local repertoire. It was applied to stirrup jars, alabastra (both rounded and straight-sided), pyxides (= ring based straight-sided alabastra), amphoriskoi and lekythoi.

Successive banding of vases was executed in two ways: The bands were either of equal width (Figs. 4–5), or the surface of the vase was covered with successive groups of broad bands alternating with multiple thin lines (Figs. 6; 8:1–3).

II.2.1. **Vases decorated with bands of equal width** (Figs. 4–5). – This decorative system is not just linear. It consists of bands of equal width by which the vase is covered from the shoulder down to well below the largest diameter or two-thirds of the body, or all down to the base.

This kind of banding had no forerunners in LH III A and III B at Elateia. In fact, it was not even a standard feature of Mainland Mycenaean pottery until late in LH III B: First occurrences in LH III B have been reported e.g. from Elis (cf. *RMDP*, fig. 134:54,58) and Achaia (*RMDP*, fig. 145:44). In Boeotia the first vases decorated with successive bands of equal width were found in contexts of LH III B2 (Thebes Palace: ANDRIKOU 2006, 40, pl. 18:295). It has been observed that the pattern is reminiscent of Minoan pottery styles, particularly with regard to the stirrup jars (cf. ANDRIKOU 2006, 40. – For an actual Minoan import in LH III B see *RMDP*, fig. 257:135 [Thebes-Kolonaki]). In fact, it may well have been another Minoan feature as detected by J. Rutter in earliest LH III C assemblages of the Mainland (RUTTER 2003). At any rate, from LH III C Early onwards it was widely used in the Mycenaean regions, preferably for the decoration of stirrup jars and alabastra.[21] In Achaia closed shapes decorated with bands of equal width even became one of the typical features of the local pottery styles until the very end of Mycenaean pottery tradition (*East Achaia*: PETROPOULOS this volume. – DEGER-JALKOTZY 2003, fig. 5:1. *West Achaia*: MOSCHOS forthcoming and handout [cf. above, n. 17]).[22] In contrast, vases decorated with bands of equal width seem to have remained unknown in the Argolid until LH III C Middle (PODZUWEIT 1983, 383–384. – PODZUWEIT 1992, chapter "Amphoriskos").

At Elateia this decorative pattern was almost absent in LH III C Early, probably due to the general scarcity of pottery assignable to this period (see above, p. 129). Only for the three-handled piriform jar/stemmed amphoriskos of Fig. 5:1 a date in LH III C Early has been suggested (BÄCHLE 2003, 25, with comparative material[23]). The body is covered all over with bands. Width and spacing of the bands are not entirely even, but the intention is clear.

The date of all other vases illustrated in Figs. 5:2–6 and of the stirrup jars in Fig. 4 is LH III C Middle, or Middle to Late. The stirrup jar T. XXIV/23v (Fig. 4:1) has a striking parallel from the tombs at Nikoleika near Aigion (PETROPOULOS this volume, fig. 26), even with regard of the pale yellowish colour of the clay. In both cases the shape is clumsy, the decoration of the shoulder (foliate band?) unskilful. M. Petropoulos has dated his vase to LH III C Middle/Developed (PETROPOULOS this volume). For T. XXIV/23v from Elateia this date is precluded. It is true that, due to the flat base, the shape is FS 174 rather than FS 175, and the banding only covers two-thirds of the body: On the other hand the straight and tall spout touches the disc of the false mouth. Therefore a date in LH III C Middle/Advanced appears more adequate.

---

[21] *Phocis*: MÜLLER 1995, pls. 49:A55; 67:A247 (Medeon). *RMDP*, fig. 304:183 (Delphi). – *Boeotia*: ANDRIKOU 2006, pl. 18:295. *RMDP*, fig. 261:179 (Thebes). *RMDP*, fig. 260:164 (Eutresis). – *Attica*: IAKOVIDIS 1969/70, vol. 3, pl. 98γ (Perati). *RMDP*, fig. 209:332 (Perati-Steiria). *RMDP*, fig. 211:353 (Hymettos Cave). – *Laconia*: *RMDP*, fig. 94:158 (Sykea). – *Elis*: *RMDP*, fig. 135:70 (Renia). – *Euboea*: POPHAM – SCHOFIELD – SHERRATT 2006, figs. 2.2.1; 2.32.6 (Lefkandi). – *Skyros*: PARLAMA 1984, figs. 47:54; 53:61–62; 54:63; pl. 69:17. – For *Cyclades* and *Dodecanese* see e.g. KOEHL 1984, fig. 6:1 (Paros). *RMDP*, figs. 450:85; 451:86 (Kos). BENZI 1992, pls. 94o–p; 113a. *RMDP*, 426:171 (Rhodes: III C Early–Middle/Developed).

[22] The new evidence presented by Petropoulos and Moschos does not affect P. Mountjoy's observations on the late manifestations of this style (MOUNTJOY 1990, 267–270), except for the fact that regular banding of closed shapes was already introduced in LH III C Early and remained in fashion throughout LH III C.

[23] As distinct from the monochrome stemmed amphoriskos of Fig. 9:1, this vase was most probably set on top of a kylix stem. For stemmed amphoriskoi of this type see JUNG 2002, 167–169, fig. 62.

The disc of T. XXIV/23v deserves attention. It is decorated with a stemmed spiral which may be described either as painted fat or as reserved thin. This pattern – which is also found on the stirrup jar T. XLIV/10ai (Fig. 3:1) and on the cylindrical stirrup jar T. XLIX/16k (Fig. 3:2) – is also attested by stirrup jars of LH III C Early–Middle from Rhodes (*RMDP*, figs. 431:208; 432:215; 433:217) and from Attica (*RMDP*, fig. 211:353).[24] Above all, a fair number of stirrup jars of LH III C Middle from Medeon in Phocis carry this spiral pattern not only on the disc but also on the base. Sylvie Müller has included this feature in what she describes as "Style de Médéon" (MÜLLER 1995, 273–274, and, e.g., pls. 50:A57,60–62; 56:A131,133,135–137,139). At Elateia the motif may well have been borrowed from there.

The sparse decoration of T. LVI/23ka (Fig. 4:2) and the shaping of spout and false mouth might suggest a date in LH III C Developed. However, the widest diameter is placed well above the middle of the vase, and the lower body is pronouncedly conical. Therefore a general date in LH III C Middle is to be preferred. The elliptic shape and the oblong – albeit idiosyncratic – arrangement of the decoration of the false mouth are reminiscent of the OSJ T. XV/A5 (cf. Fig. 2:5).

The two alabastra of Fig. 5:3 (straight-sided) and 5:6 (rounded) should be assigned to LH III C Middle in general (for discussion see BÄCHLE 2003, 37–38, 41–42), and the same is true of the lekythos Fig. 5:4. – For the stirrup jar T. XV/A4 (Fig. 4:3) and T. VI/A3 (Fig. 4:4) a date in LH III C Middle/Advanced may be suggested on account of their well-balanced shapes (T. XV/A4: globular-conical; T. VI/A3: globular-biconical) with slightly sloping shoulders. T. XV/A4 moreover has monochrome handles, an early feature. On the other hand, their straight and tall spouts are generally considered to be a feature of LH III C Late. However, in some regions such as Achaia (cf. *RMDP*, fig. 148:79), Phocis (cf. *RMDP*, fig. 304:182–183,185) and Rhodes (*RMDP*, figs. 432:209; 439:269) tall spouts meeting the false mouth already occurred from LH III C Early onwards. It may also be remembered that T. XV/A4 was one of the vases found in niche Z of Tomb XV/86 and dated to LH III C Advanced, cf. above, p. 135. – The pyxis (based straight-sided alabastron) Fig. 5:5[25] and the amphoriskos Fig. 5:2 could be assigned either to LH III C Advanced or to an early phase of LH III C Late. As we have seen this ambiguity in classification applies to many LH III C Middle/Advanced vases from Elateia. – Finally, the two stirrup jars of Fig. 4:5–6 may be classified as LH III C Late on account of their shoulder decoration; it should be noted, however, that Fig. 4:5 displays earlier features such as a low ring base and monochrome decoration of handles and false mouth. In contrast, the shape of Fig. 4:6 is definitely LH III C Late.

In sum, vases decorated with bands of equal width were remarkably popular at Elateia. The decorative system was perhaps first stimulated by contacts with regions such as Phocis, Achaia and Skyros where it had already been amply practised in LH III C Early. In fact, there are some other features, too, which the banded vases of Elateia shared with the pottery of these regions: Monochrome discs of stirrup jars occur at Elateia (Fig. 4:4–5),[26] at Nikoleika near Aigion (PETROPOULOS this volume, figs. 15; 22)

---

[24] At Tiryns a reserved version of this spiral was applied on the inside of a monochrome deep bowl dated to LH III C Advanced (PODZUWEIT 1983, 375, fig. 5:14).

[25] For a close parallel dated to LH III C Middle or Middle/Late from Nikoleika see PETROPOULOS this volume, figs. 10; 36.

[26] On the vases from Elateia the monochrome discs have a reserved centre. The same decoration recurs on the discs of stirrup jars from Perati-Steiria (*RMDP*, fig. 220:448) and from Ialysos (*RMDP*, fig. 433:216). According to *RMDP*, 572 it is a Minoan feature.

and in Kephallonia (SOUYOUDZOGLOU-HAYWOOD 1999, 68, fig. 10B,g),[27] and the decoration of the disc of the stirrup jar of Fig. 4:1 has close parallels at Medeon in Phocis, as already mentioned. Moreover, the LH III C pottery from Elateia had much in common with the ceramics from East Achaia (cf. PETROPOULOS this volume), Phocis (*RMDP*. – MÜLLER 1995) and Skyros (PARLAMA 1984), as will be demonstrated on further occasions. However, the continuing frequent use of evenly spaced banded decoration at Elateia in LH III C Middle and Late was only paralleled in Achaia (PAPADOPOULOS 1978/79. – PETROPOULOS this volume). In Phocis (*RMDP*, figs. 311:285; 312; 313:294), Skyros (PARLAMA 1984, cat. nos. 5, 79, 82) and Kephallonia (SOUYOUDZOGLOU-HAYWOOD 1999, pls. 3:A1143; 4:1313) it was used until LH III C Late, but on a much more reduced scale.

II.2.2. **Vases covered with successive groups of bands alternating with thin horizontal lines.** – The basic system of covering stirrup jars and other vases with a sequence of bands alternating with multiple thin horizontal lines (Figs. 6; 8:1–3) clearly took its origin from the decorative patterns of closed vessels in LH III A and III B. Like in most other regions, it had been used during these periods at Elateia, too (cf. Fig. 6:2, LH III B–C after BÄCHLE 2003, 50). In the course of LH III C the broad-thin-broad pattern was applied more densely until the vessel was more or less entirely covered. In fact, even the shoulder decorations of stirrup jars were often reduced to a minimum (cf. Fig. 6:5,7) or edged out (Fig. 6:3–6,8) in order to emphasise the banded decoration.

According to A. Bächle who has studied a series of these vases (BÄCHLE 2003, 51–56) the typological sequence of the stirrup jars of Fig. 6 begins with T. XVI/A20 (Fig. 6:2. – BÄCHLE cat. no. 27: LH III B–C), and continues with T. VI/A9 (Fig. 6:1. – BÄCHLE 2003, cat. no. 15: LH III C Early), T. XXXVI/44x (Fig. 6:3. – BÄCHLE 2003, cat. no. 136: LH III C Early–Middle/Developed), T. LXII/18st and T. VI/A7+A8 (Fig. 6:4–5. – BÄCHLE 2003, cat. nos. 197, 14: LH III C Middle) and T. LIII/32a (Fig. 6:6. – BÄCHLE 2003, cat. no. 166: LH III C Advanced. For discussion of tall spouts see above, p. 139). – To these six vessels we add the two stirrup jars of LH III C Advanced to Late (Fig. 6:8) and LH III C Late (Fig. 6:7).

The decorative scheme of covering vases with successive groups of broad bands alternating with multiple thin lines was not confined to stirrup jars. It is also attested with the shapes of lekythos (Fig. 8:1), alabastron (Fig. 8:2 = BÄCHLE 2003, cat. no. 137) and amphoriskos (Fig. 8:3).

The same decorative system was used in other parts of the Mycenaean world, too. This does not come as much of a surprise, considering that the pattern was well rooted in the traditions of LH III A and III B. Moreover, from LH III C Early onwards a tendency towards covering a vase with successive broad-thin-broad groups of bands and lines can be observed in regions such as Attica (*RMDP*, figs. 220:443,445,447; 221:449), the Argolid (*RMDP*, figs. 45:344; 46:345,347), Achaia (PAPADOPOULOS 1978/79, figs. 70; 79. – PETROPOULOS this volume, fig. 15. – DEGER-JALKOTZY 2003, fig. 3:5. – DEGER-JALKOTZY – ALRAM-STERN 1985, 416, fig. 16:4; 421, fig. 19:4), Phocis (MÜLLER 1995, e.g. pls. 49:A54,58–59; 50:A60,62), Boeotia (*RMDP*, figs. 260:165; 261:178), Thessaly (*RMDP* 344:112–113,119), Rhodes (*RMDP*, e.g. figs. 430–432), Kos (*RMDP*, fig. 450:74–75), Skyros (PARLAMA 1984, figs. 51:57; 54:63; 57:69) and Kephallonia (SOUYOUDZOGLOU-HAYWOOD 1999, pl. 15:A1491,1346). However, in contrast to Elateia, vessels which were completely covered with successive groups of broad-thin-broad bands and lines were rare in other regions. There are only an amphoriskos from Kladeos/Trypes (*RMDP*, fig. 135:66), a

---

[27] In Achaia and Kephallonia these discs are completely monochrome, and the same applies to those of five stirrup jars from Perati (IAKOVIDIS 1969/70, vol. 2, 156, fig. 26:1).

straight-sided alabastron from Tiryns/Prophitis Elias (*RMDP*, fig. 43:331) and a few stirrup jars from Phocis (MÜLLER 1995, pl. 62:A205), Boeotia (*RMDP*, fig. 261:178) and Rhodes (BENZI 1992, pls. 9:d–e; 69:e,h. – *RMDP*, fig. 432:211). In many other regions the broad-thin-broad bandings often served as subsidiary ornament on vases decorated in the pleonastic style. In this function they were often combined with single broad lines, zones with linear pattern decoration, or monochrome zones with multiple thin reserved lines. – In contrast, in Achaia the decorative system of evenly spaced stripes of equal width prevailed.

In sum, the complete covering of a comparatively large number, as well as of a considerable variety of vessels with the broad-thin-broad banding system must be regarded as a specific feature of the pottery from Elateia. In LH III C Middle it reached a pinnacle which may have lasted into an early phase of LH III C Late. After that, it disintegrated and declined.

II.3. Local vases of "elaborate" decoration (Figs. 2:6; 3)

It has already been emphasised that the flamboyant decorative styles of LH III C Middle were not adopted at Elateia. Therefore the pottery from this site has a rather uninspired and dull appearance. However, this verdict does not apply to all vases from Elateia-Alonaki. Apart from the imports, there are a fair number of vessels which stand out by their more elaborate ornamentation of shoulder and body zones, as well as by the successful interplay of well-balanced shape and decoration. In the following a few examples will be presented.

T. XLIV/10ai (Fig. 3:1): The light ground decoration of this stirrup jar compares well with Sylvie Müller's "Style de Médéon" vases from Phocis (cf. MÜLLER 1995, 273–276). The false mouth and the base carry the characteristic spiral motif already mentioned above, p. 139. Secondly, a diagonal cross is painted on the handles. Moreover, the body is decorated with various arrangements of bands and small zones with linear patterns (zigzag, chevrons), a system also found on several vases from Medeon (cf. MÜLLER 1995, pls. 50:A57; 67:A249–A250). Furthermore, the decoration of the shoulder combines the favourite motifs of the stirrup jars from Medeon, namely triangles of all kinds, concentric arcs and semicircles.

However, none of the stirrup jars published so far from Medeon can compare with the complex shoulder decoration of the vase from Elateia: The spout is flanked on both sides by an incurved triangle with angle-filling curves. The main facial side shows an elaborate triangle built of joining arcs and filled with curves and bars, and supplemented with concentric semicircles. The same syntax recurs on other stirrup jars from Elateia (see Fig. 3:2–3) so that T. XLIV/10ai may be viewed as a local product rather than an import from Phocis or elsewhere. The chronology is clearly LH III C Middle.

T. XLIX/16k (Fig. 3:2): The cylindrical form of this stirrup jar may well have been borrowed from the straight-sided alabastron, a shape which was well represented at Elateia (cf. BÄCHLE 2003, 38–42). The disc carries the "Medeon" spiral, and the syntax of the shoulder decoration resembles that of the stirrup jar mentioned above: The spout is flanked by slightly incurved stacked triangles and the main facial decoration consists of an elaborate triangle with angle-filling curves, isolated semicircles and a motif formed by concentric loops with solid central filling. This "almond" motif was a decorative element of the pleonastic styles of LH III C Middle: In Naxos it is found among the filling motifs between the octopus tentacles of octopus stirrup jars (cf. *RMDP*, 940, fig. 382b. – KARDARA 1977, fig. 3, pls. 11; 18; 23γ). Moreover, the famous outlined rosettes of the mature Close Style (cf. e.g. Fig. 1:3) and other copious decorative systems, too, were composed of "almonds". However, in other cases "almonds" were used as main motifs of shoulder decorations, e.g. on stirrup jars of Phase II from Perati (IAKOVIDIS 1969/70, vol. 2, 123, fig. 57:174,842. – See also *RMDP*, fig. 220:447).

On the whole, a date in LH III C Middle appears appropriate for the shape and the shoulder decoration of the vase from Elateia. More precisely the later part of the period, LH III C Middle/Advanced, is indicated by the monochrome paint of the cylindrical body interspaced with three reserved stripes of equal width: According to the chronological sequence of the Argolid, monochrome coating of vases with reserved bands and/or thin lines first occurs in LH III C Advanced when it is often found on the lower part of vases decorated in the Close Style or other pleonastic styles.[28] The pattern is continued in LH III C Late, but the spacing of the reserved lines becomes irregular. – It should be added that a date in LH III C Middle/Advanced of our stirrup vase harmonises well with that of the imported vase T. XLIX/16m (Fig. 1:1) found in the same tomb and in the same context (see above, p. 130).

T. XXXVIII/10d (Fig. 3:3): This vase was found together with the narrow-necked amphoriskos (or "two-handled jug") of our Fig. 1:2 in the central pit in the chamber of Tomb XXXVIII/88. It is a beautiful specimen of FS 175. The ring base is raised, the slightly ovoid shape of the body is well balanced, and a moderately coned disc is set on top of a slim neck. The spout is not preserved, but the orientation of its lowest part suggests that it did not touch the false mouth. Handles and neck are monochrome, and the disc carries a densely coiled spiral. The body is monochrome except for a reserved band around the edge of the foot and for three reserved bands – each interspaced with two thin dark lines – placed between the shoulder and the belly zone. The adornment of the shoulders follows that of the two stirrup jars described above: The spout is flanked by slightly incurved stacked triangles, while the main facial side carries a complex triangle pattern filled with dots and concentric arcs and bars grouped around a large "almond". Apart from this elaborate ornamentation, there is no other pattern decorated zone, neither at the outer edge of the shoulder nor on the belly of the vase. Thus the contrast between the copious adornment of the shoulder and the darkground decoration of the body lends a both austere and elegant appearance to the vase.

As for chronology, the vase should be assigned to LH III C Advanced. However, an overlap with the incipient phase of LH III C Late cannot be excluded.

T. XVI/A22 (Fig. 3:4): This vase has a ring base, the body is globular-conical and the shoulder is slightly sloping. The spout is equal in height with the wide, flat and slightly coned disc. This shaping of spout and false mouth is reminiscent of stately LH III C Middle vases from Rhodes (*RMDP*, 1044, figs. 432:209; 439:269) or from the Argolid (*RMDP*, figs. 44:340; 46:346). The decoration of the body is darkground with groups of small reserved lines. Above the belly there is a band filled with groups of chevrons. It may have been borrowed from the Close Style. The shoulder decoration consists of cross-hatched triangles flanking the spout and of antithetic horns linked with chevrons on the main decorative face. Antithetic horns were extremely popular in Rhodes, particularly in Ialysos (see the stirrup jars, amphoriskoi, straight-sided alabastra, jugs, strainer jugs and a stemmed skyphos [most of them LH III C Early–Developed] as presented in BENZI 1992, *passim*), while in other regions such as Attica, Euboea and the Cyclades the motif of antithetic streamers was preferred. However, there are stirrup jars from Thebes-Kolonaki which also carry shoulder decorations of antithetic horns and triangles, one of them in combination with a darkground decoration of the body (cf. *RMDP*, fig. 265:211 [LH III C Middle]; see also figs. 261:178 [LH III C Early];

---

[28] PODZUWEIT 1992. In Rhodes this decorative pattern is said to have started slightly earlier, in LH III C Early to Developed (*RMDP*, 988), but the synchronisation of this phase with LH III C Middle in the Mainland still remains problematic (*RMDP*, 985–988).

624:210 [LH III C Middle]). It may be remembered that we have already detected a connection between Elateia and Boeotia for the narrow-necked amphoriskos T. XXXVIII/9g (Fig. 1:2) (see above, p. 130), as well as in the case of vases with banded body decoration (see above, paragraph II.2). As for chronology, it is true that cross-hatched triangles were very popular LH III C Late. However, they already occurred on stirrup jars of LH III C Early–Middle/Developed in Ialysos (BENZI 1992, pl. 36e,g. – *RMDP*, fig. 433:218), and of LH III C Middle in the Argolid (*RMDP*, figs. 45:344; 46:347). Considering the general affinity of the vase to the stately vessels of other regions, it should be viewed as a candidate for LH III C Middle/Advanced.

T. XXI/A78 (Fig. 3:5): The false mouth of this vase still carries the "Medeon" spiral, the dark coating of the body is still evenly interspaced by multiple reserved lines, and the shoulder is decorated with five incurved triangles filled with FM 42 "patch". The vase has a wide conical body, the shoulder is flat. A very close parallel of this vessel is provided by a stirrup jar from Perati (IAKOVIDIS 1969/70, vol. 2, fig. 57:1127) which is dated to Phase II, LH III C Middle. However, the spout of our vase is trumpet shaped and the false mouth has a high cone, features which are generally assigned to LH III C Late. On the whole, a date of LH III C Late seems adequate for this vase, but the regular spaced decoration of the body points to an early stage rather than to the later part of that period.

T. XV/A6 (Fig. 2:6): Although straight-sided alabastra are well attested in Elateia (BÄCHLE 2003, 34–42), the based type ("pyxis", FM 97) is rare. The shape was very popular in the Dodecanese and on Naxos, but it is also attested in various regions of the Mainland such as Achaia (PETROPOULOS this volume), Skyros (PARLAMA 1984, fig. 52:59) and Perati (IAKOVIDIS 1969/70, vol. 2, fig. 79Δ–E). As we have already noted, the striped pyxis of Fig. 5:5 has a close parallel in Nikoleika in Achaia (cf. above, n. 25). Its shape is also very similar to that of the present vessel, except for the ring base of the latter. Moreover, in both cases the neck is monochrome and the handles are cross-barred. Otherwise the decoration of the banded vessel is common to the pottery produced at Elateia, while the ornamentation of the present vase seems to meet the desire for a more elaborate style. The decoration of the cylindrical body – joining concentric lozenges – recurs on the shoulder of an evenly striped straight-sided alabastron from Skyros (PARLAMA 1984, fig. 47:54). The shoulder is decorated with isolated concentric semicircles with solid centre and framed with dots, and the lower edge of the zone is framed with joining semicircles. The motif of the dotted isolated semicircles is attested on vases of LH III C Middle in Laconia (*RMDP*, fig. 98:220), Perati (*RMDP*, fig. 220:448) and on Naxos (*RMDP*, fig. 388:42). In LH III C Late it gained even more popularity. However, in view of the excellent quality of the shape and the decoration of this vase, and given the general chronology of the group to which it belonged (on niche Z of Tomb XV/86 see above, p. 135), there is no need to date it later than LH III C Middle.

To sum up, there is a fair number of burial vases from Elateia which may be aptly called "typical LH III C Middle" according to the terminology of P. Mountjoy (*MDP*, 169).

CONCLUSIONS

In order to understand and interpret the pottery assemblages of LH III C Middle from Elateia, the geographical situation of the site has to be considered. The upper valley of the Boeotian Kephissos formed a branch of the so-called "Great Isthmos Corridor" leading from the Corinthian Gulf to the Thermopylae and further north. Moreover, at the top of the Kephissos valley the main inland route to the north from Attica via Boeotia joined the "Isthmos Corridor". Thus Elateia was situated at the main roads which connected northern and southern Greece. Moreover, there is a route of communication which runs from the upper Kephissos valley via Kalapodi into East Locris, where Kynos and Mitrou controlled the coastal region and the sea routes across the northern gulf of Euboea.

Thus, situated on the main routes of the Mainland from north to south and from east to west, it comes as no surprise that Elateia received not only items of exchange from various directions, but also cultural influences. In particular, finds at Elateia of amber (EDER 2003), glass beads of similar composition to contemporary Italian glasses (NIKITA – HENDERSON 2006. – NIKITA – HENDERSON – NIGHTINGALE forthcoming) and Italic metal objects (DAKORONIA 2004) demonstrate that the people of Elateia were involved in the transportation of goods of transadriatic origin along the "Great Isthmos Corridor" route. Against this background, the stylistic affinities, as pointed out in this paper, between the pottery from Elateia with the ceramics of Achaia, Phocis, Boeotia, Thessaly and Skyros can be easily explained.[29] On the other hand, features shared with the ceramics of Rhodes and Naxos may have been transmitted along the route from Attica via Boeotia, or along the Euboean gulf and via the East Locris.[30] In a similar fashion, pottery imports from Achaia (including perhaps an octopus stirrup jar, cf. above, p. 131–132) and from Kynos were presumably brought by ways of direct contacts, while others such as the "Cretan" stirrup jars (if such, indeed, they were, cf. above, p. 132–133) and the Close Style stirrup jar (cf. above, p. 130) may have been obtained through intermediate exchange. Closer links with the pottery finds from Kalapodi are seemingly lacking. However, since the pottery finds from Kalapodi mainly consist of open shapes, this picture is likely to change when the remains of open shapes from the dromos fills of the Elateia tombs will be published.

A LOCAL STYLE OF LH III C MIDDLE?

Under these premises, decorative elements and shapes coming from various directions were blended at Elateia into what may be called a local style of LH III C Middle. A first description of its characteristics has been attempted in this paper. Some features such as reserved body zones of monochrome vases or multiple groups of reserved bands set in monochrome surfaces were common to all regions of the Mycenaean world from LH III C Advanced onwards. Others such as a certain predilection for the elaborate triangle motif or vessels covered with stripes (cf. above, paragraph II.2.1.) or broad-thin-broad banding (cf. above, paragraph II.2.2.) covering all the body were shared by the neighbouring regions of Phocis, Boeotia and Thessaly. There were also considerable resemblances to the pottery products of Skyros and of East Achaia. However, nowhere did the banded decorations extend to such a wide range of shapes. Moreover, there is no other site from which such a large amount of vases of this decorative system(s) have been published. On the other hand, the ceramics found at Elateia outnumber those published from the other regions of Central Greece. Therefore at present we prefer to think that the we are dealing with a local variety of regional LH III C Middle style of Central Greece in general, rather than with a local style of the area of Elateia.

---

[29] Stylistic affinities with the pottery of the Ionian Islands, particularly of Kephallonia, made themselves felt during the later phases of LH III C Late rather than in LH III C Middle.

[30] G. Nightingale kindly reminded me of this alternative which will certainly become more apparent when the finds from Kynos and Mitrou will be published.

CHRONOLOGY

At the end of this paper it should be stressed again that with many closed vases from Elateia it is difficult to differentiate stylistically between LH III C Middle and LH III C Late. They often display features for which a first appearance in LH III C Middle/Advanced can be put forward, but which also continued in LH III C Late. On the other hand, in the case of banded vases the assignment to LH III C Middle often is quite clear. Moreover, there are a large number of vases which demonstrate what pottery of LH III C Late looked like, particularly during the later stretch of that period (cf. DAKORONIA – DEGER-JALKOTZY – FABRIZII-REUER 2002).

Thus the chronological development of the later pottery phases from Elateia resembles that of Achaia as presented by I. Moschos (cf. above, n. 17): LH III C Middle (= Developed–Advanced) – LH III C Advanced to III C Late – LH III C Late – LH III C Late to Submycenaean. The pottery presented in this paper comprises the phases LH III C Middle (Developed–Advanced) and LH III C Advanced to Late. It was contemporaneous with the transitional period of LH III C Advanced–Late in Achaia as defined by Aigeira II (DEGER-JALKOTZY 2003), the material from Nikoleika as shown by PETROPOULOS this volume and Phases 4 and 5 in the chronological scheme of I. Moschos.

At the beginning of the paper it has been stated that Elateia's time of greatest prosperity started in LH III C Middle. We may now finish with observing that the pinnacle of this development was reached during a phase which comprised the pottery phases of LH III C Advanced to Late. However, most remarkable is the continuation of this period of greatest prosperity beyond the end of the Mycenaean period and the transition to the Early Iron Age.

Bibliography

ALRAM-STERN, E. – G. NIGHTINGALE (eds.)
2006 *Keimelion. Elitenbildung und elitärer Konsum von der mykenischen Palastzeit bis zur homerischen Epoche. The Formation of Elites and Elitist Lifestyles from Mycenaean Palatial Times to the Homeric Period. Akten des internationalen Kongresses vom 3. bis 5. Februar 2005 in Salzburg* (DenkschrWien 350 = Veröffentlichungen der Mykenischen Kommission 27). Vienna.

ALZINGER, W. UND MITARBEITER
1985 "Aigeira-Hyperesia und die Siedlung Phelloë in Achaia. Österreichische Ausgrabungen auf der Peloponnes 1972–1983. Teil I: Akropolis", *Klio* 67, 389–451.

ANDRIKOU, E.
2006 "The Late Helladic III Pottery", 11–179 in: ANDRIKOU ET AL. 2006.

ANDRIKOU, E. – V. L. ARAVANTINOS – L. GODART – A. SACCONI – J. VROOM
2006 *Thèbes. Fouilles de la Cadmée II.2. Les tablettes en Linéaire B de la Odos Pelopidou. Le contexte archéologique. La céramique de la Odos Pelopidou et la chronologie du Linéaire B.* Pisa – Rome.

BÄCHLE, A. E.
2000 "Zur Chronologie der Anlage des Friedhofs von Elateia: Die früheste Keramik", 191–197 in: BLAKOLMER 2000.
2003 *Mykenische Keramik des 14. bis 12. Jahrhunderts vor Christus aus der Nekropole von Elateia-Alonaki. Ein Beispiel regionaler mykenischer Keramikentwicklung.* Ph.D. Diss., Universität Salzburg.
2006 "Eliten in Elateia? Überlegungen ausgehend von der frühen mykenischen Keramik", 15–30 in: ALRAM-STERN – NIGHTINGALE 2006.

BASSIAKOS, Y. – E. ALOUPI – Y. FACORELLIS (eds.)
2001 *Αρχαιομετρικές μελέτες για την Ελληνική προϊστορία και αρχαιότητα. Archaeometry Issues in Greek Prehistory and Antiquity.* Athens.

BENZI, M.
1992 *Rodi e la Civiltà Micenea* (Incunabula Graeca 94). Rome.

BLAKOLMER, F.
2000 *Österreichische Forschungen zur Ägäischen Bronzezeit 1998. Akten der Tagung am Institut für Klassische Archäologie der Universität Wien, 2.–3. Mai 1998* (Wiener Forschungen zur Archäologie 3). Vienna.

DAKORONIA, F.
1999 "Representations of Sea-Battles on Mycenaean Sherds from Kynos", 119–128 in: TZALAS 1999.
2003 "The Transition from Late Helladic III C to the Early Iron Age at Kynos", 37–51 in: *LH III C Chronology and Synchronisms*.
2004 "Special Elateia Day. Elateia in Central Greece: Excavation and Finds", *BICS* 47, 185–186.

DAKORONIA, F. – S. DEGER-JALKOTZY – S. FABRIZII-REUER
2002 "Beisetzungen mit Leichenbrand aus der Felskammernekropole von Elateia-Alonaki, Griechenland", *ArchAustr* 84–85, 2000/01 [2002] (= *Festschrift für Egon Reuer zum fünfundsiebzigsten Geburtstag*), 137–153.

DEGER-JALKOTZY, S. – E. ALRAM-STERN
1985 "Die mykenische Siedlung", 394–426 in: ALZINGER und MITARBEITER 1985.

DEGER-JALKOTZY, S. – F. DAKORONIA
1991 "Elateia (Phokis) und die frühe Geschichte der Griechen: Ein österreichisch-griechisches Grabungsprojekt", *AnzWien* 127, 1990 [1991], 77–86.

DEGER-JALKOTZY, S.
1999 "Elateia and Problems of Pottery Chronology", 195–202 in: Περιφέρεια.
2003 "Stratified Pottery Deposits from the Late Helladic III C Settlement at Aigeira/Achaia", 53–75 in: *LH III C Chronology and Synchronisms*.
2004 "Special Elateia Day. Elateia-Alonaki: The Mycenaean and Early Iron Age Pottery and the History of the Cemetery", *BICS* 47, 187–188.
2006 "Late Mycenaean Warrior Tombs", 151–179 in: DEGER-JALKOTZY – LEMOS 2006.

DEGER-JALKOTZY, S. – I. E. LEMOS (eds.)
2006 *Ancient Greece: From the Mycenaean Palaces to the Age of Homer* (Edinburgh Leventis Studies 3). Edinburgh.

EDER, B.
2003 "Patterns of Contact and Communication between the Regions South and North of the Corinthian Gulf in LH III C", 37–54 in: KYPARISSI-APOSTOLIKA – PAPAKONSTANTINOU 2003.

EVELY, D. (ed.)
2006 *Lefkandi IV. The Bronze Age. The Late Helladic III C Settlement at Xeropolis* (BSA Suppl. 39). London.

FELSCH, R. C. S. (ed.)
1996 *Kalapodi. Ergebnisse der Ausgrabungen im Heiligtum der Artemis und des Apollon von Hyampolis in der antiken Phokis. Vol. I.* Mainz.

FURTWÄNGLER, A. – G. LOESCHCKE
1886 *Mykenische Vasen. Vorhellenische Thongefässe aus dem Gebiete des Mittelmeeres*. Berlin.

IAKOVIDIS, S. E.
1969/70 Περατή. Το νεκροταφείον (Βιβλιοθήκη της εν Αθήναις Αρχαιολογικής Εταιρείας 67). Athens.

JACOB-FELSCH, M.
1996 "Die spätmykenische bis frühprotogeometrische Keramik", 1–213 in: FELSCH 1996.

JUNG, R.
2002 *Kastanas. Ausgrabungen in einem Siedlungshügel der Bronze- und Eisenzeit Makedoniens 1975–1979. Die Drehscheibenkeramik der Schichten 19 bis 11* (Prähistorische Archäologie in Südosteuropa 18). Kiel.

KANTA, A.
1980 *The Late Minoan III Period in Crete. A Survey of Sites, Pottery and their Distribution* (SIMA 58). Göteborg.

KARDARA, C.
1977 Απλώματα Νάξου. Κινητά ευρήματα τάφων Α και Β (Βιβλιοθήκη της εν Αθήναις Αρχαιολογικής Εταιρείας 88). Athens.

Koehl, R. B.
1984   "Observations on a Deposit of LC III C Pottery from the Koukounaries Acropolis on Paros", 207–224 in: MacGillivray – Barber 1984.

Kyparissi-Apostolika, N. – M. Papakonstantinou (eds.)
2003   Η περιφέρεια του Μυκηναϊκού κόσμου. Β' διεθνές διεπιστημονικό συμπόσιο, 26–30 Σεπτεμβρίου, Λαμία 1999. Athens.

MacGillivray, J. A. – R. L. N. Barber (eds.)
1984   The Prehistoric Cyclades: Contributions to a Workshop on Cycladic Chronology. Edinburgh.

Mee, C.
1982   Rhodes in the Bronze Age. An Archaeological Survey. Warminster.

Mommsen, H. – A. Hein – D. Ittameier – J. Maran – F. Dakoronia
2001   "New Mycenaean Pottery Production Centres from Eastern Central Greece Obtained by Neutron Activation Analysis", 343–354 in: Bassiakos – Aloupi – Facorellis 2001.

Moschos, I.
forthc. "Evidences of Social Re-organization and Re-construction at LH III C Achaia and Patterns of Contacts and Exchanges via the Ionian Sea", in: P. C. Guida (ed.), Dall'Egeo all'Adriatico: organizazzioni sociali, modi di scambio e interazione in età post-palaziale (XII–XI sec. a. C.), Seminario internazionale, Udine 1–2 dicembre 2006.

Mountjoy, P. A.
1990   "Regional Mycenaean Pottery", BSA 85, 245–270.

Müller, S.
1995   Les tombes mycéniennes de Médéon de Phocide. Architecture et mobilier. Ph.D. Diss., Université Lumière, Lyon.

Nikita, K. – J. Henderson
2006   "Glass Analyses from Mycenaean Thebes and Elateia: Compositional Evidence for a Mycenaean Glass Industry", Journal of Glass Studies 48, 71–120.

Nikita, K. – J. Henderson – G. Nightingale
forthc. "An Archaeological and Scientific Study of Mycenaean Glass from Elateia-Alonaki, Greece", in: 17e Congrès de l'Association Internationale pour l'Histoire du Verre, Antwerp September 4–8, 2006.

Papadopoulos, Th. J.
1978/79 Mycenaean Achaea (SIMA 55,1–2). Göteborg.

Parlama, L.
1984   Η Σκύρος στην εποχή του χαλκού. Athens.

Perdrizet, P.
1908   Fouilles de Delphes V. Monuments figurés, petits bronzes, terres-cuites, antiquités diverses. Paris.

Περιφέρεια
1999   Η περιφέρεια του Μυκηναϊκού κόσμου. Α' διεθνές διεπιστημονικό συμπόσιο, Λαμία, 25–29 Σεπτεμβρίου 1994. Lamia.

Podzuweit, C.
1983   "Bericht zur spätmykenischen Keramik. Ausgrabungen in Tiryns 1981. Die Phasen SH III C Fortgeschritten bis Spät", AA, 359–402.
1992   Studien zur spätmykenischen Keramik, vorgelegt der Philosophischen Fakultät der Rheinischen Friedrich-Wilhelms-Universität zu Bonn als Habilitationsschrift (Bonn 1992; in press for the Tiryns series).

Popham, M. R. – E. Milburn
1971   "The Late Helladic III C Pottery of Xeropolis (Lefkandi): A Summary", BSA 66, 333–352.

Popham, M. – E. Schofield – S. Sherratt
2006   "The pottery", 137–231 in: Evely 2006.

Rutter, J. B.
2003   "The Nature and Potential Significance of Minoan Features in the Earliest Late Helladic III C Ceramic Assemblages of the Central and Southern Greek Mainland", 193–216 in: LH III C Chronology and Synchronisms.

Souyoudzoglou-Haywood, C.
1999   The Ionian Islands in the Bronze Age and Early Iron Age 3000–800 BC. Liverpool.

Tzalas, H. (ed.)
1999   *Tropis V. 5th International Symposium on Ship Construction in Antiquity, Nauplia, 26, 27, 28 August 1993.* Athens.

Vikatou, O.
1999   "Το μυκηναϊκό νεκτοταφείο της Αγίας Τριάδας Ν. Ηλείας", 237–255 in: *Περιφέρεια*.

Weiss (Bächle), A. E.
1993   *Fragmente bemalter mykenischer Keramik aus den Gräbern von Elateia-Alonaki.* Diplomarbeit, Universität Salzburg.

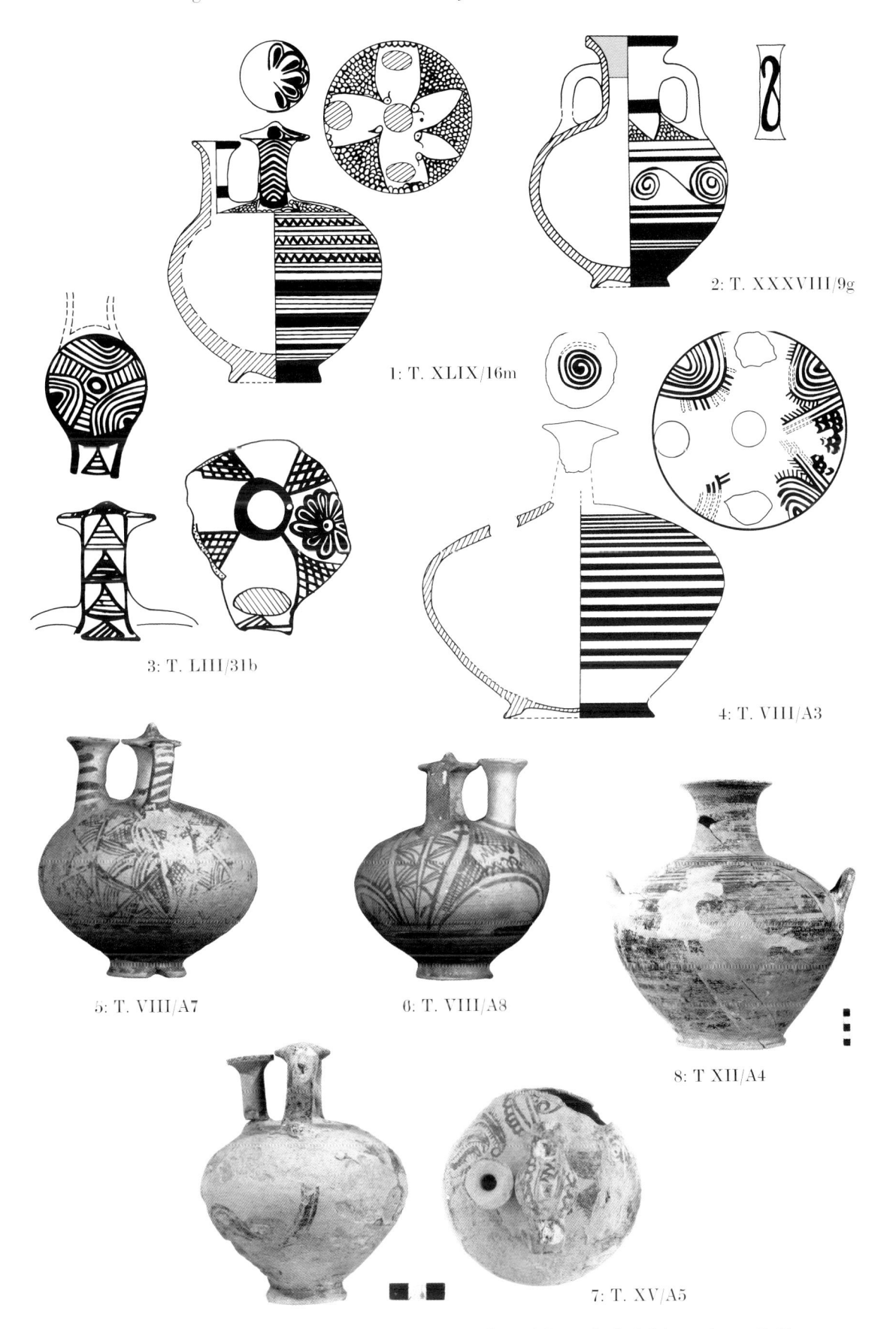

Defining LH III C Middle at the Cemetery of Elateia-Alonaki in Central Greece

1: T. XLIX/16m
2: T. XXXVIII/9g
3: T. LIII/31b
4: T. VIII/A3
5: T. VIII/A7
6: T. VIII/A8
8: T XII/A4
7: T. XV/A5

Fig. 1 Elateia: Imported vases of LH III C Middle and Late. Scale 1:3 (except nos. 7, 8)
(Drawings: B. Eder, E. Held. Ink drawings: E. Held. Photographs: St. Alexandrou, E. Held)

150 Sigrid Deger-Jalkotzy

1: T. XV/A1

2: T. XV/A2

3: T. XV/A3

4: T. XV/A4

5: T. XV/A5

6: T. XV/A6

Fig. 2 Elateia, Tomb XV/86: Vases from dromos niche Z. Scale 1:3
(Drawings: B. Eder, E. Held. Ink drawings: E. Held)

1: T. XLIV/10ai

2: T. XLIX/16k

3: T. XXXVIII/10d

4: T. XVI/A22

5: T. XXI/A78

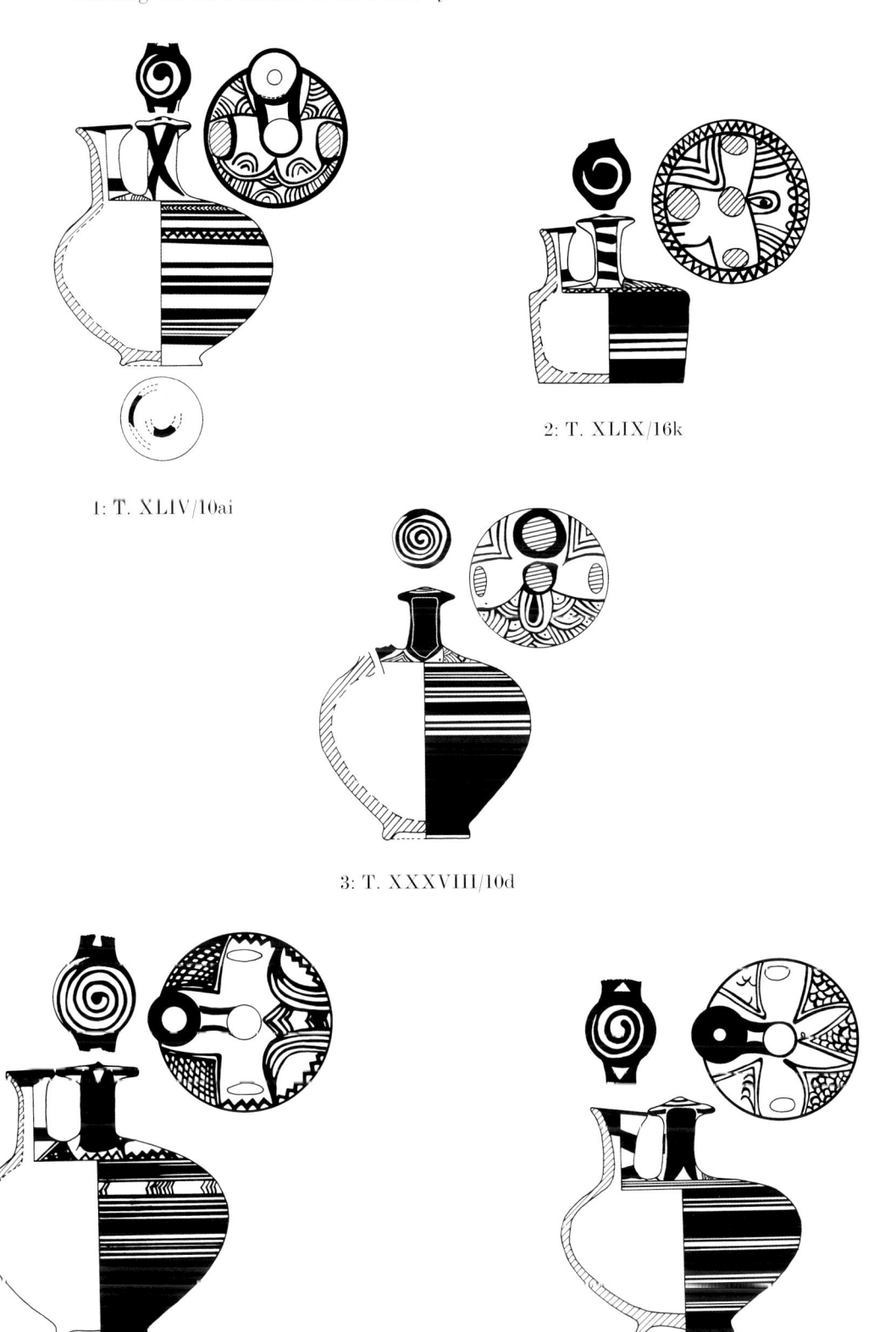

Fig. 3 Elateia, LH III C Middle and Late: Stirrup jars with elaborate decoration. Scale 1:3
(Drawings: B. Eder, E. Held. Ink drawings: E. Held)

1: T. XXIV/23v

2: T. LVI/23ka

3: T. XV/A4

4: T. VI/A3

5: T. XI/A2

6: T. VIII/A4+A11

Fig. 4 Elateia: Stirrup jars decorated with evenly spaced stripes. Scale 1:3
(Drawings: B. Eder, E. Held. Ink drawings: E. Held)

Defining LH III C Middle at the Cemetery of Elateia-Alonaki in Central Greece 153

1: T. XXI/A75

2: T. XXXI/18h

3: T. XXI/A70

4: T. LVI/23kb

5: T. XXI/A73

6: T. II/AB

Fig. 5 Elateia: Various vases decorated with evenly spaced stripes. Scale 1:2
(Drawings: B. Eder, E. Held. Ink drawings: E. Held)

1: T. VI/A9

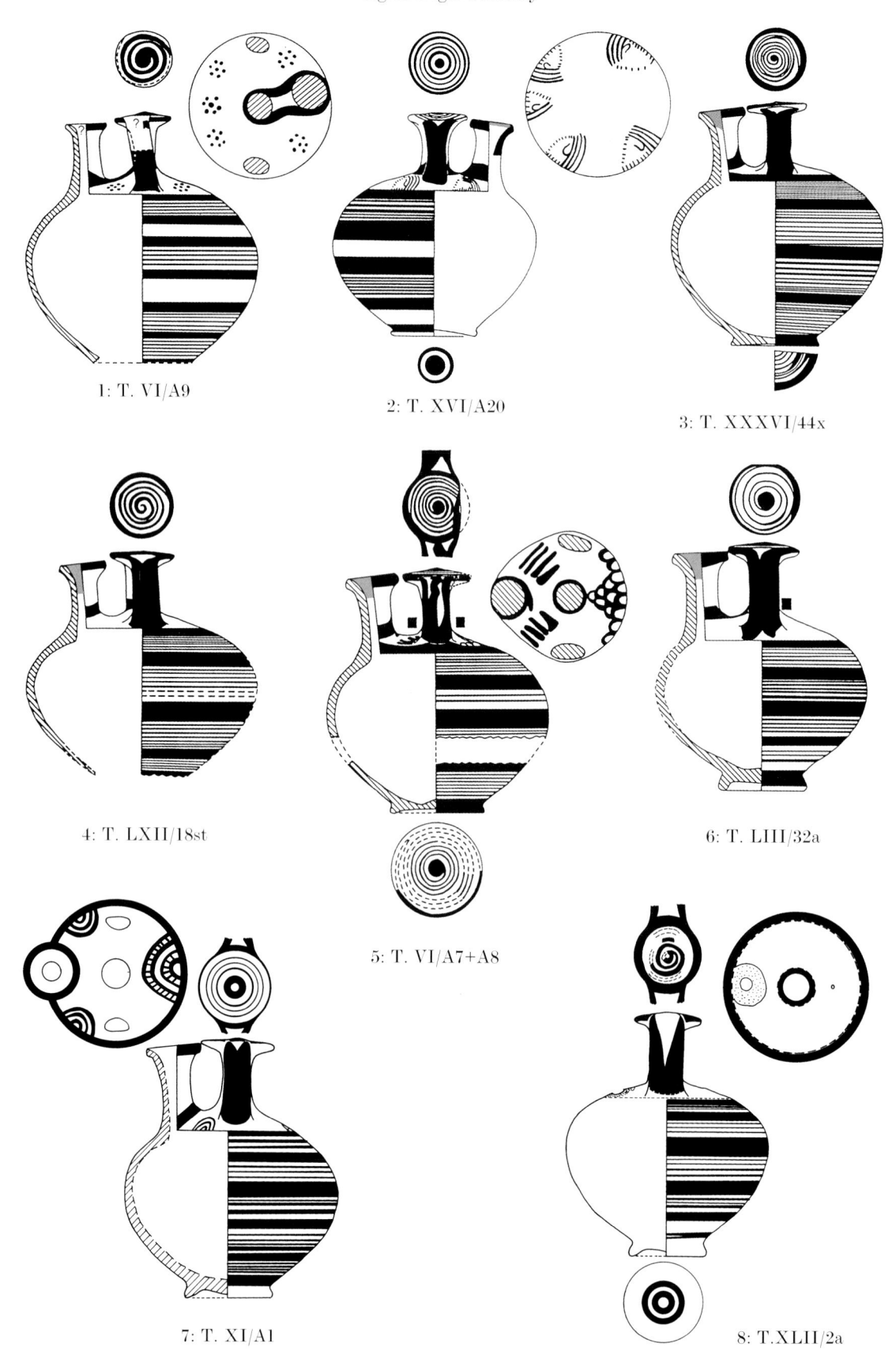

2: T. XVI/A20

3: T. XXXVI/44x

4: T. LXII/18st

5: T. VI/A7+A8

6: T. LIII/32a

7: T. XI/A1

8: T. XLII/2a

Fig. 6 Elateia, LH III C: Banded stirrup jars. Scale 1:3
(Drawings: B. Eder, E. Held. Ink drawings: E. Held)

1: T. XXVIII/33eta

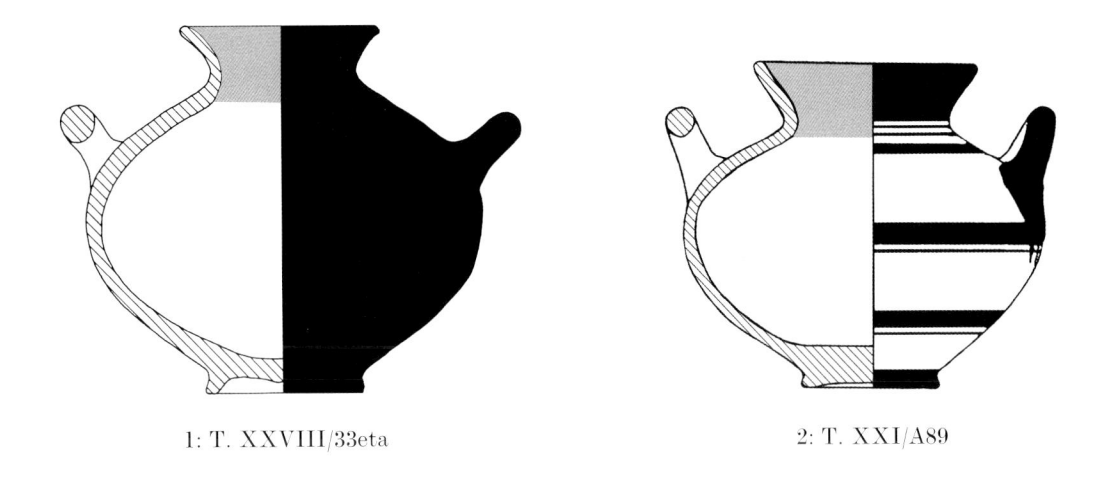

2: T. XXI/A89

3: T. XII/AB

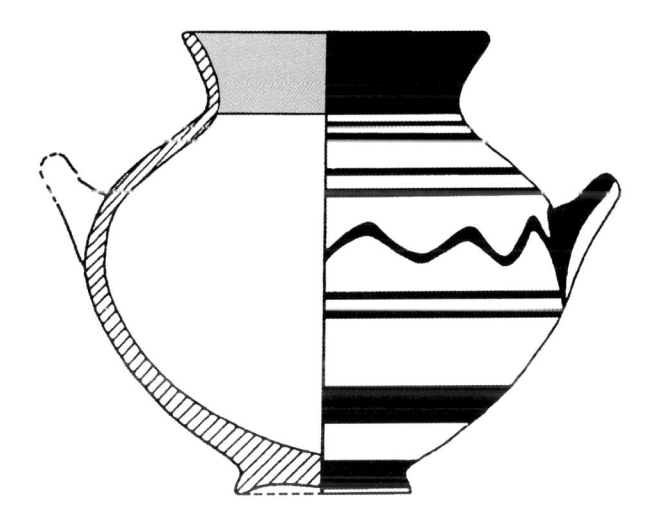

4: T. XXIV/23t

Fig. 7 Elateia, LH III C Middle: Amphoriskos FS 59. Scale 1:2
(Drawings: A. Bächle, B. Eder, E. Held. Ink drawings: A. Bächle, E. Held)

1: T. LXII/31d

2: T. XXXVI/44z

3: T. LIX/16ab

4: T. XXXIII/13e

5: T. LXVI/13p

6: T. XXXVI/38d1

Fig. 8 Elateia. LH III C Middle–Advanced: Lekythos, alabastron, amphoriskos. Scale 1:2
(Drawings: B. Eder, E. Held. Ink drawings: E. Held)

1: T. XXIV/23g

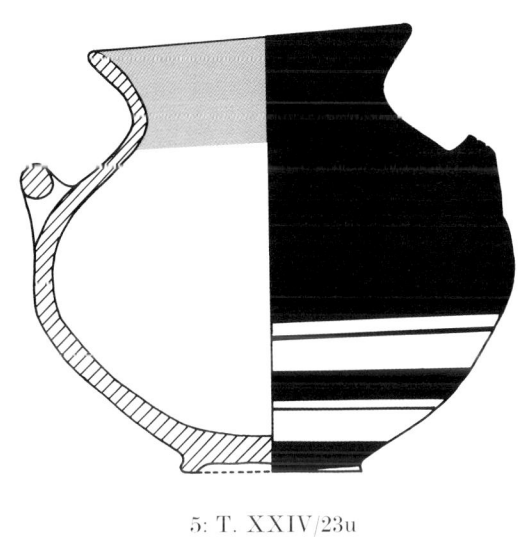

2: T. XXXVI/38b

3: T. XXXIII/9a+12b

4: T. XXXVI/38e

5: T. XXIV/23u

Fig. 9 Elateia, LH III C: Monochrome amphoriskoi. Scale 1:2
(Drawings: B. Eder, E. Held. Ink drawings: E. Held)

158 Sigrid Deger-Jalkotzy

Fig. 10 Elateia, LH III C Middle: Pottery fragments from dromos fills.
Scale 1:3 (Drawings: B. Eder, E. Held. Ink drawings: E. Held)

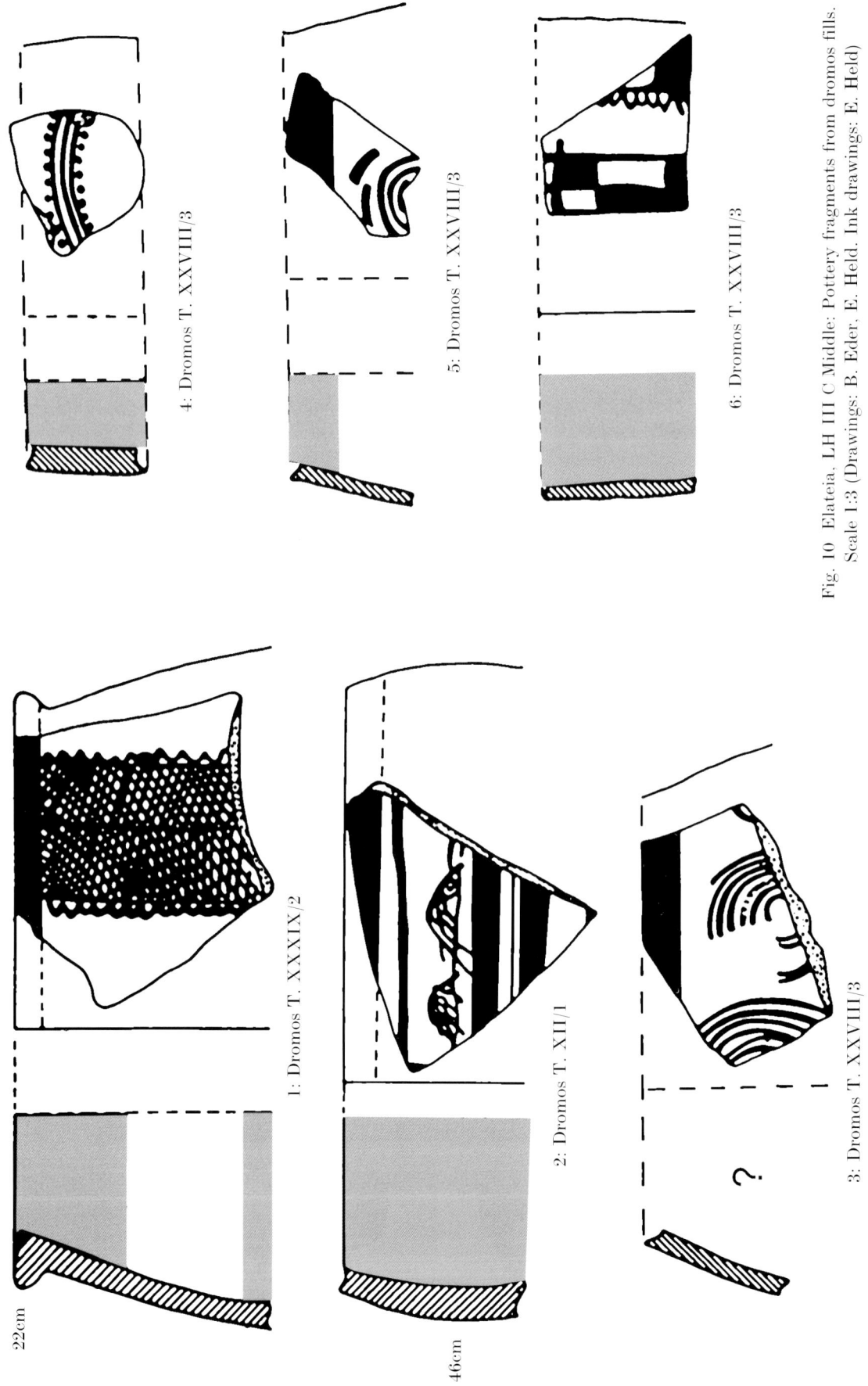

1: Dromos T. XXXIX/2

2: Dromos T. XII/1

3: Dromos T. XXVIII/3

4: Dromos T. XXVIII/3

5: Dromos T. XXVIII/3

6: Dromos T. XXVIII/3

Fig. 11 Elateia, T. VI/86: Fragments of a LH III C Middle crater from the dromos fill.
D. (rim) ca. 50 cm (Photograph: A. Bächle)

KATIE DEMAKOPOULOU

LACONIA AND ARCADIA IN LH III C MIDDLE: POTTERY AND OTHER FINDS

INTRODUCTION

This paper is an attempt to examine the LH III C Middle phase in Laconia and Arcadia on the basis of pottery and other finds. The material under discussion comes from early excavations in both regions, mostly in cemeteries. In two cases only, the material was recovered from non-funerary contexts. Of the more recent discoveries, the bulk of which is as yet unpublished, only a very limited number could be included. It must be noted that the majority of the pottery, which consists for the most part of closed shapes since it comes from tombs, can be dated by stylistic criteria rather than stratigraphy.

Laconia, in the south-east Peloponnese, was one of the regions in Mainland Greece, which remained important from the beginning until the end of the Mycenaean Age with a number of significant inland sites and the port of Epidauros Limera on the east coast[1] (Fig. 1). Finds from all these sites show connections with other regions of the Mainland, Cyclades and Crete (*RMDP*, 244–252). In Arcadia the most important site is Palaiokastro in the north-west part of this region (Fig. 2), where an extensive cemetery of chamber tombs, dating from LH II A to LH III C Late was located in early and recent excavations. The LH III C material from Palaiokastro shows a marked similarity with Elis and Achaea. There are also connections with Laconia and other parts of the Mainland, as well as with the Cyclades and Crete (*RMDP*, 296–299).

LACONIA

We will start our survey with Laconia, for which an old theory maintained that the whole region suffered a general decline after 1200 B.C. (ÅLIN 1962, 97, 148. – DESBOROUGH 1964, 90. – SNODGRASS 1971, 29–30). However, recent research with the publication of old material and the newer finds from recent excavations shows that Laconia continued to be occupied throughout almost the entire area during the LH III C period with prosperous communities that had connections with other parts of the Mycenaean world (DEMAKOPOULOU 1982). Abundant LH III C pottery from all three subdivisions of this pottery phase, Early, Middle and Late, and some Submycenaean, have been found in different sites of Laconia.

Most of the Laconian LH III C Middle pottery comes from two sites: Epidauros Limera, a flourishing port on the south-east coast, a few kilometres north of Monemvasia, and Pellana north of Sparta, at the end of the Eurotas valley. Important finds of

---

[1] The survey of prehistoric Laconia by H. Waterhouse and R. Hope Simpson (WATERHOUSE – HOPE SIMPSON 1960. – WATERHOUSE – HOPE SIMPSON 1961) is still very useful for the Bronze Age occupation of this region.

LH III C Middle have also been retrieved from the site of the Amyklaion, south of Sparta, while some pottery of this phase is known from three sites near the south coast of Laconia: Krokeai, Asteri and Phoiniki.[2]

Epidauros Limera

The material from Epidauros Limera was recovered from an extensive cemetery of chamber tombs arranged in three groups in the areas of Ayia Triada, Bambakia and Palaiokastro (WATERHOUSE – HOPE SIMPSON 1961, 136–137). The cemetery was partly excavated in three seasons, first in 1935 and later in 1953 and 1956.[3] The tombs are oval with a short dromos, which, sometimes, has steps and, in some cases, a side chamber. Burials were found on the floor and in pits in the floor. The cemetery was in use for a long period from LH I to Submycenaean. Most of the chamber tombs had been robbed; only Tomb B at Ayia Triada was intact. It was richly furnished with more than 30 clay vases, two bronzes, a dagger and a knife, as well as glass beads and steatite spindle whorls. Three burial pits in the floor of the main chamber of Tomb A at Ayia Triada were found intact, too (DEMAKOPOULOU 1968, 147).

The abundant LH III C pottery from Epidauros Limera includes a substantial group of LH III C Middle vases. They are of importance because they show the existence of distinctive local workshops, the products of which seem to have been influenced by strong external connections.

Noteworthy among them are the stirrup jars, medium and large, FS 174, 175, 176. One of them is decorated in the Close Style (DEMAKOPOULOU 1982, 118, pl. 60:136. – *RMDP*, 290). The decoration with lozenge and triangular patch on the shoulder and zones of zigzag and semi-circles on the body is very well preserved especially on the shoulder (Fig. 3). The vase, although it has been restored from fragments, is one of the finest specimens of the Close Style. Its decoration is very similar to that of a stirrup jar from Asine (*RMDP*, 165 no. 340, fig. 44) and to another from Mycenae (VERDELIS 1966, 78, pls. 84β; 85β). This similarity and the fabric of the stirrup jar from Epidauros Limera strongly suggest that this vessel is an Argive import.

There are two stirrup jars from Epidauros Limera decorated in the Octopus Style. One (Fig. 4) has no shoulder zone and the octopus with four tentacles and a long almond-shaped sac covers the whole surface of shoulder and body. There is a deep fringe painted over its head and another fringe and foliate band on the back of the vase between the tentacles (DEMAKOPOULOU 1968, 166–168 no. 37, pl. 74δ-ε. – DEMAKOPOULOU 1982, 118, pl. 61:138). It has been suggested that this vessel is a Minoan import and it may be dated to the III C Early phase rather than Middle (*RMDP*, 283 n. 151). The decoration of

---

[2] A great amount of the Laconian LH III C pottery from Epidauros Limera, Pellana and other sites, including that of the LH III C Middle phase, has been studied and published by the author of this paper, see DEMAKOPOULOU 1968. – DEMAKOPOULOU 1982. P. Mountjoy has more recently thoroughly examined the LH III C pottery from Laconia, see *RMDP*, 251–252, 282–293.

[3] All three excavations were made in emergency after the severe plundering of the Mycenaean chamber tombs. The excavation in 1935 was conducted by Th. Karachalios and is unpublished. Twelve vases from this excavation were recently presented by E. Kountouri (KOUNTOURI 1996/97). This first sounding was followed by a small salvage excavation by N. Drandakis in 1953, with few finds, which are still unpublished, apart from some vases (DEMAKOPOULOU 1982, 119–120, pl. 64:144–145). A more extensive excavation was made in 1956 by C. Christou (CHRISTOU 1961). The abundant pottery and some other finds from this excavation have been published by K. Demakopoulou (DEMAKOPOULOU 1968. – DEMAKOPOULOU 1982, 117–119, pls. 60–62). Much of the Mycenaean pottery from Epidauros Limera has also been discussed by P. Mountjoy (*RMDP*, 247–294, passim).

this stirrup jar indeed shows a prominent Minoan influence and has similarities with that on LM III C Early vessels.[4] However, I should like to draw attention to the similarity of the decorative elements of our vase to two other LH III C Middle stirrup jars, one from Perati (IAKOVIDIS 1969/70, vol. 2, 181–182, fig. 66:198), and the other from Aplomata, Naxos (KARDARA 1977, 18–19 no. 914, pls. 20–21α; 36β), likewise with an octopus with two pairs of tentacles and fringe over the head and along the top of the tentacles.[5] Furthermore, a LH III C Middle date for our stirrup jar is supported by the fact that it was found in one of the intact burial pits in Chamber Tomb A in the Ayia Triada area at Epidauros Limera together with another stirrup jar of clearly LH III C Middle date (Fig. 6).

The second Octopus Style stirrup jar from Epidauros Limera (Fig. 5. – DEMAKOPOULOU 1982, 118, pl. 60:137. – *RMDP*, 287, 290 no. 219, fig. 98) has a more elaborate decoration. Again there is no shoulder zone, but the lower body is banded. The octopus, the fill with fringed scale between the tentacles and the ovals display strong similarities to some Minoan decorative elements, but also to other ornate scenes on Octopus Style stirrup jars especially from Naxos (KARDARA 1977, 12–13 no. 951, pls. 11–12; 37δ) and Perati (IAKOVIDIS 1969/70, vol. 2, 181–187, figs. 66–73). Although it has been restored from fragments and much has been completed with plaster, this vase is a good specimen of the LH III C Middle Octopus Style and it seems to be a local product.

Another remarkable stirrup jar from Epidauros Limera (Fig. 6) was found in the intact burial pit of Chamber Tomb A in the area of Ayia Triada, together with the stirrup jar decorated with the octopus with two pairs of tentacles (Fig. 4). It is a fine specimen of LH III C Middle with a striking decoration of dot-fringed semi-circles on the shoulder and a starfish flanking a ray pattern on both sides of the belly filled with fine wavy lines, scale, and solid triangles (DEMAKOPOULOU 1968, 165–166 no. 36, pl. 74α–β. – *RMDP*, 290 no. 220, fig. 98). There are two close parallels to the decoration of the ray pattern, one from Kamini, Naxos (ZAPHEIROPOULOS 1966, 339 n. 2, pl. 274β. – *RMDP*, 955 no. 43, fig. 388) and another from Palaia Epidauros on the east coast of the Argolid (ARAVANTINOS 1977, 79–83, fig. 1, pl. 45. – *RMDP*, 165 no. 341, fig. 44). The similarity is notable, although the rays on the Epidauros Limera and Naxos stirrup jars have rounded ends, while the rays on the vessel from Palaia Epidauros are pointed (Fig. 7). Two pairs of pointed rays have also been painted on the shoulder of the Palaia Epidauros vase, which has an octopus on one side of the body. The close similarity of the decoration on the three vessels, especially between those from Epidauros Limera and Naxos, suggests that the two or even all three vases may well be Laconian products (cf. *RMDP*, 252). There are no similar decorative elements such as the starfish and rays on Naxian or Argive pottery of this period. It must also be noted that the foliate band in the central panel of the ray pattern on the back of the Palaia Epidauros vessel (Fig. 7) is similar to the motif on one of the octopus stirrup jars from Epidauros Limera (Fig. 4) and this adds additional support for its Laconian origin.

There is another striking LH III C Middle stirrup jar from Epidauros Limera (Fig. 8) decorated with a large fish on one side of the body and a pattern with pointed rays on the other (DEMAKOPOULOU 1968, 170–171 no. 41, pl. 76α–β. – *RMDP*, 252, 290 no. 221, fig. 98). There are remains of a foliate band on the shoulder. The ray pattern, which is repeated here and also on a krater fragment of the same period from a settlement context at Asteri in South Laconia (*RMDP*, 252, 290 no. 223, fig. 99),

---

[4] For this point see also HALLAGER this volume.
[5] This stirrup jar from Naxos (Aplomata no. 914) has been considered Minoan (KARDARA 1977, 18), but it may well have a Mainland origin (see *RMDP*, 955).

shows that this pattern is a common Laconian motif and provides further evidence for the Laconian origin of the three vases with the same motif from Epidauros Limera, Palaia Epidauros and Naxos. The imposing fish has a large dark head with reserved eye and horizontal wavy lines along the rounded body; it looks almost as if it were swimming (VERMEULE – KARAGEORGHIS 1982, 219, X.117. – GÜNTNER 2000, 297 no. 124, 305). Some other fish on the shoulder of a LH III C Middle stirrup jar from Perati (IAKOVIDIS 1969/70, vol. 2, 175 no. 909, fig. 62) and on a vessel from Tiryns (VERMEULE – KARAGEORGHIS 1982, 219, X.112) of the same period are good parallels.

There is a stirrup jar from Epidauros Limera dated to the III C Middle phase that seems to imitate closely a Minoan vase or even to be a Minoan import (Fig. 9). It has a broad shoulder zone with the rich decoration of arcs and fringe common on Minoan vessels of this period. The bands on handle and spout are also a Minoan feature (DEMAKOPOULOU 1968, 163–164 no. 32, pl. 73α,γ. – RMDP, 290 no. 222, fig. 99).

Other shapes of LH III C Middle pottery from Epidauros Limera include the amphoriskos, FS 59 (Fig. 10) and the lekythos, FS 122 (Fig. 11). The amphoriskos is monochrome with narrow reserved bands on the shoulder and on the lower body (DEMAKOPOULOU 1968, 181 no. 66, pl. 79γ). It is a decoration characteristic of this phase with parallels from Asine and Perati (RMDP, 251, 287 no. 215, fig. 97). The lekythos with linear decoration (DEMAKOPOULOU 1968, 184–185 no. 78, pl. 82α) also has parallels from the same sites (RMDP, 251, 287 no. 217, fig. 97). A LH III C Middle strainer jug, FS 155 (Fig. 12) has a twisted handle and is decorated with triangular patch on the shoulder area (DEMAKOPOULOU 1982, 119, pl. 63:143. – KOUNTOURI 1996/97, 503–505, fig. 13. – RMDP, 287 no. 218, fig. 97). This shape is more common in the Dodecanese and Cyclades than on the Mainland, but our vase seems to be locally made (RMDP, 251–252). The twisted handle is typical of this phase but is found mostly on jugs, although one of the strainer jugs with snakes on the belly from Perati likewise has a twisted handle (IAKOVIDIS 1969/70, vol. 2, 232–233; vol. 3, pl. 102γ, no. 280). There is also a trefoil-mouthed jug, FS 137, from Epidauros Limera, although its stomion is not preserved (Fig. 13). It is decorated with spirals on the shoulder and bands on the lower body (DEMAKOPOULOU 1968, 183 no. 74, pl. 81α). It could be dated to LH III C Middle or Late, although the ridge at the base of the neck makes a LH III C Middle date more probable (RMDP, 252, 291 no. 237, fig. 100). The feeding bottle, FS 162 (Fig. 14), which is monochrome with a narrow reserved zone on the spout area could also be dated to this phase or to LH III C Late (DEMAKOPOULOU 1982, 119, pl. 63:142. – KOUNTOURI 1996/97, 500–501, fig. 9. – RMDP, 287). The small straight-sided alabastron, FS 96 (Fig. 15), with foliate band on the shoulder and banded lower body, can be assigned to LH III C Middle (DEMAKOPOULOU 1968, 180 no. 62, pl. 78γ right. – RMDP, 287 no. 216, fig. 97).

Amyklaion

We may move now to the Amyklaion in the central Spartan plain on the west bank of the river Eurotas (Fig. 1). The discovery of two fragments of exceptionally large terracotta human figures and of a great number of wheelmade animal figures and Psi-type figurines with elaborate decoration on the hill of Ayia Kyriaki suggests the existence of a cult at this site datable from LH III B2 to LH III C Late/Submycenaean (DEMAKOPOULOU 1982, 43–68, 79–96). In addition to the terracottas, fragmentary pottery was found, including some LH III C Middle pieces. One of them is the fragment of a deep bowl, FS 285, which is monochrome inside (Fig. 16). It is decorated in the Close Style: the main decoration consists of two streamers with antithetic spirals flanking a bivalve panel, and triangular patch as a subsidiary motif (DEMAKOPOULOU 1982, 68, pl. 51:119. – RMDP, 290). The fine decoration, which recalls that on Close Style deep bowls from Mycenae (cf. *RMDP*, 172), and the good fabric suggest that the original vase should be an Argive import.

Some of the wheelmade bovid figures from the Amyklaion are finely decorated in the Close Style, such as the bull fragment with rosettes and triangular patch (DEMAKOPOULOU 1982, 59–60, pl. 34:79). The fragment of another LH III C wheelmade bovid figure with rosettes, found in one of the Syringes at Tiryns, is a close parallel (VERDELIS 1965, 73, pl. 86γ). There is an almost complete wheelmade bull figure (Fig. 17) and some fragments of others from the Amyklaion, which are richly decorated with typical motifs of LH III C Middle such as fringed semi-circles, zigzag and elaborate triangles with bird heads (DEMAKOPOULOU 1982, 59–60, pls. 27:69; 32:57α; 34:80–80α). It is noteworthy that these elaborate motifs were used not only for the decoration of vases but also of terracotta figures.

Two fragments of ring-based kraters, FS 282, from the Amyklaion might also be dated to LH III C Middle. Both are monochrome inside; one is decorated with joining semi-circles and a stem, the other with half-rosette and antithetic spiral (DEMAKOPOULOU 1982, 70–71, pl 50:117. – *RMDP*, 290 nos. 224–225, fig. 99). Another fragment comes from a krater with a pictorial scene (DEMAKOPOULOU 1982, 69–70, pl. 50:116. – VERMEULE – KARAGEORGHIS 1982, 113, 217, X.36). It is a battle scene, and what remains of it now shows parts of three men drawn in silhouette in different scale and on different levels; they are taking part in the battle. This krater fragment might be dated to LH III C Middle like other pictorial vessels with battle scenes (cf. GÜNTNER 2000, 203 no. 116). It can be compared with pictorial krater fragments with similar figures and of the same date from Lefkandi, Amarynthos (VERMEULE – KARAGEORGHIS 1982, 137, 223, XI.66; 135, 223, XI.56), and Kalapodi (FELSCH 1981, 86, fig. 7).

Pellana

One of the most important Mycenaean sites in Laconia is Pellana located in the north Eurotas valley, 25 km north of Sparta (Fig. 1). Excavations there, first in 1926 (KARACHALIOS 1926. – WATERHOUSE – HOPE SIMPSON 1961, 125–127) and more recently by Spyropoulos (SPYROPOULOS 1989), revealed a chamber tomb cemetery which was in use from LH II A to Submycenaean (*RMDP*, 244). Some of the tombs are large tholos-shaped tombs and contained rich finds, although they had been looted. The LH III C pottery from the earlier excavation in one of the large tombs includes quite a few vases from all three phases of the period, Early, Middle and Late, and even some Submycenaean. The shapes and decoration of the LH III C pottery from Pellana show not only internal connections with other Laconian sites, but also contacts with other Mycenaean centres and Crete. A LM III C Middle or Late stirrup jar, FS 175, was imported from Crete (DEMAKOPOULOU 1982, 115–116, pl. 57:129. – *RMDP*, 293 no. 242, fig. 100), probably via the port of Epidauros Limera. Of the LH III C Middle pottery from Pellana, noteworthy is a complete kalathos, FS 291 (Fig. 18), with a conical shape and linear decoration inside and out (DEMAKOPOULOU 1982, 115, pl. 57:127. – *RMDP*, 290 no. 226, fig. 99). There are some good parallels of LH III C Middle from Attica, notably from Athens, and Naxos (cf. *RMDP*, 602 nos. 497–499, fig. 224 [Athens]; 959 nos. 72–73, fig. 392 [Naxos]).

Other Laconian sites

A Mycenaean cemetery of chamber tombs was discovered on the side of a hill near the village Krokeai (WATERHOUSE – HOPE SIMPSON 1960, 103–105. – DEMAKOPOULOU 1982, 108). The site of Krokeai is known from the quarries of *lapis lacedaemonius* which were located in this area.[6] A remarkable composite vase comes from a robbed chamber tomb of this cemetery (DEMAKOPOULOU 1982, 108–109, pl. 55:123). It is a triple askoid vessel decorated with circles and semi-circles, stripes and triangle with fringe fill (Fig. 19). It might be dated to LH III C Middle,[7] although a LH III C Late date is also possible (*RMDP*, 293).

Another Laconian site is Phoiniki opposite Epidauros Limera near the west coast (Fig. 1). Among the stray finds coming from looted tombs in this area is an intact stirrup jar, FS 175 (Fig. 20), which might be of LH III C Middle date, although the rude decoration points rather to LH III C Late. The shoulder area is decorated with wavy lines and a careless net pattern, with barred handles and a rudely painted spiral on the top disk, while the lower body is banded (DEMAKOPOULOU 1982, 110, pl. 56:125. – *RMDP*, 293 no. 239, pl. 100).

ARCADIA

After Laconia we pass to Arcadia where the most important site is Palaiokastro (Fig. 2). The site is located in north-west Arcadia close to the border with Elis and near the river Alpheios. An extensive cemetery of chamber tombs has been excavated, first in 1957 by C. Christou, then Ephor of Laconia and Arcadia, who investigated six tombs; and in the 1980s by Th. Spyropoulos who dug over 100 tombs.[8] Although many of the tombs had been robbed, a great amount of pottery was found, which dates the cemetery from LH II A to LH III C Late (DEMAKOPOULOU – CROUWEL 1998, 281. – *RMDP*, 296). Some of the rock-cut chamber tombs were tholos-shaped with circular and vaulted chambers like the tombs at Pellana. Similar chamber tombs imitating tholos tombs are also found at Volimidia in Messenia. One of the tombs, found in the first excavation at Palaiokastro, has a carved triangular space above the entrance recalling the relieving triangle of Mycenaean tholoi (DEMAKOPOULOU – CROUWEL 1998, 271–274, fig. 5, 282 n. 54, with references). The settlement to which the cemetery belonged has not as yet been located.

Most of the pottery from Palaiokastro belongs to the LH III C Middle and Late phases. However, it should be noted that it is frequently difficult at Palaiokastro to distinguish between these two phases. The pottery from this site has close similarities to that from the neighbouring regions of Elis and Achaea, with which the settlement of Palaiokastro must have been closely connected. Furthermore, it reveals links with pottery from Attica (Perati), Naxos and Crete (DEMAKOPOULOU – CROUWEL 1998, 281–283. – *RMDP*, 296). The Minoan influence is prominent and it is especially apparent in the shapes used, such as the tall straight-sided alabastron, and in the decoration of the Octopus Style stirrup jars (*RMDP*, 296–297). Contacts with Crete might have come via Laconia, where the Minoan influence has also been prominent, and especially via the port of Epidauros Limera. Imported vessels, however, are not many and most of the pottery, apart from the affinities in shape and decoration with other regions, display also local characteristics that form a unique local style.

---

[6] For the location of the quarrying area of *lapis lacedaemonius* and the use of this distinctive stone in Minoan and Mycenaean times for the manufacture of seals and vessels, see WARREN 1992.

[7] For a LH III C Middle multiple vase consisting of six small amphoriskoi and a single high-swung handle (for the most part missing), see *RMDP*, 1233, pl. 3a. For composite vases of LH III C Middle cf. also *MDP*, 170, fig. 217.

[8] The finds from the first excavation at Palaiokastro by Christou have been published, see DEMAKOPOULOU – CROUWEL 1998. The material from the excavations by Spyropoulos is still unpublished, but it is extensively displayed in the Tripolis Archaeological Museum; see a short excavation report and illustrations of some of the finds in FRENCH 1989/90, 1, cover illustration (Tomb 10), and BLACKMAN 1996/97, 33–34, figs. 42–45.

Most impressive of the vases found in Palaiokastro are the stirrup jars, FS 175, some of which are very large. A finely made one, which comes from the early excavation, is 0.35 m high (Fig. 21). It has a rich and complex decoration with fringed octopus motifs on the shoulder and zones of semi-circles, zigzag and chevrons adorning the upper body and the top disk, while the lower body is covered with zones of fine lines (DEMAKOPOULOU – CROUWEL 1998, 276–277 no. P1, pl. 53a–d. – *RMDP*, 298–299, pl. 1b,d). The execution of the decoration and the various elaborate motifs are similar to those on LH III C Middle stirrup jars with ornate decoration from Perati and Naxos, while the stylised octopuses are derived from Minoan prototypes (DEMAKOPOULOU – CROUWEL 1998, 277–282 with references. – *RMDP*, 299). It is noteworthy that the fringed, stylised octopuses on the Palaiokastro stirrup jar are reminiscent of those on the stirrup jars from Epidauros Limera (Fig. 4) and Naxos (KARDARA 1977, 18–19 no. 914, pls. 20–21α; 36β). It is notable that the inspiration from the decorated pottery of other parts of the Aegean is treated here in such a manner that the overall result is a vigorously and imaginatively decorated vessel. It is surely the product of an important LH III C Middle local pottery workshop that made good use of decorative elements drawn from the pottery of other regions. Finds from the earlier excavation include the fragments of another large stirrup jar of LH III C Middle, likewise with rich and finely painted decoration of elaborate triangles and other motifs typical of the period (DEMAKOPOULOU – CROUWEL 1998, 280–281 no. P8, pl. 57a–b).

The extensive recent excavations at Palaiokastro brought to light more octopus stirrup jars, some of them also large (BLACKMAN 1996/97, 33, fig. 42). Other stirrup jars of this type have elaborate decoration, which includes pictorial motifs. A few have been illustrated in preliminary reports. One is very impressive, almost 0.40 m high with plaited handles; it is decorated with elaborate triangles with bird heads on the shoulder and panels on the body containing fish and elaborate antithetic spirals (FRENCH 1989/90, cover illustration. – *RMDP*, 298, pl. 1a). A large stirrup jar has an elaborate decoration on the belly including a pair of heraldic birds in a panel (BLACKMAN 1996/97, 33, fig. 43).

Another shape is the four-handled jar. One is decorated with octopus and another with stemmed spirals on the shoulder and a loop around the central vertical handle terminating in hooked tails (BLACKMAN 1996/97, 33, fig. 44). This is a local decorative motif, while the shape of the four-handled jar is characteristic of Achaea and Elis. From the early excavation comes another four-handled jar with floral motifs on the shoulder (DEMAKOPOULOU – CROUWEL 1998, 277 no. P3, pl. 54b). The recent excavations brought to light a few tall straight-sided alabastra, FS 96–97, and some straight-sided stirrup jars, likewise a common shape in Achaea and Elis (*RMDP*, 297–299). Another typical feature of Achaea is the frequent use of trimmed krater and kylix bases as lids, a phenomenon occurring also at Palaiokastro. Other common shapes from the recent excavations are the belly-handled amphora, FS 58, and the amphoriskos, FS 59.

A fragmentary hydria, FS 128, from the early excavation, with antithetic spiral motif on the shoulder may be dated to LH III C Middle (DEMAKOPOULOU – CROUWEL 1998, 279–280 no. P12, pl. 56c). Quite a few small stirrup jars decorated in the Argive Close Style were found in the early and more recent excavations at Palaiokastro. From the early excavation comes a restored stirrup jar richly decorated in the Close Style, as well as fragments which belong to one or possibly two more Close Style stirrup jars (DEMAKOPOULOU – CROUWEL 1998, 278–279 nos. P8, P9a–c, pl. 55a–c). The original vessels could have been imported from the Argolid.

In addition to the pottery, some bronzes were recovered in the tombs at Palaiokastro. A type II sword, two spearheads, a knife, and a pin were found in the earlier excavations, associated with burials (DEMAKOPOULOU – CROUWEL 1998, 274–276 nos. B1–B5, figs. 6–9, pl. 52a–c). A second sword of type II, a dagger, a knife, some bronze pins, and violin bow fibulae come from the recent excavations.[9] These warrior burials may well be of LH III C Middle date. Warrior burials with similar swords and spears dated to about the same phase were found in the Patras region of Achaea (PAPAZOGLOU-MANIOUDAKI 1994, 177–184, 200, figs. 3–5). This is another link between LH III C Palaiokastro and Achaea, apart from that indicated by the pottery. The tombs at Palaiokastro and their finds show the existence of a prosperous community in north-western Arcadia close to Elis during LH III C times. It has been suggested that Palaiokastro belonged to a western Greek cultural *koine* at this time (*RMDP*, 243–296). The pottery, however, shows clear connections with Laconia and the Aegean, as well.

CONCLUSION

The survey of the LH III C Middle pottery and other finds from Laconia and Arcadia has demonstrated that both areas participated in the revival or final flourishing phase of the Mycenaean civilisation around the middle of the 12th century B.C. However, the whole corpus of the pottery, which comes mostly from cemeteries, does not help us to distinguish in these two regions two sub-phases within LH III C Middle, termed Developed and Advanced, detectable in other major settlement sites. Yet the pottery found so far is of great significance because it shows strong internal and external relations and interregional interactions. The finds from Palaiokastro in Arcadia and from Epidauros Limera, the Amyklaion, and Pellana in Laconia show that these important centres were closely connected with other areas of the Mycenaean world including the Cyclades and Crete. The prosperity of these centres at this time is shown not only by the abundant and fine pottery, but also by the monumental chamber tombs imitating tholoi and the bronzes which accompanied some of the burials. The key and the most important site for contacts with the external world was of course Epidauros Limera with its strategic coastal location. Influence from Crete and other parts of the Aegean, so evident in Epidauros Limera, could well have reached the Amyklaion in central Laconia and Pellana in the north, as well as Palaiokastro in north-western Arcadia through this important port. The LH III C Middle period was a flourishing time in most regions of the Aegean. This was primarily owing to the extensive connections between them with exchange of goods and ideas.

Bibliography

Ε' Συνέδριο Πελοποννησιακών Σπουδών
1996/97 *Πρακτικά του Ε' Διεθνούς Συνεδρίου Πελοποννησιακών Σπουδών, Άργος – Ναύπλιον, 6–10 Σεπτεμβρίου 1995* (Peloponnesiaka 22). Athens.

ÅLIN, P.
1962 *Das Ende der mykenischen Fundstätten auf dem griechischen Festland* (SIMA 1). Lund.

ARAVANTINOS, V.
1977 "Μυκηναϊκά εκ Παλαιάς Επιδαύρου", *ArchDelt* 29, 1974 [1977], Mel 70–87.

BLACKMAN, D. J.
1996/97 "Archaeology in Greece 1996–97", *AR* 43, 1996/97.

CHRISTOU, C.
1961 "Ανασκαφή εν Μονεμβασία. Νεκροταφείον Αγ. Ιωάννου", *Prakt* 1956 [1961], 207–210.

---

[9] The bronzes from the recent excavations at Palaiokastro are displayed in the Archaeological Museum at Tripolis; see BLACKMAN 1996/97, 33.

DEMAKOPOULOU, K.
1968 "Μυκηναϊκά αγγεία εκ θαλαμοειδών τάφων περιοχής Αγίου Ιωάννου Μονεμβασίας", ArchDelt 23, Mel 145–194.
1982 Το Μυκηναϊκό ιερό στο Αμυκλαίο και η ΥΕ III Γ περίοδος στη Λακωνία. Athens.

DEMAKOPOULOU, K. – J. H. CROUWEL
1998 "Some Mycenaean Tombs at Palaiokastro, Arcadia", BSA 93, 269–283.

DESBOROUGH, V. R. D'A.
1964 The Last Mycenaeans and Their Successors. An Archaeological Survey c. 1200–c. 1100 B.C. Oxford.

FELSCH, R. C. S.
1981 "Mykenischer Kult im Heiligtum bei Kalapodi?", 81–89 in: HÄGG – MARINATOS 1981.

FRENCH, E. B.
1989/90 "Archaeology in Greece 1989–90", AR 36, 1–82.

GÜNTNER, W.
2000 Figürlich bemalte mykenische Keramik aus Tiryns (Tiryns. Forschungen und Berichte 12). Mainz.

HÄGG, R. – N. MARINATOS (eds.)
1981 Sanctuaries and Cults in the Aegean Bronze Age. Proceedings of the First International Symposium at the Swedish Institute in Athens, 12–13 May 1980 (Skrifter utgivna av Svenska Institutet i Athen, 4°, 28). Stockholm.

IAKOVIDIS, S. E.
1969/70 Περατή. Το νεκροταφείον (Βιβλιοθήκη της εν Αθήναις Αρχαιολογικής Εταιρείας 67). Athens.

KARACHALIOS, TH.
1926 "Θολωτός τάφος εν Καλυβίοις (Πελλάνης)", ArchDelt 10, Parartema, 41–44.

KARDARA, C.
1977 Απλώματα Νάξου. Κινητά ευρήματα τάφων Α και Β (Βιβλιοθήκη της εν Αθήναις Αρχαιολογικής Εταιρείας 88). Athens.

KOUNTOURI, E.
1996/97 "Ένα σύνολο Μυκηναϊκών αγγείων από την Επίδαυρο Λιμηρά Λακωνίας", 491–513 in: Ε' Συνέδριο Πελοποννησιακών Σπουδών.

MOUNTJOY, P. A.
1990 "Regional Mycenaean Pottery", BSA 85, 245–270.

PAPAZOGLOU-MANIOUDAKI, L.
1994 "A Mycenaean Warrior's Tomb at Krini near Patras", BSA 89, 171–200.

SANDERS, J. M. (ed.)
1992 ΦΙΛΟΛΑΚΩΝ. Lakonian Studies in Honour of Hector Catling. London.

SNODGRASS, A. M.
1971 The Dark Age of Greece. Edinburgh.

SPYROPOULOS, TH. G.
1989 "Πελλάνα", ArchDelt 37, 1982 [1989] Chron 112–114.

VERDELIS, N.
1965 "Ανασκαφή Τίρυνθος. Αποκάλυψις δύο νέων συρίγγων", ArchDelt 18, 1963 [1965], Chron 66–73.
1966 "Ανασκαφή Μυκηνών", Prakt 1962 [1966], 67–89.

VERMEULE, E. – V. KARAGEORGHIS
1982 Mycenaean Pictorial Vase Painting. Cambridge (Mass.) – London.

WARREN, P.
1992 "Lapis Lacedaemonius", 285–296 in: SANDERS 1992.

WATERHOUSE, H. – R. HOPE SIMPSON
1960 "Prehistoric Laconia: Part I", BSA 55, 67–107.
1961 "Prehistoric Laconia: Part II", BSA 56, 114–175.

ZAPHEIROPOULOS, N. S.
1966 "Ανασκαφαί Νάξου", Prakt 1960 [1966], 329–340.

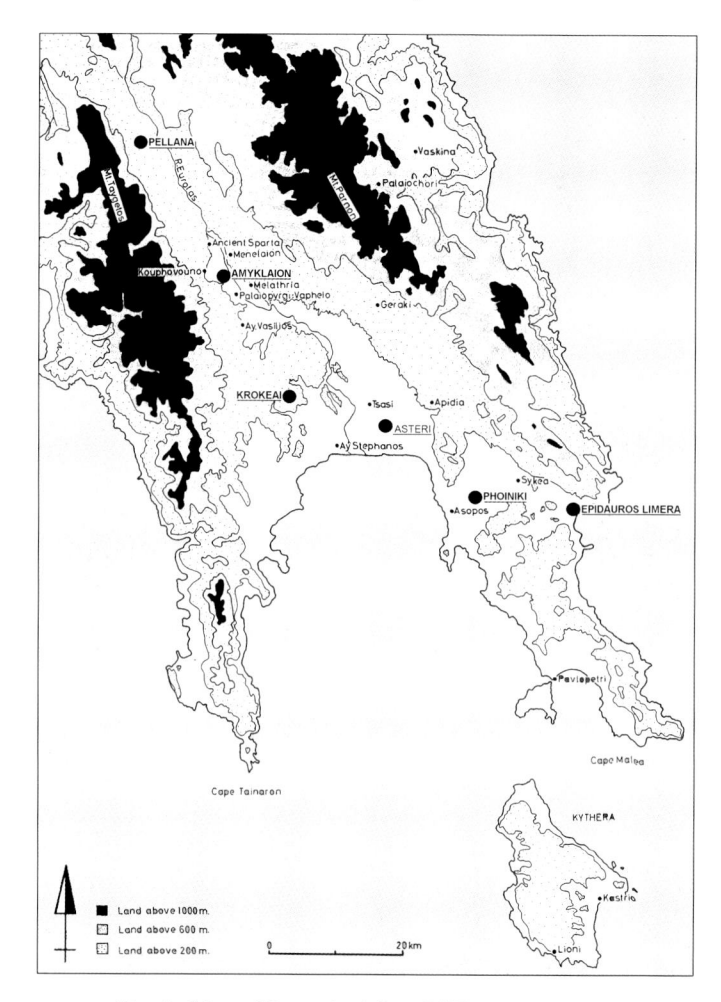

Fig. 1 Map of Laconia (after *RMDP*, 245, fig. 81)

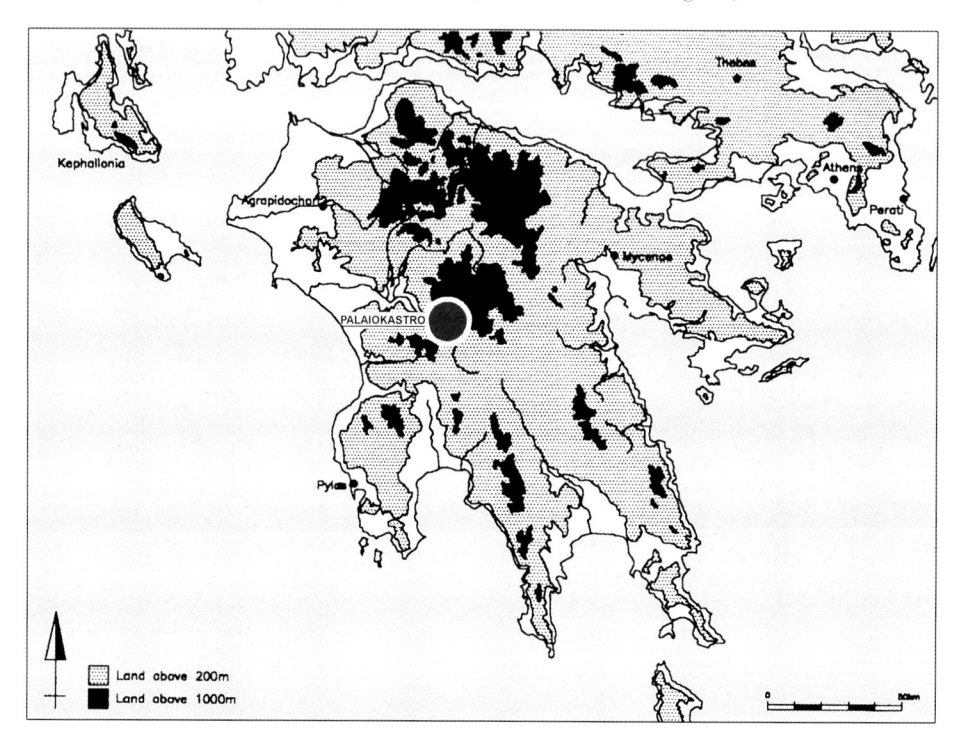

Fig. 2 Map of the Peloponnese showing Palaiokastro (after MOUNTJOY 1990, 250, fig. 7)

Fig. 3 Stirrup jar with Close Style decoration from Epidauros Limera

Fig. 5 Stirrup jar with Octopus Style decoration from Epidauros Limera

Fig. 4 Stirrup jar with Octopus Style decoration from Epidauros Limera

Fig. 6 Stirrup jar with starfish and ray pattern from Epidauros Limera

Fig. 8 Stirrup jar with fish and ray pattern from Epidauros Limera

Fig. 7 Stirrup jar with octopus and ray motif from Palaia Epidauros

Fig. 10 Darkground amphoriskos from Epidauros Limera

Fig. 9 Stirrup jar with curvilinear decoration from Epidauros Limera

Fig. 11 Lekythos with linear decoration from Epidauros Limera

Fig. 12 Strainer jug from Epidauros Limera

Fig. 13 Fragmentary trefoil-mouthed jug from Epidauros Limera

Fig. 14 Monochrome feeding bottle with narrow reserved shoulder zone from Epidauros Limera

Fig. 15 Straight-sided alabastron from Epidauros Limera

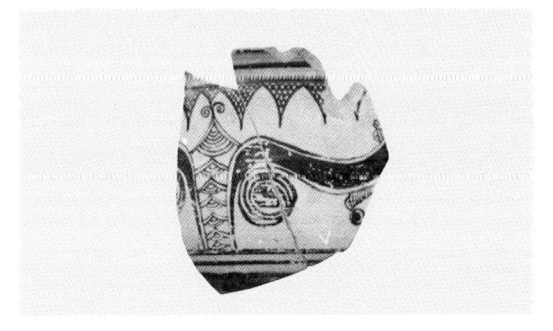

Fig. 16 Fragment of a deep bowl with Close Style decoration from the Amyklaion

Fig. 17 Fragmentary terracotta bull figure with elaborate decoration from the Amyklaion

Fig. 18 Kalathos with linear decoration from Pellana

Fig. 19 Triple askoid vessel from Krokeai

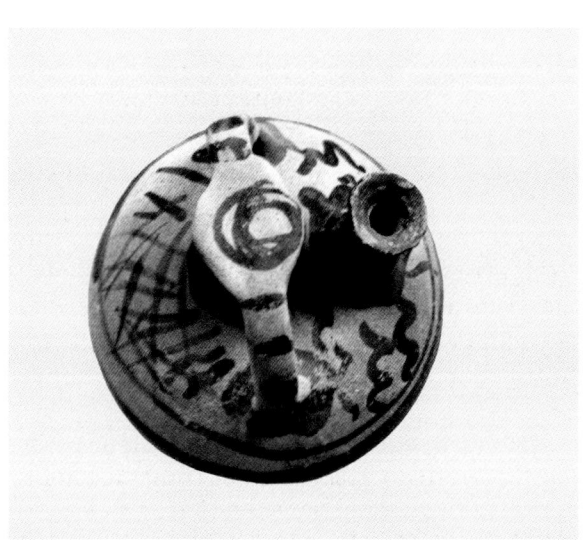

Fig. 20 Stirrup jar from Phoiniki

Fig. 21 Large stirrup jar with elaborate decoration from Palaiokastro

ELIZABETH FRENCH

LATE HELLADIC III C MIDDLE AT MYCENAE

1. BACKGROUND

The original definitions of this period for the whole of Mycenaean Greece were based on the material excavated in 1920 from the destruction level of the building called the Granary at Mycenae. This remained the prime source through the work of Furumark in *The Chronology of Mycenaean Pottery* (published in 1941) and is still the largest unit of stratified material on which our definitions are based.

The search for more information on LH III C was one of our prime interests in the excavation of the Citadel House Area (1953–69) though at first we were confused by the fact that Hellenistic terracing had cut down to LH III B/C Transitional levels at the east of the site. It was with great joy therefore that we found a small destruction deposit apparently of this period on a floor at the very end of the third major season of work (1960). In the next season (1962) more material of this phase was recovered from good contexts and much more from stray sherds in the overlying wash levels to the south.

By 1964 work had extended to the West Citadel Wall and we discovered much deeper wash levels held up by the wall. There appeared to be stylistic development in the pottery from level to level; that from the lowest strata at that time excited the most interest as it had not been previously isolated (FRENCH 2007). The whole of one section of this material was assigned to Susan Sherratt as the nucleus of a PhD study (SHERRATT 1981).

The Mycenae definitions are the result of Susan's work combined with the study of the pottery of similar type from other parts of the site. She divided the material partly by the stratigraphy but also partly *stylistically* into five phases. We are concerned here now with two of her phases: Developed and Advanced (Fig. 1). Little if anything in the definitions has changed since her thesis.[1]

The Mycenae material was made available to Penelope Mountjoy when she was compiling *Mycenaean Decorated Pottery* (*MDP*) though some of the contextual details have been refined since then. Though in her chart (*MDP*, 133. MOUNTJOY this volume) she gives the names of the Mycenae phases, the periods which she defined are much longer and thus comprise a much greater amount of internal development. It has already proved useful to re-divide LH III C Early into the two component sections and I would like to do the same for LH III C Middle (Fig. 1). However for both convenience and clarity I use here the Mycenae names rather than the titles.

What must be emphasised is that Developed is defined *stylistically* on sherd evidence; Advanced is defined *stratigraphically* by whole pots on floors in the Granary and Rooms

---

[1] Presented in 1981. Though as yet unpublished, it is available for consultation in Oxford and Athens (and apparently elsewhere). I have edited the Mycenae sections for publication in *Well Built Mycenae, Fasc. 16/17. The Post-Palatial levels* with the other material of those strata from the site. Much of the detailed information in the text presented here is taken almost *verbatim* from the edited version of Sherratt's original. The illustrations used here are the copyright of Mycenae Publications and used with full authorisation.

xlii and xliii at the east of the site (overlying Room 7 of the South House Annex) but similar material lies above Developed in the wash layers at the west. Over this in some places were layers of LH III C Late, some pure, some contaminated with the overlying material but the evidence is scanty. There is of course stratigraphic evidence from the Granary and the Lion Gate Strata.

It is also important to realise that we have no idea of the source on the site for almost all of this material. We have **no** buildings of this period preserved except the Granary, Rooms **xlii** and **xliii** and the series of floors beside the Hellenistic Tower (IAKOVIDIS 2003, 121 and 119, fig. 2).

2. THE DEVELOPED PHASE

As Penelope Mountjoy explains (MOUNTJOY this volume), Developed has been isolated so far mainly at Mycenae and so this material requires explicit description. Because of its stylistic definition, this phase is most visible in the shapes commonest in settlement debris, the deep bowl, the krater and other open shapes, and in the use and nature of the patterning. The examples illustrated (Figs. 2–3) are from Susan Sherratt's work chosen to reemphasise the points that she made. They come mainly from a large group of sherds[2] in Trench Γ32 (Γ32'66/12–14), not completely stylistically pure.

On **amphorae, jugs and hydriae** (Fig. 2:1–3) linear decoration is frequently accompanied by tassel pattern, while handle decoration still normally consists of a vertical wavy band. The rims of these vessels are now more distinctly hollowed.

Linear **cups** (Fig. 2:4) still appear to be represented in much the same proportion as in the previous (Tower) phase. A few painted **kylikes** (Fig. 2:5–6) and monochrome **carinated cups** (FS 240) are in use.

Found only in this phase are **carinated kraters** (Fig. 3:8. – *MDP*, fig. 224:1 = MOUNTJOY this volume, fig. 2:4), a shape not listed by Furumark. The ring-based bell **krater** with rounded rim is still found. Although unfortunately most of the best examples of kraters from the Mycenae wash layers come from units which also contain some Advanced phase material, there are sufficient hints to suggest that some move towards the more elaborate abstract patterns based on spiraliform, panelled and antithetic tongue/streamer motifs (though perhaps not the elaborate pictorial decoration of men, birds and animals) which are certainly features of Advanced phase kraters, may be already underway at this earlier stage. Some of the carinated examples have also additional ornamentation in the form of patterns along the top of the rim. They invariably have monochrome interiors and the lower body may be monochrome or banded.

Particularly characteristic of this phase is the apparent introduction of monochrome **deep bowls** with a single reserved line inside the rim and a reserved base and lower body (Fig. 3:1). Monochrome deep bowls without reserved lines continue to be represented, however, in much larger quantities than before (Fig. 3:2). The type of pattern decorated deep bowl typical of the Tower phase (with a medium band at the rim and running or antithetic spiral motifs, Fig. 3:4,6–7) appears to continue as before, with the difference that running spiral decoration is now almost as well represented as antithetic spiral. Some of the spiral patterns are quite elaborate (Fig. 3:5). Medium band deep bowls without patterned decoration remain the dominant type and are possibly now at the height of their popularity (Fig. 3:3).

---

[2] There are almost no restorable pots from this phase and it would be misleading to attempt to give a definitive shape chart though the shapes identified are illustrated in Fig. 1.

Linear decorated **shallow angular bowls** (Fig. 2:9–10) appear for the first time in the highly standardised form (with sharply defined carination high up on the body, bands inside and a single shallow band at the rim outside) in which they are to become noticeably well-represented in the Advanced phase. These almost all have a spiral in the interior base. This shape is apparently beginning to replace, though it has probably not superseded, the linear decorated rounded bowl with horizontal strap handle (Fig. 2:7–8). Together they would seem to form a considerable proportion of the painted (?) drinking vessels in use at this time.

The proportion of unpainted pottery (39%) has declined slightly from the Tower phase and very little information is available about the shapes represented. Of the painted pottery there is a greater proportion of sherds with monochrome interiors than in the Tower phase. The range of shapes produced in wheelmade **cooking wares** remains similar, while the **handmade burnished ware** continues to occur.

One additional shape found elsewhere on the site should be noted – the **kalathos** – though a collar-necked jar found in these levels seems more likely to be residual.

3. THE GRANARY

The Granary was originally excavated under the designation "House i".[3] The original notebooks and a numerical catalogue of registered pots and small finds exist and can provide details additional to the published account particularly with regard to the detailed find locations. The find spots are given in some detail though the descriptions of the vessels are short, inconsistent and often non-existent. The presence of the actual pot with its original number is thus vital for its correct assignment to a *locus*.

The area comprised ten major *loci* (Table 1 and Fig. 4) from which pottery was registered. These pots were all "made up" from sherds and some are considerably more complete than others. Several groups were found on floors. Wace in the original publication treated the portion of the material from the East Basement as a single unit rather than by the three relevant major individual *loci*. Based on them and the material from the fill of the Corridors he gave a clear definition of the Granary class of pottery (WACE 1921–23, 40–41) and emphasised that this style was contemporary with the Close Style (which had first been defined by BLEGEN 1921, 61–62). Recently question had arisen as to how definitively the Close Style pieces were associated with the rest, particularly because some of the unpainted ware appeared to be of very poor quality having suffered extraordinary kiln damage. Detailed reassessment seemed called for. In the spring of 2004 all the surviving pottery (69 of the original 79 items[4]) was checked and examples of the major types were drawn[5] (by Jacke Phillips) to supplement earlier example drawings by Penelope Mountjoy for her two studies (*MDP*, figs. 206:1; 212:1; 229:1. – *RMDP*, Argolid nos. 330, 358, 365–367).[6]

It is now clear that Wace was entirely justified in his deduction that the Close Style was in use with the Granary class of material. The original definitions stand. The characteristic features of the material found in the Granary (Figs. 5–9) are the Close Style

---

[3] All the new areas excavated in 1920 were lettered in continuation of that on the plan in KARO 1915, pl. 15, an article of which Karo himself had given Wace a proof copy before he left Athens in November 1916.

[4] One further pot was found in October 2004.

[5] In the 1920s recording was by photograph with a couple of colour restorations.

[6] It should be noted that all these are identified by the Nauplion Museum numbers which are now obsolete following the transfer of the material to Mycenae. A full set of indices to the various numbering systems in use will appear in *Well Built Mycenae* 16.

represented by three vessels of greatly differing size (large four-handled jar [Fig. 5:1], stirrup jar [Fig. 5:2], deep bowl [Fig. 6:1]), small neat deep bowls with various types of monochrome decoration alleviated with fine reserved lines (Figs. 6:2–3; 7:1), sharply articulated shallow angular bowls with banding on the inside only (Fig. 7:6), and large amphorae, hydriae and jugs with bands and simple curvilinear decoration (Fig. 9). Both cups and kalathoi are found in painted and unpainted version (Fig. 7:4+7 and Figs. 7:5+8:1). The unpainted dipper (Fig. 8:2) is not unusual but the kylix (Fig. 8:4) is; it has a deep piercing up the whole stem similar to Cretan examples (HALLAGER 1997, *passim*). The ill-fired unpainted ware found (kalathos [Fig. 8:1], cup [Fig. 7:7] and some of the ill-turned stemmed bowls [e.g. Fig. 8:5]) gives a false impression for there is no other obvious decline in production technique. There are two pots of cooking ware, a tripod vessel with shallow bowl (Fig. 8:6) and a small jug (Fig. 8:7).

4. THE ADVANCED PHASE

There is a great deal more new sherd evidence of the Advanced phase than of the Developed. The patterned and painted material was easily identified and was of excellent quality. It exhibited all the features that have been described from the Granary and will be only briefly summarised here. Fig. 10 shows examples of shapes and types not represented in the Granary.

The most obvious feature of this phase as a whole is the **Close Style** and the other decorative styles related to it. It had a very limited application, referring specifically to a stylistically uniform group of pots covering a very limited range of shapes (**small deep bowls, stirrup jars, trefoil-lipped jugs**). More recently the term has come to be used increasingly loosely. This wider use serves only to confuse the issue. The style is in many ways a miniaturist one, and it seems, with few exceptions, to be found only in the Argolid and Corinthia; the stylistic unity is such that they are almost certainly the product of one workshop.

Akin to the Close Style but not of it, are the large group of **kraters** with elaborate decoration (e.g. *MDP*, fig. 225:1 = MOUNTJOY this volume, fig. 7:2). These are in a heavy oatmeal[7] fabric and often have additional features such as protome handles and a slashed rib below the rim. Several pieces have polychrome decoration with added red and/or yellow as well as added white. The Warrior Vase is a typical example.

Many more simple **deep bowls** share features with those of the Close Style, e.g. dots on the rim and multiple internal reserved lines. An interesting group of these are the "negative" deep bowls where the same decorative features are employed but in reverse – black on white rather than reserved white on black (e.g. *MDP*, fig. 229:1). Other plain deep bowls continue but the medium band type would seem to be out of fashion.

The very sharply angled **shallow angular bowl** now accounts for almost 4% of the total painted pottery; the earlier rounded form has disappeared. The fabric of these is uniformly good, with well refined and fired clay and the paint evenly and neatly applied. Other open shapes include **cups, mugs, carinated cups, kylikes and kalathoi**. None is present in any very great quantity. The carinated cups are now decorated on the upper body (generally with concentric arcs) and often have a protome handle.

---

[7] The term "oatmeal" was coined to describe one type of heavy ware (the term generally used for the ware of transport stirrup jars and large vats) in which surface treatment gives an additional fine slip finish through which the inclusions can still be seen. It resembles the surface of a bowl of good porridge.

Large closed shapes, **amphorae, jugs and hydriae**, are very frequent. Tassel decoration is common but scroll and whisker appear and these motifs are often found on the same pot. Handles continue to be decorated with vertical wavy bands but crossed loop or a diagonal cross also occur. There are a few examples of **neck-handled amphorae**, an innovation which becomes common in the next phase. These shapes are generally made of either "oatmeal" or a finer pink, sandy fabric.

Unpainted buff ware forms only 36% of the total material. Some new shapes are found, e.g. the small kalathos and the three-handled cup with short stem so prevalent in the Granary.

Little information is available for **cooking ware** shapes though there is no indication of major change and the proportion (16%) remains the same. **Handmade burnished ware** continues to be represented.

A final notable feature is the popularity of **pithoi** decorated often elaborately in relief. It is frequently stamped or moulded and applied. The underlying surface is unusually smooth and well finished.

5. CONCLUSION

What is now clear is that the period as originally defined is preceded by another in which we can see these characteristics developing, hence the name given to it at Mycenae: "Developed"; the Granary material thus became an "Advanced" stage. The nature and function of all this material with its very diverse components are certainly still not clear and this remains a most intriguing problem.

Bibliography

BIETAK, M. – E. CZERNY (eds.)
2007   *The Synchronisation of Civilisations in the Eastern Mediterranean in the Second Millennium BC. III. Proceedings of the SCIEM 2000 – 2nd EuroConference, Vienna, 28th of May–1st of June 2003* (Österreichische Akademie der Wissenschaften, Denkschriften der Gesamtakademie 37 = Contributions to the Chronology of the Eastern Mediterranean 9). Vienna.

BLEGEN, C. W.
1921   *Korakou. A Prehistoric Settlement near Corinth*. Boston – New York.

FRENCH, E. B.
2007   "The Impact on Correlations to the Levant of the Recent Stratigraphic Evidence from the Argolid", 525–536 in: BIETAK – CZERNY 2007.

FURUMARK, A.
1941   *The Chronology of Mycenaean Pottery*. Stockholm.

HALLAGER, B. P.
1997   "Terminology – The Late Minoan Goblet, Kylix and Footed Cup", 15–47 in: *Late Minoan III Pottery*.

IAKOVIDIS, S.
2003   "Late Helladic III C at Mycenae", 117–123 in: *LH III C Chronology and Synchronisms*.

KARO, G.
1915   "Die Schachtgräber von Mykenai", *AM* 40, 113–230.

SHERRATT, E. S.
1981   *The Pottery of Late Helladic III C and its Significance* (unpublished Ph.D. thesis). Oxford.

WACE, A. J. B.
1921–23 "Excavations at Mycenae § VII. – The Lion Gate and Grave Circle Area", *BSA* 25, 9–126.

GRANARY								
Locus	5	6	7	8	9		10	
	Nest	Lower Floor	With Duck	Upper Floor	i3 Floor	Etc	Upper levels	TOTAL
	---- Wace's EAST BASEMENT ----							
SHAPE								
All painted wares except where indicated								
58 Amphora						CS 1		1
65 Amphora						1		1
115 Jug			1 CW					1
128 Hydria		3						3
175 Stirrup Jar			CS 1					1
216 Cup	2 + 1 UP				1			4
236 Dipper				1 UP				1
240 Carinated Cup					?1 Mono			1
275 Kylix		1 UP						1
282 Krater							1	1
284 Deep Bowl	4	CS 1			2		2	9
291 Kalathos	1 + 1 UP	1						3
295 SAB	1	1						2
320 Tripod Vessel						1 CW		1
334 Lid							1	1
Stemmed Bowl UP	20	6	9	4				39
Unidentified	2	3	2	1		1		9
TOTAL	**32**	**16**	**13**	**6**	**4**	**4**	**4**	**79**

Table 1 The Granary: find *loci*

Late Helladic III C Middle at Mycenae

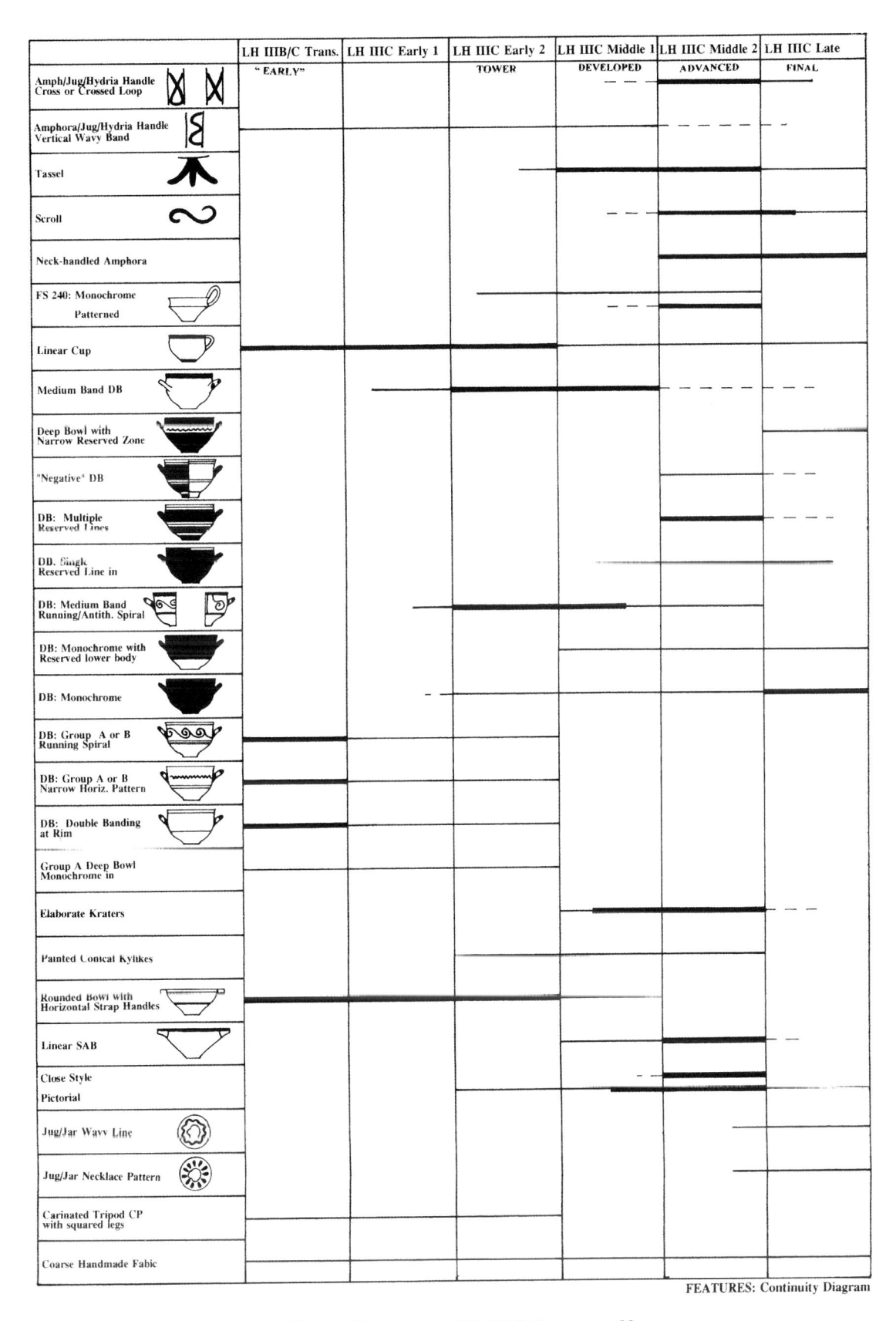

	LH IIIB/C Trans.	LH IIIC Early 1	LH IIIC Early 2	LH IIIC Middle 1	LH IIIC Middle 2	LH IIIC Late
		"EARLY"		TOWER	DEVELOPED	ADVANCED	FINAL
Amph/Jug/Hydria Handle Cross or Crossed Loop						
Amphora/Jug/Hydria Handle Vertical Wavy Band						
Tassel						
Scroll						
Neck-handled Amphora						
FS 240: Monochrome Patterned						
Linear Cup						
Medium Band DB						
Deep Bowl with Narrow Reserved Zone						
"Negative" DB						
DB: Multiple Reserved Lines						
DB: Single Reserved Line in						
DB: Medium Band Running/Antith. Spiral						
DB: Monochrome with Reserved lower body						
DB: Monochrome						
DB: Group A or B Running Spiral						
DB: Group A or B Narrow Horiz. Pattern						
DB: Double Banding at Rim						
Group A Deep Bowl Monochrome in						
Elaborate Kraters						
Painted Conical Kylikes						
Rounded Bowl with Horizontal Strap Handles						
Linear SAB						
Close Style Pictorial						
Jug/Jar Wavy Line						
Jug/Jar Necklace Pattern						
Carinated Tripod CP with squared legs						
Coarse Handmade Fabric						

FEATURES: Continuity Diagram

Fig. 1 Chart of features in LH III C Pottery at Mycenae

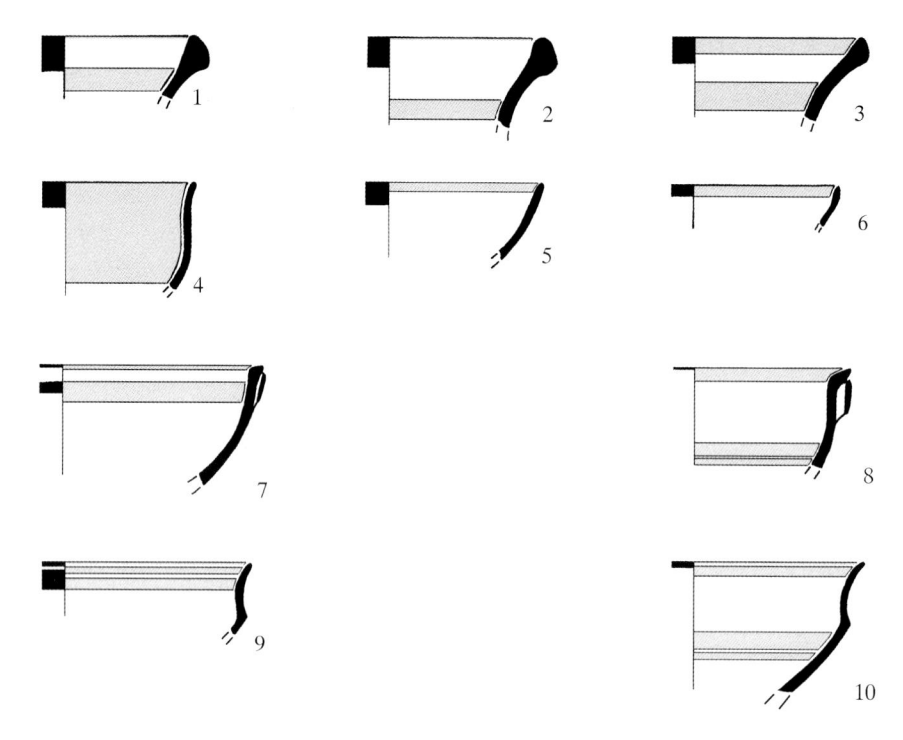

Fig. 2 Sherds of the Developed phase from Γ32˙66/12,13,14 (scale 1:3)

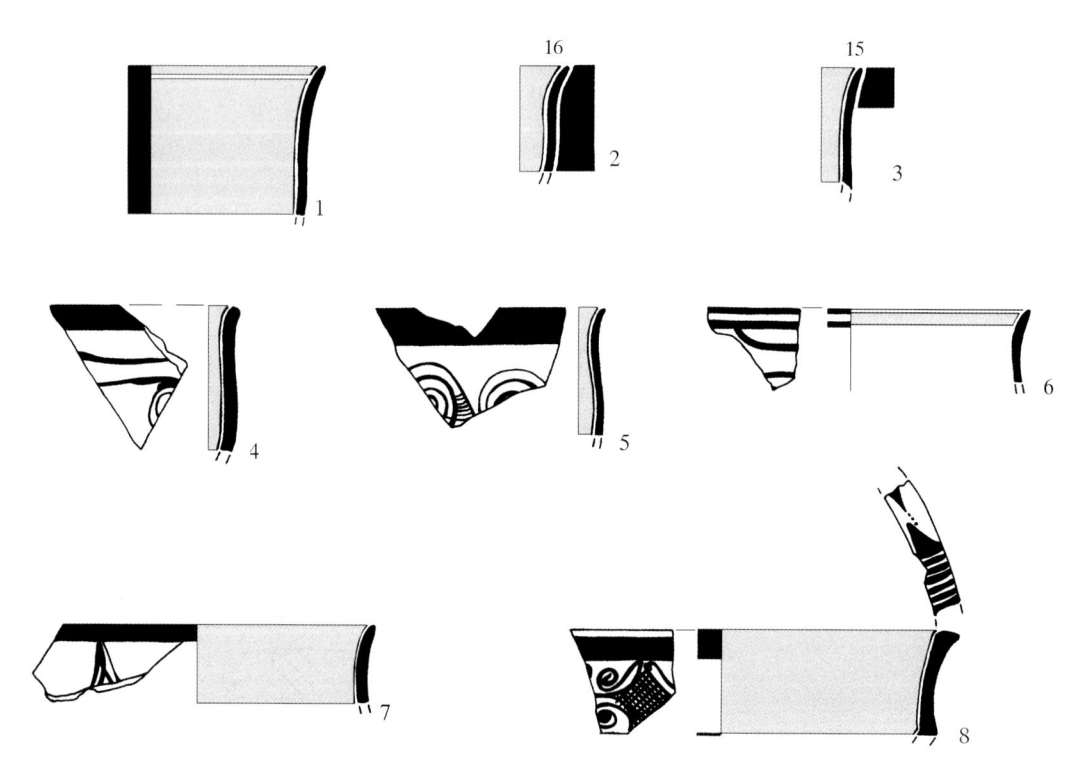

Fig. 3 Sherds of the Developed phase from Γ32˙66/12,13,14 (scale 1:3)

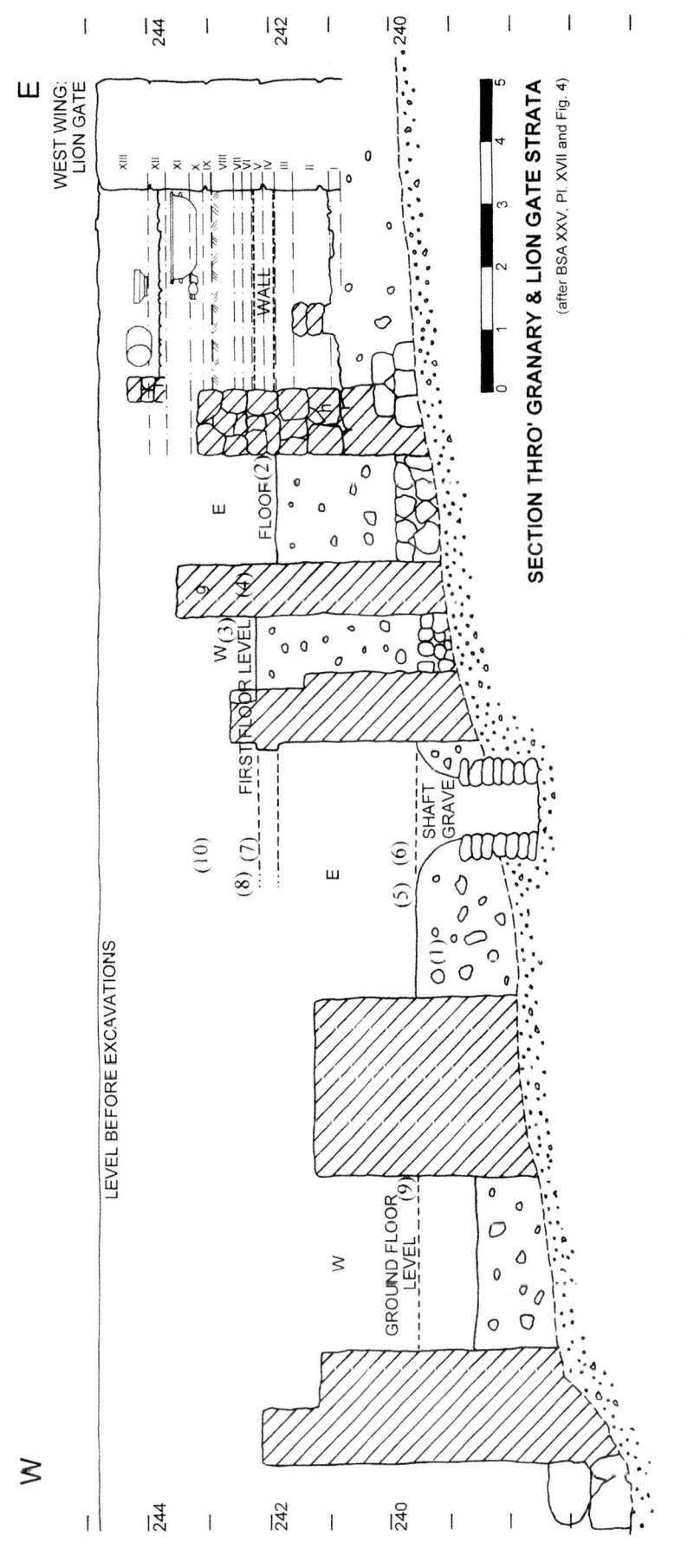

Fig. 4 Section of the Granary and Lion Gate Strata

Fig. 5 Granary: Close Style. **1**: Four-handled jar Athens NM 1126; **2**: Stirrup Jar 20-41

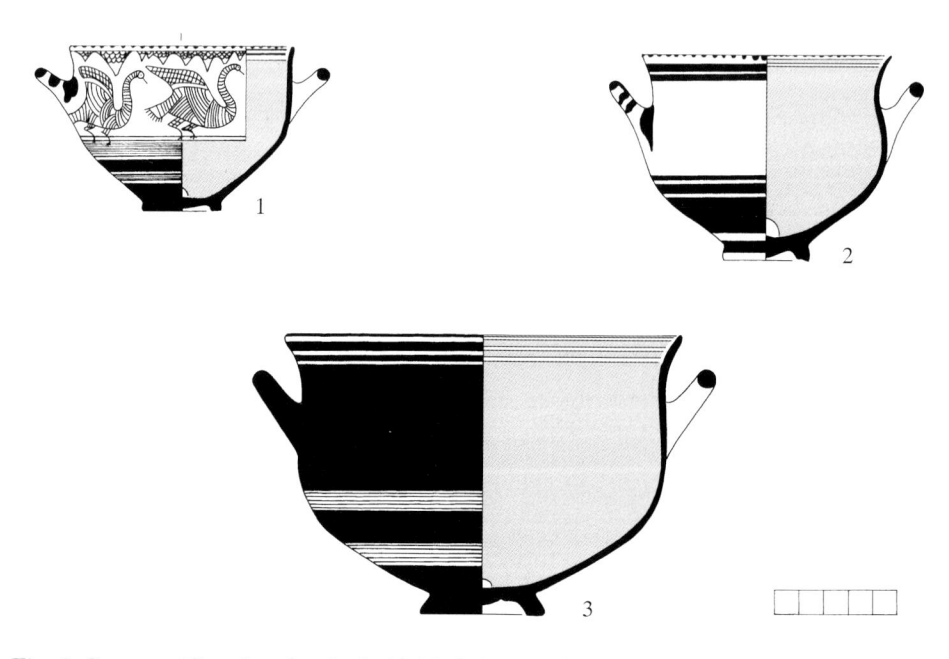

Fig. 6 Granary: Fine deep bowls: **1**: 20-28; **2**: 20-102; **3**: 20-18 (drawings by P. A. Mountjoy)

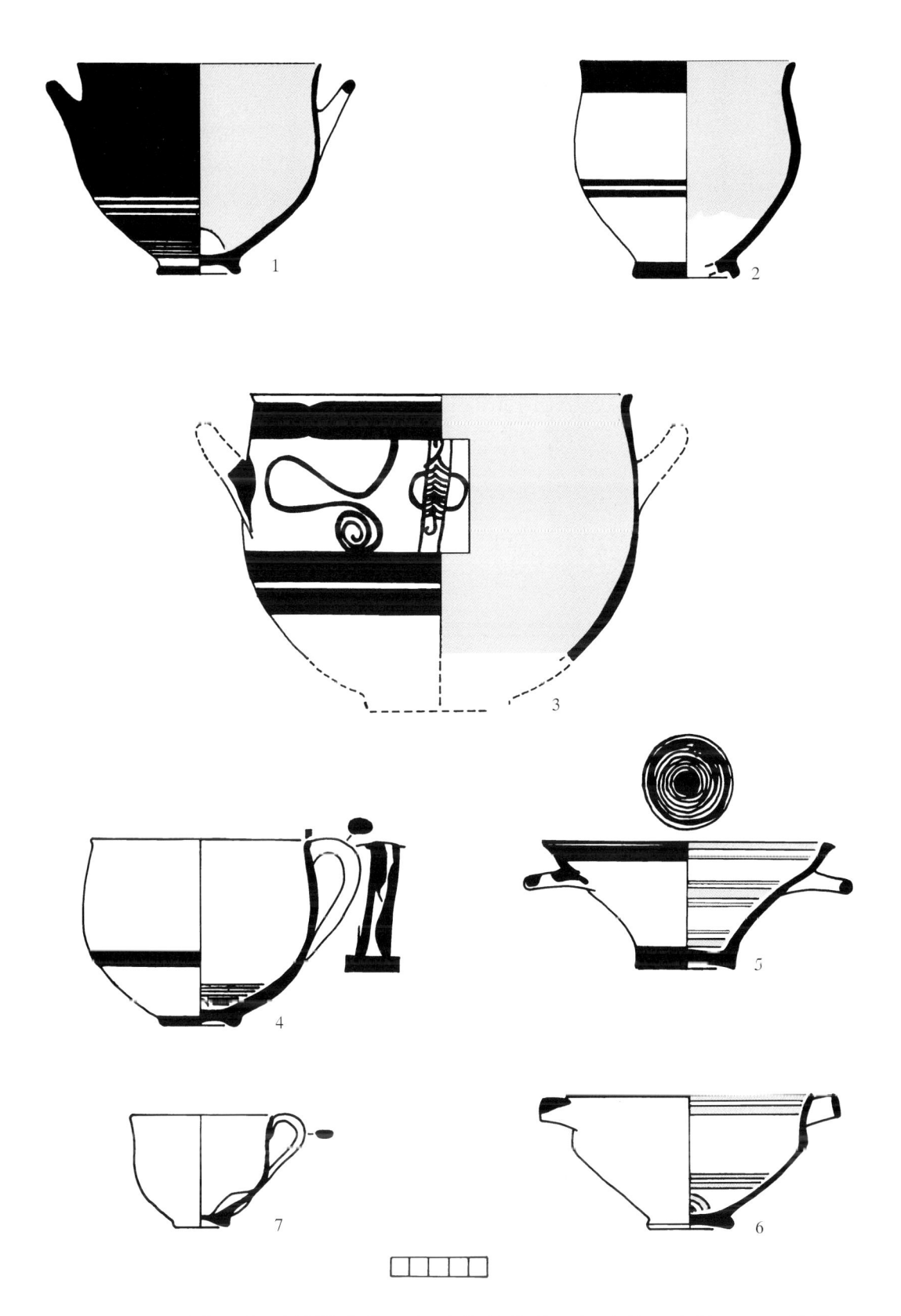

Fig. 7 Granary: **1**: Deep bowl 20-78. **2**: Deep bowl 20-24; **3**: Deep bowl 20-26; **4**: Linear cup 20-23;
5: Linear kalathos 20-77; **6**: Linear shallow angular bowl 20-52; **7**: Unpainted cup 20-85

Fig. 8 Granary: **1**: Unpainted kalathos 20-98; **2**: Unpainted dipper 20-42; **3**: Monochrome carinated cup, ?stemmed 20-25; **4**: Unpainted kylix 20-58; **5**: Unpainted three-handled stemmed bowl 20-86; **6**: Tripod vessel 20-49; **7**: Jug 20-29

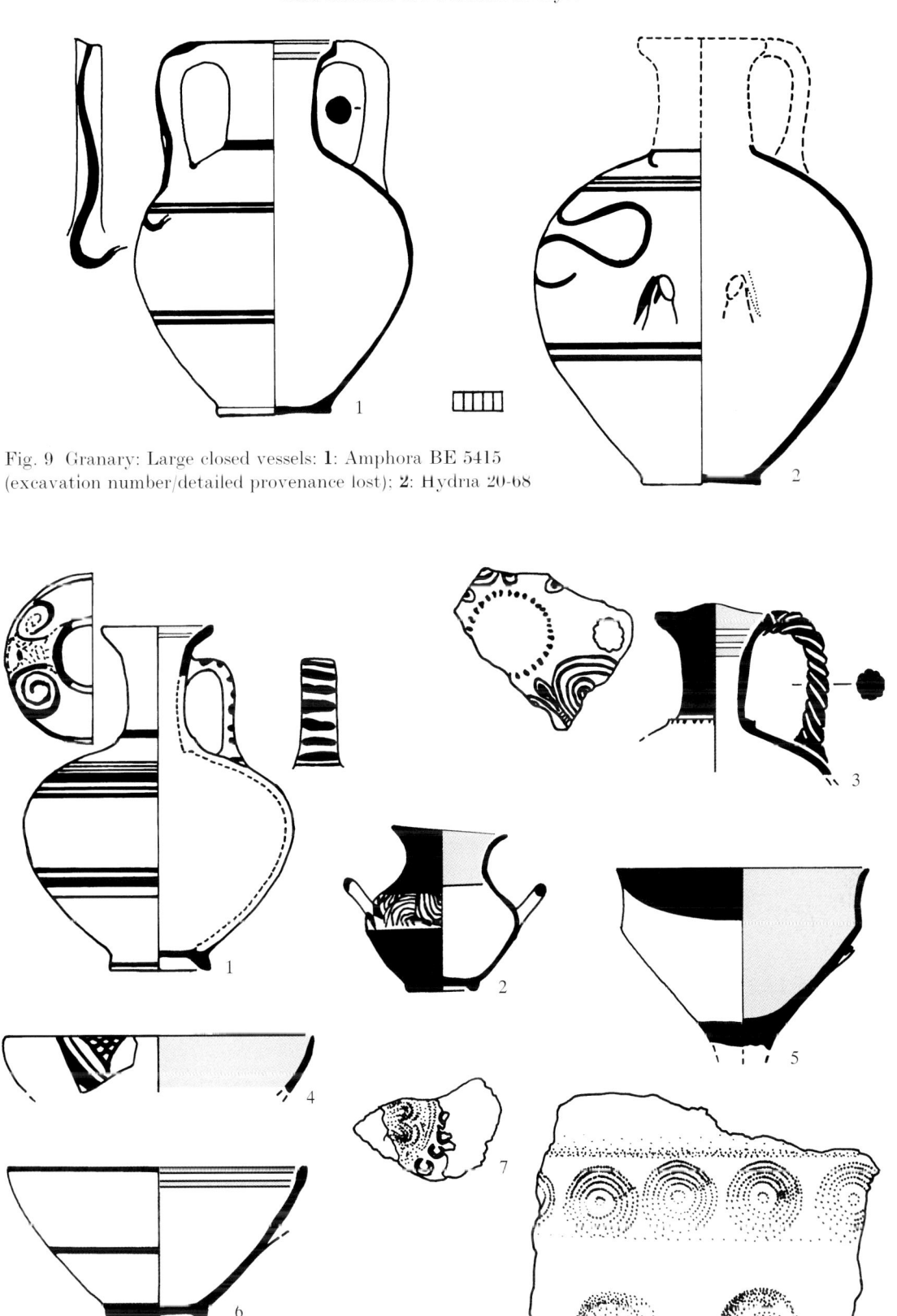

Fig. 9 Granary: Large closed vessels: **1**: Amphora BE 5415 (excavation number/detailed provenance lost); **2**: Hydria 20-68

Fig. 10 Other shapes of LH III C Advanced. **1**. Jug 60-319. **2**. Amphoriskos 60-401; **3**: Trefoil lipped jug 61 1406; **4**: Kylix Γ32'64/21; **5**: Kylix 68-481; **6**: One-handled conical bowl 64-431; **7**: Pithos 59-209; **8**: Pithos 59-225

BIRGITTA P. HALLAGER

PROBLEMS WITH LM/LH III B/C SYNCHRONISMS*

"It is worth noting the absence of references to Furumark classification in the publication of LM III C material from Khania in HALLAGER 2000, where the continental influence on Crete in this period tends to be played down", so A. L. D'Agata (D'AGATA 2003, 25 n. 3). In a paragraph in this publication (*GSE II*, 172–173) the obvious Mainland influence on the LM III C pottery is listed and it is concluded that it was not as strong as in the previous LM III B2 period. As a matter of fact, if we do *not* date Minoan pottery according to Furumark, but follow the Cretan pottery sequence, it seems that the influence is rather the reverse. Some 30 years ago Popham briefly commented upon this subject, which he called "the unexpected renewal of Cretan influence on the pottery of the Cyclades and Mainland Greece [in III B2] and in early III C" (POPHAM 1970, 88 n. 97).

The synchronisms between the Mainland and Crete are fairly well established for the LM III A and early LM III B period (POPHAM 1970, 81–84. – KANTA 1980, 298–301. – HALLAGER 1988, 1993). Fortunately they are not based only on similar stylistic features, but more importantly on mutual imports. Local imitation and adoption of certain features of the Mycenaean pottery are known throughout LM III. Furthermore they have appeared without much delay as a result of close contacts between the two areas. When we enter the LM III B2 period the best synchronisms – the Mycenaean imports – seem to disappear in Crete (HALLAGER 1993, 265. – *GSE III*, 252. – HALLAGER 2005, 289) and the influence slowly starts going the other way. But now there seems to be some delay if we assume that the periods run parallel. What was the reason for this delay? The contacts did not slow down or disappear in III B2 – on the contrary, they seem to have been intensified as for example demonstrated by the transport stirrup jar trade. In III C the Cretan influence became intensified. But with the present chronology, it takes some 70 to 100 years before a Cretan invention such as the reserved rim band, reached the workshops of the Mycenaean potters. Again I wonder – why this long delay? Could there be something wrong with the synchronisms? To be able to answer this question I intend to 1) have a look at some LM III B2 and III C Early features and their appearance in the Mycenaean relative chronology and to 2) investigate the contexts of the LM III B and LM III C vessels found on the Mainland.

SOME MINOAN INFLUENCE ON THE MAINLAND POTTERY IN LH III C EARLY AND MIDDLE

The banded cup (Fig. 1a) and the carinated cup (Fig. 1c) are type fossils in the LM III B2 period (*GSE III*, 201–202. – HALLAGER 2003, 106–108). Both of them appear on the Mainland as new shapes – *not* in the corresponding LH III B2 period – but in LH III C Early: FS 215, the deep semiglobular cup (Fig. 1b), and FS 240, the carinated cup with high-

---

* My warm thanks to Penelope Mountjoy for reviewing the English text. The drawings in Figs. 1–2 are in scale 1:3 unless otherwise stated.

swung handle (Fig. 1d). A new type of spoutless Minoan juglet (Fig. 1e) was noted in LM III B2 (KANTA 1980, 261 – a shape which continued in LM III C) and this also has a parallel in the lekythos FS 122 (a small narrow-necked jug, Fig. 1f), which was a new shape in LH III C Early.

When we come to LM III C Early, the traceable influence on the Mainland pottery becomes much stronger – not on the corresponding LH III C Early but on the LH III C Middle pottery. The very beginning of LM III C sees the introduction of two important decorative features: the reserved interior rim band (Fig. 1g) and the tricurved streamer (Fig. 1i. – *GSE II*, 139–142. – HALLAGER 2003, 109). Both features appeared all over Crete mainly on bowls and kraters. And both features were adopted by the Mainland potters (Fig. 1h,j) but – quite surprisingly – not before LH III C Middle (*MDP*, 155). Kraters with a double handle and with a bull's head, known from the end of LM III B1 to LM III C Early at Khania (*GSE III*, 219) and in eastern Crete in LM III C Early (*GSE II*, 147. – SEIRADAKI 1960, 22, type 10), appeared for the first time as a new feature in LH III C Middle (*MDP*, 155). Small stirrup jars with a marked cone top on the disc (Fig. 2b) are also characteristic for LH III C Middle (*MDP*, 155). Similar stirrup jars are known, but not very common, from the very end of LM III C Early (Fig. 2a. – *GSE II*, 146). Trefoil-mouthed jugs, particularly appreciated at eastern Cretan sites at least since LM III A2 (Fig. 2c. – KANTA 1980, 262), are introduced in LH III C Middle as FS 137 (Fig. 2d. – *MDP*, 155). Some jars, jugs and kraters in LH III C Middle have twisted handles (*MDP*, 155), a feature found on the amphora FS 69 already in LH III B (Fig. 2f. – *RMDP*, 145). The same type of handles existed *both* on jugs and amphorae in LM III C Early (Fig. 2e. – SEIRADAKI 1960, 13–14, fig. 8:4). LM III C Early neck-handled amphorae are known from both Karphi in the eastern part of the island and Khania in the western (Fig. 2g. – *GSE II*, 151 83-P0447, pls. 43; 69:d.1. – SEIRADAKI 1960, fig. 8:4). Neck-handled amphorae (FS 70) on the Mainland cannot be traced back prior to the second half of LH III C Middle (Fig. 2h. – *MDP*, 155, 181).

In the early part of LH III C Middle the *Pictorial Style* on kraters was introduced (*MDP*, 155). The motifs used on Pictorial Style vases had by this time had a long history within Minoan vase painting. Elaboration and simplicity of decoration coexisted in the second half of LH III C Middle, but these features were both found on LM III C Early pottery. On Crete the so-called *Close Style* was preferred on kraters, stirrup jars and kylikes. On the Mainland the "Close Style" is a miniature style used principally on stirrup jars and deep bowls but it also appears on other shapes such as kylikes and kraters (see MOUNTJOY this volume for the term Pleonastic Style). The third style flourishing in LH III C Middle – the *Octopus Style* – is generally considered to have had its roots in Crete. One small and final addition to this: the main important *Mycenaean* influence on LM III C Early pottery was the Mycenaean technique of making stirrup jars, a technique which surprisingly was adopted by the Cretan potters although they had a long tradition of making them in the Minoan way (*GSE II*, 144).

LM III B AND LM III C VESSELS FOUND ON THE MAINLAND

Can the above noted discrepancies in the present relative chronology also be noted in connection with the contexts of the Minoan vases found on the Mainland?

Leaving aside the LM III A imports, which at present come mainly from tombs in Attica and the Argolid,[1] I will here concentrate on the LM III B and C imports and their find contexts. Owing to the lack of Mycenaean III B2/C imports in Crete, they are our

---

[1] The following list of LM III A imports is mainly based on the information given by Popham (POPHAM 1970, 81–84) and Kanta (KANTA 1980, 298–299). A globular flask found in a tomb in Faliron Road (NIKO-

best evidence for the synchronisms during this period. The Minoan vases so far reported or published most probably constitute only the very tip of the iceberg. They are mainly, and not unexpectedly, found at (or near) coastal sites along the Peloponnese and Attica and as far up as the strait between Euboea and Boeotia.

Ships leaving western Crete could most probably have gone via **Kythera**, albeit the Minoan vases or sherds from LM III B2 and III C are still to be found. From the settlement at Kastri and a rubbish dump in one of the tombs, twelve sherds – including large stirrup jars – are reported and they are all dated to LM III A2 and III B1 (COLDSTREAM – HUXLEY 1972, 304–305, pls. 41–43).[2]

Concerning the southern Peloponnese, Mountjoy has carefully detected and remarked upon the widespread, numerous Minoanisms present over a longer period of time in the area (MOUNTJOY 1997, 123, 127–128, 131). And Rutter concluded that they may be "the results of more frequent and regular interactions between Crete, and particularly the western part of that island, and the geographically closest portions of the Greek Mainland, Laconia and Messenia in particular" (RUTTER 2003, 200).

The area around Olympia had been in contact with Crete for some considerable time before LM/LH III B (KANTA 1980, 299). In this connection the contents of three tombs in the area are of some interest. At the location **Kladeos Stravokephalo** a LM III B juglet (Fig. 3b) was found in a chamber tomb (BUCHHOLZ – KARAGEORGHIS 1971, 75, 326, no. 981). It is decorated with an elaborate triangle which, according to Kanta, is common in west Crete (KANTA 1980, 300). Seven chamber tombs were excavated at this site in the 1960s and mentioned in a brief report (YALOURIS 1965, 103, pls. 137–138). The cemetery had been in use for a long period; LH III C vases were present. Among the ten vases illustrated in the report is a hydria (FS 128) decorated with a thick wavy band (YALOURIS 1965, pl. 137γ), which may be dated to LH III C Middle (*MDP*, 203). Further one vase from this site has subsequently been published: a collar-necked jar (FS 64) with a lid (BUCHHOLZ – KARAGEORGHIS 1971, 75, 326, nos. 986–987) which is dated to LH III C Early by Mountjoy (*RMDP*, 390). As the remaining illustrated vases are of earlier date and we have no closer find context for the Minoan juglet, unfortunately no conclusions concerning the synchronisms can be drawn at the moment.

At the location **Phloka** a figurine and three vases were found, perhaps deriving from a destroyed tomb (YALOURIS 1965, 103, pl. 135α. – YALOURIS 1968, pl. 1:1–2). The bell-skirted figurine is of a well-known Minoan type with close parallels to, among others, the figurines from the Shrine of the Double Axes in the Palace at Knossos (EVANS 1921–36, vol. 2, 340, fig. 193). The thelastron with a knob at the handle attachment (Fig. 3a) is also of Minoan origin (KANTA 1980, 300). Both can be dated to LM III B and probably late in this period. The remaining two vases, an amphoriskos FS 59 and a small jug FS 115 seem to be of LH III C Early date.

POULOU 1970, pl. 174, fig. 6); a basket vase in a tomb at Vourvatsi (STUBBINGS 1947, 58, pl. 18:6); a basket vase in a tomb at Varkiza (THEOCHARIS 1960, 266–269, pl. 35a); sherds from Mycenae (FRENCH 1964, 253–254, pl. 70:b2. – FURTWÄNGLER – LOESCHCKE 1886, pl. XXX no. 262); a pyxis from tomb 7 at Mycenae (XENAKI-SAKELLARIOU 1985, 62, pl. 4:2257); fragments of a Palace Style jar from a tomb at Mycenae (MACKENZIE 1903, 194, fig. 10); a jug, two cups and a pyxis in the Prosymna tombs (BLEGEN 1937, tomb XXIV, no. 304, fig. 174; tomb XVI, no. 203, fig. 97; tomb VIII, no. 824, figs. 402, nos. 834–835; fig. 405); a jug from the Berbati tholos tomb (POPHAM 1970, 82); a stirrup jar from a tomb at Dendra (PERSSON 1931, 66, fig. 46. – KANTA 1980, 298); a piriform jar and a jug from tombs at Argos (DESHAYES 1953, fig. 16 no. 2. – DESHAYES 1966, pl. 65:1–2); a stirrup jar from a tomb at Olympia (YALOURIS 1966, pl. 183β).

[2] A sherd from the rubbish dump (COLDSTREAM – HUXLEY 1972, p 25, pl. 42), however, may be part of a locally produced LM III B2 cup. A parallel to it can be found in *GSE III*, pl. 45:71-P0895.

At the third location, **Agrapidokhori Kotrona**, the interest is confined to a single chamber tomb with LH III A2–B inhumations and at least one LH III C cremation (PARLAMA 1972). The cremation burial, a closed group, had 14 vases as grave gifts, among them a small, Minoan globular stirrup jar (Fig. 3c). The elaborate triangles on the shoulder "make an early LM III C attribution certain" according to Kanta (KANTA 1980, 300, fig. 97:1–3. – *RMDP*, 390 no. 70, fig. 135). In the publication the 13 Mycenaean vases have been dated to LH III C1/2, Mountjoy, however, dates twelve of the vases to LM III C Late and one to LH III C Early (*RMDP*, 366).

The Minoan connections with Achaia in LM III have also been pointed out (PAPADOPOULOS 1981. – MOUNTJOY 1997, 128). In **Patras** a large chamber tomb was excavated in 1978 in odos Germanou 134 (PAPAPOSTOLOU 1985, 80). The tomb contained eight undisturbed inhumations in two successive levels and altogether 24 vases. Two Minoan stirrup jars and four Argive imports from this tomb have subsequently been published (PAPAZOGLOU-MANIOUDAKI 1993, 209–215). A squat stirrup jar (Patras mus. no. 3945), made in the Local Kydonian Workshop (Fig. 3d), was found together with three Argive stirrup jars, two of which were dated to LH III B2, in the same grave in the upper level. Another Minoan stirrup jar (Patras mus. no. 3950) with a shape imitating FS 182 (Fig. 3e) was found in the lower level and in the same grave as an Argive stirrup jar dated to LH III B1.

The squat Kydonian stirrup jar is decorated with a variant of the Minoan flower motif which was applied, not only to small stirrup jars but also to, e.g., kylikes and mugs made in this workshop (KANTA 1980, fig. 120:1. – *GSE III*, pl. 105:c.1. – TZEDAKIS 1969, fig. 6). It can be dated to LM III B2. The second Minoan stirrup jar from the lower level is decorated with flowers both on the upper part and in the belly zone. The shape and especially the presence of the belly zone date the vase to the very end of LM III B1. Here the synchronisms between III B1 and the beginning of III B2 seem to be confirmed.

Other ships sailed up along the eastern coast of the Peloponnese. Some 5 km north of Monemvasia lies the acropolis of ancient **Epidauros Limera**, situated above a long and partially sheltered beach. Mycenaean chamber tombs dating from LH II A to LH III C2 were found at three spots in the neighbourhood (DEMAKOPOULOU 1968). Here Tomb A, a chamber tomb with a circular side chamber from the dromos and with three pits in the main chamber, is of interest. The tomb had been plundered, but the pits were intact. In one in the western part of the chamber four vases were found: two stirrup jars, an open and a closed vessel (CHRISTOU 1961, pl. 103β). The smaller globular stirrup (Fig. 3f. – Sparta mus. no. 5421) was recognised as a Minoan import with parallels to vases found at Mouliana and Isopata in Crete.[3] The LM III C Early date is certain. The second and larger stirrup jar (Sparta mus. no. 5419) is dated to LH III C1a–b by Demakopoulou – with present terminology LH III C Middle (DEMAKOPOULOU 1968, 165–166, pl. 74α–β. – *RMDP*, 290).[4]

---

[3] A further two parallels can be added: a stirrup jar from Tourloti (BETANCOURT 1985, 183, fig. 130) and one from Khania (*GSE II*, 146 80-P0260+, pls. 38; 69:a.10).

[4] Another stirrup jar from these tombs may be of some interest (DEMAKOPOULOU 1968, 163–164, pl. 73α,γ; Sparta mus. no. 5426). Its upper part is decorated in a "closed style" which has close parallels in Crete. In particular the additional features like the rough spiral on the false neck/disc and the bars both on the handles and on the spout may be found on stirrup jars in Knossian tombs (HOOD – HUXLEY – SANDARS 1958/59, 242, fig. 28 – stirrup jars from tomb VIA on Upper Gypsades). These stirrup jars are dated to LM III C Advanced by Popham. There seems, however, to be some disagreement whether the stirrup jar from Epidauros Limera is locally produced (DEMAKOPOULOU 1968, 164) or a Minoan import (*RMDP*, 290 no. 222, fig. 99).

If we continue up to the Argolic Gulf, the two palatial centres, Tiryns and Mycenae, must have been of vital interest for the merchants. It was in this Gulf that the well-known Point Iria wreck sank sometime at the end of the 13th century B.C.; among other vases it had eight Minoan transport stirrup jars on board. If we disregard the many Minoan transport stirrup jars in the area (HASKELL ET AL. forthcoming. – SHELMERDINE 2001, 347–348), the reported finds of other Minoan vessels are quite meagre at the moment. In a LH III B stratum at the Lion Gate in **Mycenae**, a single Minoan sherd has been found.[5] Lisa French kindly showed it to me many years ago and according to my preserved notes it was a sherd from a large open vessel made in the Kydonian Workshop and decorated with vertically connected lozenges (Fig. 3g). Subsequently I have found a somewhat more elaborate version of the motif on a LM III C Early krater in Khania (*GSE II*, pl. 41:84-P0304); the sherd from Mycenae, however, may be dated to LM III B2. There may be a second Kydonian sherd from Mycenae. It is published by Furtwängler and Loeschcke and comes from a large vessel with "yellow slip" (FURTWÄNGLER – LOESCHCKE 1886, 61, pl. XXXI no. 293). The sherd, which may derive from an amphoroid krater (Fig. 3h), is decorated with a palm tree, FM 15:18, for which Furumark gives only this single sherd as a reference. The motif, however, is well-known in the Kydonian workshop's repertoire where we find it during the period LM III B1 late and in LM III B2 (*GSE III*, 213, kylix 84-P1303+, pls. 54; 117:e.6. – HATZIDAKIS 1913, 49, fig. 11. – KANTA 1980, fig. 90:5). The excavators at **Tiryns** have identified four sherds from a single LM III B stirrup jar (GROSSMANN – SCHÄFER 1975, 71 no. 63, pl. 49:63). It was found in Building 3 in the Unterburg, a building which was destroyed by fire in LH III B2. The stirrup jar, decorated with an octopus (Fig. 3i), was made in the Local Kydonian Workshop and could very well have been produced in LM III B2. A good Kydonian parallel comes from Kritsa (KANTA 1980, fig. 55:1,3).

When we come to **Athens** we find, quite surprisingly, possible Minoan pyxides (Fig. 3j) among the prehistoric finds from the Acropolis and its northern slope. During the last workshop in Vienna J. Rutter mentioned the Athenian version of the straight-sided alabastron FS 98 – the one with a low straight neck and long handle attachments[6] – among his Minoan features and he was unable to find convincing parallels for it on the Mainland – except for the linear pyxis in Eutresis which does not have the long attachments and has a more rounded body (RUTTER 2003, 194 and n. 6, 196 and n. 12, fig. 3). The reason for this is perhaps that the Athenian vases are not Mycenaean straight-sided alabastra but rather Minoan pyxides. Two more or less complete basket-handled pyxides have been published and fragments of a further three are mentioned by Broneer (FURTWÄNGLER – LOESCHCKE 1886, pl. XVI no. 104. – BRONEER 1933, 367–368 and n. 3, fig. 39a). Broneer was well aware of the Cretan parallels. Stubbings, some fourteen years later, mentioned that this particular shape was only known from the Athenian Acropolis and referred to Broneer's Cretan parallels (STUBBINGS 1947, 43–44) and finally some twenty years ago Kanta recognised the vessel published by Furtwängler and Loeschcke as a Minoan pyxis (KANTA 1980, 299). The characteristic very long handle attachments are very common on kraters and pyxides in LM III C Crete.[7] To my knowl-

---

[5] My note for its context is the following: M. no 12, Gp 17, Lion Gate III. The Lion Gate stratigraphy is presented in WACE 1921–23, 9–38. – MOUNTJOY 1993, 145. According to Lisa French (pers. comm.), the Lion Gate III is LH III B2, possibly/probably going into Transitional LH III B2/III C Early.

[6] FS 98 is an LH III C Early feature (MOUNTJOY 1997, 116 no. 10, fig. 2:10); there seem to be two types of it: one with a low straight neck and one with a short concave neck.

[7] KANTA 1980, 299 mentions the Acropolis pyxis as "a Cretan shape common in late LM III B and in LM III C", but I have so far been unable to find any with the long handle attachments in LM III B (see *GSE II*, 153).

edge LM III C pyxides have not been found anywhere else outside the island, and why they were especially appreciated in Athens is somewhat of an enigma. The prehistoric finds from the LH III Acropolis include many of a rather late III B date and there are indications for "quite a substantial settlement in LH III C" (HOPE SIMPSON – DICKINSON 1979, 198–199). The decoration of stylised ivy leaves and branches on the published pyxides is in accordance with a LM III C Early date – as pyxides very soon became a favourite vessel for the so-called Close Style decoration.

On the way from Athens to **Porto Raphti**, some two to three kilometres from Markopoulo/Ligori, a purely LH III C chamber tomb was excavated in the late 1920s (KYPARISSIS 1930. – HOPE SIMPSON – DICKINSON 1979, 211–212). Among the finds in the tomb was a globular Minoan stirrup jar decorated with an octopus (Fig. 3k. – KYPARISSIS 1930, fig. 18. – STUBBINGS 1947, 23, fig. 8, pl. 2:3). Kanta dates the vase to LM III C (KANTA 1980, 300), but although it has some added "tongues" and shells, the drawing of the octopus – without fringes on the head – seems more in accordance with a LM III B2 date.

Close by at **Perati** on the north side of Porto Raphti Bay, a large chamber tomb cemetery of over 200 tombs has been excavated in the 1960s and subsequently published (IAKOVIDIS 1969/70). Two globular stirrup jars were identified as Minoan imports from these tombs: no. 198 from Tomb 12 and no. 1088 from Tomb 146 (IAKOVIDIS 1969/70, vol. 2, 196–197). No. 198 was found in a tomb in use during Perati Phases I–III i.e. LH III C Early to Late. On one side it is decorated with an octopus with fringes (Fig. 3l) which can be compared to the one on the stirrup jar at Epidauros Limera mentioned above. On the other side the lower tentacles end in large rosettes, the space in between being filled with, among others motifs, net and chess patterns (IAKOVIDIS 1969/70, vol. 2, pl. II and 182, fig. 66). The vase does not belong to one of the highlights in Crete, but its date seems indisputably LM III C Early. The second stirrup jar, no. 1088, was found in a tomb used in Phase II, i.e. LH III C Middle. A drawing of the motif on the upper body (Fig. 3m. – IAKOVIDIS 1969/70, vol. 2, pl. IV and 197, fig. 75) reveals that it belongs to the so-called Close Style stirrup jars which appear in LM III C Early in Crete. The broad ondulating band on the upper body of the Perati vase is very often combined with a "Close Style" decoration on Minoan stirrup jars, such as at Milatos and Mouliana (KANTA 1980, figs. 53:4–5; 82:4,7). The latter vase has a similar conical foot to that of the Perati stirrup jar – a feature which seems to appear in the last phase of LM III C Early or perhaps even slightly later.

A third vase, however, is far more interesting due to its unique pictorial decoration: a small globular stirrup jar (no. 892. – Fig. 3n) found in Tomb 124 which was used in Phase I, i.e. LH III C Early (IAKOVIDIS 1969/70, vol. 2, pl. II and 181, fig. 65). This stirrup jar has been described as "unique Mycenaean" (IAKOVIDIS 1969/70, 181) with "perhaps the most powerfully naturalistic representation in Mycenaean vase-painting" (SAKELLARAKIS 1992, 67). The vase, however, is not Mycenaean but undoubtedly Minoan, as has been pointed out by Kanta. She argues that it is "quite possible that the vase's provenance is east Cretan" (KANTA 1980, 301). This is probably not its origin. In spite of east Cretan references, the unique pictorial scene has more numerous and closer parallels in west Crete: the wild goat is found on larnakes at Armenoi (TZEDAKIS 1971, figs. 5–6), the birds (80-P0882 in *GSE IV* forthcoming), the palm and the rendering of the hindquarter of the goat are found on pottery at Khania (*GSE III*, 221 83-P0400+, pls. 67; 120:c.6) and finally the palm tree (the lower part of the tree, HALLAGER E. – VLASAKIS – HALLAGER B. 1992, fig. 4d [90-P1786], pl. 2B. – *GSE III*, pls. 54:84-P1303+; 117:e.6), the drawing of the large bush (TZEDAKIS 1968, pl. 463β). – KANTA 1980, fig. 117:4) and the spiral at its base (TZEDAKIS – MARTLEW 1999, 271 no. 281) are features typical for the Local Kydonian Workshop.[8] The stirrup jar cannot have been produced later than LM III B2.

If we continue up the strait between Euboea and Boeotia, a LM III A2/B1 stirrup jar (Fig. 3o) in a tomb in **Khalkis** with Mycenaean vases of similar date (CHOREMIS 1972, 249–250, pl. 216δ. – *RMDP*, 708 no. 49, fig. 271) and a fragmentary Local Kydonian octopus stirrup jar from **Lefkandi** (POPHAM 1979, 184 n. 7) bear witness to the presence of merchants.[9] One Minoan vessel reached far inland. In Phocis, within the settlement of **Krisa**, which had a large LH III B fortification wall, one sherd of a closed vessel (Fig. 3p) has been identified as Minoan (DOR – JANNORAY – VAN EFFENTERRE H. – VAN EFFENTERRE M. 1960, 97–98, pl. 34j).[10] We have no information about its precise find context, but the sherd, possibly from a small LM III B2 octopus stirrup jar, had probably reached the settlement before its destruction and abandonment by the end of LH III B2 (HOPE SIMPSON – DICKINSON 1979, 257).

The end station of the merchant's journey seems to have been **Thebes**. Except for the large transport stirrup jars in the Kadmeion, reports of other Minoan vessels are at the moment restricted to two. One small stirrup jar found in Kolonaki Tomb 7 has been identified as Minoan by Kanta (KANTA 1980, 299). Only part of the chamber seems to have been preserved. Thirteen vases are described, six of which are shown in fig. 102 in the publication (KERAMOPOULLOS 1917, 137–141). The squat stirrup jar decorated with a panelled pattern (Fig. 3q. – *RMDP*, 675 no. 135, fig. 257) Kanta dates to LM III B and none of the Mycenaean vases on the somewhat unclear photo seem to be of a later date. In his article on the Local Kydonian Workshop, Tzedakis mentions a second stirrup jar found in a tomb excavated by Faraklas and exhibited in the museum (TZEDAKIS 1969, 414 n. 3). It is made in the Kydonian Workshop and decorated with Minoan flowers of a kind which have several parallels, among others, to those on a Kydonian stirrup jar from Armenoi dated to LM III B (TZEDAKIS – MARTLEW 1999, 240 no. 217). The vases in the tomb were contemporary according to Tzedakis. The large number of LM III B transport stirrup jars found within the palace area is well known. Among them not less than 78 were inscribed with personal names; Cretan places names appear on some of them. These stirrup jars and their contents, found in the larger Mycenaean centres along the merchant sea routes, were probably the main reason for the long journey.

This short survey gives us the following information: if we omit Kythera, five settlements and twelve tombs on Mainland sites are involved:[11] 15 complete Minoan vases and seven identifiable sherds from 18 contexts. Six types of LM III B/III C vases were found on the merchant shipping routes: except for the large transport stirrup jars, the second most common shape, small stirrup jars, were found at sites like Olympia,

---

[8] A few days before I came to Vienna I had the opportunity to examine the vase owing to the kind generosity of the director of the Prehistoric department of the National Museum in Athens, Mrs. Heleni Papazoglou. The vase is undoubtly a west Cretan product and I am almost convinced that it is product of the Kydonian Workshop.

[9] Elizabeth Schofield has kindly informed me that the unpublished stirrup jar from Lefkandi is very fragmentary. It has inv. no. LK 66/P248 and it is illustrated and catalogued in the forthcoming *Lefkandi IV*. It is there included among the material of LH III C Phase 1a, but, according to Mervyn Popham, the context is predominantly LH III B.

[10] KANTA 1980, 299 identified a further sherd as Minoan (DOR – JANNORAY – VAN EFFENTERRE H. – VAN EFFENTERRE M. 1960, pl. 34e), but Penelope Mountjoy has convincingly demonstrated that it belongs to a locally produced cup (*RMDP*, 781 no. 235, fig. 306).

[11] Settlements: Mycenae, Tiryns, Athens, Lefkandi, Krisa; tombs: Olympia (3 tombs), Patras, Monemvasia, Porto Raphti, Perati (3 tombs), Khalkis, Thebes (2 tombs).

Patras, Epidauros Limera, Tiryns, Porto Raphti, Perati, Lefkandi, Krisa, and Thebes. Pyxides were, for some reason, appreciated in Athens; a figurine, thelastron and juglet were found as funerary gifts in the area of Olympia and large courtesy vessels like a krater and a possible amphoroid krater were found at Mycenae.

The synchronisms are fairly good for the LM/LH III B1 periods.[12] In III B2 five LM III B2 vessels were found in LH III B2 contexts, while two were connected with vases of a LH III C Early date. In III C, the LM III C Early vases seem mainly to be connected with vases of LH III C Middle date. These observations indicate that there may be possible dislocations between the LM/LH III B2 and C periods, but they are, admittedly, far from convincing proof. It may, of course, be argued that vessels earlier than the date of the burial they were found with (and I stress, that I am *not* talking about tombs in general but individual burials), are present as heirlooms. On the other hand, the evidence is not speaking *against* a slight adjustment of the relative chronology since there is also the Minoan influence on the Mainland pottery mentioned above.

Therefore I will, almost fearlessly, stick my head out and suggest the following adjustments be taken into consideration and discussion: 1) LM/LH III B2 began roughly at the same time but LH III C Early may have started before the end of LM III B2. 2) LM III C Early began sometime after LH III C Early began and may have ended after LH III C Middle had begun (Table 1).

Concerning the end of the Bronze Age, there are some slight disagreements among scholars about the LM III C sequence after the end of LM III C Early until the end of the "Subminoan" period. Until now we have operated with three periods: early and late LM III C and the "Subminoan" period. But the question has been raised: Is it possible to separate three LM III C periods in Crete? Until we have a reliable and convincing stratified settlement sequence for the whole period involving more than one site and preferably including sites from different geographical areas in Crete, I am afraid we have to postpone the problem of synchronisms during this period.

CRETE	MAINLAND
LM III A1	LH III A1
LM III A2	LH III A2
LM III B1	LH III B1
LM III B2	LH III B2
LM III C Early	LH III C Early
LM III C Late	LH III C Middle
	LH III C Late

Table 1

---

[12] This is also valid for the Mycenaean sherds found in Crete, but, as mentioned in the text, for some reason Mycenaean vases or sherds dated post III B1 are, with our present knowledge, very rare in Crete (HALLAGER 2005).

Index to illustrations

Fig. 1   **a**: LM III B2 banded cup (after *GSE III*, pl. 47); **b**: LH III C Early deep semiglobular cup FS 215 (after *MDP*, fig. 183:2); **c**: LM III B2 carinated cup (after *GSE III*, pl. 69); **d**: LH III C Early carinated cup FS 240 (after *MDP*, fig. 185:1); **e**: LM III C juglet (after NOWICKI 1994, fig. 19:4); **f**: LH III C Early lekythos FS 122 (after *MDP*, fig. 177); **g**: LM III C Early bowl with reserved rim band (after *GSE II*, pl. 35); **h**: LH III C Middle krater with reserved rim band (after *MDP*, fig. 228:1); **i**: LM III C Early krater with tricurved streamer (after *GSE II*, pl. 39, scale 1:5); **j**: LH III C Middle krater with tricurved streamer (after *MDP*, fig. 223:2, scale 1:5)

Fig. 2   **a**: LM III C Early stirrup jar with cone top (after *GSE II*, pl. 38); **b**: LH III C Middle stirrup jar with cone top (after *MDP*, fig. 216:3); **c**: LM III A2 trefoil-mouthed jug (after TSIPOPOULOU 1990, 80, fig. 1); **d**: LH III C Middle FS 137 (after *MDP*, fig. 213:1); **e**: LM III C Early amphora with twisted handles (after SEIRADAKI 1960, fig. 8:4, scale 1:5); **f**: LH III B amphora FS 69 with twisted handles (after *RMDP*, fig. 37:278, scale 1:5); **g**: LM III C Early neck-handled amphora (after *GSE II*, pl. 43, scale 1:5); **h**: LH III C Late neck-handled amphora FS 70 (after *MDP*, fig. 239:1, scale 1:5)

Fig. 3   LM III B and C vessels found on the Mainland. **a**: Phloka (thelastron); **b**: Kladeos Stravokephalo (juglet); **c**: Agrapidokhori Kotrona (globular stirrup jar after *RMDP*, fig. 135, no. 70); **d**: Patras (squat stirrup jar after PAPAZOGLOU-MANIOUDAKI 1993, fig. 2α–β); **e**: Patras (stirrup jar imitating FS 182 after PAPAZOGLOU-MANIOUDAKI 1993, fig. 2γ–δ); **f**: Epidauros Limera (globular stirrup jar); **g**: Mycenae (sherd of an open vessel); **h**: Mycenae (sherd of a closed vessel); **i**: Tiryns (fragmentary stirrup jar); **j**: Athens (pyxis after *RMDP*, 557, fig. 203:274); **k**: Porto Raphti (globular stirrup jar after STUBBINGS 1947, 23, fig. 8); **l**: Perati (globular stirrup jar no. 198 after IAKOVIDIS 1969/70, 182, fig. 66); **m**: Perati (globular stirrup jar no. 1088 after IAKOVIDIS 1969/70, 197, fig. 75); **n**: Perati (globular stirrup jar no. 892 after IAKOVIDIS 1969/70, 181, fig. 65); **o**: Khalkis (stirrup jar after *RMDP*, fig. 271, no. 49); **p**: Krisa (sherd of a closed vessel); **q**: Thebes (squat stirrup jar after *RMDP*, fig. 257, no. 135)

Bibliography

Δ' Κρητολογικό Συνέδριο
1981   Πεπραγμένα του Δ' διεθνούς Κρητολογικού Συνεδρίου (Ηράκλειο, 29 Αυγούστου – 3 Σεπτεμβρίου 1976). Vol. 2. Athens.

Atti e Memorie del 1° Congresso Internazionale di Micenologia
1968   *Atti e Memorie del 1° Congresso Internazionale di Micenologia. Roma 27 settembre – 3 ottobre 1967* (Incunabula Graeca 25). Rome.

BETANCOURT, PH. P.
1985   *The History of Minoan Pottery*. Princeton NJ.

BLEGEN, C.
1937   *Prosymna. The Helladic Settlement Preceding the Argive Heraeum*. Cambridge.

BRONEER, O.
1933   "Excavations on the North Slope of the Acropolis in Athens, 1931–1932", *Hesperia* 2, 329–417.

BUCHHOLZ, H.-G. – V. KARAGEORGHIS
1971   *Altägäis und Altkypros*. Tübingen.

CHOREMIS, A. K.
1972   "Οικόπεδον Αντ. Μάτσα εις θέσιν Παναγίτσα", *ArchDelt* 25, 1970 [1972], Chron 248–250.

CHRISTOU, C.
1961   "Ανασκαφή εν Μονεμβασία. Νεκροταφείον Αγ. Ιωάννου", *Prakt* 1956 [1961], 207–210.

COLDSTREAM, J. N. – G. L. HUXLEY (eds.)
1972   *Kythera. Excavations and Studies Conducted by the University of Pennsylvania Museum and the British School at Athens*. London.

COULSON, W. – M. TSIPOPOULOU
1994   "Preliminary Investigations at Halasmenos, Crete, 1992–93", *Aegean Archaeology* 1, 65–97.

CULLEN, T. (ed.)
2001   *Aegean Prehistory. A Review* (American Journal of Archaeology Suppl. 1). Boston.

D'AGATA, A. L.
2003   "Late Minoan III C–Subminoan Pottery Sequence at Thronos/Kephala and its Connections with the Greek Mainland", 23–35 in: *LH III C Chronology and Synchronisms*.

DEMAKOPOULOU, K.
1968 "Μυκηναϊκά αγγεία εκ θαλαμοειδών τάφων περιοχής Αγίου Ιωάννου Μονεμβασίας", *ArchDelt* 23, 1968, Mel 145–194.

DESHAYES, J.
1953 "Les vases mycéniens de la Deiras (Argos)", *BCH* 77, 59–89.
1966 *Argos. Les fouilles de la Deiras* (Études Péloponnésiennes 4). Paris.

DOR, L. – J. JANNORAY – H. VAN EFFENTERRE – M. VAN EFFENTERRE
1960 *Kirrha. Étude de Préhistoire Phocidienne*. Paris.

EVANS, A. J.
1921-36 *The Palace of Minos*. London.

FRENCH, E.
1964 "Late Helladic III A1 Pottery from Mycenae", *BSA* 59, 241–261.

FRENCH, E. B. – K. A. WARDLE (eds.)
1988 *Problems in Greek Prehistory. Papers Presented at the Centenary Conference of the British School of Archaeology at Athens, Manchester April 1986*. Bristol.

FURTWÄNGLER, A. – G. LOESCHCKE
1886 *Mykenische Vasen. Vorhellenische Thongefässe aus dem Gebiete des Mittelmeeres*. Berlin.

GROSSMANN, P. – J. SCHÄFER
1975 "Tiryns: Unterburg 1968. Grabungen im Bereich der Bauten 3 und '4'", 55–96 in: *Tiryns. Forschungen und Berichte* 8. Mainz.

HALLAGER, B. P.
1988 "Mycenaean Pottery in LM IIIA1 Deposits at Khania, Western Crete", 173–181 in: FRENCH – WARDLE 1988.
1993 "Mycenaean Pottery in Crete", 263–269 in: *Wace and Blegen*.
2003 "Late Minoan III B2 and Late Minoan III C Pottery in Khania", 105–116 in: *LH III C Chronology and Synchronisms*.
2005 "The Synchronisms Mainland – West Crete in the LM III A2–IIIB Period", 277–292 in: *Ariadne's Threads*.

HALLAGER, E. – M. VLASAKIS – B. P. HALLAGER
1992 "New Linear B Tablets from Khania", *Kadmos* 31, 1992, 61–87.

HASKELL, H. W. *et al.*
forthc. *Transport Stirrup Jars of the Bronze Age Aegean and East Mediterranean* (Fitch Laboratory Occasional Papers 5). Athens.

HATZIDAKIS, J. A.
1913 "Kretische Gräber", *AM* 38, 1913, 43–50.

HOOD, M. S. F. – G. HUXLEY – N. SANDARS
1958/59 "A Minoan Cemetery on Upper Gypsades (Knossos Survey 156)", *BSA* 53/54, 194–262.

HOPE SIMPSON, R. – O. T. P. K. DICKINSON
1979 *A Gazetteer of Aegean Civilisation in the Bronze Age I: The Mainland and Islands* (SIMA 52). Göteborg.

IAKOVIDIS, S. E.
1969/70 Περατή. Το νεκροταφείον (Βιβλιοθήκη της εν Αθήναις Αρχαιολογικής Εταιρείας 67). Athens.

KANTA, A.
1980 *The Late Minoan III Period in Crete. A Survey of Sites, Pottery and Their Distribution* (SIMA 58). Göteborg.

KERAMOPOULLOS, A.
1917 "Ζ' Μυκηναϊκοί τάφοι Κολωνακίου η Αγ. Άννης", *ArchDelt* 3, 123–209.

KYPARISSIS, N.
1930 "Μυκηναϊκοί τάφοι εις Πόρτο-Ράφτη", *ArchDelt* 11, 1927/28 [1930], Chron 59–60.

MACKENZIE, D.
1903 "The Pottery of Knossos", *JHS* 23, 157–205.

MOUNTJOY, P.
1993 *Mycenaean Pottery. An Introduction* (Oxford University Committee for Archaeology. Monograph 36). Oxford.
1997 "The Destruction of the Palace at Pylos Reconsidered", *BSA* 92, 109–137.

NIKOPOULOU, Y.
1970 "Νεκροταφείον παρά την προς Φάληρον οδόν", *AAA* 3, 171–179.

NOWICKI, K.
1994 "Katalimata", 94–97 in: COULSON – TSIPOPOULOU 1994.

PAPADOPOULOS, T. J.
1981 "Μυκηναϊκή Αχαΐα και Κρήτη", 407–415 in: Δ' Κρητολογικό Συνέδριο.

PAPAPOSTOLOU, I.
1985 "Αρχαιότητες και μνημεία Αχαΐας", ArchDelt 33, 1978 [1985], Chron 79–102.

PAPAZOGLOU-MANIOUDAKI, L.
1993 "Εισηγμένη κεραμεική στους Μυκηναϊκούς τάφους της Πάτρας", 209–215 in: Wace and Blegen.

PARLAMA, L.
1972 "Θαλαμοειδής τάφος εις Αγραπιδοχώρι Ηλείας", ArchEphem 1971 [1972], 52–60.

PERSSON, A. W.
1931 The Royal Tombs at Dendra near Midea (Skrifter utgivna av Kungl. Humanistiska Vetenskapssamfundet i Lund 15). Lund.

POPHAM, M. R.
1970 The Destruction of the Palace at Knossos. Pottery of the Late Minoan III A Period (SIMA 12). Göteborg.
1979 "Connections between Crete and Cyprus between 1300–1100 B.C.", 178–191 in: Relations between Cyprus and Crete.

Relations between Cyprus and Crete
1979 Acts of the International Archaeological Symposium "The Relations between Cyprus and Crete, ca. 2000–500 B.C.", Nicosia 16th April–22nd April 1978. Nicosia.

RUTTER, J. B.
2003 "The Nature and Potential Significance of Minoan Features in the Earliest Late Helladic III C Ceramic Assemblages of the Central and Southern Greek Mainland", 193–216 in: LH III C Chronology and Synchronisms.

SAKELLARAKIS, J. A.
1992 The Mycenaean Pictorial Style in the National Archaeological Museum of Athens. Athens.

SEIRADAKI, M.
1960 "Pottery from Karphi", BSA 55, 1–37.

SHELMERDINE, C. W.
2001 "Review of Aegean Prehistory VI: The Palatial Bronze Age of the Southern and Central Greek Mainland", 329–381 in: CULLEN 2001.

STUBBINGS, F. H.
1947 "The Mycenaean Pottery of Attica", BSA 42, 1–75.

THEOCHARIS, M. D.
1960 "A Knossian Vase from Attica", Antiquity 34, 266–269.

TSIPOPOULOU, M.
1990 "Ταφική σπηλιά στον Άγιο Σπυρίδωνα Σητείας", ArchDelt 38, 1983 [1990] Mel 78–104.

TZEDAKIS, Y.
1968 "Αρχαιότητες και μνημεία Δυτικής Κρήτης", ArchDelt 21, 1966 [1968], Chron 425–429.
1969 "L'atelier de céramique postpalatiale à Kydônia", BCH 93, 396–418.
1971 "Λάρνακες Υστερομινωικού νεκροταφείου Αρμένων Ρεθύμνης", AAA 4, 216–222.

TZEDAKIS, Y. – H. MARTLEW (eds.)
1999 Minoans and Mycenaeans. Flavours of their Time. National Archaeological Museum, 12 July–27 November 1999. Athens.

WACE, A. J. B.
1921–23 "Excavations at Mycenae § VII. – The Lion Gate and Grave Circle Area", BSA 25, 9–126.

XENAKI-SAKELLARIOU, A.
1985 Οι θαλαμωτοί τάφοι των Μυκηνών. Ανασκαφής Χρ. Τσούντα (1887–1898). Les tombes à chambre de Mycènes. Fouilles de Chr. Tsountas (1887–1898). Paris.

YALOURIS, N.
1965 "Αρχαία Ολυμπία", ArchDelt 18, 1963 [1965], Chron 102–104.
1966 "1. Ηλεία", ArchDelt 19, 1964 [1966], Chron 174–179.
1968 "Trouvailles mycéniennes et premycéniennes de la région du sanctuaire d'Olympie", 176–182 in: Atti e Memorie del 1º Congresso Internazionale di Micenologia.

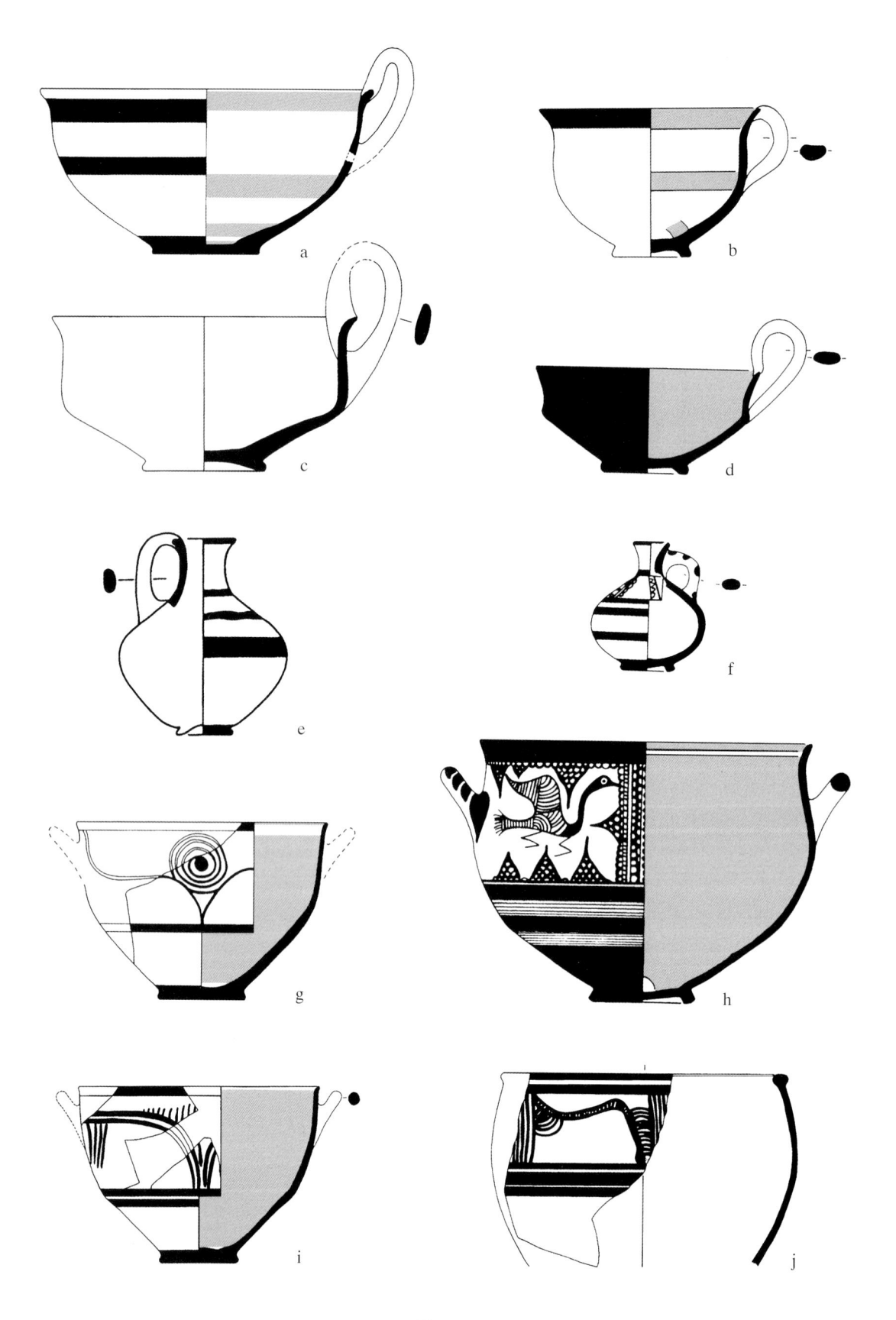

Fig. 1

Fig. 2

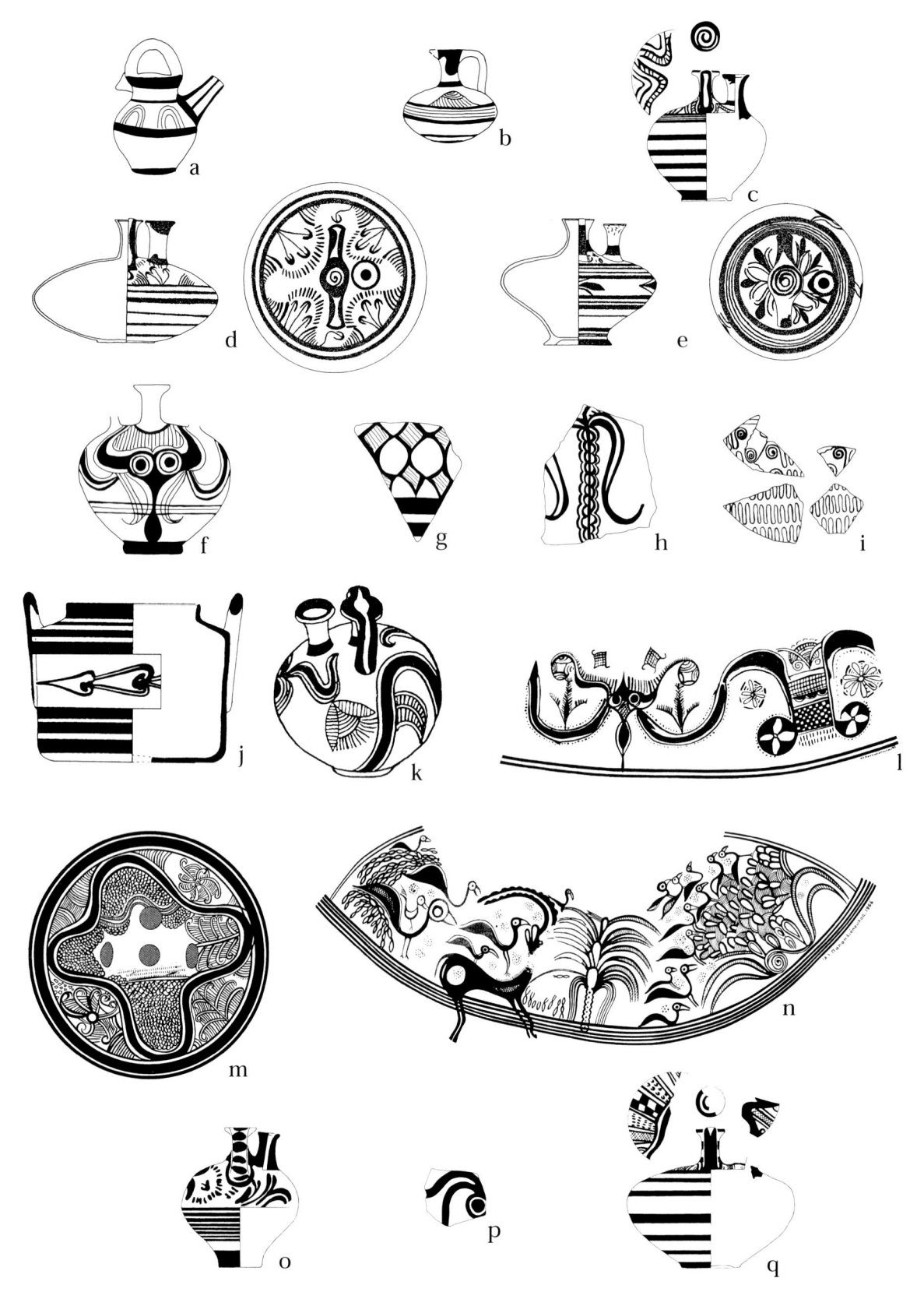

Fig. 3 LM III B and C vessels found on the Mainland

REINHARD JUNG

LH III C MIDDLE SYNCHRONISMS ACROSS THE ADRIATIC*

Traditionally, the two LH III C Middle phases Developed and Advanced are regarded to be contemporary with the Italian Final Bronze Age (FBA). Accordingly, these especially rich cultural phases of the Late Mycenaean civilisation would coincide with a period of gradual decline in trans-Adriatic contacts (cf. PERONI 1996, 384–388. – BETTELLI 2002, 96–98 with figs. 44A–B), although especially the south of Apulia (the Salento) still shows impressively intense relations with the Aegean during FBA 2 (see e.g. GUGLIELMINO 2005, 641–650. – JUNG 2007). In the traditional synchronisation the peak of Mycenaean acculturation processes during the Recent Bronze Age (RBA) in Southern Italy was paralleled with the final palatial and early post-palatial period, i.e. with the later phases of LH III B and with LH III C Early (BETTELLI – LEVI – VAGNETTI 2001/02, 67, 71. – BETTELLI 2002, 96) Following this model would mean that during their main phase of political and economic power (in LH III C Advanced) the small Late Mycenaean chiefdoms/kingdoms would not have been able to maintain fruitful processes of exchange with the coasts to the west on a regular basis and on an economically and politically significant level.

This paper aims to challenge this model and to propose a different synchronisation between the Italian and the Mycenaean chronological sequences (for a first presentation of this comparative chronology see JUNG 2005). It is possible to demonstrate that the first of the two phases of the Italian RBA, RBA 1, must have already straddled the line between LH III B Final and LH III C Early – that is to say between the last stage of the palatial society and the post-palatial reconstruction phase. Here I must stress, that in the present state of research only very few sites in Southern Italy provide us with a stratigraphical sequence for the two successive phases of the Recent Bronze Age (RBA 1 and 2). Here one may name Broglio di Trebisacce and Torre Mordillo in Calabria and Rocavecchia in Apulia. At the latter site, in addition to already known MBA and FBA deposits, an impressive RBA sequence with Late Minoan and Mycenaean pottery has been uncovered. However, these findings are the results of excavations in very recent years and most of the material has not been published yet (but see GUGLIELMINO 2005, 640–641, pl. 166a. – ID. in: SETTIS – PARRA 2005, 307 cat. nos. II.185–II.187).

So, let us start with Broglio di Trebisacce. There are only few classifiable Aegean-type sherds from the layers of RBA 1. The typologically and stylistically latest pieces are of interest for determining the end of RBA 1 in Aegean chronological terms, the prob-

---

* This article presents some of the results of a research project, that was supported by the Austrian Science Fund (FWF) from 2002 to 2004. A full presentation can be found in the monograph entitled "Χρονολογία comparata. Vergleichende Chronologie von Südgriechenland und Süditalien von ca. 1700/1600 v.u.Z." Veröffentlichungen der Mykenischen Kommission 26 (Vienna 2006). Marion Frauenglas was responsible for the processing of the illustrations.
I would like to thank Jeremy Rutter and Elisabetta Borgna for very useful discussions and advice, and I gratefully acknowledge the correction of the English text by Emily Schalk.

lem which concerns us here. Elsewhere (JUNG 2005, 478) I referred to a small, slightly carinated deep bowl A with a rim diameter of 11 cm, two bands in the lower zone of the interior wall and a horizontal zigzag motif on the outer wall (Fig. 1:1. – PANICHELLI in: VAGNETTI – PANICHELLI 1994, 382 no. 85, 384, pl. 75:12). I suggested identifying it as type 3 in Penelope Mountjoy's typology of deep bowls FT 284/285 (MOUNTJOY 1997, 111, 129, fig. 11:65–72. – *RMDP*, 37, fig. 3:177) with parallels from the destruction layer of the palace at Pylos (Fig. 1:2. – *RMDP*, 351–352, fig. 120:110,112). This would mean that it falls into Mountjoy's "Transitional LH III B2–LH III C Early" phase, which encompasses LH III B Final (palace destructions in the Argolid) and the beginning of LH III C Early (reconstruction-phase in the Argolid) of the Tiryns phasing system. To distinguish between LH III B Final and the beginning of LH III C Early is difficult even on the Greek Mainland. In order to make this differentiation, one needs stratified sequences and type counts per stratum as points of reference (cf. JUNG 2005, 478).

There is one published example of a type 3 deep bowl from the Tiryns Palace debris (Fig. 1:3. – VOIGTLÄNDER 2003, pls. 55:TA 9; 117:TA 9[1]), also called "επίχωσις" or "West Wall deposit", which is in fact the debris of the ultimate palace destruction that occurred during LH III B Final (see recently: JUNG 2006b). Christian Podzuweit argued that at Tiryns Lower Citadel deep bowls FT 284/285 A with bands in the lower zone of the interior do not start earlier than the LH III C Early layers (PODZUWEIT 1992, chapter "Skyphos A"). However, the earliest pieces with such bands and regular deep bowl profiles (without knobbed or everted rim) are found in the layer between the LH III B Final destruction and the levelling for the LH III C Early reconstruction. Finally, narrow zonal motifs (such as zigzag, U-pattern, V-pattern, etc.) like on the Broglio piece were more common on deep bowls A in LH III C Early than in LH III B Final.[2] Thanks to the permission of Joseph Maran and the 4th Ephorate of Prehistoric and Classical Antiquities I was able to check these stratigraphical data in the Tiryns storerooms in 2004. I am grateful to Tobias Mühlenbruch, who provided me with the stratigraphical assignation of the relevant find contexts, i.e. the assignations of the context numbers written on the sherds to the respective architectural horizons. I then dated these horizons according to the Podzuweit phasing system (not according to the Kilian system, for which see MÜHLENBRUCH this volume), because the pottery dates at Tiryns Lower Citadel are based thereupon.

These quantitative data indicate a higher probability for dating the Broglio deep bowl to LH III C Early rather than to LH III B Final. This dating gives more weight to the main production phase than to the first innovative appearances of the typological features discussed above – a procedure that seems appropriate in a region outside the Aegean. Other deep bowls A from Broglio also show interior bands, but no carination. They were found in contexts assigned to RBA 1–2 and in pure RBA 2 contexts as well (VAGNETTI 1984, pl. 45:7. – PANICHELLI in: VAGNETTI – PANICHELLI 1994, 388, pl. 78:2–3 [interior decoration of no. 2 omitted]; 389 nos. 108–109). One of them is probably a local product according to an AAS analysis using ten chemical elements for provenance determination (VAGNETTI 1984, pl. 45:7. – JONES in: JONES ET AL. 1994, 419, tab. 2 no. E36; 446, fig. 146; 448).

---

[1] VOIGTLÄNDER 2003, 80 no. TA 9, published as a cup, but no handle attachment is preserved which would prove this classification.

[2] For the narrow zonal motifs see PODZUWEIT 1978, 476 with n. 76, 490, fig. 38 (Tiryns, Town Northwest). – ID. 1992, chapter "Skyphos A", Beil. 3 (Tiryns, Lower Citadel: 7.3% in LH III B, 21.5% in LH III C Early).

In the debate during this conference Jeremy Rutter and Elisabetta Borgna expressed the view, that the deep bowl in question should be Minoan in type rather than Mycenaean. The main argument in favour of this identification would be the lines close to the right edge of the fragment. It was proposed that these lines belong to a Minoan handle-framing device – a loop descending around the base of the handles from the rim – very common on semiglobular cups but less so on deep bowls during the LM III A and B phases (*GSE III*, pl. 49:71-P0527: LM III B2. – D'AGATA 2005, 122, fig. 5: LM III B, with a line on the interior wall). The slightly carinated profile finds parallels on Cretan deep bowls from LM III B (*GSE III*, pl. 50:80-P0497[+84-P1452]: LM III B2, with line on interior. – RUTTER 2003, 214, fig. 14:3) and LM III C contexts (e.g. *GSE II*, 139, pl. 35 with monochrome interior).

Certainly, the Minoan factor must generally be taken into consideration when dealing with Italo-Mycenaean pottery. Lucia Vagnetti has shown on several occasions that there is Minoan influence in the local wheelmade pottery production in Southern Italy (see VAGNETTI 2003, 56–57 with bibliography). However, with the proposed Minoan interpretation of the Broglio sherd some difficulties emerge: The Minoan handle loops are regularly U-shaped loops drawn with a single brush stroke around the handle attachment, although some exist which were painted in two movements.[3] On the Broglio sherd the alleged handle-framing device would have a vertical stroke turning outwards, which is an especially rare phenomenon on Minoan pots (WATROUS 1992, 100 nos. 1724 and 1729, pl. 44:1724,1729: cups from late LM III B layers). To my mind, another explanation of the traces of paint on that sherd seems much more plausible. What we see is the horizontal zigzag that ends in a downward turn to the right and is crossed by a short stroke starting from the handle attachment down towards the left (cf. similar features on deep bowls with wavy bands from Tiryns Palace debris: VOIGTLÄNDER 2003, pls. 49:SW 1,SW 13,SW 14; 109:SW 1,SW 13, 110.SW 14). Thus, there is no real need to interpret the Broglio vessel in Minoan terms.

A closed vessel of medium dimensions (Fig. 1:4), which was also found in a RBA 1 layer at Broglio di Trebisacce, has an entirely black monochrome exterior (PANICHELLI in: VAGNETTI – PANICHELLI 1994, 380, pl. 73:12; 382 no. 76). Monochrome decoration of closed vessels (usually in black) was particularly en vogue in Achaea during LH III C Early, since Aigeira phase Ia, LH III C Early (DEGER-JALKOTZY 2003, 56–57, fig. 2:14–15; 64). The vessel in question was sampled for chemical analysis, but the AAS method employed does not allow an exact provenance ascription (for the method see above). A central Cretan or alternatively a central Greek origin was proposed (JONES in: JONES ET AL. 1994, 420, tab. 2 no. E49; 448). Good typological parallels are not available on Crete, as monochrome medium-sized or large closed vessels seem to be rare in LM III B and III C contexts (cf. *GSE III*, 26 no. 71-P0858, pl. 60:71-P0858: red monochrome).

Surprisingly, some additional evidence for a synchronisation of the borderline between RBA 1 and 2 with LH III C Early can be found in coastal Thessaly, at Dhimíni. In the Mycenaean settlement closed contexts with rich, well-preserved pottery assemblages have been found, which include regular Mycenaean pottery with good parallels in the Argolid and Boeotia and two special pottery classes that can be best compared to south Italian potters' products. In the case of these two special classes we are dealing with wheel-thrown Grey Ware and Handmade Burnished Ware. Both were stratigraph-

---

[3] Thanks to Eleni Hatzaki's permission I was able to verify this impression based on illustrations in literature with the Knossian material from the Little Palace North excavations, which she was so kind to show me.

ically confined to the limited reoccupation phase of the so-called Megaron A and the courtyard, which postdates the destruction of both "Megara A and B" (ADRIMI-SISMANI 2003, 84, 88–89, fig. 10; 97. – EAD. 2006, 86–87, 104, fig. 3). The Mycenaean pottery from this reoccupation phase has parallels in the final palace destruction contexts of the Argolid (compare e.g. ADRIMI-SISMANI 2006, 109, figs. 15–16; 110, fig. 17:bottom; fig. 19 with WARDLE 1973, 316, fig. 11:65; 317 no. 65. – VOIGTLÄNDER 2003, 73–75, 88 no. Si 38; 97 nos. Si 169–171, pls. 69:Si 169–171; 109–110; 124:Si 38; 131:Si 169–171. – PODZUWEIT 1992, chapter "Skyphos B"), but the destruction deposits of Dhimíni preceding the reoccupation phase also contain very similar Mycenaean pottery.[4] Thus, the destruction of Dhimíni may be chronologically placed in LH III B Final – contemporary with the palace destructions in southern Greece – setting the reoccupation at the beginning of LH III C Early.

Amongst the Handmade Burnished Ware from the reoccupation are two small carinated cups of special interest (ADRIMI-SISMANI 2006, 92, 108, figs. 12–13:BE 35896, BE 36013), first, because they represent a type that is absent in northern Greece and the neighbouring Balkan regions, second, because one of them can be dated with some precision in Italian chronological terms. Carinated cups are a hallmark of the *Subappennine facies* of the RBA in Italy, and the small types are provided with high-swung handles with round section like BE 36013 from Dhimíni. Moreover, the Dhimíni cup shows two cylindrical protrusions in a horn-like arrangement at the highest point of the handle. Cups with this typological feature occur in many regions of continental Italy and are regarded as typical for the second RBA phase (COCCHI GENICK 2004b, 46–47, fig. 10:7–11). The closest parallels for the Dhimíni variation come from Apulia, Calabria and Lipari. Not all are stratified; one may cite examples from RBA 2 layers at Motta near Cirò Marina (AISA – TUCCI 2004, 849, 851, fig. 2:1,4[5]), at Coppa Nevigata (Group L: MOSCOLONI in: CAZZELLA – MOSCOLONI 1987, 146, 161, fig. 80:1) and at Torre Santa Sabina (Structure 1, fill during the second phase of use: COPPOLA – RAIMONDI 1996, 384, pl. 55:6,13. – CINQUEPALMI in: COPPOLA – CINQUEPALMI 1998, 158 no. 9.034; 160 no. 9.043). Numerous pieces from the Ausonio I settlement on the acropolis of Lipari are roughly contemporary with these Mainland examples (BERNABÒ BREA – CAVALIER 1980, 578–579, pl. 205:4).

The Grey Ware pots from Dhimíni display some Mycenaean typological influence, but compare much better with the southern Italian Grey Ware (distribution map for Italy: LEVI in: BELARDELLI ET AL. 2005, 508, pl. 112C).[6] As in the case of the Handmade Burnished Ware, the carinated Grey Ware cups with high-swung handles are the most interesting vessels. They occur in two sizes: a larger one with a rim diameter of around 20 cm and a strap-handle, and a smaller one with a rim diameter of ca. 10 cm and a round handle (ADRIMI-SISMANI 2003, 88–89, fig. 10. – EAD. 2006, 106, figs. 6–7). The same

---

[4] ADRIMI-SISMANI 2006 stresses the great similarity between the two successive pottery assemblages, but remarks also on some differences. A large collar-necked jar FT 63 from the destruction layer of "Megaron B" (ADRIMI-SISMANI 2003, 89–90, fig. 12) does not necessarily postdate LH III B Final, because a parallel is already present in the Tiryns Palace debris (cf. VOIGTLÄNDER 2003, pl. 142:G 20; for the wavy line of the Thessalian jar cf. another large closed vessel IBID., pl. 143:G 42). A deep bowl FT 284/285 A from the destruction layer shows a band in the lower zone of the interior wall (ADRIMI-SISMANI 2006, 109 fig. 14:BE 36007), a feature already discussed in this article.

[5] The authors also report *impasto* types of the Final Bronze Age from this settlement layer (AISA – TUCCI 2004, 849, 851–852, fig. 2:5–6), therefore it does not seem to be a closed context.

[6] Here I wish to express my sincerest gratitude to Vassiliki Adrimi-Sismani, who kindly showed me the pottery finds from her excavations at Mycenaean Dhimíni on several occasions.

two size classes with the same morphological characteristics are present in the southern Italian Grey Ware production, too (see in general BETTELLI – DE ANGELIS in: BETTELLI 2002, 72–95. – CASTAGNA in: BETTELLI 2002, 248–249). A large carinated cup with vertical strap handle (ADRIMI-SISMANI 2006, 106, fig. 7:BE 24312), while remotely similar to the larger version of the painted Mycenaean FT 240 (PODZUWEIT 1992, pls. 59:5,9; 60:1), finds its best parallel in a RBA 1 context at Torre Mordillo in Calabria (ARANCIO ET AL. 2001, 140, fig. 76:21 [with ring base!]; 142. – For the stratigraphic date see TRUCCO in: TRUCCO – VAGNETTI 2001, 54, fig. 24; 59). The small carinated cups with vertical round handles (ADRIMI-SISMANI 2006, 106, figs. 6–7:BE 35738–BE 35895) are closer to the small Grey Ware cups from the RBA 2 Central House at Broglio di Trebisacce (CASTAGNA in: BETTELLI 2002, 235, fig. 100:7–8,10–11) than to the small version of FT 240 with its flattened handle and usually steeper lower body (cf. RUTTER 1974, 116, fig. 33:3; 192, fig. 71:3; 214, fig. 90:3–4,6; 226, fig. 99:26; 240, fig. 106:3; 327, fig. 119:2. – PODZUWEIT 1992, pls. 60:11–12,14; 61:1).

We can summarise this discussion in noting that the Grey Ware and the Handmade Burnished Ware from the LH III C Early reoccupation phase at Dhimíni have good parallels in southern continental Italy and that these parallels are found in layers of RBA 1 and 2 date. If we combine this evidence with the date of the Mycenaean-type pottery from RBA 1 contexts at Broglio di Trebisacce, it suggests, that the border between RBA 1 and 2 should be placed somewhere at the beginning of LH III C Early.

Having said that, one may ask now, when does RBA 2 end in Mycenaean terms? At Broglio di Trebisacce the contexts, which can be ascribed to the period of use of the so-called Central House yielded some important fragments of large closed vessels (PANICHELLI in: VAGNETTI – PANICHELLI 1994, 378 no. 46; 379, pl. 72:3; 387, pl. 77:2; 389 no. 116; 390 nos. 133–134; 391, pl. 79:5,13), which do not represent the local belly-handled amphoroid krater, an Italo-Mycenaean type typical for Broglio di Trebisacce (Fig. 2:1–4). Rather, they can be compared with regular Mycenaean amphoras FT 58 and FT 69, jugs FT 106, collar-necked jars FT 63 or hydrias FT 128 (JUNG 2005, 479 with n. 48). Three vessels show antithetic spirals or loops FM 50 and a fourth one has hanging antithetic stemmed spirals FM 51:27 on its shoulder. The chemical analysis (using the AAS method, see above) seems to indicate that at least one of the pieces with antithetic spirals/loops (Fig. 2:1) is an import from the Peloponnese (PANICHELLI in: VAGNETTI – PANICHELLI 1994, 378 no. 46; 379, pl. 72:3. – JONES in: JONES ET AL. 1994, 419 tab. 2 no. 40; 448). All these arguments show that it is feasible to date this group of vessels according to Peloponnesian parallels, even if some of them were produced locally in Calabria. Some Cretan closed vessels with antithetic spirals have been introduced into the discussion (ALBERTI – BETTELLI 2005, 551), although they cannot help in settling the chronological issues of these fine-ware vessels from Broglio di Trebisacce. The LM III B vessels in question are large storage stirrup jars, and the decoration of this vessel type followed different trends in fashion than did the decoration of amphoras, jugs etc. During LM/LH III B in Crete and on the Greek Mainland large stirrup jars FT 164 were decorated with several motifs like antithetic spirals FM 50 and tassel FM 72, which were used only later (in LH III C) for the painted decoration of amphoras, hydrias and jugs (RAISON 1968, 36 n. 133; 87 no. Thèbes 903; pls. 15; 27:61. – ONASSOGLOU 1995, 80 no. η; 110 nos. κ, μ; figs. 46:1; 50:3,4. – Cf. also *RMDP*, 33, 220–222).

Parallels for the large closed vessels with hanging stemmed spirals (sometimes also called stemless spirals) FM 51:27 can be found all over the Aegean, where they are attested since LH III C Advanced (PODZUWEIT 1992, chapter "Amphoren"). As examples one may cite a hydria FT 128 from the East Basement of the Granary at Mycenae (LH III C Advanced: WACE 1921–23, 51, pl. 10d), a trefoil-mouthed jug FT 137 from tomb 143 at

Peratí (phases II–III, LH III C Advanced–Late: IAKOVIDIS 1969/70, vol. 1, 219–220 no. 1034; vol. 2, 239, fig. 100:7; 400 tab.; vol. 3, pl. 63:ε1034) and a jug FT 106 (Fig. 2:6) from tomb B at Aplómata on Naxos (LH III C Advanced–Late: KARDARA 1977, 42 nos. 919–920, pls. 53–54. – *RMDP*, 942, 946 no. 27, 948 fig. 386:27).

Concerning the large closed vessels with antithetic loops or spirals FM 50, one may refer to an exceptional piece from a context as early as the beginning of LH III C Early. It is a collar-necked jar FT 63 from the fill of the so-called bothros at Íria, which is connected with the destruction of the site (DÖHL 1973, 144 no. B 1, pl. 62:1). However, large closed vessels decorated with these motifs became common only during LH III C Advanced and Late. This is illustrated, among others, by one hydria FT 128 (Fig. 2:5) from LH III C Advanced layers at Tiryns, Lower Citadel (PODZUWEIT 1983, 382, fig. 7) and one or two collar-necked jars FT 63 from LH III C Late layers of the same site (PODZUWEIT 1992, chapter "Kragenhalsamphore", pl. 79:2–3), as well as by a hydria FT 128 from the East Basement of the Granary at Mycenae (LH III C Advanced: WACE 1921–23, 51, pl. 10e) and a collar-necked jar FT 63 from tomb 145 at Peratí (phases II–III, LH III C Advanced–Late: IAKOVIDIS 1969/70, vol. 1, 138 no. 1055; vol. 2, 400 tab.; vol. 3, pl. 41:α1055).

This list of more or less complete vessels is backed up by sherd statistics based on the stratigraphical sequence of Tiryns, Lower Citadel. Again, it was possible to check the Tiryns fragments in the storerooms at the site. Both motif groups, antithetic loops/spirals and antithetic stemmed spirals, are first attested on large closed vessels by LH III C Advanced and occur even more often on these shapes by LH III C Late. In the Mycenae Citadel House sequence there are no parallels for these patterns on large closed vessels (personal information E. French).

These data from Broglio di Trebisacce suggest that the RBA 2 lasted until LH III C Advanced. Supporting evidence for this long duration of RBA 2 is found at Torre Mordillo. The typologically latest pieces from the RBA 2 layers of this Calabrian settlement include a rim sherd of a carinated cup FT 240 and a globular cup FT 215/216. The carinated cup displays a monochrome decoration with reserved upper part showing a patterned decoration (VAGNETTI 2001, 313 no. 103; 315, fig. 99:103; 320, fig. 102:103; 324), whereas the globular cup has a linear decoration with an outer band in the handle zone, which might alternatively be interpreted as a broad wavy band which has nearly no oscillation (VAGNETTI 2001, 306, fig. 96:52; 307 no. 52). The carinated cup has parallels in Mycenaean Greece from LH III C Advanced onwards. Semiglobular cups with a decoration like on the cup from Torre Mordillo had a similar production period, ranging from LH III C Developed until Late (for the discussion of these dates see JUNG 2005, 479–480, pl. 105f–g).[7]

We may conclude that the Mycenaean pottery found in Italy supports a low date for the end of RBA 2 during LH III C Advanced. Again some finds of Handmade Bur-

---

[7] Another open vessel from an insecure MBA/RBA 1 context at Torre Mordillo (VAGNETTI 2001, 306, fig. 96:46; 307 no. 46. – For the stratigraphic date see TRUCCO in: TRUCCO – VAGNETTI 2001, 22, fig. 22 and ARANCIO ET AL. 2001, 73) has been interpreted as a product of LH III C Advanced. However, it should be left out of this discussion, for it is uncertain whether we are really dealing here with a small krater FT 281/282 with an antithetic loop motif FM 50 (as suggested by ALBERTI – BETTELLI 2005, 551, pl. 124:14,16 and already by VAGNETTI 2001, 307 no. 46; 324). In my opinion it seems more likely, that it is a sherd from a stemmed bowl FT 304/305 (or a deep bowl with thickened rim) with the right end of a horizontal wavy band FM 53:25 and the rest of what could be a splash at a handle attachment (cf. VOIGTLÄNDER 2003, pls. 49:SW 2, SW 7, SW 8, SW 10, SW 13, SW 14; 50:SW 20). If the motif was indeed an antithetic loop pattern, we would expect to see the lower incurving part of the loop. But this is clearly missing on the sherd.

nished Ware found on the Peloponnese can corroborate this synchronisation. They appear in layers dated to LH III C Advanced. Two carinated cups from Tiryns have already been discussed on another occasion (JUNG 2005, 481, pl. 106e–h). A third one from House P at Korákou (Fig. 3:1) may also contribute to this discussion (RUTTER 1974, 226, fig. 99:28; 235. – ID. 1975, 22 no. 13; 28 pl. 2:fig. 14). These three carinated cups share some morphological features that characterise the *impasto* pottery production of the FBA in southern and central Italy. The part above the carination is more concave and the carination itself is more pronounced and sharp than in the case of the RBA forerunners of this shape, which were cited above as parallels for the small cups in Dhimíni. The new typological features made their first appearance in FBA 1 and are especially typical for that early phase, although their presence continued in FBA 2 contexts (ALESSANDRI – CASSETTA – GATTI 2004, 396–397, fig. 2:A1,3; 401. – PERONI 2005, 727, fig. 3:A4–5,8–10; 728–729, fig. 4:A5,13,15).

The cup from Korákou belongs to the last occupation phase of House P and was found in context with typical LH III C Advanced pottery (for the stratigraphy see RUTTER 1974, 136, 138, 143, 546–548. – For the Mycenaean pottery IBID., 214, fig. 90:6; 226, fig. 99; 542–543).[8] It has a maximum diameter of ca. 15 cm and finds parallels in Calabria, in FBA 1 layers at Torre Mordillo (Fig. 3:3–4. – ARANCIO ET AL. 2001, 78, 90, fig. 44:4; 138–139, fig. 75:16) and in FBA 2 layers at Broglio di Trebisacce (Fig. 3:2. – BUFFA 1994, 459, pl. 83:1,18. – For a recent seriation of FBA contexts from these two sites see ALESSANDRI – CASSETTA – GATTI 2004, esp. 394, fig. 1). It has become clear once again that Handmade Burnished Ware found in Greece can be used for cross-dating with Italy.

The last part of this paper deals with a special group of metal objects, which may be equally useful. Metal types form the backbone of the Italian Bronze Age chronology – just as they do in central and northern Europe. Let us focus on the swords. The typological family of Naue II swords is characteristic for the Italian RBA and FBA. One can differentiate between two basic types, which have exact counterparts in Mycenaean Greece (JUNG 2005, 484, pl. 106j. – EDER – JUNG 2005, 494–495, pls. 107–108). The first one is called type Cetona in Italy and corresponds to Imma Kilian-Dirlmeier's type A of the Naue II swords (BIANCO PERONI 1970, 62–64. – KILIAN-DIRLMEIER 1993, 94–96). This type is attested since the beginning of RBA 1 in Italy and most probably LH III B Middle in Greece.[9] The second one is called type Allerona or type C of the Naue II swords (BIANCO PERONI 1970, 66–70. – KILIAN-DIRLMEIER 1993, 94, 96–99). The absence or presence of a pommel spur is the determining difference between these two types. Both, in Greece and in Italy these two types appear in chronological succession, type A/Cetona being the earlier and type C/Allerona the later one. Usually the same chronological succession is generally assumed for the other European regions of their distribution as well, where the Cetona type is called Reutlingen or Nenzingen and the Allerona type is referred to as Stätzling (see e.g. HARDING 1995, 35–38, 49–52, pl. 67:74,172,179). However, one must admit that in central and northern Europe it is frequently not possible to reach a

---

[8] There is one floor level, but almost no architecture, which can be connected with this settlement phase (RUTTER 1974, 547). The relevant excavation levels (P I–II) were the first two below the modern ground level (IBID., 223). Thus, the context of the carinated cup is not a closed one; however, Rutter stresses that *"there is no evidence for any occupation of the site between the advanced LH III C period and the end of the seventh century B.C."* (IBID., 548).

[9] This earliest piece from Mycenae is only classifiable as Naue II in general, because the ivory hilt plates do not show the upper part of the handgrip. However, all the other early Naue II swords from the Aegean and Cyprus belong to type A (see JUNG 2005, 476, pl. 106j – with bibliography).

very fine dating, which would allow an exact synchronisation with the Italian RBA subphases let alone the Aegean LH III phases.[10]

In Italy, the Allerona type with pommel spur is characteristic for FBA 1 and 2, but its earliest specimens may be dated a little earlier (CARANCINI – PERONI 1999, 18, 58 no. 44, pls. 28:44; 29:44. – Cf. also EDER – JUNG 2005, 494 nos. 2–3, pl. 107:4–5). These attestations are found in a large hoard find from Pila del Brancón in the Po valley, in the north Italian region of Veneto. The hoard is probably constituted by two groups of bronzes, found in 1993 and 1997 respectively, and some additional small fragments, which were surface finds. It could be established that both groups were originally buried in a layer of turf on the right bank of an old creek of the Tartaro river, but only the six fragmentary swords discovered in 1997 were found more or less in situ (SALZANI 1994, 83. – ID. 1998, 66, 69). While it is possible that all the bronzes belong to a single hoard find, the alternative possibility cannot be ruled out that we are dealing here with two separate depositions. However, the identical treatment of the bronzes prior to deposition is remarkable. It includes various processes of intentional destruction such as bending, beating and burning. This may indicate the unity of the hoard complex and thus act as an argument for its interpretation as a closed find, as favoured by the excavator (SALZANI 1998, 69, 71).[11] Four Naue II swords, of which two belong to the Cetona (Fig. 3:6) and two to the Allerona type (Fig. 3:5), were part of the 1993 discovery (SALZANI 1994, 83–84, fig. 1:1–2,5–6). The weapons found in 1997 include one Cetona-type sword, four Naue II swords with incomplete hilts and another, even more fragmentary sword blade (SALZANI 1998, 67, fig. 1:144–146; 68, fig. 2:147–148). The 1993 complex includes a number of typical RBA metal types, such as daggers assignable to the types Pertosa, Var. B (Fig. 3:7) and Merlara (SALZANI 1994, 83, 85–86, fig. 2:8–9. – Cf. BIANCO PERONI 1994, 149–152, 154–156). Gian Luigi Carancini and Renato Peroni dated the first hoard group from Pila del Brancón to the RBA. A few objects in this group (mainly spearheads) represent types or variations of types, which are also present in FBA 1 hoard finds (CARANCINI – PERONI 1999, pl. 29). Therefore, the date of the deposition may be placed at the end of RBA or the beginning of FBA (in this respect Pila del Brancón resembles some of the hoard finds from neighbouring Friuli-Venezia Giulia, cf. BORGNA 2000/01, 305, 311–313). It follows that the production of the Allerona type started by RBA 2 or FBA 1 at the latest.

On the other side of the Adriatic one can find a number of closed contexts, which fortunately comprise Naue II swords of Allerona type in association with Mycenaean pottery. These are mainly warrior burials equipped with Allerona swords and Mycenaean ceramic vessels in chamber tombs, which can be isolated from the rest of the interments in the chambers.

---

[10] A dating of the Stätzling sword from the so-called Spandau hoard to the transition from Nordic Bronze Age Period II to III (SCHAUER 1971, 146) would make this piece as early as the earliest Reutlingen swords (cf. IBID., 132–144), but this context is by no means a closed one. It is probably a ritual site, where metal objects were deposited in a broad area over a longer period of time (SCHWENZER 1997). The sword seems to be a northern European variation of the central European type. Other Stätzling swords from northern central Europe date to Period III, i.e. contemporary with central European Bronze Age D and Hallstatt A1 or Italian RBA and early FBA (WÜSTEMANN 2004, 55–56). For the date of the Reutlingen type in central Europe to the phases BA D and Ha A1 see recently CLAUSING 2005, 19–21 (for the synchronisation with the Italian chronology see CARANCINI – PERONI 1999, 16–20, pl. 35). The Stätzling type is not known in graves in southern central Europe, which makes its exact dating very problematic in that region.

[11] Admittedly, this identical treatment of all the bronzes could also be due to ritualised behaviour, which might have been compulsory for ideological reasons and therefore observed during every act of deposition.

At Krini, chamber tomb 3, the warrior buried with an Allerona sword unfortunately is not accompanied by pottery (PAPAZOGLOU-MANIOUDAKI 1994, 174, fig. 2:upper; 175, fig. 3; 178 figs. 4–5; 181, pls. 24b–c; 26; 27a). The pottery assemblage from the relevant burial layer ranges in date from LH III C Early to LH III C Advanced. According to Lena Papazoglou-Manioudaki the sword burial D is not the earliest interment in the sequence of that layer. A group of LH III C Early vessels accompanied the alleged earliest interment A (IBID., 181, 188–190, figs. 10–14). In view of this stratigraphic situation Papazoglou-Manioudaki concludes: *"a more advanced date may be suggested for the Krini sword"* (IBID., 181). The latest amongst the vessels in the tomb are two stirrup jars, which were found between the heads of burials A and B. Their barred handles and the groups of wiggly lines upon the shoulder are indications for a date not earlier than LH III C Advanced, if we judge by the Argive settlement sequences (PAPAZOGLOU-MANIOUDAKI 1994, 174, fig. 2:upper; 188 nos. 9–10; 191, figs. 17:9; 18:10, pl. 33. – Cf. stratified pieces from Tiryns, Lower Citadel, in LH III C Advanced and III C Late layers: PODZUWEIT 1992, chapter "Kleine Bügelkanne", Beil. 60: "Henkel no. 4"[12]). However, the warrior with the Allerona-type sword may be even later in date than the latest pots in the chamber, if he was buried without ceramic vessels after the other persons who were given ceramic grave goods.

In the single grave 18 in Tumulus I at Barç in southern Albania a skeleton was found together with a very short version of an Allerona-type sword and a Mycenaean amphoriskos, probably imported from Achaea (ANDREA 1985, 23, pls. 3:V.18:1–2; 43:2. – KILIAN-DIRLMEIER 1993, 100 no. 269 [erroneously ascribed to Tumulus II], pl. 40:269). The pommel spur of the sword is broken off now, but there is no doubt that it once existed. The amphoriskos with a height of 11.5 cm, a belly diameter of 11 cm and a rim diameter of 6.2 cm (ANDREA 1985, 23, tomb 18 no. 1) shows a banded decoration that belongs to those heavy variants that were common – mainly on stirrup jars – since LH III C Developed and were especially popular during LH III C Advanced and Late (at Tiryns, Lower Citadel,[13] and at Perati, Phases II and III[14]). I refer here in particular to the upper part of the amphoriskos. Sigrid Deger-Jalkotzy demonstrates that this decoration is especially typical for central Greece (DEGER-JALKOTZY this volume). Judging by its decoration the amphoriskos from Barç may be dated from LH III C Developed to Late, probably to LH III C Advanced. Its shape has parallels in Achaea – as usual for the Late Mycenaean pots in Albania – and seems to belong to the later phases of LH III C, i.e. Advanced or rather Late. However, there are no stratigraphic sequences available in publication which would provide good parallels.

---

[12] The closed grave contexts from the necropolis at Voúdeni may eventually show if in Achaea the use of these motifs on stirrup jars started at the same time as in the Argolid.

[13] Broad zones alternating with groups of thin lines on stirrup jars: PODZUWEIT 1983, 383, 385, figs. 8 (LH III C Advanced); 9 (LH III C Late instead of "Advanced"). – PODZUWEIT 1992, chapter "Kleine Bügelkanne", pls. 83:2 (LH III C Late); 87:8 (LH III C Late); 88:5 (LH III C Advanced). – Broad zones alternating with single thin lines on stirrup jars: PODZUWEIT 1983, 383, 393, fig. 13:14. – PODZUWEIT 1992, chapter "Kleine Bügelkanne", pl. 83:1 (LH III C Late).

[14] Broad zones alternating with groups of thin lines on stirrup jars in chamber tombs at Perati: Chamber tomb 10, burial in the centre (phase II, LH III C Advanced): IAKOVIDIS 1969/70, vol. 1, 263, 265 nos. 162, 164; vol. 2, 400 tab.; vol. 3, pl. 76:β164,γ162. – Chamber tomb 36, burial in the SW corner (phases II–III, LH III C Advanced–Late): IAKOVIDIS 1969/70, vol. 1, 275–276, 278 no. 414; vol. 2, 400 tab.; vol. 3, pl. 79:414. – Chamber tomb 148, burial along the western wall (phase II): IAKOVIDIS 1969/70, vol. 1, 129, 131 nos. 124–125; vol. 2, 400 tab.; vol. 3, pl. 39:β1124,1125. – Chamber tomb 92, probably belonging to the last burial (phase III, LH III C Late): IAKOVIDIS 1969/70, vol. 1, 201–203 nos. 708, 710; vol. 2, 400 tab.; vol. 3, pl. 60:γ708,710.

The sword from chamber tomb A at Kallithéa-Spénzes is also most probably a type C/Allerona specimen (KILIAN-DIRLMEIER 1993, 98). Unfortunately the warrior equipped with this weapon received only one ceramic vessel which can be ascribed securely to his grave goods (YALOURIS 1960, 43–44, Beil. 27–29; 30:1. – PAPADOPOULOS 1978/79, vol. 2, 89, fig. 113d; 182, fig. 206d; 288–290, figs. 312a–314a; 296, fig. 320a[lower],b[lower]; 323, fig. 347; 324, fig. 348a–b; 326, fig. 350a; 331, fig. 355c–d). It is a rare variety of a globular stirrup jar on a stemmed foot, which has been dated to LH III C Middle by Mountjoy because of the lozenge and zigzag patterns that reoccur on Close Style stirrup jars.[15] That would be LH III C Advanced according to the stratigraphic data for Close Style vessels from Tiryns (PODZUWEIT 1992, chapters "Krater"; "Kleine Bügelkanne"; "Charakterisierung der Phasen"). If however the monochrome Achaea amphora with elaborate spiral patterns in the reserved belly and shoulder zone originally belonged to this burial in chamber tomb A (YALOURIS 1960, 43 no. 3, Beil. 30:2. – PAPADOPOULOS 1978/79, vol. 2, 34, fig. 56d), a date of the sword burial to a rather late stage of LH III C Advanced or even to LH III C Late must be considered. This is the case, because the monochrome decoration with reserved zones carrying different motifs was introduced no earlier than LH III C Advanced and became more common by LH III C Late (PODZUWEIT 1992, chapters "Monochromer Skyphos"; "Amphoriskos"; "Charakteri-sierung der Phasen". – Cf. IAKOVIDIS 1969/70, vol. 2, 402).

Chamber tomb 2 at Spaliaréika-Lousiká provides us with a number of good burial contexts, for which a whole sequence may be reconstructed. Two burials in the tomb were equipped with Naue II swords, one with a type A or Cetona specimen along the western chamber wall and one with a type C or Allerona sword in pit 2 in the north-eastern corner of the chamber. The older burials of the chamber were found along the south wall of the chamber (PETROPOULOS 2000, 68–69, drawing 4; 82, fig. 5). They consist of the groups A, B, Γ and Δ. The pottery of groups B and Γ can be dated to LH III C Early (PETROPOULOS 2000, 75, 86, fig. 24:π9879,π9881,π10429; 88, figs. 30–32; 33:π9883, π9887,π9888), while group A may fall into LH III C Developed (PETROPOULOS 2000, 75, 86, figs. 22–23 and 24:π10433).[16] Group Δ in the south-western corner of the chamber includes three stirrup jars. At least two of them seem to exhibit Minoan influence or are even Cretan imports, probably of LM III C Early (PETROPOULOS 2000, 75, 88, fig. 33:π9880; 89, fig. 34:π10434).[17]

The next burial in the sequence would be the warrior in pit 2 in the north-eastern corner of the chamber. This deposition includes amongst other things a type C/Allerona sword (Fig. 3:9) and a stirrup jar, the sole piece of pottery (PETROPOULOS 2000, 76, 86, fig. 21:π4161; 87, fig. 28:μ4651; fig. 29:μ4957; 90, fig. 41:μ4650; fig. 42; 91 figs. 43–46). This biconical stirrup jar has horizontally barred handles and a shoulder pattern con-

---

[15] *RMDP*, 427–428 with fig. 150:96. – For this kind of zigzag body pattern see examples in LH III C Advanced (PODZUWEIT 1983, 385, fig. 8. – PODZUWEIT 1992, pl. 88:5) and Late (PODZUWEIT 1983, 379, fig. 5:1; 385, fig. 9 [both LH III C Late instead of "Advanced"]. – PODZUWEIT 1992, pls. 83:2; 86:1).

[16] The neck-handled amphora FT 70 (no. π10620) is the main argument in favour of a date later than LH III C Early, as this type (in its painted version) starts in LH III C Developed in the Tiryns sequence (PODZUWEIT 1992, chapter "Amphoren"). However, the angular alabastron and the Achaea amphora do not seem to be far from LH III C Early style. Therefore it seems plausible to assign group A to LH III C Developed.

[17] MOSCHOS 2002, 26, 41, pl. 1:3, has already suggested a Cretan provenance for π10434. π9880 may also be Minoan by the criterion of the triple shoulder loop connecting handle and neck attachments. At present group Δ cannot be dated in Mycenaean terms, because these two stirrup jars are the only published pottery items in this complex. Only mention is made of a third stirrup jar, and a small bronze knife is not closely datable (cf. PETROPOULOS 2000, 75, 87, fig. 28:μ4644). The excavator suggests a dating to LH III C Middle for this group.

sisting of complex filled triangles (Fig. 3:8). The whole body is decorated with evenly spaced thin bands of equal width, which is the characteristic decoration scheme of closed vessels produced in Achaea and Elis. Outside this region the earliest attestation of this decoration is found on an imported (probably Achaean) stirrup jar in the last stratigraphic horizon (21a1) of LH III C Developed in the Lower Citadel of Tiryns (PODZUWEIT 1983, 369, fig. 3:3; 383–384. – ID. 1992, pl. 88:4[18]). Judging by its stylistic details the stirrup jar found at Tiryns might be somewhat earlier than the densely banded one from Spaliaréika. Another example from Aigeira, Phase II (LH III C Advanced [–Late]), is closer in style to the one from Spaliaréika (DEGER-JALKOTZY 2003, 70, fig. 6:2). A seemingly locally produced closed vessel from Thebes, Pelopídhou Street, layer 1a (ANDRIKOU 2006, 45, 88 cat. no. 355, 122, pl. 22:355), shows the same kind of decoration and is dated to LH III C Advanced by the accompanying pottery from that layer.[19] A date to LH III C Advanced for the grave gift of the Achaean warrior would also be in good agreement with the handle decoration (cf. above) and the complex shoulder pattern.

The last burial in the chamber tomb is said to be the warrior along the western chamber wall (PETROPOULOS 2000, 68, 71, 75–76, 87, fig. 28:μ4646,μ4647; fig. 29:μ4648,μ4649; 89, fig. 34:π10435; figs. 35–37; 90, fig. 38:π9885,π9890,π9892; figs. 39–40; fig. 41:μ4645). He had a type A/Cetona sword and a number of ceramic vessels which date to LH III C Advanced or even more probable LH III C Late, in view of the frequent reserved patterned or unpainted zones on monochrome pots in this assemblage (cf. above). It is noteworthy that the stirrup jars with evenly spaced bands now have a monochrome lower body. The date of the pottery thus confirms the classification of this burial as the last one in the tomb.

Chamber tomb 3 at Pórtes in Achaea contained a warrior burial with bronze body armour and an Allerona sword. On the published photos a kalathos with dotted rim and evenly spaced bands on the exterior and interior can be discerned. It is located close to the head of the deceased, while the sword lies to the left of his feet (KOLONAS 2000, 96 with fig. 3:22. – KOLONAS – MOSCHOS 2000, 218, pl. 83β). This vessel points to a date of the burial to LH III C Advanced according to the production period of Achaean stirrup jars decorated in the same way (cf. above).[20]

To sum up, the Allerona type of Naue II swords is attested in the Aegean since the phase LH III C Advanced. There is no context that might securely be dated earlier than this. In Italy the type is present since RBA 2 (or possibly FBA 1). If we combine the results of the discussions of pottery and bronze artefacts, we can draw now the line between RBA 2 and FBA 1 during the phase LH III C Advanced. Thus, LH III C Advanced would encompass both the end of RBA 2 and FBA 1. This is entirely possible, since FBA 1 seems to have been a rather short phase in Italy (CARANCINI – PERONI 1999, 18), while LH III C Advanced – judging by the settlement horizons at Tiryns – was a lengthy phase indeed (cf. PODZUWEIT 1992, chapters "Die Stratigraphie von Tiryns"; "Geschlossene Komplexe Unterburg", Beil. 86). Thus, the flourishing Late Mycenaean phase LH III C Advanced would coincide with an intensification of transadriatic/Mycenaean – Italian contacts at the end of the Recent and the beginning

---

[18] LXII 44/9, Ofl. X, R 127 (inscription on the sherd: "LXII 44/9, Ofl. X, R 127a"), stratigraphic assignation to horizon 21a1 according to a personal information by Tobias Mühlenbruch, pottery date according Podzuweit's pottery phases for the horizons of Tiryns, Lower Citadel.

[19] Cf. ANDRIKOU 2006, 14, 32, tab. 6, 38–39, tab. 7B, 44–49, 122–124, pl. 22–24, 155–167, pl. 55–67, 175 pl. 75:146–150: monochrome deep bowls with reserved bands on the belly or with a reserved decorative zone, Close Style motifs, krater with slashed rib below the rim etc.

[20] I would like to thank Ioannis Moschos for sending me a photo of that kalathos. My earlier discussion of its decoration based on the published excavation photographs (JUNG 2006, 205) has to be corrected.

of the Final Bronze Age. In some regions this intense contact continued into FBA 2/ LH III C Late–Submycenaean. That, however, is yet another story (for the comparative chronology of the later phases see JUNG 2005. – For the post-palatial Mycenaean – Italian contacts see amongst others EDER – JUNG 2005. – JUNG 2007).

Index to illustrations

Fig. 1 Deep bowl and closed vessel from Broglio di Trebisacce, RBA 1 (**1**, **4**), from Pylos, palace destruction (**2**) and from Tiryns Palace debris, LH III B Developed–Final (**3**) (after VAGNETTI – PANICHELLI 1994, 384, pl. 75:12; 380, pl. 73:12. – *RMDP*, 351, fig. 120:112. – VOIGTLÄNDER 2003, pl. 117:TA 9)

Fig. 2 Large closed vessels from Broglio di Trebisacce, RBA 2 (**1–4**), from Tiryns, Lower Citadel, LH III C Advanced (**5**) and from Aplómata, Tomb B, LH III C Advanced–Late (**6**) (after VAGNETTI – PANICHELLI 1994, 379, pl. 72:3; 387, pl. 77:2; 391, pl. 79:5,13. – PODZUWEIT 1983, 382, fig. 7. – *RMDP*, 948, fig. 386:27)

Fig. 3 Carinated Handmade Burnished/*impasto* cups from Korákou, House P (**1**), from Broglio di Trebisacce, FBA 2 (**2**) and from Torre Mordillo, FBA 1 (**3**, **4**). Naue II swords, type C/Allerona (**5**) and type A/Cetona (**6**), and Pertosa-type dagger (**7**) from Pila del Brancón; stirrup jar (**8**) and Naue II sword, type C/Allerona (**9**), from Spaliaréika-Lousiká, tomb 2, scale 1:3 (after RUTTER 1975, 22 no. 13. – BUFFA 1994, 459, pl. 83:1. – ARANCIO ET AL. 2001, 90, fig. 44:4; 138, fig. 75:16 – SALZANI 1994, 84, fig. 1:1–2; 85 fig. 2:8. – PETROPOULOS 2000, 90, fig. 41:μ4650; 91 fig. 46)

Bibliography

ADRIMI-SISMANI, V.
2003 "Μυκηναϊκή Ιωλκός", *AAA* 32–34, 1999–2001 [2003], 71–100.
2006 "Η γκρίζα ψευδομινύεια και η στιλβωμένη χειροποίητη κεραμική από τον Μυκηναϊκό οικισμό Διμηνίου", 85–110 in: *Αρχαιολογικό Έργο*.

AISA, M. G. – A. M. TUCCI
2004 "L'età del Bronzo nel territorio di Cirò Marina (KR)", 849–853 in: *Istituto Italiano di Preistoria e Protostoria: Atti della XXXVII Riunione Scientifica "Preistoria e protostoria della Calabria", Scalea, Papasidero, Praia a Mare, Tortora, 29 settembre – 4 ottobre 2002*. Florence.

ALESSANDRI, L. – I. CASSETTA – D. GATTI
2004 "Il Bronzo finale nella Calabria settentrionale", 393–402 in: *Istituto Italiano di Preistoria e Protostoria: Atti della XXXVII Riunione Scientifica "Preistoria e protostoria della Calabria", Scalea, Papasidero, Praia a Mare, Tortora, 29 settembre – 4 ottobre 2002*. Florence.

ALBERTI, L. – M. BETTELLI
2005 "Contextual Problems of Mycenaean Pottery in Italy", 547–559 in: LAFFINEUR – GRECO 2005.

ALRAM-STERN, E. – G. NIGHTINGALE (eds.)
2007 *Keimelion. Elitenbildung und elitärer Konsum von der mykenischen Palastzeit bis zur homerischen Epoche. The Formation of Elites and Elitist Lifestyles from Mycenaean Palatial Times to the Homeric Period. Akten des internationalen Kongresses vom 3. bis 5. Februar 2005 in Salzburg* (Veröffentlichungen der Mykenischen Kommission 27). Vienna.

ANDREA, Z.
1985 *Kultura ilire e tumave në pellgun e Korçës*. Tirana.

ANDRIKOU, E.
2006 "The Late Helladic III Pottery", 11–179 in: ANDRIKOU – ARAVANTINOS – GODART – SACCONI – VROOM 2006.

ANDRIKOU, E. – V. L. ARAVANTINOS – L. GODART – A. SACCONI – J. VROOM
2006 *Thèbes. Fouilles de la Cadmée II.2. Les tablettes en linéaire B de la Odos Pelopidou. Le contexte archéologique. La céramique de la Odos Pelopidou et la chronologie du linéaire B*. Pisa – Rome.

ARANCIO, M. L. – V. BUFFA – I. DAMIANI – F. TRUCCO
2001 "3. Catalogo delle unità stratigrafiche e dei reperti", 61–153 in: TRUCCO – VAGNETTI 2001.

Αρχαιολογικό Έργο
2006   Αρχαιολογικό Έργο Θεσσαλίας και Στερεάς Ελλάδας. Πρακτικά επιστημονικής συνάντησης, Βόλος 27.2–2.3.2003. Volos 2006.

BELARDELLI, C. – M. A. CASTAGNA – I. DAMIANI – A. DE GUIO – A. DI RENZONI – S. T. LEVI – R. PERONI – A. SCHIAPPELLI – A. VANZETTI
2005   "L'impatto miceneo sulle coste dello Jonio e dell'Adriatico e l''Alta Congiuntura' del Bronzo recente italiano", 507–513 in: LAFFINEUR – GRECO 2005.

BERNABÒ-BREA, L. – M. CAVALIER
1980   Meligunìs Lipára IV. L'acropoli di Lipari nella preistoria. Palermo.

BETTELLI, M.
2002   Italia meridionale e mondo miceneo. Ricerche su dinamiche di acculturazione e aspetti archeologici, con particolare riferimento ai versanti adriatico e ionico della penisola italiana (Grandi contesti e problemi della Protostoria italiana 5). Florence.

BETTELLI, M. – S. T. LEVI – L. VAGNETTI
2001/02 "Cronologia, topografia e funzione dei siti con testimonianze micenee in Italia meridionale", Geografia Antiqua 10/11, 65–95.

BIANCO PERONI, V.
1970   Die Schwerter in Italien / Le spade nell'Italia continentale (Prähistorische Bronzefunde IV 1). Munich.
1994   I pugnali nell'Italia Continentale (Prähistorische Bronzefunde VI 10). Stuttgart.

BORGNA, E.
2000/01 "I ripostigli del Friuli: proposta di seriazione cronologica e di interpretazione funzionale", Rivista di Scienze Preistoriche 51, 289–335.

BUFFA, V.
1994   "8. I materiali del Bronzo finale e della prima età del ferro", 455–569 in: PERONI – TRUCCO 1994.

CARANCINI, G. L. – R. PERONI
1999   L'età del bronzo in Italia: per una cronologia della produzione metallurgica (Quaderni di Protostoria 2). Città di Castello.

CAZZELLA, A. – M. MOSCOLONI
1987   "I materiali dell'età del Bronzo di Coppa Nevigata", 146–188 in: Coppa Nevigata e il suo territorio. Testimonianze archeologiche dal VII al II millennio a.C. Rome.

CINQUEPALMI, A. – F. RADINA
1998   Documenti dell'età del bronzo. Ricerche lungo il versante adriatico pugliese. Fasano di Brindisi.

CLAUSING, C.
2005   Untersuchungen zu den urnenfelderzeitlichen Gräbern mit Waffenbeigaben vom Alpenkamm bis zur Südzone des Nordischen Kreises. Eine Analyse ihrer Grabinventare und Grabformen (BAR-IS 1375). Oxford.

COPPOLA, D. – P. RAIMONDI
1996   "L'insediamento dell'età del Bronzo di Torre S. Sabina (scavi 1990)", Taras 15,2, 1995 [1996], 375–394.

COPPOLA, D. – A. CINQUEPALMI
1998   "Torre Santa Sabina", 147–162 in: CINQUEPALMI – RADINA 1998.

COCCHI GENICK, D.
2004a   (ed.) L'età del bronzo recente in Italia. Atti del Congresso Nazionale di Lido di Camaiore, 26–29 ottobre 2000. Viareggio.
2004b   "Le ceramiche nel ruolo di indicatori cronologici e regionali", 22–52 in: COCCHI GENICK 2004a.

D'AGATA, A. L.
2005   "Central Southern Crete and its Relations with the Greek Mainland in the Postpalatial Period", 109–130 in: Ariadne's Threads.

DEGER-JALKOTZY, S.
2003   "Stratified Pottery Deposits from the Late Helladic III C Settlement at Aigeira/Achaia", 53–75 in: LH III C Chronology and Synchronisms.

DÖHL, H.
1973   "Iria. Die Ergebnisse der Ausgrabungen 1939", 127–194 in: Tiryns. Forschungen und Berichte 6. Mainz.

EDER, B. – R. JUNG
2005 "On the Character of Social Relations between Greece and Italy in the 12th/11th C. BC", 485–495 in: LAFFINEUR – GRECO 2005.

GRECO, E. (ed.)
2002 *Gli Achei e l'identità etnica degli Achei d'Occidente. Atti del Convegno Internazionale di Studi, Paestum, 23–25 febbraio 2001* (Tekmeria 3). Paestum – Athens.

GUGLIELMINO, R.
2005 "Rocavecchia: Nuove testimonianze di relazioni con l'Egeo e il mediterraneo orientale nell'età del Bronzo", 637–651 in: LAFFINEUR – GRECO 2005.

HÄNSEL, A. – B. HÄNSEL (eds.)
1997 *Gaben an die Götter. Schätze der Bronzezeit Europas* (Freie Universität Berlin und Museum für Vor- und Frühgeschichte, Staatliche Museen zu Berlin, Bestandskataloge Band 4). Berlin.

HARDING, A.
1995 *Die Schwerter im ehemaligen Jugoslawien* (Prähistorische Bronzefunde IV 14). Stuttgart.

IAKOVIDIS, S. E.
1969/70 Περατή. Το νεκροταφείον (Βιβλιοθήκη της εν Αθήναις Αρχαιολογικής Εταιρείας 67). Athens.

JONES, R. E. – L. LAZZARINI – M. MARIOTTINI – E. ORVINI
1994 "7.4. Appendice: studio minero-petrografico e chimico di ceramiche protostoriche da Broglio di Trebisacce (Sibari)", 413–454 in: PERONI – TRUCCO 1994.

JUNG, R.
2005 "Πότε; Quando? Wann? Quand? When? – Translating Italo-Aegean Synchronisms", 473–484 in: LAFFINEUR – GRECO 2005.
2006a *Χρονολογία comparata. Vergleichende Chronologie von Südgriechenland und Süditalien von ca. 1700/1600 v.u.Z.* (DenkschrWien 348 = Veröffentlichungen der Mykenischen Kommission 26). Vienna.
2006b "Review of Walter Voigtländer, Die Palastkeramik. Tiryns. Forschungen und Berichte 10. Mainz 2003", *Germania* 84, 189–195.
2007 "Goldene Vögel und Sonnen: ideologische Kontakte zwischen Italien und der postpalatialen Ägäis", 219–255 in: ALRAM-STERN – NIGHTINGALE 2007.

KARDARA, C.
1977 Απλώματα Νάξου. Κινητά ευρήματα τάφων Α και Β (Βιβλιοθήκη της εν Αθήναις Αρχαιολογικής Εταιρείας 88). Athens.

KILIAN-DIRLMEIER, I.
1993 *Die Schwerter in Griechenland (außerhalb der Peloponnes), Bulgarien und Albanien* (Prähistorische Bronzefunde IV 12). Stuttgart.

KOLONAS, L.
2000 "Μυκηναϊκές εγκαταστάσεις στην ορεινή Δυμαία Χώρα", 93–98 in: RIZAKIS 2000.

KOLONAS, L. – Y. MOSCHOS
2000 "Πόρτες", *ArchDelt* 50, 1995 [2000], Chron 217–218.

LAFFINEUR, R. – E. GRECO (eds.)
2005 *Emporia. Aegeans in the Central and Eastern Mediterranean. Proceedings of the 10th International Aegean Conference/10e Rencontre égéenne internationale, Athens, Italian School of Archaeology, 14–18 April 2004* (Aegaeum 25). Liège – Austin.

MOSCHOS, I.
2002 "Western Achaea during the LH III C Period. Approaching the Latest Excavation Evidence", 15–41 in: GRECO 2002.

MOUNTJOY, P. A.
1997 "The Destruction of the Palace at Pylos Reconsidered", *BSA* 92, 109–137.

ONASSOGLOU, A.
1995 Η οικία του τάφου των τριπόδων στις Μυκήνες (Βιβλιοθήκη της εν Αθήναις Αρχαιολογικής Εταιρείας 147). Athens.

PAPADOPOULOS, TH. J.
1978/79 *Mycenaean Achaea* (SIMA 55,1–2). Göteborg.

PAPAZOGLOU-MANIOUDAKI, L.
1994 "A Mycenaean Warrior's Tomb at Krini near Patras", *BSA* 89, 171–200.

PERONI, R.
1984 (ed.) *Nuove ricerche sulla protostoria della Sibaritide*. Rome.
1996 *L'Italia alle soglie della storia*. Rome – Bari.
2005 "Il Bronzo finale e la prima età del ferro nelle Marche", 721–738 in: *Istituto Italiano di Preistoria e Protostoria: Atti della XXXVIII Riunione Scientifica "Preistoria e protostoria delle Marche", Portonovo, Abbadia di Fiastra 1–5 ottobre 2003*. Florence.

PERONI, R. – F. TRUCCO (eds.)
1994 *Enotri e Micenei nella Sibaritide I. Broglio di Trebisacce*. Taranto.

PETROPOULOS, M.
2000 "Μυκηναϊκό νεκροταφείο στα Σπαλιαρέϊκα των Λουσικών", 65–92 in: RIZAKIS 2000.

PODZUWEIT, C.
1978 "Ausgrabungen in Tiryns 1976. Bericht zur spätmykenischen Keramik", *AA*, 471–498.
1983 "Ausgrabungen in Tiryns 1981. Bericht zur spätmykenischen Keramik: Die Phasen SH III C Fortgeschritten bis Spät", *AA*, 359–402.
1992 *Studien zur spätmykenischen Keramik, vorgelegt der Philosophischen Fakultät der Rheinischen Friedrich-Wilhelms-Universität zu Bonn als Habilitationsschrift* (Bonn 1992; in press for the *Tiryns* series) (plates are referred to according to the forthcoming printed edition).

RAISON, J.
1968 *Les vases à inscriptions peintes de l'âge mycénien et leur contexte archéologique* (Incunabula Graeca 19). Rome.

RIZAKIS, A. D. (ed.)
2000 *Αχαϊκό τοπίο II. Δύμη και Δυμαία Χώρα. Πρακτικά του Συνεδρίου "Δυμαία-Βουπρασά", Κάτω Αχαΐα, 6–8 Οκτωβρίου 1995. Paysages d'Achaïe II. Dymé et son territoire. Actes du colloque international: Dymaia et Bouprasia, Katô Achaïa 6–8 Octobre 1995* (Meletemata 29). Athens.

RUTTER, J. B.
1974 *The Late Helladic III B and III C Periods at Korakou and Gonia in the Corinthia*. (Ph.D. dissertation, University of Pennsylvania [Ann Arbor Nr. 48106]).
1975 "Ceramic Evidence for Northern Intruders in Southern Greece at the Beginning of the Late Helladic III C Period", *AJA* 79, 17–32.
2003 "The Nature and Potential Significance of Minoan Features in the Earliest Late Helladic III C Ceramic Assemblages of the Central and Southern Greek Mainland", 193–216 in: *LH III C Chronology and Synchronisms*.

SALZANI, L.
1994 "Nogara. Rinvenimento di un ripostiglio di bronzi in località «Pila del Brancón»", *Quaderni di Archeologia del Veneto* 10, 83–94.
1998 "Segnalazioni di rinvenimenti archeologici nel Veronese", *Quaderni di Archeologia del Veneto* 14, 66–71.

SCHAUER, P.
1971 *Die Schwerter in Süddeutschland, Österreich und der Schweiz I (Griffplatten, Griffangel- und Griffzungenschwerter)* (Prähistorische Bronzefunde IV 2). Munich.

SCHWENZER, ST.
1995 "‚Wanderer kommst Du nach Spa…'. Der Opferplatz von Berlin-Spandau. Ein Heiligtum für Krieger, Händler und Reisende", 61–66 in: HÄNSEL A. – HÄNSEL B. 1997.

SETTIS, S. – M. C. PARRA (eds.)
2005 *Magna Grecia – archeologia di un sapere. Exhibition Catalogue, Catanzaro*. Martellago (Venice).

STAMPOLIDIS, N. C. (ed.)
2001 *Πρακτικά του Συμποσίου 'Καύσεις στην Εποχή του Χαλκού και την πρώιμη Εποχή του Σιδήρου', Ρόδος, 29 Απριλίου – 2 Μαΐου 1999*. Athens.

STAMPOLIDIS, N. C. – V. KARAGEORGHIS (eds.)
2003 *Sea Routes ... Interconnections in the Mediterranean 16th–6th c. BC. Proceedings of the International Symposium Held at Rethymnon, Crete in September 29th–October 2nd 2002*. Athens.

TRUCCO, F. – L. VAGNETTI (eds.)
2001 *Torre Mordillo 1987–1990. Le relazioni egee di una comunità protostorica della Sibaritide* (Incunabula Graeca 101). Rome.

VAGNETTI, L.
1984 "2.5. Ceramica di importazione egea e ceramica dipinta dell'età del bronzo", 169–196 in: PERONI 1984.
2001 "10. Le ceramice egeo-micenee", 299–328 in: TRUCCO – VAGNETTI 2001.
2003 "The Role of Crete in the Exchange between the Aegean and the Central Mediterranean in the Second Millennium BC", 53–61 in: STAMPOLIDIS – KARAGEORGHIS 2003.

VAGNETTI, L. – ST. PANICHELLI
1994 "7. Ceramica egea importata e di produzione locale", 373–413 in: PERONI – TRUCCO 1994.

VOIGTLÄNDER, W.
2003 *Die Palastkeramik* (Tiryns. Forschungen und Berichte 10). Mainz.

WACE, A. J. B.
1921–23 "Excavations at Mycenae § VII. – The Lion Gate and Grave Circle Area. 2. The Granary", *BSA* 25, 38–61.

WARDLE, K. A.
1973 "A Group of Late Helladic III B2 Pottery from within the Citadel at Mycenae – 'The Causeway Deposit'", *BSA* 68, 297–348.

WATROUS, L. V.
1992 *Kommos III. The Late Bronze Age Pottery*. Princeton.

WÜSTEMANN, H.
2004 *Die Schwerter in Ostdeutschland*. Prähistorische Bronzefunde IV 15. Stuttgart.

YALOURIS, N.
1960 "Mykenische Bronzeschutzwaffen", *AM* 75, 1960, 42–67.

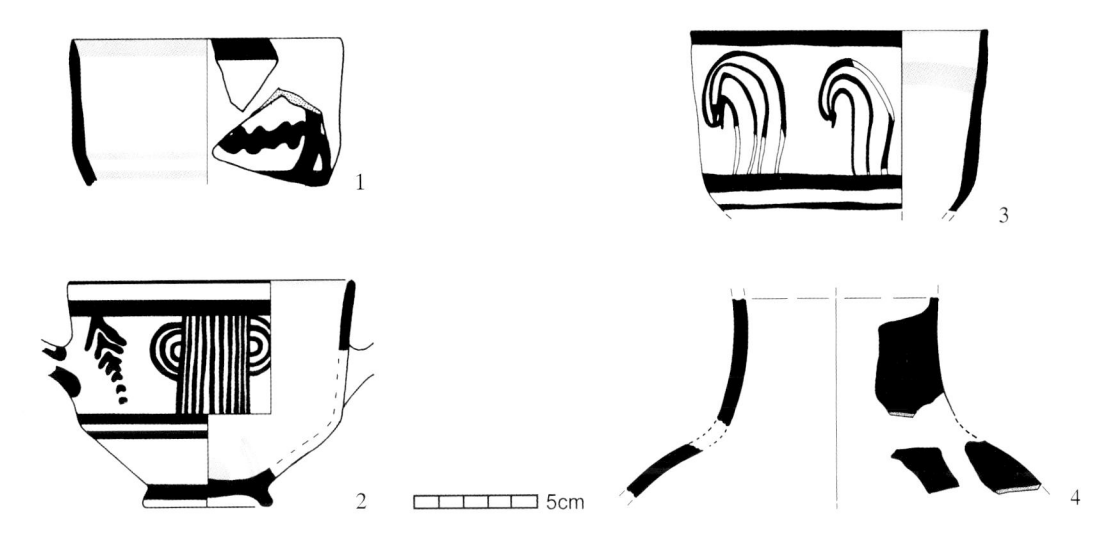

Fig. 1 Deep bowl and closed vessel from Broglio di Trebisacce, RBA 1 (1, 4), from Pylos, palace destruction (2) and from Tiryns Palace debris, LH III B Developed-Final (3) (scale 1:3)

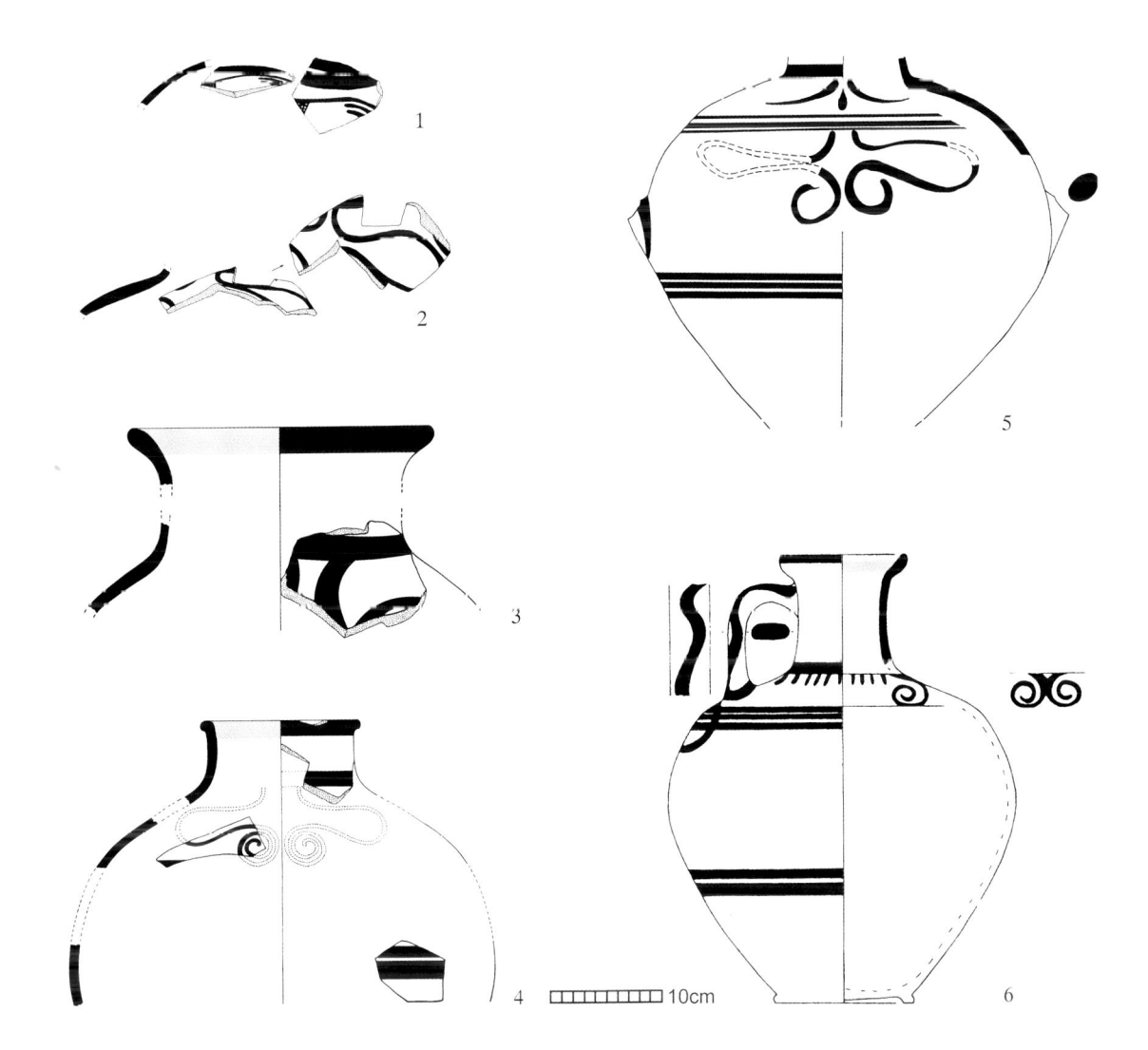

Fig. 2 Large closed vessels from Broglio di Trebisacce, RBA 2 (1–4), from Tiryns, Lower Citadel, LH III C Advanced (5) and from Aplómata, Tomb B, LH III C Advanced–Late (6) (scale 1:6)

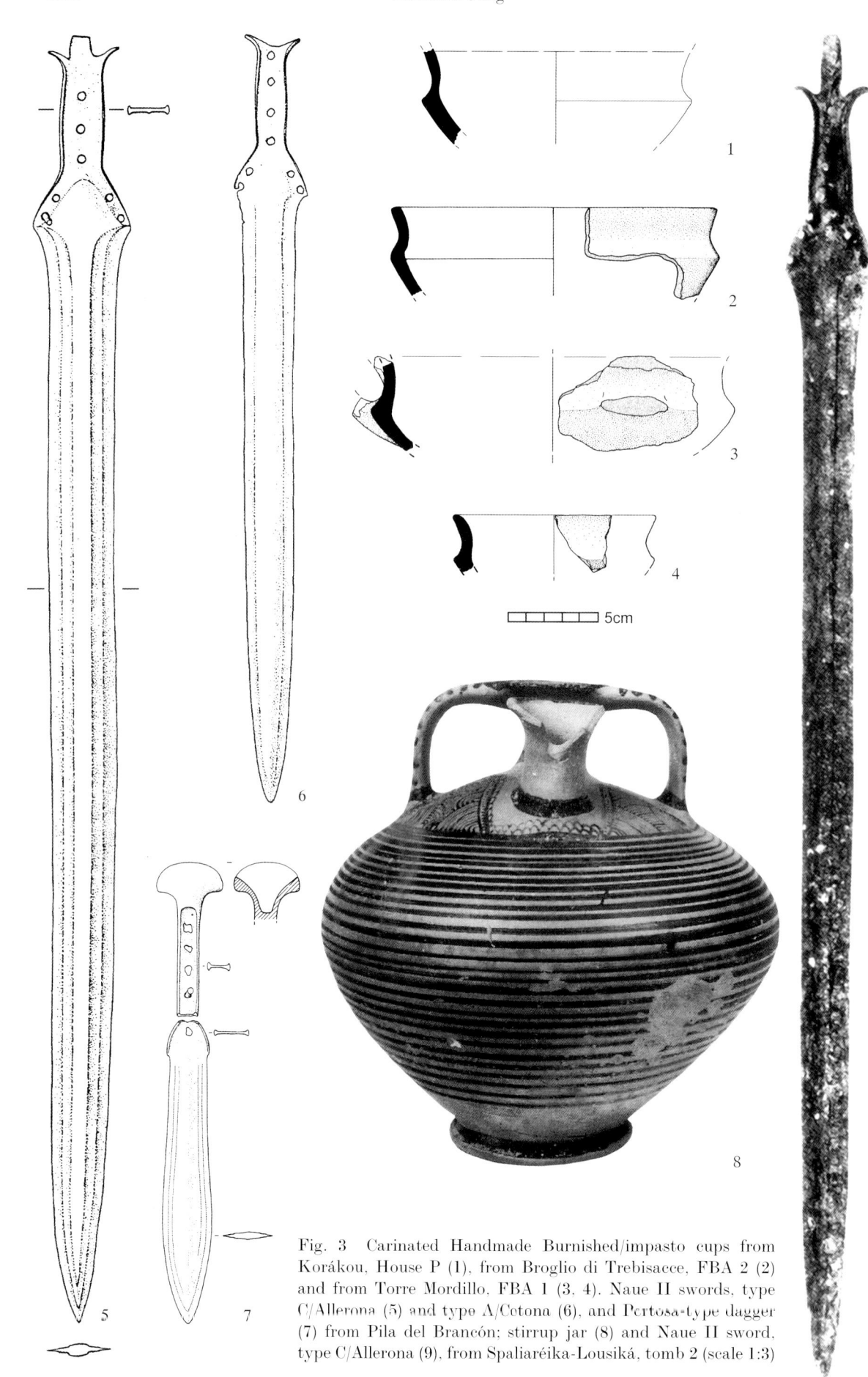

Fig. 3 Carinated Handmade Burnished/impasto cups from Korákou, House P (1), from Broglio di Trebisacce, FBA 2 (2) and from Torre Mordillo, FBA 1 (3, 4). Naue II swords, type C/Allerona (5) and type A/Cetona (6), and Pertosa-type dagger (7) from Pila del Brancón; stirrup jar (8) and Naue II sword, type C/Allerona (9), from Spaliaréika-Lousiká, tomb 2 (scale 1:3)

PENELOPE A. MOUNTJOY

A DEFINITION OF LH III C MIDDLE

LH III C Middle is difficult to define owing to the lack of stratified deposits, although there are characteristic types and styles. No settlement material is comprehensively published apart from that from the Granary at Mycenae (WACE 1921–23, 38–61), the small deposits from Iria (DÖHL 1973) and Korakou House P (RUTTER 1974, 134–316) and the unstratified Athens Fountain House fill (BRONEER 1939), but the preliminary publication of the material from Lefkandi (POPHAM – MILBURN 1971) provides much information. Most of the corpus, however, comes from re-used chamber tombs and can only be differentiated stylistically; some stratigraphy can be seen in the LH III C cemetery at Perati (IAKOVIDIS 1969/70), which was a new foundation at the end of LH III B, but in this cemetery some of the material from burials assigned to Phase III is identical to that of Phase II suggesting some overlap.

The definition of LH III C Middle has changed slightly from that published in 1986 (*MDP*, 133 table II, 155–180), where I followed Rutter's definition (RUTTER 1977. – RUTTER 1978) (Fig. 1). In *RMDP*, 38–41, I reassigned the Lefkandi phases because stylistic reassessment of the material suggested that Lefkandi Phase 2b should belong to LH III C Late rather than to LH III C Middle advanced and that Lefkandi Phase 2a begins late in LH III C Middle developed, but equates almost entirely to LH III C Middle advanced, not to LH III C Middle developed, as stated in *MDP*. This conclusion is based on the fact that features of Lefkandi 2a, such as kraters with slashed ribs, kalathoi with interior pictorial decoration, trefoil-mouthed jugs, trays, streamers and antithetic loops begin in LH III C Middle (advanced) at Mycenae together with the Close Style. No Close Style has been published from Lefkandi, but a kylix sherd with triangular patch and streamers looks like a poor imitation of it (POPHAM – MILBURN 1971, pl. 55:3 right). Since this pottery appears in the advanced phase of LH III C Middle at Mycenae not in the developed phase, it suggests that Lefkandi Phase 2a should also equate to this phase. In contrast the decoration of Lefkandi Phase 2b is more sparse and the Pictorial Style may not have survived. This does not correspond at all with the lively pottery styles of LH III C Middle (advanced) in the Argolid. Even allowing for regionalism contacts between the different areas were close and ideas moved fast. The pottery of Lefkandi Phase 2b is most akin to that of LH III C Late. This reassignment seems to have met with general acceptance.

Thus LH III C Middle is now defined by the developed and advanced phases at Mycenae, that is Phases XIa and XIb, Lefkandi Phases 1b and 2a and Perati Phase II. However, it is difficult to apply the division elsewhere, since the developed phase is elusive.

LH III C MIDDLE DEVELOPED

This phase was originally defined at Mycenae (see FRENCH this volume), but is best illustrated by Phase 1b at Lefkandi (Fig. 2). Since it is treated in detail in this volume (FRENCH this volume. – SCHOFIELD this volume), only a few points are noted here. The phase is described by the excavators as monotonous, generally with monochrome or linear decoration. The LH III C hollow lip can be seen on the jug and amphora (Fig. 2:1–2), that on the amphora already quite deep. Scroll pattern and tassel are now present (Fig. 2:1–2). They actually appear in Phase 1a at Lefkandi, but are rare (I thank E. Schofield for this information). The linear cup still has a medium rim band (SCHOFIELD this volume, fig. 2:1–2). The carinated conical cup FS 240 appears earlier, in LH III C Early at Mycenae (*MDP*, 135) and in Lefkandi Phase 1a (POPHAM – MILBURN 1971, 333, 338, fig. 3:5,7); it continues into Phase 1b at Lefkandi, but is rare. At Lefkandi it is generally monochrome (for a variant which appears in Lefkandi Phase 2a see SCHOFIELD this volume). The conical kylix (Fig. 2:3) is either monochrome or linear, with a slightly inturning rim. There may be a reserved circle in the centre of the interior base (SCHOFIELD this volume, fig. 1:9). The carinated krater (Fig. 2:4) is from the Citadel House at Mycenae. It appears in this phase at Mycenae. The everted rim is typical, as also the groups of decoration on the rim and the monochrome lower body; the upper body is shallow resulting in a narrow decorative zone. Linear and monochrome deep bowls are also typical at Lefkandi and Mycenae, monochrome being in the majority. At Mycenae the medium band deep bowl is still popular, but the monochrome deep bowl with reserved lower body and single interior rim band now appears (*MDP*, 156). At Lefkandi this type appears in Phase 2a (POPHAM – MILBURN 1971, 340). Phase 2a correlates to late LH III C Middle developed and to LH III C Middle advanced at Mycenae.

LH III C MIDDLE ADVANCED

The phase can be defined by Lefkandi 2a, Mycenae Phase XIb, Perati II and Asine Tomb 5, the dromos niche. The latter, a small hollow in the upper wall of the dromos, had three pots fitted into it, a deep bowl, a belly-handled amphora and a carinated conical cup FS 240, acting as a lid on the amphora (FRÖDIN – PERSSON 1938, 175–179). They are a closed find group dated to advanced LH III C Middle by the patterned FS 240.

Shapes

There are three new shapes (Fig. 3:1–3), the trefoil-mouthed jug FS 137, the one-handled conical bowl FS 242 and the tray FS 322. They do not first appear in LH III C Middle developed, as stated *MDP*, 155, on the old correlations. On Crete FS 242 is not present, the tray is rare and the trefoil-mouthed jug appears later, in Subminoan, but only the type with high handle FS 138 (HOOD – HUXLEY – SANDARS 1958/59, pl. 57b centre [Gypsades T. VII.9]. – CATLING 1996, 301 [T. 40.18, T. 121.4]).

There are three characteristic shapes in this phase (Fig. 3:4–6), the carinated conical cup FS 240, the linear shallow angular bowl FS 295 and the kylix FS 275, which may now have a swollen stem. The carinated cup (Fig. 3:4) dates the Asine dromos niche deposit (FRÖDIN – PERSSON 1938, 175–179).

There is regional variation in that FS 240 appears again at Lefkandi in this phase (SCHOFIELD this volume contra POPHAM – MILBURN 1971, 338), but continues at Mycenae (present in sherd material, see FRENCH this volume, fig. 1) and at Tiryns (PODZUWEIT 1983, 379, fig. 5:7,9) and is now patterned; FS 242 is very rare at Mycenae, but is present at Tiryns (PODZUWEIT 1983, 379, fig. 5:13, unfortunately illustrated with two handles and described 375 as a deep bowl) and Lefkandi (POPHAM – MILBURN 1971, pl. 53:5); FS 295 is not found at Lefkandi, but is present at Mycenae (*MDP*, fig. 233) and Tiryns (PODZUWEIT 1983, 373, fig. 4:4–5). The upper body on FS 295 is deep and concave. On Crete FS 240 and FS 295 do not appear. The kylix is present (Fig. 4:1), but it has a short carinated upper body with a conical bowl. This type has already appeared in LM III C

Early (Kavousi: MOOK – COULSON 1997, 344, fig. 8:1, 346, fig. 11:31), but kylikes with swollen stems do not seem to appear on Crete until LM III C Late/Subminoan (Vrokastro: HALL 1914, 150–151, fig. 89A,C).

Apart from the shapes discussed above, some Mycenaean shapes do not correspond to the parallel Minoan shape, or do not appear on Crete, or appear later in LM III C Late/Subminoan. The amphoriskos (Fig. 5:1): a Minoan version seems to appear in late LM III B or early LM III C (Fig. 4:5), but the type with proportions similar to the Mainland type does not appear until Subminoan (CATLING 1996, 303 [T. 40.2, T. 2.3]). The collar-necked jar (Fig. 5:2): the true collar-necked jar does not seem to appear on Crete. The lekythos (Fig. 5:3) becomes more popular on the Mainland in this phase, but on Crete it is always very rare, as the stirrup jar is preferred. The airhole on the shoulder begins now on the lekythos and on the stirrup jar, but it is not common in this phase (*RMDP*, lekythos Attica no. 427, stirrup jar Attica nos. 443, 446, 450). On Crete airholes first seem to appear on Subminoan stirrup jars (CATLING 1996, 298 incl. T. 200). The kalathos (Fig. 5:4) is a conical shape with cylindrical lower body and straight or incurving upper body. The Minoan kalathos is a wide-based straight-sided type (for example *GSE II*, pl. 54:71-P1378 [+71-P0188]). A shape corresponding to the Mycenaean one does not appear on Crete until Subminoan (WARREN 1982/83, 87, fig. 66 right). Mainland and Aegean kalathoi are often decorated on the interior (*RMDP*, Argolid no. 369, Kos no. 190, Kalymnos nos. 30 31), but this is not the case on Crete.

Decoration

There are several styles which are characteristic of LH III C Middle advanced. The **Pictorial Style** (Fig. 6) flourished in this phase. The straight-sided alabastron from Lefkandi is painted in white on dark, another feature of this phase, but not very common. The vase has an unusually tall neck and a down-sloping rim. This type of alabastron is also present on Crete, but with the usual collar-neck (Fig. 4:3). The alabastron FS 98, (Fig. 4:2), with handles extending down the sides of the body is current on the Mainland from Transitional LH III B–III C Early (*RMDP*, Attica nos. 274–276) and on Crete from LM III A2 (SAPOUNA-SAKELLARAKI 1990, 82, fig. 25). The **Close Style** (Fig. 7:1) is a miniature style with finely drawn motifs. The decorative zone is completely filled, with much use made of triangular patch. Close Style may also be used on the shoulder of stirrup jars, when the main decoration is in another style, such as the **Octopus Style**, for example on a stirrup jar from Perati (*MDP*, fig. 216:3). The **Pleonastic Style** (Fig. 7:2) is not to be confused with the Close Style. Some of the same motifs are used, but they are large not miniature. The slashed rib on the krater (Fig. 7:2) is typical of this phase.

The **Granary Style** (Figs. 7:3; 8) is a complete contrast to the above styles. It is named from the decoration of vases found on the floor of the East Basement of the Granary at Mycenae (WACE 1921–23, 38–61). Decoration is generally linear or monochrome, but a small corpus of motifs is also used (Fig. 9). Some, such as tassel (Fig. 2:2), scroll (Fig. 2:1) and wavy line (Fig. 8:4) have been in use during the LH III C Middle developed phase; others, such as antithetic loops (Fig. 8:1), and necklace and stemless spirals (Fig. 8:2) become popular now. Antithetic loops and necklace are new in this phase at Lefkandi (POPHAM – MILBURN 1971, 340, 342) and Mycenae (Fig. 8:1: antithetic loops. – FRENCH this volume, fig. 1: necklace), but stemless spirals appear at Mycenae in LH III C Late (*MDP*, fig. 244:2) and at Lefkandi not at all. On Crete the wavy line is present throughout LM III C, the tassel is found at Palaikastro Kastri (SACKETT – POPHAM – WARREN 1965, 296, fig. 16:P31) and at Kavousi Kastro Phase II (MOOK – COULSON 1997, 354, fig. 21:91), scroll appears at Thronos on an amphora dated to LM III C Early

(D'AGATA 2003, 27, fig. 2:1), while necklace appears in LM III C Late (D'AGATA 2003, 27, fig. 2:3[1]); antithetic loops seem to be replaced by streamers and the stemless spiral seems not to be present. Hooks are common below handles throughout LH III C, especially single ones (Fig. 7:3), but in this phase and in LH III C Late the hooks may be double (Fig. 8:2), and often appear as coils (Fig. 8:3). Single hooks below the handle appear on Crete in LM III C Late (D'AGATA 2003, 27, fig. 2:8. – CATLING 1996, fig. 128:200.4). Half-moon decoration is a feature at Perati (IAKOVIDIS 1980, 62 [pendant half-ovals]) as on the cup (Fig. 8:5). There are corresponding half-moons on interior and exterior. This deep cup shape with half-moon appears at Thronos in Pit 3 dated to LM III C Early (D'AGATA 1999, 190, fig. 5:3.17), but otherwise the shape seems not to be common on Crete until LM III C Late/Subminoan (D'AGATA 2003, 27, fig. 2:6. – WARREN 1982/83, 85, fig. 60a–b. – CATLING 1996, fig. 83:40.19).

Apart from examples with Close Style decoration (Fig. 7:1), the deep bowl, which is very common in this phase, is often monochrome, but may have a narrow reserved band on the interior just below the lip and a reserved lower body (Fig. 8:6[2]). This type appears on Crete, for example in Thronos Pit 41 (D'AGATA 2003, 27, fig. 2:5,7), which has been dated to Subminoan. Another type is monochrome with multiple reserved lines or with reserved areas on exterior (*MDP*, fig. 229). A range of patterns is also used on deep bowls in this phase (*MDP*, fig. 228. – *RMDP*, LH III C Middle passim). They include antithetic streamers (Fig. 6:1), which are now popular on the deep bowl and many other shapes (POPHAM – MILBURN 1971, pl. 55:1–5), but on Crete they have been popular since LM III C Early. On Crete the deep bowl has a carinated body (Fig. 4:4). This type appears alongside the type with rounded body in LM III C Early (*GSE II*, pls. 35–36). Both types should continue into LM III C Middle; stratified examples are needed to know how long they lasted.

This definition of LH III C Middle on the Greek Mainland is based on material from stratified sites in the Argolid, Attica and Euboea. Elsewhere on the Mainland there are problems, particularly in separating LH III C Middle from LH III C Late as no stratified deposits are fully published, except that of Kalapodi in Phthiotis (JACOB-FELSCH 1996). Here the stratigraphy is good, but the material is so scrappy it does not add much to the general picture. Most areas do not have much published pottery of these periods. The exceptions are Phocis, where Delphi has much LH III C Late tomb material and Medeon a local LH III C Middle style, Achaia and north Elis which have large amounts of tomb material and the site of Palaiokastro in west Arcadia, which combines the west Peloponnesian style with Minoan elements (*RMDP*, Phocis 782–796, Achaia 424–441, Elis 392–398, Arcadia 296–299).

CORRELATIONS BETWEEN THE MAINLAND AND CRETE

It now seems to be generally agreed that the deep bowl with interior reserved band below the rim (Fig. 10:2), which begins in LH III C Middle advanced on the Mainland, starts in LH III C Early on Crete (Fig. 10:1). The Minoan version is also wider than the Mycenaean one, as a comparison of Fig. 10:1 with Fig. 10:2 makes clear. Streamers (Fig. 10:1)

---

[1] Pit 31 is dated to close to the first half of LM III C Early (D'AGATA 2003, 28–29), but necklace first appears in LH III C Middle advanced on the Mainland; it should not be earlier on Crete. The vase does not have the Perati banding, as stated in D'AGATA 2003, 29 n. 13. Perati banding consists of a broad band flanked by a narrow band, that is with a narrow band on each side of the broad band.

[2] The example dates to Lefkandi 2b as I have no drawing of a stratified complete vase for this phase.

are also in use on Crete in LH III C Early, but appear on the Mainland in LH III C Middle advanced. On Crete in the later LM III C phases it is possible streamers are used in preference to antithetic loops, which are popular on the Mainland. The use of the term Close Style by Minoan pottery specialists for Minoan LM III C Early vases decorated in the Pleonastic Style (Fig. 10:3–4) still causes confusion.[3] This Minoan decoration has nothing to do with the Mainland LH III C Middle advanced Close Style (Fig. 10:2). It is chronologically misleading to give them the same name (MOUNTJOY 1999).

There is a problem with Minoan/Mycenaean correlations in that motifs which would be LH III C Middle advanced on the Mainland seem to be LM III C Early/Middle developed on Crete. At Kastelli Chania three deposits could be assigned stratigraphically as a little later than the first LM III C Early levels, suggesting a later LM III C Early or a LM III C Middle developed date (*GSE II*, 135). The deposit from the pit in Room I has the most instructive pottery, (*GSE II*, 41–44). The deposit includes a storage stirrup jar with deep wavy band round the body, which is a Knossian import (*GSE II*, 163–164, pl. 50:71-P0736/0763/0779/77-P0719); it has a parallel in LH III C Early Phase 2 at Tiryns (MARAN 2005), which would fit a later LM III C Early date for the deposit. However, the kraters from the deposit (*GSE II*, pls. 38:71-P0782; 39:71-P0733, 71-P0730/1424 [+73-P0726; 77-P1644], 71-P0734) (Fig. 10:4) would be LH III C Middle advanced on the Mainland. This dichotomy has repercussions elsewhere.

CYPRUS

The so-called hippocamp krater (Fig. 11) from Hala Sultan Tekke (ÅSTRÖM 1988) is a good example of the dichotomy. It should equate to Sinda Phase III and Enkomi Level IIIB Early. These settlement phases equate stratigraphically to LH III C Middle developed in Mainland terms, but stylistically to LH III C Middle advanced. The barred filling motif between the streamer and rim on the right side (Fig. 11A–B) is close to that from Kastelli Pediada (Fig. 10:3), which should be LM III C Early and to one of the kraters from the Kastelli Chania later deposit (Fig. 10:4). The motif has probably developed from LM III A2 concentric arcs, (Fig. 12:1) and (Fig. 12:2), a later rendering (Fig. 12:3) depicts one of the kraters from the later deposit from Kastelli Chania and Fig. 12:4–5 two more Cypriote sherds with the barred filling motif, together with a krater from Ekron Level VIIa (Fig. 12:6). The Cypriot and Ekron sherds date to LH III C Middle developed in Mainland terms, but stylistically on the Mainland they would be LH III C Middle advanced. However, the parallels from the Chania deposit are LM III C Early Phase 2 or LM III C Middle developed. It would seem that this motif, which is popular in Sinda III and the last phase of Hala Sultan Tekke, has gone from Crete to Cyprus and then on from Cyprus to Philistia. A krater (Fig. 13:1) from the Knossos Stratigraphical Museum Extension excavations from the Trench T Pit, which is thought by the excavator to be slightly earlier than the main deposit (but see now WARREN this volume, Trench T), has decorative parallels to a slightly more ornate krater from Sinda Phase III (Fig. 13:2) On the latter the double-axe (lower half not extant) is elaborated by a zone of chevrons across the centre. The Cypriote pottery seems to go chronologically with that from Crete rather than with that from the Mainland.

---

[3] I suggested this name for the style (MOUNTJOY 1999, 513), based on a term used by Schachermeyr to describe his Noble Ware vases (SCHACHERMEYR 1979, 206), but suggested the term Noble Ware not be used.

THE EAST AEGEAN – WEST ANATOLIAN INTERFACE

The same difficulty of correlation is apparent in this area. A krater (Fig. 14), from the recent excavations at Bademgediği Tepe in coastal west Turkey emphasises the difficulties of dating stylistically. It is from unstratified wash and is locally made. On the left is a ship with a row of warriors standing on the deck with a shield in the left hand and the right hand raised to throw a spear; they wear Sea Peoples' feathered helmets. On the right another row of warriors, presumably on a second ship, faces those on the left. The iconography of the rowers is LH III B but the heads of the warriors are similar to those from Kos dated stylistically to LH III C Middle in Mainland terms (*RMDP*, 1080[4]). There are no Minoan parallels to them. There is no other LH III B pottery from the site, so the earliest possible date for the krater is Transitional LH III B2–LH III C Early. This suggests the feathered helmets from Kos (*RMDP*, Kos nos. 102–104, 170), and perhaps some of the other Koan pictorial pieces with birds and goats, should also move back from LH III C Middle at least to LH III C Early. Indeed, the birds and goats (*RMDP*, for example Kos no. 101) would not be out of place on Crete at this earlier date.

The degenerate octopus in a double-axe (Fig. 13:3), from the same excavations, again from unstratified wash, sums up the problem of correlations. It is LM III C Early or Middle developed in Minoan terms and LH III C Middle advanced in Mainland terms. How is it to be dated?

Index to illustrations

Fig. 1   after *MDP*, 133. – *RMDP*, 39

Fig. 2   *RMDP:* **1)** Amphora FS 69 Euboea no. 66; **2)** Jug FS 106 Euboea no. 67; **3)** Kylix FS 274 Euboea no. 73; **4)** Carinated krater FS 282 Argolid no. 362

Fig. 3   **1)** Trefoil-mouthed jug FS 137 (*RMDP*, Argolid no. 338); **2)** One-handled conical bowl FS 242 (after POPHAM – MILBURN 1971, fig. 4:9)
RMDP: **3)** Tray FS 322 Euboea no. 83; **4)** Carinated cup FS 240 Argolid no. 359; **5)** Kylix FS 275 Euboea no. 80; **6)** Shallow angular bowl FS 295 Argolid no. 371

Fig. 4   Karphi: **1)** Kylix unpublished
SEIRADAKI 1960: **2)** Alabastron FS 98 K22 fig. 12:2; **3)** Alabastron FS 96 K8 fig. 12:1; **4)** Deep bowl K27 fig. 14:3; **5)** Amphoriskos K116 fig. 3:10

Fig. 5   *RMDP:* **1)** Amphoriskos FS 59 Euboea no. 78; **2)** Collar-necked jar FS 63 Attica no. 405; **3)** Lekythos FS 122 Attica no. 427; **4)** Kalathos FS 291 Attica no. 602

Fig. 6   Alabastron, straight-sided FS 98 (*RMDP*, Euboea no. 79)

Fig. 7   **1)** Deep bowl FS 285 (*RMDP*, Argolid no. 365); **2)** Krater FS 282 (*MDP*, fig. 225:1); **3)** Amphora FS 69 (*RMDP*, Argolid no. 330)

Fig. 8   **1)** Hydria FS 128 (*MDP*, fig. 212:1)
RMDP: **2)** Hydria FS 128 Attica no. 428; **3)** Coiled hooks Attica no. 433; **4)** Cup FS 216 Argolid no. 358; **5)** Cup FS 216 Attica no. 459; **6)** Deep bowl FS 285 Euboea no. 89

Fig. 9   Motifs

Fig. 10 **1)** MOUNTJOY 1999, pl. CXIIIb3; **2)** MOUNTJOY 1999, pl. CXIIIa1; **3)** (after RETHEMIOTAKIS 1997, 322, fig. 33b); **4)** (after *GSE II*, pl. 39:71-P0735 [+71-P0762; 77-P0739])

Fig. 11 Krater Hala Sultan Tekke (ÅSTRÖM 1988, 173, fig. 1)

Fig. 12 **1)** Knossos South House (MOUNTJOY 2003, no. 728); **2)** Kastelli Pediada (after RETHEMIOTAKIS

---

[4] I noted *RMDP*, 1080 n. 733 that some of the Koan pictorial might be LH III C Early as similarly decorated amphoroid kraters, which seem to have been exported from this area, were found in the destruction level at Ugarit dated to c1186.

1997, 309, fig. 10b); **3)** Kastelli Chania (after *GSE II*, pl. 39:71-P0733); **4)** Hala Sultan Tekke F6122 (ÖBRINK 1979, 53, fig. 175); **5)** Sinda (FURUMARK – ADELMAN 2003, pl. 17 Px112); **6)** Ekron (DOTHAN – ZUKERMAN 2004, fig. 16:6)

Fig. 13 **1)** Knossos (after WARREN 1982/83, fig. 43); **2)** Sinda (FURUMARK – ADELMAN 2003, pl. 15 Px89); **3)** Bademgediği Tepe

Fig. 14 Bademgediği Tepe (MOUNTJOY 2005)

Bibliography

ÅSTRÖM, P.
1988   "The Hippocampus Krater", *RDAC*, 173–176.

BRONEER, O.
1939   "A Mycenaean Fountain on the Athenian Acropolis", *Hesperia* 8, 317–433.

CATLING, H. W.
1996   "The Subminoan Pottery. The Subminoan Phase in the North Cemetery at Knossos", 295–310 in: COLDSTREAM – CATLING 1996, vol. II.

COLDSTREAM, J. N. – H. W. CATLING (eds.)
1996   *Knossos North Cemetery: Early Greek Tombs. Vol. I–IV* (BSA Suppl. 28). London.

D'AGATA, A. L.
1999   "Defining a Pattern of Continuity during the Dark Age in Central-Western Crete: Ceramic Evidence from the Settlement of Thronos/Kephala (Ancient Sybrita)", *SMEA* 41, 181–218.
2003   "Late Minoan III C–Subminoan Pottery Sequence at Thronos/Kephala and its Connections with the Greek Mainland", 23–35 in: *LH III C Chronology and Synchronisms*.

DAVIS, E. N. (ed.)
1977   *Symposium on the Dark Ages in Greece*. New York.

DÖHL, H.
1973   "Iria. Die Ergebnisse der Ausgrabungen 1939", 127–194 in: *Tiryns Forschungen und Berichte* 6, Mainz.

DOTHAN, T. – A. ZUKERMAN
2004   "A Preliminary Study of the Mycenaean III C:1 Pottery Assemblages from Tel Miqne-Ekron and Ashdod", *BASOR* 333, 1–54.

FELSCH, R. C. S. (ed.)
1996   *Kalapodi. Ergebnisse der Ausgrabungen im Heiligtum der Artemis und des Apollon von Hyampolis in der antiken Phokis. Vol. I*. Mainz.

FRÖDIN, O. – A. W. PERSSON
1938   *Asine. Results of the Swedish Excavations 1922–1930*. Stockholm.

FURUMARK, A. – C. ADELMAN
2003   *The Swedish Excavations at Sinda, Cyprus*. Stockholm.

HALL, E. H.
1914   *Excavations in Eastern Crete. Vrokastro* (University of Pennsylvania. The Museum Anthropological Publications 3). Philadelphia.

HOOD, S. – G. HUXLEY – N. SANDARS
1958/59 "A Minoan Cemetery on Upper Gypsades (Knossos Survey 156)", *BSA* 53/54, 194–262.

IAKOVIDIS, S. E.
1969/70 *Περατή. Το νεκροταφείον* (Βιβλιοθήκη της εν Αθήναις Αρχαιολογικής Εταιρείας 67). Athens.
1980   *Excavations of the Necropolis at Perati*. Los Angeles.

JACOB-FELSCH, M.
1996 "Die spätmykenische bis frühprotogeometrische Keramik", 1–213 in: FELSCH 1996.

LAFFINEUR, R. – E. GRECO (eds.)
2005 *Emporia. Aegeans in the Central and Eastern Mediterranean. Proceedings of the 10th International Aegean Conference/10e Rencontre égéenne internationale, Athens, Italian School of Archaeology, 14–18 April 2004* (Aegaeum 25). Liège – Austin.

MARAN, J.
2005 "Late Minoan Coarse Ware Stirrup Jars on the Greek Mainland. A Postpalatial Perspective from the 12th Century BC Argolid", 415–431 in: *Ariadne's Threads*.

MOOK, M. – W. COULSON
1997 "Late Minoan III C Pottery from the Kastro at Kavousi", 337–365 in: *Late Minoan III Pottery*.

MOUNTJOY, P. A.
1999 "Late Minoan III C/Late Helladic III C: Chronology and Terminology", 511–516 in: *Meletemata*.
2003 *Knossos. The South House* (BSA Suppl. 34). London.
2005 "Mycenaean Connections with the Near East in LH III C: Ships and Sea Peoples", 423–427 in: LAFFINEUR – GRECO 2005.

ÖBRINK, U.
1979 *Hala Sultan Tekke 5. Excavations in Area 22 1971–1973 and 1975–1978* (SIMA 45.5). Göteborg.

PODZUWEIT, C.
1983 "Ausgrabungen Tiryns 1981. Bericht zur spätmykenischen Keramik. Die Phasen SH III C Fortgeschritten bis Spät", *AA*, 359–402.

POPHAM, M. R. – E. V. MILBURN
1971 "The Late Helladic III C Pottery of Xeropolis (Lefkandi): A Summary", *BSA* 66, 333–352.

Relations between Cyprus and Crete
1979 *Acts of the International Archaeological Symposium "The Relations between Cyprus and Crete, ca. 2000–500 B.C.", Nicosia 16th April–22nd April 1978*. Nicosia.

RETHEMIOTAKIS, G.
1997 "Late Minoan III Pottery from Kastelli Pediada", 305–326 in: *Late Minoan III Pottery*.

RUTTER, J. B.
1974 *The Late Helladic III B and III C Periods at Korakou and Gonia in the Corinthia* (Ph.D. dissertation, University of Pennsylvania [Ann Arbor Nr. 48106]).
1977 "Late Helladic III C Pottery and Some Historical Implications", 1–20 in: DAVIS 1977.
1978 "A Plea for the Abandonment of the Term 'Submycenaean'", *TUAS* 3, 58–65.

SACKETT, L. H. – M. R. POPHAM – P. M. WARREN
1965 "Excavations at Palaikastro VI", *BSA* 60, 248–315.

SAPOUNA-SAKELLARAKI, E.
1990 "Archanès à l'époque mycéniénne", *BCH* 114, 67–102.

SCHACHERMEYR, F.
1979 "The Pleonastic Pottery Style of Cretan Middle III C and its Cypriote Relations", 204–214 in: *Relations between Cyprus and Crete*.

SEIRADAKI, M.
1960 "Pottery from Karphi", *BSA* 55, 1–37.

WACE, A. J. B.
1921–23 "Excavations at Mycenae § VII. – The Lion Gate and Grave Circle Area", *BSA* 25, 9–126.

WARREN, P. M.
1982/83 "Knossos: Stratigraphical Museum Excavations, 1978–82. Part II", *AR* 29, 63–87.

MDP	RUTTER 1977, 1978	Mycenae Citadel House	Lefkandi Xeropolis	Perati
LH III C Early	1	Early	(LH III B)	
	2	Early/Tower	1a	I
	3	Tower	1b	
LH III C Middle	4 early	Developed	2a	II
	4 late	Advanced	2b	
LH III C Late	5 early	Final	3	III
Submycenaean	5 late	Submycenaean	Skoubris Submycenaean	–

RMDP	RUTTER 1977, 1978	Mycenae Citadel House	Lefkandi Xeropolis	Perati
Transitional LH III B2–III C Early	1	?		
LH III C Early	2	Early	1a	I
	3	Tower	1b	
LH III C Middle	4 early	Developed	2a	II
	4 late	Advanced		
LH III C Late	5 early	Final	2b	III
			3	
			Chaliotis	
Submycenaean	5 late	Present	Skoubris	

Fig. 1 Chronological chart

Fig. 2 LH III C Middle developed

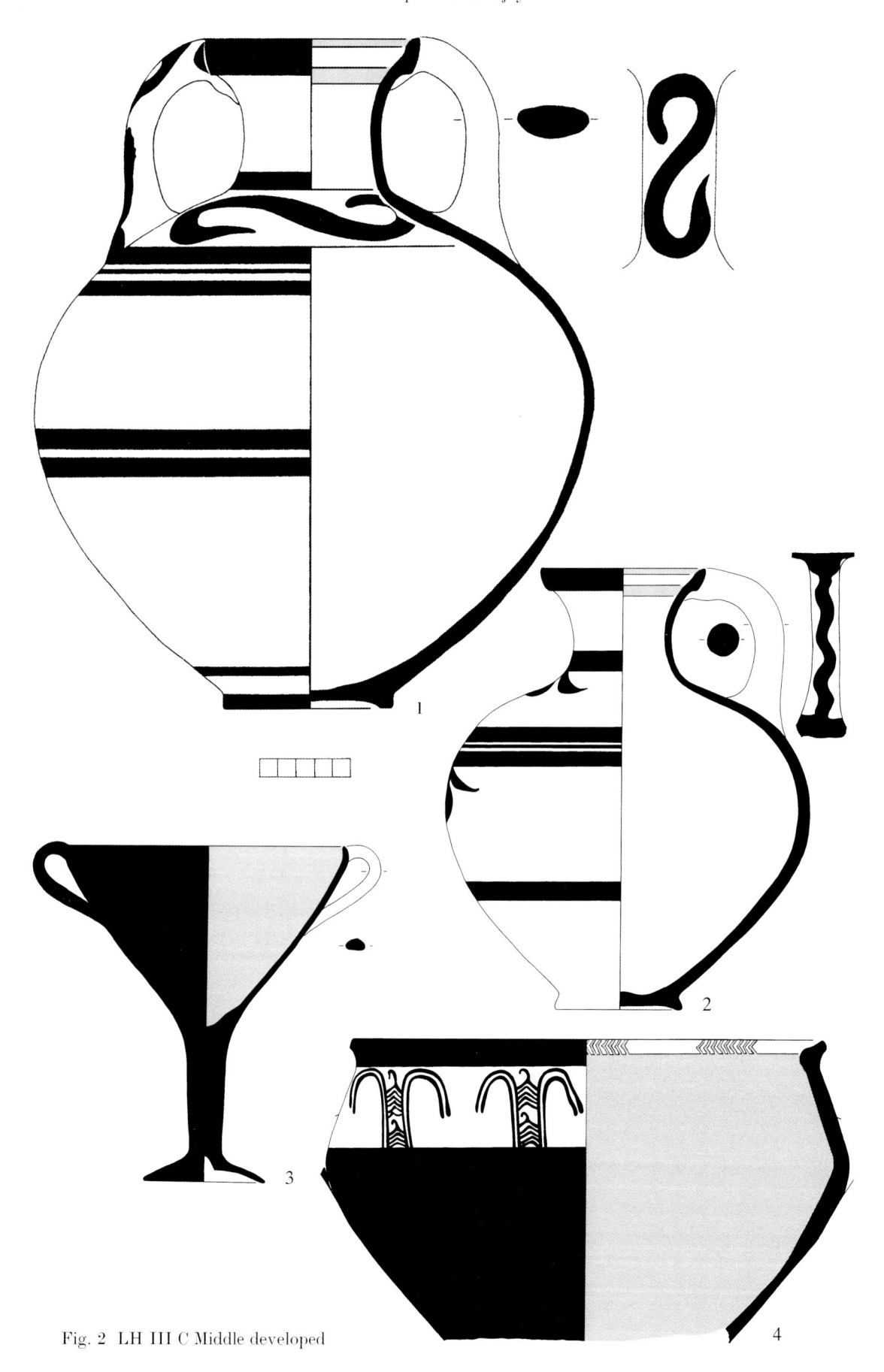

A Definition of LH III C Middle

New Shapes

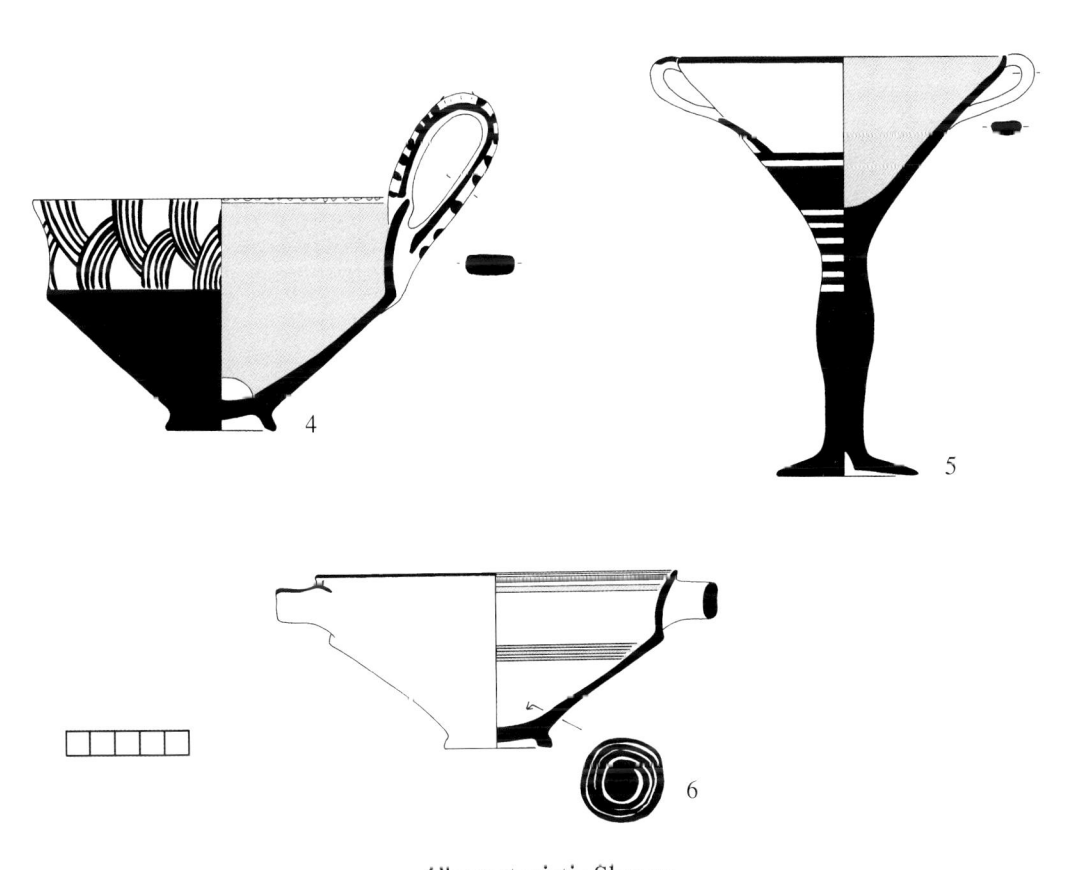

Characteristic Shapes

Fig. 3 LH III C Middle advanced

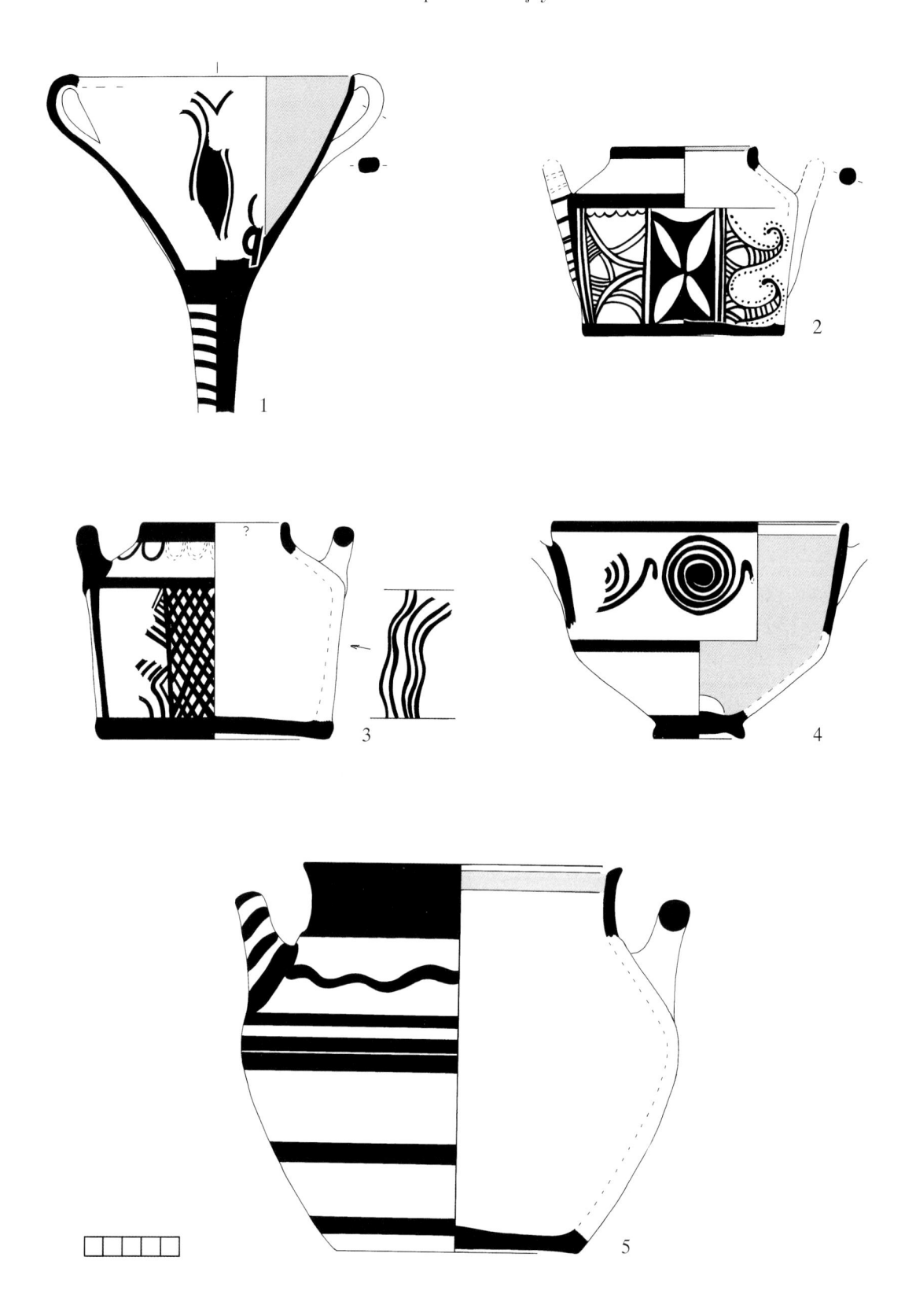

Fig. 4 Late Minoan III C pottery from Karphi

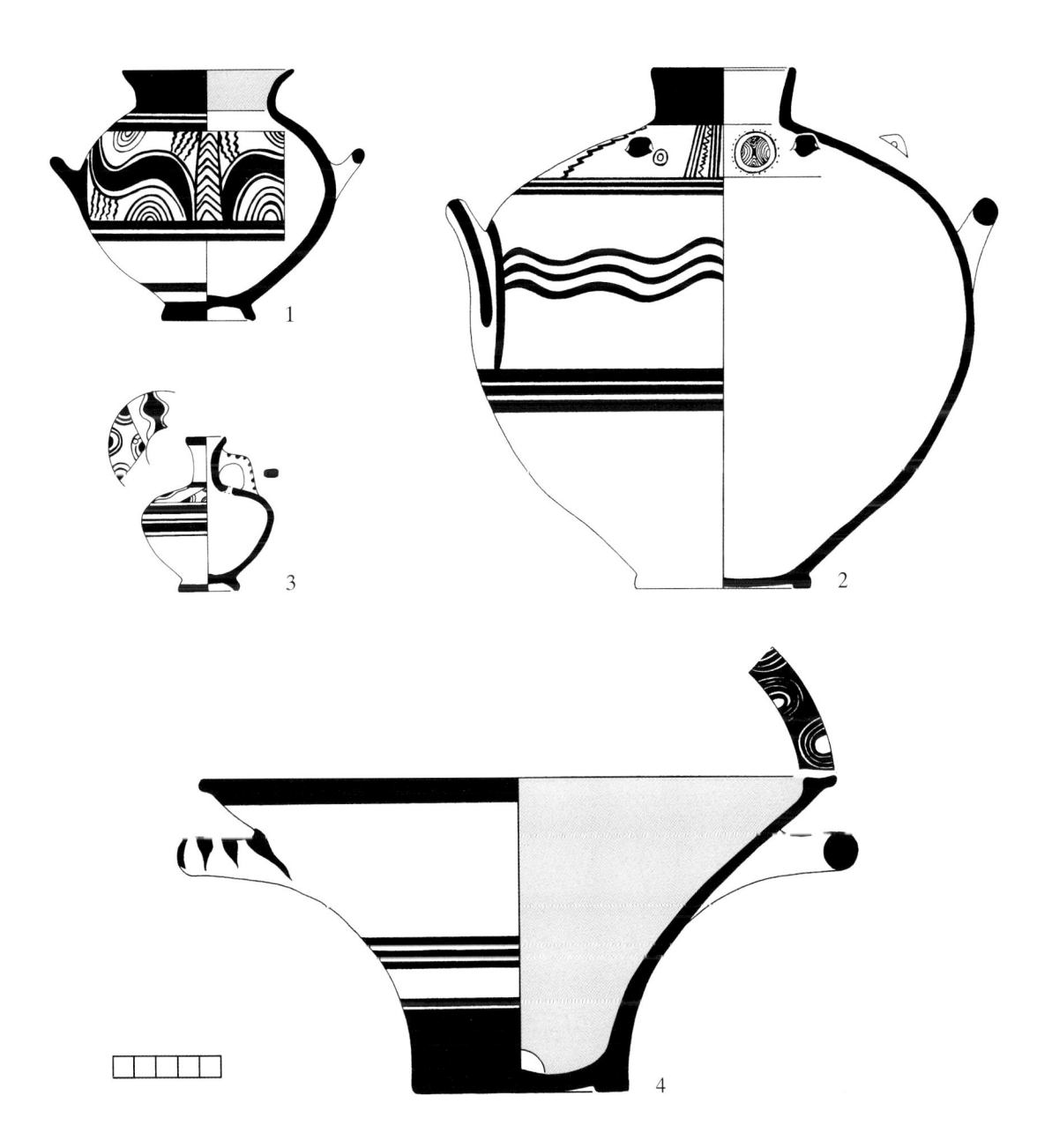

Fig. 5 LH III C Middle advanced

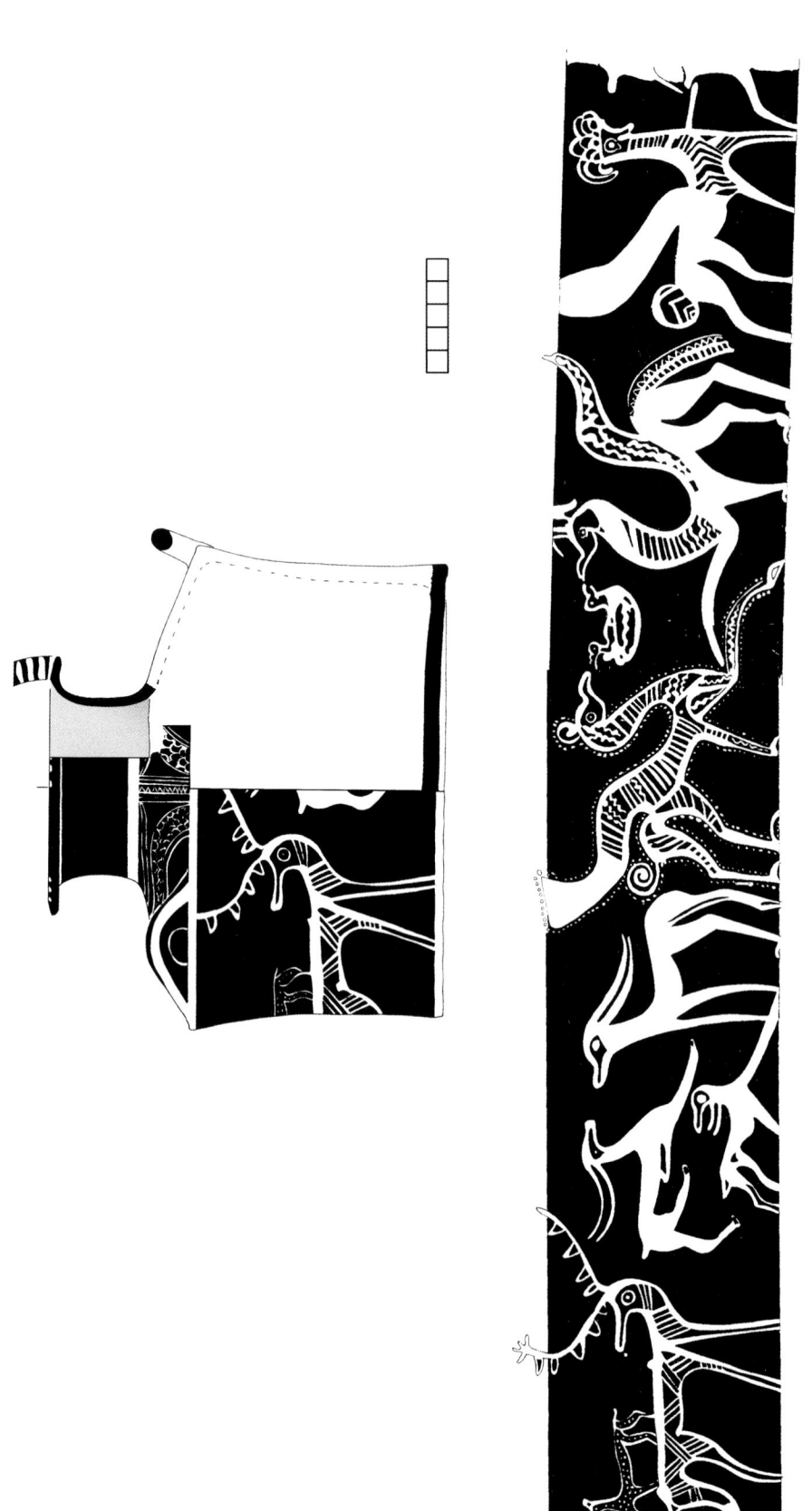

Fig. 6 LH III C Middle advanced: Pictorial Style

A Definition of LH III C Middle 235

Close Style

Pleonastic Style

Granary Style

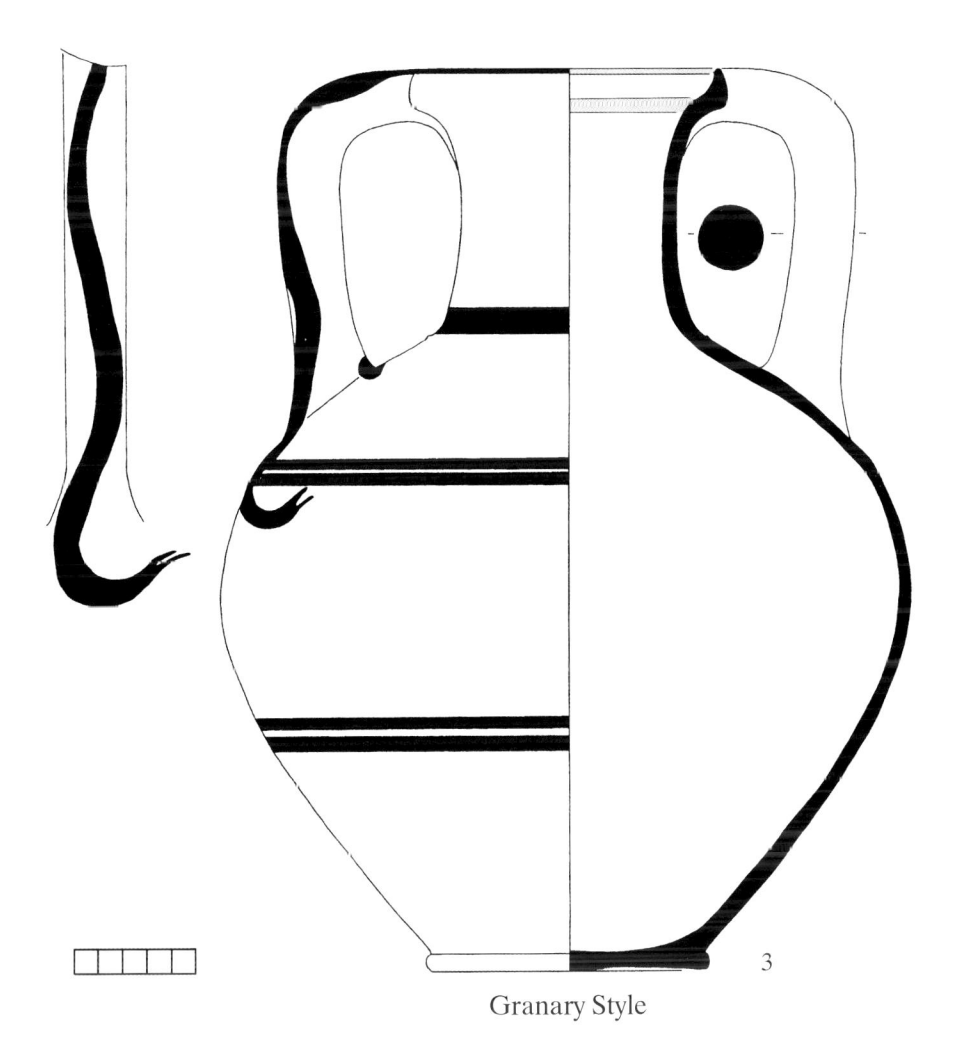

Fig. 7 LH III C Middle advanced

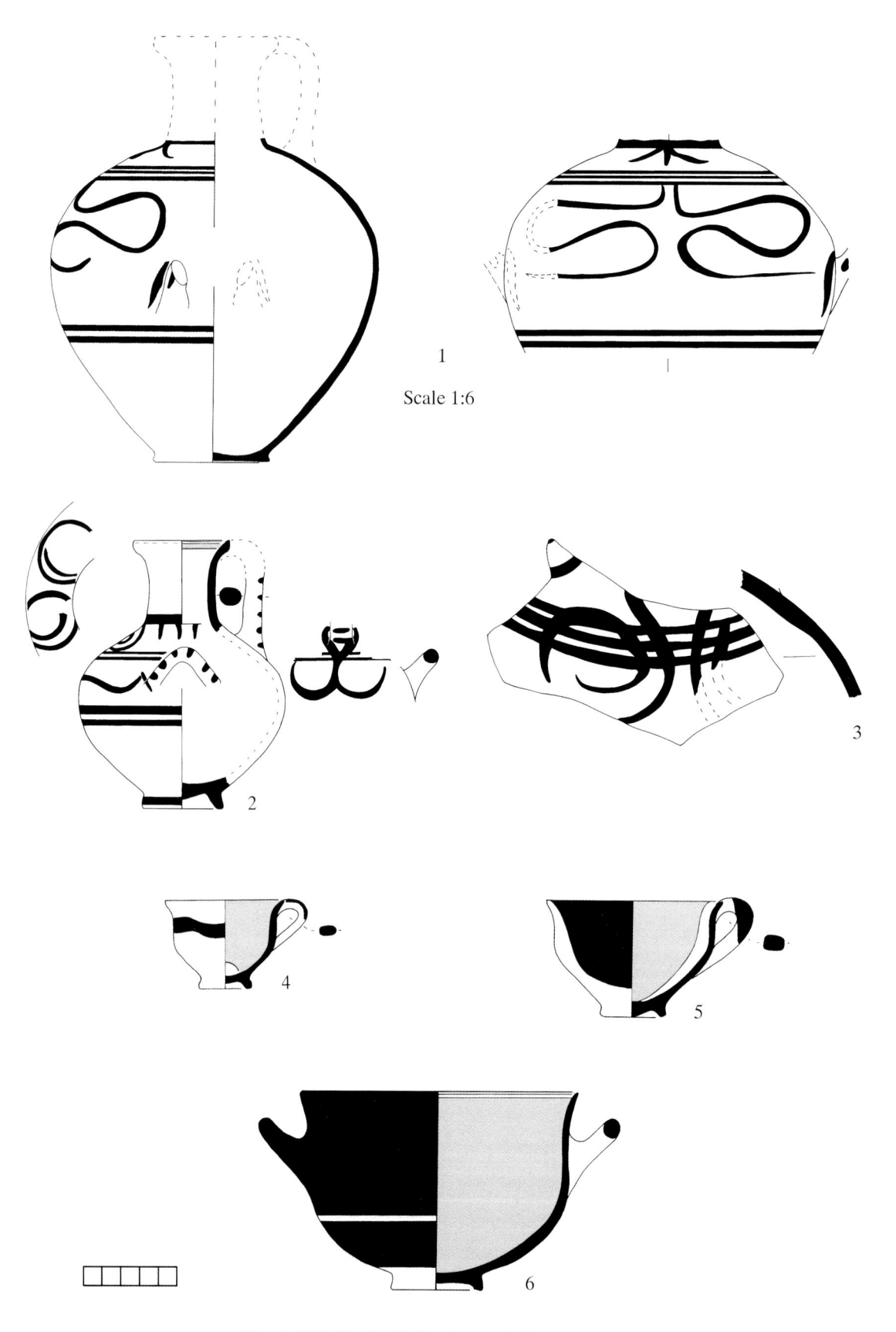

Fig. 8 LH III C Middle advanced: Granary Style

MOTIFS: MYCENAE, LEFKANDI, PERATI. CRETE

	Lefkandi	Stemless spiral	Tassel	Necklace	Scroll	Antithetic loops	Streamers	Hooks below handle
III C Early 1	1a		Lefk.		Lefk.		Crete	
III C Early 2	1b		Cit.Hse		Thronos Pit 54			
III C Middle Dev 1			Kavousi: Kastro; PK:Kastro		Cit.Hse			
III C Middle Adv 2	2a	Perati II	Perati II	Lefk. Perati II Cit.Hse		Lefk. Cit.Hse	Lefk. Perati II Cit.Hse	Lefk. Perati II Cit.Hse
III C Late	2b	Cit.Hse	x		x			
III C Late	3			Thronos Pit 31	KMF T.200			Thronos Pit 41 KMF T.200
SubMyc/Min								

Fig. 9 The floruit of LH III C motifs used in the Granary Style and their LM III C correlations

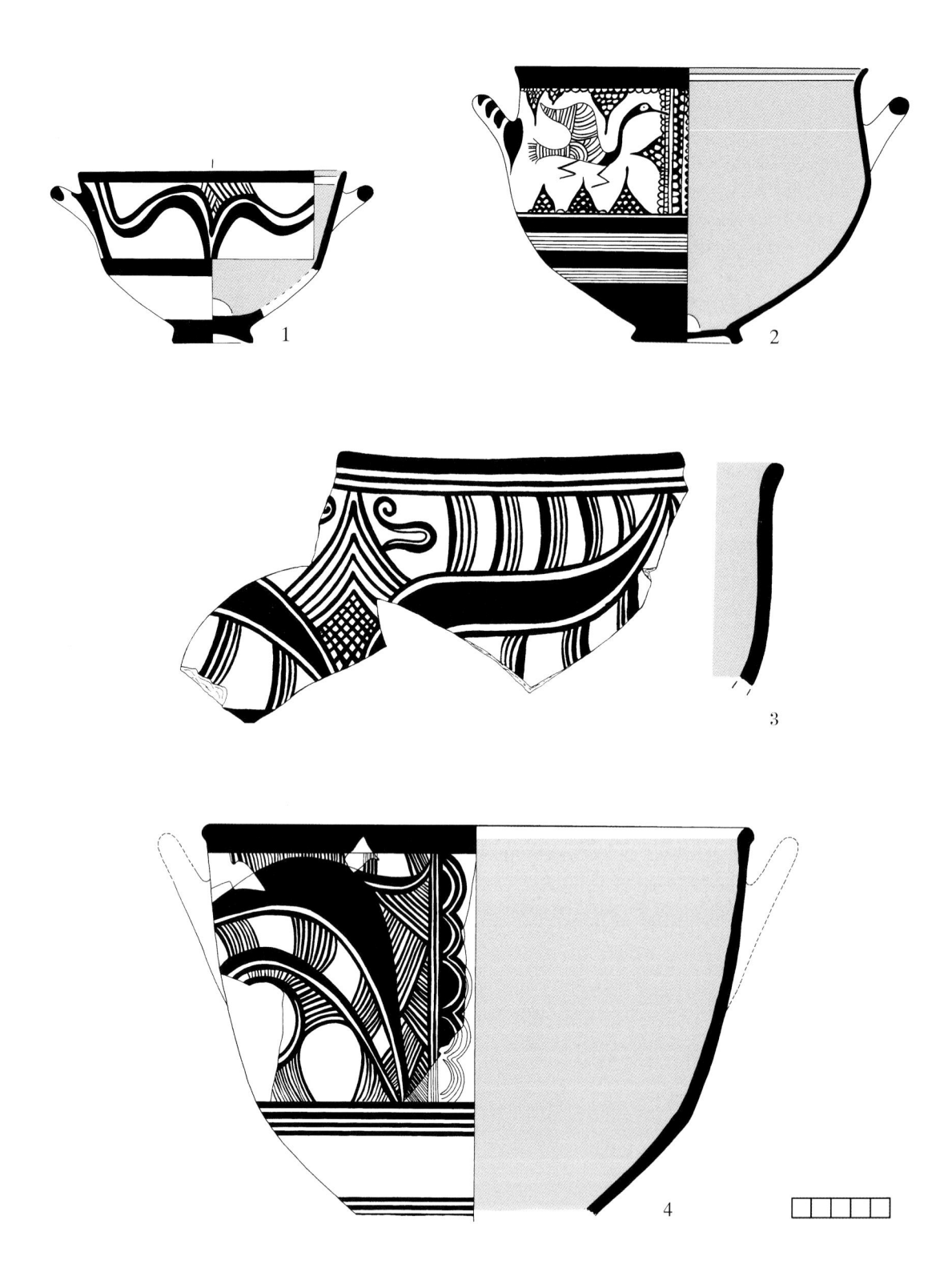

Fig. 10 Mycenaean-Minoan correlations

Fig. 11 Hala Sultan Tekke: the Hippocamp krater

Knossos

Kastelli: Pediadha

Kastelli: Chania

Hala Sultan Tekke

Sinda

Ekron

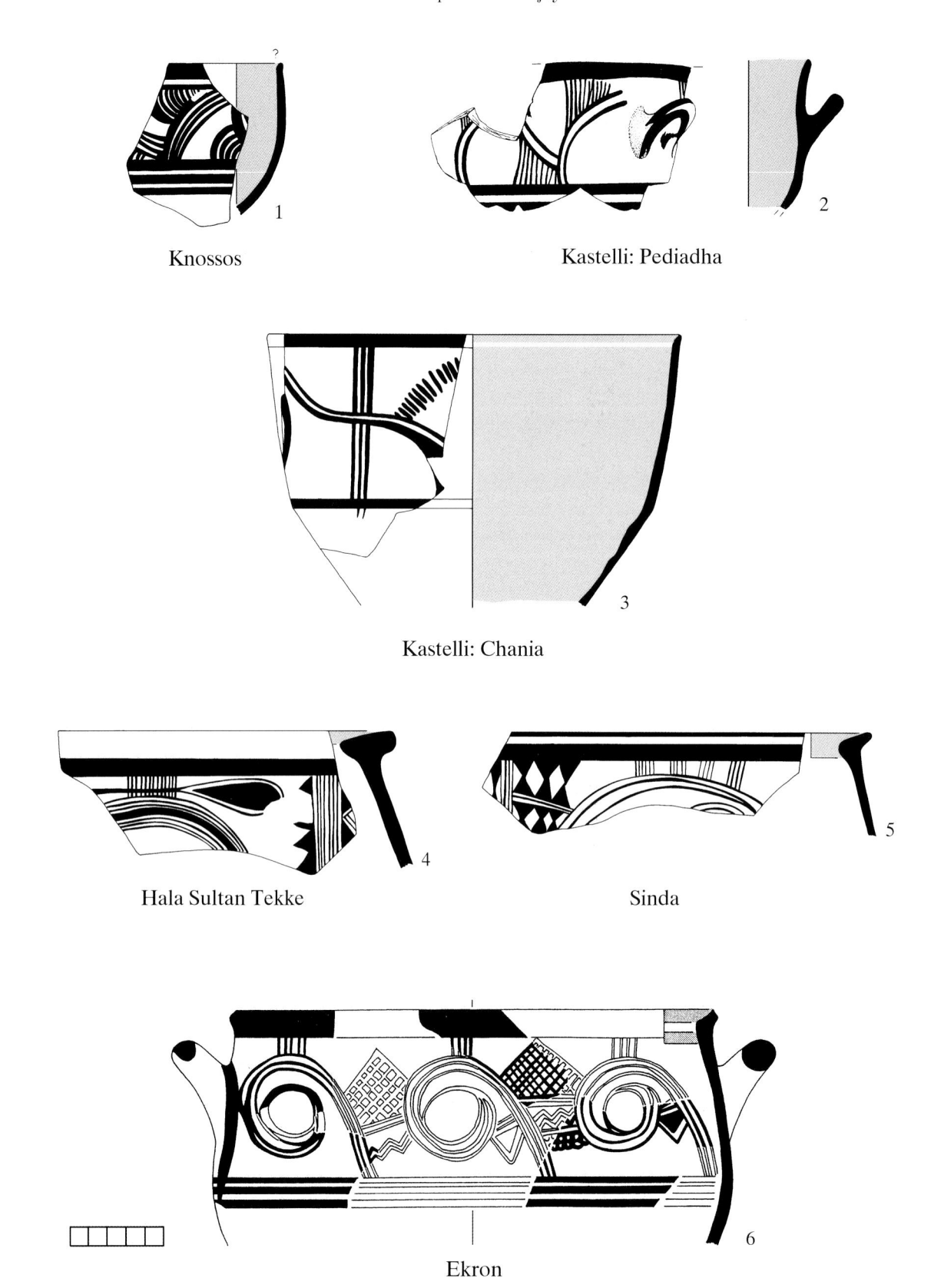

Fig. 12 The development of the barred filling motif

Knossos

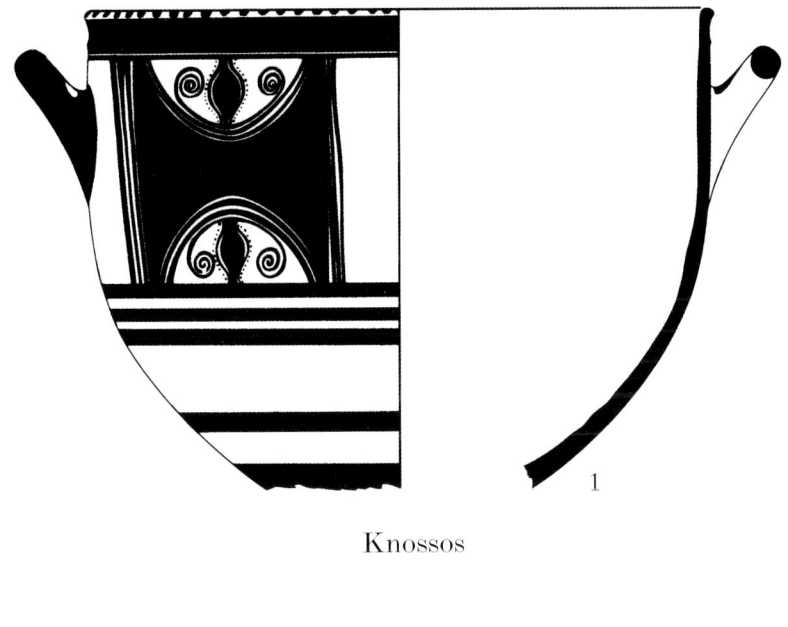

Sinda

Bademgediği Tepe

Fig. 13 The double-axe motif

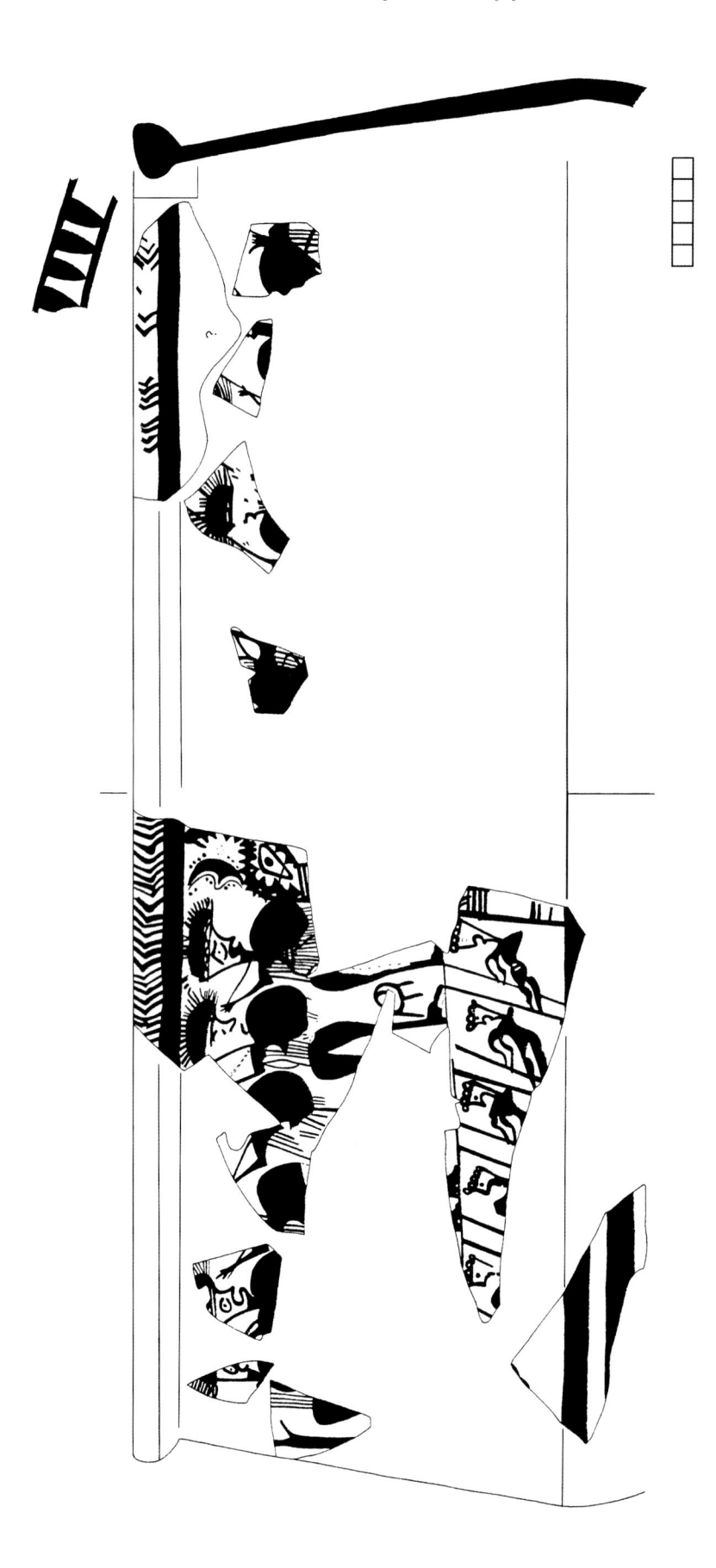

Fig. 14 Bademgediği Tepe krater

TOBIAS MÜHLENBRUCH

THE POST-PALATIAL SETTLEMENT IN THE LOWER CITADEL OF TIRYNS*

Tiryns was first investigated by Friedrich Thiersch and Rizo Rangabe for one day in 1831, before Heinrich Schliemann in 1876 and Schliemann together with Wilhelm Dörpfeld in 1884/85 excavated the best preserved Mycenaean palace known so far. They also cut trenches in the Lower Citadel and proved the existence of a settlement in this area (DÖRPFELD 1886, 200). Further excavations in the Lower Citadel were carried out by the German Archaeological Institute at Athens, conducted by Wilhelm Dörpfeld, Georg Karo and Kurt Müller together with Heinrich Sulze until World War II. After the war, Nikolaos Verdelis discovered, in 1962/63, the Syringes, which led to new excavations in the Lower Citadel. In 1965 the German Archaeological Institute participated in Verdelis' campaign, and since 1967 the German Archaeological Institute has been in charge of the excavations at Tiryns. In the following years Ulf Jantzen and his colleagues uncovered palatial and post-palatial structures in the area south of the Syringes (GROSSMANN 1975a, 43–44, fig. 12. – HIESEL 1975), but it was Klaus Kilian, who proved, with his large-scale excavation between 1976 and 1983, the existence of not only a palatial settlement in the Lower Citadel, but also a unique sequence of LH III C settlements, which covered the whole post-palatial period (KILIAN 1978. – KILIAN 1979. – KILIAN 1981. – KILIAN 1982. – KILIAN 1983. – KILIAN 1988).

After Kilian's death and the death of his successor, Christian Podzuweit (FITTSCHEN 1993, 7), Joseph Maran became director of the excavations at Tiryns.

The ridge of Tiryns, which was also surrounded by a settlement, the Lower Town, rises only 26 m above the plain and can be divided into three sections: The Upper Citadel as the highest point in the south, where a sequence of the most important buildings of Tiryns has been found, the Middle Citadel, slightly lower, and the Lower Citadel in the north, separated from the Middle Citadel by a terrace-wall (MARAN 2000a).

In LH III B Developed, the Lower Citadel (Fig 1) was fortified by a Cyclopean wall with 28 casemates, which had partly been used even in post-palatial times. Accesses to the Lower Citadel have been located in the north, the so called North Gate, in the south-west and – to the Upper Citadel – in the south-east. The Syringes in the

---

* Special thanks to Sigrid Deger-Jalkotzy for inviting me to this workshop and for the possibility to talk about a part of my doctoral thesis, which was supervised by Joseph Maran in Heidelberg (MÜHLENBRUCH 2004). I also wish to thank Joseph Maran and Bernd Päffgen for reviewing the English text.

"Bau" means "building" and is primarily used for the palatial houses in Tiryns, so I refrained from a translation. "Kw"/"Ko" is the German abbreviation for "casemate west"/"casemate east". Some Rooms (Room 87 = "R") have two numbers. "Room 127a.b" is the abbreviation of "Room 127a and Room 127b" etc. Whereas Kilian numbered "his" rooms all the way through ("Room 97"), Maran's findings are only counted within one campaign ("Room 3/02" means the third room found in 2002).

north-western part of the fortification wall served for ensuring the water-supply (MARAN 2000a).

The roughly ovoid settlement area measured ca. 135 x 50 m. At the time of the construction of the fortification wall and the last palace at the Upper Citadel, the Lower Citadel was levelled and organised in several north-south-orientated terraces. After that, the palatial buildings were erected on different levels, ascending from west to east (MARAN 2000a). Because we know isolated houses of LH III B from the eastern part of the Lower Citadel, where they were found immediately beneath the modern surface, it is possible that LH III C structures above them have eroded since the Late Bronze Age. Buildings of the post-palatial period are nearly exclusively known from the lower west terraces. There we have a sequence from LH III C Early to LH III C Late.

Concerning the history of the settlement in the Lower Citadel,[1] first of all it is necessary to have a look at the situation at the end of the palatial period. At that time, large rectangular buildings, often with an upper storey such as the so-called corridor-houses, stood on the north-south-orientated terraces. Some of them gave access to casemates in the fortification. There was only little space for the courtyards except the so called "Zwinger", which seemed to be an official courtyard because it offered access to the casemate Kw 7 with a cult-function. There probably existed a way in the middle of the Lower Citadel from the North Gate to the Upper Citadel, a second from the North Gate to the Syringes, and another one from the "Zwinger" to the central way (DAMM-MEINHARDT unpublished. – MÜHLENBRUCH 2001, 22–23).

It seems plausible that the Lower Citadel in LH III B was a part of the palace-system and that, therefore, the access to this area was restricted. Corridor-houses, which likely served for residential and storage purposes, as workshops and in the administration and cult, are only known from LH III B and mostly from palatial contexts, so that there was no necessity for building such houses after the end of the palatial period.[2]

Immediately after the destruction of the palace, the survivors began, in the beginning of LH III C Early, with the construction of first buildings (see Fig. 2[3] for the LH III C settlement in general). Kilian called this horizon 19a "Ruinenbewohnung"/"squattering" because of the temporary character of the houses, such as Room 10a, and the state of the Lower Citadel with its depressions, ruins and debris. It is of special interest that in this situation the inhabitants built a kiln and a first shrine, Room 119 (MÜHLENBRUCH 2001, 24–25. – KILIAN 1981, 162–166).

Only Room 119 was still in use in the following horizon 19ba. Like the "squattering", the horizon 19ba in middle LH III C Early has been noticed only in a restricted area on the western terrace. The small Room 86 with its kiln has to be seen together with Room 87 = "R", which had an uneven floor and a hearth. Room 97 had an irregular ground-plan and rested on a slope. Room 119 served north of the new courtyard, Hof 1, furthermore as a shrine and demonstrates the importance of religion for the people. But still in this horizon we have to stress the provisional impression of the settlement.

I have called the end of LH III C Early, the horizon 19b1, "initial horizon", because it is the first post-palatial settlement, which covered nearly the whole western part of

---

[1] We cannot mention the time of construction and abandonment of all rooms in the Lower Citadel.

[2] KILIAN 1982, 428. – KILIAN 1983, 327. The existence of the archives in Bau VIa has not been proven (MARAN 2000a. – DAMM-MEINHARDT unpublished).

[3] R 134.135, as marked on the plan, were not rooms, but only terrace-walls (R 134 here does not mean R 134 = R 140 from horizon 21c1); R 138 is uncertain.

the Lower Citadel and whose principal plan remained unchanged in Mycenaean times. In the north-western area, Room 224 gave access to Kw 14, and the Syringes still served for the water-supply. The use of Bau II in LH III C is uncertain.

Above Bau I first the irregular complex Room 93–96 was built, its inhabitants may have also used Kw 10.11. To the south were Room 86 and Room 87 = "R", in the east Room 97.

The corridor of Bau V was used as a passage from the northern to the central western Lower Citadel. It is likely that at the same time parts of Bau VI were reconstructed as Bau VIa, which may have had an upper storey. Opposite was the shrine Room 117 in the area of the courtyard Hof 1 at the place of the former cult-casemate Kw 7 in LH III B. Also the elaborate architecture of Room 117 recalled palatial elements.

Slightly lower in the south-western part of the Lower Citadel was the irregular complex Room 74–77 with a kiln, and courtyard Hof 3. Later in horizon 19b1, after the destruction of Room 74–77, courtyard Hof 2 was established. At that time, the Rooms 87 = "R", 93–96.97 were built over Room 83 = 89a.86.88.89. Now Room 119 was levelled, too.

We can sum up that the settlement of the Lower Citadel was completely reconstructed in horizon 19b1. Most of the simple built houses were single storey, and only in LH III C Early were buildings with more than two rooms built. The principal plan of the settlement remained unchanged until LH III C Late.

In my opinion, only a basic planning existed for the rebuilding of the site. Between the new types of houses space remained for passage-ways and several courtyards. The area of the courtyard Hof 1 is of special interest. Hof 1 may have had a central meaning in the social, economical, political and – because of the shrine – religious life of the inhabitants after the end of the palace-system. However, only the existence of courtyard Hof 1, not its form, seems to have been crucial. The shrine Room 117 was erected on courtyard Hof 1 at the place, where in LH III B Developed/End the cult-casemate Kw 7 was situated above the "Zwinger". The eastern boundary of courtyard Hof 1 was marked by Bau VIa, an exceptional building in LH III C following a palatial tradition.

So maybe Bau VIa belonged to an elite, which organised the wide-scale rebuilding after the great catastrophe in Tiryns, and which was responsible for the points of contact in cult and settlement planning to the late palatial period.

After the "initial horizon" 19b1, there were not many modifications in horizon 20a1, the beginning of LH III C Developed. For the first time in the post-palatial period the use of the North Gate can be substantiated. Room 110, a new shrine, was built over Room 117. The casemate Ko 4 was used, and Room 133 shows building activity in the south-eastern part of the Lower Citadel for this horizon.

Horizon 20a3, the end of LH III C Developed, was also a period without major alterations. The use of Bau VIa is indicated by the fragment of a floor in the entrance area.

At the beginning of LH III C Advanced, horizon 21a1, Room 11.12 was a new feature to the south of Room 224, and Room 81.82, which was built over Room 83 = 89a. The courtyard Hof 2 was terraced by walls of "Room" 125. Room 127, the largest one in the post-palatial Lower Citadel, with a hearth and canal, is important. Probably the formation of courtyard Hof 3 with a new access and a small terrace-wall has to be seen in the context of the building of Room 127. The pottery found in this building may testify to the storage of valuable substances, and the quantity of drinking-vessels points to significant feasting activities. Maybe this was the house of another important group, that gained prosperity in the early post-palatial period. In this case, we may contrast the inhabitants of Room 127 as possibly belonging to a new elite with the people living in Bau VIa, whose house gives the impression of conservatism.

Therefore, after a phase of consolidation in LH III C Developed, we can recognise more building activity at the beginning of LH III C Advanced, maybe with the emergence of a new elite which occupied the south-western part of the Lower Citadel.

After horizon 21a1, in the middle of LH III C Advanced (horizon 21b1), Room 127 was reconstructed after a fire, but did not lose its prominent position with several hearths and a great quantity of pottery. Room 137 was newly constructed with a kiln south-east of courtyard Hof 3.

In horizon 21c1, at the end of LH III C Advanced, Room 135 was inhabited in the north-western area. Room 115 with probably two rows of posts and a figurine found next to a platform, served partly for cult purposes and was above Room 88 to the south of Room 86.89 and immediately to the north of the shrine Room 110. Room 134 = Room 140 was built and used just in this horizon on the slope east of courtyard Hof 2, while the northern wall of Room 126 separated the courtyards Hof 1.2. Room 127 was now enlarged and divided into Room 127a.b, but kept several hearths. Room 136 replaced Room 137.

At the end of LH III C Advanced, several buildings were destroyed by a fire, which was probably caused by an earthquake, which was also responsible for the damage of the Granary at Mycenae.[4] Room 115 may have been a hall for the cult of the elite.

At the beginning of LH III C Late, horizon 22a1, Room 11.12 and Room 135 were abandoned. Room 99 was erected south of Room 81.82, and a new shrine, Room 110a, succeeded Room 110, which had been destroyed at the end of LH III C Advanced together with Room 115. In the building Room 127a.b with one hearth in every room, a larnax in Room 127b – maybe for keimelia (FISCHER 1973. – MARAN 2006) – demonstrates another special feature of the house. Room 132 was erected on courtyard Hof 3 and may have been used in the context of Room 127a.b.

Still at the end of LH III C Late, in horizon 22c1, there was a lot of building-activity in the Lower Citadel. The complex Room 100.a succeeded Room 99, and Room 112 was erected south of the shrine. The complex Room 106.a.124, which was superimposed over Room 126, is of special interest. It contained a kiln for metalworking and several storage bins. It also possibly had an upper storey (KILIAN 1979, 383–385). With the erection of Room 106.a.124, the courtyards Hof 1.2 were separated like the courtyards Hof 2.3 at the time of Room 127a.b. But now, this building had been given up and had been built over by Room 129, so that the passage between the courtyards Hof 2.3 in horizon 22c1 was reminiscent of one of the courtyards Hof 1.2 at the time of Room 126.

Although the south-western part of the Lower Citadel was rearranged at the end of LH III C Late, the principal plan of the settlement continued. After the abandonment of Room 127a.b the complex Room 106.a.124 can be seen as the house of an important family at Tiryns.

The horizon 22d in Kilian's stratigraphy does not mark a real settlement-horizon, but a layer of debris. But also in this stratum there were indications for a small settlement in the Lower Citadel. Room 104.a was built over the northern part of Bau VIa. Its two phases of use marked the end of the Late Bronze Age at Tiryns.

Room 102a in the Lower Citadel and the important grave of a warrior in the former Lower Town testify to the Submycenaean period in Tiryns (GROSSMANN 1975b).

---

[4] KILIAN 1980, 186. Until 1983 (PODZUWEIT 1983, 360), the subphase "Developed" still contained the subphase "Advanced".

In summary, after the destruction of the palace in Tiryns, in the Lower Citadel there were horizons with more and less building activity. The settlement started with temporary houses, but also a shrine belonged to the first buildings in LH III C Early. At the end of this subphase there must have been people, who had the responsibility for the settlement. In my opinion, they must have been members of the former palatial system, because only they could have adopted the corresponding knowledge. The result can be seen in the plan of the settlement of horizon 19b1, which was continued until LH III C Late. Characteristic for LH III C were houses for residential functions, for storage and working (KILIAN 1979, 383–385) with one or two rooms and without an upper storey. Often they were built against the fortification wall, so that they could give access to the casemates. Buildings with a complicated internal structure and rooms with a specific purpose belonged to the past, so that there was a change in the function of the buildings. The houses had an influence on the form of the courtyards, but not on their existence: Especially courtyard Hof 1 served with an "altar", the shrine and fire-places as an important part in the daily life of the people. The significance of courtyards may demonstrate the meaning of the consent between the elite as the responsible body and the community.

All shrines in front of the former cult-casemate Kw 7 were unique in their form and elaborate furnishings. Their positions bordering to the courtyard also enabled a more common cult praxis than in the palace period (ALBERS 1994, 105–111. – MÜHLENBRUCH 2001, 38).

Ruins of LH III B still existed in the settlement of the early post-palatial period, but the position of the courtyard Hof 1 and the shrines Room 117.110.a also demonstrate a reminiscence of the palatial times. This is particularly striking in the case of Bau VIa and may give an indication for important inhabitants, perhaps former functionaries of the palatial system.

In comparison to the late LH III C Early, the alterations in LH III C Developed were minimal. Room 110 served as a new shrine.

In LH III C Advanced, the construction of the complex Room 127.a.b attracts attention not only because of its size, its furnishment and its findings, but also because of the forming of courtyard Hof 3 as a possibly "private" area. Room 127.a.b could have been the seat of a risen elite. Room 115 may have served for the cult of the various prominent groups in Tiryns.

The end of LH III C Advanced is marked by a destruction horizon, perhaps caused by an earthquake. Afterwards there were new building activities in the Lower Citadel, and with the rebuilding of complex Room 127a.b and, after its abandonment, with the erection of Room 106.a.124, the existence of prominent houses until the second part of LH III C Late can be established. At the end of the Late Bronze Age and in the Submycenaean phase, isolated houses were still inhabited.

Maran has been able to prove Kilian's assumption that the "Antenbau" on the Upper Citadel was a post-palatial building with reminiscences to the former Megaron (MARAN 2000b). Because of the duration of LH III C Early, in my opinion it is highly probable that it was built in this subphase, and served as a meeting-house for the prominent groups at Tiryns (MÜHLENBRUCH 2001, 48). These persons, who may have been officials in the former palace administration, could have summoned up all their experience to rebuild the site. Perhaps one of these groups lived in Bau VIa in the Lower Citadel, but it is plausible that there were several important groups, likely families. Others may have lived in the buildings Room 127.a.b in LH III C Advanced/Late and in Room 106.a.124 in LH III C Late, so that we have to take into account the rise and fall and – above all – the rivalry among these groups, maybe for the throne in the Antenbau. In addition, we have to take into account the settlement in the Lower Town, an area I left aside in this paper.

The competition of the elite was, in my opinion, instrumental for the flourishing during the post-palatial times. In the Lower Citadel of Tiryns, the beginning of the flourishing can be dated to the end of LH III C Early, and it lasted, maybe with a break in LH III C Developed, until late in LH III C Late. But this only applies to Tiryns, and we have to stress that a flourishing period in the archaeological and especially in the architectural record may merely be the result of former prosperity.

Bibliography

ALBERS, G.
1994 *Spätmykenische Stadtheiligtümer. Systematische Analyse und vergleichende Auswertung der archäologischen Befunde* (BAR-IS 596). Oxford.

DAMM-MEINHARDT, U.
unpublished *Architekturbefunde und Stratigraphie der Phase Späthelladisch (SH) III B und der beginnenden Phase SH III C in der Unterburg von Tiryns.*

DEGER-JALKOTZY, S. – I. S. LEMOS (eds.)
2006 *Ancient Greece: From the Mycenaean Palaces to the Age of Homer* (Edinburgh Leventis Studies 3). Edinburgh.

DEUTSCHES ARCHÄOLOGISCHES INSTITUT (ed.)
2000 *Archäologische Entdeckungen. Die Forschungen des Deutschen Archäologischen Instituts im 20. Jahrhundert* (Sonderbände der Antiken Welt). Mainz.

DÖRPFELD, W.
1886 "Die Bauwerke von Tiryns", 200–352 in: SCHLIEMANN 1886.

FISCHER, F.
1973 "ΚΕΙΜΗΛΙΑ. Bemerkungen zur kulturgeschichtlichen Interpretation des sogenannten Südimports in der späten Hallstatt- und frühen Latène-Kultur des westlichen Mitteleuropa", *Germania* 51, 436–459.

FITTSCHEN, K.
1993 "Klaus Kilian – Leben und Werk", *AM* 108, 1–7.

GROSSMANN, P.
1975a "Die Unterburg: Die Befestigung", 43–47 in: JANTZEN 1975.
1975b "Die Dunklen Jahrhunderte", 95 in: JANTZEN 1975.

HIESEL, G.
1975 "Geschichte der Ausgrabungen", 112–113 in: JANTZEN 1975.

JANTZEN, U. (ed.)
1975 *Führer durch Tiryns*. Athens.

KILIAN, K.
1978 "Ausgrabungen in Tiryns 1976. Bericht zu den Grabungen", *AA*, 449–470.
1979 "Ausgrabungen in Tiryns 1977. Bericht zu den Grabungen", *AA*, 379–411.
1980 "Zum Ende der mykenischen Epoche in der Argolis", *RGZM* 27, 166–195.
1981 "Ausgrabungen in Tiryns 1978. 1979. Bericht zu den Grabungen", *AA*, 149–194.
1982 "Ausgrabungen in Tiryns 1980. Bericht zu den Grabungen", *AA*, 393–430.
1983 "Ausgrabungen in Tiryns 1981. Bericht zu den Grabungen", *AA*, 277–328.
1988 "Ausgrabungen in Tiryns 1982/83. Bericht zu den Grabungen", *AA*, 105–151.

MARAN, J.
2000a "Tiryns – Mauern und Paläste für namenlose Herrscher", 118–123 in: DEUTSCHES ARCHÄOLOGISCHES INSTITUT 2000.
2000b "Das Megaron im Megaron. Zur Datierung und Funktion des Antenbaus im mykenischen Palast von Tiryns", *AA*, 1–16.
2006 "Coming to Terms with the Past: Ideology and Power in Late Helladic III C", 123–150 in: DEGER-JALKOTZY – LEMOS 2006.

MÜHLENBRUCH, T.
2001 *Mykenische Architektur. Studien zur Siedlungsentwicklung nach dem Untergang der Paläste in der Argolis und Korinthia* (unpublished MA dissertation). Heidelberg.
2004 *Ein dunkles Zeitalter? Untersuchungen zur Siedlungsstruktur der Unterburg von Tiryns in der mykenischen Nachpalastzeit* (unpublished Ph.D. thesis). Heidelberg.

PODZUWEIT, C.
1983 "Bericht zur spätmykenischen Keramik. Ausgrabungen in Tiryns 1981. Die Phasen SH III C Fortgeschritten bis Spät", *AA*, 359–402.

SCHLIEMANN, H.
1886 *Tiryns. Der prähistorische Palast der Könige von Tiryns. Ergebnisse der neuesten Ausgrabungen*. Leipzig.

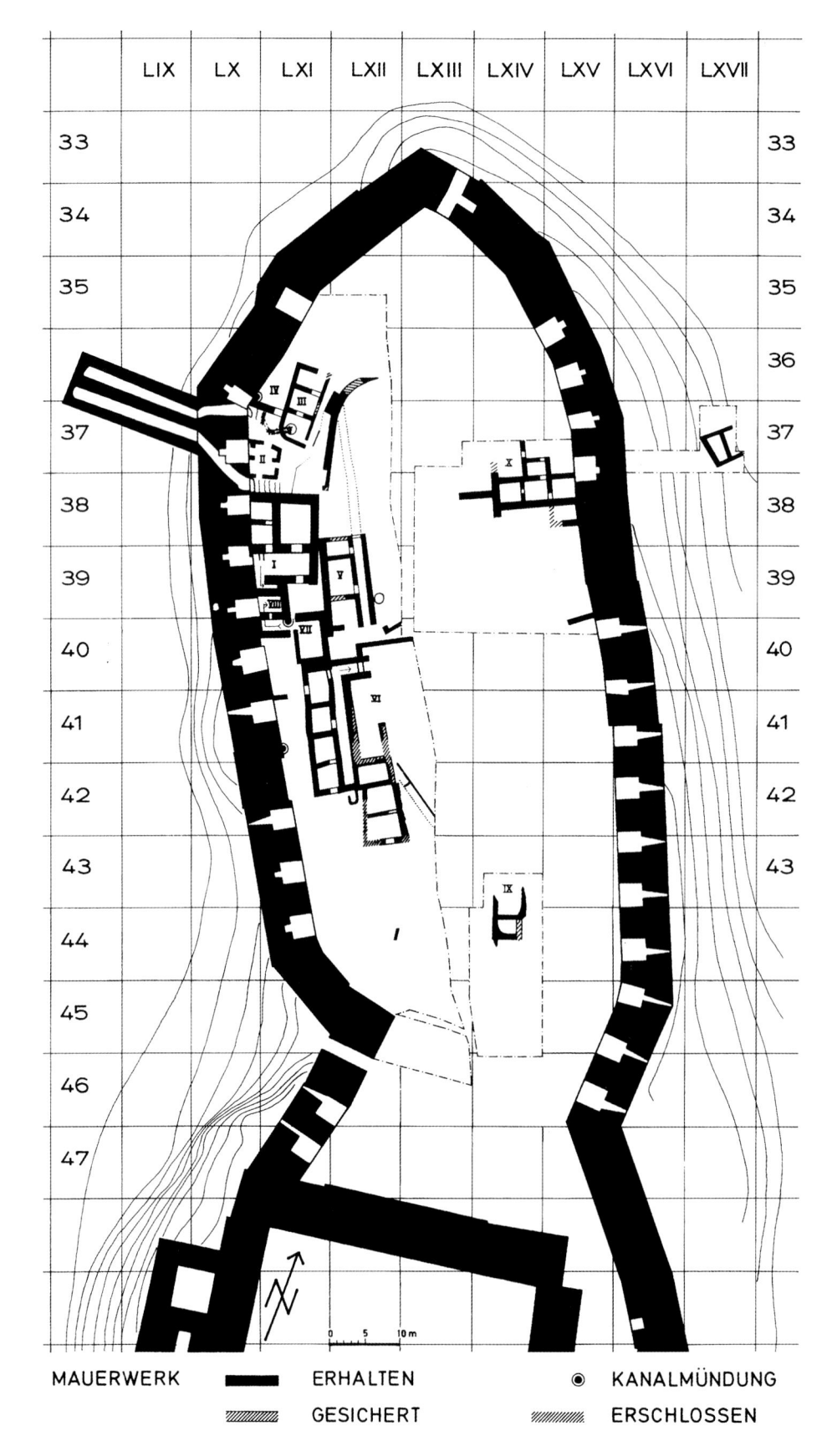

Fig. 1 Tiryns, Lower Citadel. Buildings from LH III B Developed/End (after Kilian 1982, fig. 23)

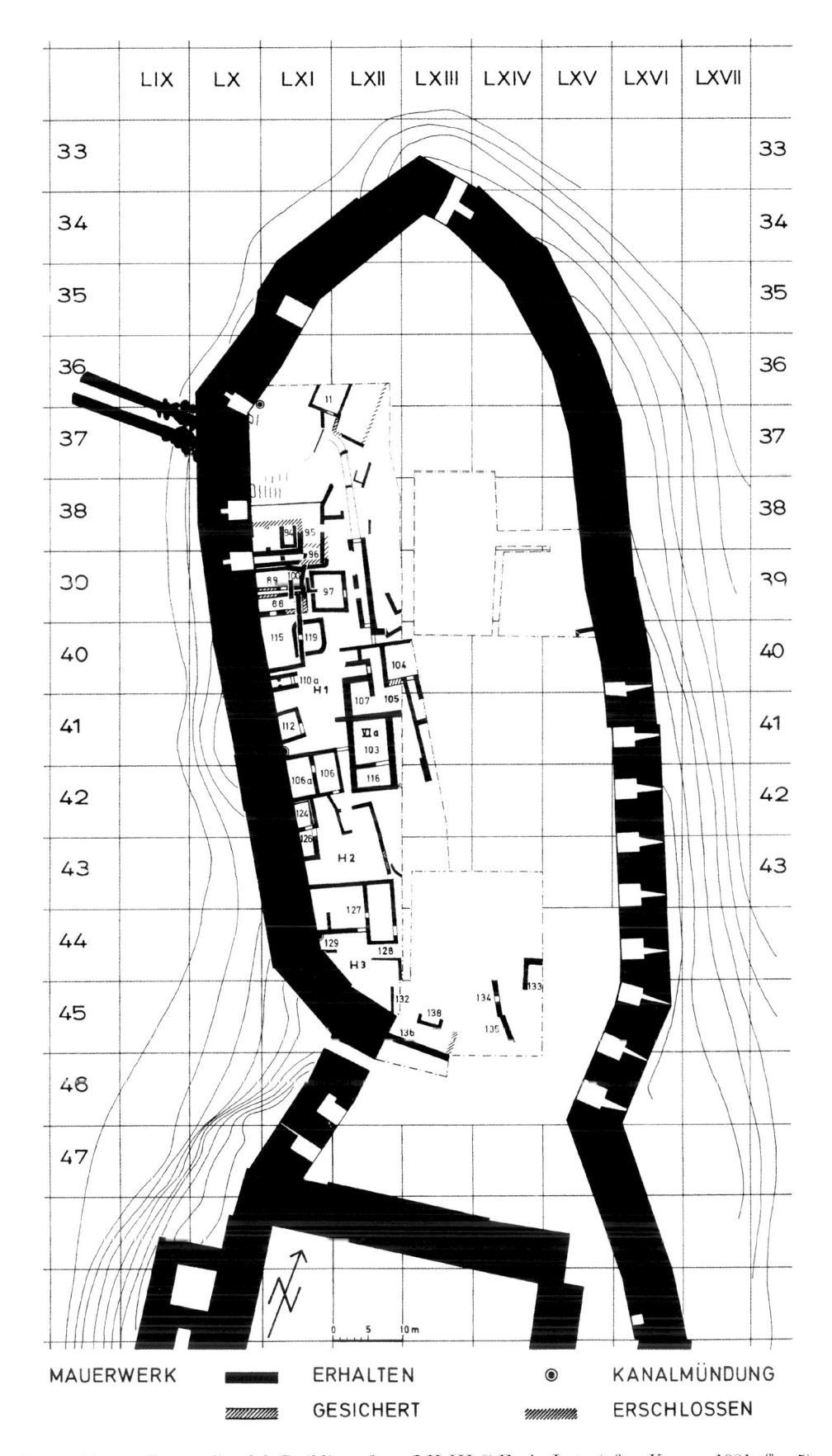

Fig. 2 Tiryns, Lower Citadel. Buildings from LH III C Early-Late (after KILIAN 1981, fig. 5)

MICHALIS PETROPOULOS

A MYCENAEAN CEMETERY AT NIKOLEIKA
NEAR AIGION OF ACHAIA*

During 1995 at Nikoleika, south-east of Aigion in Achaia (Fig. 1), on account of some public works, a Mycenaean cemetery of chamber tombs on the northern slope of mount Agios Ilias came to light (Fig. 2. – PETROPOULOS 2000b, 233–236. – PETROPOULOS 2001, 240). Based on surface observations we assume that there are at least 70 tombs. We excavated only three, because they were in danger, while a fourth one was completely destroyed during the works. The cemetery lies in the region between the rivers Selinous and Kerynitis, which in the classical period constituted the *chora* of ancient Helike. The classical city has not yet been found, although systematic investigations, which started in 1989 are still continuing today (PETROPOULOS 2004. – PETROPOULOS 2002, 148).[1] But the most remarkable element of this research is the finding of an EH II settlement in the plain, under the hill of the Mycenaean cemetery.[2]

Helike was one of the 12 or 14 cities of Achaia, as the written sources inform us (PETROPOULOS 1999, 37 n. 162). According to these sources the Achaian cities were created, or existed, during the Mycenaean period (Hdt. 1.145, 1.148. – Strab. 8.383. – Polyb. 2.41.4. – Paus. VII, 2,18.8, 2,38.1, 3,13.4 and 22.6, 5,1.1, 6,1). This information seems to be confirmed by the excavations, because in almost all of the classical cities identified elements of the Mycenaean period have been found.[3] Where the excavations were of a more systematic nature, settlements of the EH or the MH periods have been found in deeper layers.[4] The same seems to have happened in Helike. The Mycenaean settlement is not in the plain any more, as the EH one was, but on the hill of Agios Georgios, to the west of the cemetery (PETROPOULOS 1990, 511). The large distance between the settle-

---

* I would like to thank Prof. Jalkotzy, an old and good friend of mine, for her kind invitation to come to Vienna and present the finds of the Mycenaean cemetery, which I excavated some years ago. My warmest thanks also go to my colleague I. Moschos for his help; to the architect T. Stamatopoulou for the drawings of the tombs; to my wife Maria for the drawings of the vases, and to my colleague M. Gazis for the revision of the English text.

[1] Except our Ephorate, another Scientific Group is also searching in the region for the location of the ancient city. The American School of Classical Studies of Athens tried to solve the problem between 1989 and 1998. The search is continued by the Geological School of the University of Patras, with the contribution of Dr. D. Katsonopoulou.

[2] One grave of the MH period was found near the Mycenaean cemetery on the small hill Psoriarou or Kallithea (PETROPOULOS 2000b, 234). We had supposed that the EH settlement would also be found on the same small hill. However, Dr. D. Katsonopoulou announced that an EH settlement was found in the plain during their investigations (KATSONOPOULOU 2002, 207–209).

[3] In Aigion, Aigeira, Rhypes, Patras (in two places), Pharai, Olenos, Tritaia, Dyme, etc.

[4] As for example in Aigion, Aigeira, Aigai, Patras and Dyme. But generally more than twenty EH II sites are known in Achaia. Only in the wider region of ancient Helike are finds from two EH II sites exposed in the Archaeological Museum of Aigion: From Aigion and from Akrata (ancient Aigai). This density of the EH sites in Achaia is absolutely normal, because the EH inhabitants passed from Northern Greece to

ment and the cemetery is due to the fact that there is no suitable rock for the opening of chamber tombs in the hill of the settlement. Among the excavated tombs, Tomb 1 was the one completely destroyed by the works. Tomb 3 was almost completely destroyed; only the skeleton of a child was found.

CHAMBER TOMB 2

Chamber Tomb 2 had an irregular, circular shape (Figs. 3–5). Its dromos was almost completely destroyed by the works. A large number of bones of removed skeletons were found on the chamber floor. The number of the skulls shows that they belonged to 27 individuals. Most of them were pushed aside along the back inner wall of the tomb. The grave offerings show that the first use of it took place during the LH III A period. One naturalistic female figurine of this period and a small tongued dagger, which may be dated in LH II B, stand out among the older finds. The use of the tomb continued without interruption until the LH III C period.

Only a part of a primary burial (T2/A) was found on the chamber floor, in which four pit-graves were also opened. One of them contained one removed skeleton, the second only some offerings and each of the third and the fourth one primary burial (Λ1/A, Λ1/B). The primary burials belong to the last period of use of the tomb, which contained a total of 58 clay vases, two bronze daggers (Fig. 9), four bronze tweezers, three bronze knives, one bronze razor, one whetstone, a great number of glass beads, 14 buttons of steatite, seven clay whorls, one bronze needle, two bronze rings, three sea shell-pendants, parts of one bronze spearhead, half of a naturalistic clay figurine of a woman, and four seals (Fig. 30), one of glass and three of steatite (PETROPOULOS – PINI 2004, 89–92).

The three primary burials belong to the LH III C period and these are of interest to us.

Primary Burial T2/A on the floor of the tomb

Only the skull and some parts of the thighbones were preserved, which show that the dead person was buried in a contracted position. A large number of vases[5] were found around the burial, but it is not sure that they belonged to it. It is possible that they rather belonged to the removed burials, which were around it.
Four vases were found to the north of the skeleton:

The **stirrup jar Π 9**[6] (inv. no. AΠ 1803, H. 0.18 m, FS 175, Fig. 31a–b), dates to LH III C Middle/Late.[7] The decoration on the shoulder consists of panels with FM 50

---

the Peloponnese not only through Corinth, but also through Rion–Antirrion. So, instead of searching for suitable sites to stay at in the rest of the Peloponnese, they preferred to exploit the small plains of Achaia, the first land they saw after the crossing, and the hills around them. Nearly every year during the past decade the Ephorate has located a new EH II settlement. The most recent site was found two years ago near ancient Aigeira, by the river Krios, during the survey, which is carried out by the Ephorate, in cooperation with the Italian School of Athens and the University of Salerno (PETROPOULOS – PONTRANDOLFO-RIZAKIS 2004, 955–959). The EH II settlement of the current year was located at Kato Kastritsi, a small village north of Patras.

[5] Only the height of the vases and a small description, where it is needed, are given in the text, because it is a preliminary presentation, but there are photos of all of them and many drawings.

[6] The Greek letter "Π" characterises the excavation number.

[7] RMDP, 169 no. 349, fig. 46, from the Argolid, LH III C Middle. The philosophy of the decoration of the shoulder is near the stirrup jar, RMDP, 435 no. 129, fig. 157, from Klauss, LH III C Late.

and lozenges with four concentrated semicircles in the inner corners. A zone of chevrons alternating with foliate bands is found below the shoulder.

The **double kernos**, or **multiple vase Π 10** (inv. no. ΑΠ 2301, H. 0.097 m, Fig. 33) consists of two handleless straight-sided alabastra, FS 330, LH III C Middle/Late.[8] The few traces of the decoration are composed of chevrons.

The **based askos Π 11** (inv. no. ΑΠ 2295, H. 0.095 m, FS 195, Fig. 32a–b) dates to LH III C Early/Middle developed. Although its shape is very rare, it has a parallel in Tomb 4 of Nikoleika (cf. based askos Π 49, comments).

The **one-handled jug Π 12** (inv. no. ΑΠ 2296, H. 0.049 m, FS 115, Fig. 34) with linear decoration, although having the biconical body known from Delphi (*RMDP*, 787 nos. 270–272, fig. 310), cannot be dated to LH III C Late, because it was found with the askos (the two vases perhaps accompanied the dead). So it must date to LH III C Early/Middle developed, like the askos. If it did not belong to the offerings of the primary burial, which date to this period, then it could date with the group of the vases Π 9, Π 10 and Π 15 of LH III C Late.

The only things that certainly belonged to the primary burial and were found along the left side of the dead, are:

The **stirrup jar Π 14** (inv. no. ΑΠ 2289, H. 0.088 m, FS 174, Fig. 37a–b), has a dumpy narrow-based body and zigzag on the shoulder, which can be dated to LH III C Early or at least Middle developed (*RMDP*, 421 no. 81, fig. 148, from Chalandritsa in western Achaia, and *RMDP*, 429 no. 100, fig. 151), and three small finds, a bronze razor, bronze tweezers, and a whetstone.

The **large monochrome narrow-necked jug Π 15** (inv. no. ΑΠ 2300, H. 0.19 m, FS 121, Fig. 35) cannot be associated to this primary burial with certainty. It has the shape of the FS 175 stirrup jars of western Achaia (PAPADOPOULOS 1978/79, 71),[9] and a chronology in the LH III C Middle/Late period may be possible.

The **straight-sided alabastron Π 13** (inv. no. ΑΠ 2297, H. 0.084 m, Figs. 10; 36), was found near the jug. The base is popular on the island of Rhodes[10] and generally in the Dodecanese, but there are also some examples from Mainland Greece (see the examples given by *RMDP*, 1099: Attica 333, Skyros 29, Argolid 331. – Cf. BENZI 1992, 41–42. – KARANTZALI 2001, 61). It belongs to a local workshop because it does not have the usual decoration of the islands on the body (wide and narrow bands). The decoration of the lip, small lines instead of dots, is also a local characteristic. The shape FS 97, although seldom, is also found in western Achaia.[11] The small lines on the handles and the horizontal lines on the body, although they are not dense, are connected with the typical decoration of the vases of the LH III C Middle/Late. A very similar shape, with the same decoration, foliate band on the shoulder zone and bands on the vertical sides, comes from Aigion. This decoration is the most popular pattern in Achaia

---

[8] An almost similar vase comes from Elis (*RMDP*, 391 no. 76, fig. 136, LH III C Middle), and two others from Attica (*RMDP*, 574 no. 357, fig. 212, LH III C Early and *RMDP*, 596 no. 457, fig. 222, LH III C Middle). A triple multiple kernos comes from Kladeos (Elis), VIKATOU 2004, 232 (tomb 9), pl. 96α:Π7628 (LH III C).

[9] A stirrup jar from Asine, Argolid, LH III C Middle (*RMDP*, 169 no. 346, fig. 46) has a similar shape.

[10] One from Pylona was imported from the Mainland (Argolid) (KARANTZALI 2001, 60–61, fig. 41, pl. 43d [no. 16775]). Four more vases come from Ialysos (IBID., 61. Cf. *RMDP*, 1038 nos. 168–170, fig. 425). Also from Kos (*RMDP*, 1102 no. 77, fig. 450, 1112 no. 127, fig. 155).

[11] *RMDP*, 418 does not include FS 97 in the shapes of Achaia, as there is only one unpublished example from Portes.

and A. Papadopoulos dates the vase from Aigion to the LH III C:1a period (PAPADOPOULOS 1978/79, 89 no. 13, LH III C:1a). Chronology: LH III C Middle or Middle/Late.

The primary burial T2/A was not the last, as we can suppose from its disturbance. The vases Π 9, Π 10, perhaps Π 15 and one more stirrup jar Π 8, that were found on the floor near the entrance of the tomb, belonged to a later burial (burial T 2/B) of LH III C Middle/Late, the skeleton of which was moved for the digging of Pit 1 or 2.

Primary Burial Λ1/A (pit)

This rectangular pit was found in the centre of the chamber tomb. Its dimensions were 1.43 × 0.40 × 0.60 m. It contained the disturbed skeleton of a primary burial. Three vases were found on the waist of the skeleton: The **stirrup jar Π 63** (inv. no. ΑΠ 1805, H. 0.073 m, Fig. 38a–b), partly preserved, the **small lekythos Π 64** (inv. no. ΑΠ 2286, H. 0.092 m, Figs. 11; 39a–b) and the **stirrup jar Π 62** (inv. no. ΑΠ 1784, H. 0.10 m, Fig. 40a–b). They date to LH III C Late, close to the Submycenaean period.

The stirrup jar Π 62 and the small lekythos Π 64 have the same zone of decoration on the shoulder, which consists of chevrons. On the small lekythos the decoration is completed with the figure of a griffin (?) or scorpion (?) with a long tail (Figs. 11; 39b). The fringed high triangle on the stirrup jar Π 63 is very common in the LH III C period (PAPADOPOULOS 1978/79, 130) and usual during the Submycenaean period in western Achaia. This decoration continues during the Protogeometric period (GADOLOU 2000, plan 11 [ΑΜΠ 1578Θ/K44], plan 32, figs. 23ζ; 35. – PAPADOPOULOS 1978/79, 137).

Primary Burial Λ2/A

The pit was opened in the left part of the Tomb. Its dimensions were 1.10 × 0.40 × 0.65 m. The dead was buried in a contracted position. Four vases were found along the right side of the dead: The **two-handled small amphora (amphoriskos) Π 65** (inv. no. ΑΠ 2299, H. 0.11 m, Fig. 41), the **stirrup jar Π 66** (inv. no. ΑΠ 1794, H. 0.30 m, Fig. 42a–b), the **stirrup jar Π 67** (inv. no. ΑΠ 1804, H. 0.108 m, Fig. 43), and the **stirrup jar Π 68** (inv. no. ΑΠ 1801, H. 0.11 m, Fig. 44). The burial dates to the LH III C Late period.

Comments

The use of the tomb during the LH III A period is proved by the following vases:[12] The **piriform jar Π 38** (inv. no. ΑΠ 1779, H. 0.15 m, Fig. 45),[13] the small **stirrup jar Π 39** (inv. no. ΑΠ 1792, H. 0.08 m, Fig. 46a–b),[14] the **stirrup jar Π 40** (inv. no. ΑΠ 1800, H. 0.10 m,

---

[12] My colleague Dr. Helen Papazoglou-Manioudaki examined the earliest periods of the cemetery (PAPAZOGLOU-MANIOUDAKI 1998, vol. 1, 103–105; vol. 2, pls. 1.3, 1–4).

[13] A similar vase comes from Aigion (PAPADOPOULOS 1976, 30–31 no. 6, pl. 93b, LH III A:2a–B1[–2?]).

[14] *RMDP*, 140 no. 252, fig. 34, from the Argolid. For an almost identical stirrup vase from western Achaia (Patras), but with a more conical body, which was imported from western Crete and dates to LH III B, see PAPAZOGLOU-MANIOUDAKI 1993, 211, fig. 2γ, pl. 23c–d. The shoulder decoration of our vase, with chevrons in the form of a five-radial star, is found on another vase from Aigeira of the LH III B period (*RMDP*, 414 no. 48, fig. 145).

Fig. 47a–b) (*RMDP*, 415 nos. 44–45, fig. 145, from Achaia), the **stirrup jar Π 42–Π 59** (inv. no. ΑΠ 1799, H. 0.095 m, Fig. 48a–b) (*RMDP*, 415 no. 45, fig. 145, from Aigion) and the **stirrup jar Π 60** (inv. no. ΑΠ 1808, H. 0.10 m, Fig. 49a–b) (*RMDP*, 415 no. 45, fig. 145, from Aigion).

The use of the tomb during the LH III B period is proved by the following vases: The **stirrup jar Π 26** (inv. no. ΑΠ 1790, H. 0.146 m, Fig. 50a–b) (*RMDP*, 140 nos. 251–252, 255, figs. 33–34, from the Argolid), the **stirrup jar Π 27** (inv. no. ΑΠ 1782, H. 1.13 m, Fig. 51a–b) (*RMDP*, 140 no. 250, fig. 33, and 147 no. 285, fig. 37, from the Argolid), the **three-handled alabastron Π 30** (inv. no. ΑΠ 1788, H. 0.16 m, Fig. 52) (*RMDP*, 386 no. 57, fig. 134, from Elis) with net pattern on the shoulder and the **three-handled alabastron Π 35** (inv. no. ΑΠ 1780, H. 0.14 m, Fig. 53) (*RMDP*, 386 no. 57, fig. 134, from Elis). The stirrup jar Π 27 was imported from the Argolid, and an absolutely similar vase was found in Patras,[15] dated to the LH III B period. These stirrup jars from the Argolid are also found in Aigion and in Teichos Dymaion (PAPAZOGLOU-MANIOUDAKI 1993, 211).[16]

The following vases confirm the use of the tomb during the LH III C Early period: The stirrup jar **Π 25** (inv. no. ΑΠ 2290, H. 0.105 m, Fig. 55a–b) (*RMDP*, 155 no. 310, fig. 40, from the Argolid) and the stirrup jar **Π 37+59** (inv. no. ΑΠ 1798, H. 0.14 m, Fig. 54) (*RMDP*, 421 no. 81, fig. 148, from Achaia).

The earlier burial in situ is burial T2/A (LH III C Early to LH III C Middle developed). Burial T2/B follows (LH III C Middle/Late). Some vases which were removed during the digging of Pit 1 or 2 remained in the area around the burial. The burials of the Pits Λ1/A and Λ2/A are dated to the LH III C Late, probably at the end of the period.

CHAMBER TOMB 4

Chamber Tomb 4, like Tomb 2, has an irregular shape (Figs. 6–8). This deformation is due to the fact that the initial, circular shape, was changed, because there was need for more room for the later burials. So some niches with pits were opened in the periphery of the tomb. Another reason was also the bad quality of the rock, which resulted in the frequent falling of big parts of the lateral walls and of the roof onto the floor. So, the pits were also opened for the protection of the skeletons (for the same conclusion, see MOSCHOS 2002, 28). During the last period of its use the floor of the tomb was used as an ossuary. No primary burial was found on it, only a great number of removed skeletons. The bones belonged to at least twenty people, as can be assumed by the number of the skulls. 37 vases were found in the layer of the removed skeletons, along with nine beads of glass and two of cornelian, one bone comb, two small bronze nails with gilt heads, one bronze pin, one bronze bracelet, one bronze ring, three clay whorls, seven steatite buttons, and some other smaller finds. Seven pits (Λ1–Λ7) were opened in the floor. They contained one or two skeletons in situ. Two of them also contained removed skeletons of earlier burials, which were perhaps primary burials on the floor. 23 clay vases, nine glass beads, two steatite buttons, one bronze needle, one bronze knife, one bronze sword of Naue II type and one clay whorl were found in the pits.

Tomb 4 was in use from LH II B until LH III C.

---

[15] PAPAZOGLOU-MANIOUDAKI 1993, 211, pl. 23e–f. The shoulder decoration, Mycenaean flowers, is the same and from the same hand. Another stirrup jar, FS 173, with the same shoulder decoration comes from Achaia, without place provenance (*RMDP*, 415 no. 44, fig. 145).

[16] My colleague, I. Moschos, has informed me that similar stirrup jars have been also found in Voudeni.

Floor

Some vases on the floor are of special interest. These are the **stirrup jar Π 39** (inv. no. ΑΠ 2287, H. 0.093 m, Fig. 56a–b), which was possibly imported from Voudeni, an important Mycenaean centre of western Achaia, near Patras. The cemetery of Voudeni has been completely studied by L. Kolonas.[17] The **squat jug Π 27** (inv. no. ΑΠ 1834, H. 0.07 m, FS 87, Fig. 57) dates to the LH II B period.[18] A **hole-mouthed jar** (without number of excavation, inv. no. ΑΠ 1765, H. 0.269 m, FS 101, Fig. 58) dates to LH II A, and may have been imported from the Argolid (*RMDP*, 89 no. 37, fig. 13 [LH II A], and 100 no. 82, fig. 17 [LH II B]). A similar jar comes from Thermon of Aitolia and also dates to the LH II A period (*RMDP*, 799 no. 2, fig. 319). The **stirrup jar Π 34** (inv. no. ΑΠ 2293, H. 0.105 m, FS 175, Figs. 12; 59a–b) dates to LH III C Late and is imported from western Achaia (*RMDP*, 435 nos. 120–124, fig. 155. – PETROPOULOS 2000a, fig. 38, no. 9890 [LH III C Middle to Late]). Another **stirrup jar Π 21** (inv. no. ΑΠ 2292, H. 0.098 m, Figs. 13; 60a–b), of LH III C Middle/Late belongs to a local workshop which shows influence from Phokis (*RMDP*, 790 no. 285, fig. 311 [LH III C Late, from Delphi]). A third **stirrup jar** from Pit 6 (**Τ4/Λ6/ΟΜ 29**, inv. no. ΑΠ 1817, H. 0.092 m, Figs. 14; 61a–b) also belongs to the same workshop and to the same craftsman, such as the **stirrup jar Π 36** (inv. no. ΑΠ 1821, H. 0.112 m, Figs. 15; 62a–b). They date rather to LH III C/Middle. The **stamnos Π 35** (inv. no. ΑΠ 1763, H. 0.24 m, Fig. 63a–b) was found with the stirrup jar Π 34 and can be dated to the LH III C Middle/Late period.[19]

Removed skeleton

One removed skeleton, which was found in a niche at the back part of the tomb, over Pit Λ2, is also of special interest. A group of seven vases was found among the bones, which initially belonged to more primary burials. The group consists of the following vases:

The **stirrup jar Π 12** (inv. no. ΑΠ 1829, H. 0.13 m, FS 175, Figs. 16; 64) rather belongs to LH III C Middle/Late. The decoration in a zone below the shoulder is unique and obscure (row of X-X-pattern? Crosses? Simplified net pattern? N-pattern? Joining semicircles? Quirk or rather lozenge in a chain?). The vase belongs rather to the local workshop.[20]

---

[17] KOLONAS 2007 (in press). His book (three-volumes) is in press and will give us many new elements for Mycenaean Achaia. The information is owed to my colleague I. Moschos. For the identification of Voudeni with ancient Messatis, see PETROPOULOS 2001/02, 406–407.

[18] The shape of the vase and the system of decoration is very close to the alabastra from the Argolid of this period (*RMDP*, 98 nos. 75, 77–78, fig. 17). But our vase is closer to the squat jug (*RMDP*, 209 no. 46, fig. 65, from Corinthia [Galataki], LH II B). A similar vase comes from Aigion (PAPADOPOULOS 1976, pls. 76a; 79c: LH II B). L. Papazoglou characterises some almost similar vases from Vrysari, modern southern Achaia but ancient northern Arcadia, as one-handled alabastron and dates them to LH II B (PAPAZOGLOU-MANIOUDAKI 1999, 274–275, figs. 20–27). Another squat jug with the same shape comes from the region of Patras (Petroto) and dates to LH II B (PAPAZOGLOU-MANIOUDAKI 2003, 448, fig. 10:11–12). For the vase from Nikoleika see also PAPAZOGLOU-MANIOUDAKI 1998, vol. 1, 104, pl. A.3, 3, who dates it to the LH II B period.

[19] The system of the decoration is like that of a four-handled jar from Chalandritsa (*RMDP*, 425 no. 85, fig. 149), of a stirrup jar from Achaia (*RMDP*, 429 no. 100, fig. 151. – PAPADOPOULOS 1978/79, fig. 66e–f), both of LH III C Middle, and a stirrup jar from Klauss (*RMDP*, 435 no. 127, fig. 156. – PAPADOPOULOS 1978/79, fig. 67c), dated to LH III C Late. See also PETROPOULOS 2000a, figs. 22–23, from Spaliareika in western Achaia, LH III C Middle to Late.

[20] The stirrup jar PAPADOPOULOS 1978/79, figs. 98–99, in Berlin, comes from Aigeira, a city near Helike, and the decoration on the shoulder is a little similar. It is dated to LH III C:1a.

The **three-handled straight-sided alabastron Π 13** (inv. no. ΑΠ 1823, H. 0.083 m, FS 96, Figs. 17; 66) with opened linear triangles belongs to LH III C Middle developed.[21]

The **three-handled straight-sided alabastron Π 14** (inv. no. ΑΠ 2298, H. 0.071 m, FS 96, Fig. 67) belongs to LH III C Early.[22]

The **two-handled straight-sided alabastron Π 15** (inv. no. ΑΠ 1826, H. 0.09 m, FS 96, Figs. 18; 68) belongs to LH III C Early/Middle.[23]

The **amphoriskos Π 16** (inv. no. ΑΠ 1832, H. 0.08 m, FS 59, Figs. 19; 65) belongs to LH III C Late.

The **stirrup jar Π 17** (inv. no. ΑΠ 1824, H. 0.18 m, Figs. 20; 69a–b) belongs to LH III C Early/Middle?[24]

The **two-handled rounded alabastron Π 18** (inv. no. ΑΠ 1833, H. 0.08 m, FS 86, Figs. 21; 70), with net decoration,[25] belongs to LH III C Early.

Comments on some vases from the floor

The **stirrup jar Π 36** (Figs. 15; 62a–b) belongs rather to the LH III C Middle period.

The **stirrup jar Π 21** (Figs. 13; 60a–b) was made in eastern Achaia and imitates vases of western Achaia. The shape is close to FS 174–175, the first still in use in western Achaia during LH III C Middle developed, while the latter (FS 175) made its appearance in the same period. The angular base is a typical feature of FS 175 stirrup jars in western Achaia. It is possible that the broad band in the wider part of the body harks back to the decoration of the body with broad bands, framing thinner ones. The horizontal small lines on the handles follow the typical characteristic of the Middle/Late style in western Achaia. The shoulder decoration is rather an evolution of the early style, which L. Papazoglou has established in the tomb of the warrior at Krini of Patras (PAPAZOGLOU-MANIOUDAKI 1994, 189–193).[26] The curved motifs are frequent on the vases from Nikoleika and it can be said that they are characteristic of the decoration of LH III C in eastern Achaia or Aigialeia, corresponding with the concentric semicircles of western Achaia.[27] The three-curved compact motif with the dots in the semicircles is rather a tassel. The stirrup jar FS 175 from Delphi of LH III C Late (*RMDP*, 790 no. 285, fig. 311) is similar. Chronology: LH III C Middle/Advanced to LH III C Late.

The **stirrup jar Π 34**, FS 175 (Figs. 12; 59a–b), has fringed semicircles on the shoulder. Bands run all down the body. It was found on the upper layer of the floor of the tomb with

---

[21] P. MOUNTJOY (*RMDP*, 427) does not assign any Achaian FS 96 vase to this period.

[22] *RMDP*, 418. An evolution of the motif of the shoulder is found on the oinochoe Π 12415 from Spaliareika (PETROPOULOS 2000a, fig. 36) of LH III C Middle to Late. For earlier three-handled alabastra from western Achaia (LH III A2) and their origin from the Argolid, see PAPAZOGLOU-MANIOUDAKI 1993, 212, fig. 2ε, pl. 24d.

[23] P. MOUNTJOY (*RMDP*, 418) includes this shape in the LH III C Early period. But the decoration is more familiar in LH III C Middle.

[24] The same decoration system of the body is found on the stirrup jars Π 9880 and Π 9887 from Spaliareika (PETROPOULOS 2000a, fig. 33), of the LH III C Middle. It is also found on a square-sided alabastron from Aigion (PAPADOPOULOS 1976, 30 no. 5, pl. 93a, LH III A:2a).

[25] The same decoration is found on the based two-handled alabastron Π 9881 from Spaliareika (PETROPOULOS 2000a, fig. 24), LH III C Middle to Late. It is also found from LH III A1 onwards on vases from Elis (*RMDP*, fig. 131) and from the Argolid (Prosymna) (*RMDP*, 106 no. 106, fig. 20).

[26] A stirrup jar with similar decoration on the shoulder comes from Spaliareika of Lousika and dates to LH III C Middle (PETROPOULOS 2000a, 73, tomb 1, fig. 14).

[27] For the concentric semicircular motifs of western Achaia, see PAPADOPOULOS 1978/79, 77. – *RMDP*, 44. – MOSCHOS 2002, 24.

the stamnos Π 35, and represents the last use of the tomb. It was imported from western Achaia (*RMDP*, 435 nos. 122–123, fig. 155. – PAPADOPOULOS 1978/79, fig. 88g–h) and shows the relations with it even in LH III C Late, since the sword (inv. no. AM 842, Fig. 87), LH III C Middle, from Pit 7, may also have been imported from western Achaia, a very important region during the LH III C period and with many warrior's tombs (PAPADOPOULOS 1999, 273). The same seems to be the case with the sword from Paliokastro in Arcadia (DEMAKOPOULOU 1969. – PAPAZOGLOU-MANIOUDAKI 1994, 179). The sword from Nikoleika, the first which is certainly from eastern Achaia,[28] shows that warrior's tombs also existed there and not only in western Achaia.[29] With the other two swords, possibly from Aigeira, today in Berlin, the total number of the swords in eastern Achaia reaches three. So, it is not easy to believe that the swords are the rule for western Achaia and the exception for eastern.[30] It is possible that more swords will be found in future excavations.[31]

Pits 1–7

Pit 1 contained two primary burials, one over the other, without grave offerings.

Pit 2 was opened in a niche. Removed bones were found over it. It contained one skeleton without grave offerings.

Pit 3 was also opened in a niche. It contained two primary burials, one over the other. Only the upper burial contained **jug Π 40** (inv. no. ΑΠ 1768, H. 0.14 m, FS 110, Fig. 72), which possibly belongs to LH III A–B.[32]

Pit 4 contained a primary burial and the **stirrup jar Π 41** (inv. no. ΑΠ 1835, H. 0.108 m, FS 175.4, Fig. 76). The shoulder is without any decoration. Wide and narrow alternating bands cover the body. This decoration is like that of the amphoriskos Π 65 of Tomb 2, which dates to LH III C Late, but this jar dates to LH III C Early/Middle.[33]

Pit 5 contained one primary burial without grave offerings.

Pit 6 was the most interesting. It contained one primary burial on the bottom and over it many removed bones and eleven vases from the earlier use of the tomb:

The **small stirrup jar Π 42** (inv. no. ΑΠ 2285, H. 0.097 m, FS 174, Fig. 71a–b) dates to LH III C Early/Middle. The decoration consists of two concentric circles of small vertical lines on the shoulder[34] and foliate band on the body. The decoration system is similar to the stirrup jar Π 9890 from Spaliareika in western Achaia, LH III C Middle to Late (PETROPOULOS 2000a, fig. 38).

---

[28] PAPADOPOULOS 1999, 267 also refers to some other plundered warrior's tombs in Aigeira, without any details. It is obvious that he refers to the two swords later published by KONTORLI-PAPADOPOULOU 2003, 38, 43–45, who ascribes them to Aigeira. They were found in 1904 and are now in Berlin.

[29] For the two swords found last from western Achaia and some thoughts about the reason for their appearance in Achaia, see PETROPOULOS 2000a, 72, 76. – See also MOSCHOS 2002, 29–30.

[30] EDER 2003, 41. She believes that the warrior burials belong to the upper stratum of the social pyramid, and PAPAZOGLOU-MANIOUDAKI 1994, 180, to the local elites. On this topic see also DEGER-JALKOTZY 2002, 59–60. – PAPAZOGLOU-MANIOUDAKI 1998, vol. 1, 103.

[31] Two more swords of Naue II type come from Mavriki, a place near Aigion, and date to the Late Geometric/Early Archaic period (BOZANA-KOUROU 1980, 314–317).

[32] It may be placed stylistically between the two jugs illustrated by Papadopoulos: PAPADOPOULOS 1978/79, fig. 154d (LH III A:2b) and fig. 154e (LH III B1).

[33] Stirrup jars with similar decoration come from Delphi (*RMDP*, 775 nos. 185–186, fig. 304, LH III C Early), and Mycenae (*RMDP*, 155–156 nos. 310–311, fig. 40, of the same period). The same decoration appears on a straight-sided alabastron from Tiryns (*RMDP*, 161 no. 331, fig. 43, LH III C Middle).

[34] A single circle of small lines is seen on the shoulder of a LH III C Early stirrup jar from Klauss (*RMDP*, 421 no. 82, fig. 148. – PAPADOPOULOS 1978/79, fig. 101h–i).

The **small stirrup jar Π 43** (inv. no. ΑΠ 2291, H. 0.11 m, FS 175, Fig. 73a–b) belongs to LH III C Middle. The decoration consists of spirals on the shoulder and sophisticated zigzag on the body.[35]

The **small stirrup jar Π 44** (inv. no. ΑΠ 1828, H. 0.13 m, FS 175, Figs. 22; 74a–b), which dates to LH III C Middle/Late, has elaborate triangles on the shoulder.[36] The black body is common in western Achaia in LH III C Late (PAPADOPOULOS 1978/79, figs. 66b; 89d–e; 149a–b,f. – *RMDP*, 432–433 nos. 110–112, fig. 153, 435 nos. 113–114, fig. 154).

The **multiple vase Π 45** (inv. no. ΑΠ 1767, H. 0.085 m, Fig. 75a–b), with four small amphoriskoi,[37] dates possibly to LH III C Middle.

The **rounded alabastron Π 46** (inv. no. ΑΠ 1772, H. 0.03 m, Fig. 77) has a decoration with rock pattern,[38] LH II B.

The **jug Π 47** (inv. no. ΑΠ 1771, H. 0.158 m, Fig. 78) has a decoration with spirals,[39] LH II B.

The **small stirrup jar Π 48** (inv. no. ΑΠ 2284, H. 0.131 m, FS 175, Figs. 23; 79a–b), LH III C Middle (cf. *comments*).

The **based askos Π 49** (inv. no. ΑΠ 2288, H. 0.106 m, FS 195, Figs. 24; 80a–b), LH III C Early/Middle developed (cf. *comments*).

The **small stirrup jar Π 50** (inv. no. ΑΠ 2294, H. 0.11 m, FS 195, Figs. 25; 81a–b), LH III C Middle (cf. *comments*).

The **kylix Π 51** (inv. no. ΑΠ 1770, H. 0.105 m, Fig. 82), LH III A–B.[40]

The **small stirrup jar T4/Λ6/OM 29** (inv. no. ΑΠ 1817, H. 0.092 m, Figs. 14; 61a–b). Decoration with horizontal bands on the body and zigzag on the shoulder, LH III C Middle to Late.[41]

These vases date to LH II B, LH III A2, LH III C Early–Middle, LH III C Middle and possibly to LH III C Middle/Late.

The **primary burial**, in contracted position, contained the **stirrup jar Π 57** (inv. no. ΑΠ 2282, H. 0.11 m, Figs. 26; 84a–b), which dates to LH III C Early/Middle developed (cf. *comments*).

Pit 7 contained two primary burials (Λ7/Θ, Λ7/Η), which were disturbed by later use, when the removed bones of eight individuals were put inside it. Three vases were found among these bones:

---

[35] The decoration harks back to the stirrup jars from the Argolid of the LH III C Middle period (*RMDP*, 166–167).

[36] Stacked triangles on vases from western Achaia of LH III C Middle: *RMDP*, 427 no. 93, fig. 149, 430 no. 101, fig. 151. PAPADOPOULOS 1978/79, fig. 136b. Achaia, LH III C Late: *RMDP*, 432 no. 110, fig. 153. – PAPADOPOULOS 1978/79, fig. 149h.

[37] Similar but with triple amphoriskoi from Perati (*RMDP*, 596 no. 456, fig. 222).

[38] This decoration is more common in eastern Achaia. It is found on vases from Aigion (*RMDP*, 405 no. 2, fig. 142, 107 nos. 3–5, fig. 142). For the vase from Nikoleika see also PAPAZOGLOU-MANIOUDAKI 1998, vol. 1, 104; vol. 2, pl. A.3, 1. She dates it to the LH II B period. For similar vases (decoration or shape) of western Achaia (region of Patras) of the LH II B/III A period, see PAPAZOGLOU-MANIOUDAKI 2003, 446, figs. 5–6.

[39] Similar decoration on a squat jug from Prosymna (Argolid) (*RMDP*, 98 no. 80, fig. 17), LH II B, and an askos from Galataki (Corinthia) (*RMDP*, 211 no. 60, fig. 66), LH II B. Similar decoration is found on an amphoriskos from Vrysari in southern Achaia (ancient northern Arcadia) (PAPAZOGLOU-MANIOUDAKI 1999, 270, figs. 7–8), LH II B/III A1. The shape of the bodies of the two vases is very similar. For the vase from Nikoleika, see PAPAZOGLOU-MANIOUDAKI 1998, vol. 1, 104; vol. 2, pl. A.3, 4.

[40] A similar kylix from Teichos Dymaion in western Achaia dates to LH III B2 (PAPADOPOULOS 1978/79, fig. 179). Another from Laconia (*RMDP*, 274 no. 130, fig. 91) to LH III A2.

[41] It is almost similar to the stirrup jar Π 21, which was found on the floor of Tomb 4. See there for comments.

The **squeezed or depressed alabastron Π 53** (inv. no. ΑΠ 1787, H. 0.05 m, Fig. 85a–b), with rock pattern,[42] dates to LH II B.

The **small stirrup jar Π 55** (inv. no. ΑΠ 2283, H. 0.089 m, FS 175, Figs. 27; 86a–b) belongs to LH III C Middle. Horizontal bands and two zones with isolated semicircles and zigzag or opposite triangles on the body, zigzag on the handle, isolated semicircles, S– or wavy lines on the shoulder.[43]

The **feeding bottle Π 56** (inv. no. ΑΠ 1786, H. 0.117 m, FS 162, Figs. 28; 83) dates to LH III C Early.[44]

Some grave offerings of a warrior were found on the bottom of the pit: The **sword** of the type Naue II (Fig. 87), the **sickle-shaped knife** (inv. no. AM 843, Fig. 88), and **the stirrup jar Π 58** (inv. no. ΑΠ 1820, H. 0.092 m, Fig. 29) of the LH III C Middle period. The stirrup jar Π 55, because of the same chronology, seems to belong to the same burial.

Comments on some vases of Pit 6

a) **Stirrup jar Π 48**, FS 175 (Figs. 23; 79a–b). Decoration: FM 43, semicircles, joined semicircles, wavy lines. It was found between the removed bones of the pit. It is possible that it belonged to the same primary burial with the **based askos Π 49**. These two vases are the last before the final use of the tomb and help to determine the chronology of the burial of the warrior with the sword Naue II. Date: LH III C Middle. The double ribbon that comes down from the handle is found on stirrup jars from the Argolis, LH III C Middle, Achaia and Elis, LH III C Late (*RMDP*, 163 no. 337, fig. 44, 393 no. 78, fig. 137, 435 no. 125, fig. 156).

b) The **stirrup jar Π 44** (Figs. 22; 74a–b) seems to belong to the same hand. The decoration has the same philosophy.

c) **Based askos Π 49**, FS 195 (Figs. 24; 80a–b). Decoration: wavy lines, joined semicircles. It was found between the bones of the removed skeleton in the upper layer of the pit. The vases of the removed burial date to the LH II B–III C Middle period. The shape of the based askos Π 49 was not very common. It is actually a variation of the stirrup jars. Similar vases with the handle on the upper part of the body are known from Delphi and dated by Mountjoy to the LH III A2 period (*RMDP*, 756 no. 51, fig. 292), from Thessaly (also LH III A2) (*RMDP*, 842 no. 78, fig. 339), and from Corinthia, at Galataki (LH II B) (*RMDP*, 212 no. 60, fig. 66) and Korakou (LH III B) (*RMDP*, 222 no. 132, fig. 70). An early example comes from Portes in western Achaia and another one from Voudeni.[45] Th. Papadopoulos has also published some vases from Aigialeia (eastern Achaia) which are not exactly similar and he dates them to the LH III B2/C:1a period.[46]

---

[42] Exactly the same decoration is found on an alabastron from Asine (Argolid) (*RMDP*, 98 no. 74, fig. 17). PAPADOPOULOS 1978/79, fig. 127 dates another rounded alabastron with rock pattern from Vrysari (Achaia; ancient Arcadia) to LH III A1. A third alabastron from Aigion, with the same decoration, but with more globular body (PAPADOPOULOS 1976, 16 no. 3, pls. 46; 55), dates to LH II B. For the vase from Nikoleika, see PAPAZOGLOU-MANIOUDAKI 1998, vol. 1, 104, pl. A.3, 2.

[43] The decoration system, bands and zone on the body, is very similar to the decoration on vases from Argolid of LH III C Middle (*RMDP*, 167, fig. 46). The shape of the vase is almost similar to the shape of the stirrup jar PAPADOPOULOS 1978/79, fig. 100c, LH III C:1a from Chalandritsa.

[44] A feeding bottle from Laconia of LH III C Early (*RMDP*, 283 no. 188, fig. 96) is similar in shape and system of decoration. A feeding bottle from Elis (*RMDP*, 390 no. 69, fig. 135) belongs to the same period.

[45] As my colleague I. Moschos informed me.

[46] From Achladies (Chatzi) (PAPADOPOULOS 1978/79, 101, fig. 162c–d). The stirrup vases, PAPADOPOULOS 1978/79, figs. 106e; 111a–b, which have a similar decoration, date to LH III C:1a, and come from Klauss in western Achaia. A globular flask from Aigion, with almost the same decoration on the shoulder, joining semicircles (PAPADOPOULOS 1976, 11 no. 10, pl. 32), dates to LH III B1.

The decoration of the shoulder, zone of joining semicircles, is similar to the decoration of stirrup jar Π 48, which was found in the same pit.[47] It is possible that they belonged to the same primary burial.

The based askos from Nikoleika could be dated to LH III C Early/Middle advanced. If this chronology is correct, then the vase from Delphi must date to LH III B/III C Early and the vase from Thessaly in LH III C Early. Due to its decoration, the vase from Galataki (Corinthia) must be ascribed to LH II B/III B. Our vase shows contacts between eastern Achaia and mainly Phokis,[48] Thessaly, Corinthia and perhaps western Achaia.

d) **Stirrup jar Π 50**, FS 175 (Figs. 25; 81a–b). Decoration on the shoulder: net lozenge, FM 43 semicircles, panelled lozenge in a chain. Chronology: LH III C Middle. The elements that speak for the dating to the LH III C Middle period, and not to LH III C Late, are the following:

i) The net lozenge, a motif known on LH III C Middle jars shoulders from Achaia (PAPADOPOULOS 1978/79, figs. 219 [LH III C:1a]; 220 [LH III C:1b]) and Phokis (*RMDP*, 783 no. 254, fig. 308).

ii) The sparse semicircles without dots or fringes,[49] and

iii) the presence of a central motif (panelled lozenge) between the semicircles (PAPADOPOULOS 1978/79, figs. 217 [LH III C:1a]; 211 [LH III C:1b]).

e) **Stirrup jar Π 57**, FS 174? (Figs. 26; 84a–b). It was an offering of the primary burial on the bottom of Pit 6. Its careless construction does not offer help for a precise chronology. The wide base and the lightly squeezed body bring this shape close to the shape FS 174, with a possible chronology in the LH III Early/Middle period.[50]

The three thin bands on the upper part of the body, which are framed by a larger one in the centre of the body, are possibly an imitation of the narrow-wide bands of the vases of the LH III Early/Middle period. The horizontal lines on the handles are common during the LH III C Middle period. The decoration on the shoulder possibly imitates the foliate band. These bands are common on the stirrup jars of western Achaia during the LH III C Early and Middle developed. Chronology: LH III C Early advanced/Middle developed?

Comments on the vases of Pit 7: The warrior burial

a) **Stirrup jar Π 55**, FS 175 (Figs. 27; 86a–b). Decoration: Shoulder: isolated semicircles, wavy lines, fringe beneath the spout. Body: Zones of zigzag and isolated semicircles. Chronology: LH III C Middle. Since its decoration and chronology are similar to the stirrup jar Π 58, it is possible that it also belonged to the primary burial of the warrior.

---

[47] The decoration of the stirrup jar, PAPADOPOULOS 1978/79, fig. 111, is very similar and dates to LH III C1:a.

[48] A road from Arcadia to Phokis through Aigion is known during the Geometric period. It is possible that the connection of the port of Aigion with Phokis existed from the Mycenaean period onwards (PETROPOULOS 1996/97, 172–175. – PETROPOULOS 2002, 157). The main ports for the communication are the port of Aigion in Achaia and the ports of Kirrha and Medeon in Phokis (EDER 2003, 41. – DEGER-JALKOTZY 2002, 62–63). For the road from Arcadia to Aigion see also PAPAZOGLOU-MANIOUDAKI 1998, 157.

[49] PAPADOPOULOS 1978/79, figs. 98–99 (LH III C:1a) from Aigeira in eastern Achaia, fig. 103a–b (LH III C:1a) from Chalandritsa in western Achaia and fig. 114 (LH III C:1a) from Achladies in eastern Achaia.

[50] The shape of the body is close to a stirrup jar from Chalandritsa (LH III C:1a): PAPADOPOULOS 1978/79, fig. 104g. The decoration on the body is close to the decoration of the stirrup jar, PAPADOPOULOS 1978/79, fig. 106f (LH III C:1a), and the decoration on the shoulder, two concentric circles with small vertical lines between them, is close to the decoration of the stirrup jar, PAPADOPOULOS 1978/79, fig. 114 (LH III C:1a), with a similar decoration also on the body.

b) **Stirrup jar Π 58**, FS 175 (Fig. 29). Chronology: LH III C Middle.

c) **Feeding bottle Π 56**, FS 162 (Figs. 28; 83). Chronology: LH III C Early. It is not certain that this vase was an offering of the warrior's burial, because its chronology is slightly different from the stirrup jars Π 55 and Π 58.

CONCLUSIONS

It was not possible to present, in detail, all the vases of the two tombs from Nikoleika, because it would take too long. We commented only on some characteristic and special features of the period we are interested in.[51]

What can be said is that the ceramic from the earlier phases to the last ones shows a normal evolution without interruption. During the three phases of the LH III C period, as the ceramic of the tombs proves, life continues without problems and no sign of any destruction can be proved at the end of LH III C, as in other regions, or movements of peoples (DEGER-JALKOTZY 2004, 54–56). But only the excavation of the settlement can provide the answer to these questions.[52]

This cemetery had more contacts with the north-eastern Peloponnese (Corinthia and Argolid) and the northern coast of the Corinthian Golf, and only in the last period did it have more obvious relations with western Achaia.[53] The relations with Corinthia and Argolid seem to be direct, and this is logical, because during the Mycenaean period eastern Achaia was part of the Kingdom of Agamemnon (Hom. *Il.* II 575. – Paus. VII, 1.4). The relations with western Achaia and the northern coasts of the Corinthian Golf on the contrary are rather commercial.[54] L. Papadopoulou-Kontorli in her last article about the Late Mycenaean Achaian vases from Aigeira, another eastern Achaian city, now in Berlin, reaches the same conclusion, that the finds from Aigeira, exclusively dated to LH III A–B, show connections with western Achaia, but more closely with the Argolid (KONTORLI-PAPADOPOULOU 2003, 47). L. Papazoglou-Manioudaki proves the same for the earlier periods of the cemetery of Nikoleika (PAPAZOGLOU-MANIOUDAKI 1998, vol. 1, 104, 151, 155). These conclusions, which apply especially to Helike, are with the written sources in accordance, which refer to the conquest of Helike by Tisamenos, the son of Orestes and grandson of Agamemnon, after the Dorian invasion in the Peloponnese (Polyb. 2.41.5. – Paus. VII, 1.7–8). This tradition shows that Tisamenos did not go to a place unknown to him and to Mycenae. The division in western and eastern Achaia can be explained by the fact that Mount Panachaikos, situated at the centre of the whole region, acts as a barrier between them (PETROPOULOS 2002, 144). L. Papazoglou-Manioudaki testifies, using archaeological documents, that during the Early Mycenaean

---

[51] There are also further LH III C vases, which have not been presented here.

[52] The best-excavated prehistoric settlement in eastern Achaia is Aigeira: ALRAM-STERN 2003a. – ALRAM-STERN 2003b. The systematic excavation offered useful observations for the stratigraphy of the Mycenaean period.

[53] For the earlier LH II B period and the connections of the cemetery with Argolid, see PAPAZOGLOU-MANIOUDAKI 1998, 104.

[54] DEGER-JALKOTZY 2002, 62–63, and EDER 2003, 41–42 show the commercial relations of Achaia, mainly of its western part, with the neighbouring regions, even with Albania and Southern Italy, based on the exported characteristic western Achaian vases of LH III C. If the vases of western Achaia were exported to Albania, it was much easier to be exported to eastern Achaia, mainly by sea. But the vases of western Achaia were exported rather through Rion–Antirrion and not through eastern Achaia and the port of Aigion. For the relations of Achaia and Skyros during the last Mycenaean period see PAPADOPOULOS – KONTORLI-PAPADOPOULOU 2003, and of Achaia with Elateia DEGER-JALKOTZY 1999, 195, 197.

period (LH II B–III A1) Achaia was part of the north-eastern Peloponnese, while the presence of the tholos tombs in western Achaia shows the rising of local leading social groups. But during the post-palatial period western Achaia had an autonomous development (PAPAZOGLOU-MANIOUDAKI 1998, vol. 1, 155. – PAPAZOGLOU-MANIOUDAKI 2003, 440–441).

The eastern part of Achaia continued to have closer relations with the north-eastern Peloponnese even during the Geometric period, as the ceramic shows (PETROPOULOS 2002, 144–145).

Bibliography

Ε' Συνέδριο Πελοποννησιακών Σπουδών
1996/97 Πρακτικά του Ε' Διεθνούς Συνεδρίου Πελοποννησιακών Σπουδών, Άργος – Ναύπλιον, 6–10 Σεπτεμβρίου 1995 (Peloponnesiaka 22). Athens.

ΣΤ' Συνέδριο Πελοποννησιακών Σπουδών
2001/02 Πρακτικά του ΣΤ' Διεθνούς Συνεδρίου Πελοποννησιακών Σπουδών, Τρίπολις, 24–29 Σεπτεμβρίου 2000 (Peloponnesiaka 24). Athens.

ALRAM-STERN, E.
2003a "Aigeira – Acropolis: The Stratigraphy", 15–21 in: *LH III C Chronology and Synchronisms*.
2003b "The Acropolis of Aigeira before the Mycenaean Settlement", 437–454 in: BIETAK 2003.

BENZI, M.
1992 *Rodi e la Civiltà Micenea* (Incunabula Graeca 94). Rome.

BIETAK, M. (ed.)
2003 *The Synchronisation of Civilisations in the Eastern Mediterranean in the Second Millennium B.C. II. Proceedings of the SCIEM 2000 – EuroConference, Haindorf, 2nd of May–7th of May 2001* (Österreichische Akademie der Wissenschaften. Denkschriften der Gesamtakademie 29 = Contributions to the Chronology of the Eastern Mediterranean 4). Vienna.

BOZANA-KOUROU, N.
1980 "Ταφικό σύνολο από την περιοχή Αιγίου", 303–317 in: ΣΤΗΛΗ.

BRAUN-HOLZINGER, E. A. – H. MATTHÄUS (eds.)
2002 *Die nahöstlichen Kulturen und Griechenland an der Wende vom 2. zum 1. Jahrtausend v. Chr. Kontinuität und Wandel von Strukturen und Mechanismen kultureller Interaktion. Kolloquium des Sonderforschungsbereiches 295 "Kulturelle und sprachliche Kontakte" der Johannes Gutenberg-Universität Mainz, 11.–12. Dezember 1998*. Möhnesee.

DEGER-JALKOTZY, S.
1999 "Elateia and Problems of Pottery Chronology", 195–202 in: Περιφέρεια.
2002 "Innerägäische Beziehungen und auswärtige Kontakte des mykenischen Griechenland in nachpalatialer Zeit", 17–74 in: BRAUN-HOLZINGER – MATTHÄUS 2002.
2004 "Das Ende der mykenischen Palastära: Überlegungen zur Chronologie", 51–58 in: HEFTNER – TOMASCHITZ 2004.

DEMAKOPOULOU, K.
1969 "A Mycenaean Bronze Sword from Arcadia", *AAA* 2, 226–228.

EDER, B.
2003 "Patterns of Contact and Communication between the Regions South and North of the Corinthian Gulf in LH III C", 37–51 in: KYPARISSI-APOSTOLIKA – PAPAKONSTANTINOU 2003.

GADOLOU, A.
2000 *Η Αχαΐα στους πρώιμους ιστορικούς χρόνους. Κεραμική παραγωγή και έθιμα ταφής* (unpublished Ph.D. thesis). Athens.

GRECO, E. (ed.)
2002 *Gli Achei e l'identità etnica degli Achei d'Occidente. Atti del Convegno Internationale di Studi, Paestum 23–25 febbraio 2001* (Tekmeria 3). Paestum – Athens.

HEFTNER, H. – K. TOMASCHITZ (eds.)
2004 *Ad Fontes! Festschrift für Gerhard Dobesch zum fünfundsechzigsten Geburtstag am 15. September 2004.* Vienna.

KARANTZALI, E.
2001 *The Mycenaean Cemetery at Pylona on Rhodes* (BAR-IS 988). Oxford.

KATSONOPOULOU, D.
2002 "Helike and her Territory in the Light of New Discoveries", 205–216 in: GRECO 2002.

KOLONAS, L.
2007 (in press) *Βούντενη, ένα σημαντικό μυκηναϊκό κέντρο της Αχαΐας.*

KONTORLI-PAPADOPOULOU, L.
2003 "Late Mycenaean Achaean Vases and Bronzes in Berlin", *AM* 118, 23–47.

KYPARISSI-APOSTOLIKA, N. – M. PAPAKONSTANTINOU (eds.)
2003 *Η περιφέρεια του Μυκηναϊκού κόσμου. Β΄ Διεθνές Διεπιστημονικό Συμπόσιο, 26–30 Σεπτεμβρίου, Λαμία 1999.* Athens.

LAFFINEUR, R. (ed.)
1999 *Polemos. Le contexte guerrier en Égée à l'âge du Bronze. Actes de la 7e Rencontre égéenne internationale, Université de Liège, 14–17 avril 1998* (Aegaeum 19). Liège – Austin.

MOSCHOS, I.
2002 "Western Achaea during the LH III C Period. Approaching the Latest Excavation Evidence", 15–40 in: GRECO 2002.

PAPADOPOULOS, A. J.
1976 *Excavations at Aigion – 1970* (SIMA 46). Göteborg.
1978/79 *Mycenaean Achaea* (SIMA 55). Göteborg.
1999 "Warrior Graves in Achaean Mycenaean Cemeteries", 267–274 in: LAFFINEUR 1999.

PAPADOPOULOS, A. – L. KONTORLI-PAPADOPOULOU
2003 "Δυτικοπελοποννησιακές σχέσεις με Θεσσαλία και Σκύρο στην Υστερομυκηναϊκή εποχή", 455–461 in: KYPARISSI-APOSTOLIKA – PAPAKONSTANTINOU 2003.

PAPAZOGLOU-MANIOUDAKI, L.
1993 "Εισηγμένη κεραμεική στους Μυκηναϊκούς τάφους της Πάτρας", 209–215 in: *Wace and Blegen.*
1994 "A Mycenaean Warrior's Tomb at Krini near Patras", *BSA* 89, 171–200.
1998 *Ο Μυκηναϊκός οικισμός του Αιγίου και η πρώιμη Μυκηναϊκή εποχή στην Αχαΐα* (unpublished Ph.D. thesis). Athens.
1999 "Πήλινα και χάλκινα της πρώιμης Μυκηναϊκής εποχής από την Αχαΐα", 269–283 in: *Περιφέρεια.*
2003 "Ο θολωτός τάφος του Πετρωτού Πατρών. Τα πρώτα στοιχεία της έρευνας", 433–453 in: KYPARISSI-APOSTOLIKA – PAPAKONSTANTINOU 2003.

Περιφέρεια
1999 *Η περιφέρεια του Μυκηναϊκού κόσμου. Α΄ Διεθνές Διεπιστημονικό Συμπόσιο, Λαμία, 25–29 Σεπτεμβρίου 1994.* Lamia.

PETROPOULOS, M.
1990 "Αρχαιολογικές έρευνες στην Αχαΐα", 495–537 in: *Τιμητικός τόμος Τριανταφύλλου.*
1996/97 "Νεώτερα στοιχεία από την ανασκαφή γεωμετρικού ναού στο Άνω Μαζαράκι (Ρακίτα)", 165–192 in: *Ε΄ Συνέδριο Πελοποννησιακών Σπουδών.*
1999 *Τα εργαστήρια των ρωμαικών λυχναριών της Πάτρας και το λυχνομαντείο* (Δημοσιεύματα του Αρχαιολογικού Δελτίου 70). Athens.
2000a "Μυκηναϊκό νεκροταφείο στα Σπαλιαρέικα των Λουσικών", 65–92 in: RIZAKIS 2000.
2000b "Νικολέικα Αιγίου. Καλλιθέα (μυκηναϊκό νεκροταφείο)", *ArchDelt* 50, 1995 [2000], Chron 233–236.
2001 "Νικολέικα", *ArchDelt* 51, 1996 [2001], Chron 240.
2001/02 "Η αρχαία Μεσάτις της Πάτρας", 399–422 in: *ΣΤ΄ Συνέδριο Πελοποννησιακών Σπουδών.*
2002 "The Geometric Temple at Ano Mazaraki (Rakita) in Achaia during the Period of Colonisation", 143–160 in: GRECO 2002.
2004 "Αρχαία Ελίκη", *ArchDelt* 53, 1998 [2004], Chron 279.

PETROPOULOS, M. – I. PINI
2004 "Äjion", *CMS V*, Suppl. 3,1, 89–92.

PETROPOULOS, M. – A. PONTRANDOLFO – A. D. RIZAKIS
2004 "Prima campagna di ricognizioni archeologiche in Egialea, settembre–ottobre 2002", *ASAtene* 80, 939–965.

RIZAKIS, A. D. (ed.)
2000 *Αχαϊκό τοπίο ΙΙ. Δύμη και Δυμαία Χώρα. Πρακτικά του Συνεδρίου "Δυμαία-Βουπρασία", Κάτω Αχαΐα, 6–8 Οκτοβρίου 1995. Paysages d'Achaïe II. Dymé et son territoire. Actes du colloque international: Dymaia et Bouprasia, Kato Achaïa 6–8 Octobre 1995* (Meletemata 29). Athens.

ΣΤΗΛΗ
1980 *ΣΤΗΛΗ. Τόμος εις μνήμην Νικολάου Κοντολέοντος*. Athens.

Τιμητικός τόμος Τριανταφύλλου
1990 *Τιμητικός τόμος Κ. Ν. Τριανταφύλλου*. Vol. 1. Patras.

VIKATOU, O.
2004 "Κλαδέος", *ArchDelt* 53, 1998 [2004], Chron 230–233.

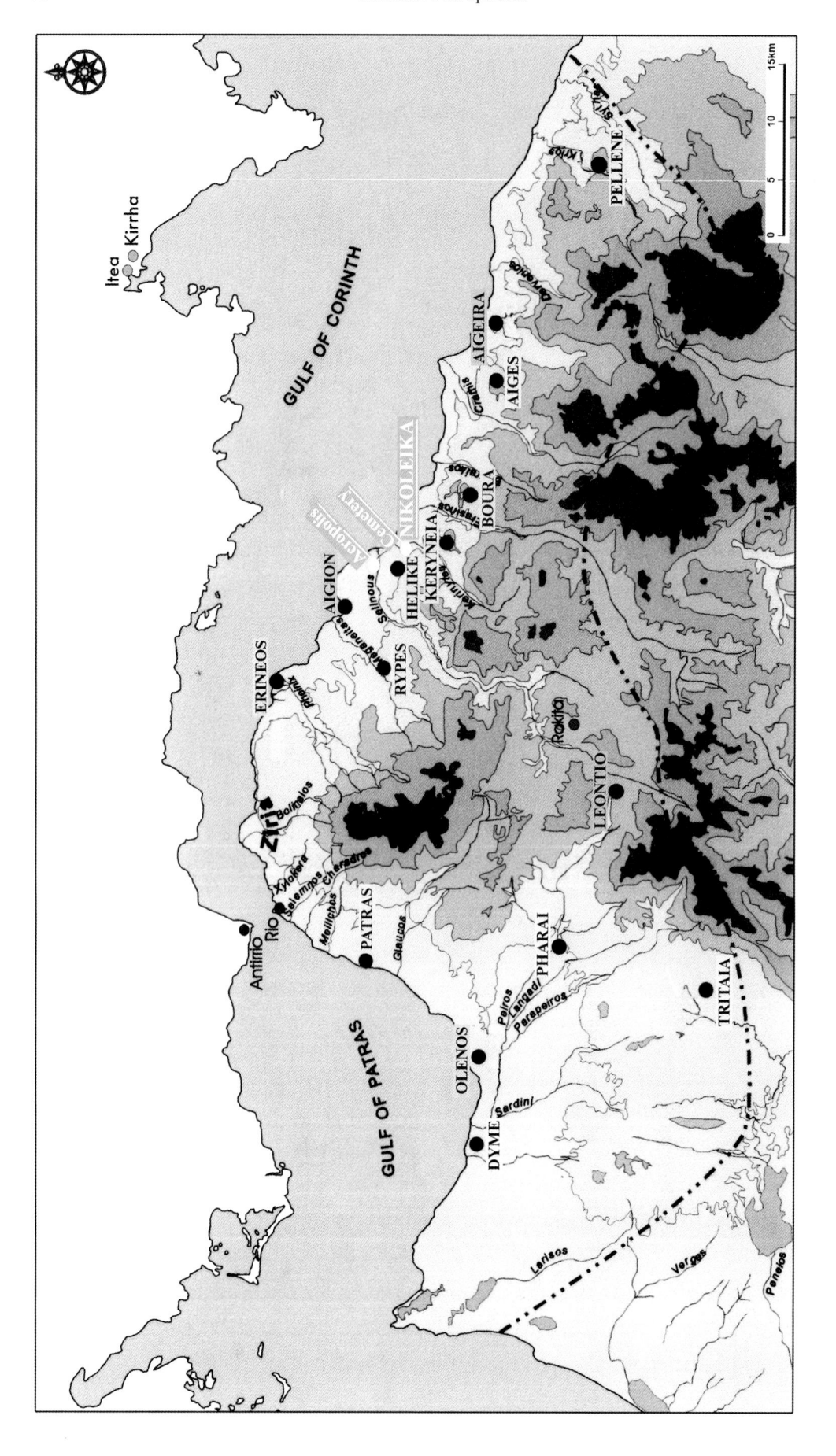

Fig. 1 Map of ancient Achaia

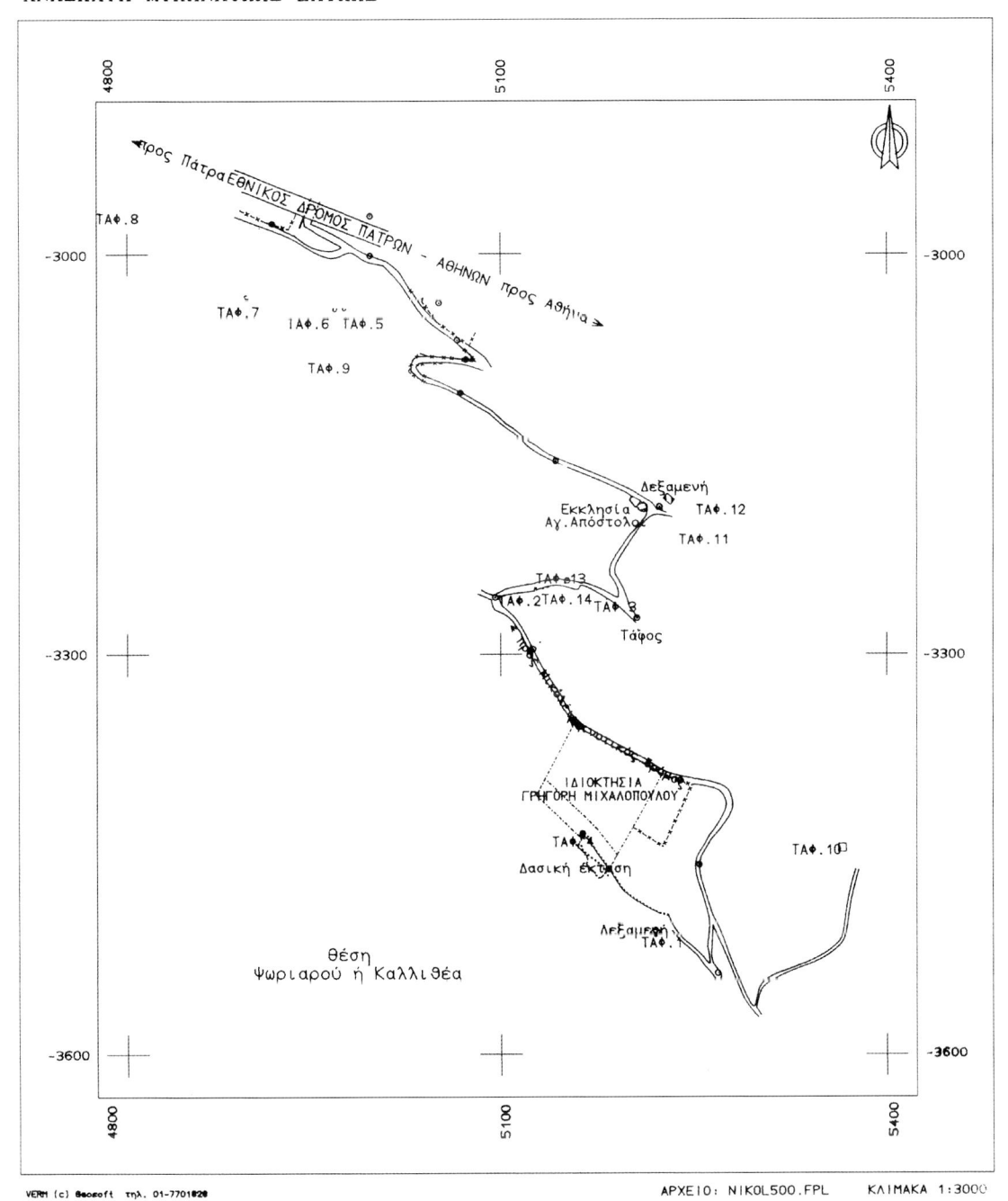

Fig. 2 The region of the Cemetery

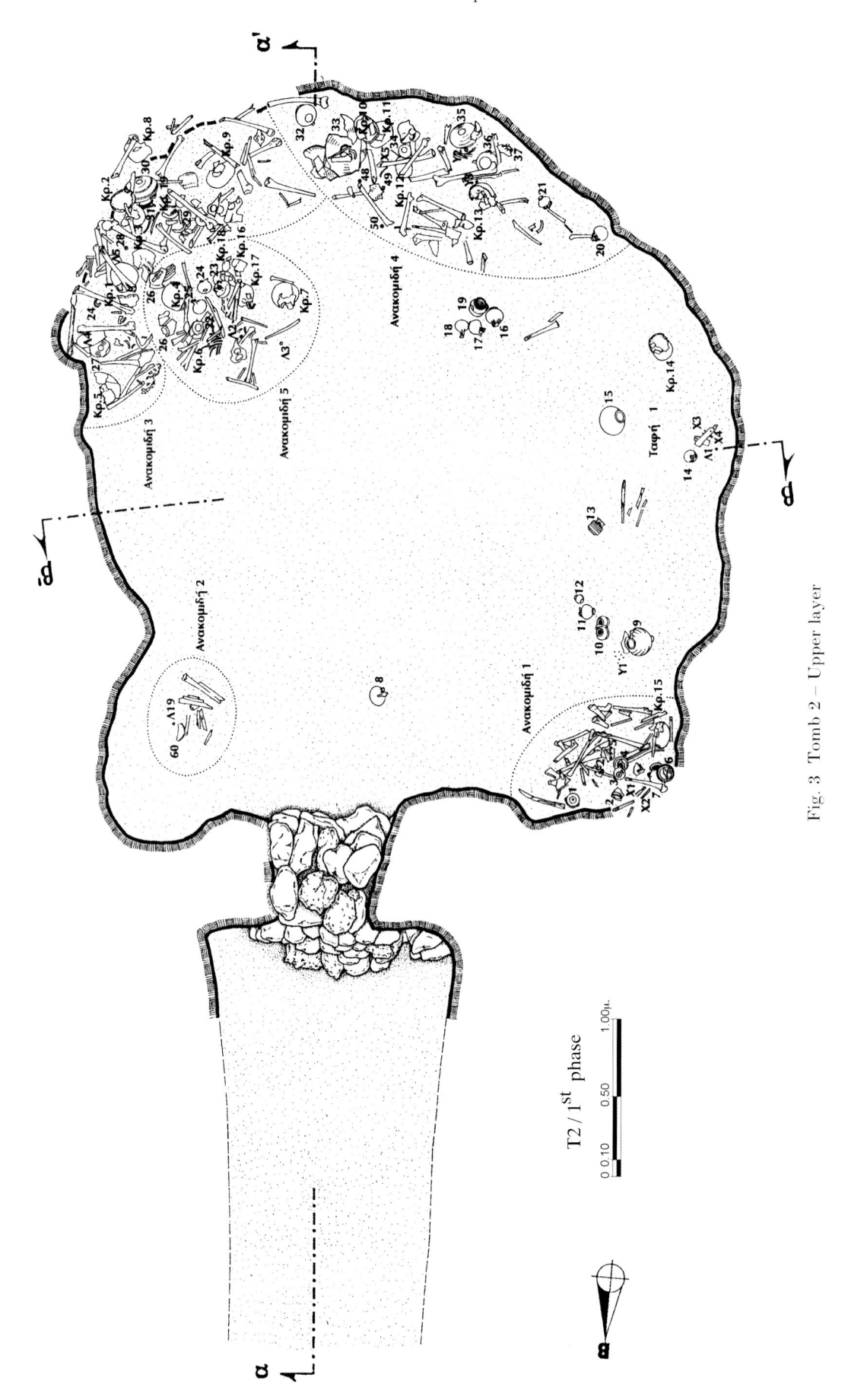

Fig. 3 Tomb 2 – Upper layer

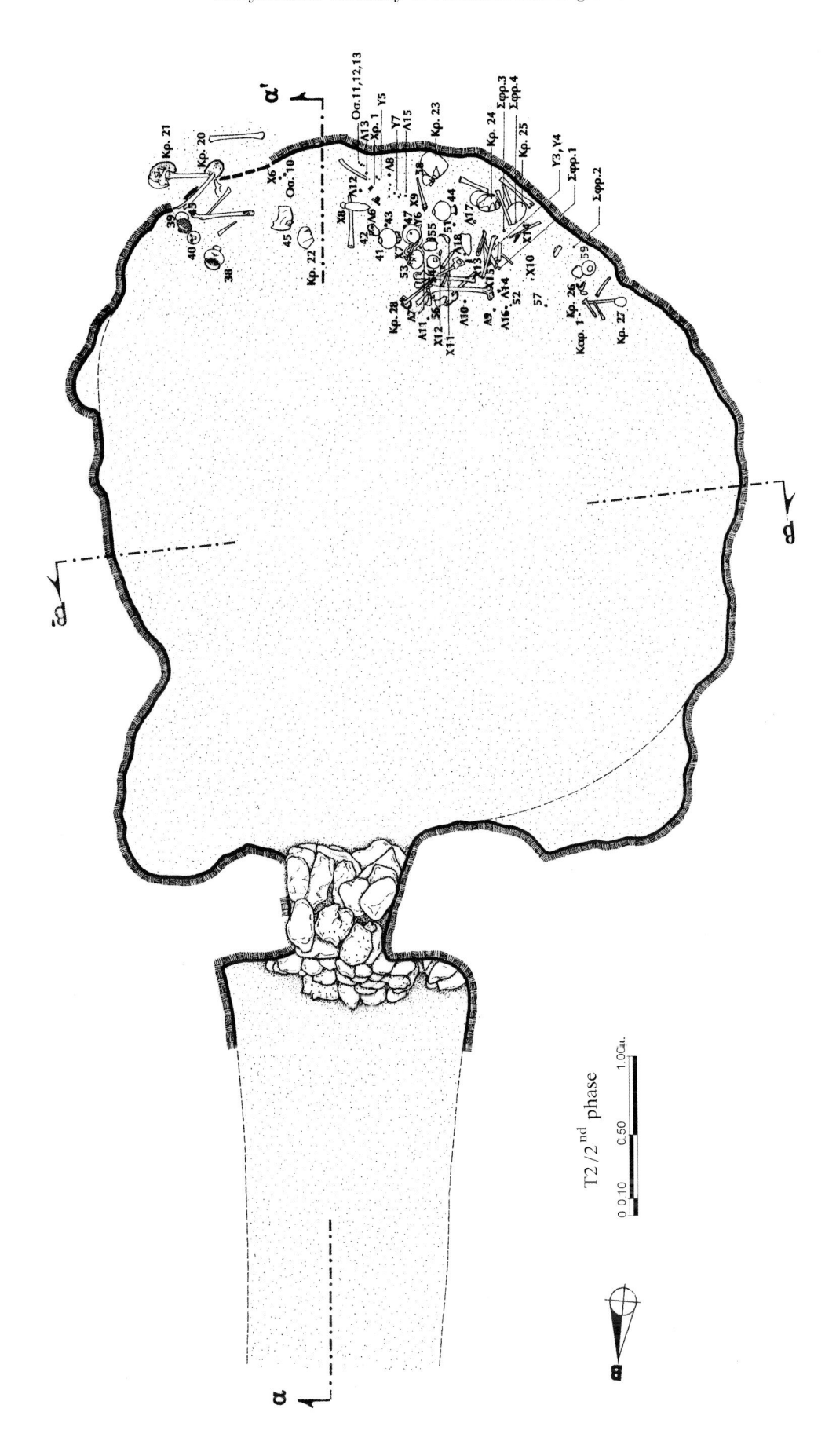

Fig. 4 Tomb 2 – Middle layer

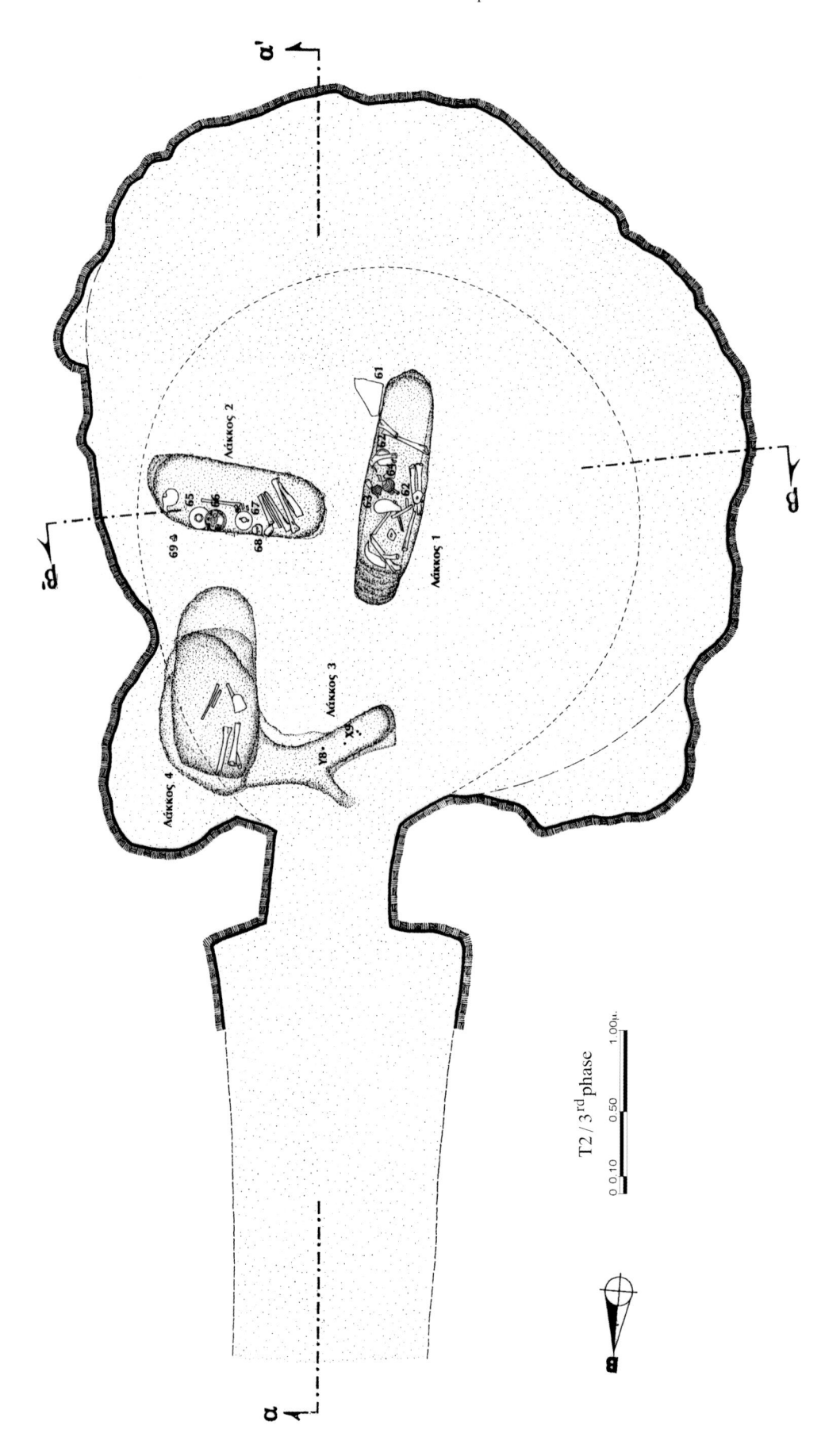

Fig. 5 Tomb 2 – Lower layer

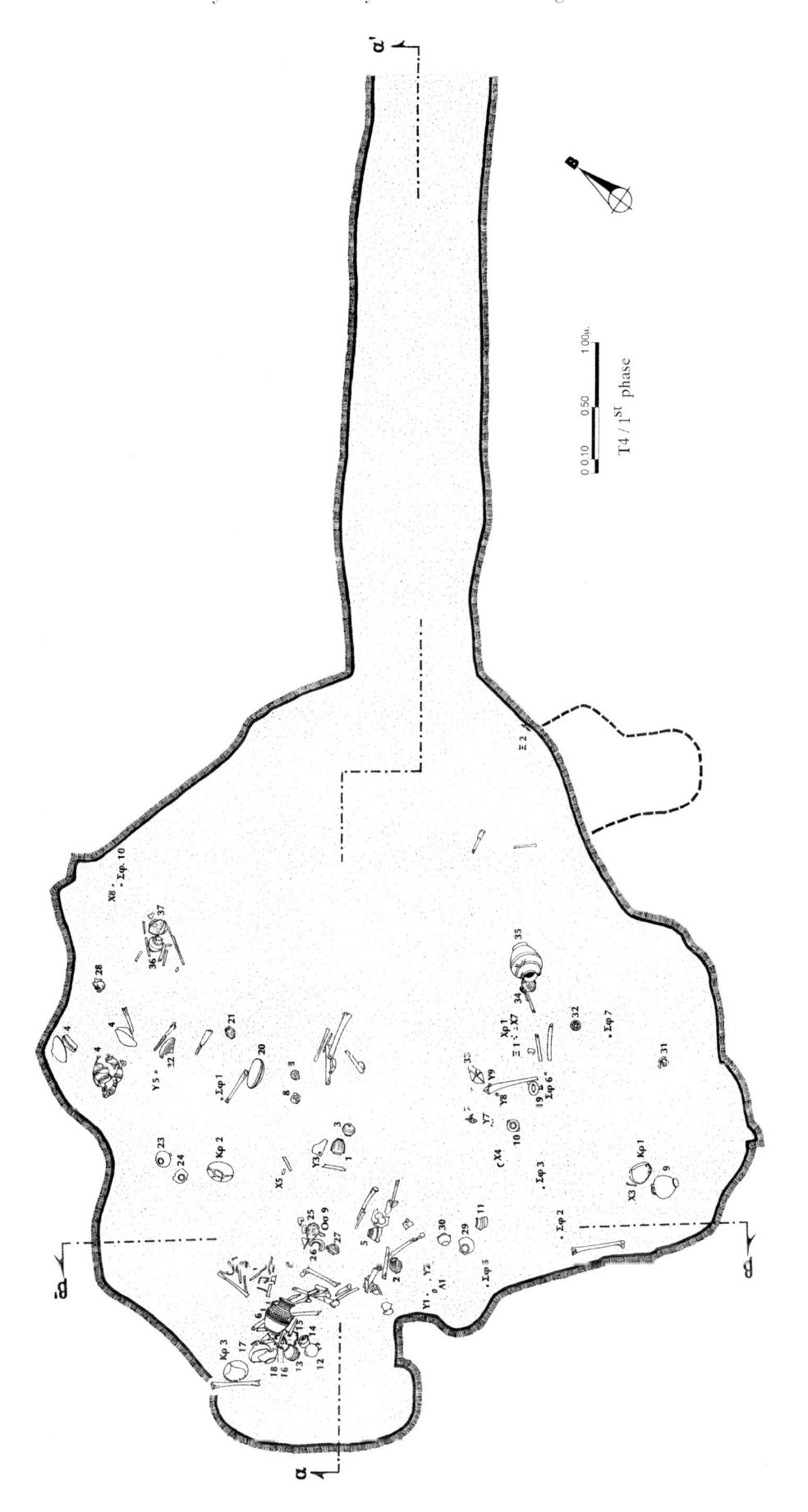

Fig. 6 Tomb 4 – Upper layer

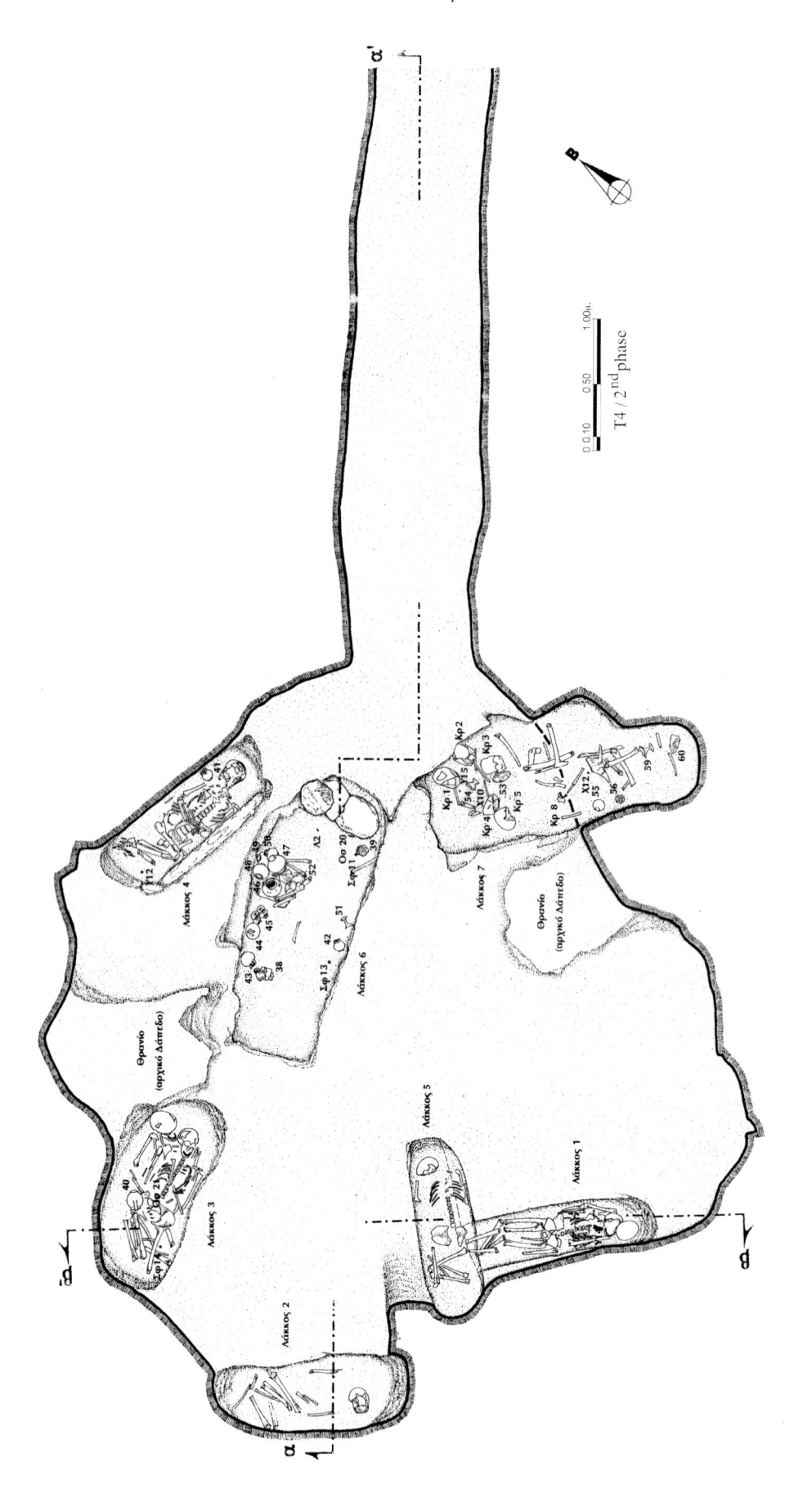

Fig. 7 Tomb 4 – Middle layer

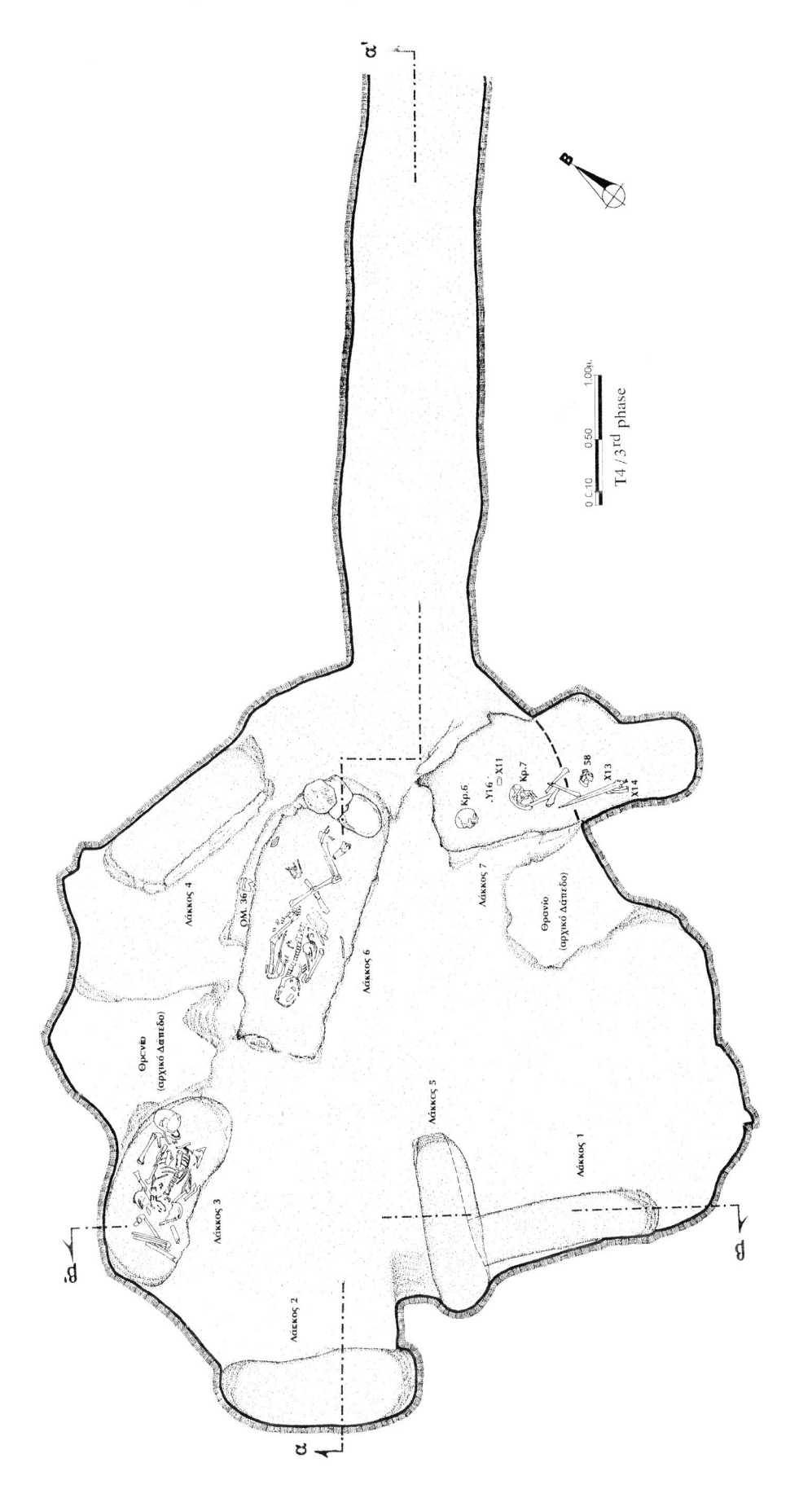

Fig. 8 Tomb 4 – Lower layer

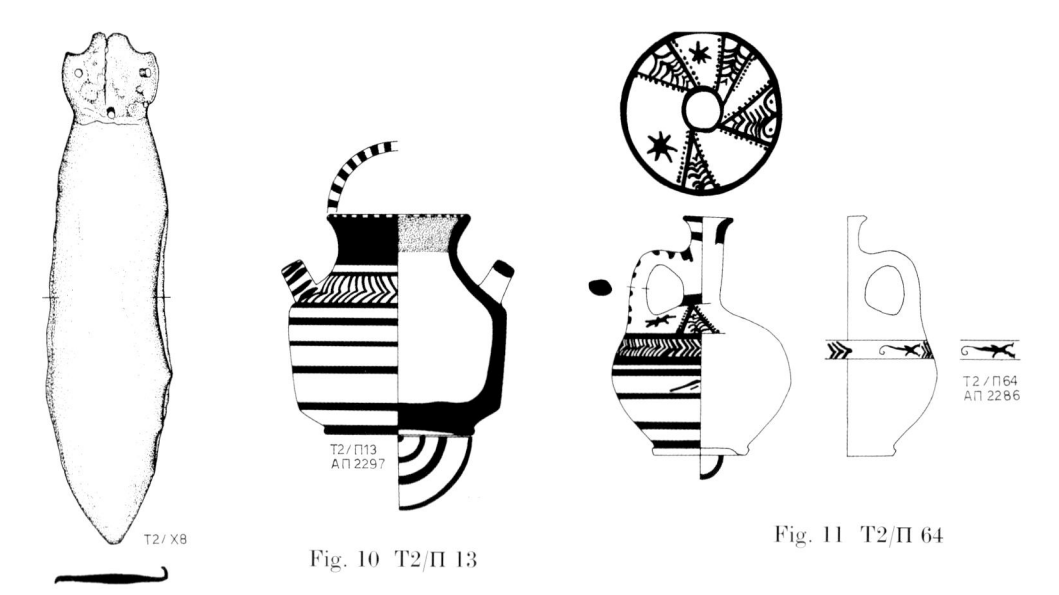

Fig. 9 T2/ dagger

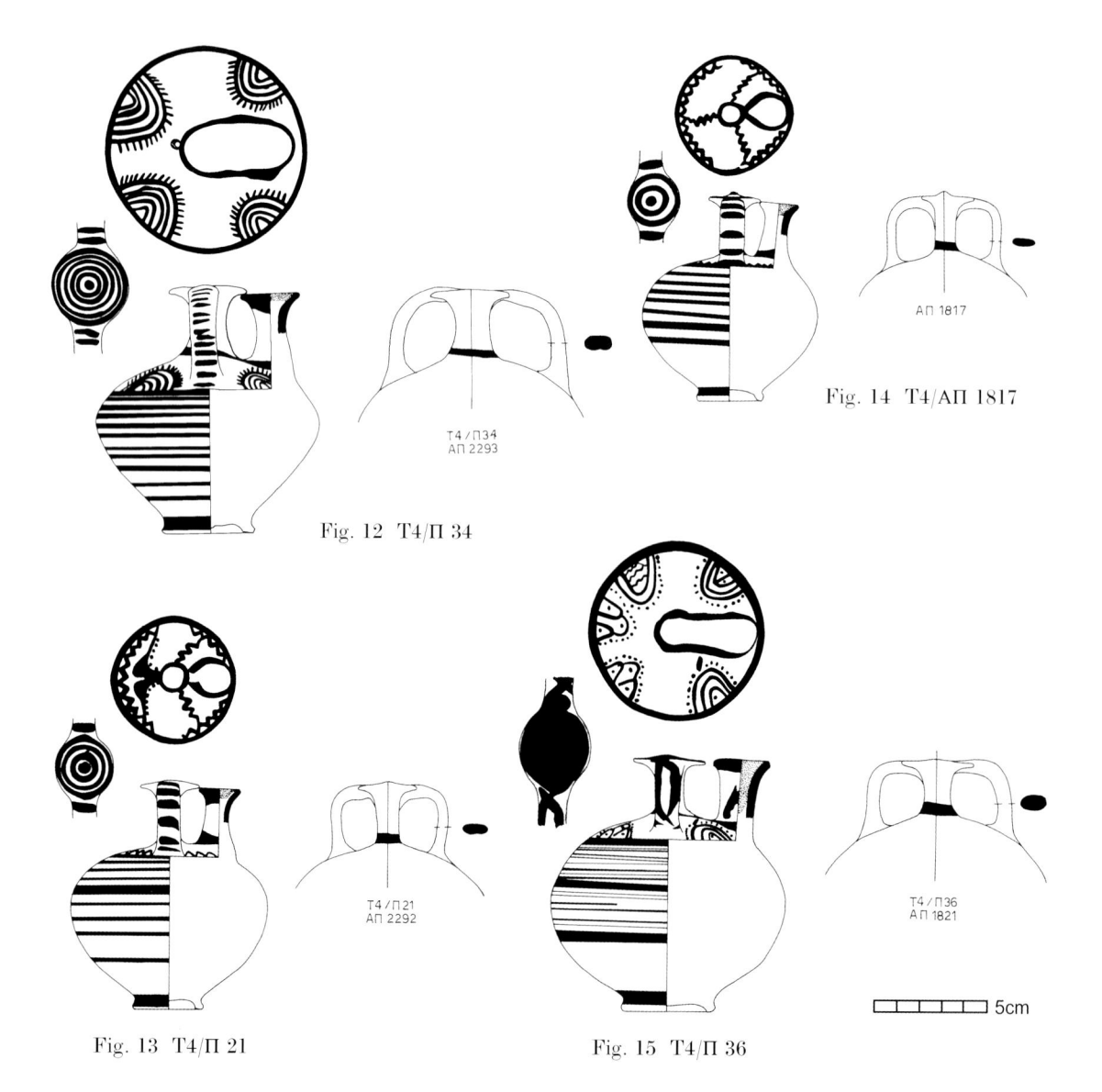

Fig. 10 T2/Π 13

Fig. 11 T2/Π 64

Fig. 12 T4/Π 34

Fig. 14 T4/ΑΠ 1817

Fig. 13 T4/Π 21

Fig. 15 T4/Π 36

Fig. 16 T4/Π 12

Fig. 17 T4/Π 13

Fig. 18 T4/Π 15

Fig. 19 T4/Π 16

Fig. 21 T4/Π 18

Fig. 20 T4/Π 17

278   Michalis Petropoulos

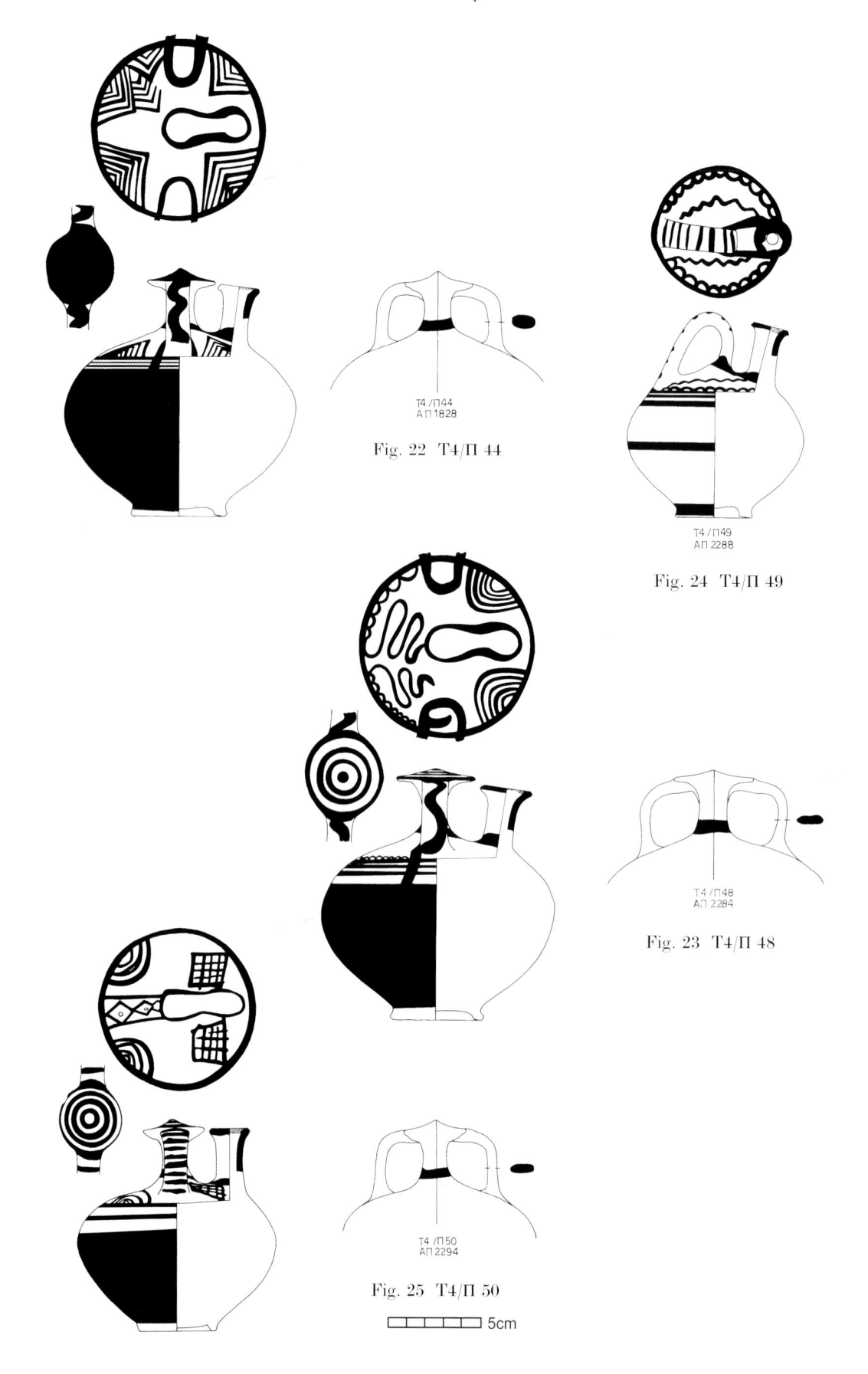

Fig. 22 T4/Π 44

Fig. 24 T4/Π 49

Fig. 23 T4/Π 48

Fig. 25 T4/Π 50

5cm

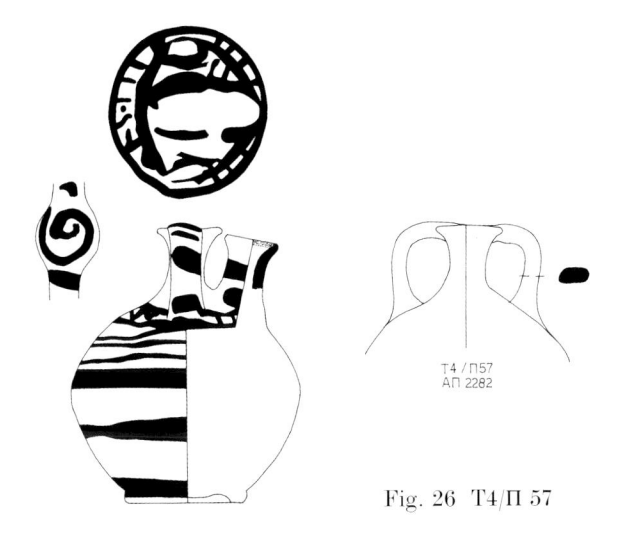

Fig. 26 T4/Π 57

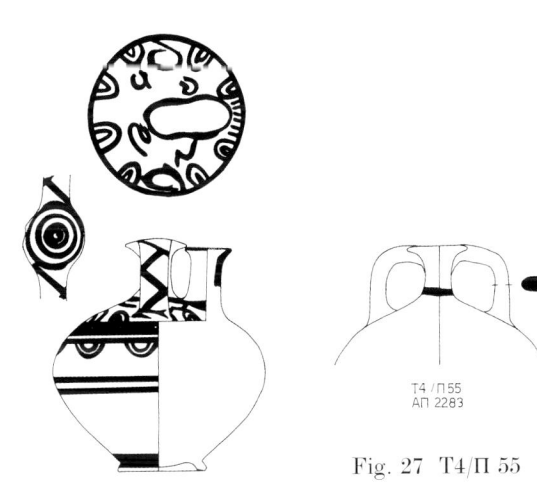

Fig. 27 T4/Π 55

Fig. 28 T4/Π 56

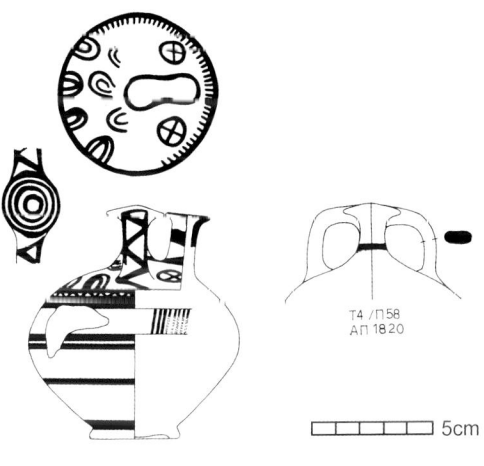

Fig. 29 T4/Π 58

Fig. 30

Fig. 31a

Fig. 32a

Fig. 33

Fig. 31b

Fig. 32b

Fig. 34

Fig. 35

Fig. 36

Fig. 37a

Fig. 38a

Fig. 39a

Fig. 37b

Fig. 38b

Fig. 39b

Fig. 40a

Fig. 42a

Fig. 40b

Fig. 41

Fig. 42b

Fig. 43

Fig. 44

Fig. 45

Fig. 46a

Fig. 47a

Fig. 48a

Fig. 46b

Fig. 47b

Fig. 48b

Fig. 49a Fig. 50a Fig. 51a

Fig. 49b Fig. 50b Fig. 51b

Fig. 52 Fig. 53 Fig. 54

Fig. 55a Fig. 56a Fig. 57

Fig. 55b Fig. 56b Fig. 58

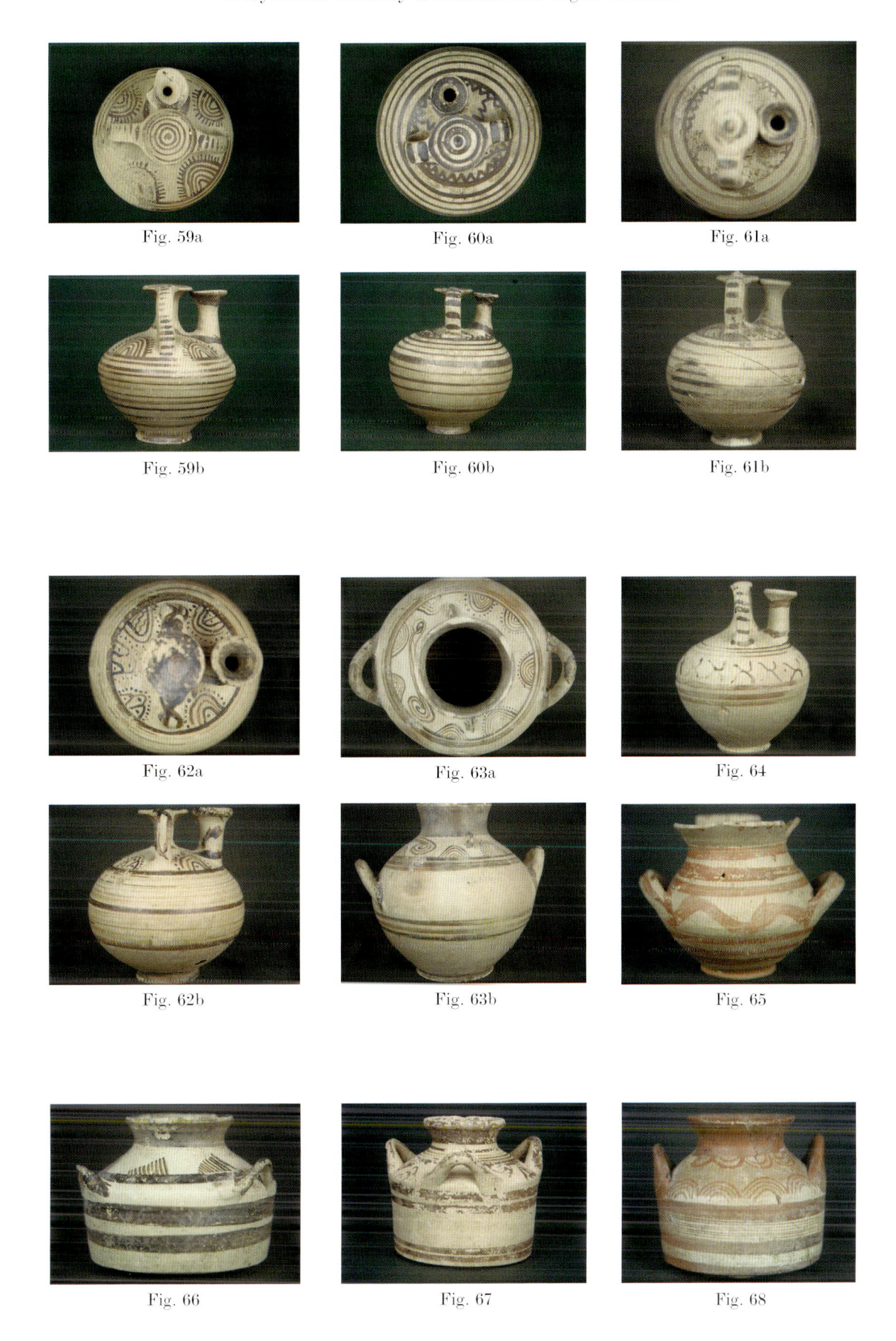

A Mycenaean Cemetery at Nikoleika near Aigion of Achaia 283

Fig. 59a

Fig. 60a

Fig. 61a

Fig. 59b

Fig. 60b

Fig. 61b

Fig. 62a

Fig. 63a

Fig. 64

Fig. 62b

Fig. 63b

Fig. 65

Fig. 66

Fig. 67

Fig. 68

Fig. 69a

Fig. 70

Fig. 71a

Fig. 69b

Fig. 72

Fig. 71b

Fig. 73a

Fig. 74a

Fig. 75a

Fig. 73b

Fig. 74b

Fig. 75b

Fig. 76

Fig. 77

Fig. 78

Fig. 79a

Fig. 80a

Fig. 81a

Fig. 79b

Fig. 80b

Fig. 81b

Fig. 82

Fig. 83

Fig. 84a

Fig. 85a

Fig. 86a

Fig. 84b

Fig. 85b

Fig. 86b

Fig. 87

Fig. 88

JEREMY B. RUTTER

HOW DIFFERENT IS LH III C MIDDLE AT MITROU? AN INITIAL COMPARISON WITH KALAPODI, KYNOS, AND LEFKANDI

The first of a projected series of five seasons of excavation took place from June 21 through July 30 2004 at the prehistoric site of Mitrou in the region that in Classical times was known as eastern Lokris. This program of fieldwork is a Greek-American *synergasia* co-directed by Eleni Zachou of the 14th [ΙΔ´] Ephoreia of Prehistoric and Classical Antiquities headquartered in Lamia and by Aleydis Van de Moortel of the Department of Classics at the University of Tennessee at Knoxville.[1] The site is located on what is now a small tidal islet just off the central Greek Mainland's east coast, near the southern boundary of the modern nome of Phthiotida and immediately east of the village of Tragana, some 11 km almost due south of Kynos/Livanates and an equal distance southeast of Atalanti, the capital of the modern eparchy of Lokrida. As the crow flies, Mitrou is almost exactly centered on a line running between Lamia at the north-west and Lefkandi in the south-east and lies about 65 km from each.

The findings of an intensive surface survey of the site conducted in 1988 and 1989 under the auspices of the Cornell Halai and East Lokris Project have been reported by Margaretha Kramer-Hajós, briefly in a paper delivered at the Archaeological Institute of America's annual meetings in 2002 and in considerably greater detail in her recently completed Cornell Ph.D. dissertation entitled "Mycenaean Civilization in East Lokris" (KRAMER-HAJÓS 2002. – KRAMER-HAJÓS 2005). Among the enormous quantities of pottery littering the site's surface, substantial numbers of diagnostic sherds of all phases of the Mycenaean era as well as of the subsequent Protogeometric period suggested that the transition from the Late Bronze to the Early Iron Age ought to be richly documented at the site in the form of stratified settlement debris. At the same time, comparatively little Geometric material was found, and even less of the Archaic or later periods. Furthermore, there was abundant evidence that the site had been ploughed for years, indeed deep-ploughed in many of the more than 20 fields into which the 3.8 hectares of the islet is presently subdivided among different owners. These two facts indicated that there was a strong possibility that strata of the Late Bronze/Early Iron transition might have been

---

[1] I am very grateful to Aleydis Van de Moortel and Eleni Zachou for their permission to present the material from Mitrou included in this article so soon after its excavation. The drawings are the work of Giuliana Bianco (Fig. 1) and the team of Roxana Docsan and Tina Ross (Figs. 2–11). My thanks also go to Penelope Mountjoy for helpful correspondence following the October 2004 workshop in Vienna on the subject of the LH III C ceramic sequence at Kalapodi; she is intimately familiar with the material, inasmuch as she was responsible for drawing it all for publication. The web site of the Mitrou Archaeological Project may be found at http://sunsite.utk.edu/mitrou/. The project's international staff during the 2004 field season, numbering almost 50, included members with the following nationalities: Belgium, Canada, Greece, Holland, Hungary, Ireland, Poland, Romania, the United Kingdom, and the United States.

largely destroyed, thus accounting for the large amounts of later Mycenaean through Protogeometric pottery to be found on the surface. An electronic resistivity survey conducted over much of the north-eastern quadrant of the site late in 2003 as a preliminary to making a decision as to where to locate our initial trenches produced a pattern of subsurface anomalies that appeared to be unmistakable evidence for a dense gridwork of walls separated by empty strips interpretable as streets or roads. The portion of the site surveyed in this fashion had not been intensively surveyed fifteen years earlier because of the dense herbaceous ground cover that here reduced surface visibility during the summer to almost zero. We were confident that excavation in this quadrant of the site would be productive, but we had no idea to what period the walls revealed by the resistivity survey would date. Indeed, we had no idea how deeply buried they might be within the uppermost meter of deposit that was the practical limit of the survey's capacity to detect subsurface anomalies. Being the kinds of archaeologists who naturally hope for the best but from bitter experience have a habit of fearing the worst, we imagined that we would probably be unlucky and lose the Late Helladic III C/Protogeometric interface.

Imagine our delight, then, when in the first series of four trenches that we opened up, each measuring four meters by four meters separated from the next by baulks one meter wide, we discovered that the ploughzone in this area of the site was no more than about 25 cm deep! Unfortunately, our first set of trenches turned out not to be located where we had expected they would be with reference to the gridwork of walls suggested by the resistivity survey. Some clever detective work by the project's architect, Giuliana Bianco, soon established what the problem was: we were digging about ten meters west of where we really wanted to be. Once we relocated to a fresh set of trenches, we immediately came down upon the apsidal innermost room of a large, MPG building (tentatively called Building A) set within and partially buttressed by a rectangular network of LH III C walls (belonging to a structure tentatively called Building B). Two rows of flat-topped fieldstone bases, of which at least two remain to be exposed because they fall within the baulks of our excavation grid, run *across* the apse (Fig. 1), instead of in a single row running *along* the apse's major axis. This peculiarity disturbed us, as did the depth at which these bases appeared to be founded below the Protogeometric floor level. But at last we realised that the bases, in fact, belong to the rectilinear LH III C predecessor and were re-used in the MPG building. I draw attention to this point because of the strong impression of continuity it communicates. No other example of such continuity in settlement architecture across the Late Bronze/Early Iron divide on the Mycenaean Greek Mainland, with the possible exception of some of the buildings at Thermon in Aetolia (HOPE SIMPSON – DICKINSON 1979, 103–104), is known to me.

On the floor of the large apsidal room – its internal width is roughly 5.4 m – lay a substantial deposit of MPG pottery for which numerous close parallels exist with the pottery recovered from the so-called Heróon at Lefkandi (e.g. Fig. 2). How much earlier this impressive apsidal building at Mitrou was constructed is at present uncertain, but two small groups of sherd material from fills associated with its predecessor suggest that the apsidal structure was built later than an advanced stage of LH III C Middle, perhaps not before the beginning of the PG period. As for when the rectilinear predecessor was constructed, at present I can only suggest a *terminus post quem*. The north-west wall of this building appears to have been built as a terrace wall against a comparatively gentle slope down from north-west to south-east. Its width is highly irregular and it has only a single finished face, that toward the south-east. At least one orthogonally oriented wall of this LH III C complex abuts against rather than bonding with this finished south-eastern face, and this abutting wall overlies a floor that has been revealed at several points on the downhill side of the terrace wall and that clearly belongs to the earliest stage of the rectilinear complex's use, since its level slopes slightly down from north-east to south-west in parallel with the base of the wall, itself sloping down gradually in this direction. The pottery from the fill behind the north-west terrace wall is quite different from that to the south-east, not only in date but in character. The latest material from this terrace fill dates from LH III C Early, while the sherd material overlying both of two floor levels identified in the north-easternmost angle of the rectangular building thus far exposed appears to be LH III C Middle to LH III C Late in date. Although it is regrettable that we cannot be more precise about these chronological assignments, we have simply not excavated enough at this point to be able to make more definitive statements. Indeed, much of what I am reporting here must be considered provisional, pending further excavations planned for the summer of 2005 and beyond. The basic points I wish to make are simply these: first, the apsidal Building A is likely to date entirely from the Early Iron Age; however, its rectilinear forerunner, Building B, the internal support bases of which the apsidal building re-uses, is of LH III C date, and quite possibly no earlier than LH III C Middle.

Aside from the stratified LH III C deposits recovered from just north and outside of the apsidal building in Trench LN784, we have also found stratified LH III C material between 5 and 7 meters to the north in Trench LN786 and also immediately to the west of this in the south-east corner of the adjoining Trench LM786. It is only in the last-mentioned trench that anything more than an occasional mendable or largely restorable LH III C vessel has been recovered, so the assessment of the LH III C Middle pottery that follows is based largely on sherd material coming from stratified fills rather than on the substantial floor deposits that we hope to discover in future seasons. The only potential destruction level so far noted is one containing burnt mud-brick and mendable LH III C Middle pottery from the south-east corner of Trench LM786 previously mentioned; this stratum has yet to be explored in full, however, or to be associated with a particular series of walls.

Thanks to the admirably full and comprehensive publication by Margrit Jacob-Felsch of the well-stratified and superbly excavated LH III C to EPG ceramic sequence recovered in Trenches K25 and K25N at Kalopodi between 1976 and 1982, it is possible to compare pottery from the LH III C Middle contexts so far encountered at Mitrou in considerable detail with what is known of east Lokrian Mycenaean pottery from a site located just 20 km to the west. The generous number of drawings published by Jacob-Felsch, in tandem with the wealth of quantitative data she has presented in an extensive series of charts and tables, allows us to assess the date and character of our LH III C Middle pottery from Mitrou not only in terms of a handful of significantly decorated pieces but also in light of the full range of this period's ceramic assemblage. Some of the quantitative data from Kalapodi is presented here in a modified format for purposes of comparison (Tables 1–2).

The excavators of Kalapodi were able to distinguish, in their Trench K25, a total of 23 distinct levels above sterile soil which spanned the time period from a comparatively early stage of LH III C through the EPG phase. Of these 23, only the lowest twelve were dated to LH III C; the excavators assigned the three strata immediately overlying these twelve to what they termed a "Submycenaean" phase, above which two further levels spanning the transition to EPG underlay a total of six EPG strata.[2] Formal and quanti-

---

[2] FELSCH 1996b, xvi. For a minor re-dating of strata 16–17 to EPG rather than to a transitional "Submycenaean" to EPG phase, see FELSCH 2001, 193 n. 3. I use the term "Submycenaean" in inverted commas because I continue to be skeptical about the existence of such a ceramic phase that can be defined satisfactorily in both typological and stratigraphic terms that has more than purely local (i.e. site-specific) or regional (i.e. at a scale corresponding to a modern Greek nomos) significance (RUTTER 1978; for an altogether different view, see RMDP, 55–58, 811, 816 [with respect to Kalapodi]).

Horizon	Stratum	Total Sherds in K25 [K25N]	Cat. Nos. in Kalapodi I [Total]	Fine Wheel-made (No./%)	Wheelmade Cooking Pots (No./%)	Handmade Cooking Pots (No./%)	Wheelmade Kitchen Ware (No./%)	Handmade Kitchen Ware (No./%)	Pithoi (No./%)	Other [Pre-Mycenaean and Unidentifiable] (No./%)
2	2	374	#8–35 [28]	245 / 65.5	53 / 14.2	27 / 7.2	5 / 1.3	9 / 2.4	16 / 4.3	19 / 5.1
2	Upper 2	198	#36–48 [13]	130 / 65.7	20 / 10.1	20 / 10.1	—	1 / 0.5	18 / 9.1	9 / 4.5
2	3	438	#49–69 [21]	299 / 68.3	54 / 12.3	42 / 9.6	5 / 1.1	7 / 1.6	22 / 5.0	9 / 2.1
2	Upper 3	184	#70–78 [9]	116 / 63.0	16 / 8.7	22 / 12.0	—	—	22 / 12.0	8 / 4.3
HORIZON 2 TOTALS		1194	70	790 / 66.2	143 / 12.0	111 / 9.3	10 / 0.8	17 / 1.4	78 / 6.5	45 / 3.8
3	4	1700 [224]	#79–130 [52]	1122 [156] / 66.0 [69.6]	223 [25] / 13.1 [11.2]	120 [16] / 7.1 [7.1]	8 [1] / 0.5 [0.4]	24 [9] / 1.4 [4.0]	140 [13] / 8.2 [5.8]	63 [4] / 3.7 [1.8]
4	Upper 4	444	#131–140 [10]	335 / 75.5	46 / 10.4	36 / 8.1	2 / 0.5	5 / 1.1	18 / 4.1	2 / 0.5
4	5	175	#141–142 [2]	133 / 76.0	11 / 14.7	9 / 5.1	—	3 / 1.7	8 / 4.6	11 / 6.3
4	Upper 5	1376	#143–159 [17]	1169 / 85.0	88 / 6.4	69 / 5.0	11 / 0.8	9 / 0.7	17 / 1.2	13 / 0.9
4	6	1525	#160–176 [17]	1201 / 78.8	104 / 6.8	104 / 6.8	4 / 0.3	33 / 2.2	56 / 3.7	23 / 1.5
4	7	400 [126]	#177–180 [4]	294 [81] / 73.5 [64.3]	31 [16] / 7.8 [12.7]	37 [13] / 9.3 [10.3]	1 [–] / 0.3 [–]	3 [3] / 0.8 [2.4]	30 [8] / 7.5 [6.3]	4 [5] / 1.0 [4.0]
4	8	2086	#181–208 [28]	1526 / 73.2	178 / 8.5	190 / 9.1	—	19 / 0.9	154 / 7.4	19 / 0.9
HORIZON 4 TOTALS		6132	78	4739 / 77.3	474 / 7.7	458 / 7.5	18 / 0.3	75 / 1.2	291 / 4.7	77 / 1.3
5	9	1207	#209–225 [17]	780 / 64.6	81 / 6.7	203 / 16.8	—	9 / 0.7	125 / 10.4	9 / 0.7
5	10	1821	#226–263 [38]	1097 / 60.2	114 / 6.3	337 / 18.5	—	21 / 1.2	233 / 12.8	19 / 1.0
HORIZON 5 TOTALS		3028	55	1877 / 62.0	195 / 6.4	540 / 17.8	—	30 / 1.0	358 / 11.8	28 / 0.9
6	11	138	#264–268 [5]	82 / 59.4	8 / 5.8	23 / 16.7	—	10 / 7.2	15 / 10.9	—
6	12	394	#269–275 [7]	199 / 50.5	24 / 6.1	67 / 17.0	—	26 / 6.6	73 / 18.5	5 / 1.3
HORIZON 6 TOTALS		532	12	281 / 52.8	32 / 6.0	90 / 16.9	—	36 / 6.8	88 / 16.5	5 / 0.9

Table 1 Kalapodi Trenches K25 and K25N: Horizons 2–6 (LH III C Middle–Late): Ceramic Assemblage Characterisation by Fabric and Mode of Manufacture

	HORIZON 2 [LH III C Middle] [No./%]	HORIZON 3 [LH III C Middle] [No./%]	HORIZON 4 [LH III C Middle] [No./%]	HORIZON 5 [LH III C Middle] [No./%]	HORIZON 6 [LH III C Late] [No./%]
TOTAL OPEN SHAPES IDENTIFIED	**189**	**197**	**554**	**272**	**49**
Semiglobular Cup FS 215	26 **13.8**	17 **8.6**	56 **10.1**	19 **7.0**	3 **6.1**
FS 215 Semiglobular Cup or FS 284 Deep Bowl	13 **6.9**	25 **12.7**	62 **11.2**	29 **10.7**	13 **26.5**
Deep Bowl FS 284, linear or patterned	21 **11.1**	13 **6.6**	19 **3.4**	11 **4.0**	2 **4.1**
Deep Bowl FS 284, monochrome painted	49 **25.9**	71 **36.0**	217 **39.2**	122 **44.9**	16 **32.7**
TOTAL FS 215 SEMI-GLOBULAR CUPS AND FS 284 DEEP BOWLS	**109** **57.7**	**126** **63.9**	**354** **63.9**	**181** **66.6**	**34** **69.4**
Unpainted kylikes (FS 267, 274, etc.)	13 **6.9**	13 **6.6**	7 **1.3**	4 **1.5**	3 **6.1**
Painted kylikes (FS 275 only)	27 **14.3**	21 **10.7**	90 **16.2**	34 **12.5**	2 **4.1**
Mug FS 226	– –	1 **0.5**	3 **0.5**	– –	– –
Dipper FS 236	7 **3.7**	1 **0.5**	5 **0.9**	7 **2.6**	– –
Carinated Cup FS 240	– –	2 **1.0**	1 **0.1**	– –	– –
Conical Bowl FS 242	– –	– –	4 **0.7**	2 **0.7**	– –
Stemmed Bowl FS 305/306	6 **3.2**	6 **3.0**	6 **1.1**	1 **0.4**	1 **2.0**
Tray FS 322	– –	– –	12 **2.2**	13 **4.8**	2 **4.1**
Krater FS 282	22 **11.6**	23 **11.7**	55 **9.9**	23 **8.5**	7 **14.3**
Kalathos FS 291	– –	1 **0.5**	4 **0.7**	2 **0.7**	– –
Basin FS 294	3 **1.6**	– –	3 **0.5**	3 **1.1**	– –
Other	2 **1.1**	3 **1.5**	10 **1.8**	2 **0.7**	– –

Table 2 Kalapodi Trench K25: Horizons 2–6 (LH III C Middle–Late): Frequencies of Fine Wheelmade Open Shapes

tative analyses of the pottery from each of these strata allowed Jacob Felsch to group them into a smaller number of "horizons". In view of the specific concerns of the October 2004 workshop held in Vienna, my focus in the commentary that follows is on Jacob-Felsch's Horizons 2 through 5, comprising strata 2 through 10, although I have appended some information about Horizon 6 (= strata 11 and 12) so as to indicate how LH III C Middle in this part of the Greek Mainland is to be distinguished from LH III C Late.

The beauty of the Kalapodi data from our point of view at Mitrou is that this information not only comes from a nearby site but also consists precisely of the kind of material that we have ourselves been finding – that is, badly broken and incomplete settlement pottery rather than complete vases recovered from tombs (like the finds from Elateia recovered by S. Deger-Jalkotzy and F. Dakoronia [DEGER-JALKOTZY 1999. – Also DEGER-JALKOTZY this volume]) or large deposits of broken but mendable pottery from one or more seismic destruction levels (such as the rich finds made at Kynos by F. Dakoronia [DAKORONIA 2003. – Also DAKORONIA this volume]). Thanks to the high quality of both the excavation and the publication of the Kalapodi material, all of us working in eastern Lokris and nearby Phokis should be able to correlate our post-palatial and early Dark Age findings with comparative ease in the future. As a result, we will have the luxury of being able to compare the findings from a sanctuary (Kalapodi), a cemetery (Elateia), and two town and harbour sites (Kynos and Mitrou) in seemingly continuous use during the critical two centuries which witnessed the transition from the Bronze to the Iron Age in perhaps a more comprehensive as well as nuanced way than has yet been possible in any other region of the Greek Mainland to date.

Of the four ceramic "horizons" at Kalapodi of principal interest here, Horizon 2 is dated by Jacob-Felsch to LH III C Entwickelt (or Developed) in terms of the Mycenae stratification, or Phase 4 early in the terminology for the subdivisions of LH III C that I proposed in 1977 (Table 4) (JACOB-FELSCH 1996, 93–94. – RUTTER 1977). Horizons 4 and 5 are dated to the later Fortgeschritten (or Advanced) stage of LH III C Middle, or what I have called Phase 4 late (JACOB-FELSCH 1996, 95–97. – RUTTER 1977). The intervening stratum 4 that defines Horizon 3 features joins with strata both above and below and is viewed as truly transitional (JACOB-FELSCH 1996, 94–95). The later Horizon 6, comprised of strata 11 and 12, is considered to represent LH III C Late, a phase which like LH III C Early is quite sparsely represented at Kalapodi, possibly because at this point the sanctuary was in a state of decline relative to the flourishing stages which both precede and follow (JACOB-FELSCH 1996, 97–98). Throughout the LH III C Middle period at Kalapodi, the dominant open shapes, a category that itself accounts for roughly three-quarters of the fine wheelmade pottery that can be assigned to a shape, are the deep semiglobular cup FS 215, the deep bowl FS 284, and the conical kylix FS 275 (Table 2). Together, these three shapes account for 72% of the identifiable fine wheelmade open shapes in Horizon 2, for 74.6% in Horizon 3, and for 79–80% in Horizons 4 and 5. What distinguishes the later from the earlier phase within LH III C Middle at Kalapodi is the sparing appearance of the conical bowl FS 242, a comparatively large version of the carinated cup FS 240, and the kalathos FS 291, the appearance in significantly larger numbers of the tray FS 322, and fairly abrupt declines in frequency of both unpainted kylikes and decorated stemmed bowls (Table 2). Cooking pots at Kalapodi during LH III C Middle consist, when wheelmade, exclusively of one-handled wide-mouthed jugs (FS 65) or the closely related two-handled shape FS 66 (JACOB-FELSCH 1996, pls. 24:34; 29:121–123), the only fragments of tripod cooking pots identified in these early levels coming from Early Iron Age levels (JACOB-FELSCH 1996, 74–75). Handmade and burnished cooking pots are found at Kalapodi right from the beginning of the LH III C sequence in Horizon 1. In their shape, these differ little in basic concept from the wheelmade vessels just described in that they, too, are wide-mouthed, feature one or perhaps occasionally two vertical strap handles from rim to shoulder, and have short flaring or steeply spreading necks (JACOB-FELSCH 1996, pls. 24:35; 26:67; 27:77; 30:142; 31:156; 32:175; 35:224). Not all of these handmade cooking pots are burnished, however (JACOB-FELSCH 1996, 122, pl. 23:7, 126, pl. 25:48). Moreover, beginning in Horizon 3 and probably a feature only of the more advanced phase of LH III C Middle, appear other kinds of handmade vessels such as unburnished shallow bowls or saucers, deep cups, kraters, vats, and amphorae.[3] Likewise characteristic of

---

[3] JACOB-FELSCH 1996, pls. 29:126; 32:176 (shallow bowls or saucers), pls. 29:127; 31:158; 35:225 (vats or tubs), 38:260 (deep cup), 38:261 (krater), 31:159 (amphora). A handmade body sherd from a cooking pot featuring a trapezoidal ledge-lug is described as both burnished and unburnished (JACOB-FELSCH 1996, 76, 135, pl. 29:125). The only handmade and unburnished vessel to be decorated, with impressed circles on both the top of its flattened rim and the exterior of its neck, is perhaps more likely to come from a pithos than from the bowl suggested by Jacob-Felsch (JACOB-FELSCH 1996, 135 no. 128, pls. 21; 29).

	Fine Wheelmade (No./%)	Cooking Pots[i] (No./%)	Kitchenware[ii] (No./%)	Pithoi (No./%)	TOTALS
Sherd Count	132 **65.0**	41 **20.2**	28 **13.8**	2 **1.0**	203
Weight (in g)	865 **35.5**	500 **20.5**	560 **23.0**	510 **20.9**	2435

---

[i] The figures for cooking pottery include both handmade and burnished as well as wheelmade and unfinished cooking pots, the latter distinctly in the majority.

[ii] The figures for kitchenware (= pale-firing, medium coarse wheelmade vessels) include both plain and painted (linear and solidly coated) sherds

Table 3 Mitrou Trench LM786 Stratigraphic Units 25–26:
Ceramic Assemblage Characterisation by Gross Fabric and Decorative Distinctions

RMDP, Phases of LH IIIC	RUTTER 1977, 1978	Mycenae [Argolid]	Lefkandi [Euboea]	Kalapodi [Phokis]	Mitrou [Lokris]	Kynos (Livanates) [Lokris]
LH III C Early	2	Early	1a			
	3	Tower	1b	Horizon 1		
LH III C Middle	4 early	Developed		Horizon 2	LM786 lower floor	
	4 late	Advanced	2a	Horizon 3	LM786 upper floor	Phase 5 [earthquake/ fire]
				Horizon 4		
			2b	Horizon 5		
LH III C Late	5 early	Final		Horizon 6		Phase 4 [earthquake]
			3			
"Sub-Mycenaean"	5 late		Skoubris Cemetery	Horizon 7	Graves	Phase 3 (?)

Table 4 Suggested Relative Chronology of Kalapodi, Kynos, Lefkandi, and Mitrou
during LH III C Middle and LH III C Late

the more advanced stage of LH III C Middle is the appearance of a reinforcing plastic band at the junction of neck and shoulder on wheelmade cooking pots of Horizons 4 and 5 (JACOB-FELSCH 1996, 74, pls. 32:174; 35:223; 38:258).

Thus far only one small context from Mitrou has produced sufficient mendable LH III C Middle pottery from a pure enough deposit to lend itself to meaningful comparison with these data from Kalapodi Trenches K25 and K25N. The small body of material in question comes from a floor in Trench LM786 already alluded to that is sealed above by collapsed building debris containing for the most part much earlier sherd material and then by a second LH III C Middle floor overlain by a pure LH III C pottery unit. The profile of the small corpus of pottery from the lower floor (Table 3) invites comparison with Horizon 2 at Kalapodi by virtue of the relatively low percentage of fine wheelmade pottery, the comparative frequency of unpainted kylix fragments, the significantly higher quantity of wheelmade than handmade and burnished cooking pots, and the prominence of wheelmade medium coarse kitchenware (what Jacob-Felsch refers to as Küchengeschirr), even if most of this last is due to numerous sherds from a single large closed vase. The small group of inventoried pottery from this deposit – a monochrome coated deep bowl, a large linear jug or hydria, a patterned closed vase (possibly a collar-necked jar) decorated with running spirals linked by dot-filled tangents (Fig. 3), and a patterned krater with two superposed rows of isolated spirals (Fig. 4) – supports the assignment of this group to the same regional phase of LH III C represented by Horizon 2 at Kalapodi. The patterned krater has reasonably close parallels in the stacked spiral decoration of two kraters from Kalapodi from Horizon 2 and 3 contexts (JACOB-FELSCH 1996, pls. 23:19; 28:91), and the remaining three vessels seem more at home in Horizon 2 at Kalapodi than in Horizons 4 and 5. From the *very* small excavation unit representing the fill above the upper LH III C floor identified in this trench come sherds of a small patterned mug and a patterned kalathos, two indicators that this later level is likely to represent an advanced stage of LH III C Middle contemporary with Kalapodi Horizons 4 or 5.

As the above very preliminary comparison of our findings at Mitrou with those from Kalapodi suggests, the LH III C Middle ceramic repertoires at the two sites are very similar. Visual inspection of the patterned kraters from the two sites suggests that they could easily have been produced at the same locale, even in the same workshop. Furthermore, handmade and burnished rim-handled cooking pots occur together with wheelmade and unburnished versions of the same basic form at both sites. There are, however, some differences between the pottery of this period recovered from these two sites that are worth drawing attention to. For example, although the most popular fine painted open shapes at Mitrou are, as at Kalapodi, the deep bowl and the deep semiglobular cup, the conical kylix is rare at Mitrou. The most popular patterned shapes at both sites are kraters, deep bowls, stirrup jars, and collar-necked jars, in that order, but carinated cups and trays have so far not been recognised at Mitrou. It is possible that some of these differences may simply be due to the fact that the later stage of LH III C Middle – Advanced/Fortgeschritten or what I have called Phase 4 late – is so far poorly attested at Mitrou, but this will not account for the dearth of linear and monochrome painted conical kylikes at our site. Moreover, among the handmade, dark-surfaced, and medium-coarse to coarse pottery at Mitrou, shapes other than wide-mouthed rim-handled cooking pots appear in burnished form already in the earlier stage of LH III C Middle, rather than regularly *unfinished* as at Kalapodi and only in *later* LH III C Middle contexts. Finally, although we have found a fair number of pithoi decorated with broad plastic bands embellished with incised and impressed ornament of the sort found at Kalapodi, we have yet to see anything that we would be willing to call White Ware (as this fabric has been defined at Lefkandi and recognised in the case of nine sherds at Kalapodi).

A quick look at the evidence from Kynos just 10 km to the north of Mitrou provides further food for thought. The large destruction deposit of Dakoronia's phase 5 containing the by now very well-known pictorial kraters decorated with ships, some of them unmistakably engaged in battle, has produced a wealth of other LH III C Middle pottery that she has illustrated extensively in her contribution to the proceedings of the

2001 Vienna workshop on LH III C ceramic chronology and synchronisms (DAKORONIA 2003, 45–47, figs. 24–38). Despite a host of similarities linking LH III C Kynos with Mitrou, including the fact that painted conical kylikes appear to be equally rare at both sites, there are also a few important differences. Neither in LH III C Middle nor in LH III C Late levels at Kynos is there any evidence for handmade and burnished pottery; instead, this makes its initial appearance at Kynos contemporaneously with the first evidence for compass-drawn circles and semicircles, in a phase that Dakoronia has identified as "Submycenaean" on the basis of parallels with Kalapodi Horizon 8 (DAKORONIA 2003, 43, 47). White Ware has been identified in LH III C Late (DAKORONIA 2003, 45) as well as LH III C Middle (DAKORONIA this volume) levels at Kynos.

Whatever differences may exist between the LH III C Middle ceramic repertoires at Mitrou and contemporary Kalapodi and Kynos, they are comparatively minor in comparison to the much more substantial disparities between Mitrou and Lefkandi. The absence of White Ware at Mitrou may be due to the popularity there of the same shapes as typify White Ware at Lefkandi – that is, kraters, basins, and especially large closed shapes – but produced in a finer reddish yellow fabric decorated with broad bands in dull orange paint. If this dully painted fabric represents, as seems likely, a locally produced alternative to White Ware, the absence of the latter at Mitrou is perfectly intelligible. But cooking habits at LH III C Mitrou seem to have been quite different than at Lefkandi, where burnished cooking pottery is unattested in LH III C levels and where tripod cooking pots are common. The frequency of both conical kylikes and conical bowls as painted shapes at Lefkandi is quite unlike the situation at Mitrou, where semiglobular cups and deep bowls were overwhelmingly the preferred forms of painted tableware for drinking and eating. The two sites nevertheless have in common the popularity of very plain decoration on the commonest open and closed shapes, either banding or solid coatings of coloured slip, coupled with a fondness for pictorial ornament on kraters and some closed forms. They also share a common aversion to painted cups and bowls with carinated profiles, both of which are quite popular in the north-eastern Peloponnese at this time. Whether or not Mitrou will turn out to be a production centre for a distinctive school of pictorial vase-painting as both Lefkandi and Kynos appear to have been is something that only further excavation at the site will reveal. But we have already made two discoveries that provide important links with other sites during other phases of the post-palatial Bronze Age that should be mentioned here. One, a surface find, is the rim of a deep handmade-and-burnished jar decorated with a finger-impressed plastic band interrupted at one point by a prominent lug (Fig. 5) that belongs to a vessel of precisely the same sort as numerous fragments and fully restorable pots from Korakou, Mycenae, Tiryns, and above all the Menelaion but which have heretofore not been represented in central Greece. The second is a group of crudely handmade, reddish-brown but unburnished, medium coarse imitations of small Mycenaean shapes (Figs. 6–9) of precisely the same sort as are typical of the "Submycenaean" levels of Horizon 7 at Kalapodi (JACOB-FELSCH 1996, 79, pls. 38:260; 39:286; 40:302–304,307; 41:334; 43:371). The Mitrou pieces unfortunately were all found at a level very close to the surface in the north-easternmost corner of Trench LN784, the trench in which the LH III C levels underlying our MPG apsidal building are best represented. We are therefore not at all sure how their chronological context at Mitrou should yet be described. Possibly to be associated with these handmade miniatures in date is a sizeable fragment from a small stirrup jar (Fig. 10) that was found in a mixed surface level, almost certainly part of a tomb deposit disturbed by the plough and decorated in a fashion that is reminiscent of "Submycenaean" tombs in Athens. And finally, at least some of the cooking pots from LH III C Middle or Late contexts at Mitrou appear to be both wheelmade and burnished (Fig. 11).

ADDENDUM

Discoveries made during an additional season of excavation at Mitrou in June and July 2005 require some corrections to, and enable some amplifications of, the picture of the site's LH III C through MPG occupational sequence presented above.

The twin rows of fieldstone bases running across the apse of Building A turn out to be of PG date after all. The only base that can be convincingly associated with the preceding LH III C Building B is a roughly circular and possibly worked support for a post or column which directly underlies one of Building A's fieldstone bases, the two bases in question both lying on the main NW-SE axes of their respective buildings.

The set of four crudely handmade, medium coarse, small-scale imitations of Mycenaean shapes (Figs. 6–9) with close parallels at "Submycenaean" Kalapodi turned out to be only a small part of a much larger group of between 22 and 26 such handmade and unburnished miniatures representing eight or more different open shapes,[4] almost all intact and found within a small rectangular room (preliminarily labelled Building C) that was built over Building B's north-west corner. Together with these miniatures was found a complete wheelmade and unburnished cooking pot (LN784-018-014) provided with a base fragment from a large painted krater as a lid. Inside the cooking pot, a pair of femurs from a young pig (3–5 months old) had been laid carefully on top of a stack of four additional pairs of femora from even smaller, foetal piglets.[5] This extremely unusual context has yet to be studied in detail, but appears to date from the very end of the LH III C period at Mitrou.

Two additional discoveries at Mitrou in 2005 are worth reporting. First, immediately to the south-west of Building A, a deposit of mixed LH III C Late to EPG pottery in square LN782 provided welcome confirmation that a full LH III C through LPG ceramic sequence will be recoverable in this portion of the site.[6] Secondly, two unmistakable examples of dark-surfaced handmade and burnished kylix stems[7] were recovered from this area, unfortunately in neither case from narrowly datable contexts. To my knowledge, these may be the first examples of this quintessentially Mycenaean ceramic form to have been recognised in this markedly non-Mycenaean ceramic class at a Mainland Greek site.

---

[4] In addition to the four miniatures found in 2004 (LN784-018-016, 019, 023, and 026; Figs. 6–9), 18 more such vases were found in 2005 within the walls of Building C (LO-784-041-012, 013; LO-784-048-011, 036, 037, 040, 041, 042, 043, 044, 047, 048, 050, 055, 056, 057, 059; LO-784-050-015). Four more were found nearby (LO784-013-013; LO785-005-014; LO785-030-014; LN786-005-013) and are likely to represent disturbed parts of the same deposit.

[5] The identifications of these bones and the age estimates for the animals to which they belonged were generously provided by Thanos Webb, the zooarchaeologist working at Mitrou in 2005, and are reported here with the kind permission of Aleydis Van de Moortel.

[6] This deposit has been preliminarily analysed by Bartek Lis of the University of Warsaw whose work is cited here with his kind permission.

[7] The inventory numbers of these two pieces are LO784-007-013 and LN784-049-014. The latter has a perforated stem (diameter of perforation 1.0 cm) and may conceivably be an exceptionally long and thick-walled tubular spout. The former, however, is unquestionably the upper stem and lower bowl of a dark-surfaced handmade and burnished kylix, the interior bowl of which is black-burnished.

Bibliography

DAKORONIA, F.
2003 "The Transition from Late Helladic III C to the Early Iron Age at Kynos", 37–51 in: *LH III C Chronology and Synchronisms*.

DAVIS, E. N. (ed.)
1977 *Symposium on the Dark Ages in Greece*. New York.

DEGER-JALKOTZY, S.
1999 "Elateia and Problems of Pottery Chronology", 195–202 in: *Περιφέρεια*.

FELSCH, R. C. S. (ed.)
1996a *Kalapodi. Ergebnisse der Ausgrabungen im Heiligtum der Artemis und des Apollon von Hyampolis in der antiken Phokis*. Vol. I. Mainz.
1996b "Vorwort des Herausgebers", ix–xvii in: FELSCH 1996a.
2001 "Opferhandlungen des Alltagslebens im Heiligtum der Artemis Elaphebolos von Hyampolis in den Phasen SH III C – Spätgeometrisch", 193–199 in: LAFFINEUR – HÄGG 2001.

HOPE SIMPSON, R. – O. T. P. K. DICKINSON
1979 *A Gazetteer of Aegean Civilisation in the Bronze Age I: The Mainland and Islands* (SIMA 52). Göteborg.

JACOB-FELSCH, M.
1996 "Die spätmykenische bis frühprotogeometrische Keramik", 1–213 in: FELSCH 1996a.

KRAMER-HAJÓS, M.
2002 "Bronze Age Mitrou in East Lokris, Greece", *AJA* 106, 278.
2005 *Mycenaean Civilization in East Lokris* (unpublished Ph.D. dissertation). Cornell University.

LAFFINEUR, R. – R. HÄGG (eds.)
2001 *POTNIA. Deities and Religion in the Aegean Bronze Age. Proceedings of the 8th International Aegean Conference/8e Rencontre égéenne internationale, Göteborg, Göteborg University, 12–15 April 2000* (Aegaeum 22). Liège – Austin.

Περιφέρεια
1999 *Η περιφέρεια του Μυκηναϊκού κόσμου. Α΄ διεθνές διεπιστημονικό συμπόσιο, Λαμία, 25–29 Σεπτεμβρίου 1994*. Lamia.

RUTTER, J. B.
1977 "Late Helladic III C Pottery and Some Historical Implications", 1–20 in: DAVIS 1977.
1978 "A Plea for the Abandonment of the Term 'Submycenaean'", *TUAS* 3, 58–65.

298   Jeremy B. Rutter

Fig. 1 Mitrou. General plan at end of 2004 excavation season (G. Bianco)

Fig. 2 Mitrou. MPG Krater LN783-022-026 from floor of apsidal Building A (R. Docsan/T. Ross)

Fig. 3 Mitrou. LH III C Middle closed shape (collar-necked jar?) LM 786-025-013 (R. Docsan/T. Ross)

Fig. 4 Mitrou. LH III C Middle krater LM 786-025-012 (R. Docsan/T. Ross)

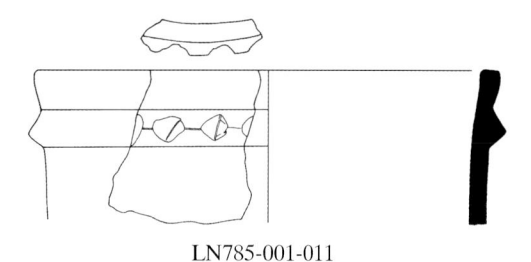

LN785-001-011

Fig. 5 Mitrou. LH III C handmade and burnished jar LN 785-001-011 found on surface (R. Docsan/T. Ross) (scale 1:3)

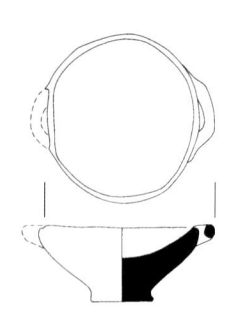

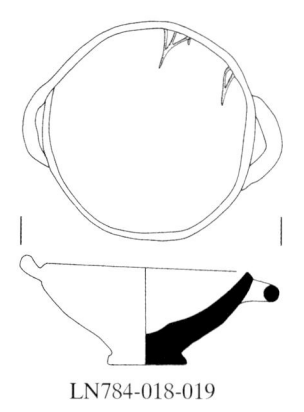

LN784-018-019

Fig. 6 Mitrou. Medium coarse handmade and unburnished miniature cup LN 784-018-019 of terminal LH III C or "Submycenaean" date (scale 1:3)

LN784-018-016

Fig. 7 Mitrou. Medium coarse handmade and unburnished miniature cup LN 784-018-016 of terminal LH III C or "Submycenaean" date (scale 1:3)

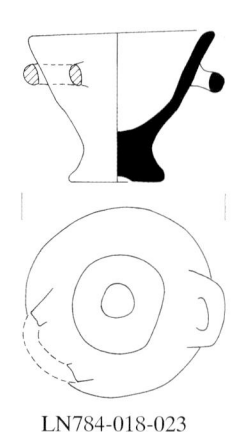

LN784-018-023

Fig. 8 Mitrou. Medium coarse handmade and unburnished miniature stemmed cup LN 784-018-023 of terminal LH III C or "Submycenaean" date (scale 1:3)

LN784-018-026

Fig. 9 Mitrou. Medium coarse handmade and unburnished tray LN 784-018-026 of terminal LH III C or "Submycenaean" date (scale 1:3)

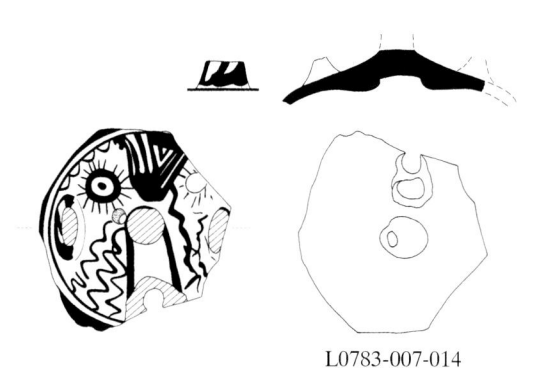

L0783-007-014

Fig. 10 Mitrou. Top of "Submycenaean" stirrup jar LO 783-007-014 found in ploughzone, probably from a disturbed grave (scale 1:3)

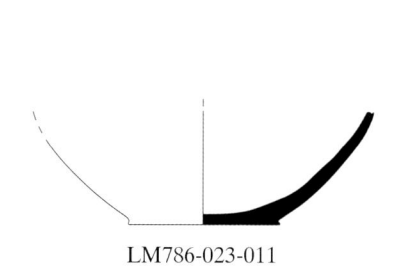

LM786-023-011

Fig. 11 Mitrou. Lower half of a wheelmade dark-surfaced cooking pot with a burnished exterior surface LM 786-023-011, of LH III C Middle or Late date (scale 1:3)

ELIZABETH V. SCHOFIELD †

LEFKANDI IN LATE HELLADIC III C MIDDLE*

Excavations at the site of Xeropolis at Lefkandi were conducted in the 1960s by Mervyn Popham and Hugh Sackett for the British School at Athens. The site is notable for its deep and well-stratified deposits of LH III C, associated with three architectural phases. Each of these major phases can be subdivided into an earlier and a later phase (Table 1). Phases 1b and 2a terminate in destructions, and it is these two that Penelope Mountjoy has assigned to LH III C Middle (*RMDP*, 38–40).

Final publication of the excavations was well advanced at the time of Popham's death, and the volume is now complete (EVELY 2006). Popham assigned the analysis of the III C pottery to himself, Susan Sherratt, and me, with Joost Crouwel writing on the pictorial vases. Popham himself undertook Phase 1, Phases 2a and 3 were assigned to me, and 2b to Susan Sherratt. He did not live to complete Phase 1b, and I undertook to do so. I shall necessarily repeat information contained in our preliminary summary (POPHAM – MILBURN 1971), but I shall add to it in some detail. The figures illustrate the standard types, but not the rarer shapes, nor the variety of ornamentation.

PHASE 1b

The Phase 1b destruction deposits produced a good number of whole or nearly whole pots. There is much less material of Phase 1a, and not all is well stratified. They are in many ways very similar, but Phase 1a has some distinctive features and some survivals from LH III B which do not continue into Phase 1b.

The commonest open vessels in 1b are the cup FS 216 and the deep bowl FS 285, probably in almost equal numbers. The most favoured **cup** is the type we call the lip-band cup (Fig. 1:1–2), usually with a banded interior, but sometimes with just a spiral at the base. Two unpainted types are also well represented, one rounded and shallow (Fig. 1:3), the other carinated (Fig. 1:4). The monochrome carinated cup with high handle FS 240, which was one of the characteristic features of Phase 1a, may by now have gone out of use; at any rate, there are only a few sherds.

Deep bowls (Fig. 1:6–8) are nearly all linear or monochrome, but, unlike Phase 1a when the linear type predominated, monochrome is now more popular. Decorative motifs such as the antithetic spiral with central panel are infrequent, and most sherds in the Phase 1b deposits may be earlier throw-ups. Decorative motifs certainly do occur in

---

* This paper is published by permission of the British School at Athens. I am grateful to Penelope Mountjoy, Elizabeth French and Anne Jackson for editorial assistance, and to Jacke Phillips for drawing the new illustrations presented here. [Elizabeth Schofield saw the completed version of this text before her death in July 2005 (Eds.).]

Phase 1a. Interiors of deep bowls are always monochrome, often with a reserved disc at the interior base.

Kylikes FS 274, 275 (Fig. 1:9) are always conical with solid stems, and may be painted or plain. Painted examples are sometimes monochrome, but more often have a lip band, reserved upper body, and painted lower body down to the foot (Fig. 1:9). Interiors are monochrome, sometimes with a reserved disc at the base. The conical kylix occurred in Phase 1a, when it could be plain or monochrome; the plain carinated kylix of LH III B type FS 267, which continued into Phase 1a, does not survive into Phase 1b; and nor does the plain shallow angular bowl FS 295.

Kraters FS 282 are apparently not particularly popular. No nearly complete example was found, and the smaller sherds may be throw-ups. They did not occur frequently in Phase 1a either, when they favoured panel designs on the whole.

Other open shapes that are found in fairly large numbers are the plain **scoop** or **ladle** FS 236, and the large **shallow basin** FS 294, 302, with or without bridged spout, having linear decoration inside and out (Fig. 1:5). They occur also in Phase 1a.

Of the closed shapes, **jugs** FS 106, 110, **amphorae** FS 69, 70 and **hydriae** FS 128 form the largest group (Fig. 2:4–5). Nearly all are lip-handled, a very few are neck-handled, and very occasionally twisted handles occur. Lips may be more noticeably hollowed, whereas in Phase 1a they were only slightly hollowed, if at all. Decoration is mostly linear, with common use of a triple group of thick-thin-thick bands, unlike the bands of equal width current in Phase 1a. Shoulder ornaments are found much more frequently than earlier, usually either tassel (POPHAM – MILBURN 1971, 335, fig. 1:7) or scroll (Fig. 2:4), and very occasionally both, or two tassels, at shoulder and belly. Handles are decorated with an S or figure 8, or, less frequently, a vertical wavy line.

Amphoriskoi FS 59 are much the same in both phases: a globular body, with either loop handles or lugs at the belly (Fig. 2:2). All have a monochrome neck and banding on the body, often a combination of thick and thin in Phase 1b, but thick only in Phase 1a. Additional decoration, such as a wavy line or tassel, is rare.

Dipper jugs with arching high handle are quite frequent (Fig. 2:3). They are always unpainted.

Small globular **stirrup jars** FS 174, 175 are not common (Fig. 2:1). The decoration may be entirely linear, but the sherd material includes a few patterned pieces, such as chevrons and lozenges. A large storage stirrup jar has tassels on the shoulder.

Other shapes are very rare.

Storage vessels are well represented, including a variety of **pithoi,** and **tubs** are very popular (Fig. 3:4). There are also a good many **cooking pots** (Fig. 3:1–3). They comprise one-handled jugs, two-handled jars, and **tripod vessels** of two types: one is carinated with a tall concave rim, the other rounded with inturned rim. Both types have quite a shallow bowl, and differ from the tripod vessel of Phase 1a, which has a deep rounded body and everted rim.

PHASE 2a

An early and a mature stage have been identified. There is little material of the early stage, which shows marked continuity from Phase 1b, but some innovations, such as more decorated kraters. The mature stage produced a variety of restorable pots from partially preserved destruction deposits. Many are still almost indistinguishable from Phase 1b, but some new shapes appear, bands are used in a more decorative fashion, there is greater use of ornamental motifs, especially on kraters, less frequently on deep bowls and other shapes, and added white paint is an innovation, particularly but not exclusively on pictorial kraters.

Cups FS 216 are still popular, but are greatly outnumbered by deep bowls. The lip-band type predominates, mostly indistinguishable from Phase 1b, but sometimes the broad band is set lower and a very narrow band runs round the top of the lip (Fig. 4:3); rarely a wavy line decorates the upper body. Interiors are usually plain except for a circle or spiral at the base, but several have solid paint, sometimes with a reserved disc. A few cups are monochrome, and a very few of those are carinated, similar to the carinated cup FS 240 of Phase 1a, but smaller and with a more elegantly arched handle (Fig. 4:2).

Conical kylikes FS 274, 275 are quite few in number, a little smaller and with a shallower bowl than those of Phase 1b (Fig. 4:4–6). A minority have a swollen stem, which first appears in Phase 2a early. The norm is the banded kylix (also an innovation of Phase 2a early), with bands just above and on the stem. Interiors are monochrome, sometimes with a reserved disc. A very few kylikes have abstract decoration in the handle zone.

Deep bowls FS 285 are much the most popular open shape. Dimensions vary more than in Phase 1b and include miniatures, which first appear in Phase 2a early (Fig. 5:1–3). Monochrome bowls predominate, though there are some with linear decoration. The great majority have a solid-painted interior, sometimes with a reserved disc at the base, and occasionally with a reserved line at the lip, another innovation of Phase 2a early. Some are indistinguishable from Phase 1b, but on some the whole lower body is unpainted. More rarely, one or two reserved bands are added just below the belly. Decorative motifs reappear in Phase 2a early, chiefly variations on the running spiral. They remain very much in the minority throughout Phase 2a. The most popular patterns are antithetic motifs (spirals, loops, streamers) with or without a central triglyph (Fig. 5:4–5). The running spiral still occurs, and a few other motifs, such as the wavy line. Most schemes are quite simple.

Conical bowls FS 242, which perhaps were invented in Phase 1b, are quite few in number. In Phase 2a early they are quite large, with a rounded body and sometimes an incurving rim (Fig. 4:8). By the mature phase the sides are less rounded, and the canonical form probably evolved quite quickly. They have a few bands on the exterior; interiors are usually painted solid, sometimes with a reserved disc at the base.

One-handled bowls, probably introduced in the mature stage, are not frequent. In effect, they are small one-handled deep bowls, with a rounded profile and a short everted lip. No complete profile with handle has survived, but there is a probable candidate lacking the handle (Fig. 4:7), with simple linear decoration and a banded interior with spiral at the base. But interiors may also be monochrome, sometimes with a reserved disc.

Kraters FS 282 (Figs. 6–7) are the third most popular open shape, but yet not in large numbers. Only a couple are nearly complete. They prefer abstract decorative motifs, but include a splendid collection of pictorial scenes. The decorated krater above all distinguishes Phase 2a from 1b. Most are either bell-shaped with rounded rim, or with straighter sides and usually a squared ledge rim, which may be accompanied by one or two slashed ribs. Interiors are mostly painted solid, but some have interior bands. There are also two types of carinated krater: one with a very incurving upper body, and a series of horizontal grooves at the level of the carination (Fig. 6:3); the other, which sometimes also is grooved, has a straight neck above the carination, which may be sharp or more gently curving (Fig. 6:1–2). Monochrome or linear exterior decoration seems to be confined to carinated kraters; very occasionally they have abstract or pictorial ornamentation.

Abstract motifs on standard kraters are nearly all spiral types and antithetic patterns. Antithetic spirals, loops, and streamers are often in a panelled arrangement of greater or lesser complexity (Fig. 7:1), and pictorial kraters with birds or animals are also sometimes in antithetic arrangements (Fig. 7:2). Other pictorial fragments include human figures engaged in various activities (CROUWEL 2006).

Kalathoi FS 291 are very few in number and mostly very fragmentary. Exterior decoration is usually linear. The interior decorative zone at the flaring top of the vessel can contain abstract or pictorial patterns, either of which can occur in a panel arrangement. There is only one restorable example; it is very idiosyncratic (POPHAM – MILBURN 1971, 343, fig. 6:3).

Trays FS 322 are a new shape in the mature stage of Phase 2a, but are few in number. They can be decorated both on the exterior and interior (Fig. 4:1). Others have solid-painted interiors, occasionally with added white bands.

Shallow basins FS 294, 302, sometimes bridge-spouted, continue from Phase 1b, with exterior decoration nearly always linear, interiors banded or monochrome (Fig. 8:4).

Plain scoops FS 236 occur in most deposits, but are quite few in number. They are essentially the same as in Phase 1b. The plain dipper jug has almost ceased to exist.

Standard **amphorae** FS 69, 70, **hydriae** FS 128 and **jugs** FS 106, 110 are well represented, but mostly fragmentary. In the early stage, lips may still be rounded or slightly hollowed, but throughout Phase 2 there is a tendency towards a markedly hollow lip (Fig. 8:1). Almost all are lip-handled, but there are two or three neck-handled jugs. Twisted handles have become more popular, but are still uncommon; there is an unusual case with grooved handles (Fig. 8:2). The standard decoration is indistinguishable from Phase 1b. Handles frequently have a figure 8, but the wavy line occurs more often than before. Not all have shoulder decoration. The tassel is still favoured, followed by the scroll, with just a few other motifs appearing. Decoration on the belly is rare. Novelties include droplets around the neck of some jugs, and the first appearance of the **trefoil-mouthed jug** FS 137.

Amphoriskoi FS 59 are quite few (Fig. 8:5). Most are small, with a globular body, two small round horizontal handles, and a ring or raised base. Most are decorated with a variety of motifs from the standard repertoire of this phase.

Alabastra FS 96 are very rare indeed. The well-known light-on-dark griffin vase is, of course, unique (see MOUNTJOY this volume, fig. 6).

Stirrup jars FS 174, 175 are not very common. There are a couple of big storage jars, but most others are of the globular type, with much variation in size. Most are extremely fragmentary, but there is one intact jar with elaborate decoration and added white paint (POPHAM – MILBURN 1971, pls. 53:7; 56:1). The top disk may be flat or coned; it is usually decorated with a spiral. The normal decorative scheme comprises an ornamental shoulder zone, multiple bands on the body, and usually a reserved zone on the lower body. Shoulder decoration is often simple, such as isolated concentric semicircles. Sometimes one or more decorative zones are inserted on the body with, for example, chevrons and zigzag.

Tubs for storage are lacking in the mature phase; **tripod cooking vessels** also rapidly go out of style. One- and two-handled jars are preferred for cooking, more or less the same as those of Phase 1b (Fig. 8:3).

Postscript

I was particularly requested to indicate where we have changed our minds from what was said in previous publications. For the most part it has been more a matter of adding further details. But there has been one major change resulting from study of the stratigraphy: the reassignment to Phase 2a of some contexts originally assigned to Phase 2b. A result of this is that some new features once thought to have appeared in 2b have been pushed forward into 2a. These include one-handled bowls, possibly the neck-handled amphora, and small quantities of White Ware, usually deep bowls, kraters, amphorae and jugs, a few of which may be intrusive.

LEFKANDI XEROPOLIS in LH III C PHASES 1 and 2

PHASE 1a
 	
  Filling below floors; yard refuse
 	
PHASE 1b
 	
  Destruction deposits

PHASE 2a
 	
  Early stage
 	
    Under-floor fill; yard refuse
 	
  Mature stage
 	
    Partially preserved destruction deposits
 	
PHASE 2b
 	
  Repair and modification of buildings

Table 1

Bibliography

CROUWEL, J. H.
2006 "Late Mycenaean Pictorial Pottery", 233–255 in: EVELY 2006.

EVELY, D. (ed.)
2006 *Lefkandi IV. The Bronze Age. The Late Helladic III C Settlement at Xeropolis* (BSA Suppl. 39). London.

POPHAM, M. R. – E. V. MILBURN
1971 "The Late Helladic III C Pottery of Xeropolis (Lefkandi): A Summary", *BSA* 66, 333–352.

Fig. 1 Phase 1b. 1–4 cups, 5 basin, 6–8 deep bowl, 9 kylix

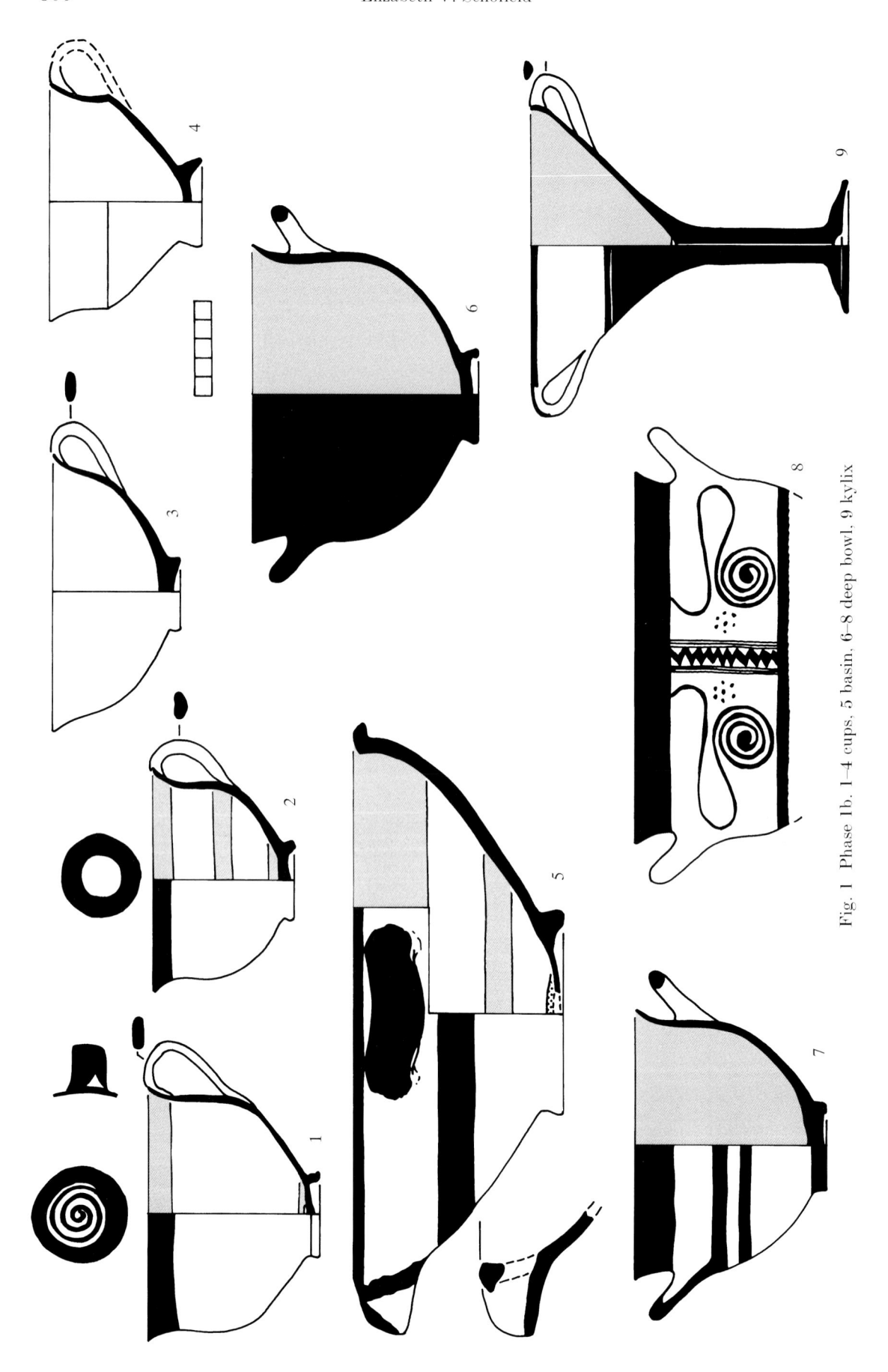

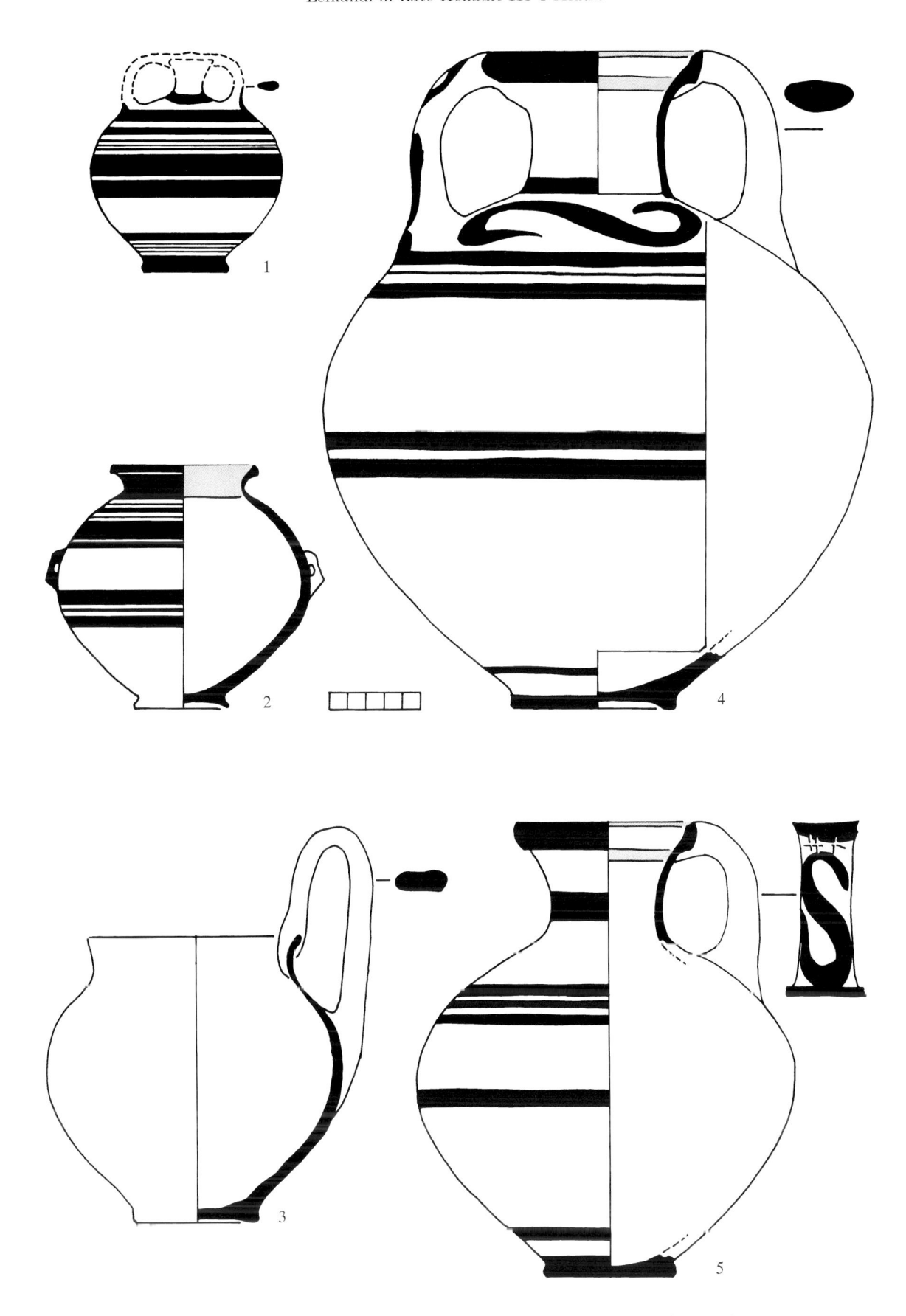

Fig. 2 Phase 1b. 1 stirrup jar, 2 amphoriskos, 3 dipper jug, 4 amphora, 5 jug

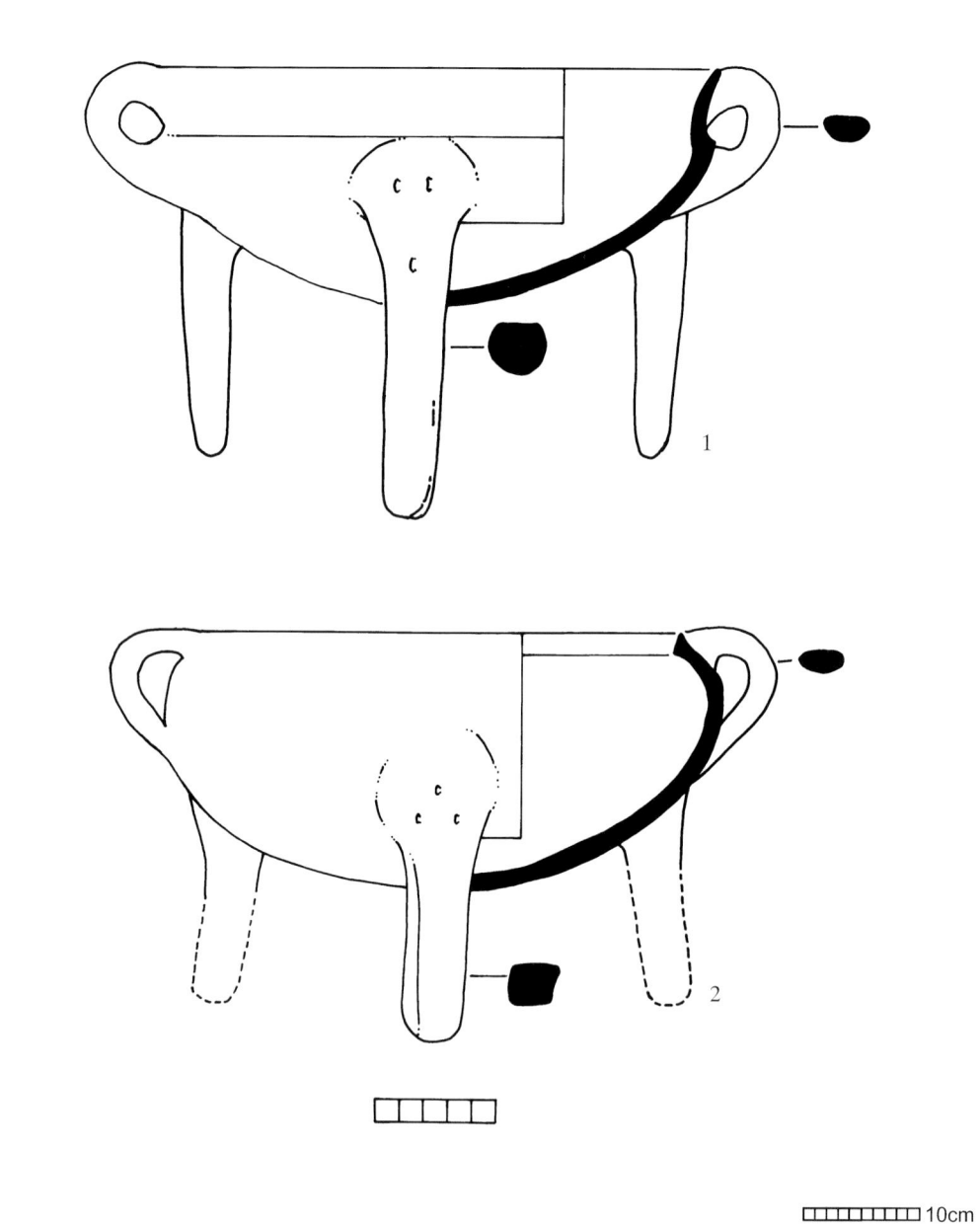

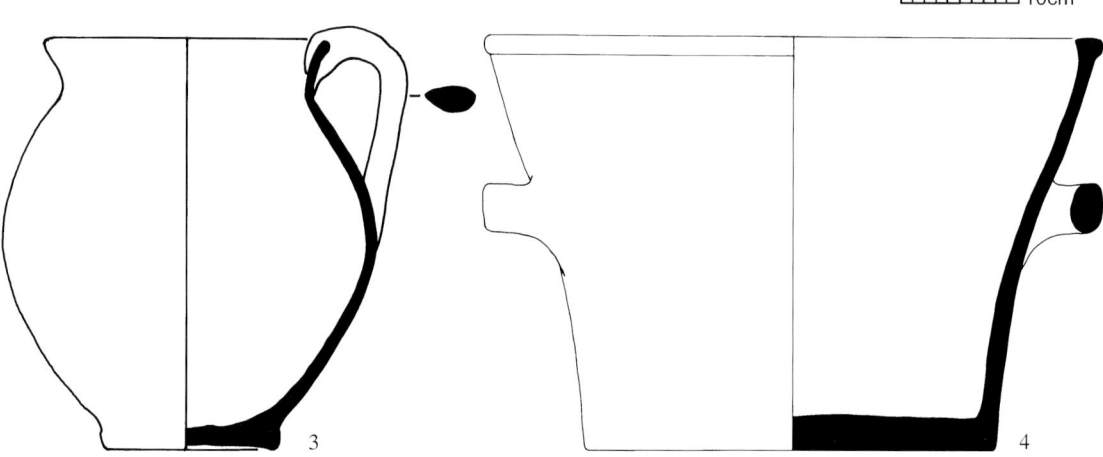

Fig. 3 Phase 1b. 1–2 tripod cooking pot, 3 cooking jug, 4 tub

Fig. 4 Phase 2a. 1 tray, 2 carinated conical cup, 3 cup, 4–6 kylix,
7 one-handled bowl, 8 one-handled conical bowl

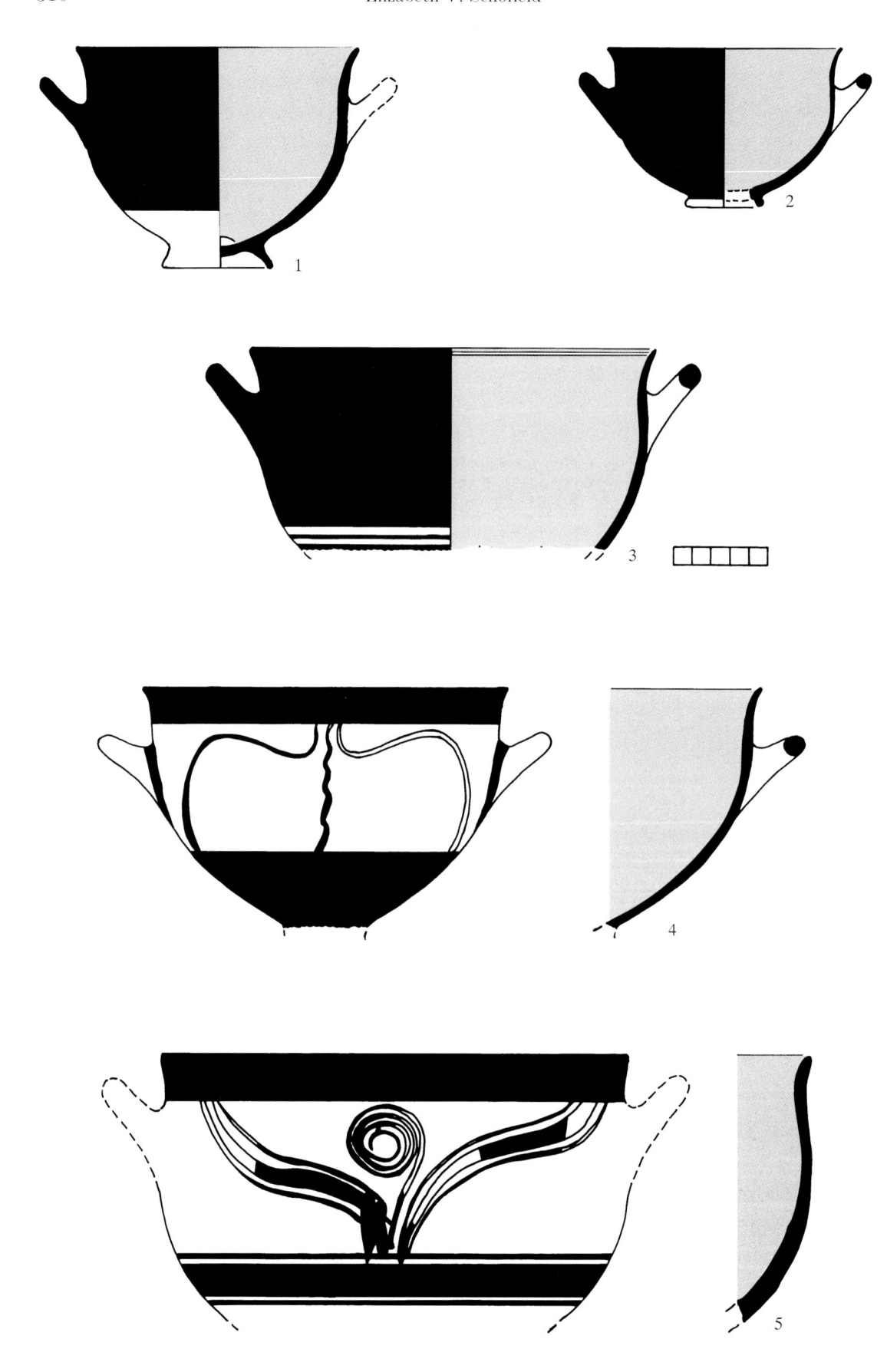

Fig. 5 Phase 2a. Deep bowl

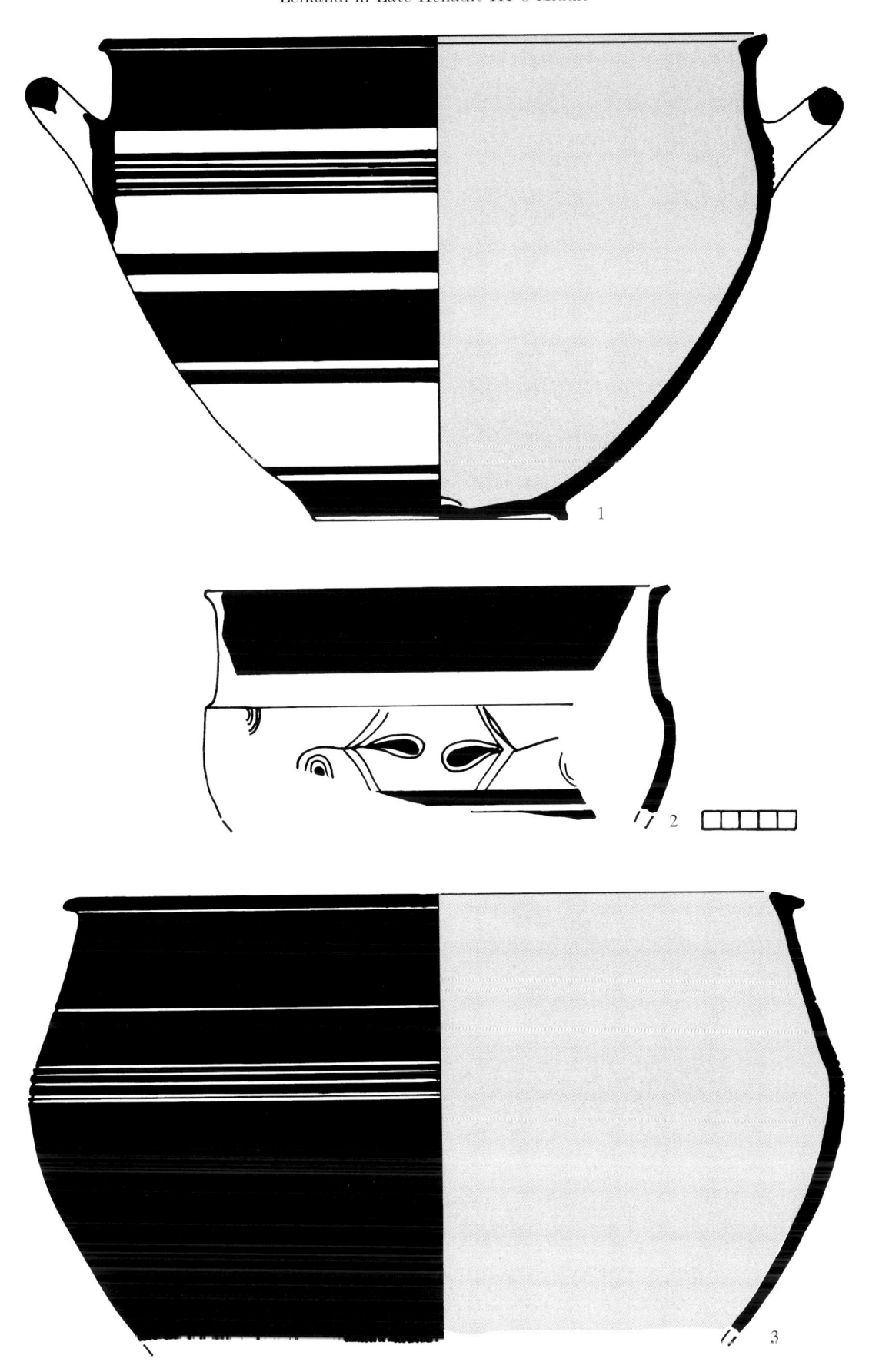

Fig. 6 Phase 2a. Carinated krater

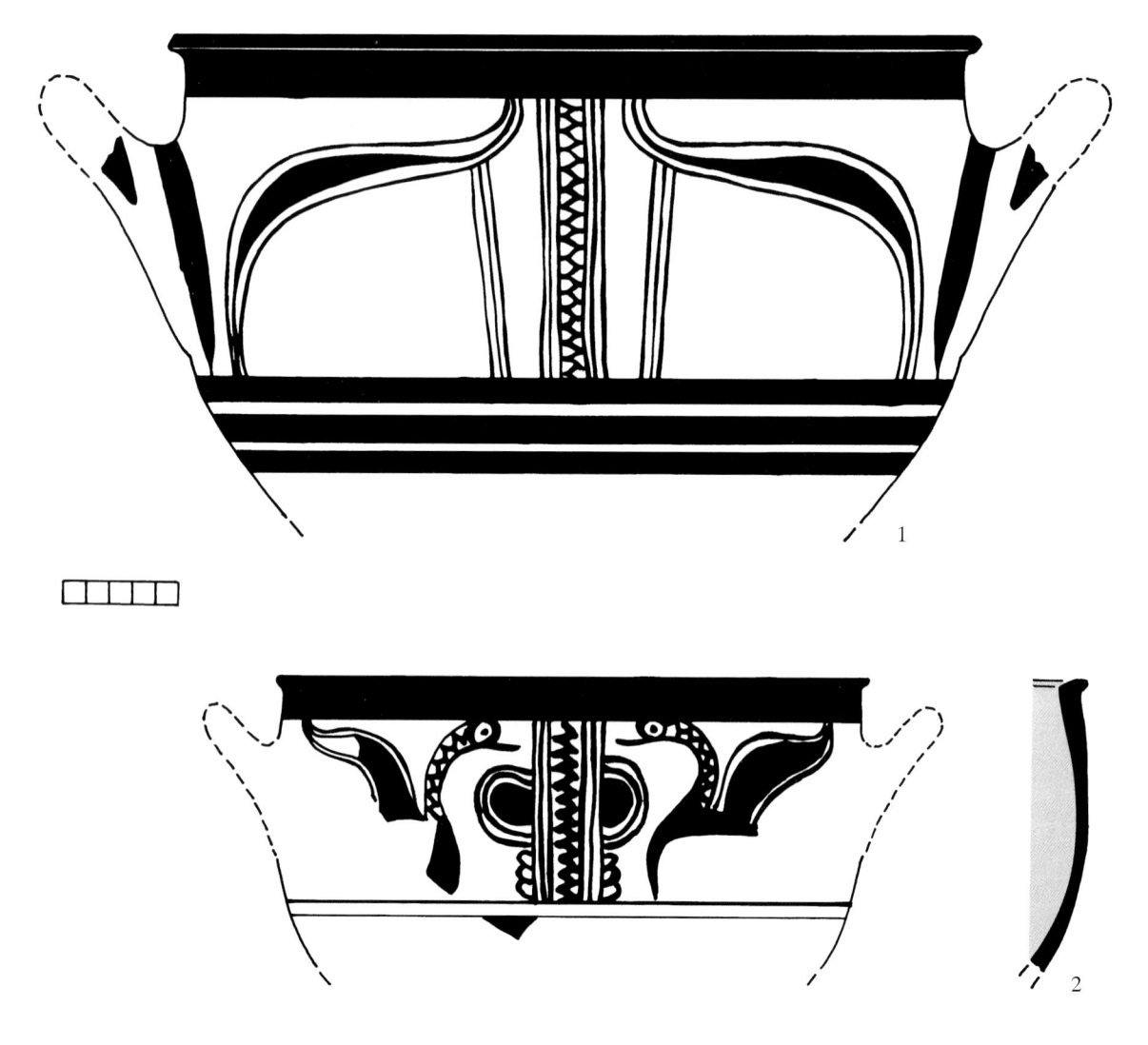

Fig. 7 Phase 2a. Krater

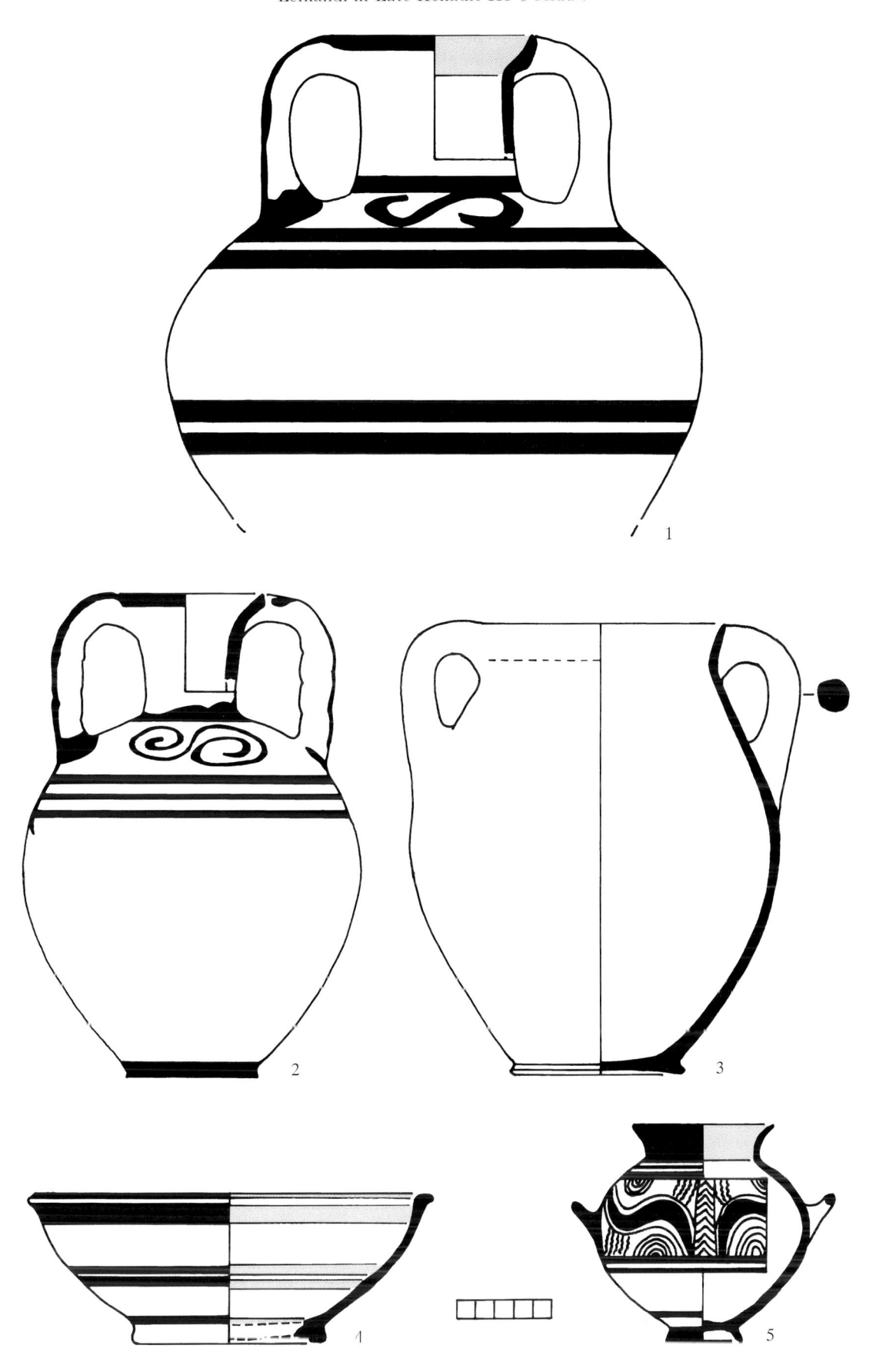

Fig. 8 Phase 2a. 1–2 amphora, 3 two-handled cooking jar, 4 basin, 5 amphoriskos

MARINA THOMATOS

KOINE AND SUBSIDIARY *KOINES*: COASTAL AND ISLAND SITES OF THE CENTRAL AND SOUTHERN AEGEAN DURING LH III C MIDDLE*

INTRODUCTION

The LH III C Middle phase has been recognised at numerous sites throughout Greece, yet most contemporary academic literature focuses on local trends and definitions rather than examining the phase as a whole whilst taking into account the numerous geographical areas. This paper originates from an examination of the LH III C Middle period in the Argolid, Corinthia, Attica, Euboea, the Cyclades and the Dodecanese (THOMATOS 2006). Even though this research has been based on published material, I believe the synthetic nature of the study, which allows for an examination of a wide geographical area, can contribute to our study and search for answers to the crucial questions that arise when examining the post-palatial phase in the history of the Late Bronze Age.

Three questions will be addressed:
- Can the term *koine* be used in relation to the post-palatial Aegean?
- How does one define the term *koine*?
- What factors contributed to the prosperity of certain areas in this period?

CURRENT NOTIONS

A main issue for this work has been whether the regions examined can be considered independent of each other or to what extent they maintained contact and, thus, interconnectedness. In *Last Mycenaeans and their Successors*, Desborough identifies a "miniature Mycenaean *koine*" during LH III C, which encompasses the Central and South Aegean, embracing the Dodecanese, Naxos, Miletus and Perati (DESBOROUGH 1964, 20, 228). The significance of the identification of such a *koine* lies within the implications it provides for contacts during this post-palatial period whose primary characteristic feature is regionalism. This connection is identified not only through the similarities of the pottery, which will be discussed below, but also in burial customs and religious practices.

---

* Acknowledgements: I would like to thank Prof. S. Deger-Jalkotzy for the opportunity to participate in this workshop; many thanks are due to Dr. I. S. Lemos, Dr. A. Papadimitriou and Dr. M. Iacovou for their support and suggestions and to C. Trejo for proofreading my manuscript.

In his examination of the material evidence from Rhodes, Mee agrees with the existence and geographical positioning of Desborough's *koine* and acknowledges comparisons in the pottery of Perati, Ialysos, Aplomata, Eleona, Langada and Kalymnos (MEE 1982, 90–91). Other scholars, however, disagree. Mountjoy recognises an East Aegean *koine* between Kos, Kalymnos, Chios and possibly Miletus. Characteristic shapes of this *koine* are the amphoroid kraters with large globular bodies and tiny bases, ovoid piriform jars and kalathoi. Characteristic motifs are horizontal wavy lines, double stemmed spirals, a lively Pictorial Style and other elaborate decoration. She believes that Desborough's Aegean *koine* is "based on general ceramic features rather than on specific ones" (*RMDP*, 51).[1]

Deger-Jalkotzy also disagrees with Desborough, noting that "despite the uniformity which can be observed in pottery of everyday use and unassuming objects, the artistic styles of LH III C Middle of the islands should not be called an 'Aegean *koine*'. Nor is this term adequate for the culture of Mycenaean LH III C in general" (DEGER-JALKOTZY 1998, 115). Based upon his examination of the pottery from Naxos, Vlachopoulos is also an advocate of this opinion. He argues that "the multifarious, singular and heterogeneous picture of the central Aegean during LH III C is at variance with the picture of the 'Small Mycenaean Koine', as elaborated by Desborough in the 1960s, a term that no longer applies to the diverse picture that emerges from each island in the Cyclades" (VLACHOPOULOS 2003, 231).

According to Sherratt, in LH III C Middle a uniformity of style in a "strict sense" (SHERRATT 1981, 507) does not exist. She attributes two regional groupings to the early phase. The first includes the Argive plain, Corinthia, Attica, Euboea and Achaea whilst the second incorporates the Dodecanese, Crete, Cyprus, and to a lesser degree the Cyclades and Messenia. During the middle phase, the links between these two groups become stronger, particularly between coastal sites of the Mainland and the islands. Sherratt writes, "the distinction between a clear Mainland grouping, on the one hand, and an Aegean grouping on the other has been largely obliterated, and the links between these two groups are now as strong as the links within them" (SHERRATT 1981, 508). She attributes two small regional groupings as well as a larger intermediate group to this middle phase. Group A includes the Argive plain and Corinthia and is characterised by deep bowls with multiple reserved bands and the Close Style. Group B includes coastal and island sites, and is characterised by trays and amphoroid kraters. Sherratt identifies an intensified connection between Attica and the Dodecanese whilst at the same time acknowledging "enhanced links" between coastal sites such as Asine, with Attica and Euboea rather than with other Argive sites such as Mycenae and Tiryns. She also recognises, that the Dodecanese, Attica and the Cyclades share the conical bowl, strainer-jugs and the high cylindrical pyxis, whilst the Dodecanese and Cyclades share the belly-handled amphora and the amphoroid krater. Furthermore, Sherratt points out that the combination of the decorated trays and the amphoroid kraters occurs only in the Dodecanese and Euboea, showing a relation between these two areas. Sub-groupings between Groups A and B unite the Dodecanese and the Cyclades, the Dodecanese and Crete, the Dodecanese, Cyclades and Attica, and, finally, the Argolid and Corinthia and, more rarely, Attica (SHERRATT 1981, 507–510, figs. 205–208). These types of groupings prove pertinent for understanding contact patterns during LH III C Middle and will be examined in more detail below.

---

[1] In her 1993 publication, Mountjoy is in agreement with Desborough's miniature Mycenaean *koine*; see MOUNTJOY 1993, 100–103.

TRACING A KOINE

It is possible that the past interpretation of the term *koine* is too confining to be safely applied in this post-palatial period. Even so, it is necessary to examine the existing common ceramic features since indications of similarities and influences are present between the various areas.

The four main shapes which Desborough used as indicators for a *koine* and which should be re-examined are the very large flasks, the kalathoi with elaborate and often pictorial decoration, the strainer-jugs and the octopus stirrup jars. Mountjoy rejects the evidence of the large flasks with concentric circles and wavy lines in the side panel since only two examples of such vessels have been found at Perati (*RMDP*, 50). She does however, point out their presence in the Cyclades and the Dodecanese where their numbers are few: on Naxos (*RMDP*, 957) only three published examples exist; on Rhodes there are only two from Ialysos (*RMDP*, 1056) and singletons from Vati (*RMDP*, 1074) and Lardos (*RMDP*, 1074); and just two examples are known from Kalymnos (*RMDP*, 1136). Thus, it is arduous to see why Mountjoy stresses the scarcity of the shape at Perati when the examples from other sites are equally few, and the sites that Mountjoy cites as having flasks are also the areas included in Desborough's *koine*.

The next form to be considered is the kalathos with its elaborate interior decoration. Mountjoy rightly points out that the kalathos is not limited to the geographical areas of Desborough's *koine*, but is found in the Argolid, Attica, Melos, Naxos, Rhodes, Kos and Kalymnos (*RMDP*, 50). Whilst all the areas appear to treat the shape similarly, there is a difference. Examples from Naxos, Rhodes, Kos and Kalymnos all have a single wavy line on the exterior whilst in Attica and Rhodes examples of the kalathos have figurines on the rim. Furthermore, whilst the presence of the fish motif on the examples from the Argolid, Melos and Athens have been compared to examples from islands, such as the elaborate examples from Kalymnos, they are very distinctive in their execution with the former containing minimal decoration.

The strainer-jug is present in Attica, Naxos, Rhodes and Kos. Although the examples may have different features – such as a narrower neck on the examples from Rhodes or a deep bowl/cup spout on those from Naxos, Rhodes and Kos as well as variations in decoration – the strainer-jug shape appears to be found only in these areas. Additionally, most of the published examples from the above-cited areas have a plastic snake feeding from the spout.

The fourth shape is the Octopus stirrup jar which Mountjoy notes as being present in the Argolid, Laconia and Arcadia, thereby indicating that this type of vessel was not limited to the geographical areas of Desborough's *koine*.[2] However, once again it should be pointed out that the majority of these vessels come from the Dodecanese, Naxos and Perati.

---

[2] *RMDP*, 50–51. Mountjoy cites the example from the Argolid as possibly being a Laconian import (*RMDP*, 290). The examples from Laconia are degenerate versions of the Octopus Style. Mountjoy notes that the one example which is most similar to the regular Octopus Style stirrup jars (*RMDP*, Laconia no. 219) also displays similarities to examples from Naxos. However, she does not believe it is an import due to its small false mouth. The two vessels, however, exhibit such similarities in decoration that I find it possible that it is a Naxian import. Mountjoy cites another example as being very similar to Minoan examples whilst another is clearly a Minoan import (*RMDP*, Laconia nos. 221–222). The examples from Arcadia are also very Minoanising and show that this area, as in the case of Laconia, had close links with Crete during this period (*RMDP*, 296, 298).

Mountjoy rightly noted the presence of certain shapes in other areas that were not included in Desborough's *koine*, however, I do not believe her points are that much more "specific" than Desborough's. Therefore, based on these four shapes, Desborough is not altogether wrong in identifying these features as being unique to these particular areas.

Returning to Sherratt's groupings, I believe much can be gained from such an examination for, like Sherratt, I have taken characteristic shapes as well as decorative motifs and have attempted to establish which geographical regions share common features. My focus has been on the published material from the geographical regions of the Argolid, Corinthia, Attica, Euboea, the Cyclades and the Dodecanese.[3] It should be noted from the outset that a few sites such as Mycenae, Tiryns, Korakou and Koukounaries have been difficult to incorporate due to the lack of published material. I will separately examine shapes and motifs below in order to conclude on whether groupings similar to Sherratt's can emerge.

Table 1 contains a summary of the distribution of shapes.[4] From this table a number of geographical groups sharing common features have been recognised: Group 1 (Perati and the Dodecanese), Group 2 (Perati, Naxos and the Dodecanese), Group 3 (Naxos and the Dodecanese), Group 4 (Eastern Mainland and Euboea).

Group 1 consists of the ring vases found at Perati, Rhodes and Kos and the multiple vases with amphoriskoi found in Perati and Rhodes. Group 2 contains the boxes found in Perati, Naxos and Rhodes, the strainer-jugs found at Perati, Naxos, Rhodes and Kos, and the legged alabastra found at Perati, Naxos, Rhodes and Kalymnos. Group 3 is comprised of the neck-handled amphorae found on Naxos, Rhodes and Kalymnos, the four-handled jars found on Naxos and Kos and the duck vases found on Naxos and Rhodes. Group 4 includes the carinated cups found in the Argolid and Euboea, the basins found in Attica and Euboea and the rim-handled amphorae found in the Argolid, Attica and Euboea.

Table 2 summarises the distribution of a number of motifs or decorative elements found on LH III C Middle pottery. Six general geographical groups have been recognised: Group 1 (Perati and the Dodecanese), Group 2 (Attica, Naxos and the Dodecanese), Group 3 (Naxos and the Dodecanese), Group 4 (Eastern Mainland and Naxos), Group 5 (Asine, Attica, Naxos and/or Dodecanese) and Group 6 (Argolid, Attica, Naxos and/or Dodecanese). One general difference between these groups and those based on shapes is that, based on the motifs used, Asine stands out from the other areas of the Argolid. It is for this reason that Asine is included in certain groups on its own rather than as part of the Argolid.

Group 1 consists of the elaborated circle found in Attica and Kos. Group 2 contains the almond motif found in Perati, Naxos and Kos, the half rosette found in Perati, Naxos, Rhodes and Kos, and the snake found in Perati, Naxos, Rhodes and Kos. Group 3 is comprised of the double stemmed spiral found on Naxos and Kos, horizontal chevrons found on Naxos, Rhodes, Kos and Kalymnos, the stacked zigzag found on Naxos and Rhodes and the simple triangle found on Naxos, Rhodes and Kos. Group 4 includes the

---

[3] These areas were chosen as the focus of my doctoral thesis not only for their interconnectivity during this period, but also because they provide the most comprehensive evidence of events and conditions during LH III C Middle.

[4] Frequency of occurrence is not indicated in these tables due primarily to the fact that many of the vessels published from settlement sites are fragmentary. Thus, I believe that if one takes frequency into account this would yield an inaccurate survey of the material in several instances. However, the inclusion of the presence of a shape or motif within a particular area is usually based upon more than one occurrence. This distribution is derived solely from published material. It may be the case that certain shapes and motifs do appear in more sites than what has been indicated here, but only published material has been utilised for the purpose of this research.

antithetic loop found in the Argolid, Corinthia and Naxos. Group 5 consists of the bivalve flower found at Asine, Attica, Naxos and Kos, the chevron fill found at Asine, Attica and Kos, fine bands flanked by wide bands found at Asine, Attica, Naxos, Rhode and Kos, the foliate band found at Asine, Attica, Rhodes, Kos and Kalymnos and a wide band flanked by single thin ones found at Asine, Attica and Naxos. Group 6 contains concentric arcs found at Tiryns, Mycenae, Asine, Attica and Rhodes, elaborate triangles found at Mycenae, Asine, Attica, Naxos, Rhodes, Kos and Kalymnos, framed zigzag found at Argos, Mycenae, Asine, Attica and Kos, the octopus found at Asine, Attica, Naxos, Rhodes, Kos and Kalymnos, the stacked triangle found at Mycenae, Asine, Attica, Naxos and Rhodes and the triangular patch found at Mycenae, Tiryns, Asine, Attica, Naxos, Rhodes, Kos and Kalymnos.

These groupings reveal that although each area has regional characteristics many also share features. The three main groups that emerge from this analysis in terms of the distribution of both shapes and motifs encompass Perati, Naxos and the Dodecanese whilst the next most popular grouping includes Asine and the above named regions. The other areas that appear to share common features are Xeropolis-Lefkandi and the areas of the Eastern Mainland such as the Argolid (namely, Tiryns and Mycenae) and Attica. These include simple motifs such as the tassel and scroll as well as the type of pictorial scenes depicted. In particular, the Euboean style of figurative pottery with the predominance of its warrior scenes has its closest parallels with that of the Argolid. Nonetheless, each area still possesses certain local characteristics such as the shallow angular bowl found at Mycenae and Tiryns but lacking at Lefkandi, or the conical bowl that appears at Lefkandi and other coastal and island sites but is lacking at Mycenae. Euboea also appears to have some ties with the Dodecanese as is evident by the presence of trays as well as the numerous animal pictorial scenes.[5]

Although many shared features do not appear to exist between Melos, Paros and other areas, some common features are exhibited amongst the areas. In the case of Phylakopi and Koukounaries, most of the pottery consists of a linear style similar to III C Early with the occasional III C Middle novelty such as deep bowls decorated with pictorial scenes or multiple interior reserved bands. Yet, for the most part, the pottery from these two areas does not seem to exhibit the sort of rich III C Middle style that is seen elsewhere. One possible reason for this could be the fact that both of these areas are settlement sites and, as such, lack the great repertoire of closed shapes that are often included in tombs. The same could apply to the material from Athens, which can, indeed, be perceived as being similar to that of Phylakopi and Koukounaries. Nevertheless, the material from Athens does share more features with areas such as Euboea and certain instances with Corinthia and the Argolid.

Returning for a moment to Sherratt's common features and feature matrix of the various shared characteristics (SHERRATT 1981, figs. 205–206), the following similarity coefficients appear: similarity coefficients between 0.5 and 0.74 are shared between

---

[5] This article was written in 2005 with reference to publications available at that time. In the summer of 2006, the Lefkandi IV volume (Evely, D. (ed.) Lefkandi IV: the Bronze Age, the late Helladic III C settlement at Xeropolis. London, 2007), which examines the Late Helladic III C deposits of Xeropolis, was published before this article went to press. I have tried to include in the two tables the shapes and decorative motifs evident from this publication. While most do not affect the similarity distribution in the tables it is interesting to note that the material from Xeropolis shares similarities with both the Mainland regions such as the Argolid but also greatly with Attica and the island sites which as has been noted above differ from the previously central regions of the Mycenaean world. While a more in depth examination of this material could not be carried out for this article, the material from Xeropolis I believe strengthens the idea of a general koine and subsidiary koines in the Aegean during LH III C middle.

Euboea and the Dodecanese, Euboea and Crete, the Dodecanese and the Cyclades, the Dodecanese and Attica, Attica and the Argolid and between Asine and Crete; similarity coefficients between 0.25 and 0.49 are shared between Attica and the Cyclades, the Cyclades and Achaea, the Cyclades and Messenia and between Euboea and Messenia. A comparison of Sherratt's feature matrix, particularly those with similarity coefficients between 0.5 and 0.74, and my groupings set out above reveals very similar results. The greatest similarities exist within the areas specified in Desborough's *koine*, including the Dodecanese, Naxos and Perati.

DEFINING THE TERM *KOINE*

The question of whether the term *koine* can be used in this post-palatial period will now be posited. When examining the term *koine* a few questions arise such as how does one define a *koine*, should there be a minimum number of common features, is a uniform ceramic style the predominant feature in defining a *koine* or can common customs and practices contribute to the definition and finally, does the presence of a *koine* imply a "political unity" or can the term be applied equally to a "community of interests"?[6]

Most scholars who study the Mycenaean civilisation have applied the term *koine* to the LH III A and LH III B periods (early uses of the term include DUSSAUD 1914, 209. – FIMMEN 1924, 89–95, 143–145. – Hall 1928, 217–218. – FURUMARK 1944, 263). Furumark used the term *koine* in reference to LH III C alongside the term *style*:

> "In order to understand the Myc. III C:I development, we must keep in mind the distinction between style in an abstract and style in a concrete sense ... The facts that there are parallel stylistic strains represented both on the Mainland and in the Rhodian region and that the stylistic development shows a tendency of convergence, justify us in speaking of the Myc. III C:I decoration as, in a general sense, one style and in regarding the regionally limited variations as variants of this style." (FURUMARK 1941, 568)

Furumark took this even further by relating this particular style to a *koine*:

> "... the Myc. III C:I ceramic decoration may – in spite of the great variations which it presents – be regarded as one style. There are not only common origins and sources, and many stylistic interconnexions [*sic*], but also a general parallelism and a progressive convergence in development. All this shows that in a certain sense the *koine* was still in existence, viz. in the form of a universality of artistic intentions." (FURUMARK 1941, 575)

We should not expect to find a common ceramic style to the extent that is seen in the earlier periods of LH III A and LH III B. However, can one truly state that, based on the available ceramic evidence from LH III C deposits, the pottery of this period is anything other than essentially one style with local variants? When defining the Mycenaean *koine* Fimmen noted that "die mykenische Koine gilt im eigentlichen Sinne erst zur Zeit, als man in Mykenä, Knossos und Milet Vasen genau derselben Technik, Form und Dekoration gebrauchte" (FIMMEN 1924). For the most part, all of these areas use the same techniques, forms and decorations during LH III C. Each area has certain regional characteristics and certain geographical groups which appear to have close contact with one another and, consequently, seemingly more similar pottery than with other areas.

---

[6] In reference to East Attica, the Dodecanese and Miletus, Desborough comments on whether the close connections seen in these areas are to be interpreted as a "political unity" or a "community of interests" (see DESBOROUGH 1964, 228).

Nonetheless, in the general sense, the pottery of Mycenaean Greece during LH III C is still comparable between the various geographical regions.

Another very crucial point to consider is the context of the finds. For example, in both the groups examined above and Sherratt's groupings, what becomes apparent is that although these regions have common shapes or motifs, they usually share a common context; being either cemeteries or settlements with the appearance of a particular shape or motif in the respective context. Could this be a factor in identifying regions that share common features? For example, the legged alabastron, strainer jug and box appear at Perati, Naxos and the Dodecanese and come from cemetery contexts.[7] This could also account for the fact that unlike other Argive sites, Asine is grouped with the coastal sites of Perati, Aplomata, Kamini and Ialysos and not its neighbouring palatial sites of Mycenae and Tiryns; the published material from the former are all cemeteries whilst the latter are mainly settlements. A similar phenomenon occurs when comparing the evidence of Athens with that of Koukounaries, which has similar forms and decorative treatment. Once again, both of these sites are settlements. In the preceding periods of LH III A and LH III B, making a comparison of the total ceramic corpus and concluding on the presence of a cultural *koine* was easier because the published ceramic material came from tombs and settlements. Perhaps if a greater corpus of pottery existed from both settlements on coastal and island sites and cemeteries on the Mainland, we would be able to more confidently conclude on the existence of a *koine* in LH III C.

A *koine* or common culture is also apparent when one takes into account other pieces of evidence such as burial customs and religion. For the most part, burials are chamber tombs with multiple interments. There exist occasional cremations as seen at Perati, Ialysos, Langada, Achaia, Argos, Chania and Thebes (CAVANAGH – MEE 1998, 93–94. – PITEROS 2001), as well as a traceable, although not drastic, increase in single burials such as at Perati, a few examples at the Deiras cemetery at Argos, a few intramural burials at Tiryns, Livanates and Xeropolis-Lefkandi, and some cist graves at Thebes (CAVANAGH – MEE 1998, 90–91). Religious customs also appear to be similar amongst the areas; figurines continue to be deposited in tombs of all areas and a continuation of religious beliefs and practices is present in the areas where sanctuaries are preserved such as Phylakopi (RENFREW 1981) or the small shrine at Tiryns (KILIAN 1978, 460–465. – MARAN 2001).

In LH III C there is a shift in the distribution of wealth which, no longer limited to the large palatial centres, spreads more widely yet thinly across the population base. Newly flourishing areas such as Perati in Attica, Kamini and Aplomata on Naxos, numerous cemeteries in the Dodecanese and the settlement of Xeropolis-Lefkandi on Euboea are the best candidates for this new distribution of wealth. For example, many burials at the cemetery of Perati are treated in the same manner. Namely, similar and rich finds of jewellery and ornamentation demonstrate that more than a few members of this community had both the means and necessity to display their wealth. The overall wealth in the few excavated tombs at Aplomata and Kamini on Naxos arguably illustrates, since an apparent differentiation of rank is not present within the tombs, that a broad-based group in society used the cemetery. The placement of precious gold objects in the child burial of Tomb E at Kamini may attest to this observation. Other sites such as Langada and Pilona have tombs that are adorned with rare imported items and appear to display a preference for faience, a material imported from Egypt. Finally, the cemetery

---

[7] Other examples of the legged alabastron also appear in a tomb context at Boeotia (*RMDP*, 687). Although in Laconia at Epidauros Limera (*RMDP*, 287) the strainer jug appears in a settlement/port context.

of Ialysos should be mentioned, for it clearly belongs to a flourishing community and contains imports not only from areas within Greece but also Cyprus and Anatolia.

It is interesting to note that all the areas mentioned above fall within Desborough's miniature *koine*. These communities, as Desborough rightly points out, may belong to a community of interests rather than a political unity. Such a community of interests shared usage of the sea and sea routes throughout the Aegean. The inhabitants of the settlements and those who buried their dead in the tombs and cemeteries of the period were consciously aware of their historic past and, in many ways, followed the traditions that had been established. However, one should not interpret this as a desire to return to what once was. The population now sought a new form of prosperity, and the sea became the means through which this prosperity was achieved.

CONCLUSIONS

Although the Argolid has evidence for continuity and possibly some degree of prosperity in this period, it now becomes clear that it is not at the centre of the post-palatial activities of the above-mentioned areas. This is a definitive factor in the formation of a culturally unified group. A *koine* that emerges out of a particular centre will sustain a general uniformity as long as the centre continues to function as a controlling body. However, once this controlling body begins to recede, its influence diminishes.

In reference to the Pictorial Style Furumark comments, "In a certain sense the whole category may be called a *koine* style … dependent on the same prototypes and developing according to the general rules of the Mycenaean stylistic evolution" (FURUMARK 1941, 462). This "definition" can be applied to all LH III C pottery that develops throughout Greece according to the same prototypes and the general rules of the Mycenaean stylistic evolution. I believe that the geographical groupings described above reveal intensified contacts within these areas. However, if one examines the overall distribution of shapes and motifs in Tables 1 and 2 along with the evidence of burial and religious practices, what emerges amongst all of the examined areas is a shared common culture – a cultural *koine*. Whilst there is a general *koine* encompassing most of the Mycenaean world during this period, smaller, *miniature koines* or subsidiary *koines* also emerge, differentiating this period from the previous periods of LH III A and LH III B. The regions which form subsidiary *koines* share many common features with other areas, but the intensified contacts with one other, primarily via the sea, distinguishes them from the larger geographical world of the Mycenaean culture. This should not be construed to mean that they are at variance with the "general rules" of the Mycenaean evolution. As Fimmen has noted, the formation of a *koine* is deeply rooted in commercial activities (FIMMEN 1924, 92–94). These subsidiary *koines* are formed between the coastal sites examined above precisely because these areas were involved in trade and commerce.

As Desborough notes, "The sea protected them, and they pursued their way in security and prosperity; closely united, they probably constituted one of the last strongholds of the Mycenaean way of life." (DESBOROUGH 1964, 229). Nonetheless, the numerous destructions that transpired throughout LH III C should not be overlooked for although a recovery does occur, unrest is still a recurring feature; and this unrest goes on to become a defining feature in the succeeding phase. The evolving changes that begin to take place during LH III C, mark the transition from the palace administrative system of the Mycenaean era to that of the city-states of the Early Greek period.

Bibliography

CAVANAGH, W. – C. MEE
1998   *A Private Place: Death in Prehistoric Greece* (SIMA 75). Jonsered.

DEGER-JALKOTZY, S.
1998   "The Aegean Islands and the Breakdown of the Mycenaean Palaces around 1200 B.C.", 105–119 in: KARAGEORGHIS – STAMPOLIDIS 1998.

DESBOROUGH, V. R. d'A.
1964   *The Last Mycenaeans and Their Successors. An Archaeological Survey c. 1200–c. 1000. B.C.* Oxford.

DUSSAUD, R.
1914   *Les civilisations préhelléniques dans le bassin de la mer Égée*. Paris.

FIMMEN, D.
1924   *Die kretisch-mykenische Kultur*. Leipzig – Berlin.

FURUMARK, A.
1941   *The Mycenaean Pottery: Analysis and Classification*. Stockholm.
1944   "The Mycenaean III C Pottery and its Relation to Cypriote Fabrics", *OpArch* 3, 194–265.

HALL, H. R.
1928   *The Civilization of Greece in the Bronze Age*. London.

KARAGEORGHIS, V. – N. STAMPOLIDIS (eds.)
1998   *Proceedings of the International Symposium 'Eastern Mediterranean: Cyprus – Dodecanese – Crete 16th–6th Cent. B.C.' Organized by the University of Crete, Rethymnon, and the Anastasios G. Leventis Foundation, Nicosia, Rethymnon 13–16 May 1997*. Athens.

KILIAN, K.
1978   "Ausgrabungen in Tiryns 1976. Bericht zu den Grabungen", *AA*, 449–470.

LAFFINEUR, R. – R. HÄGG (eds.)
2001   *Potnia. Deities and Religion in the Aegean Bronze Age. Proceedings of the 8th International Aegean Conference/8e Rencontre égéenne internationale, Göteborg, Göteborg University, 12–15 April 2000* (Aegaeum 22). Liège – Austin.

MARAN, J.
2001   "Political and Religious Aspects of Architectural Change on the Upper Citadel of Tiryns. The Case of Building T", 113–122 in: LAFFINEUR – HÄGG 2001.

MEE, C.
1982   *Rhodes in the Bronze Age. An Archaeological Survey*. Warminster.

MOUNTJOY, P. A.
1993   *Mycenaean Pottery. An Introduction* (Oxford University Committee for Archaeology. Monograph 36). Oxford.

PITEROS, C.
2001   "Ταφές και τεφροδόχα αγγεία τύμβου της ΥΕ ΙΙΙ Γ στο Άργος", 99–120 in: STAMPOLIDIS 2001.

RENFREW, C.
1985   *The Archaeology of Cult. The Sanctuary at Phylakopi* (BSA Suppl. 18). London.

SHERRATT, E. S.
1981   *The Pottery of Late Helladic III C and its Significance* (unpublished Ph.D. thesis). Oxford.

STAMPOLIDIS, N. C. (ed.)
2001   Πρακτικά του Συμποσίου 'Καύσεις στην Εποχή του Χαλκού και την πρώιμη Εποχή του Σιδήρου', Ρόδος, 29 Απριλίου – 2 Μαΐου 1999. Athens.

THOMATOS, M.
2006   *The Final Revival of the Aegean Bronze Age. A Case Study of the Argolid, Corinthia, Attica, Euboea, the Cyclades and the Dodecanese during LH III C Middle* (BAR-IS 1498). Oxford.

VLACHOPOULOS, A.
2003   "The Late Helladic III C 'Grotta Phase' of Naxos. Its Synchronisms in the Aegean and its Non-Synchronisms in the Cyclades", 217–234 in: *LH III C Chronology and Synchronisms*.

Dodecanese	Attica, Naxos, Dodecanese	E. Mainland and Euboea	Argolid/Corinthia, Attica, Naxos and/or Dodecanese
Attica and Dodecanese	Naxos and Dodecanese	E. Mainland and Naxos	Euboea, Cyclades and Dodecanese

Shape	Argolid	Corinthia	Attica	Euboea	Melos	Paros	Naxos	Rhodes	Kos	Kalymnos
Alabastron		X		X	X	X	X	X	X	X	X
Alabastron type Multiple Vase			X			X				
Amphoriskos type Multiple Vase			X					X		
Amphoriskos	X		X	X			X	X	X	
Amphoroid Krater								X	X	X
Askos							X			
Basin	X		X	X						
Belly-Handled Amphora	X			X		X	X		X	
Bird Vase							X	X		
Box			X				X	X		
Carinated Cup	X			X						
Carinated Spouted Cup							X			
Collar-Necked Jar	X		X	(X)		X	X	X		X
Cup	X		X	X		X	X	X		
Deep Bowl	X	X	X	X	X	X	X	X	X	X
Deep Bowl with vertical handles			X	X			X			
Duck Vase							X	X		
Feeding Bottle	X		X	(X)			X	X	X	
Flask			X		X		X	X		X
Four-Handled Jar							X		X	
Hydria	X		X	(X)			X			
Jug	X		X	X		X	X	X	X	
Jug with Cutaway Neck							X			
Kalathos	X		X	(X)	X		X	X	X	X
Krater	X	X	X	X	X	X		X		
Kylix	X	X	X	X	X	X		X	X	
Legged Alabastron			X				X	X		X
Lekythos	X		X				X	X	X	
Mug			X	X	X	X	X	X	X	X
Narrow-Necked Jug			X	(X)		X		X	X	
Neck-Handled Amphora				(X)			X	X		X
One-Handled Conical Bowl	X		X	X	X		X	X	X	
Piriform Jar	X					X		X	X	
Rim-Handled Amphora	X		X	X						
Ring Vase			X	(X)				X	X	
Shallow Angular Bowl	X		X			X	X	X		
Spouted Cup							X	X	X	
Spouted Krater				X						
Stemmed Bowl								X		
Stirrup Jar	X	X	X	X	?	X	X	X	X	X
Strainer Jug			X				X	X	X	
Tray				X	X			X	X	
Trefoil-Mouthed Jug	X	X	X	(X)			X	X	X	

Table 1

Dodecanese	Attica, Naxos, Dodecanese	E. Mainland and Naxos
Attica and Dodecanese	Naxos and Dodecanese	Asine, Attica, Naxos and/or Dodecanese
Argolid, Attica, Naxos and/or Dodecanese		

Decoration	Argolid	Corinthia	Attica	Euboea	Melos	Paros	Naxos	Rhodes	Kos	Kalymnos
almond			X				X		X	
antithetic flower								X		
antithetic foliate band								X		
antithetic loop	X	X		(X)			X			
antithetic semicircles										X
antithetic spiral	X		X	X		X		X	X	
antithetic spiral with hourglass fill			X							
apse								X		
apse with chevron			X							
arc								X		
birds	X		X	(X)				X	X	X
bivalve	X		X	X				X	X	
bivalve chain						X				
bivalve flower	X (As)		X				X		X	
bivalve foliate band									X	
chequer			X	X	X			X	X	X
chevron	X		X	(X)		X		X	X	X
chevron fill	X (As)		X						X	
Close Style	X									
concentric arcs	X		X	(X)				X		
concentric circles	X		X	(X)	X		X			X
concentric pendant semicircles	X									
crab								X		X
cross bar	X									
cross filler										X
diagonal pattern								X		
dolphin							X			
dots				(X)					X	
dotted semicircles	X (As)						X		X	
double-stemmed running spiral									X	
double-stemmed spiral							X		X	
droplet foliate band								X		
elaborate circle			X						X	
elaborate semicircles								X		
elaborate spiral		X								
elaborate triangles	X		X				X	X	X	X
fine bands flanked by wide bands	X (As)		X	(X)			X	X	X	
fish	X		X	(X)			X	X	X	
flower				(X)		X		X		
foliate band	X (As)		X					X	X	X

Table 2

Decoration	Argolid	Corinthia	Attica	Euboea	Melos	Paros	Naxos	Rhodes	Kos	Kalymnos
framed zigzag	X		X						X	
fringed chevron									X	
fringed isolated spiral									X	
fringed semicircle										X
goat	X								X	X
half moon	X		X	(X)		X		X		
half moon stemmed spiral								X		
half rossette			X				X	X	X	
hatched lozenge					X			X		
hatched triangles	X		X			X	X	X	X	
hedgehog										X
horizontal bars			X							
horizontal chevrons							X	X	X	X
horns				X			X	X		X
hybrid flower						X				
isolated semicircle								X		
isolated spiral						X				
joining semicircles	X (Ti)		X	(X)			X	X		
lozenge	X		X	(X)		X		X	X	
multiple stem spiral				(X)				X		
N pattern								X		
necklace	X		X	(X)	X		X	X	X	
netting				(X)		X		X	X	
octopus	X		X	(X)			X	X	X	X
panel	X	X	X	X	X	X	X	X	X	X
papyrus	X (As)							X		
pendant			X				X			
pictorial	X	X	X	X	X		X		X	X
quatrefoil									X	
quirk	X					X		X		X
Rhodian horns								X		
rock pattern							X			
rosette	X	X	X	(X)				X		X
runnig spiral	X	X	X	X	X	X	X	X	X	
running spiral with bar fill									X	
running spiral with open	X (As)		X							
scale pattern								X		
scorpion								X		X
scroll	X		X	X			X			
semicircles	X		X	X	X	X	X	X	X	X
semicircles with solid fill							X			
single thin band flanked by wide bands				X						
snake			X				X	X	X	
spiral	X	X	X				X	X		

Table 2 continued

Decoration	Argolid	Corinthia	Attica	Euboea	Melos	Paros	Naxos	Rhodes	Kos	Kalymnos
stacked semicircles	X									
stacked triangle	X		X				X	X		
stacked zigzag							X	X		
starfish							X			
stemless spiral							X			
stemmed spiral	X	X	X	(X)	X	X	X	X	X	X
streamer			X	X			X	X	X	
tassel	X		X	X				X	X	
tongue							X			
tree								X		
triangle							X	X	X	
tricurved arch								X		
triglyph				X		X	X	X		
triglyph concentric arcs								X		
triangular patch	X		X				X	X	X	X
U pattern										X
vertical foliate band								X		
wavy line	X		X	(X)		X	X	X	X	X
whorl shell						X				
wide band flanked by single thin bands	X (As)		X				X			
zigzag	X		X	(X)	X		X	X	X	

Table 2 continued

PETER M. WARREN

CHARACTERISTICS OF LATE MINOAN III C FROM THE STRATIGRAPHICAL MUSEUM SITE AT KNOSSOS*

It is a great pleasure to offer a contribution from Knossos to a conference on LH III C Middle, indeed an extra pleasure for a simple Minoan to observe that when a Mainland conference is organised in Vienna or Salzburg it somehow includes in its final programme a stream of Minoan papers.

The explosion of information and knowledge of LM III C pottery over the last twenty five years has been remarkable, to cite only, and alphabetically, Kastelli Pediada, Kastrokephala, Katalimata, Kavousi Kastro and Vronda, Khalasmenos, Khamalevri, Khania, Knossos, Phaistos, Sybrita, Vasilike Kephala and Vrokastro to add to the preceding publications of pottery from Karphi and the site and pottery of Palaikastro Kastri. A good overview has recently been given by Kanta (KANTA 2003). Even so we in Crete cannot yet offer such a sophisticated phasing of the sequence as has been established for LH III C. Even within the specialised world of Mycenaean ceramic studies, where outsiders greatly fear to tread, you can hardly get more specialised than an entire conference devoted to LH III C Middle.

Several of the Minoan sites have now produced III C phasing specific to the site in question, notably Kastelli Pediada (RETHEMIOTAKIS 1997), Kavousi Kastro (MOOK – COULSON 1997. – MOOK 2004) and Sybrita (PROKOPIOU 1997. – D'AGATA 2003. – D'AGATA this volume), to which the detailed publication of the LM III B2 and LM III C material from Khania Kastelli must be added (*GSE II. – GSE III*), although it seems not to extend beyond or much beyond III C Early. But at this point some caution is necessary, and it certainly applies to the Knossian material presented here. While stratigraphy has been carefully observed and recorded at the various sites the contents of the III C strata are normally in sherd form, rarely if ever are they floor deposits of complete or substantially preserved vases which are the usual bases from settlements for defining periods or subperiods. Sherd levels are rarely pure. When a piece cited is simply a fragment there must be some question whether the original whole pot had its whole life in that context, or whether it began as a whole pot in an earlier context. A second reason for caution, at least in trying to distinguish LM III C Middle from LM III C Early, is the relative homogeneity or lack of morphological and motif development, with the consequent difficulty of defining criteria exclusive to "Early" or "Middle".

---

* The author is grateful to the British School at Athens for permission to illustrate material from the Stratigraphical Museum Excavations at Knossos, directed by him for the School. The illustrations are the work of the author and his technical illustrators. They are used with the permission of the British School at Athens.

We turn now to Knossos and the area immediately behind or west of the Stratigraphical Museum, that is in the western part of the city on the ground which gradually rises up towards the acropolis (Fig. 1A). The excavations (Fig. 1B), directed by the writer for the British School at Athens, took place in 1978–1982 and in 1997, with study at all dates through to 2002 (WARREN 1980/81. – WARREN 1982/83. – WARREN 1984/85. – WARREN 1987/88. – WARREN in: BLACKMAN 1997/98, 114–115). Occupation here dated from MM I A to the 5th century A.D. The settlement in LM III C was, on the evidence uncovered, effectively a new foundation, following and usually lying directly upon rich LM III A and very scanty LM III B levels (WARREN 1982/83, 69–85. – WARREN 1997, 182–183. – WARREN 2005).

What is examined in the present paper is by no means all of our III C, but probably the best stratified part of it, principally in trenches O, P, S, W and the baulks between them (Fig. 1B–C). Although the material is abundant it is subject to the limitations just noted, namely, and in contrast to other periods on the site, it is for the most part fragmentary, sometimes with only just enough of a vase to merit its entry into the catalogue as a pot rather than its non-entry as a sherd (though all significant sherds are recorded in photographs). In the west part of the trench O building there were two floors, the upper of irregular stone paving some 30 cm above the lower one of earth; there were changes of level and a lower floor level at about the same depths (in relation to the site datum) in the trench S building. None of these are completely sealed levels, as evidenced by the fact that a few vases have fragments in both of the two levels. If a vase has a fragment in the lower level it may be reasonable to date it to that stage, so that a fragment of the same vase at a higher level would simply represent disturbance, as of course often happens. But if a fragmentary vase is represented only in the upper level we cannot be certain that it dates to that stage and did not begin life, as a whole vase, at the lower, earlier stage.

There are three stratigraphical stages.

- Stage I (earliest): LM III C material earlier than the buildings in trenches O and S, either because it was stratified below their walls or because it was used as part of the construction material in the walls.
- Stage II: material from the first level of occupation of the buildings and from equivalent levels adjacent to them.
- Stage III: material from the upper levels of these buildings, above the stone paving in and adjacent to the trench O building and at the same depth in the trench S building.

In trench T, east of trench S, a pit in a robbed out LM III A wall contained a cluster of III C vases. Its depth and level suggests it is contemporary with the Stage I material; as in trenches O and S the level underlying these vases (T level 11 zembil 1026) included fragments of LM III C deep bowls, so the vases do not mark the very earliest III C occupation. (The fragmentary decorated krater WARREN 1982/83, 70, fig. 43 came only from earth above the pit [T level 4 zembil 1012]; two vases in the pit also had fragments in this level above it. But since the krater did not it seems better taken as [slightly?] later than the pit).

A summary documentation of the illustrated pottery for each stage is as follows. Drawings are at scale 1:3 unless otherwise stated. Photograph scale is in centimetres. Decoration is not described (see drawings).

STAGE I (Fig. 2)

Cup **P 1919**, two non-joining fragments. Trench S Building north room west wall (μ) construction.

Kylix **P 1922**, three fragments, Trench S Building north room west wall (μ) construction and under wall.
Deep bowl **P 2152**, fragments, decorated with wild goats, Trench O Pit 4 under north wall (ζ) of O Building (Fig. 1C).

STAGE II

Fig. 2. Trench O Building, levels below stone paving and equivalent levels outside it including Pit 3 (Fig. 1C).
Deep bowls **P 241**, **P 251**, **P 252**, **P 253**, **P 284** (carinated), **P 285**.
Kylix **P 254**.
Fig. 3. Trench O Building and equivalent levels outside it.
Deep bowls **P 250**, **P 2149** (also in Stage III), **P 2143**, **P 2466**.
Krater, small **P 2144** (fragments scattered through the levels including in Stage III).
Krater (scale 1:6) **P 2470 + P 2510**, equivalent level in Baulk OS south of O Building.
Fig. 4. Trench S Building (Fig. 1C), levels equivalent to those below stone paving in Trench O Building.
Deep bowl, large **P 1920** (fragments also in Stage III).
Deep bowls **P 1921**, **P 1925** (fragments also in Stage III).
Bowl or Cup, carinated (missing piece could have had handle) **P 896**. This could well be an import. The fabric is light red and the vase has a pale, almost white slip, with decoration in black-red paint. If the missing piece had a handle the vase is close to FS 240. Of examples of FS 240 illustrated by Mountjoy the LH III C Middle form is the nearest (*MDP*, 171, fig. 220, especially no. 5 with slightly convex lower body. – *RMDP*, 170 no. 359). The vase was in situ beside the east wall of the main room of the Trench S Building (Fig. 1C) in Baulk WX.
Tray or Lid **P 1923**, fragment.
Tripod cooking pot **P 309**, in situ S Building south west room.
Fig. 5. Trench S Building, levels equivalent to those below stone paving in Trench O Building.
Kraters, fragmentary **P 1780** (scale 1:6), **P 1917**, **P 307 + P 662** (scale 1:6) (pieces widely scattered including in Stage III).

STAGE III

Fig. 6. Trench O Building, the curved east end in Trench P (Fig. 1C top right area), pottery at depth of the uppermost preserved wall stone.
Jug **P 3** (see below).
Trench O Building, level above stone paving and equivalent levels outside the building.
Kraters, fragmentary (scale 1:6) **P 2145**, **P 2146**, **P 2147**, **P 2469 + P 2511**.
Tub/lekane/basin (scale 1:6) **P 2468**.
Trench S Building, upper levels equivalent to those of Trench O Building.
Krater (fragments) (scale 1:6) **P 1924**.
Pyxis, body-base fragment, decorated with double axe between horns of consecration **P 308**.

STAGE I (probably, just possibly Stage II).

Figs. 7–8. Trench T Pit in robbed LM III A wall (see text).
Deep bowls **P 182**, **P 183**.
Bowl, no handle preserved on the five fragments and perhaps unlikely on such an everted rim **P 186**.

Cup **P 172**.
Tripod cooking pot with handle **P 171**.
Stirrup jar **P 173**.
Jugs **P 169**, **P 197**.

CONCLUSIONS

(1) The morphology of the above material is clear. The decorated wares comprise large numbers of deep bowls, a significant presence of kraters, shallow kylikes present but few in number, cups likewise; in coarse wares there are tripod cooking pots of more or less globular form, with circular section legs and often a thumb or finger hollow at the top and sometimes a vertical slash down the leg, trays or perhaps (on the evidence of Karphi) lids with concentric raised bands bearing thumb or finger hollows, and basins or lekanes with an everted rim and carination just below, the latter in pithos fabric. There are a few other forms.

(2) There does not appear to be clear evidence of development between Stages I and II or between II and III.

(3) With the exception of the likely import **P 896** the pottery appears to be locally made. The range of motifs on deep bowls and kraters is wide and seems Minoan. The total ceramic package is, however, new and, as a package, cannot, in my view, be derived from what precedes (from what precedes I exclude late LM III B, a question much discussed elsewhere). While I agree with Penelope Mountjoy (MOUNTJOY 1999) that the LM III C deep bowls are not exact copies of FS 284, it remains my view that their origin was not in preceding forms of Minoan deep bowl but was the Mainland deep bowl of that shape, that is the LH III B2–III C Early form rather than the essentially later more bell-like form (FS 285). A Mainland origin is also likely, too, for the globular tripod cooking pots with circular section legs, though the Minoan version prefers upright bow-handles on the shoulder to the usual vertical thick strap handles from rim to shoulder of the Mainland.

(4) The combination of kraters and scores of deep bowls suggest new eating and drinking patterns and new social arrangements. Elisabetta Borgna (BORGNA 1997. – BORGNA 2004) and Anna Lucia D'Agata (D'AGATA 2001) have both explored this difficult and profound question and, also in my view (WARREN 2005), these new arrangements are likely to have been of Mainland origin or, at the very least, to have had a strong Mainland component.

(5) How then should the Knossos material presented here be dated? Stage I in trenches O and S has few catalogued pieces; kylix **P 1922**, with its curving profile and deeper bowl than usual in III C, might represent the end of III B (the last Minoan palm ever painted?), while the deep bowl **P 2152** and other fragments must represent our stratigraphically earliest III C. The cluster of vases in trench T, taken as Stage I (see above), adds more deep bowls, a bowl, a cup, jugs, a tripod cooking pot and a stirrup jar.

Stage II has several characteristics taken as hallmarks of III C Early at Khania and Kavousi Kastro, shallow kylikes, button hook spirals, internal reserved band on deep bowls (of the fifteen catalogued deep bowls from Stage II no fewer than six have this feature) and a form of antithetic or tricurved streamer (**P 252**). It is reasonable to take our Stage II as LM III C Early (revising my preliminary view in WARREN 1982/83), with Stage I as earliest III C. Stage II goes well with Phases 1 and 2 at Kastelli Pediada (RETHEMIOTAKIS 1997) and with Palaikastro Kastri (POPHAM 1965a). At the same time we note that **P 896**, the bowl or cup from the S Building main room and a probable import, looks very close to FS 240, dated to LH III C Middle/Rutter phase 4b (see above).

Stage III, though somewhat mixed with Stage II vase fragments, is stratigraphically later; but it does not appear to show distinctive development from Stage II material. A jug level with the topmost preserved wall stone at the curved end of the O building in trench P (**P 3**) (Fig. 6) is paralleled in III C Middle? at Sybrita (D'AGATA 2003, 28–29, fig. 2:3, arguing for a Mainland origin). Equally, nothing about the Stage III material seems III C Late; while our III C as a whole does have links to Karphi (deep bowl motifs and overall krater designs, coarse ware shapes) it does not have the late kylikes or prominent raised base of the Lasithi site's deep bowls (SEIRADAKI 1960). The conclusion from these observations would therefore seem to be that Stage III is best dated within later III C Early.

Is there any case for calling it III C Middle? It is worth first repeating that Minoan specialists have found it difficult or impossible to distinguish such a period within III C, that is a period not only stratigraphically later than III C Early levels but with sufficient new ceramic features to merit a separate period designation. As noted above Khania, Kastelli Pediada, Kavousi Kastro and Thronos/Sybrita have come nearest in providing evidence, though with a majority of excavators preferring the term "the first half of III C". Even for Kavousi with its continuous stratified sequence (MOOK – COULSON 1997. – MOOK 2004), in which "the beginning of Phase II should be placed specifically in the latter part of the first half of the LM III C period, probably continuing into mid-III C" (MOOK – COULSON 1997, 357), Margaret Mook stated in discussion of the paper "The Phase I and II material could easily be lumped together" (*Late Minoan III Pottery*, 366), i.e. could be called III C Early. At Khania Kastelli the Hallagers have pointed out that the large pit cut into LM III C Room I is one of three post-initial III C deposits (*GSE II*, 39–41, 135). Kanta draws attention to a "Middle III C" krater with Close Style decoration from the pit (KANTA 2003, 515, fig. 1 O, reproducing *GSE II*, 41, 146, pl. 39:71-P0735). The Cretan Close Style (which has nothing to do with the LH III C miniaturist Close Style) is a subject well worth fuller analysis. We may note here that one form of it is exemplified by this Khania krater. The style is a complex decorative scheme based on large arcs, curves or spirals painted with a thick inner band outlined by a thin band on one or both sides, the surrounding spaces filled predominantly with concentric arc patterns to produce a densely or closely decorated field as a whole, very Minoan in its avoidance of symmetry. Though the style blends into other forms of krater decoration we may cite a few other distinct examples of it across the island: Haghia Triadha and/or Phaistos (BORDA 1946, 107, 109, pl. 37 top row centre, 2nd row centre, 4th row centre. – BORGNA 2004, fig. 8 [field left in part undecorated] [Phaistos]. – BORGNA this volume, Phase IV); Knossos (Fig. 6 [**P 1924**, **P 2469**]); Karphi (SEIRADAKI 1960, fig. 26a–b); Kastelli Pediada (RETHEMIOTAKIS 1997, 320, fig. 33a–b [based on an elaborate tricurved streamer]); Palaikastro Kastri (POPHAM 1965a, 299 KP31, fig. 13) It is, therefore, interesting to note the site dating evidence of these pieces, where available. At Khania and Knossos they are later than the earliest III C phase, at Kastelli they are from the later phase, Phase 2 (level 2) and from a phase intermediate between Phases 1 and 2 (level 5). At Phaistos at least one piece is from Borgna's Phase IV (III C Late). Karphi is later than III C Early. Palaikastro Kastri is a defining site for the first part of the III C period. With the possible exception of Palaikastro, therefore, this form of LM III C Close Style (and probably others near to it) is absent from the first part of the period and may be thought a defining characteristic of LM III C Middle. Giorgos Rethemiotakis so names it (RETHEMIOTAKIS 1997, 318, 320, 325). Clearly, however, more defining characteristics are needed.

(6) Finally we happily take up a further observation by Rethemiotakis. In presenting the Kastelli Pediada III C material he referred, as have others, to "the striking homogeneity of material coming from distant sites all over the island" (RETHEMIOTAKIS 1997,

320). I venture to go further. Surveying the published material from the fifteen sites listed at the beginning of this paper, sites of every type, coastal, lowland, mountain refuge, I find the extent of ceramic repetition astonishing, large numbers of deep bowls, with many parallels among them in the decorative repertoire, significant presence of finely decorated kraters, some kylikes, the same coarse wares. There is a strong case for claiming that such a degree of homogeneity across the island is unequalled in any period of Minoan ceramic history. As such it requires explanation. It is surely not derived, in this post-palatial age, from one single Cretan centre. I therefore think that, while the material is locally made and most of it is Minoan in decoration, the only viable explanation of the new package in its totality is external, Greek Mainland stimulus, as Popham (building on Desborough) argued (POPHAM 1965b, especially 334–335). As is the case on Cyprus and at several Levantine sites, such as Ashkelon and Tell Miqne-Ekron, we appear to have from the start of LM III C (seemingly from the end of III B at Khania) a blending of local and Mycenaean elements, in all likelihood including refugee Mycenaean presence after the collapse of the Mainland palatial system. So LM III C Early and possibly Middle, while very different in details from LH III C Early–Middle, stand quite closely parallel to those Mainland periods, giving, as many have shown (BORGNA 2004. – D'AGATA 2003. – KANTA 2003. – MOUNTJOY 1999. – RUTTER 2003), as well as receiving.

Bibliography

BIETAK, M. (ed.)
2003 *The Synchronisation of Civilisations in the Eastern Mediterranean in the Second Millennium B.C. II. Proceedings of the SCIEM 2000 – EuroConference, Haindorf, 2nd of May – 7th of May 2001* (Österreichische Akademie der Wissenschaften. Denkschriften der Gesamtakademie 29 = Contributions to the Chronology of the Eastern Mediterranean 4). Vienna.

BLACKMAN, D. J.
1997/98 "Archaeology in Greece 1997–98", *AR* 44, 1–128.

BORDA, M.
1946 *Arte cretese-micenea nel Museo Pigorini di Roma*. Roma.

BORGNA, E.
1997 "Some Observations on Deep Bowls and Kraters from the 'Acropoli Mediana' at Phaistos", 273–298 in: *Late Minoan III Pottery*.
2004 "Aegean Feasting: A Minoan Perspective", *Hesperia* 73, 247–279.

D'AGATA, A. L.
2001 "Religion, Society and Ethnicity on Crete at the End of the Late Bronze Age. The Contextual Framework of LM III C Cult Activities", 345–354 in: LAFFINEUR – HÄGG 2001.
2003 "Late Minoan III C–Subminoan Pottery Sequence at Thronos/Kephala and its Connections with the Greek Mainland", 23–35 in: *LH III C Chronology and Synchronisms*.

DAY, L. P. – M. S. MOOK – J. D. MUHLY (eds.)
2004 *Crete Beyond the Palaces: Proceedings of the Crete 2000 Conference* (Prehistory Monographs 10). Philadelphia.

KANTA, A.
2003 "The First Half of the Late Minoan III C – Correlations among Cretan Sites with Reference to Mainland and Cypriote Developments", 513–538 in: BIETAK 2003.

LAFFINEUR, R. – R. HÄGG (eds.)
2001 *Potnia. Deities and Religion in the Aegean Bronze Age. Proceedings of the 8th International Aegean Conference/8e Rencontre égéenne internationale, Göteborg, Göteborg University, 12–15 April 2000* (Aegaeum 22). Liège – Austin.

MOOK, M. S.
2004 "From Foundation to Abandonment: New Ceramic Phasing for the Late Bronze Age and Early Iron Age on the Kastro at Kavousi", 163–179 in: DAY – MOOK – MUHLY 2004.

MOOK, M. S. – W. D. E. COULSON
1997 "Late Minoan III C Pottery from the Kastro at Kavousi", 337–365 in: *Late Minoan III Pottery*.

MOUNTJOY, P. A.
1999 "Late Minoan III C/Late Helladic III C: Chronology and Terminology", 511–516 in: *Meletemata*.

POPHAM, M. R.
1965a "The Late Minoan III Pottery from Kastri", 278–299 in: SACKETT – POPHAM – WARREN 1965.
1965b "Some Late Minoan III Pottery from Crete", *BSA* 60, 316–342.

PROKOPIOU, N.
1997 "LM III Pottery from the Greek-Italian Excavations at Sybritos Amariou", 371–394 in: *Late Minoan III Pottery*.

RETHEMIOTAKIS, G.
1997 "Late Minoan III Pottery from Kastelli Pediada", 305–326 in: *Late Minoan III Pottery*.

RUTTER, J. B.
2003 "The Nature and Potential Significance of Minoan Features in the Earliest Late Helladic III C Ceramic Assemblages of the Central and Southern Greek Mainland", 193–216 in: *LH III C Chronology and Synchronisms*.

SACKETT, L. H. – M. R. POPHAM – P. M. WARREN
1965 "Excavations at Palaikastro VI", *BSA* 60, 218–315.

SEIRADAKI, M.
1960 "Pottery from Karphi", *BSA* 55, 1–37.

WARREN, P. M.
1980/81 "Knossos: Stratigraphical Museum Excavations, 1978–1980. Part I", *AR* 27, 73–92.
1982/83 "Knossos: Stratigraphical Museum Excavations, 1978–82. Part II", *AR* 29, 63–87.
1984/85 "Knossos: Stratigraphical Museum Excavations, 1978–82. Part III", *AR* 31, 124–129.
1987/88 "Knossos: Stratigraphical Museum Excavations, 1978–82. Part IV", *AR* 34, 86–104.
1997 "Late Minoan III Pottery from the City of Knossos: Stratigraphical Museum Extension Site", 157–184 in: *Late Minoan III Pottery*.
2005 "Response to Eleni Hatzaki, 'Postpalatial Knossos: Town and Cemeteries from LM III A2 to LM III C'", 97–103 in: *Ariadne's Threads*.

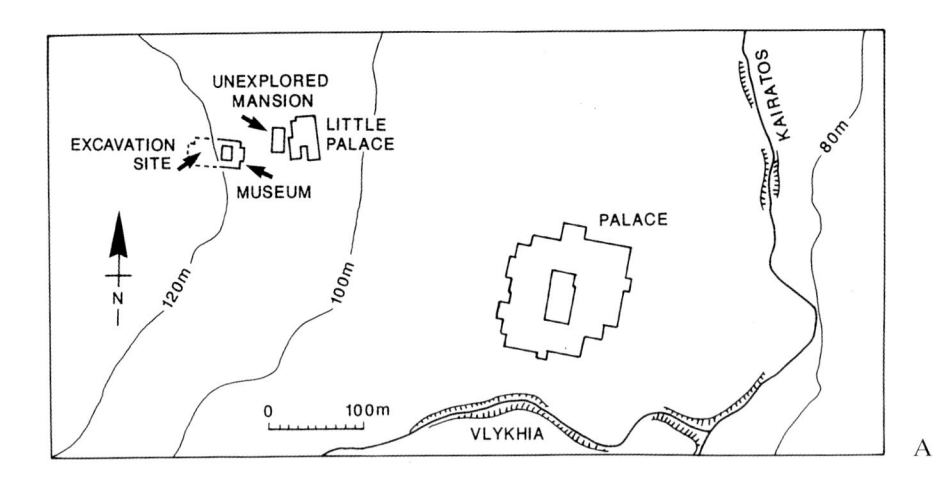

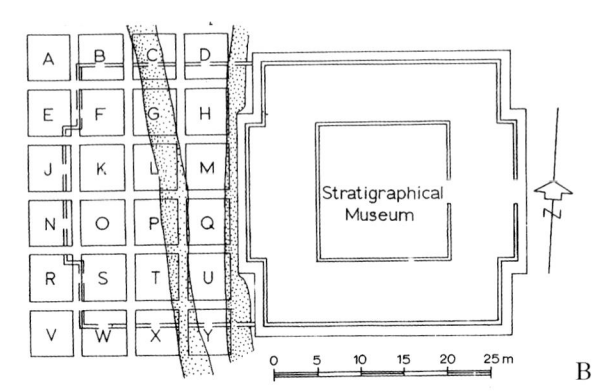

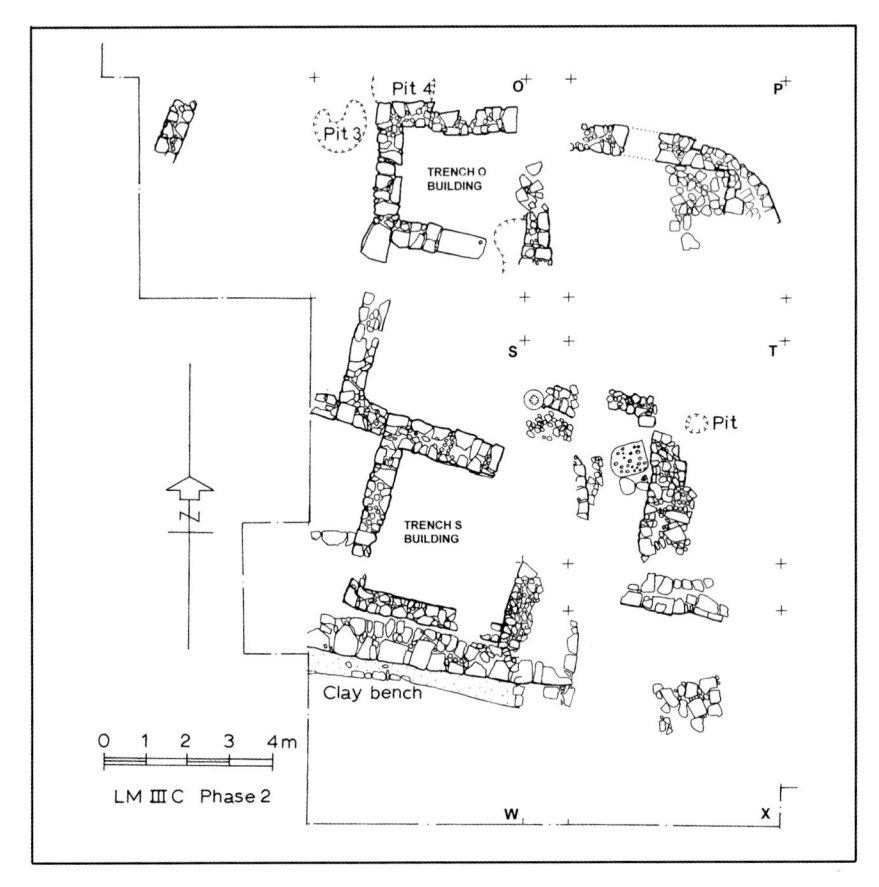

Fig. 1

Characteristics of Late Minoan III C from the Stratigraphical Museum Site at Knossos 337

STAGE I

P1919   P1922   P2152

STAGE II

P241   P251

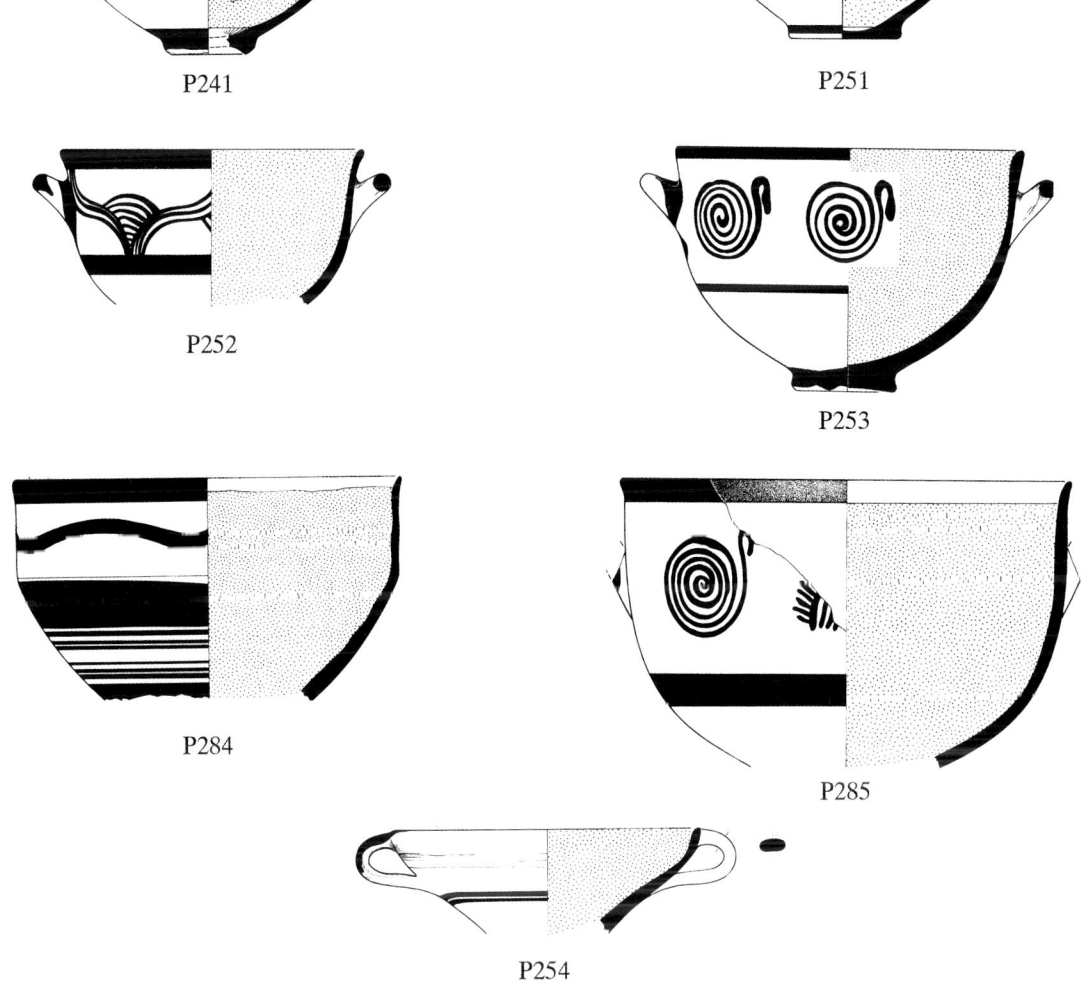

P252   P253

P284   P285

P254

Fig. 2

STAGE II

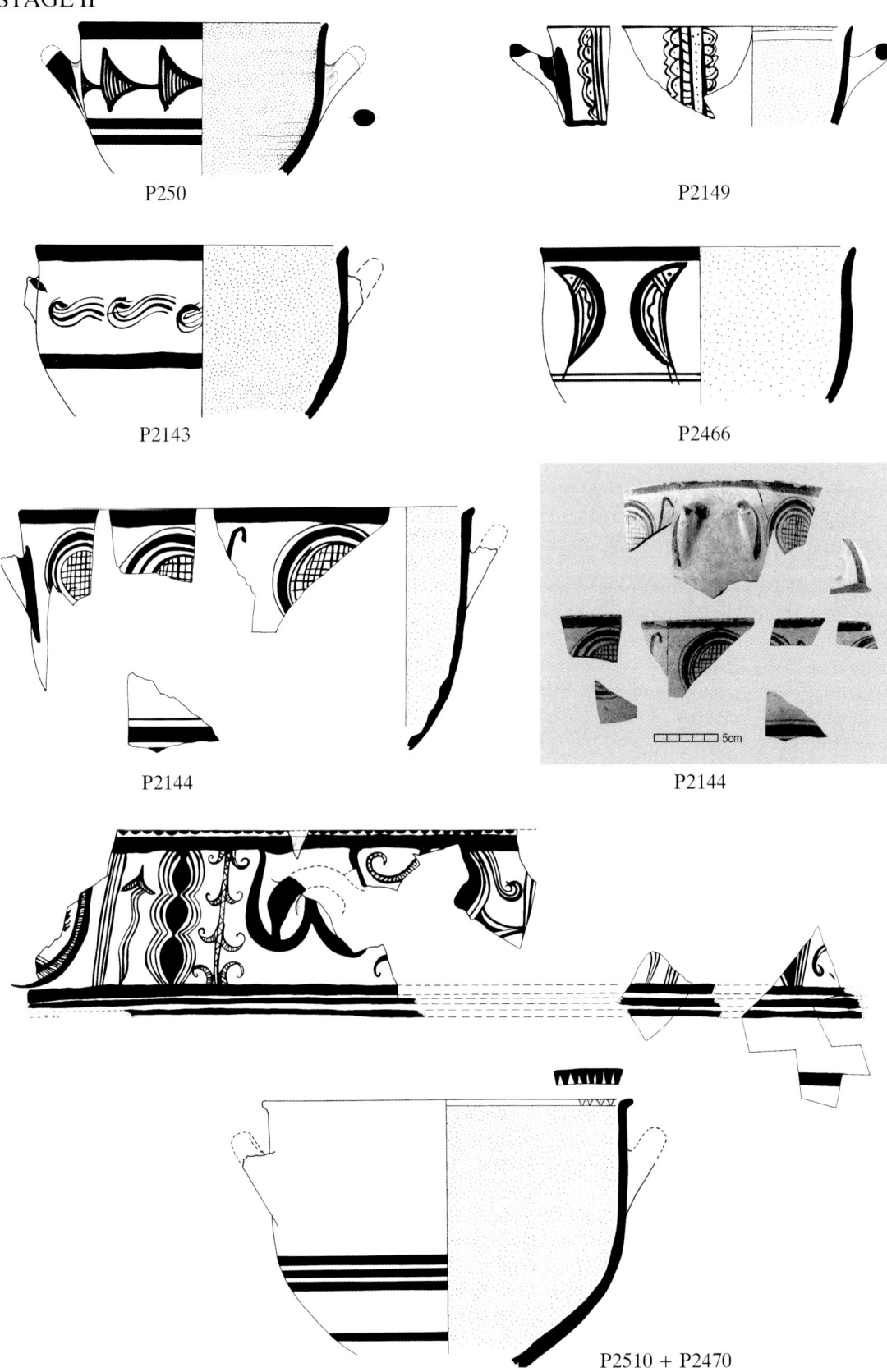

P250

P2149

P2143

P2466

P2144

P2144

P2510 + P2470

Fig. 3

STAGE II

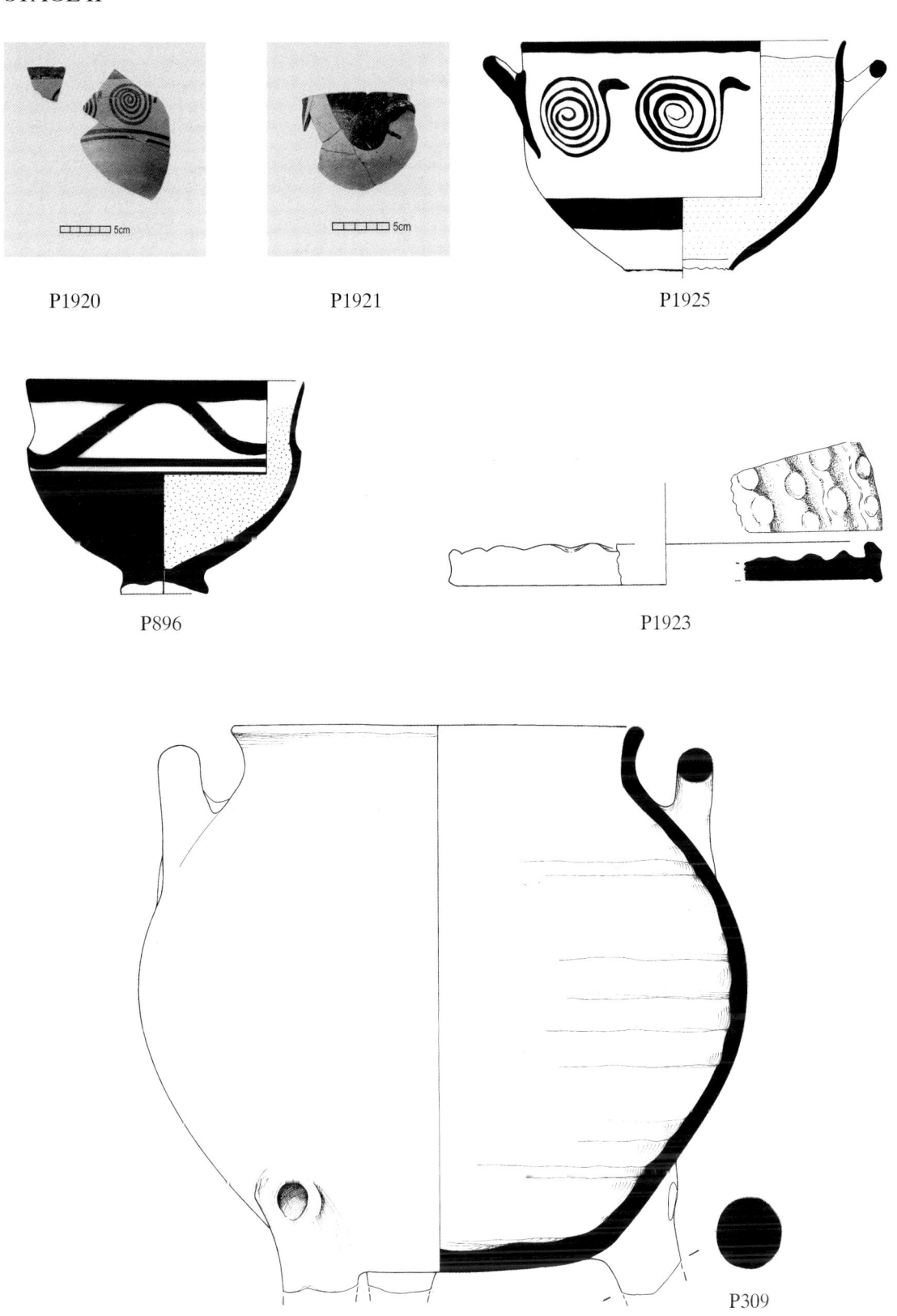

P1920

P1921

P1925

P896

P1923

P309

Fig. 4

STAGE II

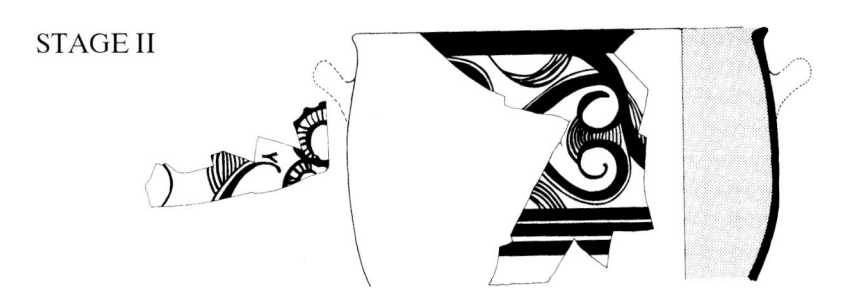

P1780

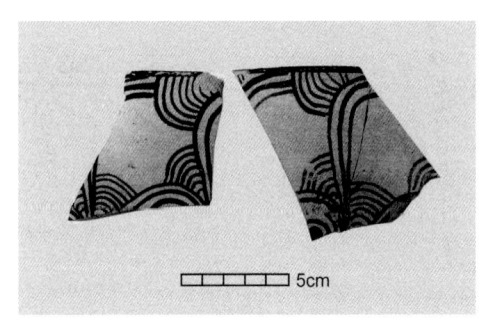

P1917

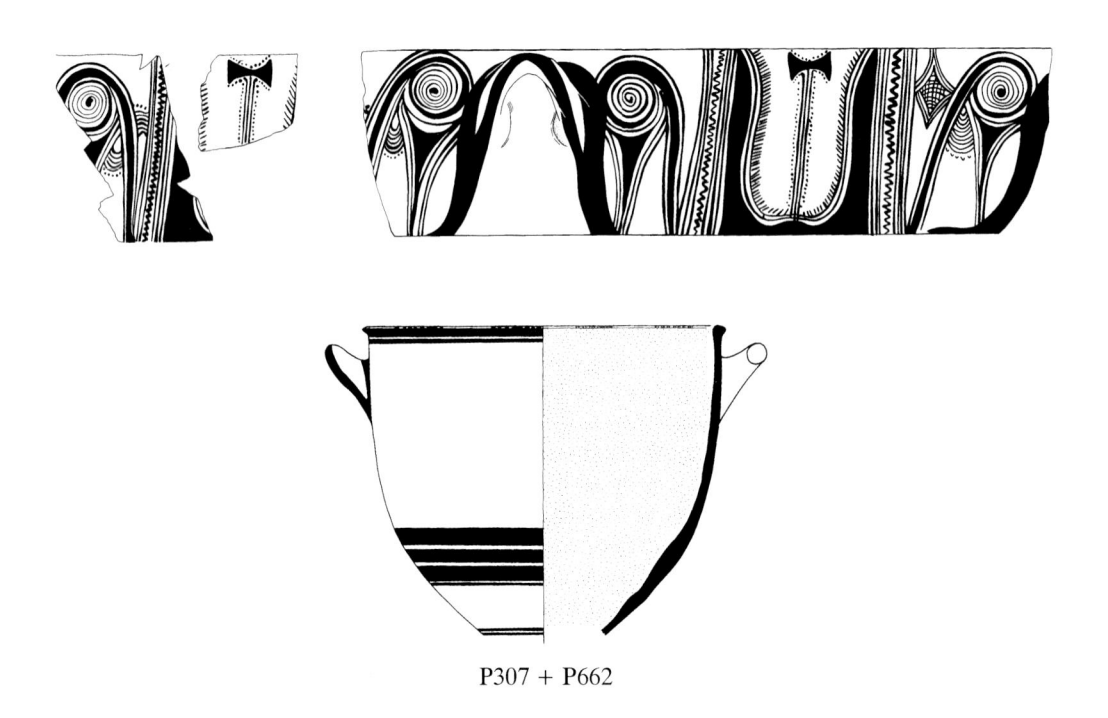

P307 + P662

Fig. 5

STAGE III

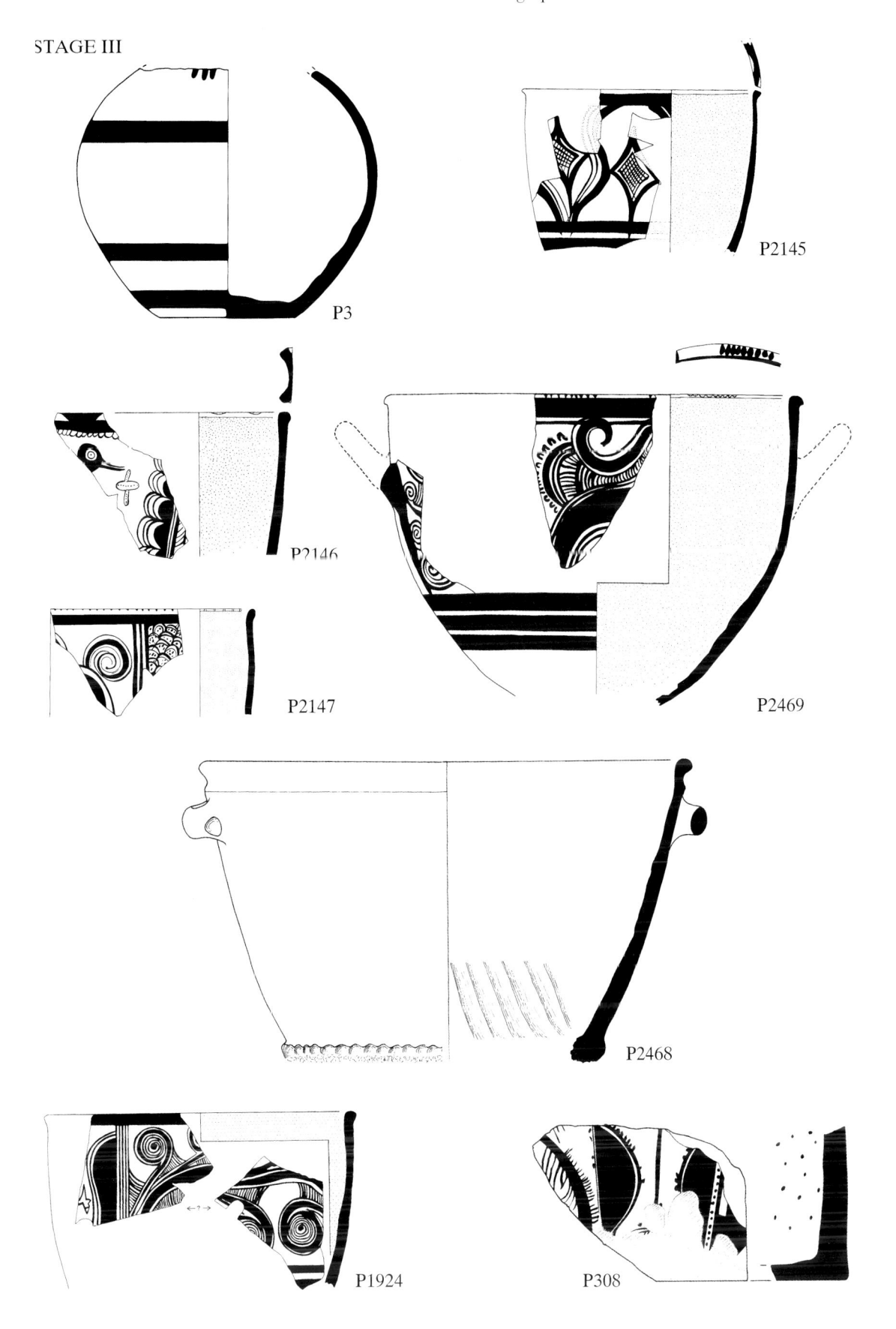

P3

P2145

P2146

P2147

P2469

P2468

P1924

P308

Fig. 6

P182

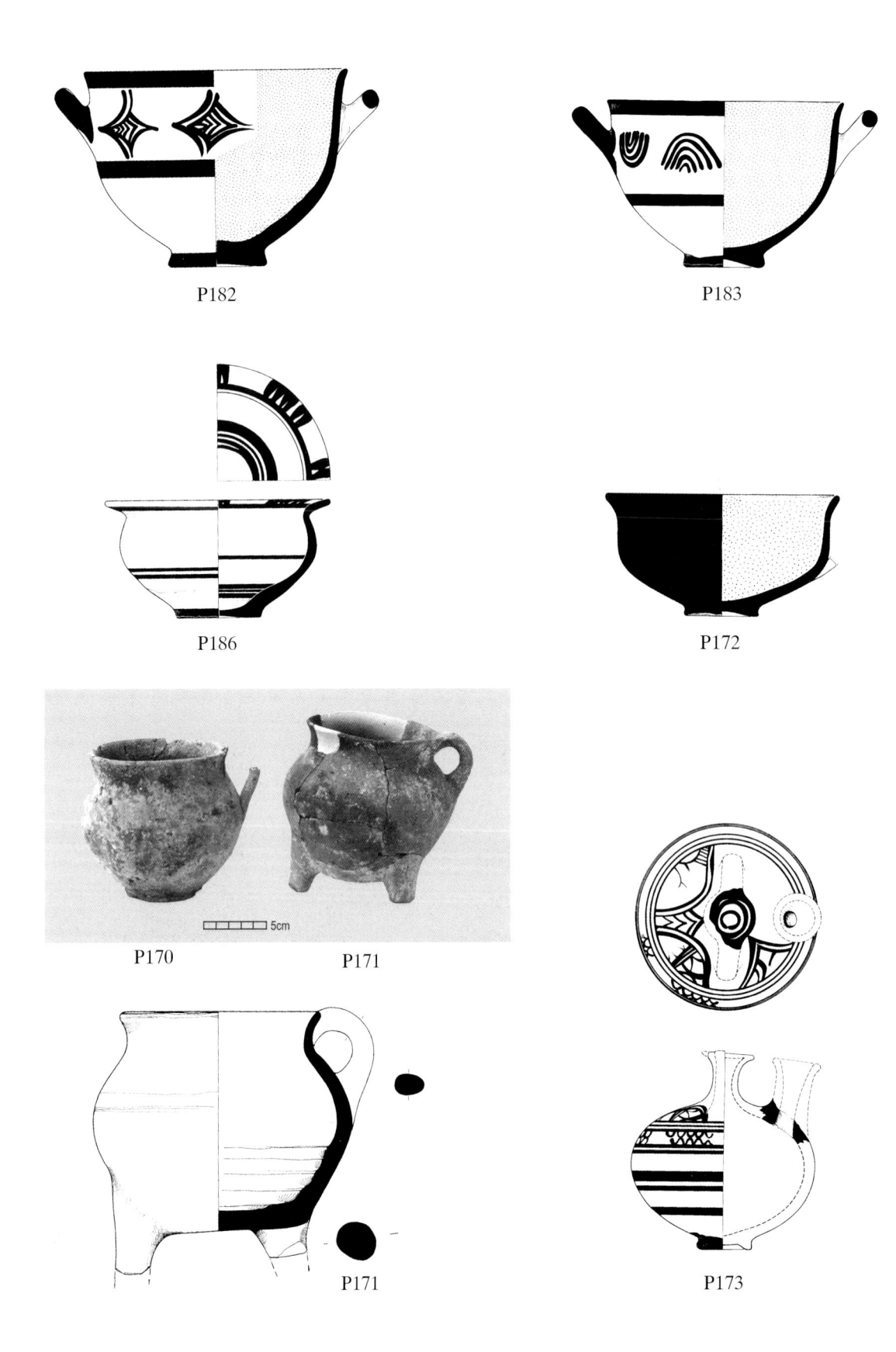

P183

P186

P172

P170 P171

P171 P173

Fig. 7

P169

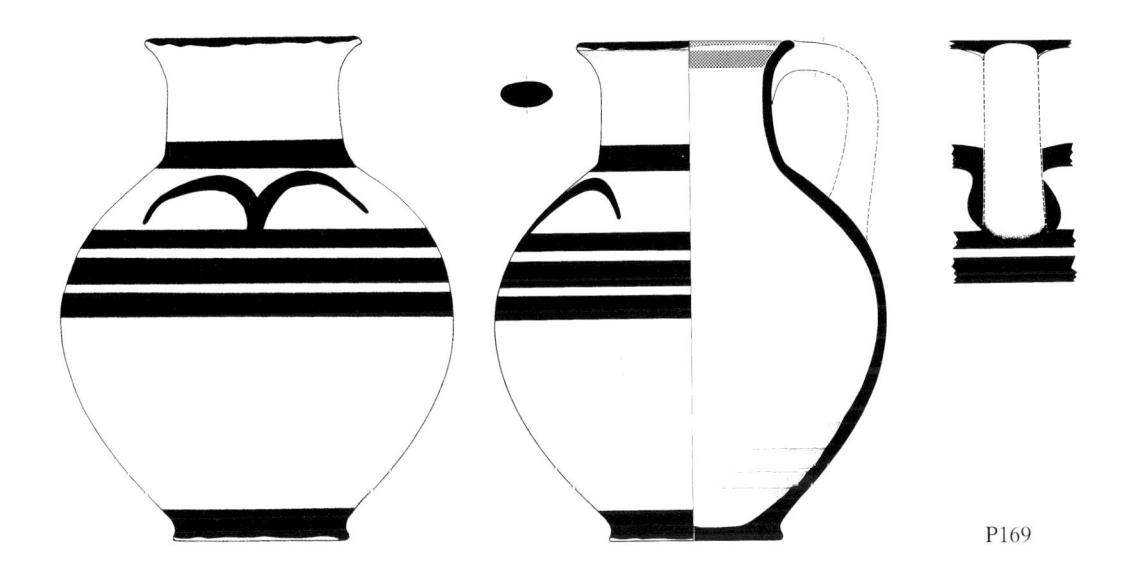

P197

Fig. 8

REPORT ON THE FINAL GENERAL DISCUSSION

JEREMY B. RUTTER

I) QUESTIONS TO BE ADDRESSED BY SPEAKERS AT VIENNA, WORKSHOP ON "LATE HELLADIC III C CHRONOLOGY AND SYNCHRONISMS II: LH III C MIDDLE" (29–30 OCTOBER, 2004)

DEFINITIONS

(A) GREEK MAINLAND

Definitions of LH III C Middle as a ceramic phase were established at the outset of the workshop on the basis of stratified settlement sequences at several sites (especially Mycenae and Lefkandi; also Kalapodi and Kynos). These definitions were extended to the rather different ceramic assemblages characteristic of Mycenaean funerary contexts by way of several major cemeteries or regional groups of cemeteries (especially Perati and the cemeteries of western Achaia; also Elateia). Two rather different approaches to the task of defining this phase ceramically were noted: first, a checklist of features initially designed by S. Sherratt for the Mycenae sequence (1981) which has subsequently been verified and modestly refined by E. French; and second, a system based on class and shape frequencies designed by M. Jacob-Felsch for the Kalapodi sequence (1996). There was general consensus in the discussion that future definitions of the phase in various regional or functionally specific (i.e. tomb vs. settlement pottery) settings should be based upon a combination of these two approaches. More attention at the workshop seemed to be focused on defining the *beginning* of LH III C Middle rather than its *end*. A distinction between two sub-phases within LH III C Middle (traditionally termed Developed [or Entwickelt] before Advanced [or Fortgeschritten]) is detectable at the major settlement sites.

Questions

1. What is the significance of the changes noted between LH III C Early and LH III C Middle? In particular, how should the decorative austerity of LH III C Early be interpreted, and what should we make of what appears to be a dramatic rise in pictorialism on ceramics in LH III C Middle?

2. How is the virtual disappearance, with the exception of a small number of comparatively unusual shapes (e.g. the three-handled cups from the Granary at Mycenae), of fine unpainted (i.e. plain) pottery in the course of LH III C Middle to be explained? Indeed, what is the history of this disappearance? That is, is it sudden or gradual? Does it occur over most of the Greek Mainland at the same time, or is there significant regional variation in this phenomenon? Is this disappearance really something that happens *during* LH III C Middle, or is it rather a development that should be added to the list of changes that distinguish LH III C Early from LH III C Middle?

3. Aeginetan cooking pots bearing potter's marks are well known from several LH III C Early contexts (e.g. Athenian Acropolis North Slope; see LINDBLOM 2001), but have so far not been documented in LH III C Middle contexts. Does the long-lived Aeginetan ceramic export industry finally die out in LH III C Middle after an existence of close to a millennium? What happens to Mainland Greek cooking pottery during LH III C Middle once the Aeginetan series of standard types are removed as models? For example, is there evidence for the development of regional cooking assemblages beginning in LH III C Middle?

4. What criteria should be used to distinguish LH III C Late from LH III C Middle? Why should Lefkandi Phase 2b be considered largely but not entirely LH III C Late (as per MOUNTJOY 1999) as opposed to defining a second major sub-phase of LH III C Middle?

(B) CRETE

Several different versions of what is likely to be the Minoan chronological equivalent of LH III C Middle were presented at the workshop. A major stumbling block to establishing a simple series of correlations between Helladic and Minoan chronological terms during the LBA III C period is caused by the traditional subdivision of the LM III C period into just two phases (Early and Late) rather than into the three principal phases of the Mainland LH III C sequence. B. Hallager proposed a tripartite division of the Minoan sequence into LM III B2, LM III C Early, and LM III C Late which together would cover the same time span as the four Mainland phases of LH III B2, LH III C Early, LH III C Middle, and LH III C Late. A. L. D'Agata suggested a tripartite sequence of LM III C Early, LM III C Late, and Subminoan I which would be roughly equivalent individually and as a group to LH III C Early, LH III C Middle, and LH III C Late; a later Subminoan II phase would be contemporary with Submycenaean. E. Borgna identified a five-stage LM III B to Subminoan sequence at Phaistos, of which the last three phases (3–5) were termed LM III C Early, LM III C Late, and Subminoan and of which the fourth (LM III C Late) was suggested to be contemporary with LH III C Middle.

There was a consensus at the workshop that establishing what the Minoan equivalent of LH III C Middle is will necessarily be a two-stage process: first, Minoan specialists must agree on a sequence of paradigmatic settlement deposits that define the various stages of LM III C, and they must also degree on a single terminology to describe these stages. LM III B2, for example, is a term and a ceramic assemblage that has so far been clearly defined only at Chania. D'Agata's subdivision of Subminoan into two stages is based principally on her discoveries at Thronos. How widely these terms will, or for that matter can, be adopted by the excavators of other Minoan sites remains to be determined. In the meantime, all participants at the workshop agreed that it would be useful to compile a list of dated Mainland Greek and Aegean island contexts in which LM III C vessels occur as imports, as well as a corresponding list of dated Minoan contexts in which LH III C ceramic imports occur. Such lists will clearly facilitate the correlation of the Mainland LH III C ceramic sequence with whatever LM III C – Subminoan sequence is eventually agreed upon by Minoan excavators.

Questions

1. Do you know of any LM III C ceramic imports in Helladic or Cycladic contexts? Please provide an excavation or museum identification number, a publication reference, the shape of the Minoan vessel in question, and a date for the context in which it was found.

TERMINOLOGY

There was widespread agreement at the workshop that the term "Close Style" has been badly abused in the scholarly literature on LBA III C ceramics over the past three decades. A better term for the complex decoration characteristic of many LH/LM III C kraters and stirrup jars, as well as smaller numbers of several other shapes, is Schachermeyr's "Pleonastic Style". This term, however, is a blanket term for all kinds of decorative complexity, and should be qualified with regional modifiers (e.g. Achaian, Cretan, Coan, etc.) whenever possible. Much the same can be said for the term "Octopus Style", which likewise should be qualified with regional adjectives (e.g. Naxian, Rhodian, east Attic, Cretan) whenever appropriate. The Close Style is a Pleonastic Style characteristic of the Argolid during the LH III C Middle phase. Genuine examples of this style were quite widely exported from their Argive center of production; the style was also to various degrees imitated by other regional Pleonastic Styles.

Question

How many individual LH III C Pleonastic Styles can presently be recognised and persuasively differentiated? What do the regional affiliations of these styles, in tandem with their shape and pattern ranges, contribute to our understanding of the Aegean economy or political order during this period? Are the various Pleonastic Styles a distinctive feature of LH III C Middle (and contemporary Crete and the islands) in particular, as opposed to the preceding LH III C Early and the succeeding LH III C Late phases? If so, how should they be interpreted as a broader cultural phenomenon?

OTHER TOPICS

Questions

1. What aspects of material culture other than changes in ceramics are likely to be most helpful in establishing more finely subdivided slices of time during the 12th and 11th centuries B.C. in the Aegean? Which of these may help to correlate developments on Crete with those on the Greek Mainland? Do any of these artifactual classes (e.g. figurines, weaponry, jewelry [including pins and fibulae], weaving equipment, etc.) serve to distinguish LH III C Middle in particular from either earlier or later phases of the LH III C period?

2. To what extent does the model of competing (aristocratic?) kin groups occupying large houses located in both the Unterburg and the Unterstadt at LH III C Tiryns (as outlined by T. Mühlenbruch) lend itself to the interpretation of the (contemporary?) rise in pictorialism in LH III C vase painting, not only at Tiryns (and elsewhere in the

Argolid?) but in regions such as Lokris (Kynos), Euboea (Lefkandi), and Attica (Athens, Perati)?

3. With the publication of larger corpora of dark-surfaced handmade and burnished pottery from LM III C (Chania) as well as LH III C (Kalapodi) sites, and with the discovery of significant quantities of comparable material at contemporary sites to the east of the Aegean (e.g. Troy in Turkey, Tell Kazel in Syria), can this class of material now be utilised more extensively than before in tracking chronological and cultural connections throughout the Aegean and beyond? Doesn't the comparative rarity of this material at some sites (Lefkandi, Perati) relative to its frequency at others (Tiryns, Menelaion, Dimini, Kalapodi) already suggest some basic differences that merit more attention than they have received? The growing importance of central Greece as a region that has much to contribute on this subject (by way of Kalapodi, Dimini, Kynos, and Mitrou) and the wealth of such material recovered for the first time at a site in the Levant at Tell Kazel are only the most recent surprises in the history of a ceramic category whose importance was first recognised by E. French in 1969.

II) ANSWERS TO THESE QUESTIONS

DEFINITIONS

(A) GREEK MAINLAND

ELIZABETH FRENCH

On Point 2

At Mycenae there is NO disappearance of fine unpainted (or of wheelmade cooking wares); only an increase in the proportion of painted ware over time. The problem is mainly one of identification as the types change little and therefore unless one is dealing with stratified material there is no way to assign such wares to their correct periods of manufacture.

SHERRATT 1981 gives rough percentages:

	Unpainted wares	Cooking ware
LH III B2 (Causeway)	73%	8%
Transitional	57%	16%
[Early]	[18%]	[18%]
Tower	48%	15%
Developed	39%	16%
Advanced	36%	16%
Late	42%	12.5%

[The figures of LH III C Early 1 are taken from the whole pots from Rm xxxiv and not from sherdage.]

On Point 3

Mycenae does not appear to have Aeginetan cooking ware bearing pot marks at any period though one ware has apparently been identified by Peter Day as from Aegina (TZEDAKIS – MARTLEW 1999, 196 no. 181). Further study of the fabrics of cooking wares from Mycenae is planned for summer 2005.

On Point 4

At Mycenae the end of LH III C Middle 2 is marked by a clear destruction in various areas. We really need another meeting to define the changes observable in the following strata. The phases at Lefkandi could then be compared. There is no point in discussing the Lefkandi divisions now.

TOBIAS MÜHLENBRUCH

On Points 1, 2, 4

From an architectural point of view, especially as the beginning of LH III C Middle was not very important with regard to the building activities in the Lower Citadel of Tiryns. In return we have the "initial horizon" 19b1 from the end of LH III C Early. In the Lower Citadel there is significant building activity at the end of LH III C Early, and other important building horizons do not date until LH III C Advanced corresponding to the later part of LH III C Middle, when the sophisticated pottery decoration (Close Style, pictoralism) reached its peak. Concerning the development of the pottery at Tiryns we have to wait for the publication of the studies by Christian Podzuweit and Philipp Stockhammer.

There is no destruction horizon that divided the settlements from LH III C Early from LH III C Developed in the Lower Citadel of Tiryns, but the earthquake that caused the destruction of the Granary at Mycenae and possibly also caused damage to houses in Tiryns, can be seen as the end of the architectural phase of LH III C Advanced.

PENELOPE A. MOUNTJOY

On Point 4

I really do not think this question should be raised. It is quite obvious from the pottery that it is different from that of III C Middle (see my discussion in *RMDP*, 38). I raised the matter with Liz Schofield when I was writing *RMDP*. She agreed with me that if Close Style were present at Lefkandi it would be in Phase 2a. When I asked her again in Vienna, she was still of this opinion. Close Style appears in LH III C Middle advanced at Mycenae and Tiryns. In terms of Rutter's 1978 division of Lefkandi Phase 2b as III C Middle advanced (see *MDP*, 133 table II), it would mean extending the LH III C Middle phase to fit in yet another phase.

(B) CRETE

ELISABETTA BORGNA

If we are to call phase 4 at Phaistos "III C Late" – since we do not recognise a middle III C phase – we should be aware of the fact that we then have to "rename" some more phases. In particular we ought to attribute proper names to the phases that precede phase 4. Indeed, after the foundation of Casa a Ovest (phase 1), I have recognised two phases, which I call "III B late" (or III B2 or III B–C Transitional) (= phase 2) and "III C Early" (= phase 3): these are both represented by large quantities of pottery and surely belong to a period of intense and rather lengthy occupation. As I understand, people in general (except possibly Birgitta Hallager?) would prefer to call my phase 2 "III C Early"; in such a case we would have an additional phase (3) between III C Early and III C Late.

ELIZABETH FRENCH

On Point 1

The peculiarity of the Granary kylix with the "Cretan" narrow vertical piercing of the stem has already been mentioned. (20-58 BE 8403 [FRENCH this volume, Fig. 8:4]. – WACE 1921–23, pl. 10c).

REINHARD JUNG

On Point 1

Argos, 27 Kofiniotou Street, grave pit 4: Subminoan stirrup jar together with EPG neck-handled amphora with groups of five compass-drawn circles on the shoulder (height 57 cm, diameter 42 cm), see PITEROS 2004, 114, pl. 64:β–γ. The find is interpreted as a cinerary urn with the stirrup jar as grave gift, but no ashes or burnt bones were found. The excavator concludes that the pit was disturbed from above by inhumation tomb 4. However, the amphora was found in an upright position in a round pit of 0.50 m diameter and the stirrup jar next to it. The stratigraphy offers no reason to doubt that these two vessels were originally deposited together inside the pit.

The EPG date of the amphora is clear (cf. e.g. KRAIKER – KÜBLER 1939, pl. 56: Inv. 556), and the stirrup jar can be dated to the Subminoan phase based on parallels from Knossos, North Cemetery. Shape, linear decoration and shoulder motif (double-outlined elaborate triangle with angle-hatching leaving a triangular area reserved at the triangle's centre) are closely paralleled by the Knossian stirrup jars (COLDSTREAM – CATLING 1996 III, figs. 112:112.2; 117:121.2; 123:2; 124:186.1). Their contexts are dated to the Subminoan phase (COLDSTREAM – CATLING 1996 I, 162–165, 190–193. – CATLING in: COLDSTREAM – CATLING 1996 II, 297–301).

This dating of the deposition of a Subminoan stirrup jar to the EPG period also reopens the question of the dating of another similar Subminoan stirrup jar from Argos in Mainland terms. I refer to the vessel found in Deiras tomb XXIX (DESHAYES 1966, 91 no. DV 151, pl. 86:4. – *RMDP*, 179, 184–185, fig. 56 no. 423), the deposition of which has already been dated to Submycenaean times based on the accompanying long dress pins with globular heads (EDER 2001, 87; pins: DESHAYES 1966, 91–92 nos. DB 17–DB 18, pls. 24:6; 87:6). This low date – as opposed to a previously suggested LH III C Late date – now may gain support from the even lower contextual date of Argos, Kofiniotou Street (unless one would dismiss the latter one as secondary context, which, however, is not likely).

PENELOPE A. MOUNTJOY

On Point 1

LM III C ceramic imports to the Mainland and Islands are listed and illustrated in *RMDP*.

ELIZABETH FRENCH

TERMINOLOGY

Personally I do not believe that true Close Style was "widely" exported. I know of very few, if any, examples which can be added to Desborough's list (DESBOROUGH 1964, 15 n. 1).

Sherratt discusses this at length and as her thesis seems to have become widely distributed in Germany at least we may as well make full use of her work.

I have always supposed that the other examples cited were Close Style derivatives and not true Close Style. It would be very useful to compile a complete list of the examples from sites other than Mycenae and make sure of their identification.

PENELOPE A. MOUNTJOY

I suggested in my Meletemata article (MOUNTJOY 1999) that Schachermeyr's term "Pleonastic Style" be adopted, particularly by Minoan archaeologists, to avoid confusion with Close Style.

"Regional modifiers" is a good idea.

Close Style has a wide distribution geographically, but may not have been exported in large quantity. The Close Style stirrup jar *RMDP*, Rhodes no. 271 from Kalavarda does not seem to be of Argive clay. It may be local Rhodian.

OTHER TOPICS

ELIZABETH FRENCH

On Point 1

Other relevant items: All present in the stratified levels at Mycenae which I am publishing.

- Figurines (though the argument is apt to become circular) (FRENCH 1971. – FRENCH in: EVELY 2006)
- Unbaked clay spools (also WACE 1921–23, 54)
- Spinning/weaving equipment
- Sherd hearths (also POPHAM – SACKETT 1968. – Tiryns pers. comm.)
- Bone pins with round heads (*Well Built Mycenae* 24, in press)
- Fibulae
- Steatite jewellery (bull's head pendant WACE 1921–23, fig. 13)

REINHARD JUNG

On Point 1

As is well known, the Aegean chronological systems are based on stylistic series and stratigraphical sequences of painted fine ware pottery. This kind of pottery was massproduced and provides a great number of typological characteristics, which were, simply put, subject to developments in taste and fashion. Because of this great number of characteristics including vessel proportions, morphological details, linear and monochrome decoration and patterned decoration with lots of possible combinations, this pottery is a very sensitive chronological indicator. The huge quantities of this painted fine ware in every Aegean excavation contribute further to its usability for answering chronological questions.

Bronze artefacts often show fewer chronologically sensitive variables than pottery. Apart from that, they are rather rare in settlement layers and occur more often in tombs – and this applies to Greece, the inner Balkan regions and Italy as well. Moreover, the Aegean Late Bronze Age tombs unfortunately very often contain multiple burials. Due to depositional practices and often also due to the lack of detailed publications, it is generally not easy to separate these multiple burials into individual closed contexts. Therefore,

352 Report on the Final General Discussion

at first sight bronze objects have certain disadvantages when used for the establishment of fine chronologies in the Aegean regions. However, some types of weapons and dress ornaments may very well act as Leitfossilien of certain phases. An exceptionally favourable case in this respect may be the separation of the phase LH III C Late from Submycenaean. From the archaeological point of view the change in burial rites towards a significant increase in single interments implies an improvement of the contextual record at hand. Additionally, more dress ornaments (fibulae, pins) are used now. These may help to identify Submycenaean burials – especially in regions, where a purely pottery based chronology meets with difficulties when defining a specific Submycenaean style.

The limitations outlined above are important, if solely the internal Aegean chronological sequences are concerned. However, in the geographical regions to the north and northwest of the Mycenaean world other systems of relative chronology are in use. These are mainly based on bronze objects, because the handmade pottery of those regions frequently shows both, a great deal of conservatism and a very strong regionalism (with certain exceptions such as the widely distributed Subapennine pottery of continental Italy), two factors which restrain its use as an interregional chronological indicator. It follows then, that bronze types of bronze artefacts can be quite helpful for linking non-Aegean chronological systems to the Mycenaean relative chronology. And indeed, they have been used in this way successfully ever since Oscar Montelius' times in the early 20th century. If, as in the case of Southern Italy, Mycenaean pottery is additionally available for synchronisation, bronzes do not lose their chronological value. They can still be used for cross-dating purposes, in order to test the synchronisms obtained by means of Mycenaean pottery chronology.

Yet, the Aegean pottery remains the most precise tool for chronological differentiation in LBA III C. And in the Aegean it is the Argolid that still provides the master sequences, although ceramic regionalism is a prominent phenomenon in LH/LM III C. This is because of two reasons. 1) Only the continuous stratigraphies of Tiryns and Mycenae allow the LH III C phases to be linked to the important socio-political turning point, which was the breakdown of the Mycenaean palace society that occurred in LH III B Final. Otherwise, the regional LBA III C phasing systems would be floating (see the problems with cross-dating Cretan LM III B–III C). In the future, Thebes with its recently excavated stratigraphies (ANDRIKOU 2006) may become the third site which allows this fundamental chronological connection to be made. 2) The Argive LH III C styles (such as the true Close Style of LH III C Advanced) show interaction with styles of other regions and, together with ceramic imports and exports, facilitate intra-Aegean cross-dating processes.[1]

TOBIAS MÜHLENBRUCH

On Point 2

As Sigrid Deger-Jalkotzy (DEGER-JALKOTZY 1994, 19–21) pointed out, the scenes on the pottery – chariot scenes, seafaring, hunting, dancing, fighting and warfare – may have

---

[1] All those regions may be called "centres" of Mycenaean pottery production, where Mycenaean pottery was the only or clearly dominating pottery class. In contrast, in "peripheral regions" Mycenaean pottery was locally produced, but it was only one pottery class among others. In those "peripheral regions" (southern Italy, Macedonia or the Levantine coast) the vessels of local types and wares outnumber the Mycenaean-type vessels. This use of "centre" and "periphery" in respect to Mycenaean pottery production (JUNG in: *LH III C Chronology and Synchronisms*, 252) was obviously misunderstood by THOMATOS 2006, 5. The Argive sites are by no means the only "centres" of Mycenaean pottery production during LH III C.

Report on the Final General Discussion 353

reflected the lifestyle of the elite. Therefore it seems to be plausible, that an elite, which we can possibly connect with important houses in the Lower Citadel of Tiryns, used the medium of the pottery to show its ideals – whether they lived these ideals or not. But we have to take into account, that e.g. we do not have so many vessels with pictorial decoration from the time of the "initial horizon" at the end of LH III C Early, because the style became more frequent in LH III C Middle (GÜNTNER 2000, 332–335). Finally we should not forget metal vessels as real "prestige objects" because we have only got few of them.

ELIZABETH FRENCH

On Point 3

Much care is needed with *Handmade Burnished Ware* as not all pieces identified truly belong to this category, e.g. much of that sent from Cyprus for NAA testing would not have been so classed at Mycenae.

REINHARD JUNG

On Point 3

First, one has to keep in mind though that "Handmade Burnished Ware" (HMB) is rather a working term born from the find situation, in which some extraordinary handmade pottery with burnished surfaces turned up within a ceramic environment dominated by wheelmade pottery with slipped or smoothed surfaces. Even if for sites such as Dhimini, Lefkandi, Tiryns and Khania it can be clearly demonstrated that the HMB there follows South Italian *impasto* typology, not all HMB must necessarily be due to external influence from outside southern and central Greece. A site like Kalapódhi provides us with HMB and other coarse handmade wares that neither include clear Italian nor clear Macedonian or even Epirotic types. Some of this handmade pottery may be interpreted in terms of a special adaptation of contemporary (LH III C–EPG) Mycenaean cooking pot and fine ware shapes in the potters' workshops producing handmade pottery (cf. JACOB-FELSCH 1996, 75–80). The geographical setting of Kalapódhi within the mountainous regions of central Greece provides a suitable background, where potters may have been working without the wheel and according to older technical traditions right up until the end of the Bronze Age and beyond (a local tradition is also suggested by JACOB-FELSCH 1996, 78). Another separate case is the handmade pottery found in the chamber tombs on Kefalonía, which mostly falls into the later phases of LH III C. Some types imitate Mycenaean shapes, others seem to belong to a local tradition, possibly partly depending on pottery types from the north-western Greek Mainland (SOUYOUDZOGLOU – HAYWOOD 1999, 75–76), from which, however, extremely few LBA deposits are sufficiently published. Specific South Italian types are missing in those tombs.

When analysing those HMB assemblages that do show external influence, one needs to address two important points: 1) It is essential to determine, in which region the specific style of a HMB assemblage originates. Only if in the southern Greek assemblages specific types can be singled out, whose main production was limited to certain distant geographical regions, may one conclude that those types do illustrate relationships with these main production regions. 2) As much handmade pottery is crudely made and shows only few well-definable typological characteristics, one needs to isolate types which constantly show clearly definable typological elements. Only these types can function as chronological indicators.

To give an example: Coarser bucket-shaped jars with applied cordons and lugs are present all over the Balkan Peninsula (including present-day northern Greece), Italy and central Europe in virtually all periods of the Bronze Age. Even more specific "types" are often not limited to smaller production regions. Moreover, the morphological variability of specific elements such as rim shape and position and morphology of applied cordons and lugs is frequently blurred to such an extent that a precise circumscription of a type and its differentiation from similar shapes gets exceedingly difficult. This is not to say that handmade coarse ware types do not merit attention. Various typological classes of cooking pots and stands for example show significantly different distribution patterns (ROMSAUER 2003, maps 2–8. – HOREJS 2005), but apart from a few exceptions coarse ware types cannot function as precise chronological indicators.

Generally speaking, one can state that handmade fine ware (as defined within the fabric categories of handmade pottery; for Southern Italy see PERONI ET AL. 2004, 167, 168 fig. 1, for Macedonia see HOREJS in press, chapter "Gattungen und Warengruppen") is more suitable for geographic and chronological differentiation than coarse ware. Carinated cups and bowls, for example, show clearly definable characteristics in profile morphology, handle shapes and plastic handle applications, which allow not only broad-scale distinctions of distribution patterns (e.g. between the south-central Balkan regions, north-western Greece and continental Italy), but also the identification of types with a rather limited distribution (for Italy see e.g. COCCHI GENICK 2004b, 32–36). The chronological significance of these types has been demonstrated in various recent settlement excavations.

Finally, there are sites, far from the Aegean that yield a HMB repertory very close to those assemblages known from the Aegean. Such a site is Tell Kazel in southern coastal Syria, where HMB was locally made – possibly according to Southern Italian *impasto* typology. Like at Dhimini, it occurs together with a specific kind of wheelmade grey ware, which also finds parallels in southern continental Italy (see BADRE 2003. – BADRE ET AL. 2005, esp. 31 with fig. 7:1.2 and n. 48 [grey ware]: 33–36 with fig. 9:1.3–5). At Tell Kazel the production of these two typologically foreign pottery classes started at the same time as the local production of a specific kind of Mycenaean pottery, which can be well dated to the very beginning of LH III C Early by Argive parallels (JUNG 2007). All of these new pottery classes are sealed below the debris of a destruction, which affected the site at the transition from LBA II to IA I (BADRE 2003. – CAPET 2003. – JUNG 2007) and may be ascribed to the Sea Peoples devastating Amurru, as reported in Ramesses' III year 8 inscription. A possible explanation for the occurrence of small percentages of HMB, grey ware and local Mycenaean pottery before this destruction may be the integration of small groups of foreign warriors from different regions in the central Mediterranean and the Aegean into Syrian society (perhaps former pirates like the Sardana in 13th century Egypt – for their integration into Egyptian society see CIFOLA 1994, 2–7). They seem to have transferred their consumption patterns together with new pottery classes to Syria (JUNG 2006). At Tell Kazel the production of HMB and local Mycenaean pottery survived the aforementioned destruction and continued right into IA I.

Bibliography

ANDRIKOU, E.
2006   "The Late Helladic III Pottery", 11–179 in: ANDRIKOU – ARAVANTINOS – GODART – SACCONI – VROOM 2006.

ANDRIKOU, E. – V. L. ARAVANTINOS – L. GODART – A. SACCONI – J. VROOM
2006   *Thèbes. Fouilles de la Cadmée II.2. Les tablettes en linéaire B de la Odos Pelopidou. Le contexte archéologique. La céramique de la Odos Pelopidou et la chronologie du linéaire B*. Pisa – Rome.

BADRE, L.
2003   "Handmade Burnished Ware and Contemporary Imported Pottery from Tell Kazel", 83–99, in: STAMPOLIDIS – KARAGEORGHIS 2003.

BADRE, L. – M.-C. BOILEAU – R. JUNG – H. MOMMSEN
2005   "The Provenance of Aegean- and Syrian-Type Pottery Found at Tell Kazel (Syria)", *Egypt and the Levant* 15, 15–47.

BIETAK, M. – E. CZERNY (eds.)
2007   *The Synchronisation of Civilisations in the Eastern Mediterranean in the Second Millennium BC. III. Proceedings of the SCIEM 2000 – 2nd EuroConference, Vienna, 28th of May–1st of June 2003* (Österreichische Akademie der Wissenschaften. Denkschriften der Gesamtakademie 37 = Contributions to the Chronology of the Eastern Mediterranean 9). Vienna.

CAPET, E.
2003   "Tell Kazel (Syrie), rapport préliminaire sur les 9e–17e campagnes de fouilles (1993–2001) du Musée de l'Université Américaine de Beyrouth, chantier II", *Berytus* 47, 63–121.

CIFOLA, B.
1994   "The Role of the Sea Peoples at the End of the Late Bronze Age: A Reassessment of Textual and Archaeological Evidence", *Orientis Antiqui Miscellanea* 1, 1–23.

COCCHI GENICK, D.
2004a   (ed.) *L'età del bronzo recente in Italia. Atti del Congresso Nazionale di Lido di Camaiore, 26–29 ottobre 2000*. Viareggio.
2004b   "Le ceramiche nel ruolo di indicatori cronologici e regionali", 22–52 in: COCCHI GENICK 2004a.

DEGER-JALKOTZY, S.
1994   "The Post-Palatial Period of Greece: An Aegean Prelude to the 11th Century B.C. in Cyprus", 11–30 in: KARAGEORGHIS 1994.

COLDSTREAM, J. N. – H. W. CATLING (eds.)
1996   *Knossos North Cemetery: Early Greek Tombs* (BSA Suppl. 28). London.

DESBOROUGH, V. R. D'A.
1964   *The Last Mycenaeans and Their Successors. An Archaeological Survey c. 1200–c. 1100 B.C.* Oxford.

DESHAYES, J.
1966   *Argos. Les fouilles de la Deiras* (Études Péloponnésiennes 4). Paris.

EDER, B.
2001   *Die submykenischen und protogeometrischen Gräber von Elis* (Βιβλιοθήκη της εν Αθήναις Αρχαιολογικής Εταιρείας 209). Athens.

EVELY, D. (ed.)
2006   *Lefkandi IV. The Late Helladic III C Settlement at Xeropolis* (BSA Suppl. 39). London.

FELSCH, R. C. S. (ed.)
1996   *Kalapodi. Ergebnisse der Ausgrabungen im Heiligtum der Artemis und des Apollon von Hyampolis in der antiken Phokis. Vol. I*. Mainz.

FRENCH, E.
1971   "The Development of Mycenaean Terracotta Figurines", *BSA* 66, 101–187.

GÜNTNER, W.
2000   *Figürlich bemalte mykenische Keramik aus Tiryns* (Tiryns. Forschungen und Berichte 12). Mainz.

HOREJS, B.
2005   "Kochen am Schnittpunkt der Kulturen – zwischen Karpatenbecken und Ägäis", 71–94 in: HOREJS ET AL. 2005.

in press *Das Prähistorische Olynth. Ausgrabungen in der Toumba Agios Mamas 1994–1996 III. Die spätbronzezeitliche handgemachte Keramik der Schichten 13 bis 1* (Prähistorische Archäologie in Südosteuropa).

HOREJS, B. – R. JUNG – E. KAISER – B. TERŽAN (eds.)
2005 *Interpretationsraum Bronzezeit. Bernhard Hänsel von seinen Schülern gewidmet* (Universitätsfor-
schungen zur Prähistorischen Archäologie 121). Bonn.

JACOB-FELSCH, M.
1996 "Die spätmykenische bis frühprotogeometrische Keramik", 1–213 in: FELSCH 1996.

JUNG, R.
2006 "ΕΧΥΤΟΝ ΠΟΤΕΡΙΟΝ: Mykenische Keramik und mykenische Trinksitten in der Ägäis, in Syrien,
Makedonien und Italien", 407–423 in: *Studi in onore di Renato Peroni*. Florence.
2007 "Tell Kazel and the Mycenaean Contacts with Amurru (Syria)", 551–570 in: BIETAK – CZERNY 2007.

KARAGEORGHIS, V. (ed.)
1994 *Proceedings of the International Symposium Cyprus in the 11th Century B.C.* Nicosia.

KRAIKER, W. – K. KÜBLER
1939 *Die Nekropolen des 12. bis 10. Jahrhunderts. Kerameikos* (Ergebnisse der Ausgrabungen I). Berlin.

LINDBLOM, M.
2001 *Marks and Makers. Appearance, Distribution and Function of Middle and Late Helladic Manufactur-
ers' Marks on Aeginetan Pottery* (SIMA 128). Jonsered.

MOUNTJOY, P. A.
1999 "Late Minoan III C/Late Helladic III C: Chronology and Terminology", 511–516 in: *Meletemata*.

PERONI, R. – A. VANZETTI – C. BARTOLI – M. BETTELLI – I. CASSETTA – M. A. CASTAGNA – A. DI RENZONI
– F. FERRANTI – D. GATTI – S. T. LEVI – A. SCHIAPPELLI
2004 "Broglio di Trebisacce (Cosenza)", 167–176 in: COCCHI GENICK 2004a.

PITEROS, C.
2004 "Όβος Κορινθιώτου 27 (Ο.Τ. 19/23, οικόπεδο Β. Πετρόπουλου – Κ. Σμυρλά)", *ArchDelt* 53, 1998 [2004].
Chron 112–114.

POPHAM, M. R. – L. H. SACKETT
1968 *Excavations at Lefkandi, Euboea, 1964–66. A Preliminary Report*. Oxford.

ROMSAUER, P.
2003 *Πυραυνοί. Prenosné pieсky a podstavce z doby bronzovej a doby železnej*. Nitra.

SHERRATT, E. S.
1981 *The Pottery of Late Helladic III C and its Significance* (unpublished Ph.D. thesis). Oxford.

SOUYOUDZOGLOU-HAYWOOD, C.
1999 *The Ionian Islands in the Bronze Age and Early Iron Age 3000–800 BC*. Liverpool.

STAMPOLIDIS, N. C. – V. KARAGEORGHIS (eds.)
2003 *Sea Routes ... Interconnections in the Mediterranean 16th–6th c. BC. Proceedings of the International Symposium Held at Rethymnon, Crete in September 29th–October 2nd 2002*. Athens.

THOMATOS, M.
2006 *The Final Revival of the Aegean Bronze Age. A Case Study of the Argolid, Corinthia, Attica, Euboea,
the Cyclades and the Dodecanese during LH III C Middle* (BAR-IS 1498). Oxford.

TZEDAKIS, Y. – H. MARTLEW (eds.)
1999 *Minoans and Mycenaeans. Flavours of Their Time. National Archaeological Museum, 12 July–27
November 1999*. Athens.

WACE, A. J. B.
1921–23 "Excavations at Mycenae § VII. – The Lion Gate and Grave Circle Area", *BSA* 25, 9–126.